Marketing Research

Seventh Edition

Carl McDaniel, Jr.
University of Texas
at Arlington

Roger Gates
DSS Research

John Wiley & Sons, Inc

Dedicated to
the market research instructors and students
who make this book a part of their
professional lives

ASSOCIATE PUBLISHER   Judith Joseph
ACQUISITIONS EDITOR   Jayme Heffler
ASSOCIATE EDITOR   Jennifer Conklin
PRODUCTION MANAGER   Pam Kennedy
SENIOR PRODUCTION EDITOR   Sarah Wolfman-Robichaud
CREATIVE DIRECTOR   Harry Nolan
SENIOR DESIGN ASSISTANT   Hope Miller
SENIOR ILLUSTRATION EDITOR   Anna Melhorn
PHOTO RESEARCHER   Elle Wagner
SENIOR MEDIA EDITOR   Allie Morris
SENIOR EDITORIAL ASSISTANT   Ame Esterline
PRODUCTION ASSISTANT   Jenna Belisonzi
COPYEDITOR   Betty Pessagno
COVER PHOTO   Todd Pearson/The Image Bank/Getty Images

This book was set in 10.5/12 Adobe Garamond by GGS Book Services and printed and bound by Quebecor World Versailles. The cover was printed by Quebecor World Versailles.

This book is printed on acid free paper.

To order books or for customer service please, call 1-800-CALL WILEY (225-5945).

ISBN-13 978-0-471-75528-9
ISBN-10 0-471-75528-1

Printed in the United States of America

10 9 8 7 6 5 4 3 2 1

CONTENTS IN BRIEF

CONTENTS

PREFACE

Making Marketing Research Work For Your Students With *Real Data/Real People/Real Research*

You are holding the only marketing research textbook coauthored by a full-time marketing researcher. Our emphasis on "being real" has made this the world's leading marketing research textbook. Being marketing research insiders enables us to provide you with the latest trends and what works and what doesn't! The difference between this text and the others is like sitting in the stands observing versus being on the field where the action is taking place. We can tell you that marketing research is much more than computing sample size, learning SPSS, or conducting a focus group. It is also about getting managers to use your findings, managing people, controlling costs, and a host of other things. Sure, like other texts, *Marketing Research* covers research design, data acquisition, and data analysis, but it does so with a dose of reality unmatched by our competitors.

Real Data

Working with Survey Sampling International, the global leader in providing samples to marketing research suppliers (www.surveysampling.com), we obtained a nationwide sample of 2,000 college-aged students that provided information for our three new data cases. These cases all focus on topics of interest to college students. They include: an Online Dating Service, an Online Student Travel Service, and a new chain of combination fast food and a convenience store located near college campuses. Not only do we have demographic and attitudinal data for each respondent, but working with Claritas, a leading provider of marketing databases (www.claritas.com), we offer students a chance to work with PRIZM NE appended to our data sets. This latest version of the original PRIZM is the most widely used target marketing system in the United States! The new PRIZM NE is a 66-segment model. These segments are arranged to make up two standard sets of groups: Social Group and Lifestage Group.

In addition to the three new data cases, we have retained the data case, Rockingham National Bank Visa Card Survey, for the 7th edition. This was done in response to many requests from our users. We know that you will enjoy working with this student favorite!

Real People

Roger Gates, President of DSS Research, is one of the authors of this text. His firm is privately held and therefore does not publicly disclose revenue. However, if it did, it would be one of the 35 largest research firms in America! DSS specializes in health care products and services. We decided to add a new feature entitled "**From the Front Line**," featuring a wide range of DSS professionals from new MBAs to Roger himself. Each person was asked to discuss a provocative question that we thought would be of interest to you. Some of the topics discussed in "From the Front Line" include:

- ☐ Secrets of Conducting Good Focus Groups
- ☐ Why Isn't All Data Collection Moving to the Internet?
- ☐ Tips on Making Sure You Have the Right Level of Scaling
- ☐ Six Secrets of Good Questionnaire Design
- ☐ How to Develop a Good Set of Tables
- ☐ Tips on Significance Testing
- ☐ How Many Factors are Enough
- ☐ Tips for Managing Difficult Clients
- ☐ How to Write a Good Report
- ☐ Secrets of Sample Management
- ☐ Courses I Wish That I Had Taken Before
- ☐ Becoming a Marketing Research and Why
- ☐ Why I Chose a Career in Marketing Research and the Biggest Surprise I have Faced Doing Research
- ☐ Get your Objectives in Order Before You Start

We are sure that you will enjoy meeting a few of the research professionals at DSS and learning the inside scoop in our new "From the Front Line" feature.

Real Research

Our new data cases were developed using 2,000 respondents from around the United States the Survey Sampling International (SSI) database. Our data cases are not student respondents from our classrooms! SSI provides samples for more than 1,200 research organizations each year! Our goal continues to be one of providing you with the most up-to-date, realistic picture possible of the tools, techniques, and trends in marketing research. Partnering with Survey Sampling International and Claritas helps us to accomplish this goal.

Classic "Real Research" Features Have Been Updated and Enhanced. In the 7th edition you will find:

- ☐ **_All New Opening Vignettes._** Every chapter-opening vignette has been either updated or replaced. The companies/products featured include Proctor & Gamble, Starbucks, Swiffer dust mops, Gap, and Coach Handbags, to name a few.

- ☐ **_New "Global Research" Vignettes._** You will find new Global Research vignettes throughout the text. Our observations of the research industry indicate that more and more companies are "going global." Multinational clients are demanding multi-country research.

- ☐ **_New "In Practice Boxes" in Every Chapter._** The 7th edition continues our emphasis on the "real world" of marketing research. You will find new "In Practice" boxes in every chapter, and we have retained the best of these vignettes from the previous edition. This text addition is equivalent to having a marketing researcher offer his or her comments about various topics in each chapter. We have received excellent feedback from both professors and students about this timely feature.

☐ *New "Real-Life Research" Cases.* You will find new end-of-chapter real-world case problems at the end of each chapter. Examples include: Digital Insights Online Customer Feedback Program, Continental Airlines Online Advertising, Managing Growth at Benson Marketing Research, DDB Worldwide research on differences between men and women, Paramount Parks, KDA Research's Parenthood Project, Decision Analyst's research on frozen pizza, Coke Test Marketing, and BIG research's look at satellite radio.

NEW—You Asked for SPSS Student Version Software with Every Text—You have SPSS 14.0! Plus SPSS Exercises and Data Sets

Many market researchers use SPSS on a daily basis. You will find new timely SPSS screen shots in the quantitative chapters. We also offer you *fully classroom-tested* new SPSS exercises and data sets. The quantitative chapters each conclude with a series of SPSS exercises. You will find that these real-world, user-oriented exercises provide great hands-on experience for your students. These SPSS exercises will feature a new database and questionnaire. The database has 500 responses from a questionnaire dealing with movie theatre attendance by college students. In addition to the SPSS Exercises in the data analysis chapters, there will also be two SPSS exercises for the chapter dealing with sample size.

The Movie Theatre Questionnaire has questions that utilize all four levels of measurement and a variety of different attitude scale formats. Students will evaluate the importance of various movie theater information sources, as well as specific movie theater amenities. The questionnaire also features an assessment of various movie ticket purchase options. The data are classified by traditional demographic lifestyle characteristics. You will find the questionnaire for generating your own data set on our companion web site at www.wiley.com/college/mcdaniel.

Of course, you can customize the exercises or use your own as you choose. Our coverage of SPSS is thorough yet balanced. Unlike other texts, we realize that you are teaching a course in marketing research, not SPSS. Our focus is on a balanced approach to contemporary marketing research.

NEW—Want the Student Exercises in Excel? We Have It

The same exercises for segmenting the college student market for movie theater attendance are available as Excel-based exercises. You can find these on our website at www.wiley.com/college/mcdaniel. Now you have the flexibility to pick which tool you prefer, SPSS or Excel. Of course, you can have both! We also provide an Excel User Guide for those students less than familiar with the Excel program. It consists of detailed step-by-step instructions for each exercise, accompanied by relative visual aids, such as "screen shots," to further serve as "road map" indicators ensuring that you are on the right track. The guide also includes periodic "troubleshooting" tips.

NEW—For the Student—Web Quizzes

The online questions are designed to be similar in type and difficulty level to the Test Bank questions. By careful review and study your students can dramatically improve their test scores.

NEW CONTENT

We have updated and streamlined the 7th edition based upon your feedback.

- ☐ *The important topic of marketing research ethics has been moved to the front of the text where it belongs.*

- ☐ *Major new section on Exploratory Research.*

- ☐ *Major new section on writing a research proposal with new appendix containing a sample proposal.*

- ☐ *Basic sampling issues and sample size determination have been combined into a single streamlined chapter.*

- ☐ *Major new section on Internet search strategies and a new appendix on Optimal Google Search strategies.*

- ☐ *Managing Marketing Research and Communicating Research Results have been integrated into a single chapter.*

OTHER NEW CONTENT IN OUR MOST EXTENSIVE AND THOROUGH REVISION EVER!

Chapter 1, The Role of Marketing Research in Management Decision Making—New AMA definition of marketing; new AMA definition of marketing research; new explanations of the descriptive, diagnostic, and predictive functions of marketing.

Chapter 2, The Marketing Research Industry and Research Ethics—Completely revised chapter with a new major section on marketing research ethics; new description and simplified diagram of the marketing research industry; detailed new explanations of research suppliers; new material on research supplier firms, new discussion of the state of the marketing research industry and current challenges; new section on ethical theories; new discussion on the ethics of "black box" branding in marketing research; new code of marketing research ethics; updated material on the European Commission's Directive on Data Protection; new discussion of marketing researcher certification.

Chapter 3, Problem Definition, Exploratory Research, and the Research Process—Major new section on exploratory research, major new section on writing the research proposal and new appendix with a research proposal.

Chapter 4, Secondary Data and Databases—Major new section on Internet search strategies, all new appendix on optimal Google search strategies; new material on identity theft, new section on blogging, new discussion of geographic information systems (GIS).

Chapter 5, Qualitative Research—New discussion of focus group usage in the U.S. and globally; new material on using the Web to find focus group participants; new section on focus group length; new material on online focus groups; new section on hermaneutic research; new section on online individual depth interviewing.

Chapter 6, Survey Research: The Profound Impact of the Internet—New material on the use of surveys; new material on in-store interviewing; new discussion of hybrid telephone interviewing techniques; new discussion on gaining respondent cooperation; new material on Internet survey research and Internet panels; new discussion of what makes a quality Internet panel; new discussion of how research suppliers work with Internet panel suppliers like SSI.

Chapter 7, Primary Data Collection: Observation—New material on ethnographic research; new section on facial action coding service (FACS); major new section on the portable people meter and Project Apollo; new material on Double Click.

Chapter 8, Primary Data Collection: Experimentation—New streamlined chapter, new material on external validity, new discussion on types of test markets, new section on ideal test markets, new discussion on global test marketing.

Chapter 9, The Concept of Measurement—New examples of ordinal measurement.

Chapter 10, Using Measurement Scales to Build Marketing Effectiveness—New example of rank-order scales; new discussion of dos and don'ts when creating scales; new material on scale balancing.

Chapter 11, Questionnaire Design—New material on coding questionnaires; new discussion on things to avoid in questionnaire design; new material on specific questions that can lead to greater insight; new discussion on the "don't know" response; new material on questionnaire software.

Chapter 12, Basic Sampling Issues—New discussion on problems with telephone samples; new material on random digit dialing.

Chapter 13, Sample Size Determination—New material on appropriate sample size, new discussion of non-response bias, discussion of call-in and infotainment polls.

Chapter 14, Data Processing and Fundamental Data Analysis—New data quality procedures to identify interviewer falsification; new discussion of text analytics software for coding open-ended responses; tips for easier cross tabulations, new professional pointers for the best graphical design of statistical data.

Chapter 15, Statistical Testing of Differences and Relationships—New material on why we need statistical tests of differences, new discussion on the practical significance of statistical significance.

Chapter 16, Bivariate Correlation and Regression—New discussion of data visualization in statistical analysis, new material on when bivariate and multivariate correlation combined give the best picture.

Chapter 17, Multivariate Data Analysis—New discussion on multiple discriminate analysis, new material on finding the right number of factor scores.

Chapter 18, Communicating the Research Results and Managing Marketing Research—New section on organizing the supplier firm; new material on the role of marketing research in the organization; new section on measuring marketing research's return-on-investment (ROI).

You Can Bring Internet Research Alive with Perseus WebResearcher

Your students can use the same marketing research Web application as professional marketing researchers. You will have the capability of assigning multiple class projects and conducting real Internet marketing research surveys. You can create, implement, and manage surveys using only a Web browser. There is nothing to download or install. Perseus question logic capabilities such as branching, linking, and piping make creating simple or complex questionnaires easy. You can even set quotas for your surveys to reach your target demographics. *In short, you can make Internet marketing research come alive for your students!*

GREAT RESOURCES TO MEET YOUR TEACHING NEEDS

Instructor's Manual

The Instructor's Manual for this edition has been designed to facilitate convenient lesson planning. Each chapter includes the following:

- ☐ *Suggested Lesson Plans.* Suggestions are given on dividing up the chapter material, based on the frequency and duration of your class period.

- ☐ *Chapter Scan.* A quick synopsis highlights the core material in each chapter.

- ☐ *Learning Objectives.* The list of learning objectives found in the text is repeated here.

- ☐ *General Chapter Outline.* The main headers provide a quick snapshot of all the content areas within the chapter.

- ☐ *List of Key Terms.* The key terms introduced to the students in the text are repeated here.

- ☐ *Detailed Chapter Outline.* This outline fleshes out the general outline given previously. It also indicates where ancillary materials fit into the discussion: PowerPoint slides, exhibits from the text, learning objectives, and review questions. Opening vignettes and boxed features are also included in this outline.

- ☐ *Summary Explaining Learning Objectives.* An explanation of how the learning objectives are satisfied by chapter material is the basis of the IM summary.

- ☐ *Answers to Pedagogy.* Suggested answers and approaches to the critical thinking questions, the Internet activities, the cases, the cross-functional questions, and the ethical dilemmas are offered at the end of each chapter or part.

    Instructors can access the electronic files on the Instructor Companion Site at www.wiley.com/college/mcdaniel.

PowerPoint Slides

For this edition, we have created a comprehensive, fully interactive PowerPoint presentation with roughly 400 slides in the package. You can tailor your visual presentation to include the material you choose to cover in class. This PowerPoint presentation gives you the ability to completely integrate your classroom lecture with a powerful visual statement of chapter material. Keep students engaged and stimulate classroom discussion! The entire collection of slides will be available for download from our Web site at www.wiley.com/college/mcdaniel.

Comprehensive Test Bank

Our test bank is comprehensive and thoroughly classroom-tested. The questions range from definitions of key terms, to basic problem-solving questions, to creative-thinking problems. This new and improved test bank includes approximately 60 questions per chapter consisting of multiple choice, true/false, and essay questions. Regardless of the type and level of knowledge you wish to test, we have the right questions for your students. A computerized version of this newly created test bank is also available on the book's companion Web site so that you can customize your quizzes and exams. Instructors can access the electronic files on the Instructor Companion Site at www.wiley.com/college/mcdaniel.

Personal Response System (PRS)

Our personal response system questions for each chapter of this textbook are designed to spark discussion and debate in the Marketing Research classroom. For more information on PRS, please contact your local Wiley representative.

New! Focus Group Video and Lecture Launches

Additional *Real Research* is offered through a new focus group video conducted by another one of our research partners, Jerry Thomas, President of Decision Analyst (www.decision analyst.com). Decision Analyst, Incorporated is a large international marketing research firm. The focus group subject is online dating and ties in with the new online dating data case. We also offer several interviews featuring Jerry Thomas and your author, Carl McDaniel, discussing key topics in marketing research. For more information on this 45-minute video, available on DVD, please contact your local Wiley representative.

Acknowledgments

This book could not have been written and published without the generous expert assistance of many people. First, we would like to thank Joshua Been for his excellent assistance in preparing the material on geographic information systems (GIS). Jerry Thomas for providing the focus group research. Elizabeth Anderson, Tammy Austin, Sarah Beck, Emily Beck, Michelle Dodd, Mike Foytik, Richard Kagel, Paul Schmiege, Suzanne Simpson, Suzanne Wagner, Krista White, and Doug Zook at DSS Research for their contributions to the "From the Front Line" boxes. We must also thank Joe Cangelosi of the University of Central Arkansas for preparing the Web Quizzes and SPSS exercises, Aron Levin of Northern Kentucky University for preparing the Test Bank, Carolyn Predmore of Manhattan University for preparing the PRS questions, David Ashley of Johns Hopkins University for the Interactive Power Points, and Barbara Oates and Craig Hollingshead both of Texas A&M University-Kingsville for preparing the Instructor's Resource Guide.

Our deepest gratitude goes to the team at John Wiley and Sons for continuing the trend of excellence established by this text. Special thanks to Jayme Heffler, Jennifer Conklin, and Ame Esterline, and to Ellinor Wagner for the photo research, and Sarah Wolfman-Robichaud, our production editor.

Finally, we'd like to thank the following reviewers for their valuable comments throughout the revision process:

Paul Boughton, Saint Louis University
Haim Mano, University of Missouri, St. Louis
Carolyn E. Predmore, Manhattan College
Louis A. Tucci, The College of New Jersey
Michael Tsiros, University of Miami
Robert Watson, Quinnipiac University

Marketing Research

Seventh Edition

THE ROLE OF MARKETING RESEARCH IN MANAGEMENT DECISION MAKING

LEARNING OBJECTIVES

1. To review the marketing concept and the marketing mix.

2. To comprehend the marketing environment within which managers must make decisions.

3. To define marketing research.

4. To understand the importance of marketing research in shaping marketing decisions.

5. To learn when marketing research should and should not be conducted.

6. To learn how the Internet is changing marketing research.

7. To understand the history of marketing research.

A great opportunity exists for automakers to target Generation Y. With the number of 16- to 25-year-olds projected to jump from 37.9 million to 42.7 million by 2010, competition for Generation Y's business will be fierce. Generation Y includes people born between the years 1977 and 1994.

Synovate Motoresearch Inc. conducted a Generation Y automotive study using an Internet research methodology. The study focused on five areas: general preferences, buyer behavior, purchase influences, brand awareness, and future vehicle considerations and aspirations.

The survey began with some general questions regarding music, television, and activities. Pop, rap, and hard rock were the most listened-to music genres with Generation Y. Among the activities participated in, watching TV, surfing the Internet, and watching videos were mentioned most. The Internet is a very large part of Generation Y's everyday life.

When asked about favorite automotive Web sites, Kelly Blue Book, Autotrader, manufacturers' Web sites, *Consumer Reports*, and *Car and Driver* were found to be most popular. Each respondent was asked what he or she owned/drove the most. Interestingly, four out of the top five models indicated were domestic brands. However, the top vehicle owned/driven was the Honda Accord.

Automakers often wonder if it is worth spending huge amounts of money sponsoring certain sporting/musical events and whether it actually affects Generation Y's automotive purchase decisions. Overall, community involvement, motor sports, sports, and concert sponsorships exhibit little influence over this group's purchase decisions.

Factors that do have influence include test drives, recommendations from family members, visiting dealerships, and *Consumer Guide*. Recommendations from friends were also very important. Peer pressure also plays an important role in Generation Y's purchase decisions.[1] ■

Understanding Generation Y will help auto manufacturers reach their sales goals. But what exactly is marketing research? And how important is it to shaping marketing decisions? How has the Internet affected marketing research? When should marketing research be conducted? These are some of the questions we will address in Chapter 1.

Nature of Marketing

> **marketing**
> The process of planning and executing the conception, pricing, promotion, and distribution of ideas, goods, and services to create exchanges that satisfy individual and organizational objectives.

> **marketing concept**
> A business philosophy based on consumer orientation, goal orientation, and systems orientation.

> **consumer orientation**
> The identification of and focus on the people or firms most likely to buy a product and the production of a good or service that will meet their needs most effectively.

> **goal orientation**
> A focus on the accomplishment of corporate goals; a limit set on consumer orientation.

> **systems orientation**
> The creation of systems to monitor the external environment and deliver the desired marketing mix to the target market.

> **marketing mix**
> The unique blend of product/service, pricing, promotion, and distribution strategies designed to meet the needs of a specific target market.

Marketing is an organizational function and a set of processes for creating, communicating, and delivering value to customers and for managing customer relationships in ways that benefit the organization and its stakeholders.[2] Good customer relationships often result in exchanges; that is, a good or service is exchanged for money. The potential for exchange exists when there are at least two parties and each has something of potential value to the other. When the two parties can communicate and deliver the desired goods or services, exchange can take place. How do marketing managers attempt to stimulate exchange? They follow the "right" principle. They attempt to get the right goods or services to the right people at the right place at the right time at the right price, using the right promotion techniques. The "right" principle describes how marketing managers control the many factors that ultimately determine marketing success. To make the "right" decisions, management must have timely decision-making information. Marketing research is a primary channel for providing that information.

The Marketing Concept

To efficiently accomplish their goals, firms today have adopted the **marketing concept**, which requires (1) a consumer orientation, (2) a goal orientation, and (3) a systems orientation. A **consumer orientation** means that firms strive to identify the people (or firms) most likely to buy their product (the target market) and to produce a good or offer a service that will meet the needs of target customers most effectively in the face of competition. The second tenet of the marketing concept is **goal orientation**; that is, a firm must be consumer-oriented only to the extent that it also accomplishes corporate goals. The goals of profit-making firms usually center on financial criteria, such as a 15 percent return on investment.

The third component of the marketing concept is a **systems orientation**. A system is an organized whole—or a group of diverse units that form an integrated whole—functioning or operating in unison. It is one thing for a firm to say it is consumer-oriented and another actually to *be* consumer-oriented. First, systems must be established to find out what consumers want and to identify market opportunities. As you will see later, identifying target market needs and finding market opportunities are the tasks of marketing research. Next, this information must be fed back to the firm. Without feedback from the marketplace, a firm is not truly consumer-oriented.

Opportunistic Nature of Marketing Research

Marriott's marketing research uncovered an opportunity to create a hotel chain that would serve business travelers, offering homey surroundings at moderate prices. That is, Marriott used marketing research to identify marketing opportunities. The Courtyard concept was aimed at a new target market for Marriott.

After the target market was identified, a marketing mix had to be created. A **marketing mix** is the unique blend of product/service, pricing, promotion, and distribution strategies designed to reach a specific target market. Marriott spent 2 years creating the marketing mix for Courtyard. Research identified the best sites for courtyard units (distribution), prices to be charged in various markets, how to position the product in the marketplace, and what features to promote. Marriott also used research to determine the size of the rooms and the features and amenities most desired by business travelers (product/service offering). Marketing research identified an opportunity, which then enabled Marriott to further use research to create a very successful addition to its product line: Courtyard by Marriott.

External Marketing Environment

Over time, the marketing mix must be altered because of changes in the environment in which consumers and businesses exist, work, compete, and make purchasing decisions. Some new consumers and businesses will become part of the target market, while others will drop out of the market; those who remain may have different tastes, needs, incomes, lifestyles, and purchase habits than the original target consumers.

Although managers can control the marketing mix, they cannot control elements in the external environment that continually mold and reshape the target market. Unless management understands the external environment, the firm cannot intelligently plan its future, and organizations are often unaware of the forces that influence their future. American auto manufacturers clearly didn't understand the demand for hybrid vehicles. In 2005, Japanese companies had captured 96 percent of the hybrid sales in the United States.[3]

Marketing research is a key means for understanding the environment. Knowledge of the environment helps a firm not only to alter its present marketing mix, but also to identify new opportunities. For example, when Ann Arbor, Michigan-based Domino's Pizza introduced its pizza delivery in Japan, a major change in Japanese consumers' behavior was needed as well. Yet Domino's managed to rise to the challenge successfully. If Domino's had merely tested the acceptability of the service it delivered in other parts of the world, it never would have entered Japan. Japanese consumers typically don't eat tomato-based food, and Asians tend to have allergies to milk products. Home delivery was not widely accepted, housewives were reluctant to give up cooking, houses were small, and finding customers in the labyrinthine streets of Tokyo seemed impossible. A market for pizza didn't exist, nor did any sign of hope in creating one.

Instead of trying to sell its existing product and service to the market, Domino's used its marketing research about customers to design a new product and service offering for Japan. It introduced toppings such as fish and sushi. To sustain its 30-minute delivery, Domino's developed a complex address database and small scooters to navigate the narrow streets in Tokyo. Through this research process this pizza-delivery service that no one asked for became a big hit in Japan.[4]

Let's Meet Some New Market Researchers

From time-to-time we are going to introduce you to an exciting group of people that have recently begun a career in marketing research. We decided to use employees of DSS Research, a very large marketing research firm owned by one of your co-authors. They will be introducing you to various aspects of marketing research from a new researcher's perspective. These managers are in the trenches every day and can tell you what works and what doesn't. We begin our series with Sarah Beck discussing, "Courses I Wish I Had Taken in College Before I Became a Marketing Researcher." We hope that you enjoy these "From the Front Line" tidbits! And, just for fun, we added a "Front Line" box from your author who is also "on the front line of marketing research" every day!

FROM THE FRONT LINE

Courses I Wish I Had Taken in College Before Becoming a Marketing Researcher, and Why.

Sarah Beck, Project Manager, DSS Research

I'm confident that my undergraduate and graduate-level coursework prepared me well for my current position as a project manager at a full-service research firm. Classes in marketing and consumer behavior helped me understand the basic principles of marketing and laid the foundation for my career in marketing research. However, there are a few courses I wish I had taken that now I believe would have strengthened my abilities as a marketing researcher.

As an undergraduate, I had the opportunity to take a course in business statistics, but I didn't. I regret not having pursued this advanced coursework in statistical analysis. At the time, I wasn't aware of the important role that statistics plays in marketing research. Although this topic is generally feared by students and may not be the most exciting course available, it is relevant to a marketing researcher. Whether you become the analyst who will answer clients' research questions or the project manager who will review the analysis that will be presented to clients, it's important to understand statistics.

As a graduate student in a master of marketing research program, I had the opportunity to take specialized courses in a variety of different areas, such as new product development, qualitative research, and multivariate data analysis. However, one course that I now believe would have helped better prepare me for a research career is project management. As a project manager, you're responsible for the success of a project from its inception to the final delivery of results. A number of people in a variety of departments, such as programming, data processing, and reporting, are directly involved in the success of a project. It's vital that a project manager possess the strong time management and communication skills necessary to keep the research on schedule and the client well informed. A course in project management, covering the life of a project from questionnaire and sampling design to reporting, prepares you to handle challenging, real-life situations with success as you begin your marketing research career.

Marketing Research and Decision Making

Marketing research plays two key roles in the marketing system. First, as part of the marketing intelligence feedback process, marketing research provides decision makers with data on the effectiveness of the current marketing mix and offers insights into necessary changes. Second, marketing research is the primary tool for exploring new opportunities in the marketplace. Segmentation research and new product research help identify the most lucrative opportunities for a firm.

Marketing Research Defined

Now that you have an understanding of how marketing research fits into the overall marketing system, we can proceed with a formal definition of the term, as stated by the American Marketing Association:

The systematic gathering, recording, and analyzing of data with respect to a particular market, where market refers to a specific customer group in a specific geographic area.[5]

We prefer another definition: **Marketing research** is the planning, collection, and analysis of data relevant to marketing decision making and the communication of the results of this analysis to management.

Importance of Marketing Research to Management

Marketing research can be viewed as playing three functional roles: descriptive, diagnostic, and predictive. Its **descriptive function** includes gathering and presenting statements of fact. What is the historic sales trend in the industry? What are consumers' attitudes and beliefs toward a product? Duracell, the "Copper Top" battery, found through marketing research that consumers had the misconception that cheaper "heavy duty" zinc batteries offer better performance than alkaline. Duracell launched a major advertising campaign to correct consumers' beliefs. The ads mention rivals Rayovac and Eveready by name. "Rayovac calls them 'heavy duty.' Rayovac calls them 'super heavy duty,'" says a narrator as animation shows the labels being slapped on the batteries. "But when it comes to performance, any heavy duty zinc is a lightweight." The ad goes on to say that Duracell provides up to four times the battery life of the others. Another ad poses the question: "If they really are so heavy duty, why are they so cheap?"[6]

The second role of research is the **diagnostic function**, wherein data and/or actions are explained. For example, what was the impact on sales when the package design was changed? How can product/service offerings be altered to better serve customers and potential customers? Since kids eat over 5 billion ounces of ketchup each year, Heinz decided that the heavy users (kids) should have a lot to say (via marketing research) about how to make ketchup fun. Heinz listened and watched children using ketchup, which resulted in a new bottle design, name selection, and color. The true ketchup connoisseurs helped create Heinz EZ Squirt green ketchup![7]

The final role of research is the **predictive function**. How can the firm best take advantage of opportunities as they arise in the ever-changing marketplace? Kraft Foods noticed in 2003 that consumers were flocking to "low-carb" diets. The company used marketing research to determine if this was a fad or long-term trend. Determining that "low carb" was more than a fad, it entered into an alliance with Arthur Agatston, the creator of *The South Beach Diet*. The result, in 2004, was certain Kraft products being labeled "South Beach Diet Recommended." Further marketing research led to a broad new line of products, in 2005, entitled "The South Beach Diet" brand. Products include cereal, meal replacement and cereal bars, refrigerated sandwich wraps, frozen entrees, and frozen pizza.[8]

The Unrelenting Drive for Quality and Customer Satisfaction

Quality and customer satisfaction have become the key competitive weapons of the decade. Few organizations can prosper in today's environment without a focus on quality, continual improvement, and customer satisfaction. Corporations across the globe have implemented quality improvement and satisfaction programs in an effort to reduce costs, retain customers, increase market share, and, last but not least, improve the bottom line.

When the concept of total quality management swept through corporate America in the 1990s, the emphasis was strictly on product improvement. But product improvement alone wasn't the answer. Since its founding in 1925, Correct Craft Inc. has focused on one thing—building the absolutely best boats in the industry. This means being a leader in boating technology as well. Gone are the days when skiers and riders can blame their wipeouts on the driver's inability to maintain the correct boat speed. Correct Craft has made maintaining your desired constant speed as easy to achieve as using the cruise control in your car. The PerfectPass Digital Pro Systems use incredibly sophisticated

> **marketing research**
> The planning, collection, and analysis of data relevant to marketing decision making and the communication of the results of this analysis to management.

> **descriptive function**
> The gathering and presentation of statements of fact.

> **diagnostic function**
> The explanation of data or actions.

> **predictive function**
> Specification of how to use descriptive and diagnostic research to predict the results of a planned marketing decision.

speed control technology that can calculate and maintain ideal speed based on the athlete's weight and strength.

Correct Craft's Ski Nautique 196 is the number one choice of professional water skiers worldwide, as well as exclusive Official Towboat for all IWSF World Water Ski Championships to be held between 2006 and 2010. Despite unsurpassed quality, Correct Craft knows that customer service and satisfaction is a key part of the equation. The company has earned a 98.1 percent outstanding customer service award among its dealers worldwide.[9] Achieving such accolades is not by accident. Marketing research plays a key role in understanding the desires of skiers and wakeboarders and in assuring that service is topnotch.

Quality that means little to customers usually doesn't produce a payoff in improved sales, profits, or market share; it represents wasted effort and expense. Today, the new mantra is **return on quality**, which means that (1) the quality being delivered is the quality desired by the target market and (2) the added quality must have a positive impact on profitability. For example, banking giant NationsBank Corporation measures every improvement in service quality, from adding more tellers to offering new mortgage products, in terms of added profitability.

> **return on quality**
> Management objective based on the principles that (1) the quality being delivered is at a level desired by the target market and (2) that level of quality must have a positive impact on profitability.

Paramount Importance of Keeping Existing Customers   An inextricable link exists between customer satisfaction and customer loyalty. Long-term relationships don't just happen; they are grounded in the delivery of service and value. Customer retention pays big dividends for firms. Powered by repeat sales and referrals, revenues and market share grow. Costs fall because firms spend less funds and energy attempting to replace defectors. Steady customers are easy to serve because they understand the modus operandi and make fewer demands on employees' time. A firm's ability to retain customers also drives job satisfaction and pride, which leads to higher employee retention. In turn, long-term employees acquire additional knowledge that increases productivity. A Bain & Company study estimates that a 5 percent decrease in the customer defection rate can boost profits by 25 to 95 percent.[10] Another study found that the customer retention rate has a major impact on the value of the firm.[11]

The ability to retain customers is based on an intimate understanding of their needs. This knowledge comes primarily from marketing research. For example, British Airways recast its first-class transatlantic service based on detailed marketing research. Most airlines stress top-of-the-line service in their transatlantic first-class cabins. However, British Air research found that most first-class passengers simply want to sleep. British Air now gives premium flyers the option of dinner on the ground, before take-off, in the first-class lounge. Then, once on board, they can slip into British Air pajamas, put their heads on real pillows, slip under blankets, and enjoy an interruption-free flight. On arrival at their destination, first-class passengers can have breakfast, use comfortable dressing rooms and showers, and even have their clothes pressed before they set off. These changes in British Air's first-class service were driven strictly by marketing research.

Understanding the Ever-Changing Marketplace   Marketing research also helps managers to understand trends in the marketplace and to take advantage of opportunities. Marketing research has been practiced for as long as marketing has existed. The early Phoenicians carried out market demand studies as they traded in the various ports on the Mediterranean Sea. Marco Polo's diary indicates he was performing a marketing research function as he traveled to China. There is evidence that the Spanish systematically conducted marketing surveys as they explored the New World, and examples exist of marketing research conducted during the Renaissance.

Today, Internet marketing research can help companies to quickly and efficiently understand what is happening in the marketplace. Internet research told AvantGo

Mobile Inc., a mobile Internet Service, that 40 percent of its users also were American Airlines frequent fliers. Armed with that information, AvantGo pitched advertising on its PDA service to the airline. Now, AvantGo offers an American Airlines channel, including flight lookup, weekly Netsaver fares, promotions, special offers, contact numbers, and the locations of airport lounges.

California-based computer accessory maker Iogear uses a sample from its opt-in panel created on its Web site (*www. Iogear.com*) to find out what its customers want. The company surveyed users to find out whether they preferred to buy a mouse for a notebook computer rather than use a touchpad. Of 9,400 users, 500 responded, and 72 percent said they preferred a mouse. That information was included in a press release, introducing three new mini-mice, that was sent to members of the technical media.[12]

The necessity of understanding the marketplace is not restricted to the United States or other industrialized markets. It is important for managers all over the world to understand the ever-changing marketplace and their customers. The Global Research below feature illustrates this point.

Proactive Role of Marketing Research

Understanding the nature of the marketing system is a necessity for a successful marketing orientation. By having a thorough knowledge of factors that have an impact on the target market and the marketing mix, management can be proactive rather than reactive. Proactive management alters the marketing mix to fit newly emerging patterns in economic, social, and competitive environments, whereas reactive management waits for change to have a major impact on the firm before deciding to take action. It is the difference between viewing the turbulent marketing environment as a threat (a reactive stance) and as an opportunity (a proactive stance). Companies like UPS, Dell, and FedEx were largely proactive in Internet marketing and customer service. A proactive position would have been to become cutting-edge Internet marketers. Marketing research plays a key role in proactive management by allowing managers to anticipate changes in the market and customer desires and then design goods and services to meet those changes and needs.

A proactive manager not only examines emerging markets but also seeks, through strategic planning, to develop a long-run **marketing strategy** for the firm. A marketing strategy guides the long-term use of the firm's resources based on the firm's existing and projected internal capabilities and on projected changes in the external environment. A good strategic plan is based on good marketing research. It helps the firm meet long-term profit and market share goals.

Asking the right questions in marketing research can be as important as getting good answers. UPS found that customers wanted more interaction with their UPS driver. Go to http://www.ups.com to find out how UPS uses marketing research to better serve its customers.

marketing strategy
A plan to guide the long-term use of a firm's resources based on its existing and projected internal capabilities and on projected changes in the external environment.

Applied Research versus Basic Research

Virtually all marketing research is conducted to better understand the market, to find out why a strategy failed, or to reduce uncertainty in management decision making. All research conducted for these purposes is called **applied research**. For example, should the price of DiGiorno frozen pizza be raised 40 cents? What name should Ford select for a new sedan? Which commercial has a higher level of recall: A or B? On the other hand,

GLOBAL RESEARCH

Sony Corporation has used marketing research to create a proactive strategy for its Aiwa division. Research has identified two different market segments for the Sony and Aiwa brands. Aiwa-brand products will be at lower price points and appeal to younger target customers. Among the products that will carry the Aiwa logo are ministereos and a lipstick-size digital camera. Again, based upon marketing research,

Sony will limit the functions of Aiwa products. Masaru Hirauchi, chief of Sony's business operations involving Aiwa-brand products, said, "We would like to make new Aiwa-brand products simple devices with a carefree image, as such products cannot be released under the brand of Sony, which has focused on making products featuring multiple functions and high performances."[13]

> **applied research**
> Research aimed at solving a specific, pragmatic problem—better understanding of the marketplace, determination of why a strategy or tactic failed, or reduction of uncertainty in management decision making.

> **basic, or pure, research**
> Research aimed at expanding the frontiers of knowledge rather than solving a specific, pragmatic problem.

basic, or **pure**, **research** attempts to expand the frontiers of knowledge; it is not aimed at a specific pragmatic problem. Basic research is conducted to validate an existing theory or learn more about a concept or phenomenon. For example, basic marketing research might test a hypothesis about high-involvement decision making or consumer information processing. In the long run, basic research helps us understand more about the world in which we live. The findings of basic research usually cannot be implemented by managers in the short run. Most basic marketing research is now conducted in universities; the findings are reported in such publications as *The Journal of Marketing Research* and *The Journal of Marketing*. In contrast, most research undertaken by businesses is applied research because it must be cost-effective and of demonstrable value to the decision maker.

Nature of Applied Research

Marketing research studies can be classified into three broad categories: programmatic, selective, and evaluative. **Programmatic research** is conducted to develop marketing options through market segmentation, market opportunity analysis, or consumer attitude and product usage studies. **Selective research** is used to test decision alternatives. Some examples are testing concepts for new products, advertising copy testing, and test marketing. **Evaluative research** is done to assess program performance; it includes tracking advertising recall, doing organizational image studies, and examining customer attitudes on a firm's quality of service.

Programmatic research arises from management's need to obtain a market overview periodically. For example, product management may be concerned that the existing market information base is inadequate or outdated for present decision making, or marketing plans may call for the introduction of new products, ad campaigns, or packaging. Whatever the specific situation, current information is needed to develop viable marketing options. Typical programmatic research questions include the following:

☐ Has its target market changed? How?

☐ Does the market exhibit any new segmentation opportunities?

"I don't *know* what I'm doing — this is pure research!"

☐ Do some segments appear to be more likely candidates than others for the firm's marketing efforts?

☐ What new product or service opportunities lie in the various segments?

Equidistant between Los Angeles and San Francisco in the Eastern Sierra Nevada Mountains, Mammoth Mountain has been serving the skiers and snowboarders of central California for 50 years. With the summit reaching above 11,000 feet and average annual snowfall hitting 400 inches, thousands of customers flock to the slopes and the lodges annually.

Yet, the resort's longstanding direct-mail program just wasn't driving the traffic. While the resort wasn't losing visitors (most resort traffic industrywide comes from existing skiers and snowboarders rather than those new to the sports), executives hoped to gain some ground in an overall stable market by injecting some life into what had become an out-of-date marketing campaign—and to increase the frequency of visits by the 900,000 customers in its database.

Resort executives used programmatic research collected from an annual survey, the National Skier and Snowboarder Opinion Survey conducted on behalf of resorts across the country, and found that 94 percent of Mammoth's users in particular acknowledge using the Internet to find information about everything from weather advisories to checking room rates at one of Mammoth's lodges.

This information led to the creation of an e-mail marketing system that reaches 18,000 subscribers. The format is chatty and informing. For example, "The weather has been beautiful here lately, and with a 12- to 14-foot base you can't go wrong anywhere on the mountain. At 1:15 P.M. the temperature is 34 degrees at Main Lodge with clear skies and moderate to gusty winds. It's extremely windy and cold on top at 17 degrees, so be sure to bundle up." Skier visit numbers have been increasing 5 percent or more annually as a result of the programmatic research![14]

Selective research typically is conducted after several viable options have been identified by programmatic research. If no one alternative is clearly superior, product management usually will wish to test several alternatives. However, selective research may be required at any stage of the marketing process, such as when advertising copy is being developed, various product formulations are being evaluated, or an entire marketing program is being assessed, as in test marketing.

The need for evaluative research arises when the effectiveness and efficiency of marketing programs must be evaluated. Evaluative research may be integrated into programmatic research when program changes or entirely new options are demanded because of present performance such as at mammoth Mountain.

Decision to Conduct Marketing Research

A manager who is faced with several alternative solutions to a particular problem should not instinctively call for applied marketing research. In fact, the first decision to be made is whether to conduct marketing research at all. In a number of situations, it is best not to conduct research.

☐ *Resources are lacking.* There are two situations in which a lack of resources should preclude marketing research. First, an organization may lack the funds to do the research properly. If a project calls for a sample of 800 respondents but the budget allows for only 50 interviews, the quality of the information would be highly suspect. Second, funds may be available to do the research properly but insufficient to implement any decisions resulting from the research. Small organizations in particular sometimes lack the resources to create an effective marketing mix. In one case, for example, the

---

▷ **programmatic research**
Research conducted to develop marketing options through market segmentation, market opportunity analyses, or consumer attitude and product usage studies.

▷ **selective research**
Research used to test decision alternatives.

▷ **evaluative research**
Research done to assess program performance.

director of a performing arts guild was in complete agreement with the recommendations that resulted from a marketing research project. However, 2 years after the project was completed, nothing had been done because the money was not available.

☐ *Research results would not be useful.* Some types of marketing research studies measure lifestyle and personality factors of steady and potential customers. Assume that a study finds that introverted men with a poor self-concept, yet a high need for achievement, are most likely to patronize a discount brokerage service. The management of Charles Schwab discount brokerage service might be hard-pressed to use this information.

☐ *The opportunity has passed.* Marketing research should not be undertaken if the opportunity for successful entry into a market has already passed. If the product is in the late maturity or decline stage of the product life cycle (such as cassette recorders or black-and-white television sets), it would be foolish to do research on new product entry. The same may be true for markets rapidly approaching saturation, such as super-premium ice cream (Häagen-Dazs, Ben and Jerry's). For products already in the market, however, research is needed to modify the products as consumer tastes, competition, and other factors change.

☐ *The decision already has been made.* In the real world of management decision making and company politics, marketing research has sometimes been used improperly. Several years ago, a large marketing research study was conducted for a bank with over $800 million in deposits. The purpose of the research project was to guide top management in mapping a strategic direction for the bank during the next 5 years. After reading the research report, the president said, "I fully agree with your recommendations because that was what I was going to do anyway! I'm going to use your study tomorrow when I present my strategic plan to the board of directors." The researcher then asked, "What if my recommendations had been counter to your decision?" The bank president laughed and said, "They would have never known that I had conducted a marketing research study!" Not only was the project a waste of money, but it also raised a number of ethical questions in the researcher's mind.

The super-premium ice cream market is reaching saturation. At this point, it might not be wise to enter this market. However, marketing research is necessary to keep products already in the market ahead of the competition.

☐ *Managers cannot agree on what they need to know to make a decision.* Although it may seem obvious that research should not be undertaken until objectives are specified, it sometimes happens. Preliminary or exploratory studies are commonly done to better understand the nature of the problem, but a large, major research project should not be. It is faulty logic to say "Well, let's just go ahead and do the study and then we will better understand the problem and know what steps to take." The wrong phenomena might be studied or key elements needed for management decision making may not be included.

☐ *Decision-making information already exists.* Some companies have been conducting research in certain markets for many years. They understand the characteristics of their target customers and what they like and dislike about existing products. Under these circumstances, further research would be redundant and a waste of money. Procter & Gamble, for example, has extensive knowledge of the coffee market. After it conducted initial taste tests, P&G went into national distribution with Folger's Instant Coffee without further research. The Sara Lee Corporation did the same thing with its frozen

EXHIBIT 1.1	Deciding Whether to Conduct Marketing Research	
Market Size	**Small Profit Margin**	**Large Profit Margin**
Small	Costs likely to be greater than benefits (e.g., eyeglass replacement screw, tire valve extension). DON'T CONDUCT MARKETING RESEARCH.	Benefits possibly greater than cost (e.g., ultra-expensive Lamborghini-type sportswear, larger specialized industrial equipment like computer-aided metal stamping machines). PERHAPS CONDUCT MARKETING RESEARCH. LEARN ALL YOU CAN FROM EXISTING INFORMATION PRIOR TO MAKING DECISION TO CONDUCT RESEARCH.
Large	Benefits likely to be greater than costs (e.g., Stouffers frozen entrees, Crest's teeth whitener strips). PERHAPS CONDUCT MARKETING RESEARCH. LEARN ALL YOU CAN FROM EXISTING INFORMATION PRIOR TO MAKING DECISION TO CONDUCT RESEARCH.	Benefits most likely to be greater than costs (e.g., medical equipment like CAT scanners, Toshiba's high-definition television). CONDUCT MARKETING RESEARCH.

croissants, as did Quaker Oats with Chewy Granola Bars. This tactic, however, does not always work. P&G thought it understood the pain reliever market thoroughly, so it bypassed marketing research for Encaprin, encapsulated aspirin. The product failed because it lacked a distinct competitive advantage over existing products and was withdrawn from the market.

☐ *The costs of conducting research outweigh the benefits.* There are rarely situations in which a manager has such tremendous confidence in her or his judgment that additional information relative to a pending decision would not be accepted if it were available and free. However, the manager might have sufficient confidence to be unwilling to pay very much for it or wait long to receive it. Willingness to acquire additional decision-making information depends on a manager's perception of its quality, price, and timing. The manager would be willing to pay more for perfect information (that is, data that leave no doubt as to which alternative to follow) than for information that leaves uncertainty as to what to do. Therefore, research should be undertaken only when the expected value of the information is greater than the cost of obtaining it.

Two important determinants of potential benefits are profit margins and market size. Generally speaking, new products with large profit margins are going to have greater potential benefit than products with smaller profit margins, assuming that both items have the same sales potential. Also, new product opportunities in large markets are going to offer greater potential benefits than those in smaller markets if competitive intensity is the same in both markets (see Exhibit 1.1).

Profound Impact of the Internet on Marketing Research

The Internet has turned the world of marketing research upside-down. Current methods of conducting some types of research soon may seem as quaint as a steam-engine train. New techniques and strategies for conducting traditional marketing research are appearing online in increasing numbers every day. In 2006, Internet marketing research will account for about 50 percent of all marketing research revenue in the United States.[15] Following are some growth drivers of such research:

☐ The Internet provides more rapid access to business intelligence and thus allows for better and faster decision making.

☐ The Internet improves a firm's ability to respond quickly to customer needs and market shifts.

☐ The Internet facilitates conducting follow-up studies and longitudinal research.

☐ The Internet slashes labor- and time-intensive research activities (and associated costs), including mailing, telephone solicitation, data entry, data tabulation, and reporting.

Internet surveys have several specific advantages:

☐ *Rapid development, real-time reporting.* Internet surveys can be broadcast to thousands of potential respondents simultaneously. The results can be tabulated and posted for corporate clients to view as the returns arrive. Thus, Internet survey results can be in a client's hands in significantly less time than traditional survey results.

☐ *Dramatically reduced costs.* The Internet can cut costs by 25 to 40 percent while providing results in half the time it takes to do a traditional telephone survey. Data-collection costs account for a large proportion of any traditional market research budget. Telephone surveys are labor-intensive efforts incurring training, telecommunications, and management costs. Using the Internet eliminates these costs completely. While costs for traditional survey techniques rise proportionally with the number of interviews desired, electronic solicitations can grow in volume with little increase in project costs.

☐ *Personalization.* Internet surveys can be highly personalized for greater relevance to each respondent's own situation, thus speeding the response process. Respondents enjoy answering only pertinent questions, being able to pause and resume the survey as their schedule allows, and having the ability to see previous responses and correct inconsistencies.

☐ *Higher response rates.* Busy respondents are growing increasingly intolerant of "snail mail" or telephone-based surveys. Internet surveys take half the time to complete than phone interviews do, can be accomplished at the respondent's convenience (after work hours), and are much more stimulating and engaging. Graphics, interactivity, links to incentive sites, and real-time summary reports make Internet surveys more enjoyable. The result: much higher response rates.

☐ *Ability to contact the hard-to-reach.* Certain of the most surveyed groups are also the most difficult to reach—doctors, high-income professionals, and top management in Global 2000 firms. Many of these groups are well represented online. Internet surveys provide convenient anytime/anywhere access that makes it easy for busy professionals to participate.

With the mushrooming number (currently over 75 percent) of Americans with Internet access, researchers are finding that online research and offline research yield the same results. America Online's (AOL) Digital Marketing Services (DMS), an online research organization, has done a number of surveys with both online and offline samples for clients such as IBM, Eastman Kodak, and Procter & Gamble. Side-by-side comparison of over 100 online and offline studies showed that both techniques led clients to the same business decisions.[16] That is, the guidance provided by both sets of data was the same.

Conducting surveys is not the sum total of the Internet revolution in marketing research. Management of the research process and dissemination of information also have been greatly enhanced by the Internet. Several key areas have been greatly affected by the Internet:

☐ *Libraries and various printed materials, which may be virtually replaced as sources of information.* On its Web site, the Bureau of Census (*http://www.census.gov*) indicates that it plans to gradually make the Internet the major means of distributing census data. The same is true for a number of other government agencies. Information from countless databases (both governmental and nongovernmental) can be called up almost instantaneously on the user's desktop, notebook, Blackberry, or even some cell phones!

☐ *The distribution of requests for proposals (RFPs) and the proposals themselves.* Companies can now quickly and efficiently send RFPs to a select e-mail list of research suppliers. In turn, the suppliers can develop proposals and e-mail them back to clients. A process that used to take days now occurs in a matter of hours.

☐ *Collaboration between the client and the research supplier in the management of a research project.* Both the researcher and the client might look at a proposal, RFP, report, or some type of statistical analysis at the same time on their computer screens while discussing it over the telephone. This is very effective and efficient, as changes in sample size, quotas, and other aspects of the research plan can be discussed and changes made immediately.

☐ *Data management and online analysis.* Clients can access their survey via the research supplier's secure Web site and monitor the data gathering in real time. The client can use sophisticated tools to actually carry out data analysis as the survey develops. This real-time analysis may result in changes in the questionnaire, sample size, or types of respondents interviewed. The research supplier and the client become partners in "just-in-time" marketing research.

☐ *Publishing and distribution of reports.* Reports can be published directly to the Web from such programs as PowerPoint and all the latest versions of leading word processing, spreadsheet, and presentation software packages. This means that results are available to appropriate managers worldwide on an almost instantaneous basis. Reports can be searched for content of specific interest, with the same Web browser used to view the report.

☐ *Oral presentations of marketing research surveys,* which now can be viewed by widely scattered audiences. Managers throughout the world can see and hear the actual client presentation on password-protected Web sites. This saves firms both time and money, as managers no longer need to travel to a central meeting site.

As we pointed out earlier, the Internet represents the present and the future of a significant portion of the world of marketing research. Its impact is limited only by the researcher's imagination.

Development of Marketing Research

The many benefits that accrue to management from using marketing research served as the initial impetus to begin conducting marketing research in the United States. In light of the competitive advantage a company can gain from engaging in marketing research, it is surprising that the industry did not move out of its embryonic stage until 1900.

Inception: Pre-1900

The first recorded marketing research survey was taken in July 1824 by the *Harrisburg Pennsylvanian.* It was an election poll in which Andrew Jackson received 335 votes; John Quincy Adams, 169; Henry Clay, 29; and William H. Crawford, 9. Later the same year, another newspaper, the *Raleigh Star,* canvassed political meetings held in North Carolina, "at which the sense of the people was taken." Perhaps the first marketing researcher was John Jacob Astor, who in the 1790s employed an artist to sketch the hats worn by fashionable New York women so that he could keep abreast of fashion trends.[17]

The first documented use of research to make informed marketing decisions was carried out by the advertising agency N. W. Ayer in 1879. That systematic effort was a simple survey of state and local officials to determine expected levels of grain production. The purpose of the research was to develop the scheduling of advertising for a producer of farm equipment. The second documented instance of marketing research appears to have been at E. I. duPont de Nemours & Company toward the end of the 19th century. It involved the systematic compilation of salespersons' reports on a variety of customer characteristics. The response to this second research effort was a harbinger of things to come. The salespersons who were responsible for obtaining and reporting the data were outraged because they didn't like the extra paperwork.

Academic researchers entered into marketing research about 1895, when Harlow Gale, a professor of psychology at the University of Minnesota, introduced the use of mail surveys to study advertising. He mailed 200 questionnaires and received 20 completed questionnaires, a 10 percent response rate. Gale's work was quickly followed by the pioneering work of Walter Dill Scott at Northwestern University. Scott introduced the use of experimentation and psychological measurement to the fledgling practice of advertising.

Early Growth: 1900–1920

It was not until after the turn of the century that consumer demand surged; the growth of mass production meant larger and more distant markets. No longer was America characterized by cottage industries where the craftsman-seller was in daily contact with the marketplace. The need arose to understand consumers' buying habits and attitudes toward manufacturers' wares. In response to this need, the first formal marketing research department was established by the Curtis Publishing Company in 1911. The research focused primarily on the automobile industry, as manufacturers had decided that everyone who had the money and inclination to buy a car had done so. The manufacturers were seeking a new group of consumers to which to target their promotions. A few years later, Daniel Starch pioneered recognition measures of advertising response, and E. K. Strong introduced recall measures and scaling to marketing research.

Adolescent Years: 1920–1950

Percival White developed the first application of scientific research to commercial problems. White's words express his realization of the need for systematic and continual marketing research:

Perhaps the greatest advantage of the company's having its own market analysis department is that the work then becomes a continuous process, or at least a process which is carried forward at periodic intervals, so that altered conditions in the market and in the industry at large are always kept in view. The necessity for regarding markets as constantly changing and not as fixed phenomena should not be lost sight of.[18]

White's book bore scant resemblance to this text. For example, the book avoided the use of statistics and mathematics, only briefly mentioning the U.S. Census.

The 1930s saw widespread use of survey research. A. C. Nielsen entered the research business in 1922. He expanded on White's earlier work by developing the "share of market" concept, plus many other services that became the foundation for one of America's largest marketing research organizations. It was not until the late 1930s that formal courses in marketing research became common on college campuses; a substantial body of knowledge developed within both the practice and academic communities. Two events—the spread of broadcast media and World War II—helped the fledgling discipline coalesce into a well-defined profession. Social scientists found that broadcast media created interesting new phenomena and increased the variability of human behavior.

By the end of the 1930s, simple examinations of respondents' replies were becoming categorized and compared across groups classified by differences in income, gender, or family status. Simple correlation analysis came into use but was not widespread; those who would use it had to be able to go directly to the statistical sources for such techniques, using texts by some of the pioneers in the field at this time, including G. Udney Yule, Mordecai Ezekiel, and Horace Sechrist.

The requirements of World War II pressed social scientists into service on a number of fronts. Tools and methods that had been novelties before the war were adopted and adapted to study the consumer behavior of soldiers and of their families on the home front. Among those tools were experimental design, opinion polling, human factors research, and operations research techniques.

In the 1940s, focus groups developed under the leadership of Robert Merton. During the late 1940s, the importance of random selection in sampling became widely recognized, and major advances were made in sampling techniques and polling procedures. A small number of psychologists who had been assigned to work in the Army Quartermaster Corps found their way into industry, where they introduced techniques for consumer tests of products.[19]

Mature Years: 1950–Present

The change from a seller's market to a buyer's market (resulting from post–World War II pent-up demand) necessitated better marketing intelligence. No longer could producers sell all of anything they made. The rising costs of production "tooling up," advertising, inventories, and other factors made the price of failure much higher than it had been in the past. Now, marketing research first determines what the market wants and then goods are crafted to meet those needs.

The mid-1950s brought the concept of market segmentation, based largely on easily identifiable demographic characteristics of customers. The same period gave rise to motivation research, with its emphasis on why consumers behave as they do. The underlying concepts of segmentation and motivation analysis, combined with the power of survey techniques, led to such innovations as psychographics and benefit segmentation. In the 1960s, mathematical models were developed for description and prediction—stochastic models, Markovian models, linear learning models. Even more significant was the development of the computer during the early 1960s, greatly enhancing the researcher's ability to quickly analyze, store, and retrieve large amounts of data. Today, of course, we have the impact of the Internet, which was discussed above.

Bill Neal, founder of SDR Consulting, discusses what's good about marketing research in the "Practicing Marketing Research" box that follows.

PRACTICING MARKETING RESEARCH

What Is Good about Marketing Research Today

William D. Neal is founder and senior executive officer of SDR Consulting in Atlanta. Bill talks about what he believes is good about marketing research today.

Looking back over the last 40 years, marketing research on the whole has contributed significantly to business success. Investments in marketing research have continued to increase far above the rate of inflation, and operational marketing managers depend more on marketing research to reduce the risks in undertaking new marketing initiatives.

Voice of the customer. More than ever, businesses and other institutions are measuring and monitoring customer satisfaction and loyalty on a continuous basis, using that information to improve processes and stem defections. Fifteen years ago, very little customer satisfaction and loyalty tracking research was supported or funded at all. Now, most major firms and many smaller firms track their customer's levels of satisfaction. And a smaller number are tracking customers' attitudinal and/or behavioral loyalty. Clearly, both the organization and the customer benefit from this revived focus on customer care.

Management metrics. Slowly, but surely, marketing research is beginning to provide some of the key metrics to senior management. Long the exclusive territory of the purveyors of financial numbers, management metrics are beginning to include marketing components—brand health measures, changes in brand equity, ad-

vertising and promotional effectiveness measures, indices of customer satisfaction, and several other measures of marketing impact.

New products. Research has often been blamed for the historically abysmal rate of new product failures. However, some of the more recent investigations into new product failures tend to exonerate at least some of the research. More often, the failures occur because (1) there were inadequate investments in research, (2) the research was ignored, (3) what was researched was not what was launched, (4) there was inadequate marketing and promotional support, or (5) there was inadequate sales or fulfillment support. We have several new tools for testing new products, from concept to prelaunch. When used properly, these newer tools greatly reduce the risks inherent in a new product launch and accurately predict trial and repurchase rates under different levels of marketing support.

Branding. After the branding debacles of the early 1990s, many firms began to recognize that their greatest asset is their brands. Unlike any other aspect of the marketing mix, brands represent a component of value that can't be replicated by a competitor. Thus it represents a unique, defensible asset for the owner and a launch pad for new product development and deployment. Unfortunately, branding has long been resistant to the imposition of scientific investigation, relying too much on the creative arts of advertising and promotion. But that is changing. There are now several research-based models for measuring brand value and brand equity and uncovering their key drivers. Quantifiable changes in brand equity represent the ultimate measure of return on marketing investment.[20]

SUMMARY

Marketing is an organizational function and a set of processes for creating, communicating, and delivering value to customers and for managing customer relationships in ways that benefit the organization and its stockholders. Marketing managers attempt to get the right goods or services to the right people at the right place at the right time at the right price, using the right promotion technique. This may be accomplished by following the marketing concept, which is based on consumer orientation, goal orientation, and systems orientation.

The marketing manager must work within an internal environment of the organization and understand the external environment over which he or she has little, if any, control. The primary variables over which the marketing manager has control are distribution, price, promotion, and product/service decisions. The unique combination of these four variables is called the *marketing mix.*

Marketing research plays a key part in providing the information for managers to shape the marketing mix. Marketing research has grown in importance because of management's focus on customer satisfaction and retention. It also is a key tool in proactive management. Marketing research should be undertaken only when the perceived benefits are greater than the costs.

A marketing research study can be described as programmatic, selective, or evaluative. Programmatic research is done to develop marketing options through market segmentation, market opportunity analysis, or consumer attitude and product usage studies. Selective research is used to test decisional alternatives. Evaluative research is done to assess program performance.

The Internet has had a major impact on the marketing research industry. The use of Internet surveys has increased dramatically because they can be quickly deployed, cost significantly less, are readily personalized, have high response rates, and provide the ability to contact the hard-to-reach respondent. Most importantly, as Internet participation by households has increased, identical online and offline surveys have been shown to produce the same business decisions.

Marketing research has also found other uses for the Internet. It serves as a major information source, aids in the distribution of RFPs and proposals, facilitates collaboration between the client and the research supplier in the management of a research project, provides data management and online analysis, and allows for the publication and distribution of reports and the viewing of oral presentations by a widely scattered audience. The Internet represents the present and the future of marketing research.

Marketing research in the United States traces its roots back to 1824, when the first public poll was taken. Its early growth period, from 1900 to 1920, was characterized by the establishment of the first formal marketing research department. Its adolescent years, from 1920 until 1950, saw the widespread use of marketing research. The maturing of marketing research began in 1950 and continues today, with growth in use of the Internet and in the number and sophistication of both quantitative and qualitative marketing research techniques.

KEY TERMS & DEFINITIONS

marketing An organizational function and a set of processes for creating, communicating, and delivering value to customers and for managing customer relationships in ways that benefit the organization and its shareholders.

marketing concept A business philosophy based on consumer orientation, goal orientation, and systems orientation.

consumer orientation The identification of and focus on the people or firms most likely to buy a product and the production of a good or service that will meet their needs most effectively.

goal orientation A focus on the accomplishment of corporate goals; a limit set on consumer orientation.

systems orientation The creation of systems to monitor the external environment and deliver the desired marketing mix to the target market.

marketing mix The unique blend of product/service, pricing, promotion, and distribution strategies designed to meet the needs of a specific target market.

marketing research The planning, collection, and analysis of data relevant to marketing decision making and the communication of the results of this analysis to management.

descriptive function The gathering and presentation of statements of fact.

diagnostic function The explanation of data or actions.

predictive function Specification of how to use descriptive and diagnostic research to predict the results of a planned marketing decision.

return on quality Management objective based on the principles that (1) the quality being delivered is at a level desired by the target market and (2) that level of quality must have a positive impact on profitability.

marketing strategy A plan to guide the long-term use of a firm's resources based on its existing and projected internal capabilities and on projected changes in the external environment.

applied research Research aimed at solving a specific, pragmatic problem—better understanding of the marketplace, determination of why a strategy or tactic failed, or reduction of uncertainty in management decision making.

basic, or pure, research Research aimed at expanding the frontiers of knowledge rather than solving a specific, pragmatic problem.

programmatic research Research conducted to develop marketing options through market segmentation, market opportunity analyses, or consumer attitude and product usage studies.

selective research Research used to test decision alternatives.

evaluative research Research done to assess program performance.

QUESTIONS FOR REVIEW & CRITICAL THINKING

1. The role of marketing is to create exchanges. What role might marketing research play in facilitating the exchange process?

2. Marketing research traditionally has been associated with manufacturers of consumer goods. Today, an increasing number of organizations, both profit and nonprofit, are using marketing research. Why do you think this trend exists? Give some examples.

3. Explain the relationship between marketing research and the marketing concept.

4. Comment on the following statement by the owner of a restaurant in a downtown area: "I see customers every day whom I know on a first-name basis. I understand their likes and dislikes. If I put something on the menu and it doesn't sell, I know that they didn't like it. I also read the magazine *Modern Restaurants* to keep up with industry trends. This is all the marketing research I need to do."

5. Why is marketing research important to marketing executives? Give several reasons.

6. What differences might you note among marketing research conducted for (a) a retailer, (b) a consumer goods manufacturer, (c) an industrial goods manufacturer, and (d) a charitable organization?

7. Comment on the following: Ralph Moran is planning to invest $1.5 million in a new restaurant in Saint Louis. When he applied for a construction financing loan, the bank officer asked whether he had conducted any research. Ralph replied, "I checked on research, and a marketing research company wanted $20,000 to do the work. I decided that with all the other expenses of opening a new business, research was a luxury that I could do without."

8. What is meant by "return on quality"? Why do you think that the concept evolved? Give an example.

9. Describe three situations in which marketing research should not be undertaken. Explain why this is true.

10. Give an example of (a) the descriptive role of marketing research, (b) the diagnostic role of marketing research, and (c) the predictive function of marketing research.

11. Using the Internet and a Web browser, visit a search engine such as Google or Yahoo! and type, "marketing research." From the thousands of options you are offered, pick a Web site that you find interesting and report on its content to the class.

(Team Exercise) 12. Divide the class into groups of four. Each team should visit a large organization (profit or nonprofit) and conduct an interview with a top marketing executive to discover how this firm is using marketing research. Each team then should report its findings in class.

13. How is the Internet changing the field of marketing research?

Courtyard by Marriott

REAL-LIFE RESEARCH • 1.1

Forget American Express. Some businesspeople don't leave home without their teddy bears. That was one of the surprising facts Courtyard by Marriott found when it commissioned research on its customer base. At Courtyard, market research is "very important to us to understand the wants and needs of our customers. We can't find out if we don't ask," said Geary Campbell, director of national public relations at Marriott.

The survey also serves as a marketing tool "to tell the media and customers what our customer base does while they are on the road," Campbell said, "and to get greater recognition for the Courtyard brand."

The Courtyard by Marriott Business Traveler Profile of 300 business travelers who had taken at least six work-related trips in the previous 12 months was conducted by D. K. Shifflet & Associates of McLean, Va. The 30-question telephone survey focused on how travelers communicated with their homes and offices, as well as what they do or what they bring with them to make life on the road feel more like home. "We also wanted to find out quirky things," Campbell said, "such as their travel behaviors."

Marriott predicted some of the results ahead of time. For example, the survey found that 58 percent of business travelers bring along a laptop computer. Other findings came as a surprise: 70 percent of those with laptops said they have games on their computer, and 7 percent of business travelers said they travel with a teddy bear or other type of stuffed animal.

Survey results confirmed that business travelers want "more than a friendly face" greeting them at the front desk, Campbell said. Business travelers who are on the road want the opportunity to purchase breakfast in advance and efficient check-ins and check-outs.

Marriott launched its Courtyard brand after 2 years of research conducted on guests of their full-service hotels, asking what features they would want in a moderately priced hotel. Courtyard's main customer base is the business traveler, Campbell said.[21]

Questions

1. How might Courtyard use these research findings?
2. Based on this study, do you think more research is needed? If so, what types of information would you look for?
3. Do you think all hotel/motel chains should conduct marketing research? Why?

REAL-LIFE RESEARCH • 1.2

I Want My Satellite Radio

Columbus, Ohio-based BIGresearch reports that 18- to 34-year-olds are satellite radio providers' No. 1 age group for current subscribers as well as for those planning on buying in the next six months.

For those 35 years of age and over, the majority say they don't plan on buying/subscribing to satellite radio at this time. These age groups also tend to be less likely to be current subscribers, according to the findings from the company's March Consumer Intentions and Actions survey of over 7,000 consumers. The satellite radio questions were developed in collaboration with MarketStar.

Education about the advantages or useful outcomes of subscribing to satellite radio appear to be necessary in order to motivate the 35+ crowd to subscribe as 22.7 percent of the 35- to 44-year-olds said they didn't know enough about the service; 24.3 percent of the 45- to 54-year-olds, 2.8 percent of the 55- to 64-year-olds, and 42 percent of the 65+ said the same. "Lack of understanding of the benefits and technological anxiety are the key hurdles that the satellite radio vendors need to overcome at this stage, especially for subsegments including older consumers," says Ryan Brock, vice president of strategic services with MarketStar Corporation. "In the retail environment, this underscores the need to target these consumer segments where they are most likely to shop, with hands-on, face-to-face educational tools to overcome these specific objections."

Of consumers 18+, 4.2 percent said they currently subscribe to one of the satellite radio services and 2.5 percent said they are planning to within the next six months. An additional 16.1 percent said they plan to subscribe someday.

Of those people who said they plan to subscribe, 28.7 percent said they would subscribe to Sirius, 16.7 percent said XM, and 54.6 percent were undecided about which service they would choose. XM was the No. 1 pick for 18–24-year-olds and Sirius was No. 1 for all other age groups.[22]

Questions

1. How might Sirius use this information?
2. Is this basic or applied research? Why?

3. What other marketing research information might Sirius want in order to better market to nonusers?

4. Go to the Internet and see if you can locate any additional marketing research data about satellite radio that might be beneficial to Sirius. Report your findings to the class.

THE MARKETING RESEARCH INDUSTRY AND RESEARCH ETHICS

LEARNING OBJECTIVES

1. To appreciate the structure of the marketing research industry.

2. To comprehend the nature of corporate marketing research departments.

3. To learn about the various types of firms and their functions in the marketing research industry.

4. To understand the impact of the Internet on the marketing research industry.

5. To learn who uses marketing research.

6. To understand the growing importance of strategic partnering.

7. To appreciate trends in global marketing research.

8. To examine unethical practices among marketing research suppliers, clients, and marketing research field services.

9. To become familiar with respondents' rights.

10. To discover methods by which the level of professionalism in marketing research can be raised.

Sitting in his company's Caracas, Venezuela, headquarters, A. G. Lafley, chief executive officer of Procter & Gamble Company, shared some advice with a group of laundry executives: "The simple principle in life is to find out what she wants and give it to her. It's worked in my marriage for 35 years and it works in laundry."

The attention to what women want reflects a philosophical shift at P&G that Mr. Lafley is urging: to look outside the company for solutions to problems, instead of insisting P&G knows best. P&G has always aimed its marketing at women. But it used to develop consumer goods in its labs and market them based on the product's best technical feature. Its market research tended to be about the pros and cons of specific products.

These days, employees spend hours with women, watching them do laundry, clean the floor, apply makeup, and diaper their children. They look for nuisances that a new product might solve. Then, they return to the labs determined to address the feature women care about most. "We discovered that women don't care about our technology and they couldn't care less what machine a product is made on," Mr. Lafley told P&G executives in Caracas, during a recent tour of Latin America. "They want to hear that we understand them."

Roughly 80 percent of the people who buy P&G products are women. And that's why on a recent morning, Mr. Lafley climbed up a steep set of concrete stairs in Caracas, into the cramped kitchen of 29-year-old Maria Yolanda Ríos, to listen to her describe how often she washes her hair, what kind of skin cream she uses, and if she wears nail polish.

For an hour, Mr. Lafley sat in the corner of Ms. Ríos's kitchen, where bright yellow paint peeled off the wall, and listened to the young mother. Avon Products Inc., which sells cosmetics through door-to-door salespeople, dominates the beauty market there, and P&G wants a foothold. Ms. Ríos, a housekeeper, told the group through a translator that she and her husband, who drives a school bus, together earn just under $600 a month.

But when a P&G executive asked Ms. Ríos to bring her beauty and hygiene products into the kitchen, she came back with 31 bottles of cream, lotion, shampoo, and perfume and placed them on the embroidered tablecloth. She has two lotions for her feet, one for her body, one for her hands and another for her face. She dug out her old Avon catalogues and showed the dog-eared pages where she marked certain products.

"It's her entertainment," Mr. Lafley said, putting his Cartier glasses case on the kitchen table and perusing the room. Every year, in different parts of the world, Mr. Lafley makes 10 to 15 visits like this where he observes women doing everything from washing their clothes to applying makeup. "Her entertainment is looking at the Avon catalogue at night, and we need to remember that," he said.

Lessons drawn from these kinds of encounters inform P&G's product development.[1] ∎

Yes, it is unusual for a CEO of one of the world's largest consumer good manufacturers to go into the field to conduct ethnographic research, a type of marketing research (discussed in Chapter 7). But it underscores just how important marketing research is to the company. P&G is somewhat rare in that it has a very large internal marketing research department. Most manufacturers, retailers, and service businesses, such as McDonald's or American Airlines, have small internal marketing research departments. These companies contract with independent marketing research firms (suppliers) to conduct their studies.

In Chapter 2 we will examine the structure of the marketing research industry and trends in the industry. In the latter part of the chapter we will turn our attention to marketing research ethics.

Evolving Structure of the Marketing Research Industry

Today, over $20 billion a year is spent on marketing/advertising/public opinion research services around the world. Spending on marketing research is $6.9 billion in the United States alone.[2] During the past two decades, the research market has become highly concentrated, with about 54 percent of the market being held by the 50 largest worldwide organizations. The other half of the market is shared by a thousand or more small research firms. The concentration is even more pronounced in the United States, where the 10 largest firms account for 64 percent of total U.S. spending for marketing research.[3]

The various types of organizations encountered in the marketing research industry are summarized in Exhibit 2.1. Exhibit 2.2 summarizes the structure of the marketing research industry.

EXHIBIT 2.1	General Categories of Organizations Involved in Marketing Research
Organization	**Activities, Functions, and Services**
Consumer and industrial goods and services producers	Firms such as Kraft General Foods, Procter & Gamble, Ford Motor, and Caterpillar
Media Companies	Advertising agencies such as J. Walter Thompson, Young & Rubicam, and Foote, Cone, & Belding. Public relations companies such as Hill and Knowlton. Sales promotion firms such as Acosta
Syndicated service firms	Marketing research data gathering and reporting firms such as ACNielsen, Arbitron, and Information Resources Incorporated, which collect data of general interest to many firms but for no one firm in particular (i.e., anyone can buy the data they collect); prominent in the media audience field and retail sales data
Custom research firms	Marketing research consulting firms such as Market Facts, DSS Research, and Burke, Inc., which do customized marketing research projects that address specific problems for individual clients
Field service firms	Firms that collect data only, on a subcontract basis, for corporate marketing research departments, ad agency research departments, custom research firms, or syndicated research firms
Specialized service firms	Firms that provide specialized support services to the marketing research industry, such as SDR in Atlanta, which provides sophisticated quantitative analysis or SSI which provides samples for marketing research suppliers
Others	Government agencies, university research bureaus, individual university professors, and database providers

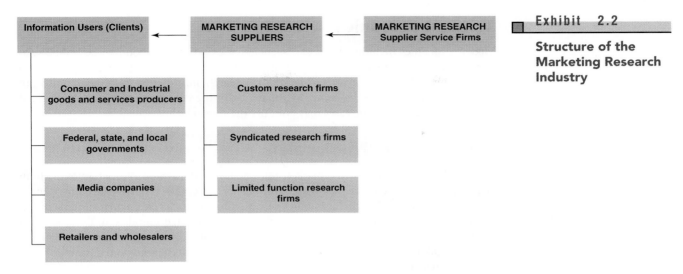

Exhibit 2.2

Structure of the Marketing Research Industry

Primary Information Users (Client Organizations) Consumer and Industrial goods and services producers

Producers of goods and services, such as Procter and Gamble and American Airlines are the ultimate users of the research data. Their primary business is the sale of products and services. They use marketing research data on an ongoing basis in a variety of ways to support the marketing decision-making process such as:

1. To determine how various target groups will react to alternative marketing mixes.
2. To evaluate the ongoing success of operational marketing strategies.
3. To assess changes in the external, or uncontrollable, environment and the implications of those changes for their product or service strategy.
4. To identify new target markets.
5. To measure the quality of customer service and level of satisfaction.

We will discuss users of marketing research in greater detail later in the chapter.

Federal, State, and Local Governments

The various branches of government are large buyers of marketing research information. This includes everything from where a new city park should be located to American's attitudes toward nutritional labeling. Although no estimates are available for marketing research expenditures at the state and local levels, federal marketing research expenditures are estimated at $4.5 billion annually.[4] Except for Westat, America's third largest market research firm, little of this money goes to traditional marketing researchers. Instead, the bulk of the work is either done in-house or conducted through academic non-profits, such as the National Opinion Research Center (University of Chicago), Institute for Social Research (University of Michigan), or Research Triangle Institute— as well as think-tank for-profits such as Rand Corporation and Mathematica Policy Research.

Media Companies

Media companies include advertising agencies, sales promotion companies, public relations agencies, and direct marketing firms. All are concerned with getting the right message to the right target market. Marketing research information is often required to accomplish this goal. Media companies may obtain the data from custom or syndicated research firms and in some cases may conduct the research themselves.

Retailers and Wholesalers

In the highly competitive retail market, understanding the customer is paramount. John Fleming, Wal-Mart's new chief marketing officer, notes, "We clearly have an opening price-point customer that has been our foundation for years. A better understanding of our customer will allow us to focus on some businesses beyond that foundation. Everyone who comes into Wal-Mart shops the consumable area, but not everyone buys their apparel [here]. I think there are ways for us to fill in the gaps by understanding our customer."[5]

Of course, marketing research is the tool for gaining knowledge about the customer.

Marketing Research Suppliers

Custom, syndicated, and limited function marketing research firms represent the front line of the research industry. They sell research services, design research studies, analyze the results, and make recommendations to their clients. They will be discussed in detail below.

Marketing Research Supplier Service Firms

As the heading above implies, these are companies that service the research industry. Services range from software providers, such as Sawtooth Software, to providers of samples, such as SSI. There are several large online panel (groups of persons willing to answer marketing surveys) providers to the marketing research industry. Harris Interactive claims to have the largest panel in the world with members from over 200 countries. Service firms will be described in more detail below.

Consumer and Industrial Corporate Marketing Research Departments

Because corporations are the final consumers and the initiators of most marketing research, they are the logical starting point in developing an understanding of how the industry operates. Most large corporations (and virtually all consumer package goods manufacturers of any size) have marketing research departments. Currently, some are melding marketing research and strategic planning, whereas others are combining marketing research and customer satisfaction departments.

The average size of marketing research departments is quite small. One recent study found that only 15 percent of service companies such as Federal Express and American Airlines had marketing research departments with more than 10 employees. Only 23 percent of manufacturers' research departments had more than 10 employees. The size of marketing research departments has been experiencing a downward trend because of mergers and reengineering. The implication of smaller internal research staffs and growing budgets is clear: companies are conducting less research internally and are outsourcing more to research suppliers. Often, persons in small corporate marketing research departments act as intermediaries between internal research users and outside suppliers.

Because we cannot cover all types of marketing research departments in this text, we will focus our attention on those found in larger, more sophisticated companies, where marketing research is a staff department and the director of the department generally reports to the top marketing executive. Most of the work of the department is with product or brand managers, new product development managers, and other front-line managers. With the possible exception of various recurring studies that may be programmed into a firm's marketing information system, the marketing research department typically does not initiate studies. In fact, the research manager may control little or no actual budget. Instead, line managers have funds in their budgets earmarked for research.

When brand managers perceive that they have a problem that requires research, they go to the marketing research department for help. Working with the marketing research manager or a senior analyst, they go through a series of steps that may lead to the design and execution of a marketing research project.

FROM THE FRONT LINE

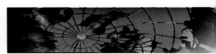

Why I Chose a Career in Marketing Research and the Biggest Surprise I Have Faced in Doing Research

Emily Beck, Project Manager, DSS Research

When I first had to select an undergraduate major, I decided to pursue a career in marketing. While many of my business school classmates focused on financial ratios or debits and credits, I was more intrigued by how consumers think and how a business can maximize the sale of its products or services. In my introductory marketing courses, I learned the basics of product, pricing, promotion, and distribution, and I realized that marketing decisions are often made on intuition and not on an analytical foundation. While intuitive and creative approaches are indispensable, I wanted to learn how to decrease the risk companies face in making pivotal decisions.

The field of marketing research allows me to apply the right balance of intuition and analytics. The principles used in marketing research combine traditional marketing skills with insights from statistical analysis, psychology, and advertising to allow a more informed and objective approach to solving business problems. I enjoy knowing that business decision makers rely on the valuable insight that my research can provide.

My role as a project manager for a full-service research supplier has given me the opportunity to learn about the entire research process—questionnaire design and sampling, data collection and analysis, reporting actionable results—and all the factors that help shape the business strategies of major corporations. My role in the research process gives me the chance to work on multiple projects simultaneously, and I'm constantly presented with exciting new challenges.

One of the most surprising things I've learned is that findings which are not actionable and clearly communicated mostly will be ignored by your clients. Clients pay for research that drives results, not for complex methodologies or flashy PowerPoint reports. You succeed when your findings are clearly communicated in terms of what they *mean* for a client's business. Only by using your skills to tell a story and answering your clients' research questions will you prove your value, drive specific action, and build client relationships.

Research Suppliers

Although the marketing research industry is characterized by hundreds of small firms, there are some giants in the industry. Exhibit 2.3 shows total revenues for the 40 largest marketing research firms. The 2 largest firms in the industry—VNU and IMS Health Inc.—are largely syndicated service firms. The remaining 38 firms are either primarily custom research firms or combination firms offering some syndicated service along with custom research services.

VNU Inc. (VNU), based in New York, and Haarlem, Netherlands, is a public company founded in 1964. VNU is a major international media and information company providing business intelligence in five main business groups: VNU Marketing Information, VNU Media Measurement & Information, VNU Business Media Inc., VNU Business Media Europe, and VNU World Directories. The largest U.S. company owned by VNU is ACNielsen. ACNielsen, in turn, is broken down into several companies. ACN (the main firm) offers the following services:

☐ *Retail Measurement:* These syndicated services provide information on competitive sales volumes, market shares, distribution, pricing, merchandising, and promotional activities to manufacturers and retailers of fast-moving consumer goods. Sales information, captured by check-out scanners or through in-store audits, is gathered from stores in more than 80 countries.

☐ *Consumer Panel:* ACN's consumer panel services are provided in 24 countries and capture consumer purchase information from more than 200,000 households across every outlet. The ACN panel in the United States, *Homescan,* consists of about 91,500 households that use in-home hand-held scanners to record bar-coded items.

☐ *Customized Research:* Available in more than 60 markets, customized research services provide information about consumer attitudes and purchase behavior. Studies include customer satisfaction measurement, brand awareness, and advertising effectiveness. Information is gathered through surveys, personal interviews, focus groups and online methodologies.

☐ *Modeling and Analytics:* These services use modeling and analytical techniques to transform information from multiple sources to optimize pricing, promotion, product mix, media spending, and other marketing activities.

VNU Media Measurement and Information (MMI)

☐ *Media Measurement Division:* This division includes Nielsen Media Research (NMR) (*www.nielsenmedia.com*), based in New York. NMR's core business is providing television audience measurement information. In the United States, the Nielsen TV ratings are the currency for more than $60 billion of transactions each year between buyers and sellers of television time.

☐ *Internet Measurement Division:* This division includes NetRatings Inc. (NR). NR, which markets its services under the Nielsen//NetRatings brand (N//NR), provides Internet audience and advertising measurement and analysis, and offers syndicated Internet and digital media research reports and custom-tailored data.

☐ *Entertainment Information Division (NE):* NE serves the entertainment industry, including the film, book, home entertainment, music, and interactive segments in 16 markets worldwide with a broad range of consulting services, information, and analytical tools. Its services include testing entertainment and promotional content; measuring sales results; tracking consumer entertainment trends in terms of overall spending, time spent, and by segment; and providing custom research information.

| EXHIBIT 2.3 | The Forty Largest Marketing Research Firms* | | |

U.S. rank	Organization	Headquarters	Web Site	U.S. Research revenue ($, in millions)
1	VNU Inc.	New York	www.vnu.com	$1,794.4
2	IMS Health Inc.	Fairfield, Conn.	www.imshealth.com	571.0
3	Westat Inc.	Rockville, Md.	www.westat.com	397.8
4	TNS U.S.	New York	www.tns-global.com	396.0
5	Information Resources Inc.	Chicago	www.infores.com	379.6
6	The Kantar Group	Fairfield, Conn.	www.kantargroup.com	365.7
7	Arbitron Inc.	New York	www.arbitron.com	284.7
8	NOP World US	New York	www.nopworld.com	213.0
9	Ipsos	New York	www.ipsos-na.com	193.9
10	Synovate	Chicago	www.synovate.com	193.5
11	Harris Interactive Inc.	Rochester, N.Y.	www.harrisinteractive.com	154.8
12	J.D. Power and Associates	Westlake Village, Calif.	www.jdpower.com	133.5
13	Maritz Research	Fenton, Mo.	www.maritzresearch.com	136.6
14	The NPD Group Inc.	Port Washington, N.Y.	www.npd.com	110.5
15	GfK Group USA	Nuremberg, Germany	www.gfk.com	93.0
16	Opinion Research Corp.	Princeton, N.J.	www.opinionresearch.com	91.5
17	Lieberman Research Worldwide	Los Angeles	www.lrwonline.com	67.2
18	Abt Associates Inc.	Cambridge, Mass.	www.abtassociates.com	41.5
19	Market Strategies Inc.	Livonia, Mich.	www.marketstrategies.com	37.9
20	Burke Inc.	Cincinnati	www.burke.com	37.1
21	comScore Networks Inc.	Reston, Va	www.comscore.com	34.9
22	MORPACE International Inc.	Farmington Hills, Mich.	www.morpace.com	31.1
23	Knowledge Networks Inc.	Menlo Park, Calif.	www.knowledgenetworks.com	29.8
24	OTX Research	Los Angeles	www.otxresearch.com	29.8
25	ICR/Int'l Communications Research	Media, Pa.	www.icrsurvey.com	29.0
26	Directions Research	Cincinnati	www.directionsrsch.com	27.3
27	National Research Corp.	Lincoln, Neb.	www.nationalresearch.com	26.7
28	Marketing Research Services Inc.	Cincinnati	www.mrsi.com	25.4
29	Lieberman Research Group	Great Neck, N.Y.	www.liebermanresearch.com	25.1
30	Peryam & Kroll Research Corp.	Chicago	www.pk-research.com	22.5
31	National Analysts Inc.	Philadelphia	www.nationalanalysts.com	22.3
32	Public Opinion Strategies LLC	Alexandria, Va.	www.pos.org	21.2
33	Walker Information Inc.	Indianapolis	www.walkerinfo.com	20.4
34	The PreTesting Co. Inc.	Tenafly, N.J.	www.pretesting.com	19.8
35	C&R Research Services Inc.	Chicago	www.crresearch.com	19.7
36	Flake-Wilkerson Market Insight LLC	Little Rock, Ark.	www.mktinsights.com	18.8
37	Data Development Worldwide	New York	www.datadw.com	18.3
38	Cheskin	Redwood Shores, Calif.	www.cheskin.com	16.5
39	RDA Group Inc.	Bloomfield Hills, Mich.	www.rdagroup.com	15.4
40	Schulman, Ronca & Bucavalas Inc.	New York	www.srbi.com	17.2

Source: Jack Honomichl, "Top 50 U.S. Research Organizations," *Marketing News* (June 15, 2005), p. H4.
* Some large privately owned firms, such as DSS Research and Decision Analysts, would be included in this list but they do not disclose financial date.

❑ *Media Solutions Division:* This division includes PERQ/HCI and Scarborough Research, as well as Standard Rate & Data Services (SRDS) and Interactive Market Systems (IMS). PERQ/HCI provides healthcare audience measurement and ad expenditure services to advertising agencies, publishers, and advertisers in the United States. Scarborough Research (SR), a joint venture between VNU and Arbitron, identifies local, regional, and national shopping patterns, and media usage for the American consumer. SRDS offers the world's largest database on media rates and information on media companies. IMS serves the media industry with products such as audience profiling, reach and frequency analysis, and campaign analysis.[6]

IMS Health Incorporated, the number two research firm, has about 8,000 employees providing services in over 100 countries. IMS's marketing research services include pharmacy and hospital audits plus the measurement of disease and treatment patterns. Westat, America's third largest research company, primarily conducts survey research for agencies of the U.S. government as well as businesses, foundations, and state and local governments. Major project areas include health, epidemiological research, education, and the environment, energy, transportation, and federal social programs.

Its major statistical surveys cover educational progress, medical expenditures and long-term follow-up surveys concerning health, education and employment.[7]

Custom Research Firms

> **custom research firms**
> Companies that carry out customized marketing research to address specific projects for corporate clients.

Custom research firms, as noted earlier, are primarily in the business of executing custom, one-of-a-kind marketing research projects for corporate clients. If a corporation has a new product or service idea, a packaging idea, an ad concept, a new pricing strategy, a product reformulation, or a related marketing problem or opportunity, it typically will go to a custom research firm for research help.

There are thousands of custom marketing research firms in the United States. Examples of large custom research firms include Market Facts, Inc., the MARC Group, Opinion Research Corp. International, Elrick and Lavidge Marketing Research, Burke, Inc., DSS Research, and Decision Analyst. However, the overwhelming majority of custom marketing research firms are small, with billings of less than $1 million and fewer than 10 employees. They may limit their client base to their local area and may or may not specialize by type of industry or type of research.

Syndicated Service Firms

> **syndicated service research firms**
> Companies that collect, package, and sell market research data to many firms.

In sharp contrast to custom research firms, **syndicated service research firms** collect and sell marketing research data to many firms. Anyone willing to pay the price can buy the data these firms collect, package, and sell. Syndicated service firms are relatively few and, compared to custom research firms, relatively large. They deal primarily with media audience and product movement data and are based on serving information needs common to many companies. For example, companies that advertise on network television want to select shows that reach their target customers most efficiently. They need information on the size and demographic composition of the audiences for various TV programs. It would be extremely inefficient for each company to collect these data itself.

Firms like NMR sell standardized TV ratings to a group of clients known as a syndicate—thus, the term *syndicated data*. Some syndicated firms, like Roper Starch Worldwide, sell lifestyle data that is both syndicated and customized. The standardized process is the same to gather the data, but some members of the syndicate may want special information just for their company. This, in fact, is quite common. An additional charge is levied for each custom question added to the syndicated survey.

GLOBAL RESEARCH

Chinese Marketing Research Comes of Age

Marketing research firms can be found in all major Chinese cities; however, Guangzhou is the cradle of the marketing research industry there, for several reasons. First, Guangzhou is near Hong Kong, the commercial center of southern China for the last 25 years. The Hong Kong market system provided a template for Guangzhou to emulate. Second, Guangzhou was one of the first cities in China to open commercial operations with the West. As early as 1985, Guangzhou Soft Science Co., under the aegis of the government, set up its own marketing department. From this department, the Guangzhou Market Research Co. (GMR) emerged in 1988, becoming the first professional marketing research company in China.

The early Chinese marketing research industry would not have survived without support from Procter & Gamble. P&G provided GMR with a full range of support, including software, hardware, and professional training in sampling and research methodology. Starting in the early 1990s, P&G invited the Chinese researchers of GMR (including one of the authors) to its internal professional training courses. In the following years, many P&G-trained marketing research professionals started their own marketing research companies.

Initially, P&G was also the main client of these early Chinese marketing research firms. In the early 1990s, more than 90 percent of GMR's revenue came from P&G.

Today the domestic marketing research industry in China comprises about 400 firms. These firms come in many flavors of ownership; however, private-owner and stock companies dominate. But government and university ownership still is at a significant level. Most of the firms are small: Almost half of Chinese marketing research firms have revenues between $10,000 and $50,000 annually.

The current customer base heavily emphasizes the advertising and broadcasting areas, which is one of the main outcomes of the changes from planned economy to market economy. Learning how and what to advertise and broadcast or print is extremely important in making this transition. Fierce market competition also taught developing enterprises the importance of marketing research to determine customer needs and wants. The next largest customer group is consumer products.[8]

Approximately 44 percent of all research monies are spent on syndicated research; the remainder is spent for custom research. Custom quantitative studies account for 39 percent of all research dollars and custom qualitative research, 17 percent.[9] Exhibit 2.4 shows a list of syndicated service firms and the specific type of marketing research they offer.

Limited Function Research Firms

Some firms specialize in one or a few activities. They may, for example, serve only one industry. Westat, for example, serves various government agencies, whereas IMS Health and DSS Research focus on healthcare. Other firms use a single research technique or a special type of research technique. Mystery Shopper organizations, such as Shop 'n Check and Speedmark, engage only in mystery shopping (discussed in Chapter 8). The Pretesting Company uses devices such as the People Reader to measure how much time is spent reading an ad in a magazine or newspaper.

Many new marketing research firms conduct research only via the Internet. A pioneer in this area is Greenfield Online, *http://www.greenfieldonline.com*, which conducts

EXHIBIT 2.4	Syndicated Service Research Firms
Firm	**Syndicated Services**
AC Nielsen Corp. Schaumberg, Illinois	Television ratings Scanner-based data Wholesale/retail audits Internet research
FIND/SVP New York, New York	Large variety of industry/product studies
Maritz Marketing Research Inc. Fenton, Missouri	Customer satisfaction studies
GfK NOP New York, New York	Public opinion surveys Lifestyle data Media/advertising effectiveness data
Information Resources Incorporated Chicago, Illinois	Scanner-based data

both quantitative research and qualitative research (research not subject to quantitative analysis). Greenfield claims to have the world's largest Internet-based marketing research panel. A **research panel** consists of a group of individuals who agree to participate in a series of research studies over time. Often, participants receive cash or gifts.

> **research panel**
> A group of individuals who agree to participate in a series of research studies over time.

Another Internet-bred marketing research firm is Keynote. Keynote evaluates customers' online satisfaction with a Web site and measures online behavior. It works in the automotive, pharmaceutical, telecom, and other industries.

Some cyberresearch firms focus on tracking the popularity of Web sites. ComScore, the pioneer in this area, now is being challenged by a newcomer—Relevant Knowledge. Nielsen Media Research, which has been rating television programs for decades, also has joined the battle as discussed above.

Marketing Research Supplier Service Firms

A number of firms service marketing research suppliers. When research departments of corporations, such as Kraft General Foods, are conducting their own research, these service firms also cater to them. The two largest categories of service firms are field service organizations and sampling firms.

> **field service firms**
> Companies that only collect survey data for corporate clients or research firms.

A true **field service firm** does nothing but collect survey data—no research design, no analysis. Field service firms are data collection specialists, collecting data on a subcontract basis for corporate marketing research departments, custom research firms, ad agency research departments, and others.

The following description of the sequence of activities undertaken by a typical field service company provides a good idea of how these firms operate:

1. *Client contact.* Custom or syndicated research firm or corporate or ad agency research department alerts field service firm, usually by e-mail, that it wants to conduct a particular type of study (telephone interview, mall interview, focus group, taste test, etc.).

2. *Interviewer training.* The day the job is to begin, a briefing or training session is held to acquaint interviewers with the requirements of the particular job or questionnaire.

3. *Interviewing status reports.* Daily progress reports are made via e-mail to the client regarding number of interviews completed and costs incurred. These reports permit the client to determine whether the job is on schedule and within budget and allow the field service to advise the client of any problems.

4. *Quality control.* The interviews are edited; that is, specially designed software is used to verify that they were completed correctly.

5. *Ship to client.* Finally, the completed, edited interviews are shipped (typically electronically) to the client.

Most custom research firms rely on field services because it is not cost-effective for them to handle the work themselves. There are too many geographic areas to cover, and it is hard to know which areas will be needed over time. On the other hand, field service firms in particular areas maintain a steady work flow by having numerous research firms and corporate and ad agency research departments as their clients.

The major field service firm of today has a permanent office. It probably has one or more permanent mall test centers, focus group facilities, a central telephone interviewing facility, as well as other specialized facilities and equipment. A recent trend among field service firms is the establishment of satellite offices in multiple cities.

Sampling Firms Sampling firms provide samples (persons to interview) to marketing research suppliers and other research creators. The largest sampling firm is Survey Sampling Inc. (SSI); this firm does nothing but generate samples for mail, telephone, or Internet surveys. SSI's Survey Spot Internet panel has over 6 million members. The firm's SSI-Lite eSample is a panel categorized by lifestyles; the panel contains over 3,500 topical lists and 12 million names. Other firms such as Harris Interactive and Decision Analyst have huge Internet panels that they use for their own research and rent to other research suppliers.

Software Firms A number of companies specialize in providing software for statistical analysis and/or Internet interviewing. The most popular statistical package, used by over two-thirds of all research suppliers, is SPSS. This is the same software that we provide you when you purchase a new text. Other companies, like Perseus and Web Surveyor, sell software for online interviewing. The firms also will host surveys on their own servers.

Other Service Companies Other service companies provide a variety of services to research firms. For example, SDR Consulting, located in Atlanta, offers sophisticated data analysis to marketing research suppliers. MarketingResearchCareers.com specializes, as the name implies, in careers in the marketing research field. Quirk's publishes a magazine, *Quirk's Marketing Research Review,* and directories such as directories of field service firms, international research companies, focus group facilities, and others. Quirk's also hosts an online forum for marketing researchers.

Using Marketing Research— A Corporate Perspective

Now that you are familiar with the marketing research industry, let's look in more detail at research users. There is a very good possibility that any future encounters that you, as a businessperson, will have with marketing research will be as a research user. Exhibit 2.5 shows some of the various types of marketing research clients. Despite the importance of

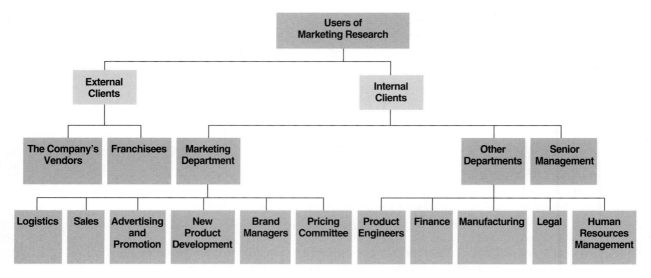

Exhibit 2.5

Using Marketing Research— A Corporate Perspective

nonmarketing, *internal* clients to the success of an organization, some firms' research departments have paid little attention to their specific marketing information needs. As you might expect, these poorly served clients have demonstrated little interest in marketing research information. It has been our experience that the most successful marketing research departments and firms are those committed to the complete satisfaction of all of their clients. Let's take a closer look at the types of information these various clients need and use.

External Clients

Because marketing research can be a valuable source of information about new or improved competitive advantages and because such information is often very expensive to gather, data gathered by a firm's research department is rarely circulated outside of the firm. Many firms don't provide any information to outsiders, such as suppliers. However, those that do usually find that it is to their mutual benefit.

> **strategic partnership**
> An alliance formed by two or more firms with unique skills and resources to offer a new service for clients, provide strategic support for each firm, or in some other manner create mutual benefits.

Vendors Manufacturers are moving into **strategic partnerships** with their vendors in order to implement just-in-time manufacturing. These alliances are based on fully integrated manufacturer–supplier logistics systems that get the component to the assembly line just when it is needed. The result is little or no raw materials inventory and significantly reduced carrying costs. The backbone of this system is shared information. Large retailers, such as Wal-Mart, have such relationships with their major vendors.

Within the framework of strategic partnering, marketing research information is fed back to a manufacturer's suppliers when consumers voice opinions about a component on the manufacturer's customer satisfaction surveys. For example, if Pioneer was supplying radios for Honda automobiles and customers were complaining about how difficult a certain model was to program, this research information would be shared with Pioneer. In one case, a major retail chain commissioned a study on changes in customer preferences for Christmas-related items such as gift wrap, cards, artificial trees, and ornaments, to help its suppliers of production materials understand the importance of making specific product changes and to provide guidance in making those changes.

Franchisees Most major franchisors of consumer goods and services provide marketing research data to their franchisees. Perhaps the most common way of gathering data is from *mystery shoppers*. A mystery shopper, posing as a customer, observes how long it takes to be waited on and/or make a purchase, the courtesy of the clerks, the cleanliness of the operation, and whether his or her purchase or order was properly prepared. Mystery shopping is discussed in detail in Chapter 7.

Franchisors also share marketing research information with their franchisees to support certain recommendations or actions. When McDonald's suggests to a franchisee that a restaurant be remodeled in a particular style, it will show research data indicating that the building is perceived as out-of-date or old-fashioned. Other data might reveal which theme or style current customers prefer. When Burger King launches a major new promotional campaign, it may share with franchisees research data showing that the selected campaign theme was preferred by customers and noncustomers over alternative themes.

A major retail chain commissioned a study on changes in customer preferences for Christmas-related items in order to help suppliers understand the need for product change and what product changes to make.

Internal Clients

Marketing Managers   Virtually every manager within an organization will, at some point, be a user of marketing research information. However, marketing managers use research data more than any other group. Recall that the marketing mix consists of decisions regarding products or services, promotion, distribution, and pricing. Marketing research helps decision makers in each of these areas make better decisions. Product managers, for example, begin by using research to define their target market. In some cases, managers use research to determine the heavy users of their product within the target market. Marketing research revealed that heavy users of Miracle Whip consume 550 servings, or 17 pounds, of the product a year. These data were used to target a $30 million promotional campaign to core users, telling them not to "skip the zip." As a result, Miracle Whip's market share went up 2.1 percent, to $305 million annual sales.[10] The ad campaign also was thoroughly tested for effectiveness by marketing research before it was launched.

New product development managers are among the heaviest users of marketing research. From qualitative research techniques that generate product ideas to concept testing, product prototype testing, and then test marketing, marketing research is the key to creating a new product. For example, Post's research on cereals had always shown that bananas are America's favorite cereal fruit. Therefore, why not a banana-flavored cereal? Post's new product manager concocted cereals with dried banana pieces, but they failed marketing research taste tests. Further research, conducted to explain why this happened, uncovered the fact that consumers saw no reason to buy a cereal with preserved bananas, as the fresh fruit is quite cheap year-round. If consumers wanted a banana-flavored cereal, they'd peel a banana and make one on the spot. One day, the new product manager had an inspiration: Consumers had said that they liked banana nut bread; it conjured up thoughts of something delicious that grandma used to make. The manager had Post's labs create a new cereal for test marketing in consumers' homes, where it received very high consumer test scores. Thus, Banana Nut Crunch, one of Post's hottest cereals, was born. It is solely a product of marketing research, created from the initial concept of a new product manager.

Marketing research also plays an important role in the distribution function. It is used to choose locations for new stores and to test consumer reactions to internal store design fixtures and features. Banana Republic, for example, has relied on marketing research to create the right atmosphere in its stores.

Within larger organizations, pricing decisions are usually made by committees composed of representatives from marketing, finance, production, and perhaps other departments. A recent marketing research study conducted by Ford Motor Company took a look at some of the new ideas generated by its engineers in order to determine first whether target customers were interested in a particular feature and then, if the concept had appeal, whether consumers would pay the suggested retail price. The research was conducted in both the United States and the United Kingdom. Twenty-eight new technology features were evaluated using computer-aided multimedia personal interviewing on desktop computers (see Exhibit 2.6). Video descriptions were integrated with a computerized

EXHIBIT 2.6	Ford's Marketing Research on Sample New Technology Features
Fingerprint Passive Entry (US $980, reg. power locks—$350 UK £504, central locks—£280)	Fingerprint Passive Entry allows the driver to gain access to vehicles equipped with power locks, without the use of a key. The driver's own fingerprint is used as a unique identification to lock and unlock the vehicle. The vehicle recognizes the driver's fingerprint through the use of a touch pad. To lock the driver's door or all the vehicle's doors, simply touch the pad for half a second. (UK VERSION) Fingerprint Passive Entry is also available for easy trunk or liftgate access. The vehicle can still be locked or unlocked with a key.
Night Vision System (US $2100/UK £1400)	The Night Vision System enhances driver visibility at night without causing glare to oncoming drivers. The system uses infrared headlamps to illuminate the road ahead. Sensors form an image of the road on a transparent display which lowers into the driver's view. An enhanced image of the road ahead is displayed on the screen, improving visibility.
Sun Tracking Visor (US $42/UK £35)	The Sun Tracking Visor slides along a track from the inside rearview mirror to the edge of both front side doors, providing more accurate coverage. This feature is easy to use and provides a wide range of coverage.
Front Impact Warning Indicator Light and Tone (US $420, UK £210) Indicator Light and Voice (US $420/UK £210) Indicator Light and Brake Tap (US $490/UK £252)	The Front Impact Warning System alerts drivers when approaching another vehicle or object. Sensors located in the bumper detect obstacles in front of the vehicle. The Front Impact Warning System combines an indicator light and audible tone to alert the driver: a combined indicator light and voice warning, or a combined indicator light and automatic brake tap.
Infinite Door Check (US $35/UK £14)	The Infinite Door Check holds the door at any open position selected. When in a cramped parking space or on an inclined surface, the door can be stopped at any position without bumping the vehicle next to you.
Skin Temperature Sensor (US $28, reg. ATC—$245 UK £14, reg. ATC—£420)	The Skin Temperature Sensor can be added to vehicles equipped with automatic temperature control to automatically cool the temperature inside the vehicle. The Skin Temperature Sensor uses an interior infrared sensor to measure a face's skin temperature. The sensor adjusts the fan and air conditioning to cool the vehicle's interior, until the skin temperature is within a normal range.

Source: Courtesy of Ford Motor Company. (Prices are not actual.)

quantitative questionnaire for all feature evaluations. Qualitative research (see Chapter 5) was conducted to clarify customer likes and dislikes of specific features.

Some concepts were perceived as a bit "gimmicky" or just "something else to break." For example, Fingerprint Passive Entry was not perceived as a benefit over current remote keyless entry systems. On the other hand, features that are inexpensive but offer high utility appeared to be desirable. Examples include the Sun Tracking Visor and the Infinite Door Check. As might be expected, consumers overestimated the manufacturer's target retail price for some items and underestimated it for others. Correspondingly, consumers were willing to pay the manufacturer's suggested retail price for some features but not for others.[11]

Top Management   Recall from the opening vignette how Procter & Gamble's CEO A. G. Lafley has brought marketing research to the forefront of the company. This, in turn, has meant rising market share, profits, and shareholder value. The president of Harley Davidson decided to create a second line of motorcycles, called Buell, after consulting marketing research data. This new strategic direction opened a whole new market segment (sport/performance) for Harley. Top executives at DuPont, Wal-Mart, Marriott, Carnival Cruise Lines, and Amazon.com look to marketing research for strategic guidance.

Other Internal Users   From time to time, other individuals besides marketing managers and senior management find a need for marketing research. As discussed earlier, Ford's engineers sometimes invent new items for which demand must be assessed. Ford's marketing research, however, feeds engineering management a steady stream of consumer desires and dislikes. Manufacturing also receives continual feedback, from customer satisfaction surveys, about loose-fitting door panels, balky sunroof openers, and the like.

Finance departments use test market data to forecast revenue streams for 1 to 3 years. Similarly, repositioning research helps financial managers forecast revenue spurts from older products. Originally, Gatorade was promoted as a drink for competitive athletes. Marketing research found that its main users were men, aged 19 to 44, who understood the product, had a good perception of what it did, and knew when to drink it. The product was repositioned toward physical activity enthusiasts as a drink that would quench their thirst and replenish the minerals lost during exercise better than other beverages did. The new positioning dramatically increased sales.

Human resource managers may call on marketing research to survey employees about a variety of topics. Quality customer service requires that employees have a positive image of the company, an attitude that they then convey to customers. Firms such as Southwest Airlines and Nations-Bank monitor employee attitudes through survey research.

Companies are increasingly turning to marketing research to win their cases in court. Recently, Schering-Plough and Pfizer went to court over physicians' perceptions about various antihistamines and sales messages used by sales reps about the products. You can read about the trial in detail in Real-Life Research 2.1 at the end of this chapter. Marketing research is also used to prove or disprove consumer perceptions regarding similar brand names.

A San Francisco jury ruled against Kendall-Jackson Winery in its case against E. & J. Gallo Winery. Kendall-Jackson claimed that Gallo copied the design of its Vintner's Reserve

Marketing research helped Gatorade position its product toward those who use it most often—men between the ages of 19 and 44. Go to *http://www.gatorade.com* to see if the company positions its Web site for this demographic.

label, which features a grape leaf with fall colors, by using a similarly styled logo on the Gallo Turning Leaf line of varietal wines. Marketing research won the case for Gallo.

When law firms, top management, or product managers decide to hire a research supplier, they must find the right company to do the job. Jerry Thomas, president and CEO of Decision Analyst, Inc., discussed what to watch out for when hiring a research supplier in the Practicing Marketing Research box below.

The State of the Marketing Research Industry

The marketing research industry is continuing to grow at a steady rate. For the past 15 years, the industry grew at about 5 percent annually. In 2004 and 2005, it grew at an annual rate of over 7 percent. Growth has attracted multinational corporations to the American marketing research industry. Today, 6 of the top 10 research firms are owned by foreign corporations.

Users The size of marketing research departments (users of research) continues to shrink as their budgets grow. This indicates that they are relying more on external research suppliers than ever before. Despite large budgets, users are more price sensitive than ever. One CEO of a supplier company told your authors, "Internet research is already becoming a commodity business." Price sensitivity and more accountability have meant that "nice to have" and "nice to know" projects have gone away. Each project must now lead to tactical or strategic decisions. In major corporations, purchasing departments are now getting involved in projects over $100,000. When purchasing managers aren't research experts, price often becomes the key decision variable. Some users are even resorting to reverse auctions to bid out their research projects! A reverse auction is where the client (user) specifies what research it wants completed and researcher suppliers submit bids. The lowest bid is the winner. This means that research is viewed as a commodity and that there is no strategic partnership between the user and the supplier.

Marketing Research Suppliers Although some strategic partnering is still going on, the trend seems to have slowed. Suppliers must therefore maintain visibility through promotion and personal interactions with users. As strategic partnering falters, suppliers cannot depend on having a cash cow as in the past. M/A/R/C, one of America's largest custom research firms, had R.J. Reynolds as its cash cow for a number of years. Suppliers are also outsourcing to reduce costs. Some firms have moved their telephone survey call centers to Canada, and others have subcontracted data processing to firms in India.[12]

Challenges Facing the Marketing Research Industry A recent survey of 1,500 marketing research executives asked them about challenges facing the industry. When asked to rank the challenges the results were as follows:

Ranked—"Very Challenging"

Maximizing survey participation and completion rates	38.7%
Reaching a representative sample of respondents	30.2%
Providing surveys in the format most desired for the respondent	10.2%
Designing or authoring the survey	12.0%
Analyzing results	17.6%
Coding or quantifying survey operations	18.6%

PRACTICING MARKETING RESEARCH

Look for the Danger Signals When Evaluating Research Suppliers

Jerry Thomas, president and CEO of Decision Analyst, says that clients should watch for these danger signs in evaluating research suppliers:

- **Magic techniques.** Exotic approaches. Revolutionary technology. Let them experiment on your competitors. **Rule One:** If you don't understand it, don't buy it.

- **Guaranteed solutions.** They know they can solve your problem. They are absolutely certain they are right. They are in possession of the Holy Grail. Let them bring salvation and ultimate truth to your competitors. **Rule Two:** Don't do business with prophets or other types of management consultants.

- **Price variance.** If the prices quoted for research are extremely high, you should be wary and careful (even if they are management consultants). Make sure you are getting extra value for the extra price. Equally risky are the companies that quote extremely low prices; be especially careful in using these companies. **Never, never** choose a research company just because its prices are the lowest. Typically, research costs are a small part of a project's budget. Don't save $2,000 or $3,000 on a research project and run the risk of making wrong decisions that could cost your company millions of dollars.

So, you've chosen a research partner. How do you get the most from the research company you choose?

- **Build a relationship.** Involve the research company in your business. Generally, the more you work with one company, the better the job that company will do for you.

- **Set forth clear objectives.** Tell the research company what decisions you wish to make. Be sure the research firm understands your objectives.

- **Look in on the research while it is in process.** Listen to some of the telephone interviews. Observe the focus groups or depth interviews.

Once a study is completed and you've reviewed a draft of the report and its recommendations, ask the research company to present the results of the study to all of your key people **in one room at one time**. This is an absolutely essential step for two reasons: First, most of your employees don't read research reports; second, even if they do read them, many people don't understand research reports. A real live presentation with all the key decision makers in one room allows the researcher to explain the results, answer all questions, and clear up any confusion or misunderstandings. A great added benefit of a presentation is that it helps your key executives reach a consensus on what the research results mean and what actions need to be taken.

Research is not the answer to every question, but if used wisely, it just might help your business avoid the next speculative meltdown. The future belongs to the informed, to the rational, to those who make decisions based on objective, research-based realities.[13]

Ranked—"Next-Most Challenging"

Maximizing survey participation and completion rates	36.0%
Reaching a representative sample of respondents	33.3%
Providing surveys in the format most desired for the respondent	23.4%
Analyzing results	28.1%
Coding or quantifying survey operations	26.3%

The survey also explored the pressures being brought to bear on marketing research that affect *how* research is conducted. The need to "reduce costs" was considered the biggest hurdle by 39.3 percent of respondents. After that the largest hurdles were:

Reduce time in achieving results	35.4%
Improve the data collection process	28.1%
Conduct effective research online	22.6%
Take advantage of technology	22.2%
Improve skill sets of internal staff	20.9%
Automate processes	20.7%
Reduce time to create a survey	20.4%
Reduce errors in data collection or coding	20.2%
Improve the process of coding data	8.6%
Hire staff	7.3%
Outsourcing	5.8%
Other	5.5%[14]

A discussion of the state-of-the-art of the marketing research industry would not be complete without mentioning ethics.

Marketing Research Ethics

ethics
Moral principles or values, generally governing the conduct of an individual or group.

The two most important factors for research clients in their relationships with research departments/suppliers are client confidentiality and honesty. Each is a question of ethics. **Ethics** are moral principles or values generally governing the conduct of an individual or group. Ethical behavior is not, however, a one-way relationship. Clients, suppliers, as well as field services, must also act in an ethical manner.

Ethical questions range from practical, narrowly defined issues, such as a researcher's obligation to be honest with its customers, to broader social and philosophical questions, such as a company's responsibility to preserve the environment and protect employee rights. Many ethical conflicts develop from conflicts between the differing interests of company owners and their workers, customers, and surrounding community. Managers must balance the ideal against the practical—the need to produce a reasonable profit for the company's shareholders with honesty in business practices, and larger environmental and social issues.

Ethical Theories

People usually base their individual choice of ethical theory on their life experiences. The following are some of the ethical theories that apply to business and marketing research.[15]

Deontology The deontological theory states that people should adhere to their obligations and duties when analyzing an ethical dilemma. This means that a person will follow his or her obligations to another individual or society because upholding one's duty is what is considered ethically correct. For instance, a deontologist will always keep his promises to a friend and will follow the law. A person who follows this theory will produce very consistent decisions since they will be based on the individual's set duties. Note that this theory is not necessarily concerned with the welfare of others. Say, for example, a research supplier has decided that it's his ethical duty (and very practical!) to always be on time to meetings with clients. Today he is running late. How is he supposed to drive? Is the deontologist supposed to speed, breaking his duty to society to uphold the law, or is the deontologist supposed to arrive at his meeting late, breaking his duty to be on time? This scenario of conflicting obligations does not lead us to a clear ethically correct resolution, nor does it protect the welfare of others from the deontologist's decision.

Utilitarianism   The utilitarian ethical theory is founded on the ability to predict the consequences of an action. To a utilitarian, the choice that yields the greatest benefit to the most people is the choice that is ethically correct. One benefit of this ethical theory is that the utilitarian can compare similar predicted solutions and use a point system to determine which choice is more beneficial for more people. This point system provides a logical and rational argument for each decision and allows a person to use it on a case-by-case context.

There are two types of utilitarianism: act utilitarianism and rule utilitarianism. *Act utilitarianism* adheres exactly to the definition of utilitarianism as described in the above section. In act utilitarianism, a person performs the acts that benefit the most people, regardless of personal feelings or the societal constraints such as laws. *Rule utilitarianism*, however, takes into account the law and is concerned with fairness. A rule utilitarian seeks to benefit the most people but through the fairest and most just means available. Therefore, added benefits of rule utilitarianism are that it values justice and doing good at the same time.

As is true of all ethical theories, however, both act and rule utilitarianism contain numerous flaws. Inherent in both are the flaws associated with predicting the future. Although people can use their life experiences to attempt to predict outcomes, no human being can be certain that his predictions will be true. This uncertainty can lead to unexpected results, making the utilitarian look unethical as time passes because his choice did not benefit the most people as he predicted.

Another assumption that a utilitarian must make is that he has the ability to compare the various types of consequences against each other on a similar scale. However, comparing material gains such as money against intangible gains such as happiness is impossible since their qualities differ so greatly.

Casuist   The casuist ethical theory compares a current ethical dilemma with examples of similar ethical dilemmas and their outcomes. This allows one to determine the severity of the situation and to create the best possible solution according to others' experiences. Usually, one will find examples that represent the extremes of the situation so that a compromise can be reached that will hopefully include the wisdom gained from the previous situations.

One drawback to this ethical theory is that there may not be a set of similar examples for a given ethical dilemma. Perhaps that which is controversial and ethically questionable is new and unexpected. Along the same line of thinking, this theory assumes that the results of the current ethical dilemma will be similar to results in the examples. This may not be necessarily true and would greatly hinder the effectiveness of applying this ethical theory.

Understanding ethical theories will help us better decide how certain unethical practices in marketing research should be resolved. Exhibit 2.8 details some of the unethical practices most common among the various groups involved in marketing research.

Research Supplier Ethics

Unethical research supplier practices range from low-ball pricing to violating client confidentiality.

Low-Ball Pricing   A research supplier should quote a firm price based on a specific incidence rate (percentage of the respondents in the sample that will qualify to complete

EXHIBIT 2.8	Unethical Practices in Marketing Research	
Research Suppliers	**Research Clients**	**Field Services**
Low-ball pricing	Issuing bid requests when a supplier has been predetermined	
Allowing subjectivity into the research	Soliciting free advice and methodology via bid requests	Using professional respondents
Abusing respondents		Not validating data
Selling unnecessary research	Making false promises	
Violating client confidentiality	Issuing unauthorized requests for proposal	
Black Box Branding		

> **low-ball pricing**
> Quoting an unrealistically low price to secure a firm's business and then using some means to substantially raise the price.

the survey) and questionnaire length (time to complete). If either of the latter two items changes, then the client should expect a change in the contract price. Low-ball pricing in any form is unethical. In essence, **low-ball pricing** is quoting an unrealistically low price to secure a firm's business and then using some means to substantially raise the price. For example, quoting a price based on an unrealistically high incidence rate is a form of low-ball pricing. Offering to conduct a focus group at $6,000 a group and, after the client commits, saying, "The respondents' fees for participating in the group discussion are, of course, extra" is a form of low-balling.

Allowing Subjectivity into the Research   Research suppliers must avoid using biased samples, misusing statistics, ignoring relevant data, and creating a research design with the goal of supporting a predetermined objective. One area of research today is so-called *advocacy studies*. These studies are commissioned by companies or industries for public relations purposes or to advocate or prove a position. For example, Burger King once used positive responses to the following question in an advocacy study in an attempt to justify the claim that its method of cooking hamburgers was preferred over that of McDonald's: "Do you prefer your hamburgers flame-broiled or fried?" When another researcher rephrased the question—"Do you prefer a hamburger that is grilled on a hot stainless-steel grill or cooked by passing the meat through an open gas flame?"—the results were reversed: McDonald's was preferred to Burger King.

Kiwi Brands, a shoe polish company, commissioned a study on the correlation between ambition and shiny shoes. The study found that 97 percent of self-described ambitious young men believe polished shoes are important. In many cases, advocacy studies simply use samples that are not representative of the population. For example, a news release for a diet products company trumpeted: "There's good news for the 65 million Americans currently on a diet." A company study had shown that people who lose weight can keep it off—the sample consisted of 20 graduates of the company's program, who also endorsed its products in commercials.

When studies are released to the news media, the methodology should be readily available to news reporters. Typically, this information is withheld, often on the ground that the material is proprietary. A survey done for Carolina Manufacturer's Service, a coupon redemption company, found that "a broad cross-section of Americans find coupons to be true incentives for purchasing products." The description of the methodology was available only at a price: $2,000.

Abusing Respondents   Respondent abuse can take several forms. Perhaps the most common is lengthy interviews. This problem stems in part from the "as long as

When studies are released to the news media, the methodology should be readily available to news reporters. A survey done for a coupon redemption company found that "a broad cross-section of Americans find coupons to be true incentives for purchasing products." The description of the methodology, however, was available only for a price of $2,000.

you're asking questions" mentality of many product managers. It is not uncommon for clients to request additional "nice to know" questions, or even exploratory questions on an entirely separate project. This leads to lengthy questionnaires, 30-minute telephone or internet interviews, and 40-minute mall-intercept interviews. As a result of long interviews and telephone sales pitches, more and more Americans are refusing to participate in survey research. The refusal rate for telephone surveys now averages 60-plus percent, an increase of 10 percent over 10 years. Forty-nine percent of the people who do participate say the surveys are "too personal."

Predictive dialers are tremendous productivity tools for survey research telephone call centers. They remove much of the idle time an interviewer would otherwise spend manually dialing numbers and recording call dispositions, such as no-answer and busy signals. By definition, predictive dialers dial phone numbers ahead of available interviewers, predicting when an interviewer will become available. Adjusting the pacing manually sets the aggressiveness of this dial-ahead capability. Obviously, there is strong motivation for call-center managers to increase the pacing and minimize the time an interviewer spends between calls. However, this action has undesirable consequences because some respondents are contacted before an interviewer is available. In most cases, the dialer than places the respondent on hold or disconnects the call. Both actions decrease respondent goodwill.[16]

Interest in a product or service is often discerned during the interviewing process, and the researcher knows the interviewees' potential purchasing power from their answers to income and other pertinent financial questions. Although the introduction phase of the questionnaire usually promises confidentiality, some researchers have sold names and addresses of potential customers to firms seeking sales leads. Individuals willing to participate in the survey research process have a right to have their privacy protected.

The state of New York sued Student Marketing Group for selling information on a broad scale to direct marketers. The survey filled out by students included age, gender, religious affiliation, career interests, and grade point average. The company said that it was gathering the data to provide to universities to help the students gain admission and financial aid. Direct marketers used the information to sell credit cards, magazines, videos, cosmetics, and other products.[17]

Selling Unnecessary Research   A research supplier dealing with a client who has little or no familiarity with marketing research often has the opportunity to "trade the client up." For example, if a project called for four focus groups and an online survey of approximately 350 consumers, the research supplier might sell eight groups and 1,000 Internet interviews, with a 400-interview telephone follow-up in 6 months.

It is perfectly acceptable to offer a prospective client several research designs with several alternative prices when and if the situation warrants alternative designs. The supplier should point out the pros and cons of each method, along with sample confidence intervals. The client, in consultation with the supplier, then can decide objectively which design best suits the company's needs.

Violating Client Confidentiality   Information about a client's general business activities or the results of a client's project should not be disclosed to a third party. The supplier should not even disclose the name of a client unless permission is received in advance.

The thorniest issue in confidentiality is determining where "background knowledge" stops and conflict arises as a result of work with a previous client. One researcher put it this way:

I get involved in a number of proprietary studies. The problem that often arises is that some studies end up covering similar subject matter as previous studies. Our code of ethics states that you cannot use data from one project in a related project for a competitor. However, since I often know some information about an area, I end up compromising my original client. Even though upper management formally states that it should not be done, they also expect it to be done to cut down on expenses. This conflict of interest situation is difficult to deal with. At least in my firm, I don't see a resolution to the issue. It is not a onetime situation, but rather a process that perpetuates itself. To make individuals redo portions of studies which have recently been done is ludicrous, and to forgo potential new business is almost impossible from a financial perspective.[18]

Black Box Branding

Marketing research suppliers have discovered branding. Synovate has over 25 branded product offerings, including Brand Vision and M2M. Maritz Research offers Loyalty Maximizer, and Harris Interactive has TRBC, a scale bias correction algorithm. Go to virtually any large marketing research firm's Web site, and you'll see a vast array of branded research products for everything from market segmentation to customer value analysis—all topped off with a diminutive SM, TM or ®.

A common denominator across some of these products is that they are proprietary, which means the firms won't disclose exactly how they work. That's why they're also known pejoratively as black boxes. A black box method is proprietary—a company is able to protect its product development investment. And if customers perceive added value in the approach, suppliers can charge a premium price to boot. (Black boxes and brand names are not synonymous. Almost all proprietary methods have a clever brand name, but there are also brand names attached to research methods that are not proprietary.)

At least two factors have given rise to this branding frenzy. First, competitive pressures force organizations to seek new ways to differentiate their product offerings from those of their competitors. Second, many large research companies are publicly held, and publicly held companies are under constant pressure to increase sales and profits each quarter. One way to do this is to charge a premium price for services. If a company has a proprietary method for doing a marketing segmentation study, presumably it can charge more for this approach than another firm using publicly available software such as SPSS or SAS.

Clients have no objective way of determining whether the results of a proprietary method would vary significantly from those of more standard approaches, and neither have we. Go to five different companies that have five different black boxes for choice modeling, for example. Each company claims its method is superior, yet it's impossible to assess, from a psychometric perspective, which possesses the highest level of validity.

Of course, no one is forcing clients to purchase a black box method, and they can always contact other organizations that have used a supplier's proprietary method to assess its effectiveness. Often clients will obtain multiple bids on a project so that they can select from a variety of approaches to help them answer their research questions.[19]

Client Ethics

Like research suppliers, clients (or users) also have a number of ethical dos and don'ts. Some of the more common client problems are requesting bids when a supplier has been predetermined, requesting bids to obtain free advice and methodology, making false promises, and issuing unauthorized RFPs.

Requesting Bids When a Supplier Has Been Predetermined

It is not uncommon for a client to prefer one research supplier over another. Such a preference may be due to a good working relationship, cost considerations, ability to make deadlines, friendship, or quality of the research staff. Having a preference per se is not unethical. It is unethical, however, to predetermine which supplier will receive a contract and yet ask for proposals from other suppliers to satisfy corporate requirements. Requiring time, effort, and money from firms that have no opportunity to win the contract is very unfair. Why more than a single RFP? Some corporations require more than one bid.

Requesting Bids to Obtain Free Advice and Methodology

Client companies seeking bargain basement prices have been known to solicit detailed proposals, including complete methodology and a sample questionnaire, from a number of suppliers. After "picking the brains" of the suppliers, the client assembles a questionnaire and then contracts directly with field services to gather the data. A variation of this tactic is to go to the cheapest supplier with the client's own proposal, derived by taking the best ideas from the other proposals. The client then attempts to get the supplier to conduct the more elaborate study at the lower price.

Making False Promises

Another technique used by unethical clients to lower their research costs is to hold out a nonexistent carrot. For example, a client might say, "I don't want to promise anything, but we are planning a major stream of research in this area, and if you will give us a good price on this first study, we will make it up to you on the next one." Unfortunately, the next one never comes—or if it does, the same line is used on another unsuspecting supplier.

Requesting Proposals without Authorization

In each of the following situations, a client representative sought proposals without first receiving the authority to allocate the funds to implement them:

1. A client representative decided to ask for proposals and *then* go to management to find out whether she could get the funds to carry them out.

2. A highly regarded employee made a proposal to management on the need for marketing research in a given area. Although managers were not too enthused about the idea, they told the researcher to seek bids so as not to dampen his interest or miss a potentially (but, in their view, highly unlikely) good idea.

3. A client representative and her management had different ideas on what the problem was and how it should be solved. The research supplier was not informed of the

management view, and even though the proposal met the representative's requirements, management rejected it out of hand.

4. Without consulting with the sales department, a client representative asked for a proposal on analyzing present sales performance. Through fear of negative feedback, corporate politics, or lack of understanding of marketing research, the sales department blocked implementation of the proposal.

Field Service Ethics

Marketing research field services are the production arm of the research industry requiring telephone or face-to-face interviews. They are the critical link between the respondent and the research supplier. It is imperative that they properly record information and carefully follow sampling plans. Otherwise, even the best research design will produce invalid information (garbage in; garbage out). Maintaining high ethical standards will aid a field service in procuring good raw data for the research firm.

Using Professional Respondents   The problem of professional respondents arises most often in the recruitment of focus group participants. Virtually all field services maintain a database of people willing to participate in qualitative discussion groups, along with a list of their demographic characteristics. Maintaining such a list is good business and quite ethical. When qualifications for group participants are easy (for example, pet owners, persons who drive SUVs), there is little temptation to use professional respondents. However, when a supplier wants, for example, persons who are heavy users of Oxydol detergent or who own a Russian Blue cat, it is not unheard of for a group recruiter to call a professional respondent and say, "I can get you into a group tomorrow with a $75 respondent fee and all you need to say is that you own a Russian Blue cat."

In an attempt to weed out professional respondents, a research supplier may specify that the participant must not have been a member of a qualitative discussion group within the past 6 months. However, dishonest field services will simply tell the professional respondent to deny having participated in a group within the past 6 months.

Data-Collection Code of Ethics

The Marketing Research Association (MRA) is an association to which many field services belong. The organization is dedicated to promoting excellence in data collection. To this end, it recently enacted the following code of ethics:

Companies Engaged in Data Collection . . .

1. will treat the respondent with respect and not influence a respondent's opinion or attitude on any issue through direct or indirect attempts, including the framing of questions.

2. will conduct themselves in a professional manner and ensure privacy and confidentiality.

3. will ensure that all formulas used during bidding and reporting during the data collection process conform with the MRA/CASRO Incidence Guidelines.

4. will make factually correct statements to secure cooperation and will honor promises made during the interview to respondents, whether verbal or written.

5. will give respondents the opportunity to refuse to participate in the research when there is a possibility they may be identifiable even without the use of their name or address (e.g., because of the size of the population being sampled).

6. will not use information to identify respondents without the permission of the respondent except to those who check the data or are involved in processing the data. If such permission is given, the interviewer must record it, or a respondent must do so, during all Internet studies, at the time the permission is secured.

7. will adhere to and follow these principles when conducting online research:

   ☐ Respondents' rights to anonymity *must* be safeguarded.

   ☐ Unsolicited e-mail *must not* be sent to those requesting not to receive any further e-mail.

   ☐ Researchers interviewing minors *must* adhere to the Children's Online Privacy Protection Act (COPPA).

   ☐ Before collecting, using, or disclosing personal information from a child, the researcher must obtain verifiable parental consent from the child's parent.

   Refer to MRA Internet Ethics Guidelines "Use of the Internet for Conducting Opinion and Marketing Research" for more educational information. http://www.mra-net. org/codes/internet_ethics_guidelines.PDF

8. for Internet research, will not use any data in any way contrary to the provider's published privacy statement without permission from the respondent.

9. will respect the respondent's right to withdraw or refuse to cooperate at any stage of the study and will not use any procedure or technique to coerce or imply that cooperation is obligatory.

10. will obtain and document respondent consent when it is known that the personally identifiable information of the respondent may be passed by audio, video, or Interactive Voice Response to a third party for legal or other purposes.

11. will obtain permission and document consent of a parent, legal guardian, or responsible guardian before interviewing children 13 years of age or younger. Prior to obtaining permission, the interviewer should divulge the subject matter, length of interview, and other special tasks that may be required of the respondent.

12. will ensure that all interviewers comply with any laws or regulations that may be applicable when contacting or communicating to any minor (18 years old or younger) regardless of the technology or methodology utilized.

13. will not reveal any information that could be used to identify clients without their written authorization.

14. will ensure that companies, their employees, and subcontractors involved in the data-collection process adhere to reasonable precautions so that multiple surveys are not conducted at the same time with a specific respondent without explicit permission from the sponsoring company or companies.

15. will consider all research materials provided by the client or generated as a result of materials provided by the client to be the property of the client. These materials will not be disseminated or disposed of without the verbal or written permission of the client.

16. will, as time and availability permit, give their client the opportunity to monitor studies in progress to ensure research quality.

17. will not represent a nonresearch activity to be opinion and marketing research, such as:

   ☐ the compilation of lists, registers, or data banks of names and addresses for any nonresearch purposes (e.g., canvassing or fund raising).

   ☐ industrial, commercial, or any other form of espionage.

   ☐ the acquisition of information for use by credit rating services or similar organizations.

- ☐ sales or promotional approaches to the respondent.
- ☐ the collection of debts.[20]

Respondents' Rights

Respondents in a marketing research project typically give their time and opinions and receive little or nothing in return. These individuals, however, do have certain rights that should be upheld by all marketing researchers. All potential participants in a research project have the right to choose, the right to safety, the right to be informed, and the right to privacy.

Right to Choose   Everyone has the right to determine whether or not to participate in a marketing research project. Some people, such as poorly educated individuals or children may not fully appreciate this privilege. A person who would like to terminate an interview or experiment may give short, incomplete answers or even false data.

The fact that a person has consented to be part of an experiment or to answer a questionnaire does not give the researcher carte blanche to do whatever she or he wants. The researcher still has an obligation to the respondent. For example, if a person participating in a taste test involving a test product and several existing products prefers the test product, the researcher does not have the right to use the respondent's name and address in a promotion piece, saying that "Ms. Jones prefers new Sudsies to Brand X."

Right to Safety   Research participants have the right to safety from physical or psychological harm. While it is unusual for a respondent to be exposed to physical harm, there have been cases of persons becoming ill during food taste tests. Also, on a more subtle level, researchers rarely warn respondents that a test product contains, say, a high level of salt. An unwitting respondent with hypertension could be placed in physical danger if the test ran several weeks.

It is much more common for a respondent to be placed in a psychologically damaging situation. Individuals might experience stress when an interviewer presses them to participate in a study. Others might experience stress when they cannot answer questions or are given a time limit to complete a task (for example, "You have five minutes to browse through this magazine, and then I will ask you a series of questions").

Right to Be Informed   Research participants have the right to be informed of all aspects of a research task. Knowing what is involved, how long it will take, and what will be done with the data, a person can make an intelligent choice as to whether to participate in the project.

Often, it is necessary to disguise the name of the research sponsor to avoid biasing the respondent. For example, it is poor research practice to say, "We are conducting a survey for Pepsi; which brand of soft drink do you consume most often?" In cases in which disguising the sponsor is required, a debriefing should take place following the completion of the interview. The debriefing should cover the study's purpose, the sponsor, what happens next with the data, and any other pertinent information. A debriefing can reduce respondent stress and build goodwill for the research industry. Unfortunately, taking the time to debrief a respondent is a cost that most companies are unwilling to incur.

In some business and academic research, the researcher may offer to provide the respondent with a copy of the research results as an incentive to obtain his or her participation in the project. When a commitment has been made to disseminate the findings to survey respondents, it should be fulfilled. On more than one occasion, we have participated in academic surveys where the carrot of research results was offered but never delivered.

Right to Privacy   All consumers have the right to privacy. All major research organizations, including the MRA (discussed above), the Council of American Survey Research Organizations (CASRO), the Internet Marketing Research Association (IMRO), the American Marketing Association (AMA), and the Advertising Research Foundation (ARF), have privacy codes. For example, with online research, lists of potential respondents must have one of two characteristics. Potential respondents must have either a prior opt-in for contact, or they must have an existing business relationship with the sender through which an e-mail contact would not be considered a random, unsolicited e-mail (spam).

Consumer privacy can be defined in terms of two dimensions of control. The first dimension includes control of unwanted telephone, mail, e-mail, or personal intrusion in the consumer's environment, and the second concerns control of information about the consumer. Consumer privacy can be viewed in the context of any interaction, profit or nonprofit, between marketer and consumer, including (but not limited to) credit and cash sales, consumer inquiries, and marketer-initiated surveys. The very nature of the marketing research business requires interviewers to invade an individual's privacy. An interviewer calls or approaches strangers, requests a portion of their limited free time, and asks them to answer personal questions—sometimes *very* personal questions. Perhaps the greatest privacy issue for consumers today is the role of marketing databases (see Chapter 4).

A number of laws have been passed in recent years dealing with various aspects of privacy as it relates to the marketing research industry. Diane Bowers, president of the Council of American Survey Research Organizations (CASRO), poses the following questions to marketing researchers:

Did you know. . . .

You may be violating the law if you interview customers of financial institutions who have not consented to that research? (Federal regulations require opt-out; some states require opt-in.)

You may be violating the law if patients you interview for health care research have not consented to that research? (Federal regulations require opt-in.)

You may be violating the law if telephone customers you interview for telecommunications research have not consented to that research? (Federal regulations require opt-out.)

You may be violating the law if you exchange personal data about respondents with someone in Europe without complying with the U.S. Safe Harbor and the EU Directive on Data Protection? (U.S. Safe Harbor principles must be verifiably adhered to, or contractually met, or you must be EU certified.)

You may be violating the law if you disclose personal information about respondents to a subcontractor, including interviewers and data processors? (Privacy laws require binding confidentiality agreements before any "onward transfer" of such information.)

*You are violating the law if you fail to comply with any material aspect of your online privacy statement or offline privacy policy? (The FTC, for example, has the ability to impose fines of up to several thousands of dollars **per day** for such violations.)*

You are legally and professionally liable for the privacy and confidentiality of your research respondents and the integrity of your research?[21]

The Global Research feature explains the Safe Harbor Program and why it is important to global marketing researchers.

Ethics and Professionalism

Today's business ethics are actually a subset of the values held by society as a whole. The values that underlie marketing decisions have been acquired through family, educational and religious institutions, and social movements (for example, women's rights, environmental

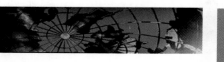

Safe Harbor in a Privacy Storm

The European Commission's Directive on Data Protection went into effect in October 1998 and prohibits the transfer of personal data to non-European Union nations that do not meet the European "adequacy" standard for privacy protection. Although the United States and the European Union share the goal of enhancing privacy protection for their citizens, the United States takes a different approach to privacy from that taken by the European Union (EU). The United States uses a sectoral approach that relies on a mix of legislation, regulation, and self-regulation. The EU, however, relies on comprehensive legislation that, for example, requires creation of government data protection agencies, registration of databases with those agencies, and in some instances prior approval before personal data processing may begin. As a result of these different privacy approaches, the Directive could have significantly hampered the ability of U.S. companies to engage in many trans-Atlantic transactions.

In order to bridge these different privacy approaches and provide a streamlined means for U.S. organizations to comply with the Directive, the U.S. Department of Commerce in consultation with the European Commission developed a "safe harbor" framework. The Safe Harbor Program—approved by the EU in 2000—is an important way for U.S. companies to avoid experiencing interruptions in their business dealings with the EU or facing prosecution by European authorities under European privacy laws. Certifying to the Safe Harbor will assure that EU organizations know that an American company provides "adequate" privacy protection, as defined by the Directive.

Organizations that participate in the Safe Harbor Program, which is voluntary, must comply with the Safe Harbor requirements and must publicly declare their adherence. To do so, an organization self-certifies annually to the Department of Commerce in writing that it agrees to adhere to the Safe Harbor Program's requirements. It must also state in its published privacy policy statement that it adheres to the Safe Harbor Program.

To qualify for the Safe Harbor Program, an organization can (1) join a self-regulatory program that adheres to the Safe Harbor's requirements and certify to the Department of Commerce or (2) develop its own self-regulatory privacy policy that conforms to the Safe Harbor and certify its adherence to the Department of Commerce.

The Safe Harbor Program consists of seven privacy principles:

1. Notice. This involves the purposes for which a company collects and uses information and how individuals can contact the organization with inquiries, the types of third parties that may receive the information, and the choices and means the organization offers for limiting its use and disclosure.

2. Choice. Choose (opt-out) whether personal information will be disclosed to a third party or used for a purpose incompatible with its original or authorized purpose. For sensitive information, affirmative or explicit (opt-in) choice must be given if the information is to be disclosed to a third party or used for another purpose.

3. Onward transfer. This is the transfer of information only to third parties who comply with Safe Harbor principles or with whom the organization has a written agreement requiring the third party to provide at least the same level of privacy protection.

4. Access. Individuals must have access to personal information about them and be able to correct or delete information that's inaccurate (except where the burden would be disproportionate to the risks of the individual's privacy or where the rights of other persons would be violated).

5. Security. Reasonable precautions must be taken to protect information from loss, misuse, unauthorized access, disclosure, alteration, and destruction.

6. Data integrity. Personal information must be relevant for the purposes for which it is to be used. An organization should take reasonable steps to ensure that data is reliable for its intended use, accurate, complete, and current.

7. Enforcement. Must have mechanisms for assuring compliance, and sanctions must be sufficiently vigorous to ensure compliance.[22]

protection). A marketing researcher with a mature set of ethical values accepts personal responsibility for decisions that affect the community. Considerations include the following:

☐ Employees' needs and desires and the long-range best interests of the organization

☐ The long-range goodwill and best interests of people who are directly affected by company activities (a bonus: good publicity for the firm)

☐ The societal values and conditions that provide the basis for the social structure in which the company exists

High standards of ethics and professionalism go hand in hand. Good ethics provide a solid foundation for professionalism, and striving for a lofty level of professionalism requires ethical behavior on the part of researchers.

Fostering Professionalism Because of the specialized knowledge and expertise they possess, members of a profession have influence and power over those for whom they provide a particular service. The tools of a doctor or lawyer cannot easily be obtained and sold in the marketplace; these professions guard their knowledge and control who has access to it. Although marketing researchers and marketers wield power and influence over their customers and even society, the marketing industry does not have a credentialing process or high entry barriers. The argument can be made that the marketers who most need to think, believe, and behave with professionalism are those in marketing research.

The distinction between a profession and professionalism is important: a **profession** and membership in it are objectively determined (for example, by medical board exams), whereas **professionalism** is evaluated on more personal and subjective levels. A study designed to measure the level of professionalism in marketing research found that researchers had autonomy in their jobs, were permitted to exercise judgment, and were recognized for their level of expertise and ability to work independently.[23] These characteristics are marks of professionalism. However, most researchers did not readily identify the contribution that marketing makes to society, nor did most firms tend to reward researchers' participation in professional organizations. These characteristics do not indicate a high level of professionalism.

Several steps have been taken recently to improve the level of professionalism in the marketing research industry. For example, CASRO has sponsored symposia dealing with ethical issues in survey research. CASRO also has created a code of ethics that has been widely disseminated to research professionals. The CASRO board has worked with groups such as the Marketing Research Association to provide input to legislatures considering antimarketing research legislation.

Researcher Certification Today, it is far too easy to begin practicing marketing research. We have seen several "fast talkers" convince unwary clients that they are qualified researchers. Unfortunately, relying on poor information to make major decisions has resulted in loss of market share, reduction in profits, and, in some cases, bankruptcy.

A profession and membership in it are objectively determined; professionalism is evaluated on more personal and subjective levels.

▷ **profession**
Organization whose membership is determined by objective standards, such as an examination.

▷ **professionalism**
Quality said to be possessed by a worker with a high level of expertise, the freedom to exercise judgment, and the ability to work independently.

Certification has generated a great deal of debate among members of the marketing research industry. It should be noted that certification is not licensing. *Licensing* is a mandatory procedure administered by a governmental body that allows one to practice a profession. *Certification* is a voluntary program administered by a nongovernmental body that provides a credential for differentiation in the marketplace. The issue of certification is sensitive because it directly affects marketing researchers' ability to practice their profession freely.

The MRA has launched a Professional Researcher Certification program. The objectives, according to the MRA, are "to encourage high standards within the profession in order to raise competency, establish an objective measure of an individual's knowledge and proficiency, and to encourage continued professional development."[24] The program allows for certification as a research user, supplier, or data collector. The process requires a series of continuing education credits and then passing an exam. Researchers can be grandfathered into certification if they meet the MRA's standards for a specific research job. The grandfathering period ends on February 28, 2007.

SUMMARY

The marketing research industry consists of (1) information users (consumer and industrial goods and services producers; federal, state, and local governments; media companies; retailers and wholesalers), (2) marketing research suppliers (custom research firms' syndicated research firms and limited function research firms), and (3) marketing research supplier service firms.

Users of marketing research can be further categorized as external or internal to the firm. External users include company vendors and franchisee. The primary internal user of marketing research is the marketing department, which seeks data for decision making in such areas as logistics, sales, promotions, new product development, brand management, and pricing. Other internal groups and departments using marketing research are senior management, product engineers, finance, manufacturing, human resources management, and legal.

The marketing research industry continues to grow at a steady rate. The size of marketing research departments, however, is shrinking despite growing budgets. This means that research users are relying on external suppliers more than ever. Some of the biggest challenges facing the research industry are maximizing survey participation and completion rates and reaching a representative sample of respondents.

Ethics are moral principles or values generally governing the conduct of an individual or group. The deontology theory says that a person will follow his or her obligations to another individual or society because upholding one's duty is what is considered ethically correct. In contrast, utilitarian ethical theory maintains that a choice yielding the greatest benefit to the greatest number of people is the choice that is ethically correct. The casuist theory holds that a decision should be made by comparing a current ethical dilemma with examples of similar ethical dilemmas and their outcomes.

Unethical practices by some suppliers include low-ball pricing, allowing subjectivity into the research, abusing respondents, selling unnecessary research, violating client confidentiality, and using black box branding. Unethical practices performed by some research clients include requesting bids when a supplier has been predetermined, requesting bids to gain free advice or methodology, making false promises, and issuing unauthorized requests for proposals. Marketing research field services have used professional respondents which is unethical.

Respondents have certain rights, including the right to choose whether to participate in a marketing research project, the right to safety from physical and psychological harm, and the right to be informed of all aspects of the research task. They should know what is involved, how long it will take, and what will be done with the data. Respondents also have the right to privacy.

The level of professionalism in the marketing research industry can be raised through the efforts of organizations such as CASRO and CMOR as well as socially concerned marketing research firms. Researcher certification has been launched by the MRA.

KEY TERMS & DEFINITIONS

custom, research firms Companies that carry out customized marketing research to address specific projects for corporate clients.

syndicated service research firms Companies that collect, package, and sell the same general market research data to many firms.

field service firms Companies that only collect survey data for corporate clients or research firms.

research panel A group of individuals who agree to participate in a series of research studies over time.

strategic partnership An alliance formed by two or more firms with unique skills and resources to offer a new service for clients, provide strategic support for each firm, or in some other manner create mutual benefits.

ethics Moral principles or values, generally governing the conduct of an individual or group.

low-ball pricing Quoting an unrealistically low price to secure a firm's business and then using some means to substantially raise the price.

profession Organization whose membership is determined by objective standards, such as an examination.

professionalism Quality said to be possessed by a worker with a high level of expertise, the freedom to exercise judgment, and the ability to work independently.

QUESTIONS FOR REVIEW & CRITICAL THINKING

1. Compare and contrast custom and syndicated marketing research firms.
2. What is the role of field service firms in marketing research?
3. Describe the marketing research industry.
4. List several key characteristics of corporate marketing research departments.
5. Discuss the various project offerings of syndicated service firms.
6. *(Team Exercise)* Divide the class into groups of five. Each group should select one section of the city in which the course is being taught (or the closest large city) and determine the zip codes for this section of the city. Next, go to *http://www.claritas.com* and follow the instructions for getting Prizm profiles by zip code. Each group should then discuss the marketing profile for its section of the city.
7. What do you see as the role of a code of ethics within an organization? What can be done to ensure that employees follow this code of ethics?
8. Who would you say has the greatest responsibility within the marketing research industry to raise the standards of ethics—marketing research suppliers, marketing research clients, or field services?
9. What role should the federal government play in establishing ethical standards for the marketing research industry? How might such standards be enforced?
10. If respondents consent to interviews after being told they will be paid $50 for their opinions, do they forfeit all respondent rights? If so, what rights have been forfeited?

11. What is the relationship between ethics and professionalism? What do you think can be done to raise the level of professionalism within the marketing research industry?

12. Explain the Safe Harbor Program and its importance.

WORKING THE NET

1. Compare the offerings of two marketing research firms, DSS Research and Burke Incorporated, by visiting their Web sites at *http://dssresearch.com* and *http://www.burke.com*.

2. Research International, which is part of the Kantar group, is a major international marketing research firm, with offices in 54 countries. Go to its Web site at *http://www.research-int.com* and report on its global research capabilities.

3. Interviewers must take special care when interviewing children or young people. The informed consent of the parent or responsible adult first must be obtained for interviews with children. Parents or responsible adults must be told some specifics about the interview process and special tasks, such as audio or video recording, taste testing, and respondent fees before permission is obtained. All researchers must adhere to all federal and state regulations regarding the interviewing of children 13 years of age or younger. All interviews conducted online must adhere to the Children's Online Privacy Protection Act (COPPA). Use these sites to gather more information about interviewing children and report the results to the class.

   http://www.ftc.gov/bcp/conline/edcams/kidzprivacy/biz.htm

   http://www.ftc.gov/privacy/coppafaqs.htm

   http://www.ftc.gov/bcp/conline/edcams/kidzprivacy/files/coppa-full_files/frame.htm

4. Go to CMOR's Web site at *http://www.cmor.org* for a discussion of the latest issue regarding respondent cooperation.

REAL-LIFE RESEARCH • 2.1

Schering-Plough and Pfizer Go Toe-to-Toe in Court with Marketing Research as Their Weapon

The dispute between Schering-Plough and Pfizer involved physicians' perceptions about various antihistamines and sales messages used by sales reps about the products. Antihistamines are drugs intended to relieve symptoms such as a runny nose, watery eyes, postnasal drip, skin rash, and itching that occur when the body releases histamine, as it often does as part of an allergic reaction to pollen, dust mites, and related irritants. Antihistamines come in two main classes: prescription products (such as Zyrtec and Allegra) and non-prescription [over-the-counter (OTC)] products (including Benadryl, Chlor-Trimeton, Drixoral, and Tavist). At the time of the research, Claritin was a prescription drug.

One of the primary, and clearly undesirable, side effects of antihistamines is the tendency of some brands to cause drowsiness. The federal Food and Drug Administration (FDA) requires that labels for most antihistamines carry a precautionary statement about possible drowsiness. Claritin and Allegra are the best products available with respect to low levels of drowsiness (essentially equal to that of a placebo). Zyrtec's drowsiness level is statistically higher than the placebo. For example, clinical trials have shown that Claritin's drowsiness level affects only 8 percent of adults, compared with 6 percent for a placebo—essentially no drowsiness at all. On the other hand, Zyrtec's drowsiness level affects 14 percent of adults compared with 8 percent for Claritin. These levels mean that Claritin (but not Zyrtec) can be promoted as nonsedating.

One of the major points was Schering's claim that, while Zyrtec's package labeling, advertising, and promotion all accurately portrayed the drug's sedation level, Pfizer sales representatives were making false claims about Zyrtec's drowsiness level in their detailing calls. (Typically, sales details are information calls, up to 10 minutes long, between the sales rep and the doctor, usually in the physician's office.) Schering alleged that some Pfizer sales reps were claiming that Zyrtec did not cause drowsiness (that is, was essentially nonsedating).

Schering based much of its claim on a market survey conducted by an outside research firm. In this survey, the firm randomly phoned a sample of physicians until it identified 200 doctors who reported that they had been detailed by a Pfizer sales rep within the prior 24 to 48 hours. The survey firm then telephoned each physician and asked three questions:

- In your recent Zyrtec detail, what did the Pfizer sales rep say to you about Zyrtec tablets?
- You may have mentioned this already, but I just want to make sure I have this right. During your recent Zyrtec detail, what did the sales rep say about Zyrtec tablets and sedation?
- Even at the risk of repeating what you have already told me, please be as complete and as specific as possible: What was said by the sales rep about Zyrtec tablets and sedation during the Zyrtec detail?

Based on the "verbatim" answers, Schering's outside research group coded each doctor's answers into common phrases for a simple frequency analysis across physicians and concluded that 14.5 percent of the physicians indicated that the Pfizer rep stated that Zyrtec is nonsedating (a claim prohibited by the FDA).

Schering had also conducted an earlier study, broadly similar to the survey, on a smaller sample of 98 physicians. In the earlier study, 16.4 percent of the doctors indicated that some sales reps said, in effect, that Zyrtec is nonsedating. Schering's outside survey expert asserted that his surveys suggested that some 15 to 20 percent of the doctors claimed their Pfizer sales rep indicated Zyrtec to be either nonsedating or essentially nonsedating.

Pfizer countered strongly that Schering's research studies were seriously flawed. None of the studies had used a control group, an essential element in marketing experiments. Also a doctor could infer "nonsedating" incorrectly from the sales rep's truthful remarks. Furthermore, the results didn't take into account the possible influence of external events (such as journal articles, doctor–patient interactions, or other information sources) and the physicians' own experience on their perceptions of Zyrtec's sedation levels. These additional sources of information could easily become confounded with what the sales rep actually said.

In preparation for further court battles, Pfizer initiated two novel surveys. The first sought to determine whether physicians really understood the sedation side effect as a continuum along which Zyrtec, even though it produces some sedation, might nonetheless be characterized by some physicians as nonsedating. The second survey tested whether physicians might mistakenly state, in response to survey questions, that the sales rep mentioned Zyrtec was nonsedating, even though the presentation never actually used that term or, indeed, any prohibited information.

A sample of 399 physicians perceived that Claritin and Allegra are no more or less sedating than a placebo. That is, the survey found no statistical difference between the mean values of these three items. Their properties were consistent with the FDA-approved labeling for these products.

The physicians also understood that the antihistamines labeled as causing drowsiness (Zyrtec, Benadryl, and Chlor-Trimeton) do in fact cause some drowsiness. All were ranked as more "sedating" than the placebo, Claritin, or Allegra by statistically significant margins. Moreover, the physicians perceived real, statistical differences among these three brands in their degree of sedation. The physicians drew the average line of demarcation between sedating and nonsedating at a point close to the average value of Zyrtec.

A second sample consisted of 578 general practitioners, family practitioners, internists, and allergists who prescribed antihistamines as part of their practice. The physicians were first shown a videotape that depicted a sales representative having a detailing discussion with a doctor. The interviewer then left the physician's office. About 24 to 48 hours after the physician saw the videotape, an interviewer contacted the physician and asked questions that essentially mirrored those used in Schering's two surveys. The 24- to 48-hour delay between exposure to the stimulus and the questions about it was intended to mimic the survey methodology of the Schering surveys, which had identified respondents by asking physicians if they had been detailed on Zyrtec within the previous one to two days.

One or two days after seeing the videotape, interviewers contacted the physicians by telephone, and asked, "What was said about (Zyrtec/Ardovac)?"; "What, if anything, was said in the video about (Zrytec/Ardovac) and side effects?"; and "What, if anything, was said in the video about (Zrytec/Ardovac) and sedation?" These questions mimicked those asked in the Schering litigation survey. The senior personnel of Guideline Research then coded the verbatim answers, and we tabulated and analyzed the responses. We found the following results:

- About 25.6 percent of survey respondents reported that the sales representative in the videotape said the product was nonsedating or words to that effect.

- There was no statistically significant difference between the Zyrtec cells and the Ardovac cells in terms of reporting that the sales representative had claimed the product was nonsedating.

- There were no statistically significant differences in responses based on the various levels of discussion of side effects. In all six cells, a substantial proportion of physicians reported that the sales representative on the tape said the product was nonsedating. Thus, the extent of commentary within the 3- to 6-minute framework had a significant effect on responses. In reality, of course, all of the video presentations contained only FDA-permitted claims.

The data from this study are similar in magnitude to the approximately 15 to 20 percent of nonsedating responses across the surveys found by Schering's survey research team. Such apparent consistency would be expected to instill confidence that "what was said" is not necessarily "what is reported." The error in this reasoning is strikingly apparent, however. None of the tapes used the term *nonsedating*. Therefore, the survey responses obviously could not be due to a stimulus (in this case, the detail session) that did not contain any prohibited message. This study demonstrates forcefully that it's incorrect to infer "what was said" (stimulus) from "what was reported" (response).

Schering's burden was to prove that Pfizer made prohibited, rather than permitted, statements. As demonstrated by a second study, the evidence by Schering didn't satisfy Schering's burden. The second study demonstrates that the Schering surveys couldn't be used reliably to discern whether the nonsedating survey responses were caused by truthful or by deceptive messages. A physician could still have concluded, based on permitted statements made by a Pfizer representative, that Zyrtec is nonsedating or "essentially nonsedating." These inferences could arise from a large variety of sources, unrelated to the sales rep's detail.

At this point, Pfizer began preparing for a full trial to contest Schering's pending motion for a permanent injunction. As part of its activities, Pfizer commissioned several additional scientific experiments to test the validity of Schering's survey evidence; for various reasons, however, the parties decided to settle the case. Schering was allowed to convert its temporary injunction against Pfizer to a permanent one. Pfizer was granted several restrictions on Schering's Claritin promotion.[25]

Questions

1. Discuss the role of marketing research in this case. Was it critical to the outcome?
2. How might lawyers attack evidence presented from marketing research data?
3. Give examples of other instances where marketing research could play a role in lawsuits.

Coke Juices Up a Market Test

For several days Dyquan Gibson and his friends had a strong incentive to study every afternoon at a neighborhood Richmond, Virginia, Boys & Girls Club. "If you finished your homework, you got a burger," says Dyquan, who is now 11 years old.

Dyquan and his friends didn't know it, but the free Whoppers came from a consultant hired by Coca-Cola Company. Officials at the Atlanta beverage company had sent the man to Richmond with $9,000. He gave cash to the clubs and other nonprofit groups and told them to treat the children to hundreds of "value meals" at Burger King.

Millions of dollars in sales were at stake for Coke. The company was trying to persuade Burger King to run a national promotion for its slushy dessert drink, Frozen Coke, which Burger King sells at all of its restaurants. But Burger King wanted to run a test promotion before it invested in a big campaign. So the Miami-based restaurant chain ran a two-week test in Richmond, offering a coupon for a free Frozen Coke when customers bought a value meal—a sandwich, fries, and drink combo. If the meals sold well enough, and enough people redeemed the coupons, Burger King would take the promotion national.

The Coke officials embarked on the buying spree because the initial test results were dismal. In the end, their efforts added only 700 value meals to the nearly 100,000 sold during the promotion. But even that small number helped bolster Coke's case for a national push. Burger King sank roughly $10 million into the campaign.

Later, Coke acknowledged that some of its employees "improperly influenced" the sales results in Richmond, and that the actions were "wrong and inconsistent with the values of the Coca-Cola Co." It issues a public apology to Burger King—and agreed to pay the company and its franchisees up to $21 million to make amends.[26]

Questions

1. Were Coke's attempts to fix the market test unethical? If so, is Coke guilty of unethical behavior, or was it just the fault of some misguided employees?
2. Burger King is Coke's second largest fountain drink customer after McDonald's. The Richmond test started out very poorly, and it was clear that unless results improved, the national Frozen Coke promotion was not going to happen. Coke was worried that without the promotion it would not make its fountain sales objectives for the year. At that point, it was decided to stimulate value-meal sales in Richmond. Did the desired end (meeting sales goals) justify the actions taken? Why or why not?
3. Use the ethics theories described in the chapter to illustrate how Coke decision makers could have reached a different decision?
4. Should Coke fire those responsible, counsel them, or do nothing?

PROBLEM DEFINITION, EXPLORATORY RESEARCH, AND THE RESEARCH PROCESS

LEARNING OBJECTIVES

1.	To understand the problem definition process.
2.	To learn the steps involved in the marketing research process.
3.	To understand the components of the research request.
4.	To learn the advantages and disadvantages of survey, observation, and experiment research techniques.
5.	To become familiar with how the marketing research process is initiated.

During a recent summer, Starbucks wanted to answer this question: Does Starbucks' out-of-home media (such as billboards, kiosk ads, vehicle wraps, vinyl signs that can be placed on cars and trucks) reach and affect people as efficiently as Starbucks' investments in television, radio, and print advertising?

Starbucks hired Bruzzone Research to measure the effects of Starbucks advertising. The Starbucks name had not been closely associated with summertime drinks; one objective of the summer advertising was to change that.

The study was conducted online. This enabled the research company to show each respondent virtually every piece of advertising that Starbucks used over the summer. The research found that virtually all of the Starbucks advertising worked. When people noticed any of it, they ended up buying more of the summer drinks being advertised than people who didn't notice the advertising. It also showed that some of the advertising worked a lot better than other advertising.

The survey came to a few other conclusions:

☐ Reminders as to the appropriateness of Starbucks' cold drinks during the summer worked well.

☐ Simple announcement of what products were now available, and where, did not work as well.

☐ Simple illustrations of the drinks with palm trees, beaches, and blue sky worked well.

☐ More complex "what is this?" graphics did not work as well.

☐ The depiction of gratification was critical. The results showed specifically what conveyed gratification and what didn't.

☐ Starbucks' green straws, featured in some advertising, produced mixed results.

☐ Limits need to be set on the amount spent on a single execution, and the results helped show where to set the limits. Starbucks found a number of cases where spending more did not produce more buyers.[1] ■

Gathering data about Starbucks' advertising fan (or any other subject) requires marketing research. Conducting marketing research involves a series of logical steps, beginning with problem definition. What are the steps in the marketing research process? How is the research process initiated? These are the issues we will address in this chapter.

Critical Importance of Correctly Defining the Problem

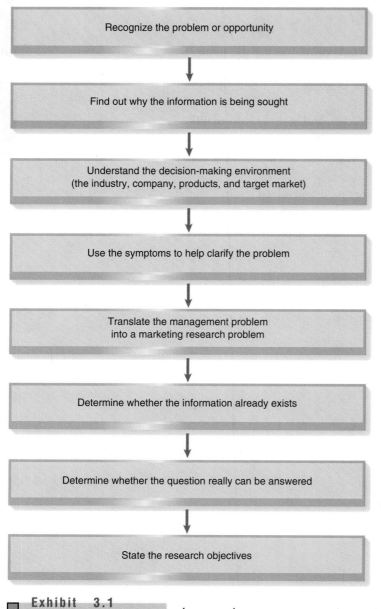

Correctly defining the problem is the crucial first step in the marketing research process. If the research problem is defined incorrectly, the research objectives will also be wrong, and the entire marketing research process will be a waste of time and money. For example, suppose a new product manager asks a marketing researcher to determine which recipe for a new peppermint and honey salad dressing consumers prefer, and the researcher correctly tells the manager that recipe A is strongly preferred over recipe B. If, in fact, target customers do not like peppermint and honey salad dressing at all, the real problem was never addressed.

The process for defining the problem is shown in Exhibit 3.1. Note that the ultimate goal is to develop clear, concise, and meaningful marketing research objectives. Researching such objectives will yield precise decision-making information for managers.

Recognize the Problem or Opportunity

The marketing research process begins with the recognition of a marketing problem or opportunity. As changes occur in the firm's external environment, marketing managers are faced with the questions "Should we change the existing marketing mix?" and, if so, "How?" Marketing research may be used to evaluate products and services, promotion, distribution, and pricing alternatives. In addition, it may be used to find and evaluate new opportunities, in a process called **opportunity identification**.

Let's look at an example of opportunity identification. In 2005, online travel spending surpassed offline travel spending for the first time. During that year, $66 billion of leisure and unmanaged business trips were bought through the Internet.[2] Yet, the landscape for consumers is confusing because there are so many sites out there. For savvy marketers, this information represents an opportunity. Marketing research can hone in and clarify where the best opportunities lie.

Exhibit 3.1

Problem Definition Process

Marketing research led to the creation of sites like Cheapflights, FareCompare, Kayak, Mobissimo, Ziso, SideStep, and Yahoo's Farechase. These so-called aggregators do what consumers have attempted with their own manual comparison shopping: open several browsers on a computer screen to check multiple travel sites. Aggregators simultaneously scour the Web sites of airlines, hotels, car rental companies, and consolidators, and present data along with the special deals.

Mobissimo, founded in 2003, noticed that other aggregators targeted the U.S. market. Again, this presented an opportunity to fill a niche in the marketplace. Mobissimo offers access to international hotels and many low-fare international carriers that the other aggregators lack. A direct flight from New York to Athens, for instance, may be too expensive. But Mobissimo can fly these travelers to Amsterdam and connect with one of Europe's 50 discount airlines. Marketing research helps firms like Mobissimo understand online travel purchasers' needs and what features they want on an online aggregator Web site. Satisfaction studies, done every quarter, help track the online travel purchasers' level of satisfaction and loyalty to a site.

Of course, marketing research doesn't always deal with opportunities. Managers may want to know, for example, "Why are we losing marketing share?" or "What should we do about Ajax Manufacturing lowering its prices by 10 percent?" In these instances, marketing researchers can help managers solve problems.

> **opportunity identification**
> Using marketing research to find and evaluate new opportunities.

Find Out Why the Information Is Being Sought

Large amounts of money, effort, and time are wasted because requests for marketing information are poorly formulated or misunderstood. For example, managers may not have a clear idea of what they want or may not phrase their questions properly. Therefore, marketing researchers often find the following activities helpful:

- ☐ Discuss what the information will be used for and what decisions might be made as a result of the research. Work through detailed examples to help clarify the issue.

- ☐ Try to get the client or manager to prioritize their questions. This helps sort out central questions from those of incidental interest.

- ☐ Rephrase the questions in several slightly different forms and discuss the differences.

- ☐ Create sample data and ask if such data would help answer the questions. Simulate the decision process.

- ☐ Remember that the more clear-cut you think the questions are and the more quickly you come to feel that the questions are straightforward, the more you should doubt that you have understood the real need.

In the Practicing Marketing Research feature, Karole Friemann, director of products and services for Marketing Research Project Management, Inc., discussed the important steps in initiating a research project.

Understand the Decision-Making Environment with Exploratory Research

Once researchers understand the motivation for conducting the research, often they need additional background information to fully comprehend the problem. This may mean simply talking to brand managers or new product managers, reading company reports, visiting production facilities and retail stores, and perhaps talking with suppliers.

PRACTICING MARKETING RESEARCH

Getting It Right the First Time

A marketing research project is effective if, and only if, it provides information that results in better business actions, decisions, products, or strategies. Executives waste time and money when they don't apply marketing research results—and waste even more time and money if results are applied inappropriately.

This first, so-called initiation phase of a marketing research project begins when the research request is made and ends when marketing research objectives are finalized. The sponsor's ownership and execution of the following six steps during the research project's initiation phase are critical to its effectiveness:

- Fully educate marketing researchers on why this marketing research is requested. Specify, in detail, the business issue prompting the research; other perspectives colleagues may have on this and their business functions or responsibilities; how this issue relates to your industry—whether it is a challenge for all companies in your industry or just your company; chief competitors with respect to this issue and what they are doing about it; the target audiences from which you need information; how marketing research is expected to help address the business issue.

- State the specific actions, decisions, or strategies that executives plan to make based on research results. The marketing researcher's understanding of how the project's results will be applied is fundamental to establishing marketing research objectives; designing research alternatives, methodologies, questions, response formats, and response scales; analyzing and interpreting data; and reporting results.

- Name the departments, business partners, or individuals who will actually take the actions or make the decisions or strategies defined above.

- Recruit project team members. Contact people identified in the third step and make them aware of the marketing research project that's been requested, its importance, and the role each is expected to play in applying research results. Recruit them or their designated representatives for the marketing research project team.

- Be present at the first project team meeting to discuss, review, and revise statements of business issues and establish and prioritize research objectives. The first project team meeting will probably be the first time that people who must apply the results will see the sponsor's preliminary statements of the business issues and expectations for the research. Their valuable perspectives should be incorporated into the statement of business issues, along with any suggestions on how research results should be applied.

- Review research alternatives, methodologies, and their respective costs and time frames and finalize research objectives and the scope of the project. Once the fifth step has been completed, marketing research professionals can design research alternatives and methodologies to meet the project's objectives. They can also provide ballpark estimates of the cost and time frame for each. When this is done, the sponsor can review the research objectives, their design alternatives and methodologies, and respective resource requirements. Sometimes the resources required to meet a given research objective will be deemed inappropriate, and that objective will be dropped from the project scope.[3]

If the industry has a trade association, researchers might peruse its Web site for information published by the association. The better the marketing researcher understands the decision-making environment, including the industry, the firm, its products or services, and the target market, the more likely it is that the problem will be defined correctly. This step may be referred to as conducting a **situation analysis**.

Sometimes informed discussions with managers and suppliers and on-site visits aren't enough. **Exploratory research** may be conducted to obtain greater understanding of a concept or to help crystallize the definition of a problem. It is also used to identify important variables to be studied. Exploratory research is preliminary research, not the definitive research used to determine a course of action.

Exploratory research can take several forms: pilot studies, experience surveys, secondary data analysis, pilot studies case analysis and focus groups. **Pilot studies** are surveys using a limited number of respondents and often employing less rigorous sampling techniques than are employed in large, quantitative studies.

Nickelodeon, for example, was well aware of the new baby boom and wanted to know what it meant for the network. Exploratory research found that a long-held assumption about kids' attitudes was not accurate: the belief that female images in TV programming generally work with girls but alienate boys. The exploratory research consisted of a small-scale pilot study on the Internet and focus groups in which children were brought together to discuss their attitudes toward television. Like Nickelodeon's research, much exploratory research is highly flexible, with researchers following ideas, clues, and hunches as long as time and money constraints permit. Often ideas are obtained from so-called experts in the field. Nickelodeon, for example, could have spoken with child psychologists.

As the researcher moves through the exploratory research process, a list of marketing research problems and subproblems should be developed. The investigator should identify all factors that seem to be related to the problem area, as these are probable research topics. This stage of problem definition requires a brainstorming-type approach, but one guided by the previous stage's findings. All possibilities should be listed without regard to the feasibility of addressing them via research. Nickelodeon ultimately decided to define the marketing research problem as determining whether a live-action show with girls as the protagonists would appeal to both sexes. Quantitative marketing research results showed that such a program would have dual appeal. Managerial action taken as a result yielded a program where the star was female, but the audience was 53 percent male.[4]

Experience Surveys Analysis A second form of exploratory research is experience surveys. **Experience surveys** involve talking with knowledgeable individuals, both inside and outside the organization, who may provide insights into the problem. Rarely do experience surveys include a formal questionnaire. Instead, the researcher may simply have a list of topics to be discussed. The survey, then, is much like an informal discussion. For example, if Jet Blue is redesigning the interior of its aircraft, it may use experience surveys to speak with interior designers, frequent flyers, flight attendants, and pilots.

Secondary Data Analysis Secondary data analysis is another form of exploratory research. Because secondary data analysis is covered extensively in Chapter 4, we will touch on it only lightly here. *Secondary data* are data that have been gathered for some purpose other than the one at hand. Today, marketing researchers can use the Internet to access countless sources of secondary data quickly and at minimal expense. There are few subjects that have not been analyzed at one time or another. With a bit of luck, the marketing researcher can use secondary data to help precisely define the problem.

---

situation analysis
Studying the decision-making environment within which the marketing research will take place.

exploratory research
Preliminary research conducted to increase understanding of a concept, to clarify the exact nature of the problem to be solved, or to identify important variables to be studied.

pilot studies
Surveys using a limited number of respondents and often employing less rigorous sampling techniques than are employed in large, quantitative studies.

experience surveys
Discussions with knowledgeable individuals, both inside and outside the organization, who may provide insights into the problem.

⮞ case analysis
Reviewing information from situations that are similar to the current one.

Case Analysis   Case analysis represents the fourth form of exploratory research. The purpose of **case analysis** is to review information from a few other situations that are similar to the present research problem. For example, electric utilities across America are scrambling to adopt the marketing concept and to become customer-oriented; these utilities are conducting market segmentation research, customer satisfaction studies, and customer loyalty surveys. To better understand the deregulation of the electric utility industry, marketing researchers are examining case studies on the deregulation of the airline industry. Researchers, however, must always take care to determine the relevancy of any case study to the present research problem.

Focus Groups   Focus groups are in-depth discussions, usually consisting of 8 to 12 participants, which are led by a moderator and are generally limited to one particular concept, idea, or theme. The general idea is to have what one person says generate thoughts and comments by others, therefore creating group dynamics. That is, the interplay of responses will yield more information than if the same number of persons had contributed in individual interviews. Focus groups are the primary topic of discussion in Chapter 5, so they will be lightly covered here. We mention them now because they are probably the most popular form of exploratory research.

Focus groups can, and do, cover just about any topic imaginable. Your authors, unlike all other marketing research text authors, have conducted over 2,000 focus group sessions. When used in exploratory research, focus groups are used to help clarify and understand the problem and issues involved. A few examples of topics that we have covered include: what creates the Harley-Davidson mystique, what happens when you discover head lice in your children, whether having a tequila made in America is a problem, what kitchen item is most difficult to clean, and the list goes on.

Using Intranets for Exploratory Research   The computer can be a very powerful tool for doing exploratory research. In very large organizations with intranets, the researcher has the capability of determining whether needed or relevant information is available somewhere inside the organization. The corporate marketing research department at Texas Instruments (TI), for example, has developed a powerful intranet application that permits TI managers worldwide to search for past research studies and those currently in progress on the basis of key words. They have immediate online access to a brief description of each study and can send email seeking permission to view the full text of reports on old projects. Permission can be granted electronically via email by the owner of the report (the person who paid for it), and the full text can be accessed online.

More and more organizations are developing similar systems to permit much more effective managerial use of information resources. In large organizations, it is not uncommon for a group in one part of the organization to conduct a research project that might have great value to managers in another part of the organization. Too often, there is no way for one group to find out what another group has already done. Intranet systems like the one at Texas Instruments will help organizations get the most mileage out of their research dollars.

While intranets provide easy access to internal data, the Internet is an invaluable resource for searching tens of millions of external sources for the information needed. At the exploratory stage, a researcher might use any one or several of the online search engines to find information needed. This type of search not only is much faster than a traditional library search but also provides access to an incredible array of information that is not available in any library. The researcher can perform an Internet search and point out or download the desired information in a matter of hours rather than the days or weeks a standard library search might require. Finally, the researcher can identify a range of discussion or special-interest groups on the Internet that may be relevant to a research project.

Completing Exploratory Research The end of exploratory study comes when the marketing researchers are convinced that they have found the major dimensions of the problem. They may have defined a set of questions that can be used as specific guides to a detailed research design. Or they may have developed a number of potential ideas about possible causes of a specific problem of importance to management. They may also have determined that certain other factors are such remote possibilities that they can be safely ignored in any further study. Finally, the researchers may end exploration because they feel that further research is not needed or is not presently possible due to time, money, or other constraints.

Use the Symptoms to Clarify the Problem

Marketing researchers must be careful to distinguish between symptoms and the real problem. A symptom is a phenomenon that occurs because of the existence of something else. For example, managers often talk about the problem of poor sales, declining profits, increased customer complaints, or defecting customers. Each of these is a symptom of a deeper problem. That is, something is causing a company's customers to leave. Is it lower prices offered by the competition? Or is it better service? Focusing on the symptoms and not the true problem is often referred to as the *iceberg principle*. Approximately 10 percent of an iceberg rises out of the ocean; the remaining 90 percent is below the surface. Preoccupied with the obstacle they can see, managers may fail to comprehend and confront the deeper problem, which remains submerged.

Ensuring that the true problem has been defined is not always easy. Managers and marketing researchers must use creativity and good judgment. Cutting through to the heart of a problem is a bit like peeling an onion—you must take off one layer at a time. One approach to eliminating symptoms is to ask "What caused this to occur?" When the researcher can no longer answer this question, the real problem is at hand. For example, when a St. Louis manufacturer of pumps faced a 7 percent decline in sales from the previous year, managers asked, "What caused this?" A look at sales across the product line showed that sales were up or about the same on all items except large, heavy-duty submersible pumps, whose sales were down almost 60 percent. They then asked, "What caused this?" Sales of the pump in the eastern and central divisions were about the same as in the previous year. However, in the western region, sales were zero! Once again they asked, "What caused this?" Further investigation revealed that a Japanese manufacturer was dumping a similar submersible pump in western markets at about 50 percent of the St. Louis manufacturer's wholesale price. This was the true problem. The manufacturer lobbied the Justice Department to fine the Japanese company and to issue a cease and desist order.

Whenever possible top management should be involved in defining the problem. This is discussed in the Practicing Marketing Research box which appears on page 69.

Translate the Management Problem into a Marketing Research Problem

Once the true management decision problem has been identified, it must be converted into a marketing research problem. The **marketing research problem** specifies what information is needed to solve the problem and how that information can be obtained efficiently and effectively. The **marketing research objective**, then, is the goal statement, defining the specific information needed to solve the marketing research problem. Managers must combine this information with their own experience and other related information to make a proper decision. Recall from our opening story that the Starbucks'

> **marketing research problem**
> A statement specifying the type of information needed by the decision maker to help solve the management decision problem and how that information can be obtained efficiently and effectively.

> **marketing research objective**
> A goal statement, defining the specific information needed to solve the marketing research problem.

marketing research problem was to gather information online to determine recall and the impact of out-of-home media. The marketing research objective was to measure recall and purchase of specific products featured in the promotions via billboards, kiosk ads, and vehicle wraps.

In contrast to the marketing research problem, the **management decision problem** is action-oriented. Management decision problems tend to be much broader in scope and far more general than marketing research problems, which must be narrowly defined and specific if the research effort is to be successful. Sometimes several research studies must be conducted to solve a broad management decision problem. The management decision problem for Starbucks was: "Does Starbucks' out-of-home media reach and affect people as efficiently as Starbucks' investments in television, radio, and print advertising?" Or, the Starbucks vice president of promotion might simply say, "How do I get the most bang for my bucks [sales] from my advertising budget?"

> **management decision problem**
> A statement specifying the type of managerial action required to solve the problem.

Determine Whether the Information Already Exists

It often seems easier and more interesting to develop new information than to delve through old reports and data files to see whether the required information already exists. There is a tendency to assume that current data are superior to data collected in the past, as current data appear to be a "fix on today's situation." And because researchers have more control over the format and comprehensiveness of fresh data, they promise to be easier to work with. Yet, using existing data can save managers time and money if such data can answer the research question.

Research objectives must be as specific and unambiguous as possible. Remember that the entire research effort (in terms of time and money) is geared toward achieving the objectives. When the marketing researcher meets with a committee to learn the goals of a particular project, committee members may not fully agree on what is needed. We have learned from experience to go back to a committee (or the individual in charge) with a written list of research objectives. The researcher should then ask the manager, "If we accomplish the objectives on this list, will you have enough information to make informed decisions about the problem?" If the reply is yes, the manager should be asked to sign off on the objectives. The researcher should then give the manager a copy and keep a copy for the research files. Putting the agreed-on objectives in writing prevents the manager from saying later, "Hey, this is not the information I wanted." In a busy and hectic corporate environment, such misunderstandings happen more frequently than one might imagine.

Avoiding the Nice-to-Know Syndrome   Even after conducting exploratory research, managers often tend to discuss research objectives in terms of broad areas of ignorance. They say, in effect, "Here are some things I don't know." A Starbucks' executive might wonder: "You know, we already sell fresh-baked goods in our stores. . . . I wonder if people would buy frozen Starbucks pastries and rolls in supermarkets?" Maybe I'll ask this question on our out-of-home advertising media study. Unfortunately, this scenario usually leads to disappointment. There is nothing wrong with interesting findings, but they must also be *actionable*. That is, the findings must provide decision-making information. Accomplishment of a research objective has to do more than reduce management's level of ignorance. Unless all the research is exploratory, it should lead to a decision. Perhaps the best way to assure that research is actionable is to determine how the research results will be implemented. Asking a single question about purchase intent of Starbucks frozen baked goods in a grocery store is not actionable. So much more would have to be known—for example, type of goods, price points, packaging design, and so forth. Numerous taste tests would also have to be conducted.

PRACTICING MARKETING RESEARCH

Importance of Top Management's Definition of the Management Problem

Researchers report that they receive incomplete, and even incorrect, answers if the person who commissions the study is not the ultimate decision maker. In one case, the commissioning agent (a midlevel manager) said the research was being conducted to learn about the market. In reality, the senior decision maker wanted to know whether version A or B would gain a bigger share of the market. The research did a great job of exploring the boundaries of the market, defining customer segments and their needs, and identifying likely competitors. But the senior decision maker found the research largely irrelevant, because it did not tell him whether to go with version A or B.

While senior decision makers may say they are too busy to talk or insist on delegating the task to someone junior, researchers who have stood firm and insisted on talking to the senior person report the effort is worth it. "First, I asked to meet the [CEO] to discuss the firm's mission and strategy and how the research would help him make better decisions. When that wasn't an option, I wrote up a one-page description of the situation and the research objectives and asked to have the CEO approve it before I designed the research. When he didn't have time to look at it, I said I couldn't waste the firm's resources by starting without clear goals. *Then* I got his full attention. We met and, believe me, the CEO's needs were quite different from what I had been told. I was really glad I had insisted. If I'd waited until the research was done, I'd never have gotten his attention, and the research would have been largely irrelevant."[5]

Determine Whether the Question Can Be Answered

When marketing researchers promise more than they can deliver, they hurt the credibility of marketing research. It is extremely important for researchers to avoid being impelled—either by overeagerness to please or by managerial macho—into an effort that they know has a limited probability of success. In most cases, you can discern in advance the likelihood of success by identifying the following:

- ☐ Instances in which you know for certain that information of the type required exists or can be readily obtained.
- ☐ Situations in which you are fairly sure, based on similar prior experiences, that the information can be gathered.
- ☐ Cases in which you know that you are trying something quite new and there is a real risk of drawing a complete blank.

State the Research Objectives

The culmination of the problem definition process is a statement of the research objectives. These objectives are stated in terms of the precise information necessary to address the marketing research problem/opportunity. Well-formulated objectives serve as a road map in pursuing the research project. They also serve as a standard that later will enable managers to evaluate the quality and value of the work by asking "Were the

FROM THE FRONT LINE

Get Your Objectives in Order before You Start

Roger Gates, President, DSS Research

We have learned through bitter experience that it is critical to get a meeting of the minds between the research team at DSS and our client on the objectives of the study. The big problem is often "forcing" our client to get specific regarding what they need to achieve with the research—what decisions they need to make, what they need to know at the end of the research that they don't know now, and what the background and context are for the research.

In a more formalized situation with a written RFP, clients are often vague regarding the research objectives and exactly why they are ordering the research. In a less formal situation where the RFP may consist of nothing more than a telephone call or brief e-mail request, the information given by the client may be even more limited. I frequently have to prod account executives and project managers to get more information from the client on the issues noted above.

The objectives are critical because they should guide every phase of the research—how we collect the data, from whom we get informa-tion, sample size, the kinds of information we need to get from target individuals, the types of analysis required, the focus of the analysis, and the nature of the report and face-to-face presen-tation. There is nothing worse than completing a project only to have a client ask, "Why didn't we ask this or why didn't we ask that?"

Failure to address the issue at the beginning of a project often produces what we call "scope creep" as the project unfolds. For example, a questionnaire is developed for a telephone sur-vey based on an initial set of objectives pro-vided in an RFP. After reviewing a draft of the questionnaire, the client might ask, "Why aren't we getting information about the image that consumers have of us and our competitors?" Our response might be that this was not cov-ered in the objectives in your RFP. The client then might respond, "Well, we need to do it."

Scope creep creates problems because an initial study costed out on the basis of a 10-minute telephone interview that would have been adequate to cover the initial objectives grows into a 17-minute survey as additional ob-jectives are uncovered along the way. At this point we have to go back to the client and say we need more money. This is usually not a very pleasant conversation, but it is a necessary one. Fortunately, deficiencies in the initial stated ob-jectives are often corrected as we go through the design process as described above, but it is much better if all of this is addressed up front.

objectives met?" and "Do the recommendations flow logically from the objectives and the research findings?"

Research Objectives as Hypotheses Often researchers state a research ob-jective in the form of a hypothesis. A **hypothesis** is a conjectural statement about a rela-tionship between two or more variables that can be tested with empirical data; it is considered to be plausible, given the available information. A good hypothesis will con-tain clear implications for testing stated relationships. For example, based on exploratory research, a researcher might hypothesize that a doubling of expenditures for billboards in cities of 300,000 or more population will increase the sales of Starbucks' summer drinks by 15 percent. Alternatively, a second hypothesis might be that spending $30,000 for ve-hicle wraps in cities of 300,000 or more will have no significant impact on the sales of Starbucks' summer drinks.

> **hypothesis**
> A conjectural statement about a relationship be-tween two or more vari-ables that can be tested with empirical data.

Marketing Research Process

We have just discussed the first step in the marketing research process: identifying the problem/opportunity and stating the marketing research objectives. The other steps in the process are creating the research design, choosing the method of research, selecting the sampling procedure, collecting the data, analyzing the data, writing and presenting the report, and following up on any recommendations that were made as a result of the report (see Exhibit 3.2). The overview of the process in this section forms the foundation for the remainder of the text. The following chapters examine specific aspects of the marketing research process.

Creating the Research Design

The **research design** is a plan for addressing the research objectives or hypotheses. In essence, the researcher develops a structure or framework to answer a specific research problem/opportunity. There is no single best research design. Instead, different designs offer an array of choices, each with certain advantages and disadvantages. Ultimately, trade-offs are typically involved. A common trade-off is between research costs and the quality of the decision-making information provided. Generally speaking, the more precise and error-free the information obtained, the higher the cost. Another common trade-off is between time constraints and the type of research design selected. Overall, the researcher must attempt to provide management with the best information possible, subject to the various constraints under which he or she must operate. The researcher's first task is to decide whether the research will be descriptive or causal.

> **research design**
> The plan to be followed to answer the marketing research objectives.

Exhibit 3.2

Marketing Research Process

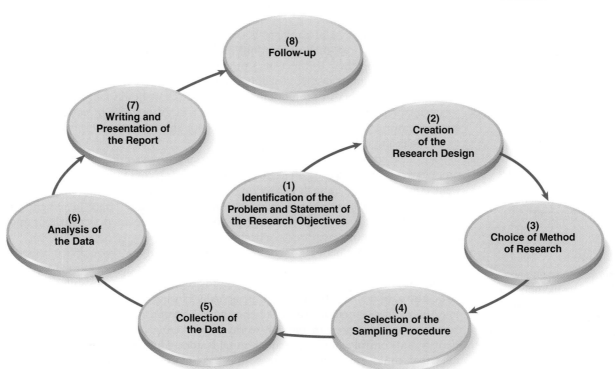

> **descriptive studies**
> Research studies that answer the questions who, what, when, where, and how.

Descriptive Studies **Descriptive studies** are conducted to answer who, what, when, where, and how questions. Implicit in descriptive research is the fact that management already knows or understands the underlying relationships among the variables in the problem. A **variable** is simply a symbol or concept that can assume any one of a set of values.

> **variable**
> A symbol or concept that can assume any one of a set of values.

A descriptive study for Starbucks might include demographic and lifestyle characteristics of typical, light, and heavy patronizers of Starbucks stores, purchasers of Starbucks baked goods, purchasers of Starbucks sandwiches, and buyers of coffee to take home. Other questions might determine drive time from work or home to the nearest Starbucks and if purchasers pay by cash or credit.

Descriptive research can tell us that two variables, such as advertising and sales, seem to be somehow associated, but it cannot provide convincing evidence that high levels of advertising cause high sales. Because descriptive research can shed light on associations or relationships, it helps the researcher select variables for a causal study.

> **causal studies**
> Research studies that examine whether the value of one variable causes or determines the value of another variable.

Causal Studies In **causal studies**, the researcher investigates whether the value of one variable causes or determines the value of another variable, in an attempt to establish linkage between them. Experiments (see Chapter 8) often are used to measure causality. A **dependent variable** is a symbol or concept expected to be explained or affected by an independent variable. In contrast, an **independent variable** is a variable that the market researcher can, to some extent, manipulate, change, or alter. An independent variable in a research project is a presumed cause of or influence on the dependent variable, the presumed effect. For example, Starbucks would like to know whether the level of advertising (independent variable) determines the level of sales (dependent variable).

> **dependent variable**
> A symbol or concept expected to be explained or influenced by the independent variable.

> **independent variable**
> A symbol or concept over which the researcher has some control and that is hypothesized to cause or influence the dependent variable.

A causal study for Starbucks might involve changing one independent variable (for example, the number of direct mailings offering a 10 percent discount on a 1 pound bag of coffee over a 6-month period to target customers) and then observing the effect on coffee sales. Here, there is an appropriate causal order of events, or **temporal sequence**; the effect follows closely the hypothesized cause. Temporal sequence is one criterion that must be met for causality.

> **temporal sequence**
> An appropriate causal order of events.

A second criterion for causality is **concomitant variation**—the degree to which a presumed cause (direct-mail promotion) and a presumed effect (coffee sales) occur together or vary together. If direct-mail promotions are a cause of increased coffee sales, then when the number of direct-mail promotions is increased, coffee sales should go up, and when the number of promotions is decreased, sales should fall. If, however, an increase in direct-mail promotions does not result in an increase in coffee sales, the researcher must conclude that the hypothesis about the relationship between direct-mail promotions and coffee sales is not supported.

> **concomitant variation**
> The degree to which a presumed cause and a presumed effect occur or vary together.

An ideal situation would be one in which sales of coffee increased markedly every time Starbucks increased its direct-mail promotions (up to a saturation level). But, alas, we live in a world where such perfection is rarely achieved. One additional bulk mailing might bring a small increase in sales and the next mailing a larger increment, or vice versa. And, during the next 6-month period, an increase in direct-mail promotions might produce no increase or even a decline in sales.

Remember, even perfect concomitant variation would not prove that A causes B. All the researcher could say is that the association makes the hypothesis more likely.

> **spurious association**
> A relationship between a presumed cause and a presumed effect that occurs as a result of an unexamined variable or set of variables.

An important issue in studying causality is recognizing the possibility of **spurious association**, in which other variables are actually causing changes in the dependent variable. In an ideal situation, the researcher would demonstrate a total absence of other causal factors. However, in the real world of marketing research, it is very difficult to identify and control all other potential causal factors. Think for a moment of all the variables that could cause sales of one pound bags of coffee to increase or decrease—for example, prices, newspaper and television advertising, coupons, discounts, and weather. The researcher may be able to lower spurious associations by trying to hold constant these other factors. Alternatively, the researcher may look at changes in sales in similar socioeconomic areas.

Choosing a Basic Method of Research

A research design, either descriptive or causal, is chosen based on a project's objectives. The next step is to select a means of gathering data. There are three basic research methods: (1) survey, (2) observation, and (3) experiment. Survey research is often descriptive in nature but can be causal. Observation research is typically descriptive, and experiment research is almost always causal.

Scanning bar code information is a means of observation research that is widely used today.

Surveys **Survey research** involves an interviewer (except in mail and Internet surveys) who interacts with respondents to obtain facts, opinions, and attitudes. A questionnaire is used to ensure an orderly and structured approach to data gathering. Face-to-face interviews may take place in the respondent's home, a shopping mall, or a place of business.

> **survey research**
> Research in which an interviewer (except in mail and Internet surveys) interacts with respondents to obtain facts, opinions, and attitudes.

Observations **Observation research** monitors respondents' actions without direct interaction. The fastest growing form of observation research involves the use of check-out terminals with scanners, which read bar codes to identify the items being purchased and/or the consumer. The potential of observation research is mind-boggling. Larry Johnston, CEO of Albertsons, the big supermarket chain based in Boise, Idaho, wants to know the brand and container size of the detergent his customers prefer and what time of day chunky peanut butter is likely to sell out at particular stores.

> **observation research**
> Typically, descriptive research that monitors respondents' actions without direct interaction.

He is getting the answers through new technology referred to as Shop 'n Scan devices now being tested at more than 100 Albertsons stores in Chicago and the Dallas-Fort Worth region. The hand-helds, which will soon be available at stores in other cities, allow customers to total expenditures and bag groceries as they shop, eliminating time on check-out lines. They also remind customers about items they may have forgotten. Shoppers who pick up a package of hot dogs, for example, are asked whether they also need pickles or rolls. At the same time, Mr. Johnston and his marketing managers get lots of information on customer buying habits—everything from how often shoppers buy a bottle of ketchup to what cookies or cosmetics they splurge on most. The information is used to target particular customers for promotions and to track store inventories.[6]

Experiments **Experiments** are the third method researchers use to gather data. Experiment research is distinguished by the researcher's changing one or more independent variables—price, package, design, shelf space, advertising theme, or advertising expenditures—and observing the effects of those changes on a dependent variable (usually sales). The objective of experiments is to measure causality. The best experiments are those in which all factors other than the ones being manipulated are held constant. This enables the researcher to infer with confidence that changes in sales, for example, are caused by changes in the amount of money spent on advertising.

> **experiments**
> Research to measure causality, in which the researcher changes one or more independent variables and observes the effect of the changes on the dependent variable.

Holding all other factors constant in the external environment is a monumental and costly, if not impossible, task. Factors such as competitors' actions, weather, and economic conditions in various markets are beyond the control of the researcher. One way researchers attempt to control factors that might influence the dependent variable is to use a laboratory experiment—that is, an experiment conducted in a test facility rather than in the natural environment. Researchers sometimes create simulated supermarket environments, give consumers scrip (play money), and then ask them to shop as they normally would for groceries. By varying package design or color over several time periods, for example, the researcher can determine which package is most likely to stimulate sales. Although laboratory techniques can provide valuable information, it is important to recognize that the consumer is not in a natural environment; how people act in a test facility may differ from how they act in an actual shopping situation. Experiments are discussed in detail in Chapter 8.

Selecting the Sampling Procedure

A sample is a subset from a larger population. Although the basic nature of the sample is specified in the research design, selecting the sampling procedure is a separate step in the research process. Several questions must be answered before a sampling procedure is selected. First, the population or universe of interest must be defined. This is the group from which the sample will be drawn. It should include all the people whose opinions, behaviors, preferences, attitudes, and so on will yield information needed to answer the research problem—for example, all persons who eat Mexican food at least once every 60 days.

After the population has been defined, the next question is whether to use a probability sample or a nonprobability sample. A **probability sample** is a sample for which every element in the population has a known nonzero probability of being selected. Such samples allow the researcher to estimate how much sampling error is present in a given study. All samples that cannot be considered probability samples are nonprobability samples. **Nonprobability samples** are those in which the chances of selection for the various elements in the population are unknown. Researchers cannot statistically calculate the reliability of a nonprobability sample; that is, they cannot determine the degree of sampling error that can be expected. Sampling is the topic of Chapter 12.

probability sample
A subset of a population where every element in the population has a known nonzero chance of being selected.

nonprobability sample
A subset of a population in which the chances of selection for the various elements in the population are unknown.

Collecting the Data

Most survey-based data is now collected on the Internet. Interviewer-based data collection is done by marketing research field services. Field service firms, found throughout the country, specialize in collecting data through personal and telephone interviewing on a subcontract basis. A typical interviewer-based research study involves data collection in several cities and requires working with a comparable number of field service firms. To ensure that all subcontractors do everything exactly the same way, detailed field instructions should be developed for every job. Nothing should be left to chance; in particular, no interpretations of procedures should be left to the subcontractors.

In addition to doing interviewing, field service firms often provide group research facilities, mall intercept locations, test product storage, and kitchen facilities for preparing test food products. They may also conduct retail audits (counting the amount of product sold from retail shelves).

Analyzing the Data

After the data have been collected, the next step in the research process is data analysis. The purpose of this analysis is to interpret and draw conclusions from the mass of collected data. The marketing researcher may use a variety of techniques, beginning with simple frequency analysis and culminating in complex multivariate techniques. Data analysis will be discussed later in the text.

Writing and Presenting the Report

After data analysis is completed, the researcher must prepare the report and communicate the conclusions and recommendations to management. This is a key step in the process because a marketing researcher who wants project conclusions acted on must convince the manager that the results are credible and justified by the data collected.

The researcher usually will be required to present both written and oral reports on a project. The nature of the audience must be kept in mind when these reports are being prepared and presented. The oral report should begin with a clear statement of the research objectives, followed by an outline of the methodology. A summary of major findings should come next. The report should end with a presentation of conclusions and recommendations for management. In today's fast-paced world of marketing research, long, elaborately written reports are virtually a thing of the past. Decision makers today typically want only a copy of the PowerPoint presentation.

Judging the Quality of a Report   Because most people who enter marketing become research users rather than research suppliers, it is important to know what to look for in a research report. The ability to evaluate a research report is crucial. As with many other items we purchase, the quality of a research report is not always readily apparent. Nor does paying a high price for a project necessarily guarantee superior quality. The basis for measuring a report's quality lies in the research proposal. Does the report meet the objectives established in the proposal? Has the methodology outlined in the proposal been followed? Are the conclusions based on logical deductions from the data analysis? Do the recommendations seem prudent, given the conclusions?

Using the Internet to Disseminate Reports   It is becoming increasingly commonplace for research suppliers and clients to publish reports directly to the Web. All of the latest versions of major word-processing, spreadsheet, and presentation packages have the capability to produce Web-ready material, which simplifies the process of putting reports on the Web. Most companies, such as Texas Instruments, locate this material not in public areas on the Web but on corporate intranets or in password-protected locations on Web sites. Publishing reports on the Web has a number of advantages:

1. The reports become immediately accessible to managers and other authorized and interested parties worldwide.
2. The reports can incorporate full multimedia presentation, including text, graphs, various types of animation, audio comments, and video clips.
3. The reports are fully searchable. Suppose a manager is interested in any material relating to advertising. Instead of manually scanning a long and detailed report for such mentions, he or she can search the report for comments relating to advertising.

Following Up

After a company has spent a considerable amount of effort and money on marketing research and the preparation of a report, it is important that the findings be used. Management should determine whether the recommendations were followed and, if not, why not. As you will learn in the next section, one way to increase the likelihood that research conducted by a corporate marketing department will be used is to minimize conflict between that department and other departments within the company.

Managing the Research Process

The Research Request

> **research request**
> An internal document used by large organizations that describes a potential research project, its benefits to the organization, and estimated costs; it must be formally approved before a research project can begin.

Before conducting a research project, a company such as Microsoft® might require approval of a formal research request. Moderate- and large-size retailers, manufacturers, and nonprofit organizations often use the **research request** as a basis for determining which projects will be funded. Typically, in larger organizations there are far more requests by managers for marketing research information than monies available to conduct such research. Requiring a research request is a formalized approach to allocating scarce research dollars.

It is very important for the brand manager, new product specialist, or whoever is in need of research information to clearly state in the formal research request why the desired information is critical to the organization. Otherwise, the person with approval authority may fail to see why the expenditure is necessary.

In smaller organizations, the communication link between brand managers and marketing researchers is much closer. Their day-to-day contact often removes the need for a formal research request. Instead, decisions to fund research are made on an ad hoc basis by the marketing manager or the director of marketing research.

Completion and approval of the request represent a disciplined approach to identifying research problems and obtaining funding to solve them. The degree of effort expended at this step in the research process will be reflected in the quality of the information provided to the decision maker because a well-conceived research request will guide the design, data-gathering, analysis, and reporting processes toward a highly focused objective. The sections of a formal research request are as follows:

1. *Action.* The decision maker should describe the action to be taken on the basis of the research. This will help the decision maker focus on what information should be obtained and guide the researcher in creating the research design and in analyzing the results.

2. *Origin.* The decision maker should state the events that led to a need for a decision. This will help the researcher understand more deeply the nature of the management decision problem.

3. *Information.* The decision maker should list the questions that she or he needs to have answered to take action. Carefully considering the questions will improve the efficiency of the research.

4. *Use.* This section should explain how each piece of information will be used to help make the actual decision. By giving logical reasons for each part of the research, it will ensure that the questions make sense in light of the action to be taken.

5. *Target groups and subgroups.* By describing those from whom information must be gathered to address the research problem, this section will help the researcher design the sample procedure for the research project.

6. *Logistics.* Time and budget constraints always affect the research technique chosen for a project. For this reason, approximations of the amount of money available and the amount of time left before results are needed must be included as a part of the research request.

7. *Comments.* Any other comments relevant to the research project must be stated so that, once again, the researcher can fully understand the nature of the problem.

Request for Proposal

> **request for proposal (RFP)**
> A solicitation sent to marketing research suppliers inviting them to submit a formal proposal, including a bid.

The research request is an internal document used by management to determine which projects to fund. A **request for proposal (RFP)** is a solicitation sent to marketing research

Internal Clients Are Not Always Easy to Deal With

Carol Graff, a partner with Minneapolis-based Graff Works Marketing Research, talks about how to handle tough, internal clients.

How many times have you fielded marketing research requests from internal clients who think they know it all? Who dictate the methodology that must be used? Who insist on being involved in every detail of the project or who play "hands-off" until the very last minute and then change everything?

Working with difficult internal clients can be challenging for any corporate marketing research department. Being on the research supplier side, we sometimes counsel clients on how they can better respond when faced with tricky situations. Here are four common situations our clients have encountered and some suggestions to consider:

Situation 1: The internal client requests expensive research which you believe is not necessary. *The client requests a project for which you already have a study and the data is less than a year old. However, the client doesn't "trust" the research.* Suggestions: *If this is a trust issue with the methodology, the person in charge of the study, or the analysis of the data, be clear on your client's objections. Exactly what or who doesn't he trust? What would make him feel more comfortable, relying on this data or funding an entirely new study?*

Get creative. Suggest an inexpensive and quick telephone study with the target audience to attempt to verify the known research results. Have him listen in or tape the interview (with the respondent's permission) and play it back for him. Your challenge is to provide the client with information he can trust.

Situation 2: The marketing research department sits on a new product committee and recognizes a need for research, but the client is unwilling to invest. Suggestions: *This is a great opportunity to demonstrate the benefit of conducting marketing research. Try saying: "By knowing the market's preference for the _____ feature, we could minimally gain a _____ percent in market share among the _____ market segment which could translate to a $_____ increase in the forecasted sales projections."*

Situation 3: The research is necessary but you want to propose a different methodology which you know your client opposes. Suggestions: *Understand the history behind your client's opposition to the methodology you have in mind. If he's been burned by unscrupulous telephone interviewers or has used online survey results that were found to be tainted, you need to be aware.*

Next, create and share a list of the pros and cons behind both the methodology he's requesting and the approach you believe is best for the request. (Note: We recommend you have this list available for all types of methods and update it frequently. Add testimonials from others in the company who have also successfully used these methods.)

If the client still balks at your method vs. his, suggest a ministudy using both types of methods to test the approaches. Yes, you may have to invest some additional funds up front. But this may pay off when you can demonstrate why the ultimate results of the methodology will be of higher value.

Situation 4: The client is laissez-faire about the project they've requested, taking a hand-off attitude until the project is under way, and then begins to challenge everything. Suggestions: *Once you've been in this situation, you promise yourself it won't happen again. The best way to manage yourself out of this one is to not point fingers at the client. Don't suggest that the client should have gotten involved from the get-go—that will only make you feel better momentarily! Instead, work to establish a rapport with the client.*

Be clear on what she is unhappy about, what's bugging her about the project. Pull out the objectives. (Are you getting sick of hearing this one?) Make certain the project is in alignment with the goals. Review the questionnaires, discussion guides, other research materials. Understand where your client is uncomfortable and work towards a quick resolution plan to diminish her level of uncertainty.

Frequently update the client on the status of her project. Identify barriers you encounter. Share the good and bad news about early findings. Make sure the communication lines are open and free flowing. Build her sense of trust in you, your department, and the supplier. The more she believes she can truly delegate to you, the less she may be inclined to continue challenging the project.[7]

suppliers inviting them to submit a formal proposal, including a bid. An actual RFP, adapted slightly for the purposes of this text, is shown in Exhibit 3.3. The RFP is the lifeblood of a research supplier. Receiving it is the initial step in getting new business and, therefore, revenue.

A typical RFP provides background data on why a study is to be conducted, outlines the research objectives, describes a methodology, and suggests a time frame. In some RFPs, the supplier is asked to recommend a methodology or even help develop the research objectives. Most RFPs also ask for (1) a detailed cost breakdown, (2) the supplier's experience in relevant areas, and (3) references. Usually, a due date for the proposal will be specified.

Suppliers must exercise care in preparing their proposals in response to the RFP. More than one client has said, "We find the quality of the proposals indicative of the quality of work produced by the firm." Thus, a research supplier that doesn't have the necessary time to adequately prepare a proposal should simply not submit a bid.

THE MARKETING RESEARCH PROPOSAL

> **research proposal**
> A document developed, usually in response to an RFP, that presents the research objectives, research design, time line, and cost of a project.

When marketing research suppliers receive an RFP, they respond to the potential client with a research proposal. The **research proposal** is a document that presents the research objectives, research design, time line, and cost of a project. We have included an actual proposal (disguised) prepared by two project managers at Decision Analyst (a large international marketing research firm) in Appendix 3-A. Most research proposals today are short (3 to 5 pages) and are transmitted back to the potential client as an e-mail attachment. A proposal for the federal government can run 50 pages or longer. The federal proposal will include a number of standard forms mandated by the government.

Most proposals contain the following elements:

I.   Title Page
     This includes the title of the project from the RFP, the names of the preparers of the proposal, and contact information; who the proposal is being prepared for; and the date.

II. Statement of the research objectives.
     These are often stated in the RFP. If not, they must be determined as described earlier in the chapter.

III. Study Design
     This presents a statement of how the data will be gathered and who will be sampled and the sample size.

IV. Areas of Questioning
     This is not found in all proposals, but in our experience we have found it to be very helpful. It is a tentative list of survey topics based on the research objectives.

V.   Data Analysis
     This states which techniques will be used to analyze the data.

VI. Personnel involved
     This provides a complete list of all supervisory and analytical personnel who will be involved in the project and a short vita of each. Each person's responsibility is also outlined. This element is typically not included when the client and supplier have an ongoing relationship. It is mandatory in most government work.

VII. Specifications and assumptions
     Most RFPs are relatively short and don't spell out every detail. In order to make certain that the supplier and potential client are on the same page, it is a good idea to list the specifications and assumptions that were made when creating the proposal (see Appendix 3-A).

Exhibit 3.3

An RFP to Conduct
an Image Benchmark
Study

Background

Mega Health has been tracking consumers' awareness and image of our plan on an annual as well as monthly basis for many years. These studies have been conducted for the purpose of understanding our brand awareness, brand image, and brand benchmarking vs. the competition. As we plan for advertising and public communication, we first need to determine how Mega Health is perceived in the marketplace. The annual Brand Image Benchmarking study allows Mega Health to assess its brand image in a competitive context.

Issue

Assess overall Mega Health brand strength by surveying individuals (in MD/DC/VA regions) in the 3rd–4th quarter of 2007, using a version of the current survey instrument.

Objectives

- Assess brand awareness and image of Mega Health in the MD/DC/VA regions.
- Benchmark Mega Health awareness and image vs. competitors in all regions.
- Determine importance of health insurance company/HMO attributes.
- Assess rating of Mega Health and competitor performance on health insurance company/HMO attributes.
- Assess reaction to attributes of Mega Health.
- Profile insured population.
- Create comprehensive brand image analysis.

Methodology

Quantitative telephone survey with the general public and business decision makers.*

Sample:
- Total interviews: 1950.
    General public: approx. 1250 interviews (may need as many as 300 over sample—1550 total—to improve representation in harder-to-recruit areas). RDD methodology. *Business decision makers:* approx. 400 interviews.
- List sources and detailed sampling methodology: to be determined.
- Quota for the study should be representative of 5 mid-Atlantic regions: Baltimore Metro, DC Metro, Eastern Shore MD, Southern MD, and Western MD (Southern and Western MD may be combined after study completion). Mega Health will provide zip codes in order to delineate regions.

Questionnaire: This study is being conducted for benchmarking and tracking purposes. Thus, the questionnaire that has previously been used to conduct this research has been included (see attachment). Some modifications to this questionnaire may be necessary for improved analysis.

Proposed Timing

Develop RFP for research	8/11/07
Select vendor	8/17/07
Sample and survey adjusted/finalized	8/30/07
Initiate interviews (including recruiting)	9/1/07
Complete interviews	10/4/07
Topline analysis	10/15/07
Final analysis[†]	11/1/07

We would like to begin the preparation for this study, so please expedite the return of proposals as soon as possible. Thank you for your consideration. Please contact Joe Bedlow at 999-998-7513 (fax: 999-998-7660; email: joebedlow@megahealth.com) with any questions or proposals.

*Sample of general public and decision makers subject to change. *Note*: The population from which to sample business decision makers is typically not very large and can be more difficult to recruit, especially larger businesses (1000+ employees).

[†]It is most important that the "general public" sample be completed within this time frame. Business decision makers' results may be afforded a later date, if needed.

Note: The real company name, contract name, and phone numbers have been disguised.

VIII. Services

This spells out exactly what the research supplier will do (see Appendix 3-A). For example, who is designing the questionnaire? Is it the client, the supplier, or is it a joint effort? Again, the purpose is to make sure that the client and the research supplier operate from the same set of expectations.

IX. Cost

This specifies the cost and payment schedule.

X. Timing

This states when various phases of the project will be completed and provides a final completion date.

Preparing proposals may be the most important function a research supplier performs in as much as proposals, and their acceptance or rejection, determine the revenue of the firm. If a research firm's proposals are not accepted, the company will have no funds and will ultimately go out of business! Moreover, if the price that is quoted is too low, the researcher may get the job but lose money. If the price is too high, the proposal may be outstanding, but the researcher will lose the work to a competitor.

What to Look for in a Marketing Research Supplier

Market Directions, a Kansas City marketing research firm, asked marketing research clients around the United States to rate the importance of several statements about research companies and research departments. Replies were received from a wide range of industries, resulting in the following top 10 list of desirable qualities in marketing researchers:

1. Maintains client confidentiality.

2. Is honest.

3. Is punctual.

4. Is flexible.

5. Delivers against project specifications.

6. Provides high-quality output.

7. Is responsive to the client's needs.

8. Has high quality-control standards.

9. Is customer-oriented in interactions with client.

10. Keeps the client informed throughout a project.[8]

The two most important qualities, confidentiality and honesty, are ethical issues; the remaining factors relate to managing the research function and maintaining good communications.

Good communications are a necessity. Four of the qualities on the top 10 list— flexibility, responsiveness to clients' needs, customer orientation, and keeping the client informed—are about good communications. A successful marketing research organization requires good communications both within the research company and with clients.

How important is communication? Consider this: Managers spend at least 80 percent of every working day in direct communication with others. In other words, 48 minutes of every hour is spent in meetings, on the telephone, or talking informally. The other 20 percent of a typical manager's time is spent doing desk work, most of which is communication in the form of reading and writing.[9] Communications permeate every aspect of managing the marketing research function.

What Motivates Decision Makers to Use Research Information?

When research managers communicate effectively, generate quality data, control costs, and deliver information on time, they increase the probability that decision makers will use the research information they provide. Yet academic research shows that political factors and preconceptions can also influence whether research information is used. Specifically, the determinants of whether or not a manager uses research data are (1) conformity to prior expectations, (2) clarity of presentation, (3) research quality, (4) political acceptability within the firm, and (5) lack of challenge to the status quo.[10] Managers and researchers both agree that technical quality is the most important determinant of research use. However, managers are less likely to use research that does not conform to preconceived notions or is not politically acceptable.[11] This does not mean, of course, that researchers should alter their findings to meet management's preconceived notions.

Marketing managers in industrial firms tend to use research findings more than do their counterparts in consumer goods organizations.[12] This tendency among industrial managers is attributed to a greater exploratory objective in information collection, a greater degree of formalization of organizational structure, and a lesser degree of surprise in the information collected.

SUMMARY

The process for correctly defining the research problem consists of a series of steps: (1) recognize the problem or opportunity, (2) find out why the information is being sought, (3) understand the decision-making environment, (4) use the symptoms to help clarify the problem, (5) translate the management problem into a marketing research problem, (6) determine whether the information already exists, (7) determine whether the question can really be answered, and (8) state the research objectives. If the problem is not defined correctly, the remainder of the research project will be a waste of time and money.

The steps in the market research process are as follows:

1. Identification of the problem/opportunity and statement of the marketing research objectives
2. Creation of the research design
3. Choice of the method of research
4. Selection of the sampling procedure
5. Collection of data
6. Analysis of data
7. Preparation and presentation of the research report
8. Follow-up

In specifying a research design, the researcher must determine whether the research will be descriptive or causal. Descriptive studies are conducted to answer who, what, when, where, and how questions. Causal studies are those in which the researcher investigates whether one variable (independent) causes or influences another variable (dependent). The next step in creating a research design is to select a research method: survey, observation, or experiment. Survey research involves an interviewer (except in mail and Internet surveys) interacting with a respondent to obtain facts, opinions, and attitudes. Observation research, in contrast, monitors respondents' actions and does not rely on direct interaction with people. An experiment is distinguished by the fact that the researcher changes one or more variables and observes the effects of those changes on another variable (usually sales). The objective of most experiments is to measure causality.

A sample is a subset of a larger population. A probability sample is one for which every element in the population has a known nonzero probability of being selected. All samples that cannot be considered probability samples are nonprobability samples. Any sample in which the chances of selection for the various elements in the population are unknown can be considered a nonprobability sample.

In larger organizations, it is common to have a research request prepared after the statement of research objectives. The research request generally describes the action to be taken on the basis of the research, the reason for the need for the information, the questions management wants to have answered, how the information will be used, the target groups from whom information must be gathered, the amount of time and money available to complete the project, and any other information pertinent to the request. The request for proposal (RFP) is the document used by clients to solicit proposals from marketing research suppliers.

Marketing research proposals are developed in response to an RFP. In some cases, the proposals are created based on an informal request such as in a telephone conversation between a client and research supplier. The research proposal gives the research objectives, research design, time line, and cost. Research proposals are the tool that generates revenue for the research firm.

Good communications are the foundation of research management and the basis for getting decision makers to use research information. The information communicated to a decision maker depends on the type of research being conducted.

KEY TERMS & DEFINITIONS

opportunity identification Using marketing research to find and evaluate new opportunities.

situation analysis Studying the decision-making environment within which the marketing research will take place.

exploratory research Preliminary research conducted to increase understanding of a concept, to clarify the exact nature of the problem to be solved, or to identify important variables to be studied.

pilot studies Surveys using a limited number of respondents and often employing less rigorous sampling techniques than are employed in large, quantitative studies.

experience surveys Discussions with knowledgeable individuals, both inside and outside the organization, who may provide insights into the problem.

case analysis Reviewing information from situations that are similar to the current one.

marketing research problem A statement specifying the type of information needed by the decision maker to help solve the management decision problem and how that information can be obtained efficiently and effectively.

marketing research objective A goal statement, defining the specific information needed to solve the marketing research problem.

management decision problem A statement specifying the type of managerial action required to solve the problem.

hypothesis A conjectural statement about a relationship between two or more variables that can be tested with empirical data.

research design The plan to be followed to answer the marketing research objectives.

descriptive studies Research studies that answer the questions who, what, when, where, and how.

variable A symbol or concept that can assume any one of a set of values.

causal studies Research studies that examine whether the value of one variable causes or determines the value of another variable.

dependent variable A symbol or concept expected to be explained or influenced by the independent variable.

independent variable A symbol or concept over which the researcher has some control and that is hypothesized to cause or influence the dependent variable.

temporal sequence An appropriate causal order of events.

concomitant variation The degree to which a presumed cause and a presumed effect occur or vary together.

spurious association A relationship between a presumed cause and a presumed effect that occurs as a result of an unexamined variable or set of variables.

survey research Research in which an interviewer (except in mail and Internet surveys) interacts with respondents to obtain facts, opinions, and attitudes.

observation research Typically, descriptive research that monitors respondents' actions without direct interaction.

experiments Research to measure causality, in which the researcher changes one or more independent variables and observes the effect of the changes on the dependent variable.

probability sample A subset of a population where every element in the population has a known nonzero chance of being selected.

nonprobability sample A subset of a population in which the chances of selection for the various elements in the population are unknown.

research request An internal document used by large organizations that describes a potential research project, its benefits to the organization, and estimated costs; it must be formally approved before a research project can begin.

request for proposal (RFP) A solicitation sent to marketing research suppliers inviting them to submit a formal proposal, including a bid.

research proposal A document developed, usually in response to an RFP, that states the research objectives, research design, time line, and cost.

QUESTIONS FOR REVIEW & CRITICAL THINKING

1. The definition of the research problem is one of the critical steps in the research process. Why? Who should be involved in this process?

2. What role does exploratory research play in the marketing research process? How does exploratory research differ from other forms of marketing research?

3. Give some examples of symptoms of problems and then suggest some underlying real problems.

4. Give several examples of situations in which it would be better to take a census of the population than a sample.

5. Critique the following methodologies and suggest more appropriate alternatives:
   a. A supermarket is interested in determining its image. Cashiers drop a short questionnaire into the grocery bag of each customer prior to bagging the groceries.
   b. To assess the extent of its trade area, a shopping mall stations interviewers in the parking lot every Monday and Friday evening. After people park their cars, interviewers walk up to them and ask them for their zip codes.
   c. To assess the potential for new horror movies starring alien robots, a major studio invites people to call a 900 number and vote yes if they would like to see such movies or no if they would not. Each caller is billed a $2 charge.

6. You have been charged with determining how to attract more business majors to your school. Outline the steps you would take, including sampling procedures, to accomplish this task.

7. What can researchers do to increase the chances that decision makers will use the marketing research information they generate?

8. Explain the critical role of the research proposal.

9. **[Team exercise]** Divide the class into teams of four or five. Half of the teams should prepare short RFPs on the following topics:

   1. food on campus
   2. role of fraternities and sororities on campus
   3. entertainment in your city
   4. your university Web site
   5. role of student internships in education
   6. online purchasing of school supplies
   7. purchasing music on the Internet

   The RFPs should state clearly and precisely the research objectives and other pertinent information. The remaining teams should create proposals in response to the RFPs.

WORKING THE NET

1. Go to the Internet and search on "intranet + future." Report your findings to the class.
2. Describe how putting research reports on the Web can benefit managers.
3. Go to a search engine and type "writing RFPs." Explain what kind of help is available to prepare RFPs.

REAL-LIFE RESEARCH • 3.1

I'll Eat Frozen Pizza But I Don't Have to Like It!

Barely an adult in the United States today has not succumbed to the combination of taste and fast-food convenience that is frozen pizza, according to a nationwide survey by Decision Analyst, Inc., Arlington, Texas. Yet despite near universal consumption (93 percent of respondents), the survey (conducted among a nationally representative sample of 15,007 adult consumers) found many Americans dissatisfied with their pizza choices.

The largest brands cannot complain of a lack of public exposure—more than half of survey respondents have eaten pizzas from Tony's, Di Giorno, Tombstone, and Red Baron (Tombstone tops the list, with 74 percent having sampled its products). Yet among these market leaders, only Di Giorno ranked among those pizzas consumers will likely purchase again. Specialist producers California Pizza Kitchen and Freschetta are, with Di Giorno, the most likely to be tried again (between 62 and 65 percent of respondents), while Tombstone and Red Baron struggle to attract half of the first-time users to return to their products.

"The data shows that no more than two in three consumers would try any frozen pizza brand again," says Decision Analyst, Inc. vice president Bruce Crandall, who supervised the study. "In other words, at least one-third of consumers will switch to another brand or refuse to buy frozen pizza again."

The reasons people buy pizza offer few consolations to the manufacturers. Taste is the No. 1 factor affecting purchases (with 36 percent), followed by prior experience (23 percent) and value for money (15 percent).

"The pizza producers have a real challenge on their hands to persuade consumers to sample, or resample, their pizzas," says Crandall. "Consumers clearly want good prices, but they also want excellent taste, and that means it's back to the test kitchens if the manufacturers—especially some of the largest sellers—want to keep their customers satisfied."[13]

Questions

1. Would you say that this is an exploratory study? If not, what are the research questions?
2. Do you think that this research is causal or descriptive? Defend your answer.
3. Explain how a marketing manager for Tombstone or California Pizza Kitchen might use this information. What might be included in an RFP to do further research?

Cessna Aircraft

REAL-LIFE RESEARCH • 3.2

Cessna Aircraft is one of the largest manufacturers of small, private-business airplanes in the United States. It is always looking for new market opportunities, which may involve cultivating existing segments or developing and exploiting new ones. Recent research by Cessna revealed that although a very small percentage of the total adult population enrolls in private pilot-training programs, about half of the individuals who enter a training program complete it. And the number of people with pilot's licenses is increasing. Eventually, about one out of five people with a private pilot's license buys a private airplane. Thus, pilot training is an important part of the total market for Cessna and its competitors.

A small percentage of pilots are women. Similarly, a small percentage of the students in training programs are women; this figure has shown only a slight increase in recent years. Moreover, there are very few women instructors in pilot-training programs. A substantial number of women have the necessary skills, time, and income to enroll in and complete the basic training program. Cessna is interested in learning why more women don't enter the program and how the program and/or promotional materials could appeal to and motivate more women to consider or inquire about such programs.

There may be several specific market segments worthy of examination. These include wives of pilots, businesswomen, women who have the income and desire to travel for pleasure, and young women who seek future employment as corporate aircraft pilots. Cessna realizes that the limiting factor may be low levels of interest or motivation and perhaps attitudes toward the desirability of women pilots. But opportunities for women are increasing in many different fields. Cessna therefore believes that a vital market may exist that is not being fully exploited.

Questions

1. What is the management decision problem?
2. Define the marketing research problem(s).
3. Develop the marketing research objectives.
4. Explain how a marketing researcher should use the problem definition process to answer the above questions.

APPENDIX 3-A
A MARKETING RESEARCH PROPOSAL

Decision Analyst, Inc. Proposal to Conduct a Brand Equity Study

Prepared For:
Fun City Gaming, Inc.

Prepared by:
Kathi McKenzie & Sally Danforth
January 2007

Background

Fun City Gaming, Inc. currently operates a multilevel dockside riverboat casino and a land-based pavilion with three restaurants and a hotel, all located on the Arlen River. The casino offers 1500 slot machines and 70 table games, and is the "flagship" of the Fun City franchise.

The Fun City Casino has four primary competitors currently operating in the area, all within a roughly 30-mile radius of the Fun City. The Fun City Casino ranks second in revenue, but first in profit among these competitors. In addition to these competitors, additional competition will be provided by the planned "River Wild" casino, which will likely begin construction in about a year. This casino will be located in St. George, minutes from the Fun City Casino.

Fun City is currently undergoing a large redevelopment, involving construction of a completely new gaming vessel, significant upgrades to the pavilion, addition of new restaurants, and a new parking garage. The gaming vessel will feature 2500 slot machines, 84 table games, high-limit gaming areas, and upgraded décor. The new Fun City will offer superior features to the current product as well as to primary competitors.

In order to be financially feasible, this project must increase business from current customers as well as attract customers from competitive casinos, some of whom may have to travel past competitive casinos to arrive at Fun City. In addition, the new offering should be especially attractive to premium casino players.

Objectives

The overall objective of this study would be to help management position the new Fun City offering. Key questions to be addressed include:

- ☐ What should be the positioning of the new casino?
- ☐ Should the Fun City name be used, or should it be rebranded?
- ☐ If rebranded, what name should be used?

Study Design

This study would be conducted using a targeted telephone survey among 800 gamblers within a 100-mile radius of the Fun City Casino location. Specifically, we will survey 400 within the Arlen Valley portion of this area and 400 in the area eastward, where the majority of current/future competition lies. Respondents will be screened based on past 12-month casino usage.

Areas of Questioning

Decision Analyst would work closely with Fun City Gaming in developing the questionnaire. Assuming that we have three to four potential positionings to test, tentative survey topics would include:

- ☐ Current casino usage and gambling behavior.
- ☐ Awareness and overall rating for Fun City name, as well as names of key competitors and other names owned by Fun City Gaming which might be used for the new casino.

- ☐ Rating of Fun City and key competitors on several (8 to 10) image attributes.
- ☐ Exposure to brief description of the "new" (redeveloped) casino. Each respondent would be exposed to the description with *one* of the potential positionings. This will result in a readable sample size for each positioning.
- ☐ Overall rating and rating on key image attributes for the "new" casino.
- ☐ Rating of Fun City name and other potential names on overall appeal and fit with this description.
- ☐ Projected use of new casino; effect on gambling habits and share of casino visits.

Data will be analyzed both by area of residence and by gambling value (high/medium/low value gamblers).

Data Analysis

Factor analysis will be conducted, and the factors that are most related to the overall rating of the casino will be identified. On the basis of these factors, a perceptual map will be created to show visually the relationship between the current Fun City and competitive brands, based on brand image. The image projected by the new casino description will also be shown on this map, and a gap analysis conducted to highlight possible differences in image projected by each of the three to four positionings.

Personnel Involved

This project will be supervised by Kathi McKenzie and Sally DanGorth. Kathi will be the overall supervisor and Sally will be responsible for the data analysis and presentation. (Note: A short bio of each person would normally be attached.)

Specifications/Assumptions

The cost estimate is based on the following assumptions:

- ☐ Number of completed interviews = 800
- ☐ Average interview length = 20 minutes
- ☐ Average completion rate = 0.62 completes per hour
- ☐ Assumed incidence = 25%
- ☐ No open-ended questions
- ☐ Type of sample: targeted random digit
- ☐ Up to two banners of statistical tables in Word format
- ☐ Factor analysis, two perceptual maps (total sample and high-value gambler), and gap analysis
- ☐ Report
- ☐ Personal presentation, if desired.

Services

Decision Analyst, Inc. would:

- ☐ Develop the questionnaire, in conjunction with Fun City Gaming management
- ☐ Generate sample within the target area
- ☐ Program the survey
- ☐ Manage and administer the project
- ☐ Monitor and oversee all telephone interviewing
- ☐ Process data, specify cross-tabulations, and compile statistical tables
- ☐ Analyze the data and prepare presentation-style report, if desired.

Cost

The cost to conduct this study, as described, would be $61,900, plus or minimum a 10 percent contingency fee, which would only be spent with specific prior approval of Fun City Gaming. This cost estimate does not include the cost of any travel outside of the Dallas-Fort Worth area. Any overnight deliveries or travel expenses would be billed at cost at the end of the study.

Decision Analyst would closely monitor data collection. If the actual data collection experience differed from the stated specifications and assumptions, we would notify you immediately to discuss the options available.

Timing

After approval of the final questionnaire, the project would require approximately five to six weeks, as outlined below:

Survey programming and quality control	3–4 days
Data collection	3 weeks
Final data tabulations	3 days
Final report	1–2 weeks

CHAPTER 4

SECONDARY DATA
AND DATABASES

		LEARNING OBJECTIVES
→	**1.**	To understand how firms create an internal database.
→	**2.**	To learn about the advantages of creating a database from Web site visitors.
→	**3.**	To become familiar with data mining.
→	**4.**	To understand the advantages and disadvantages of using secondary data.
→	**5.**	To understand the role of the Internet in obtaining secondary data.
→	**6.**	To learn about types of information management systems.

W hen Dereck Gurden pulls up at one of his customers' stores—7 Eleven, Buy N Save, or one of dozens of liquor marts and restaurants in the 800-square-mile territory he covers in California's Central Valley—he always carries his hand-held PC. "First I'll scroll through and check the accounts receivable, make sure everything's current," he says. "Then it'll show me an inventory screen with a four-week history. I can get past sales, package placements—facts and numbers on how much of the sales they did when they had a display in a certain location." After chatting up his customer, Gurden "walks the store, inputting what I see." He inputs what he sees, that is, about his *competitors'* product displays, which goes into the hand-held too. All done, Gurden jacks the hand-held into his cell phone and fires off new orders to the warehouse, along with the data he's gathered.

Gurden is a sales rep for Sierra Beverage, one of about 700 U.S. distributors that work for Anheuser-Busch. Gurden and several thousand reps and drivers serve as the eyes and ears of a data network (called Bud Net) through which distributors report, in excruciating detail, on sales, shelf stocks, and displays at thousands of outlets.

Collecting the data in a nightly nationwide sweep of its distributors' servers, Anheuser can draw a picture each morning of what brands are selling in which packages using which medley of displays, discounts, and promotions.

Today Anheuser Busch is the only major brewer to rely heavily on data from Information Resources, Inc.—which tracks every bar-coded product swiped at check-out and performs Nielsen-style consumer surveys—and to conduct its own monthly surveys to see what beer drinkers buy and why. Examining the aggregate data tells Anheuser what images or ideas to push in its ads and what new products to unveil—such as low-carb Michelob Ultra, Anheuser's most successful launch since Bud Light.

This data, crossed with U.S. Census figures on the ethnic and economic makeup of neighborhoods, also helps Anheuser tailor marketing campaigns with a local precision only dreamed of a few years ago. The data reveals trends by city (Tequiza may be hot in San Antonio, but Bud Light plays better in Peoria), by neighborhood (gay models appear on posters in San Francisco's Castro district, but not on those in the Mission), by holiday (the Fourth of July is a big seller in Atlanta, but St. Patrick's Day isn't), and by class (cans for blue-collar stores, bottles for white-collar). "They're drilling down to the level of the individual store," Thompson says. "They can pinpoint if customers are gay, Latino, 30-year-old, college-educated conservatives."[1]

Exactly what is a database? And what is data mining? Are databases derived from primary or secondary data, or both? What are the pros and cons of using secondary data? These are some of the questions we will answer in this chapter. ■

Nature of Secondary Data

> **secondary data**
> Data that have been previously gathered.

Secondary data consist of information that has already been gathered and *might* be relevant to the problem at hand. **Primary data**, in contrast, are survey, observation, and experiment data collected to solve the particular problem under investigation. It is highly unlikely that any marketing research problem is entirely unique or has never occurred before. It also is probable that someone else has investigated the problem or one similar to it in the past. Therefore, secondary data can be a cost-effective and efficient means of obtaining information for marketing research. There are two basic sources of secondary data: the company itself (internal databases, like Bud Net) and other organizations or persons (external databases).

> **primary data**
> New data gathered to help solve the problem under investigation.

Secondary information originating within the company includes annual reports, reports to stockholders, sales data, customer profiles, purchase patterns, product testing results (perhaps made available to the news media), and house periodicals composed by company personnel for communication to employees, customers, or others. Often all this information is incorporated into a company's internal database.

Outside sources of secondary information include innumerable government (federal, state, and local) departments and agencies that compile and publish summaries of business data, as well as trade and industry associations, business periodicals, and other news media that regularly publish studies and articles on the economy, specific industries, and even individual companies. When economic considerations or priorities within the organization preclude publication of summaries of the information from these sources, unpublished summaries may be found in internal reports, memos, or special-purpose analyses with limited circulation. Most of these sources can be found on the Internet.

Advantages of Secondary Data

Marketing researchers use secondary information because it can be obtained at a fraction of the cost, time, and inconvenience associated with primary data collection. Additional advantages of using secondary information include the following:

- ❑ *Secondary data may help to clarify or redefine the problem during the exploratory research process* (see Chapter 3). Consider the experience of a local YMCA. Concerned about a stagnant level of membership and a lack of participation in traditional YMCA programs, it decided to survey members and nonmembers. Secondary data revealed that there had been a tremendous influx of young single persons into the target market, while the number of "traditional families" had remained constant. The problem was redefined to examine how the YMCA could attract a significant share of the young single adult market while maintaining its traditional family base.

- ❑ *Secondary data may actually provide a solution to the problem.* It is highly unlikely that the problem is unique; there is always the possibility that someone else has addressed the identical problem or a very similar one. Thus, the precise information desired may have been collected, but not for the same purpose.

  Many states publish a directory of manufacturers (typically available online) that contains information on companies: location, markets, product lines, number of plants, names of key personnel, number of employees, and sales levels. When a consulting company specializing in long-range strategic planning for members of the semiconductor industry needed a regional profile of its potential clients, it used individual state directories to compile the profile; no primary data collection was

PRACTICING MARKETING RESEARCH

Would you pull off the road to fill your gas tank if you could already see that the needle was showing full? Probably not. However, we have found that many companies are essentially doing just that by executing surveys to gather data on questions for which they already have the answers.

A major hotel chain found that it successfully delivered clean bathrooms 99.6 percent of the time. To monitor their continued success, rather than survey 10,000 people to get back 1,000 surveys four weeks later, of which 4 would have bathroom complaints, the chain chose to put a sticker in the bathroom and on the room desk highlighting the guest services hotline.

Customers' call rates would let the chain know if quality had slipped.

In another situation, a bank was surveying customers on their satisfaction with the uptime of the ATMs. However, the bank already had internal IT metrics that measured ATM uptime to four decimal places.

In summary, make sure the data doesn't already exist. We have found that departments often operate in silos, unaware of the research being done or data being collected by their co-workers. Sharing existing research and internal metrics not only gives immediate access to actionable data but does so without incurring the costs of conducting surveys.[2]

---

necessary. John Goodman and David Beinhacker of TARP, an Arlington, Virginia, marketing research firm, note in the above Practicing Marketing Research box that secondary data may help companies save a lot of money by not conducting unnecessary surveys.

☐ *Secondary data may provide primary data research method alternatives.* Each primary data research endeavor is custom-designed for the situation at hand; consequently, the marketing researcher should always be open to sources that suggest research alternatives. For example, when we (the authors) started work on a research project for a large southwestern city's convention and visitor's bureau, we obtained a research report prepared by *Meeting and Convention Planners* magazine. In designing our questionnaire, we used a series of scales from the magazine's questionnaire. Not only were the scales well designed, but results from our study could be compared with the magazine's data.

☐ *Secondary data may alert the marketing researcher to potential problems and/or difficulties.* In addition to alternatives, secondary information may divulge potential dangers. Unpopular collection methods, sample selection difficulties, or respondent hostility may be uncovered. For example, examination of a study of anesthesiologists by a researcher planning to conduct a study of their satisfaction with certain drugs discovered a high refusal rate in a telephone survey. The researcher had planned to use a telephone study but instead switched to a mail questionnaire with a response incentive.

☐ *Secondary data may provide necessary background information and build credibility for the research report.* Secondary information often yields a wealth of background data for planning a research project. It may offer a profile of potential buyers versus nonbuyers, industry data, desirable new product features, language used by purchasers to describe the industry, and the advantages and disadvantages of existing products.

Language used by target consumers can aid in phrasing questions that will be meaningful to respondents. Sometimes background data can satisfy some of the research objectives, eliminating the need to ask certain questions; shorter questionnaires typically have higher completion rates. And secondary data can enrich research findings by providing additional insights into what the data mean or by corroborating current findings. Finally, secondary data can serve as a reference base for subsequent research projects.

☐ *Secondary data may provide the sample frame.* If a company, such as UPS, wants to track its levels of customer satisfaction each quarter, the names of customers must come from its database. Thus, the customer list is the sample frame, and the sample frame is the list or device from which a sample is drawn.

Limitations of Secondary Data

Despite the many advantages of secondary data, they also pose some dangers. The main disadvantages of secondary information are lack of availability, lack of relevance, inaccuracy, and insufficiency.

Lack of Availability For some research questions, there are simply no available data. Suppose Kraft General Foods wants to evaluate the taste, texture, and color of three new gourmet brownie mixes. No secondary data exist that can answer these questions; consumers must try each mix and then evaluate it. If McDonald's wants to evaluate its image in Phoenix, Arizona, it must gather primary data. If Ford wants to know the reaction of college students to a new two-seater sports car design, it must show prototypes to the students and evaluate their opinions. Of course, secondary data may have played a major role in the engineer's design plan for the car.

Lack of Relevance It is not uncommon for secondary data to be expressed in units or measures that cannot be used by the researcher. For example, Joan Dermott, a retailer of oriental rugs, determined that the primary customers for her rugs were families with a total household income of $40,000 to $80,000. Higher-income consumers tended to purchase pricier rugs than those Dermott carried. When she was trying to decide whether to open a store in another Florida city, she could not find useful income data. One source offered class breakdowns of $30,000 to $50,000, $50,000 to $70,000, $70,000 to $90,000, and so forth. Another secondary source broke down incomes into less than $15,000, $15,000 to $30,000, and more than $30,000. Even if the given income brackets had met Joan's needs, she would have faced another problem: outdated information. One study had been conducted in 1995 and the other in 2001. In Florida's dynamic markets, the percentages probably were no longer relevant. This is often the case with U.S. Census data, which are nearly a year old before they become available.

Inaccuracy Users of secondary data should always assess the accuracy of the data. There are a number of potential sources of error when a researcher gathers, codes, analyzes, and presents data. Any report that does not mention possible sources and ranges of error should be suspect.

Using secondary data does not relieve the researcher from attempting to assess their accuracy. A few guidelines for determining the accuracy of secondary data are as follows:

1. *Who gathered the data?* The source of the secondary data is a key to their accuracy. Federal agencies, most state agencies, and large commercial marketing research firms generally can be counted on to have conducted their research as professionally as possible. Marketing researchers should always be on guard when examining data in

which a hidden agenda might be reflected. A chamber of commerce, for instance, is always going to put its best foot forward. Similarly, trade associations often advocate one position over another.

2. *What was the purpose of the study?* Data are always collected for some reason. Understanding the motivation for the research can provide clues to the quality of the data. A chamber of commerce study conducted to provide data that could be used to attract new industry to the area should be scrutinized with a great deal of caution. There have been situations in which advertising agencies have been hired by clients to assess the impact of their own advertising programs. In other words, they have been asked to evaluate the quality of the job they were doing for their clients!

3. *What information was collected?* A researcher should always identify exactly what information was gathered and from whom. For example, in a dog food study, were purchasers of canned, dry, and semimoist food interviewed, or were just one or two types of dog food purchasers surveyed? In a voters' survey, were only Democrats or only Republicans interviewed? Were the respondents registered voters? Was any attempt made to ascertain a respondent's likelihood of voting in the next election? Were self-reported data used to infer actual behavior?

4. *When was the information collected?* A shopping mall study that surveyed shoppers only on weekends would not reflect the opinions of "typical" mall patrons. A telephone survey conducted from 9:00 A.M. to 5:00 P.M. would vastly underrepresent working persons. A survey of Florida visitors conducted during the summer probably would reveal motivations and interests different from those of winter visitors.

5. *How was the information collected?* Were the data collected by mail, telephone, Internet, or personal interview? Each of these techniques offers advantages and disadvantages. What was the refusal rate? Were decision makers or their representatives interviewed? In short, the researcher must attempt to discern the amount of bias injected into the data by the information-gathering process. A mail survey with a 1 percent response rate (that is, only 1 percent of those who received the survey mailed it back) probably contains a lot of self-selection bias.

6. *Is the information consistent with other information?* A lack of consistency between secondary data sets should dictate caution. The researcher should delve into possible causes of the discrepancy. Differences in the sample, time frame, sampling methodology, questionnaire structure, and other factors can lead to variations in studies. If possible, the researcher should assess the validity of the different studies as a basis for determining which, if any, study should be used for decision making.

Insufficiency A researcher may determine that available data are relevant and accurate but still not sufficient to make a decision or bring closure to a problem. For example, a manager for Wal-Mart may have sufficient secondary data on incomes, family sizes, number of competitors, and growth potential to determine in which of five Iowa towns Wal-Mart wishes to locate its next store. But if no traffic counts exist for the selected town, primary data will have to be gathered to select a specific site for the store.

Internal Databases

For many companies, a computerized database containing information about customers and prospects has become an essential marketing tool. An **internal database** is simply a collection of related information developed from data within the organization.

internal database
A collection of related information developed from data within the organization.

Creating an Internal Database

A firm's sales activities can be an excellent source of information for creating an internal database. A traditional starting point has been the firm's sales or inquiry processing and tracking system. Typically, such a system is built on salespersons' "call reports." A call report provides a blueprint of a salesperson's daily activities. It details the number of calls made, characteristics of each firm visited, sales activity resulting from the call, and any information picked up from the client regarding competitors, such as price changes, new products or services, credit term modifications, and new product or service features.

An internal marketing database built on sales results and customer preferences can be a powerful marketing tool. While large companies build mammoth internal databases (Yahoo! collects 400 billion bytes of information every day—the equivalent of a library of 800,000 books),[3] Ben & Jerry's uses databases to maintain the highest quality ice creams as discussed in the Practicing Marketing Research feature.

Growing Importance of Internal Database Marketing

> **database marketing**
> Marketing that relies on the creation of a large computerized file of customers' and potential customers' profiles and purchase patterns to create a targeted marketing mix.

Perhaps the fastest growing use of internal databases is database marketing. **Database marketing** relies on the creation of a large computerized file of customers' and potential customers' profiles and purchase patterns to create a targeted marketing mix.

In the 1950s, network television enabled advertisers to "get the same message to everyone simultaneously." Database marketing can get a customized, individual message to everyone simultaneously through direct mail. This is why database marketing is sometimes called *micromarketing*. Database marketing can create a computerized form of the old-fashioned relationship that people used to have with the corner grocer, butcher, or baker. "A database is sort of a collective memory," says Richard G. Barlow, president of Frequency Marketing, Inc., a Cincinnati-based consulting firm. "It deals with you in the same personalized way as a mom-and-pop grocery store, where they knew customers by name and stocked what they wanted."[4]

The size of some databases is impressive: Ford Motor Company's is about 50 million names; Kraft General Foods, 30 million; Citicorp, 30 million; and Kimberly Clark, maker of Huggies diapers, 10 million new mothers. American Express can pull from its database all cardholders who made purchases at golf pro shops in the past 6 months, who attended symphony concerts, or who traveled to Europe more than once in the past year, as well as the very few people who did all three.

The San Diego Padres baseball team used database marketing to attract 60,000 new fans and collected about $400,000 in revenues from new season ticket sales. This was accomplished by marrying the database with customer relationship marketing (CRM) software. New, powerful CRM software is helping marketers enhance their recruitment of new customers and also keep current clients.

Aided by technology, sports-specific strategies are helping marketers reconnect with their fans. Even when a team is winning and stadiums are packed, CRM helps identify those fans most likely to buy season tickets or ticket packages in advance by creating databases on fan attendance. A team can then target these prospects for season tickets the following year. Advance ticket sales are extremely valuable to sports teams since they guarantee a certain revenue level for the season.

"Club cards," similar to ATM cards, are at the heart of fan loyalty programs these days. Although programs vary slightly from team to team, the idea is pretty much the same: Each time fans use their card, they rack up attendance points redeemable for promotional coupons or items such as food, drinks, and souvenirs. The more points they

Looking for Intelligence in Ice Cream

Just beyond the souvenir shop and down the relic-filled hallways in the Ben & Jerry's factory in Waterbury, Vermont, massive pipes pump out 190,000 pints of ice cream each day. Throughout the day, tractor trailers pull up, pick up the mountains of Cherry Garcia or Chunky Monkey pints, and deliver them to depots. From there, the ice cream is shipped out to 50,000 grocery stores in the United States and 12 other countries. Once it's on the freezer shelves, it has the magical effect of curing a broken heart, satiating a sweet tooth, or possibly just heightening someone's cholesterol level.

For Ben & Jerry's, that's only the start of the journey. At the company's headquarters in Burlington, Vermont, just miles from where the founders opened their first shop 25 years ago, the life of each pint—from ingredients to sale—is tracked in a database. Once the pint is stamped and sent out, Ben & Jerry's stores its tracking number in a database; then it puts it under the microscope. Using software from a company called Business Objects, the sales team can check to see if Chocolate Chip Cookie Dough is gaining ground on Cherry Garcia for the coveted No. 1 sales position. Down the hall in the marketing department, the company checks to see whether orders online require Ben & Jerry's to make a donation to one of its philanthropies. The finance people pop the number into their journals to show results. Since they started using the software, they've sharply cut the time it takes to close their monthly books. And probably most important to a company focused on customer loyalty, the consumer affairs staff matches up the pint with the 225 calls and e-mails received each week, checking to see if there were any complaints, and if so, which supplier's milk, eggs, or cherries didn't meet the company's near obsession with quality.

Ben & Jerry's may cultivate a down-home image, but as a unit of $47-billion-a-year Unilever, it depends just as heavily on the statistics for its success. And to get those figures, it relies on business intelligence, or BI, software: a name for programs that crunch huge quantities of data in a database in search of trends, problems, or new business opportunities.

Typical BI applications first pull information out of giant databases into so-called data marts—smaller clusters of similar information that can keep financial data in one area, inventory data in another. Then the software is ready for the hunt. When a Lands' End product manager wants to know, say, what the hottest-selling turtleneck has been in the last month, the BI software first runs the request through a so-called semantic layer, which translates the query into database-speak (at Lands' End, white turtlenecks go by the number "66780," for example). Then it uses the terms to gather the relevant data from the right data mart, organize it, analyze it, translate it back, and offer an answer.

The employee sees only the last part. Just about every company now offers stand-alone or browser-based software that the industry calls "dashboards," which presents graphical displays of inventory levels, sales info, and other urgent gauges of day-to-day business.

Companies are using BI software to mine their databases not to just better understand trends and solve problems but also to eliminate false assumptions. Ben & Jerry's noticed a swell in complaints from Cherry Garcia ice cream customers, most of whom were irritated that the product had too few cherries. The company matched the complaints against the shipment records and analyzed them using Business Objects. First it eliminated the chance that this was a regional problem—complaints were coming from all over the country. Then it queried information on the manufacturing process; the recipe and ingredients all turned out to be normal. Finally, after nixing just about every possibility, the company discovered the problem: The photo on the ice-cream-pop box was not of the ice cream but of frozen yogurt—a product more laden with cherries than the paler-pink ice-cream treat. Ben & Jerry's changed the image on the box, and the complaints melted away.[5]

compile, the more "rewards" they receive. In return, the teams get a database filled with information on their fans, which could lead to additional revenue streams.[6]

Creating a Database from a Web Site— A Marketer's Dream

If a person today were opening, say, a wine shop, which of the following would give the owner the best opportunity to build a database—a traditional store or a Web retailer such as Virtual Vineyards, Incorporated?

A Web merchant like Virtual Vineyards has access to data about its clients that would make its physical-world counterparts very envious. A customer's conduit to an online store is a two-way electronic link, allowing the online merchant to gather all sorts of information, particularly if that customer has shopped with that merchant before.

Getting the customer's name, address, and purchasing history is only the beginning. A Web merchant can record the customer's actions as he or she moves through the merchant's site, taking note not only of purchases but also of window shopping. The end result is a file that allows the merchant to determine what that customer is most likely to purchase next—and then offer inducements to make it happen.

Meanwhile, back in the physical world, the wine store owner sits behind the register, eyeing the anonymous customer who just went out empty-handed. Had the customer visited the site before? If so, what did he or she buy? Did the customer even see the new Chardonnay that just came in? Unfortunately, the owner was too busy to ask those questions (and the customer would have been offended if the owner had). Maybe the customer will come back—maybe not.

Preview Travel Inc., an online travel agency based in San Francisco, determined that Las Vegas, Orlando, and Cancun were the top three vacation spots among its customers. The firm quickly purchased keywords for the three destinations on several Internet directory sites; when a Web surfer performs a search for any of the three vacation spots, a Preview Travel advertising banner accompanies the list of results. Karen Askey, senior vice president of consumer marketing at Preview Travel, says traditional travel agencies could employ the same promotional tactics, but she doubts they could spot top destinations as quickly. "When you're online, the speed at which you can get that data is basically instantaneous," she says.

Once Web surfers start clicking around the virtual aisles of an online store, merchants can monitor their every move. The best known method of doing so involves a **cookie**, a text file that sits on a user's computer and identifies that user when she or he revisits a Web site.

Even some privacy advocates admit that cookies have beneficial uses. For instance, they can store passwords, sparing users the hassle of having to identify themselves every time they go to a Web site, and they allow online shopping carts to work. Despite what some Net users believe, a site can read only the cookie that site put on the user's system, not any other cookies the user has collected from other Web sites.

Cookies are a powerful device for monitoring a user's behavior within a site, one that can tell a merchant whether the user lingers in lingerie or lawn chairs. "What it's like," says Nick Donatiello, president of Odyssey, a marketing research firm based in San Francisco, "is every time you walk into Macy's, they put a little tracker on you that follows you everywhere you go, how long you look at perfume and blue jeans."[8]

Cookies give Web merchants an advantage over their competitors in traditional retailing. Web merchants can follow window shoppers and then use the information they obtain to target promotions to them on return visits. And, unlike traditional counterparts, an online merchant can rearrange the entire layout of a store in real time, sticking an advertisement for, say, parkas on the front door when an avid skier comes calling.

> **cookie**
> A text file placed on a user's computer in order to identify the user when she or he revisits the Web site.

Database Design and Implementation

With both an MBA and an undergraduate degree in computer science, Mike Foytik, senior vice president for information science for DSS Research, exemplifies the new breed of marketing service managers with a strong background in computers. He is a proponent of the use of *relational databases*. He has designed dozens for DSS clients in direct marketing and retailing.

He notes that there are many advantages to using a relational database instead of the *traditional database approach*, sometimes referred to as the *flat-file method*. In a relational database, data are stored in several small structures, or files, rather than in a single large one. Each of the small files in a relational database contains key information that allows individual records in the database to be linked to associated data in other individual files that make up the entire database structure.

For example, a customer database might contain one file that includes customer information such as name, mailing address, and Social Security number. This information is updated occasionally. Products purchased by each customer would go into another file that is updated frequently (every time the customer buys something). The two files might be linked by the customer's Social Security number.

With each new order, a record is created that includes the product purchased, the price, other relevant information concerning the purchase, and the buyer's Social Security number. Under the traditional, flat-file approach, all this information (the product purchase information and the buyer's personal information) would have to be entered with each product purchase. Relational databases have a number of distinct advantages:

☐ *Less data storage space is required.* There is very little redundant information in a relational database. Data such as addresses are stored only once for each customer rather than being stored with every new purchase that is added. Foytik notes that "we have achieved 75 percent storage space reductions for some of our clients."

☐ *The database is more flexible.* Relational databases offer much greater flexibility and efficiency with respect to changes in the way data are stored and used. With flat-file databases, every time a new data field is added to the database, the database must be re-created in order to add the new data field to every record in the database. With a relational database, new information is stored in a new file and, therefore, has no effect on existing data in other files in the database.

☐ *Restricting access to sensitive information is easier.* Relational databases can be easily designed to restrict user access to certain areas of the database via the use of special passwords or codes while still allowing more general access to less sensitive areas. In flat-file databases, this sort of restricted access to some parts of the database is all but impossible. Users must have either total access or no access.

☐ *The database can easily be designed to accommodate many users.* Foytik notes that "most of our clients have a number of different departments with very different informational needs accessing customer data." With flat files, separate copies of the database must be created and modified to meet the needs of different users. With relational databases, the physical data remain unchanged, while the data or reports seen by the different user groups (sometimes called the logical data) can be varied.

Finally, he notes, all these advantages come at some cost. First, relational databases require much more sophisticated software and more sophisticated people to program them. Second, relational databases require much more up-front planning if the company is to reap the full benefits of this type of data. Finally, relational databases tend to require more processor horsepower. This is becoming less of an issue with the price/performance ratio of computers constantly improving.[7]

A few tips on database design are offered in the "Practicing Marketing Research" Box on page 99.

Data Mining

A few tips on database design are offered in the "Practicing Marketing Research" Box on page 99.

American Express uses a neural network to examine the hundreds of millions of entries in its database that tell how and where individual cardholders transact business. A **neural network** is a computer program that mimics the processes of the human brain and thus is capable of learning from examples to find patterns in data. The result is a set of *purchase propensity scores* for each cardholder. Based on these scores, AmEx matches offers from affiliated merchants to the purchase histories of individual cardholders and encloses these offers with their monthly statements. The benefits are reduced expenses for AmEx and information of higher value for its cardholders; American Express is engaged in data mining.

Data mining is the use of statistical and other advanced software to discover nonobvious patterns hidden in a database. The objective is to identify patterns that marketers can use in creating new strategies and tactics to increase a firm's profitability. Camelot Music Holdings used data mining to identify a group of high-spending, 65-plus customers (members of its frequent shopper club) who were buying lots of classical and jazz music and movies. Further data mining revealed that a large percentage were also buying rap and alternative music; these were grandparents buying for the grandkids. Now, Camelot tells the senior citizens what's hot in rap and alternative music, as well as in traditional music.

Data mining involves searching for interesting patterns and following the data trail wherever it leads. The discovery process often requires sifting through massive quantities of data; electronic point-of-sale transactions, inventory records, and online customer orders matched with demographics can easily use up hundreds of gigabytes of data storage space. Probability sampling, descriptive statistics, and multivariate statistics are all tools

neural network

A computer program that mimics the processes of the human brain and thus is capable of learning from examples to find patterns in data.

data mining

The use of statistical and other advanced software to discover nonobvious patterns hidden in a database.

Farmers Group Insurance used data mining to find out that, as long as a sports car wasn't the only vehicle in a household, the accident rate for sports cars wasn't much greater than that for regular cars. This information led to lower insurance rates for sports cars in this category.

of data mining that make the task manageable. (Probability sampling was discussed in Chapter 3; descriptive statistics programs and multivariate statistics will be covered in Chapters 13 through 17.) Other more advanced data mining tools, such as genetic algorithms and case-based reasoning systems, must be left for an advanced text.

Data mining has many potential uses in marketing. Those with widest application include the following:

- ☐ *Customer acquisition.* In the first stage of a two-stage process, direct marketers apply data mining methods to discover customer attributes that predict their responses to special offers and communications such as catalogues. In the second stage, attributes that the model indicates make customers most likely to respond are matched to the attributes appended to rented lists of noncustomers in order to select noncustomer households most likely to respond to a new offer or communication.

- ☐ *Customer retention.* In a typical marketing application, data mining identifies those customers who contribute to the company's bottom line but who are likely to leave and go to a competitor. With this information, the company can target the vulnerable customers for special offers and other inducements not available to less vulnerable customers.

- ☐ *Customer abandonment.* Some customers cost more than they contribute and should be encouraged to take their business elsewhere. At Federal Express, customers who spend a lot with little service and marketing investment get different treatment from, say, those who spend just as much but cost more to keep. If their shipping volume falters, "good" clients can expect a phone call, which can head off defections before they occur. As for the "bad" clients—those who spend but are expensive to the company—FedEx is turning them into profitable customers, in many cases, by charging higher shipping prices. And the "ugly" clients, those customers who spend little and show few signs of spending more in the future? They can catch the TV ads. "We just don't market to them anymore," says Sharanjit Singh, managing director for marketing analysis at FedEx. "That automatically brings our costs down."[9]

- ☐ *Market basket analysis.* By identifying the associations among product purchases in point-of-sale transactions, retailers and direct marketers can spot product affinities and develop focused promotion strategies that work more effectively than traditional one-size-fits-all approaches. The American Express strategy of selectively stuffing offers in monthly statements is an example of how market basket analysis can be employed to increase marketing efficiency.

The Farmers Group has used data mining to better understand its customers. A few years ago, owning a Porsche or a Corvette almost guaranteed that you would pay more for car insurance. Conventional wisdom and decades of data collected by insurers suggested that drivers of high-performance sports cars were more likely to have accidents than were other motorists. But, by using data mining, the Farmers Group discovered something interesting: as long as the sports car wasn't the only vehicle in a household, the accident rate actually wasn't much greater than that for a regular car. Based on that information, Farmers changed its policy that had excluded sports cars from its lowest-priced insurance rates. By eliminating that rule, "we figured out that we could almost double our sports-car market," says Melissa McBratney, vice president of personal lines at the Los Angeles insurer.[10] Farmers estimates that just letting Corvettes and Porsches into its "preferred premium" plan could bring in an additional $4.5 million in premium revenue over the next 2 years, without a significant rise in claims. The pattern Farmers discovered isn't intuitive—it had eluded most insurance veterans.

Battle over Privacy

The growth of databases both on and off the Internet is causing increasing concern about privacy issues. Recently, the U.S. Congress restricted states' sales of databases filled with personal information from drivers' licenses. And the Federal Trade Commission has investigated whether Yahoo! is complying with consumer-protection regulations in its use of users' information.

The Internet has received significant criticism from privacy advocates. The concept of privacy is changing radically as a result of our new computer-based lives. Privacy used to be achieved through the sheer friction of everyday life: distance, time, and lack of records. Information didn't travel well, and most people who wanted to escape their past could simply move to a new location. Now the picture has changed. People can escape their surroundings through the Internet, but their actions can easily catch up with them. And it's not just the Internet; it's electronic toll roads (exactly *when* did you leave that party?), credit card transactions (we know what hotel you went to), vendor databases (and what book you bought), cell phone records (and whom you called), and more. At work, employee arrival and departure times may be recorded, along with their Web searches, e-mail messages, and sick days.

What makes all this troubling to privacy advocates is the growing ability of technology to combine information: the products you bought from a variety of different merchants; your sick days plus someone else's hotel bills. It's not the routine use of this information for marketing purposes that people find troubling; it's the way someone with an agenda might put the pieces together.

Identity Theft   People have a right to be concerned. Identity theft cost $53 billion in 2005.[11] One company that has come under fire is ChoicePoint. Since spinning off from the credit bureau Equifax in 1997, it has been buying up databases and data mining operations. Businesses, individuals, even the FBI, now rely on its storehouse. Other customers: Nigerian scammers who apparently used the data to steal people's identities.

The problem was unreliable safeguards. To ensure that only certain businesses had access to its data, ChoicePoint set up certain requirements that potential customers must meet. A man named Olatunji Oluwatosin—and possibly others—used fake names and a Hollywood copy shop fax machine to create fictitious small businesses requesting ChoicePoint service. Before Oluwatosin was caught—after someone at ChoicePoint grew suspicious about one of his applications—he accessed at least 145,000 names. (Oluwatosin pleaded no contest to felony identity theft in California in February 2005; he is serving a 16-month sentence.)[12] ChoicePoint announced in March 2005 that it will no longer sell consumer data that includes drivers license numbers and Social Security numbers.[13]

Later in 2005, Citi Financial notified 3.9 million customers that computer tapes containing their personal information were missing. Data on the tapes included account information, payment histories, and Social Security numbers.[14] Were they simply lost? We did not have an answer as the book went to press.

Governmental Actions   Three key laws (one a state law) have been passed to protect consumers from identity theft. These are:

Federal Laws

> **Gramm-Leach-Bliley Act (Financial Services Modernization Act):** aimed at financial companies. Requires those corporations to tell their customers how they use their personal information and to have policies that prevent fraudulent access to it. Partial compliance has been required since 2001.

> **Health Insurance Portability and Accountability Act:** aimed at the healthcare industry. Limits disclosure of individuals' medical information and imposes penalties on organizations that violate privacy rules. Compliance required for large companies since 2003.

State Laws

California's Notice of Security Breach Law: if any company or agency that has collected the personal information of a California resident discovers that non-encrypted information has been taken by an unauthorized person, the company or agency must tell the resident. Compliance required since 2003. (Some 30 other states are considering similar laws.)

Proposed Federal Laws

Schumer-Nelson ID Theft Bill: would regulate companies that sell personal data, setting rules to prevent fraudulent access to information and requiring companies to disclose breaches in their security and the sale of personal information.

Notification of Risk to Personal Data Bill: a broader, nationwide version of California's security-breach law that carries tougher penalties for offending companies. Proposed by Senator Diane Feinstein of California.[15]

Getting Paid to Give Up Your Privacy A number of marketing research firms are paying people to participate in online surveys, to track their click streams, or to evaluate Web sites. This, of course, is legitimate research. Usually, consumers are willing to give up their right to privacy quite cheaply. A recent Jupiter report said that 82 percent of respondents would give personal information to new shopping sites to enter a $100 sweepstakes.[16]

PRACTICING MARKETING RESEARCH

Have you recently received e-mail that offers to pay you for your opinions, "turn your opinions into cash," or the like? If the answer to this question is yes, you're not alone. Many in the survey research industry have received and expressed concern over similar e-mails with offers to pay members of the public for their opinions (usually for a membership fee). In reality, these Web sites sell their "members" a database of industry members they claim will "pay" respondents for their opinions. This type of offer raises several concerns. First, a legitimate survey researcher (focus group or otherwise) never asks respondents to pay to become research participants. Second, with the publicity of these offers, respondents may become uniformly accustomed to being "paid for their opinions," rather than, in some cases, being paid as an incentive or a thank you for participation by legitimate industry members.

Moreover, although incentives may be used in focus groups, mall studies, customer satisfaction studies, Web surveys, or others, incentives normally are not used in telephone studies where telephone numbers have been randomly generated by a computer. Since telephone studies make up a considerable amount of the survey research conducted in our industry, the respondent is left with an unrealistic expectation of being offered or receiving an incentive whenever he or she participates in survey research. In addition, given the reality that all potential respondents won't fit the desired demographic for all studies, the materials (generally) don't clearly notify potential respondents that they may never be chosen to participate in any survey research and therefore may never be provided with an incentive to participate in the research process.

Lastly, as industry members have reported, one net effect of such "offers" is the creation of "professional respondents" or "professional survey takers." Such individuals who frequent group discussions have views that may not be wholly representative of the group and are more familiar with group discussion practice—which may result in uncharacteristic and unrepresentative behavior.[17]

There is also a dark side to getting paid for online surveys. Many Web sites, such as Express Paid Surveys, Get Cash for Surveys, and Opinion Paycheck, promise money for taking surveys. The catch is that you must first pay a membership fee; such fees range from $25 to $37. Donna Gillin and Jane Sheppard, both directors of the Council for Marketing and Opinion Research, discuss the membership fee in the previous Practicing Marketing Research box.

Finding Secondary Data on the Internet

Gathering secondary data from external sources, a necessity in almost any research project, has traditionally been a tedious and boring job. The researcher often had to write to government agencies, trade associations, or other secondary data providers and then wait days or weeks for a reply that might never come. Frequently, one or more trips to the library were required, and there the researcher might find that needed reports were checked out or missing. The rapid development of the Internet and World Wide Web in recent years promises to eliminate the drudgery associated with the collection of secondary data.

Finding the information that you need on the Web can be very easy, or it can require trial and error. Your Web connection provides access to over 320 million Web sites throughout the world, containing more information than any library can offer. No matter where you are on the globe, as long as you have an Internet connection you have access to all this information. There are basically two ways to find the information you need: entering a URL (Uniform Reference Locator) and using a search engine.

URLs

If you know the address of the Web site that you are searching for, you can type it directly into your Web browser. (Netscape Navigator and Microsoft Internet Explorer are the dominant browsers.) A Web address, or URL, is similar to a street address in that it identifies a particular location (server and file on that server) on the Web.

Search Engines

Sites such as Yahoo! Search, Dogpile, and Google have become popular among computer users looking for information on the Web. These organizations offer *search engines* that crawl the Web looking for sites that contain the information you are seeking. Each search engine has its own indexing system to help you locate information. All of them allow you to enter one or more keywords and search the databases of Web sites for all occurrences of those words. They then return listings of sites that you can go to immediately by clicking on the name.

Remember that the Internet is a self-publishing medium. Visits to search engines will yield files of diverse quality from a variety of sources. Be sure to try out multiple sites when you are investigating a topic.

Sites of Interest to Marketing Researchers

A number of Web sites are accessed daily by marketing researchers in search of information. The most frequently used of these sites, which offer an incredible variety of information, are listed on our Web site at *www.wiley.com/college/mcdaniel*.

Periodical, Newspaper, and Book Databases Several excellent periodical, newspaper, and book databases are available to researchers. We have also posted these on our Web site. Some can be directly accessed via the Internet and others through your local library's Web site.

Newsgroups

A primary means of communicating with other professionals and special-interest groups on the Internet is through newsgroups. With an Internet connection and newsreader software, you can visit any newsgroup supported by your service provider. If your service provider does not offer newsgroups or does not carry the group in which you are interested, you can find one of the publicly available newsgroup servers that does carry the group you'd like to read.

Newsgroups function much like bulletin boards for a particular topic or interest. A newsgroup is established to focus on a particular topic. Readers stop by that newsgroup to read messages left by other people, post responses to others' questions, and send rebuttals to comments with which they disagree. Generally, there is some management of the messages to keep discussions within the topic area and to remove offensive material. However, readers of a newsgroup are free to discuss any issue and communicate with anyone in the world who visits that group. Images and data files can be exchanged in newsgroups, just as they can be exchanged via e-mail.

With over 250,000 newsgroups currently in existence and more being added every day, there is a newsgroup for nearly every hobby, profession, and lifestyle. Both Netscape Navigator and Microsoft Internet Explorer, as well as other browsers, come with newsgroup readers. If you do not already have a newsgroup reader, you can go to one of the search engines and search for a freeware or shareware newsgroup reader. These newsgroup readers function much like e-mail programs. To find a particular newsgroup, follow these steps:

1. Connect to the Internet in your usual way.
2. Open your newsreader program.
3. Search for the topic of interest. Most newsreaders allow you to search the names of the newsgroups for keywords or topics. Some newsreaders, like Microsoft Internet Explorer, also allow you to search the brief descriptions that accompany most newsgroups.
4. Select the newsgroup of interest.
5. Begin scanning messages. The title of each message generally gives an indication of its subject matter.

Newsgroup messages look like e-mail messages. They contain a subject title, author, and message body. Unlike normal e-mail messages, however, newsgroup messages are threaded discussions. This means that any reply to a previous message will appear linked to that message. Therefore, you can follow a discussion between two or more people by starting at the original message and following the links (or threads) to each successive reply. Images, sound files, and video clips can be attached to messages for anyone to download and examine.

> **newsgroup**
> An Internet site where people can read and post messages devoted to a specific topic.

Blogs

The traditional definition of a blog, or Web log, was a frequent, chronological publication of personal thoughts and Web links. Now companies are also using blogs to talk to customers and to other businesses. Blogging gained popularity with the introduction of automated published systems, most notably Bloggeratblogger.com. Marketing researchers are finding blogs to be an important source of information on just about any topic imaginable. Researchers have also used them to recruit respondents for surveys. Although blogs can be found on most search engines, several engines, such as blogsearchengine.com are dedicated to blog searches.

Federal Government Data

Some 70 federal agencies regularly publish data, and diligent searchers are hard-pressed to wade through all the results. Federal agencies have posted a rich array of current information on the Internet, from their latest press releases to a wide range of historical results. The issue for the user is zeroing in on the information needed.

Several new hubs have been created to help solve this problem. Statistical Universe, developed by the Congressional Information Service, Inc. (CIS), is available either as a Web-based service (*http://www.cispubs.com*) or through the LEXIS-NEXIS STATIS library. Statistical Universe builds on the CIS *American Statistics Index* (ASI), which researchers have used for decades. But unlike the ASI, which is a catalogue of materials, Statistical Universe displays actual results from about 60 percent of the reports available. Material dating back to the 1970s is included, but only about 2000 of the early reports can be accessed directly. Using the Statistical Universe is like having a huge library card catalogue that delves inside the books, taking users to the precise page or table they are looking for. Once they find what they want, users can display the specific material or download the entire report. Statistical Universe is the most comprehensive and fully indexed source of federal statistics online.

Users who are looking for a particular recent report or who know which agency issued the data they are looking for might be better served by first checking with the free government Web sites. A good place to start is FedStats (*http://www.fedstats.gov*), which has links to the 70 federal agencies recognized by the Office of Management and Budget as issuing statistical data. This site's search engine covers reports from the 14 major statistical agencies, including the U.S. Census Bureau, Department of Commerce, and Bureau of Labor Statistics, and provides links to all the other agencies.

Users looking for information related to subjects in the news should try the White House Briefing Room (*http://www.whitehouse.gov/WH/html/briefroom.html*). The Federal Statistics page offers data on both economic issues (*http://www.whitehouse.gov/fsbr/esbr.html*) and social issues (*http://www.whitehouse.gov/fsbr/ssbr.html*). These pages provide an overview of the most newsworthy trends.

Internet Search Strategies

There is perhaps no single best way to search the Web, but we recommend a five-step strategy.[18]

Step One: Analyze your topic to decide where to begin. A suggested worksheet is shown in Exhibit 4.1.

Step Two: Test run a word or phrase in a search engine such as Google. Consider synonyms or equivalent terms.

Step Three: Learn as you go and vary your approach with what you learn. Don't assume that you know what you want to find. Look at the search results and see what else you might use in addition to what you thought of.

Step Four: Don't get bogged down in any strategy that doesn't work. Consider using a subject directory. A few of the best are the Librarian's Index, *http://lii.org*; Infomine, *http://infomine.ucr.edu*; Academic Info, *http://www.academicinfo.net*; Google Directory, *http://directory.google.com*; About.com, *http://www.about.com*; and Yahoo Directory, *http://dir.yahoo.com*. Many researchers switch back and forth between directories and search engines.

Step Five: If you haven't found what you want, go back to earlier steps better informed.[19]

EXHIBIT 4.1 **Internet Search Topic Worksheet**

Jot down a topic or subject you'd like to explore on the Web:

BEGIN THE PRE-SEARCHING ANALYSIS

1. **What UNIQUE WORDS, DISTINCTIVE NAMES, ABBREVIATIONS, or ACRONYMS are associated with your topic?**
   These may be the place to begin because their specificity will help zero in on relevant pages.

2. **Can you think of societies, organizations, or groups that might have information on your subject via their pages?**
   Search these as a "phrase in quotes," looking for a home page that might contain links to other pages, journals, discussion groups, or databases on your subject. You may require the "phrase in quotes" to be in the documents' titles by preceding it by **title:** (no space)

3. **What other words are likely to be in ANY Web documents on your topic?**
   You may want to require these by joining them with **AND** or preceding each by + (no space)

4. **Do any of the words in 1, 2, or 3 belong in phrases or strings—together in a certain order, like a cliché?**
   Search these as a "phrase in quotes" (e.g., "observation research" or "marketing research aggregator").

5. **For any of the terms in #4, can you think of synonyms, variant spellings, or equivalent terms you would also accept in relevant documents?**
   You may want to allow these terms by joining them by **OR** and including each set of equivalent terms in ( ) (e.g., surveys or interviews).

6. **Can you think of any extraneous or irrelevant documents these words might pick up?**
   You may want to exclude terms or phrases with—**[no space] before each term**, or **AND NOT** (e.g., surveys or interviews—job).

7. **What BROADER terms could your topic be covered by?**
   When browsing subject categories or searching sites of webliographies or databases on your topic, try broader categories (e.g., marketing research).

Effective searching on the Internet is part art, part science, and part luck. Appendix 4-A gives you tips for Googling to the max with exercises. You will find this appendix helpful not only in this course, but also during the remainder of your academic career and on the job.

Evaluating Web Pages Once you have found what you were looking for, the next step is to evaluate the quality. Things are not always as they seem. For example, recall the Web sites that want you to pay a membership fee to become an online survey respondent. There is a Web site that supposedly ranks Web sites that provide an entrée to earning cash through completing interviews. All of the sites ranked required a membership fee, and no real marketing research firms, such as Greenfield Online or Harris Interactive, were included. Of course, legitimate researchers don't charge a fee to become a panel member. The ranking site was probably created by one of the sites that charge a membership fee. No criteria were given for how the rankings were determined.

Techniques for evaluating Web pages are detailed in Exhibit 4.2.

EXHIBIT 4.2	How to Evaluate Web Pages

1. What can the URL tell you?
Techniques for Web Evaluation:
1. Before you leave the list of search results—before you click and get interested in anything written on the page—glean all you can from the URLs of each page.
2. Then choose pages most likely to be reliable and authentic.

Questions to ask:
Is it somebody's *personal page*?
- Read the *URL* carefully:
  - Look for a personal name (e.g., *jbarker* or *barker*) following a tilde (~), a percent sign (%), or the words "users," "members," or "people."
  - Is the server a commercial *ISP** or other provider mostly of Web page hosting (like aol.com or geocities.com)

What type of *domain* does it come from?
(educational, nonprofit, commercial, government, etc.)
- Is the domain appropriate for the content?
  - Government sites: look for .gov, .mil, .us, or other country code
  - Educational sites: look for .edu

What are the implications?
Personal pages are not necessarily "bad," but you need to investigate the author very carefully. For personal pages, there is no publisher or domain owner vouching for the information in the page.

Look for appropriateness, fit. What kind of information source do you think is most reliable for your topic?

2. Scan the perimeter of the page, looking for answers to these questions.
Techniques for Web Evaluation:
1. Look for links that say **"About us," "Philosophy," "Background," "Biography," "Who am I,"** etc.
2. If you cannot find any links like these, you can often find this kind of information if you
Truncate back the URL.
   INSTRUCTIONS for Truncating back a URL: In the top Location Box, delete the end characters of the URL stopping just before each / (leave the slash). Press enter to see if you can see more about the author or the origins/nature of the site providing the page. Continue this process, one slash (/) at a time, until you reach the first single / which is preceded by the domain name portion. This is the page's server or "publisher."
3. Look for the date "last updated"—usually at the bottom of a Web page.
   Check the date on all the pages on the site.
   Do not rely on a date given in IE's File|Properties or Netscape/Mozilla's View|Page Info displays. These dates can be automatically kept current and are useless in critical evaluation.

Questions to ask:
Who wrote the page?
- Look for the name of the author, or the name of the organization, institution, agency, or whatever, who is responsible for the page
  - An e-mail contact is not enough.
- If there is no personal author, look for an agency or organization that claims responsibility for the page.
  - If you cannot find this, locate the publisher by truncating back the URL (see technique above). Does this publisher claim responsibility for the content? Does it explain why the page exists in any way?

What are the implications?
Web pages are all created with a purpose in mind by some person or agency or entity. They do not simply "grow" on the Web like mildew grows in moist corners.

You are looking for someone who claims accountability and responsibility for the content.
An e-mail address with no additional information about the author is not sufficient for assessing the author's credentials.

If this is all you have, try e-mailing the author and asking politely for more information about him/her.

3. Look for indicators of quality information:
Techniques for Web Evaluation:
1. Look for a link called "links," "additional sites," "related links," etc.
2. In the text, if you see little footnote numbers or links that might refer to documentation, take the time to explore them. What kinds of publications or sites are they? reputable? scholarly? Are they real? On the Web (where no publisher is editing most pages), it is possible to create totally fake references.
3. Look at the publisher of the page (first part of the URL). Expect a journal article, newspaper article, and some other publications that are recent to come from the original publisher IF the publication is available on the web. Look at the bottom of such articles for copyright information or permissions to reproduce.

Question to ask:
Are sources documented with footnotes or links?
- Where did the author get the information?
  - As in published scholarly/academic journals and books, you should expect documentation.
- If there are links to other pages as sources, are they to reliable sources?
- Do the links work?

What are the implications?
In scholarly/research work, the credibility of most writings is proven through footnote documentation or other means of revealing the sources of information. Saying what you believe without documentation is not much better than just expressing an opinion or a point of view.

4. What do others say?
Techniques for Web Evaluation:
1. Find out what other Web pages link to this page.
   a. Use *alexa.com* URL information:
   Simply paste the URL into alexa.com's search box.
   You will see, depending on the volume of traffic to the page:
   - Traffic rank
   - Subjective reviews
   - "Site statistics" including some page history, sites that link to the page
   - Contact/ownership info for the domain name

5. Does it all add up?
Techniques for Web evaluation:
1. Step back and think about all you have learned about the page. Listen to your gut reaction. Think about why the page was created, the intentions of its author(s).
   If you have doubts, ask your instructor or come to one of the library reference desks and ask for advice.
2. Be sensitive to the possibility that you are the victim of irony, spoof, fraud, or other falsehood.
3. Ask yourself if the Web is truly the best place to find resources for the research you are doing.

Questions to ask:
Why was the page put on the Web?
- Inform, give facts, give data?
- Explain, persuade?
- Sell, entice?
- Share?
- Disclose?

So what? What are the implications?
These are some of the reasons to think of. The Web is a public place, open to all. You need to be aware of the entire range of human possibilities of intentions behind Web pages.[20]

Marketing Research Aggregators

The **marketing research aggregator** industry is a $100 million business that is growing about 6 percent a year. Companies in this field acquire, catalogue, reformat, segment, and resell reports already published by large and small marketing research firms. Even Amazon.com has added a marketing research aggregation area to its high-profile e-commerce site.

The role of aggregator firms is growing because their databases of research reports are getting bigger and more comprehensive—and more useful—as marketing research firms get more comfortable using resellers as a sales channel. Meanwhile, advances in Web technology are making the databases easier to search and deliveries speedier. And aggregators are slicing and repackaging research reports into narrower, more specialized sections for resale to better serve small- and medium-sized clients who often cannot afford to commission their own studies or buy full reports—essentially nurturing a new target market for the information.

Research aggregators are indirectly tapping new markets for traditional research firms. Selling smaller chunks of data at a lower price point is putting big research firms' results into the hands of small- and medium-sized business clients, who often cannot afford to spend more than a few hundred dollars for a report.

Prior to the emergence of research aggregators, a lot of marketing research was only available as premium-priced subscription services. For example, a $2800 report from Wintergreen Research, Inc. (based in Lexington, Massachusetts) was recently broken up and sold (on AllNetResearch.com) for $350 per chapter for the report's 17 chapters, significantly boosting the overall revenue generated by the report.

In addition to AllNetResearch.com, other major aggregators are Profound.com, Bitpipe.com, USADATA.com, and MarketResearch.com.

Information Management

Computerized databases, secondary data published or posted on the Internet, and internal databases are important parts of an organization's information system. Intelligent decision making is always predicated on having good information. The problem today is how to manage all the information available. It was sometime after the middle of the 20th century that—for the first time in human history—we began to produce information faster than we could process it. Various innovations—computers, microwave transmissions, television, satellites, and the like—have pushed us from a state of information scarcity to a state of information surplus in a very short time.

The need to make better decisions requires that emphasis move from the problems of data acquisition to the problems of effectively managing and utilizing the vast sea of data available. Everyone who has been faced with a decision recognizes that information is the single most important input influencing the quality of that decision. Information is necessary to define the problem, to determine its scope and magnitude, and to generate and evaluate alternatives. Poor decisions are usually the result of using incorrect information, making invalid assumptions, or inappropriately analyzing the information available.

Today, most managers in large and medium-size organizations and progressive smaller ones are bombarded with information. The concern at firms such as American Airlines, Pfizer, and Citicorp has shifted from the generation of information to the shaping and evaluation of information to make it useful to decision makers.

Meineke uses geographic information systems to map its stores and competitors in relation to its customer base. Go to *http://www.meineke. com* to find out how it positions its Web site based on customer information.

Geographic Information Systems

A geographic information system (GIS) provides both a means of maintaining geographic databases and a tool capable of complex spatial analysis to provide information for a decision support system. Spatial analysis is the analysis of phenomena distributed in space and having physical dimensions (the location of, proximity to, or orientation of objects, such as stores, with respect to one another). A geographic database can store and provide access to corporate data, such as customer locations, facilities, logistic routes, and competitors. As a spatial analysis tool, this corporate data can be immersed with secondary demographic data and digitized maps to analyze and maximize the effects of locations. Utilities, oil companies, large retailers, and government agencies have long used these systems. Today the technology accounts for several billion dollars a year in hardware, software, and consulting sales. There are three reasons for this boom. The cost of a GIS has fallen dramatically, the ease of use for business-related analysis has improved, and GIS data can now be transmitted over the internet fairly easily. GIS is now one of the hottest business information tools. Companies as diverse as Chase Manhattan, Domino's Pizza, Ace Hardware, Gold's Gym, and Subaru America have embraced mapping as an easier and more powerful way to manage geographic data than mind-numbing printouts, spreadsheets, and charts. GIS offers researchers, managers, and clients an intuitive way to organize data and to see relationships and patterns.[21]

Between 2001 and 2004, Avon Products, Inc.'s sales rose 29 percent to $7.7 billion. One reason for this success could be its extensive use of GIS software to identify sales opportunities, manage market penetration, and territory realignment. Avon uses a GIS product called Territory Manager from Tactician Corporation. This software assists Avon to identify new sales opportunities by combining secondary demographic data with their internal corporate sales data to segment the U.S. market. For example, the software helped Avon to pinpoint a growing Asian American population in the Southeast. The maps produced are then used to further penetrate the market and to identify new sales representatives. After using the Territory Manager software, some sales areas saw recruitment

> **geographic information system (GIS)**
> Computer-based system that uses secondary and/or primary data to generate maps that visually display various types of data geographically.

increase up to 138 percent over of the previous year during the same time period. The GIS is then used to create maps ranking sales territories to optimize the distribution and alignment of sales areas. These maps are made available to sales representatives over the Internet.[22]

GIS analysts and geographers talk about lines, points, and polygons (areas), while marketing researchers talk about roads, stores, and sales territories. But lines, points, and polygons are how business data is represented within a geographic database. Applications using lines include finding the quickest truck routes for long-haul freight companies and the shortest routes for local delivery trucks. Sears Roebuck calculates daily delivery routes, based on "estimated travel times, in-home time, truck capacity, optimal stop sequence." GPS (global positioning system) receivers in the vehicles can communicate with a GIS to receive real-time weather and road conditions to the drivers. Applications involving points focus on finding the best potential sites for retail bank branches and devising the best strategy for a network of miniwarehouses. Applications involving areas range from finding the best markets for hardware sales to identifying the best location for a new Taco Bell. A GIS can also answer detailed marketing questions. If a marketing researcher for Target wants to know how many of the company's high-performance stores have trading areas that overlap by at least 50 percent with trading areas for Wal-Mart, a GIS analyst can run a *spatial query* on a geographic database to address the question.

Aftermarket auto repair is a highly competitive $90 billion-a-year business in which dealerships have improved their services and market share. To stay ahead of the competition, Meineke Discount Muffler Corporation has turned to GIS. Meineke's 900 franchisees continuously send detailed customer and service records to Meineke headquarters in Charlotte, North Carolina. Records include customer's name and home address; vehicle make, model, and year; work performed; and payment method. They also explain how the customer learned about Meineke. This data is integrated with demographics, average commute times, market area incomes, and the like, within a geographic database. Meineke can then map its stores, competitors, and other retail outlets in relation to its customer base. GIS analysis is used to compute site selection, market share analysis, and inventory management.

Using TargetPro GIS software from MapInfo Corporation, Meineke analysts have developed GIS models (geographic formulas), allowing them to specify an actual or proposed retail location and then create an easy to understand report. Meineke can customize trade areas as it sees fit. If marketing research shows that some customers will not cross a river or a state boundary to get to the nearest outlet but will drive 2 miles farther to another Meineke franchise in a different zip code, the company can use TargetPro to create a map that reflects those shopping patterns. Meineke uses GIS to determine optimal inventory levels by analyzing demographics, commute times, and historical sales figures, which can point to short- and long-term potential business.

"We can place a store on the map, draw a radius around it, then ask the system how many vehicles are in the area," said Paul Baratta, director of real estate and international development for Meineke. "There might be 75,000 cars in a given neighborhood, but another layer of data might show that 65,000 of those are Lexus brands. How many people are going to put mufflers on a car that they're trading in every two years? [GIS] looks at the information in a different way."[23]

MapInfo is now combining GIS, data mining, and predictive analysis software to predict not only which markets offer the best potential for expansion—down to specific intersections—but also how each new store will affect revenue across the chain, generating color-coded maps of the best locales. For example, in the fast-food business, clustering with similar merchants is often beneficial, because diners typically will drive only 5 minutes for quick food and tend to go where they have myriad options. But as Arby's learned, specific products can affect behavior. MapInfo discovered that diners drove as much as 20 percent farther for an Arby's roast beef sandwich than for the chain's chicken offering. The reason? Shoppers could get chicken elsewhere but considered road beef a "destination" product.[24]

Decision Support Systems

A **decision support system (DSS)** is designed to support the needs and styles of individual decision makers. In theory, a DSS represents something close to the ultimate in data management. We say "in theory" because, for the most part, the ideal has not been realized in practice. However, there have been some notable exceptions that have provided a glimpse of how a DSS can truly support the decision-making process. Characteristics of a true DSS are as follows:

☐ *Interactive.* The manager gives simple instructions and sees results generated on the spot. The process is under the manager's direct control; no computer programmer is needed, and there is no need to wait for scheduled reports.

☐ *Flexible.* It can sort, regroup, total, average, and manipulate data in a variety of ways. It will shift gears as the user changes topics, matching information to the problem at hand. For example, the chief executive can see highly aggregated figures, while the marketing analyst can view detailed breakouts.

☐ *Discovery-oriented.* It helps managers probe for trends, isolate problems, and ask new questions.

☐ *Easy to learn and use.* Managers need not be particularly knowledgeable about computers. Novice users can elect a standard, or default, method of using the system, bypassing optional features to work with the basic system immediately. The opportunity to gradually learn about the system's possibilities minimizes the frustration that frequently accompanies use of new computer software.

Managers use a DSS to conduct sales analyses, forecast sales, evaluate advertising, analyze product lines, and keep tabs on market trends and competitors' actions. A DSS not only allows managers to ask "what if" questions but enables them to view any given slice of the data.

Here's a hypothetical example of using a DSS provided by a manager of new products:

To evaluate sales of a recently introduced new product, we can "call up" sales by the week, then by the month, breaking them out at [the vice president's] option by, say, customer segments. As he works at his terminal, his inquiries could go in several directions depending on the decision at hand. If his train of thought raises questions about monthly sales last quarter compared to forecasts, he wants his decision support system to follow along and give him answers immediately.

He might see that his new product's sales were significantly below forecast. Forecasts too optimistic? He compares other products' sales to his forecasts and finds that the targets were very accurate. Something wrong with the product? Maybe his sales department is getting insufficient leads, or is not putting leads to good use? Thinking a minute about how to examine that question, he checks ratios of leads converted to sales, product by product. The results disturb him. Only 5 percent of the new product's leads generate orders compared to the company's 12 percent all-product average. Why? He guesses that the sales force is not supporting the new product vigorously enough. Quantitative information from the DSS perhaps could provide more evidence to back that suspicion. But already having enough quantitative knowledge to satisfy himself, the VP acts on his intuition and experience and decides to have a chat with his sales manager.

➤ **decision support system (DSS)**
An interactive, personalized information management system, designed to be initiated and controlled by individual decision makers.

SUMMARY

Secondary data are previously gathered information that *might* be relevant to the problem at hand. They can come from sources internal to the organization or external to it. Primary data are survey, observation, or experiment data collected to solve the particular problem under investigation.

A database is a collection of related data. A traditional type of internal marketing database is founded on customer information. For example, a customer database may have demographic and perhaps psychographic information about existing customers and purchase data such as when the goods and services were bought, the types of merchandise procured, the dollar amount of sales, and any promotional information associated with sales. A database can even be created from recorded conversations. An internal database also may contain competitive intelligence, such as new products offered by competitors and changes in competitors' service policies and prices.

Web site databases can produce important insights. A Web merchant can track a person as he or she clicks through a site. The merchant can examine what was looked at and what was bought. The screen the customer will see first on the next visit to the site can be tailored to the customer's past purchase and browsing behavior. Cookies are an important tool for monitoring a user's behavior within a site.

Data mining has dramatically increased users' ability to get insightful information out of databases. It can be used to acquire new customers, retain existing customers, abandon accounts that are not cost-effective, and engage in market-based analyses.

The proliferation of databases on and off the Internet has raised consumer and government concerns over privacy. Several laws have been passed to protect our privacy. These include the Gramm-Leach-Bliley Act, the Health Insurance Portability and Accountability Act, and California's Notice of Security Breach Law.

Using secondary data has several advantages. Secondary data may (1) help to clarify or redefine the problem during the exploratory research process, (2) actually provide a solution to the problem, (3) provide primary data research method alternatives, (4) alert the marketing researcher to potential problems and difficulties, and (5) provide necessary background data and build credibility for the research report. The disadvantages of using secondary data include lack of availability, lack of relevance, inaccuracy, and insufficient data.

The Internet has, in many ways, revolutionized the gathering of secondary data. Now, rather than wait for replies from government agencies or other sources, users can find millions of pieces of information on the Internet. Trips to the library may become a thing of the past for many researchers. Search engines and directories contain links to millions of documents throughout the world. Special-interest discussion groups, and blogs, on the Internet can also be valuable sources of secondary data.

A five-step approach to searching the Internet is presented. This is followed by a detailed procedure that explains how to evaluate the quality of Web pages. The chapter appendix details strategies for getting the most out of Google. Geographic information systems, which consist of a demographic database, digitized maps, and software, enable users to add primary data from a current study (or secondary corporate data) to the mix. The result is computer-generated maps that can reveal a variety of strategic findings to marketing managers; for example, a map may indicate an optimal location for a new retail store.

Decision support systems are designed from the individual decision maker's perspective. DSS systems are interactive, flexible, discovery-oriented, and easy to learn; they can offer many benefits to small and large firms alike.

secondary data Data that have been previously gathered.

primary data New data gathered to help solve the problem under investigation.

internal database A collection of related information developed from data within the organization.

database marketing Marketing that relies on the creation of a large computerized file of customers' and potential customers' profiles and purchase patterns to create a targeted marketing mix.

cookie A text file placed on a user's computer in order to identify the user when she or he revisits the Web site.

neural network A computer program that mimics the processes of the human brain and thus is capable of learning from examples to find patterns in data.

data mining The use of statistical and other advanced software to discover nonobvious patterns hidden in a database.

newsgroup An Internet site where people can read and post messages devoted to a specific topic.

marketing research aggregator A company that acquires, catalogs, reformats, segments, and resells reports already published by large and small marketing research firms.

geographic information system (GIS) Provides both a means of maintaining geographic databases and a tool capable of complex spatial analysis to provide information for a decision support system.

decision support system (DSS) An interactive, personalized information management system, designed to be initiated and controlled by individual decision makers.

1. Why should companies consider creating an internal marketing database? Name some types of information that might be found in this database and the sources of this information.
2. Why has data mining become so popular with firms such as United Airlines, American Express, and Ford Motor Company?
3. What are some of the keys to ensuring the success of an internal database?
4. Why are secondary data often preferred to primary data?
5. What pitfalls might a researcher encounter in using secondary data?
6. In the absence of company problems, is there any need to conduct marketing research or develop a decision support system?
7. What is a marketing research aggregator? What role does it play in marketing research?
8. Describe a search strategy for using the Internet.
9. How can a researcher evaluate the quality of a Web page?
10. Divide the class into groups of four or five. Each team should go to the Internet and

Team Exercise) look up database marketing. Each team should then report to the class on how a specific company is effectively using databases to improve their marketing effeciency.

WORKING THE NET

1. What makes vendors' Web sites a desirable tool for creating an internal database?

2. Why has the Internet been of such great value to researchers seeking secondary data?

3. Go to *http://www.yankelovich.com*. Explain to the class the nature and scope of the Yankelovich MONITOR. How can marketing researchers use the data from this research?

4. Go to the National Opinion Research Center at *www.norc.uchicago.edu*. and describe what new reports are available for researchers.

5. You are interested in home-building trends in the United States, as your company, Whirlpool, is a major supplier of kitchen appliances. Go to *http://www.nahb.com* and describe what types of information at this site might be of interest to Whirlpool.

6. Go to *http://www.claritas.com*. Describe types of secondary data available at this site.

7. Go to *www.marketresearch.com* and explain what types of reports are available.

REAL-LIFE RESEARCH • 4.1

Michelle Olson has been a runner since high school. By the age of 25, she had already participated in 14 marathons. Now, as she contemplates her future, she has decided that she wants to combine business with her passion for running. Michelle has decided that she wants to open her own running store if there is a good market for one. She is a native of the Midwest and is willing to move to where the best opportunities might be found.

Michelle plans to open a store that will only employ dedicated runners. Unlike big box retailers, her clerks will be completely knowledgeable about all aspects of running. She even plans to have a podiatrist available 4 hours each week to work with runners with special needs. Her clothes and shoes will only be the top brands that have proven themselves in marathons.

Questions

Use the Internet to determine the following:

1. Current size of the market for running apparel

2. Market growth trends

3. Leading brands in the market today

4. Best markets for running apparel

5. Demographic trends that will affect the market over the next 10 years

6. Should Michelle enter this market? If you don't have enough information, specify what else is needed.

A Convenience Store for Rose and Bob

Fulfilling a life-long dream, Bob, a university English professor, and Rose, a university administrative assistant, will retire this year and move to the South or North Carolina coast. As both are healthy and active, they want something to occupy their time. Rose has always wanted to have her own convenience store, and after spending a year convincing Bob, he finally acquiesced.

So far they have found results from a survey by Insight Express that may help them in designing and stocking their store. For example, purchasing loyalty on behalf of Fido far exceeds that for baby Junior when it comes to the grocery store. The survey reveals that Americans report little brand loyalty when shopping for themselves or their children in the supermarket, with the most loyalty-inducing products cited by participants being soft drinks at 41 percent and condiments at 33 percent. Baby food and baby items rated just 27 percent brand loyalty. But when purchasing food for their pets, more than one-half of consumers purchasing pet food (53 percent) say they are more likely to stick with one brand (see chart for loyalty levels by product category).

Category	Percentage of Loyal Shoppers
Pet Food	53
Soft Drinks/Juices	41
Condiments	33
Baby Items and Food	27
Pasta Sauce	26
Cereal and Breakfast Foods	24
Ice Cream/Novelties	19
Cheese and Dairy	19
Household Cleaners	19
Snacks (Cookies, Chips, and Crackers)	19
Frozen Dinners/Pizza	18
Milk and Eggs	17
Pasta and Rice	16
Meats/Poultry	15
Canned Goods	14
Baking Products	14

When asked about compelling reasons to switch brands, nearly four in five consumers cited price (78 percent), followed by product quality (66 percent), an available promotional offer or coupon (40 percent), and the sheer availability of other products or brands (33 percent).

"In an attempt to affect loyalty and drive purchase behavior, stores and manufacturers have been using an ever-increasing array of tactics—not all of which are effective," says Lee Smith, president of InsightExpress. "Traditional, tangible methods should be the method of choice for marketers."

Participants indicated that weekly store flyers produced the highest level of awareness and translate into greatest level of sales, followed by in-aisle coupon dispensers and individuals offering free samples (results for other methods are shown in the following chart):

In-Store Method	Participants Citing Awareness (%)	Aware Participants Citing Purchase Impact (%)
Weekly store flyers	84	83
In-aisle coupon dispensers	79	46
Person offering free samples	74	49
Store window advertisements	49	48
Store announcements	37	37
Above-aisle product banners	35	30
Shopping cart advertisements	35	11
On-shelf flashing lights	30	24
Product trial packages	29	66
On-floor product advertisements	19	17

The survey also revealed that while 86 percent of Americans guide their shopping efforts using a grocery list, only 28 percent adhere to the list they created at home, thereby remaining uninfluenced by in-store promotional activities.

"Marketers need to recognize the tremendous power and influence they have when consumers are walking the aisles of their favorite grocery store. With shoppers spending an average of 47 minutes in the grocery store, there are enormous opportunities to induce trial," says Smith.[25]

Questions

Obviously, Rose and Bob need a lot more information before opening their store. Use the Internet to help answer the following questions:

1. Where should Bob and Rose locate their store? Why?
2. Should they position the store below, at, or above the general convenience store market? Why?
3. Should they stock national or store brands?
4. Should they sell gasoline?
5. What special features should they offer to attract more customers?

APPENDIX 4-A

Googling to the Max—Exercises   **Part 1 of Research Quality Web Searching**
Getting the most from: *http://www.google.com* The Teaching Library, SPRING 2005
University of California, Berkeley

Google Toolbars (FREE)—highlight terms, remember searches, search within a site, block pop-ups, and more:

For Internet Explorer   *http://toolbar.google.com*
For Mozilla (Netscape)   *http://googlebar.mozdev.org*

1 HOW GOOGLE "THINKS" IN DEFAULT MODE
CRAFTING BASIC GOOGLE SEARCHES

- ☐ AND automatically implied between terms
  - all your terms somewhere
    in text of pages
    in pages that link to a result page
    in other pages on the same site

Ex. 1: What is matched on?
1. Search Google for the keywords: **google page rank**
2. Click Cached: for the page titled "Google Technology" or "Google PageRank Calculator"
3. What is the explanation of the matching of your terms with these pages?

- ☐ STEMS some words
  - finds word with various endings
    search **kite flying** and get matches on **kite, kites, kiting** and **flying, fly, flies**
  - turn off with + or " " as in **+kite+flying** or **"kite flying"**
- ☐ IGNORES common or "stop" words
  - when this happens, a gray message appears below the search box in results telling you what was ignored
  - turn off with + or " " just as for stemming
- ☐ RANKING FAVORS pages with your words in PHRASES, CLOSE TOGETHER, and IN THE ORDER TYPED

Ex. 2: Word order and word choice matter	
Compare the top results for searches in Google for these three sets of keywords:	
grass snake	Mostly about a kind of snake
	By stemming also matches **snakes** and **grasses**
snake grass	Many about a kind of grass, not present in 1st search
snake in the grass	Most pages contain this expression, even though Google said *in* and *the* were ignored; also finds pages with grass snake and a few with snake grass
snake + in + the grass	Eliminates pages not containing *in* and *the* somewhere
"snake in the grass"	Most specific and precise. Requires exact phrase in all pages

- ☐ OR searching requires capitalized OR
  - Can be used between single words and phrases enclosed in quotes:
    california OR oregon OR "pacific coast"
    "global warming" OR "greenhouse effect"
    No parentheses for nesting; keep OR searches simple

- ☐ 10 WORD MAXIMUM to search length
  - Workaround: Make phrases using the wildcard for whole words: * Replacing some words with *

Ex. 3: OR searches and hitting the 10-word maximum
1. What happens if you try to perform this search? **("global warming" OR "greenhouse effect") rise "sea level" (california OR "los angeles" OR "san diego" OR "san francisco")** 2. Google ignores beyond 10 words: ~~OR "san diego" OR "san francisco"~~ 3. Substitute * for superfluous words that have little ambiguity: **("global warming" OR "greenhouse*") rise "sea level" (california OR "* angeles" OR "*diego" OR "*francisco")** = 10 words. OR not counted

> Parentheses ignored by Google

#2 EXPLOITING GOOGLE "FUZZY" SEARCH OPTIONS

- ☐ PUNCTUATION THAT IS NOT IGNORED
  - Apostrophe ('): **peoples, people's,** and **peoples'** are searched as different words
  - Hyphen (-) : **same-sex** retrieves **same-sex, same sex** and **samesex**
Always supply the – to search any word that might be used hyphenated
  - Accent marks in Roman-alphabet foreign languages: **éléphant** does not match **elephant** (and vice versa)
If searching in the language where the accent is common, the accents are not required for matches. Google assumes people writing web pages in that language may or may not put the accents in.
- ☐ SYNONYM SEARCHES (~)
  - Google will "think" of words with similar meaning:
    - **~food** matches **recipes, nutrition, cooking**
    - **~facts** matches **information, statistics**
    - **~help** matches **guide, tutorial, FAQ, manual**
- ☐ SIMILAR PAGES (in results list) or command **related:[URL]**
  - Google will "think" of pages like the one you choose, by using links to and from the page, words in the page, and the importance of pages in links.
  - Uses: evaluate a questionable page by the links in and out find comparable pages when shopping or looking for a type of site broaden a search without thinking of words that might be in pages like the one you like

Ex. 4: Exploiting "FUZZY" Google options
1. Find pages about: *The one-child law of the People's Republic of China*, knowing that some people never use apostrophes properly: **one-child law people's OR peoples "republic of china"** 2. To find out, *How do praying mantises hear?* try searching: **~ears praying mantis** 3. Find pages similar in focus to *http://www.consumerwebwatch.org* **related:www.consumerwebwatch.org** 4. Search the terms **internet hoax** In the results, find a page that seems intriguing, click *Similar pages.* How is the second page related to the first?

☐ NUMBER RANGE allowed in searches (..without spaces)
- Follow search terms with beginning and ending numbers, separated by two periods.
- Can be used one sided, as *less than* or *greater than*

Ex. 5: Number range searches

1. Find pages mentioning Babe Ruth between 1921 and 1935
    "babe ruth" 1921..1935
2. Find digital cameras priced below $300 with resolution of 4.5 to 5 megapixels (MP)
    digital camers ..$300 4.5..5 megapixels OR MP

#3 SETTING LIMITS IN GOOGLE SEARCHES

☐ Require search terms to occur in specific parts of Web pages
- intitle: Words must occur in the official title field in the head part of the page
- site: Limit to a site or domain (first part of the URL, before the first /)
- inurl: Require terms to occur anywhere in URL (URL punctuation ignored)

Can be combined with each other and with other search terms

Ex. 6: Limiting to parts of web pages

1. Find pages primarily about mileage in hybrid cars:
    intitle:mileage "hybrid cars"
2. Find pages about President Bush and either global warming or greenhouse effect:
    bush intitle: "global warming" OR intitle: "greenhouse effect"
3. Is there anything on this subject from the official White House site?
    site:www.whitehouse.gov "global warming" OR "greenhouse effect"
4. Find pages containing sheet music written to commemorate the assassination of Abraham Lincoln.
    site:memory.loc.gov lincoln "sheet music"
Searches within all Library of Congress's American Memory Project pages that are in Google.
    inurl:lincoln "sheet music"
Finds pages with "sheet music" in them and with "lincoln" somewhere in the URL.

☐ Limit to pages updated within a range of dates: **daterange:[Julian date-Julian date]**
- Matches on the date Google last visited the page without detecting any changes; Google stores the date of each visit (visible in *Cache*), but does not change the date searched in daterange, if the page has not been altered.

Ex. 7: Limiting to a range of dates visited with content changed:

Find pages about the World Trade Center that were posted to the Web on September 11 or 12, 2001, and have not been changed since:
    "world trade center" daterange:2452163-2452164
To obtain Julian dates (number of days since noon Jan. 1, 4713 B.C.):
    use *http://www.faganfinder.com/google.html*
    use Calendar Converter at http://fourmilab.to/documents/calendar

☐ Limit to type of document or file extension: **filetype:**
- Google has many types of files besides HTML pages (doc, xls, wpd, ppt and more).
- *View as HTML* link in results with these file types lets you see the document without the application and avoids any virus or worm they could contain.

Ex. 8: Limiting to type of document or file:
1. Find fact sheets and reports (not just web pages) about the death-rate for malignant mesothelioma in the United States. **filetype:xls OR filetype:pdf death-rate malignant mesothelioma "united states"** 2. Find PowerPoint presentations from reputable universities in the United States about the impact on China of its one-child policy. **filetype:ppt site:edu china one-child policy**

☐ **Google Advanced Search** does not allow *intitle:, inurl:,* or more than one *site:,* and has few date range options.

☐ **Pages from within a foreign country by building on the URL of a Google search result**
   • Use information about where the Web page server is located, as well as country coding, more comprehensive than what is available at *http://www.google.com/language_tools*
   • Search on the terms you want. In your browser's Address or URL box, append to the result (without spaces):
   &restrict=country*XX* with XX being the CAPITALIZED two-letter country code
   To find country codes: Search Google for **TLD [country name]** or list of all country codes available at *http://en.wikipedia.org/wiki/List_of_Internet_TLDS*

Ex. 9: Pages from within a country:

Find recipes for authentic Moroccan cuisine, from within Morocco
    Step 1: perform the search:
            recipes OR cuisine morocco OR moroccan
    Step 2: append to the resulting URL in the Address box **&restrict=countryMA**
        http://www.google.com/search?q=recipes+OR+cuisine+morocco+OR
        +moroccan**&restrict=countryMA**

#4 HANDY GOOGLE TOOLS AND SHORTCUTS

☐ DEFINITIONS, THESAURUS, and ENCYCLOPEDIC LOOKUPS
    ☐ **define**:[your words]   Finds Web pages about your word, Google-ranked, and often reliable
    • **define:**[your words]   Finds Web definition for the first result with link to other Web definitions; also finds Web pages with your words
    • **search and click your word in statistics bar** Access to published dictionary sources, with synonyms, antonyms, and other information. Click THESAURUS button if needed.

Ex. 10: Definitions and more:

1. Compare the results from the searches:
    define internet
    define:internet
2. Locate dictionary definitions and thesaurus terms (synonyms, antonyms, etc.) using the link in the blue statistics bar after you search:
    scholarship

□   TRANSLATIONS
- Click *Translate the page* after a page in a foreign language
- Paste a URL or a piece of text at *http://www.google.com/language_tools*

Ex. 11: Translating:

1. Go to Google Advanced Search – *www.google.com/advanced_search*
2. Limit to PAGES IN FRENCH and search
   jacques chirac avec george bush
3. Click *Translate this page* (appears with most pages in languages not in your search interface)
4. You can also translate by pasting a URL or text—www.google.com/language_tools

---

□   CALCULATOR and CONVERSIONS—parentheses accepted to sequence and clarify expressions
- **Mathematical functions** (+, -, *, /, % of, *n*th root of, sqrt(nn), ^ for exponentiation)
- **Advanced math** (Trig: sin, cos, tan, sec, csc, cot, etc.; Inverse trig: arcsin, arcos, arctan, etc.; Hyperbolic trig: sinh, cosh, tanh, etc.; Logarithms; Exponential functions; Factorials; and more)
- **Many mathematical constants** (pi, imaginary numbers, and more)
- **Units of measure and conversions**
  - MASS: kilograms or kg, grams or g, grains, pounds or lbs, carats, stones, tons, tonnes, etc.
  - LENGTH: meters or m, miles, feet, inches, Angstroms, cubits, furlongs, etc.
  - VOLUME: gallons, liters or l, bushels, teaspoons, pints, drops, etc.
  - AREA: square miles, square kilometers, acres, hectares, etc.
  - TIME: day, seconds or s, years, centuries, sidereal years, fortnights, etc.
  - ELECTRICITY: volts, amps, ohms, henrys, etc.
  - ENERGY: calories, British thermal units or BTU, joules, ergs, foot-pounds, etc.
  - POWER: watt, kilowatts, horsepower or hp, etc.
  - INFORMATION: bits, bytes, kbytes, etc.
  - QUANTITY: dozen, baker's dozen, percent, gross, great gross, score, etc.
  - NUMBERING SYSTEMS: decimal, hexadecimal or hex, binary, roman numerals, etc.
- **Physical constants** (atomic mass units or amu, Avogadro's number, Botzmann constant, Faraday constant, gravitational constant, mass of a proton, mass of each planet and of the sun, permeability of free space, etc.)

Ex. 12: Calculating and converting

1. How many carats in a pound?
   1 lb in carats
2. How many square feet in 2.5 hectares?
   2.5 hectares in square feet
3. Value of 1555 in hexadecimal?
   1555 in hex
4. The mass of an electron?
   mass of an electron
5. How many bits in a 2.5 gigabytes?
   2.5 gigabytes in bits

- ☐ SHORTCUTS to many other kinds of publicly available information
  - Area codes (U.S.), defined by maps—type **3 digit code**
  - Airport conditions—type **airport code** or **city** and the word **airport**
  - Flight tracking—type the word **airline** and the **flight number**
  - Maps—type an **address**
  - Stock info—type **one or more NYSE, AMEX, NASDAQ, or mutual fund codes**
  - White pages—type **rphonebook: name address**
  - Yellow pages—type **bphonebook: name address**
  - Zip codes—type a **zip code**
- ☐ STANDARD NUMBER LOOK-UPS
  - Parcel tracking for UPS, FedEx, USPS—type the **number**
  - U.S. patent lookup—type the word **patent** and the **number**
  - UPC product identification—type the **code**
  - VIN vehicle info, history—type the **number**

Ex. 13: Shortcuts and standard number lookups:
1. What part of the United States is in the zip code 87455? **87455** Look below the map at the town and state. 2. Are there currently any delays at O'Hare airport in Chicago? **chicago airport** or **ord airport**

- ☐ UNIVERSITY SEARCHES
  - Conduct a search within the Web site of a university—you specify the topic
  - *http://www.google.com/options/universities.html* has long list of University links to start searching from

Ex. 14: University searches:
Go to Google Advanced Search. At the bottom, click on *Universities*. Choose any university from the list and search for information on: **graduate admissions**

QUALITATIVE RESEARCH

LEARNING OBJECTIVES

1.	To define qualitative research.
2.	To explore the popularity of qualitative research.
3.	To learn about focus groups and their tremendous popularity.
4.	To gain insight into conducting and analyzing a focus group.
5.	To understand the controversy regarding online focus groups.
6.	To understand the growing popularity of Internet focus groups.
7.	To learn about other forms of qualitative research.

A few years ago, Procter & Gamble Company set out to build a better air freshener. P&G researchers learned some useful things when they asked people in focus groups to describe their "desired scent experience." Many people, after about half an hour, seem to adjust to a scent and can't smell it anymore. Most air-freshener scents don't spread evenly across a room. People complained that many scents smell artificial.

P&G took it all in and came back with a solution: a scent "player" that looks like a CD player and plays one of five alternating scents every 30 minutes. The gadget, named Febreze Scentstories and priced at $34.99, has a tiny fan inside that circulates the scent throughout the room. With it, P&G sells five different discs, each $5.99 and holding a variety of scents with trademarked names such as "Relaxing in the Hammock" and "Wandering Barefoot on the Shore."

"Nobody could have articulated Scentstories," says Steve McGowan, a product-development manager for Febreze, "but if you really watch the consumer, they'll tell you what they wish."

Ingenuity has taken an extreme turn in the high-stakes world of product development. Desperate to increase sales and market share, companies are digging deeper into shoppers' homes and habits to discover "unmet needs" and then design new products to meet them. Marketers launch about 34,000 new foods, drinks, and beauty products each year—representing more unmet needs than most people ever guessed they had.

There is no need too small for new products to address. Among the new products P&G has successfully sent out to market are Swiffer Sweep+Vac, the latest iteration in its successful Swiffer line of dust mops and disposable cloths. P&G introduced the Sweep+Vac, a small, battery-operated vacuum cleaner with a Swiffer mop head attached, during the summer, after focus group participants said they get on their hands and knees to wipe up the small pile of dirt left on the floor after mopping with a dry Swiffer cloth. "We knew that was a compensating behavior that consumers wouldn't want to do," says Joe Miramonte, a product-development manager for the Swiffer line.[1]

Introducing a new product to the market can be an expensive proposition. Development and marketing costs can easily top $50 million. The development process often begins with qualitative research. Focus groups—a form of qualitative research—were used to better understand the need for air fresheners and Swiffer cleaning products. What is qualitative research? How is it conducted? Is one form of qualitative research more popular than others? What makes qualitative research, and particularly online focus groups, controversial? These are some of the issues we will explore in this chapter. ■

Nature of Qualitative Research

> **qualitative research**
> Research whose findings are not subject to quantification or quantitative analysis.

> **quantitative research**
> Research that uses mathematical analysis.

Qualitative research is a term used loosely to refer to research whose findings are not subject to quantification or quantitative analysis. A quantitative study may determine that a heavy user of a particular brand of tequila is 21 to 35 years of age and has an annual income of $18,000 to $25,000. While **quantitative research** might be used to find statistically significant differences between heavy and light users, qualitative research could be used to examine the attitudes, feelings, and motivations of the heavy user. Advertising agencies planning a campaign for tequila might employ qualitative techniques to learn how heavy users express themselves and what language they use—essentially, how to communicate with them.

The qualitative approach was derived from the work of the mid-18th-century historian Giambattista Vico. Vico wrote that only people can understand people and that they do so through a faculty called *intuitive understanding*. In sociology and other social sciences, the concept of *Verstehen*, or the intuitive experiment, and the use of empathy have been associated with major discoveries (and disputes).

Qualitative Research versus Quantitative Research

Exhibit 5.1 compares qualitative and quantitative research on several levels. Perhaps most significant to managers is the fact that qualitative research typically is characterized by small samples—a trait that has been a focal point for criticism of all qualitative techniques. In essence, many managers are reluctant to base important strategy decisions on small-sample research because it relies so greatly on the subjectivity and interpretation of the researcher. They strongly prefer a large sample, with results analyzed on a computer and summarized into tables. These managers feel comfortable with marketing research based on large samples and high levels of statistical significance because the data are generated in a rigorous and scientific manner.

Popularity of Qualitative Research

Companies are now spending over $1.1 billion annually on qualitative research.[2] Why does the popularity of qualitative research continue to grow? First, qualitative research is usually much cheaper than quantitative research. Second, there is no better way to understand the

EXHIBIT 5.1	Qualitative versus Quantitative Research	
	Qualitative Research	**Quantitative Research**
Types of questions	Probing	Limited probing
Sample size	Small	Large
Amount of information from each respondent	Substantial	Varies
Requirements for administration	Interviewer with special skills	Interviewer with fewer special skills or no interviewer
Type of analysis	Subjective, interpretive	Statistical, summation
Hardware	Tape recorders, projection devices, video recorders, pictures, discussion guides	Questionnaires, computers, printouts
Degree of replicability	Low	High
Researcher training	Psychology, sociology, social psychology, consumer behavior, marketing, marketing research	Statistics, decision models, decision support systems, computer programming, marketing, marketing research
Type of research	Exploratory	Descriptive or causal

in-depth motivations and feelings of consumers. When, in a popular form of qualitative research, product managers unobtrusively observe from behind a one-way mirror, they obtain firsthand experiences with flesh-and-blood consumers. Instead of plodding through a computer printout or consultant's report that requires them to digest reams of numbers, the product manager and other marketing personnel observe consumers' reactions to concepts and hear consumers discuss their own and their competitors' products at length, in their own language. Sitting behind a one-way mirror can be a humbling experience for a new product-development manager when the consumer begins to tear apart product concepts that were months in development in the sterile laboratory environment.

A third reason for the popularity of qualitative research is that it can improve the efficiency of quantitative research. Reckitt Benckiser PLC, the maker of Woolite and Lysol, knew women were not happy with how glasses were cleaned in a dishwasher. Focus groups learned that, over time, glasses washed in a dishwasher tended to become cloudy and stained. The company decided to embark on a major quantitative study to determine the extent of the perceived "staining" problem among households with dishwashers. The quantitative study verified that consumers were indeed unhappy with how their glasses looked after numerous rounds in the dishwasher. They also were willing to pay a reasonable price to find a solution. Reckitt Benckiser recently introduced Finish Glass Protector, a dishwasher detergent that protects glassware from mineral corrosion. Thus qualitative research led to a well-conceived quantitative study that verified demand for the new product.

It is becoming more common for marketing researchers to combine qualitative and quantitative research into a single study or a series of studies. The Finish Glass example showed how qualitative research can be used prior to quantitative research; in other research designs, the two types of research are conducted in the reverse order. For instance, the patterns displayed in quantitative research can be enriched with the addition of qualitative information on the reasons and motivations of consumers. One major insurance company conducted a quantitative study in which respondents were asked to rank the importance of 50 service characteristics. Later, focus groups were conducted in which participants were asked to define and expound on the top 10 characteristics. Most of these characteristics dealt with client–insurance agent interactions. From these focus groups the researchers found that "agent responds quickly" may mean either a virtually instantaneous response or a response within a reasonable time; that is, it means "as soon as is humanly possible for emergencies" and "about 24 hours for routine matters." The researchers noted that had they not conducted focus groups after the quantitative study, they could only have theorized about what "responds quickly" means to customers.[3]

In the final analysis, all marketing research is undertaken to increase the effectiveness of decision making. Qualitative research blends with quantitative measures to provide a more thorough understanding of consumer demand. Qualitative techniques involve open-ended questioning and probing. The resulting data are rich, human, subtle, and often very revealing.[4]

Limitations of Qualitative Research

Qualitative research can and does produce helpful and useful information—yet it is held in disdain by some researchers. One drawback relates to the fact that marketing successes and failures many times are based on small differences in attitudes or opinions about a marketing mix, and qualitative research does not distinguish those small differences as well as large-scale quantitative research does. However, qualitative research is sometimes able to detect problems that escape notice in a quantitative study. For example, a major manufacturer of household cleaners conducted a large quantitative study in an effort to learn why its bathroom cleanser had lackluster sales when in fact its chemical compound was more effective than those used by leading competitors. The quantitative study provided no clear-cut answer. The frustrated product manager then turned to qualitative research, which quickly found that the muted pastel colors on the package did not connote "cleansing strength" to the shopper. In light of this finding and the finding that a number of people were using old toothbrushes to clean between their bathroom tiles, the package was redesigned with brighter, bolder colors and with a brush built into the top.

A second limitation of qualitative studies is that they are not necessarily representative of the population of interest to the researcher. One would be hard-pressed to say that a group of 10 college students was representative of all college students, of college students at a particular university, of business majors at that university, or even of marketing majors! Small sample size and free-flowing discussion can lead qualitative research projects down many paths. Because the subjects of qualitative research are free to talk about what interests them, a dominant individual in a group discussion can lead the group into areas of only tangential interest to the researcher. It takes a highly skilled researcher to get the discussion back on track without stifling the group's interest, enthusiasm, and willingness to speak out.

The Importance of Focus Groups

> **focus group**
> Group of 8 to 12 participants who are led by a moderator in an in-depth discussion on one particular topic or concept.

Focus groups had their beginnings in group therapy used by psychiatrists. Today, a **focus group** consists of 8 to 12 participants who are led by a moderator in an in-depth discussion on one particular topic or concept. The goal of focus group research is to learn and understand what people have to say and why. The emphasis is on getting people to talk at length and in detail about the subject at hand. The intent is to find out how they feel about a product, concept, idea, or organization; how it fits into their lives; and their emotional involvement with it.

Focus groups are much more than merely question-and-answer interviews. A distinction is made between *group dynamics* and *group interviewing*. The interaction associated with **group dynamics** is essential to the success of focus group research; this interaction is the reason for conducting research with a group rather than with individuals. One idea behind focus groups is that a response from one person will become a stimulus for another person, thereby generating an interplay of responses that will yield more information than if the same number of people had contributed independently.

> **group dynamics**
> Interaction among people in a group.

The idea for group dynamics research in marketing came from the field of social psychology, where studies indicated that, unknown to themselves, people of all walks of life and in all occupations would talk more about a topic and do so in greater depth if they were encouraged to act spontaneously instead of reacting to questions. Normally, in group dynamics, direct questions are avoided. In their place are indirect inquiries that stimulate free and spontaneous discussions. The result is a much richer base of information, of a kind impossible to obtain by direct questioning.

Popularity of Focus Groups

The terms *qualitative research* and *focus groups* are often used as synonyms by marketing research practitioners. Popular writing abounds with examples of researchers referring to qualitative research in one breath and focus groups in the next. Although focus groups are but one aspect of qualitative research, the overwhelming popularity of the technique has virtually overshadowed the use of other qualitative tools.

How popular are focus groups? Most marketing research firms, advertising agencies, and consumer goods manufacturers use them. Today, most of all marketing research expenditures for qualitative research is spent on focus groups. The majority of focus research projects in the United States take place in over 750 focus facilities and are directed by over 1,000 moderators. The most common formats of qualitative research are focus groups and individual depth interviews (IDIs). Acceptance and usage have increased consistently from 110,000 focus groups and equivalent-value IDI sessions in 1990 to over double that number in 2005 of 250,000 sessions. That is a spending level of over $7 billion.

Focus group research is a globally accepted form of marketing research. In 2005, there were an estimated 300,000 focus groups and equivalent individual depth interview sessions conducted outside the United States throughout Europe, Latin America, and Asia-Pacific. This makes a worldwide total of 550,000 sessions.[5]

Focus groups tend to be used more extensively by consumer goods companies than by industrial goods organizations, as forming industrial groups poses a host of problems not found in consumer research. For example, it is usually quite easy to assemble a group of 12 homemakers; however, putting together a group of 10 engineers, sales managers, or financial analysts is far more costly and time-consuming.

Lewis Stone, former manager of Colgate-Palmolive's Research and Development Division, says the following about focus groups:

If it weren't for focus groups, Colgate-Palmolive Co. might never know that some women squeeze their bottles of dishwashing soap, others squeeeeeze them, and still others squeeeeeeeeze out the desired amount. Then there are the ones who use the soap "neat." That is, they put the product directly on a sponge or washcloth and wash the dishes under running water until the suds run out. Then they apply more detergent.

Stone was explaining how body language, exhibited during focus groups, provides insights into a product that are not apparent from reading questionnaires on habits and practices. Focus groups represent a most efficient way of learning how one's products are actually used in the home. By drawing out the panelists to describe in detail how they do certain tasks . . . you can learn a great deal about possible need-gaps that could be filled by new or improved products, and also how a new product might be received.[6]

Thus, an "experiencing" approach represents an opportunity to learn from a flesh-and-blood consumer. Reality in the kitchen or supermarket differs drastically from that in most corporate offices. Focus groups allow the researcher to experience the emotional framework in which the product is being used. In a sense, the researcher can go into a person's life and relive with him or her all the satisfactions, dissatisfactions, rewards, and frustrations experienced when the product is taken home.

Robert L. Wehling, senior vice president of global marketing and consumer knowledge at the Procter & Gamble Company, issued the following mandate to researchers: "Know the individual consumer's heart and you will own the future! Get to know this changing consumer personally. Not as an average but as a person."[7]

Conducting Focus Groups

On the following pages, we will consider the process of conducting focus groups, illustrated in Exhibit 5.2. We devote considerable space to this topic because there is much potential for researcher error in conducting focus groups.

Setting   Focus groups are usually held in a **focus group facility**. The setting is often a conference room, with a large one-way mirror built into one wall. Microphones are placed in an unobtrusive location (usually the ceiling) to record the discussion. Behind the mirror is the viewing room, which holds chairs and note-taking benches or tables for the clients. The viewing room also houses the recording or videotaping equipment. The photo in Exhibit 5.3 illustrates a focus group in progress.

Some research firms offer a living-room setting as an alternative to the conference room. It is presumed that the informality of a living room (a typical homelike setting) will make the participants more at ease. Another variation is to televise the proceedings to a

focus group facility
Research facility consisting of a conference room or living room setting and a separate observation room with a one-way mirror or live audiovisual feed.

Exhibit 5.2

**Steps in Conducting
a Focus Group**

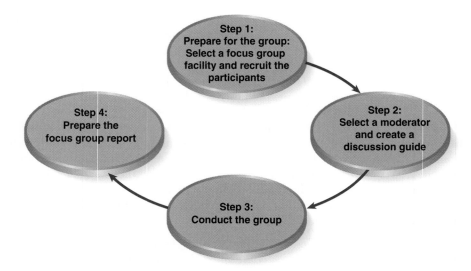

remote viewing room rather than use a one-way mirror. This approach offers clients the advantage of being able to move around and speak in a normal tone of voice without being heard through the wall. On more than one occasion, focus groups have been distracted by a flash seen through the mirror when a client moved too suddenly while watching the group.

Participants   Participants for focus groups are recruited from a variety of sources. Two traditional procedures are mall-intercept interviewing and random telephone screening. (Both methods are described in detail in Chapter 6.) Researchers normally establish criteria for the group participants. For example, if Quaker Oats is researching a new cereal, it might request as participants mothers

Exhibit 5.3

**A Focus Group
in Progress**

who have children between 7 and 12 years old and who have served cold cereal, perhaps of a specific brand, in the past 3 weeks.

Some progressive focus group researchers are now combining psychographics and demographics to recruit group participants. For example, RoperASW in New York City has studied a consumer segment it calls "the Influentials"—the one American in every 10 who has significant word-of-mouth clout. Drawing on a database of more than 10,000 questions and interviews with more than 50,000 Influentials and 500,000 other Americans, RoperASW uses its knowledge of this segment to help its clients recruit candidates for qualitative research, says RoperASW CEO Ed Keller.[8]

"Influentials are two to five years ahead of the curve in their involvement with new trends and new products and lifestyle choices. They have this bellwether nature to them," explains Keller. Recruiting Influentials is particularly useful when a marketer is trying to determine how to launch a new product or how a product's use is changing over time, he says. "We'd never say that this is a panacea for every eventuality, but to the extent that you're looking for people knowledgeable, informed and open-minded, and ahead of the curve, Influentials are very appropriate to study in qualitative research," adds Keller.[9]

Other focus group recruiters go to where the target market is to find qualified respondents. This type of recruiting means going to nursery schools to find moms with kids, health clubs to find people with active lifestyles, the home improvement center to find do-it-yourselfers, supermarkets to find primary food shoppers, and community centers to find senior citizens.

Usually, researchers strive to avoid repeat, or "professional," respondents in focus groups. Professional respondents are viewed by many researchers as actors or, at the very least, less than candid participants. Questions also may be raised regarding the motives of the person who would continually come to group sessions. Is she or he lonely? Does she or he really need the respondent fee that badly? It is highly unlikely that professional respondents are representative of many, if any, target markets. Unfortunately, field services find it much easier to use repeat respondents than to recruit a new group of individuals each time. Sample screening questions to identify repeat respondents are shown in Exhibit 5.4.

---

1. Past Participation Series

Sometimes it is important to talk with people who have participated in previous research because they have experience talking about certain topics. At other times, it is important to talk with people who have never participated in an opinion study. Often we are looking for a mix of different experiences. What type of opinion studies, if any, have you ever participated in? (DO NOT READ LIST.)

	CIRCLE ALL MENTIONS
One-on-one in-person depth interview	1
Group interview with two or more participants	2
Mock jury or trial	3
Product placement test with a follow-up interview	4
Mall interview	5
Internet survey	6
Phone survey	7
Other (SPECIFY)	8
None	9

1A. When was the last time you participated in a

_____ Group interview with two or more participants

_____ (LIST ANOTHER TYPE OF RESEARCH YOU MIGHT CONSIDER INAPPROPRIATE.)

IF WITHIN THE LAST SIX MONTHS, THANK AND TERMINATE.

1B. What were the topics of all of the group interviews in which you have participated?

_____

_____

IF ONE OF THE TOPICS LISTED BELOW IS MENTIONED, THANK AND TERMINATE.

( ) MP3 Players

( ) Camera Cell Phones

1C. Are you currently scheduled to participate in any type of market research study?

	CIRCLE	
Yes	1	→ (THANK AND TERMINATE)
No	2	→ (CONTINUE)

Exhibit 5.4

Sample Screening Questions for Identifying Professional Focus Group Participants

Source: Merrill Shugoll and Nancy Kolkebeck, "You Get What You Ask For," *Quirk's Marketing Research Review* (December 1999), pp. 61–65. Reprinted by permission.

PRACTICING
MARKETING RESEARCH

Recruiting Tricks of the Trade

Here are a few things that I have learned over the years:

1. *The multiple incentive; or, how to turn the same amount of money into more than it is, even though it isn't.*

   You have a qualified respondent who is interested in attending your session. So your recruiter offers the $75 incentive and waits for him/her to stop drooling long enough to gasp out a delighted "Yes!" But that "Yes!" doesn't come. Instead there is a refusal because the money isn't enough, along with comments like "It's too far to drive," or "Do you realize how much parking costs in that part of town?"

   What do you do? Well, here's something that has worked for me many times: Offer them a different $75. You do this by splitting the total into two components: an incentive and an allowance for gas and parking. At $75, a logical breakdown would be $50 incentive and $25 travel.

   The reason this works is because prospective group members see it as being two payoffs instead of one. They get an amount of money that, by itself, is not enough to entice them (in this regard, $50 is no different than $75). But they also get a second amount of money for gas and parking that almost certainly will exceed their actual out-of-pocket expenditure. Suddenly they're hitting for the daily double, and it feels really good. Your show rate goes up, and it didn't cost a penny more.

2. *Stealth qualifiers.*

   A very easy and very effective recruiting trick that I've used for many years is to get at least one or two qualifying criteria out of the way before the screener is actually administered.

   Let's say you need to recruit female heads of household, 25–49 years of age, who are employed outside the home, drink at least two cups of coffee a day, and use a certain brand most often. You certainly don't want to ask about the coffee usage before a security screening has been performed. That would, er, spill the beans, so to speak. But what in the world would prevent you from determining age and employment status before that security screening takes place?

   The way you do it is via judicious use of the introduction statement. Instead of simply asking to speak with the female head of the household, you would say "We are conducting a study among female heads of household, 25–49 years of age, who are employed outside their homes. If the female head of household fits this description, may I speak to her for just a few moments?"

   Voilà! If there is such a person in the household, you have met the age and employment criteria before you ever speak to her. Now you can ask all those other questions, without the prospect of losing your potential group member at the end because she is the wrong age or has the wrong employment status. And security has not been breached in any way. This makes recruiting faster, less expensive, and doesn't in any way compromise quality. Win, win, and win.

3. *A lottery that you always win.*

   I cheerfully concede that I did not personally come up with this technique. But it's so good I decided to pass it along anyway.

   You nervously check your watch again. It's 5:58 P.M., two minutes to show time. And you have three, maybe four, group members in the reception area. The client is starting to throw funny looks your way, and you're reduced to asking the hostess if she is sure your people were properly re-screened, or that they were told the right time and day, or that they weren't inadvertently spirited into someone else's group, etc.

   What's happening is that you're suffering through the fabled 6:00 P.M. Lateness Syndrome. There are a hundred excuses for people to stroll in after the start of that early-evening group—"There was too much crosstown traffic," "I had a last-minute office crisis,"—and you've heard them all.

Want to avoid this? Spring for one extra incentive and you are likely to at least lessen the problem, or even make it go away altogether. Here's how:

After a screening questionnaire has been successfully administered, interviewers, of course, tell recruited group members what day and time the session will take place. But instead of ending with "Thanks, we'll see you at the group session," they are also told that "For everyone who shows up 15 minutes or more before the session starts, their names will be put into a bowl and there will be a drawing. The winner gets a second incentive, and winds up with double the amount."

The result is astounding. Suddenly crosstown traffic evaporates, office work is completed at 5:00 P.M. on the button, and you have the maximum number of people who really, truly could get to the facility on time. Is this worth an extra incentive? You tell me.[10]

Although there is no ideal number of participants, a typical group will contain 8 participants. If the group contains more than 8 people, group members will have little time to express their opinions. Rarely will a group last more than 2 hours; an hour and a half is more common. The first 10 minutes is spent on introductions and an explanation of procedures. This leaves about 80 useful minutes in the session, and up to 25 percent of that time may be taken by the moderator. With 10 people in the group, an average of only 6 minutes per individual is left for actual discussion. If the topic is quite interesting or of a technical nature, fewer than 8 respondents may be needed. The type of group will also affect the number recruited.

Why do people agree to participate in focus groups? Research shows that the number one reason is money.[11] Other motivations, in rank order, are (2) the topic was interesting, (3) it was a convenient time, (4) focus groups are fun, (5) respondent knew a lot about the product, (6) curiosity, and (7) focus groups offer an opportunity to express opinions. The study also found that participants who came only for the money were less committed to research and tended to fulfill their roles in a more perfunctory way.

Ken Berwitz, president of Ken Berwitz Marketing Research, offers a few hints on how to get qualified respondents to attend focus groups in the Practicing Market Research feature.

Using the Web to Find Focus Group Participants

The Internet is proving to be an excellent tool to locate group participants that fit a very specific set of requirements. Researchers are tapping online bulletin boards such as Craigslist, which attracts 5 million visitors each month to its classified advertisements. The site is most useful "when you're trying to find niche users to a small population of users that is hard to find," says Tim Plowman, an anthropologist who works at Redwood Shores, California's Cheskin, a marketing consulting firm.

Point Forward, Inc., a Redwood City, California, marketing research firm, has used Craigslist to find people who fit very specific categories, such as people who travel frequently between the United States and Mexico, says Vice President Michael Barry.

A recent Craigslist posting by a different marketing research firm offered $350 to $900 to New York residents willing to give researchers a tour of their liquor cabinets, take them on a liquor-shopping trip, or make a video-based documentary of a social event they were planning.

Screening questions included: "When you are out for drinks or purchasing alcohol in a store, do people tend to ask for your advice on which brands of liquor to buy? If yes, how often does that happen?"

A downside of using the Internet is that researchers often must sift through hundreds of responses to find appropriate subjects. What is more, the Internet can bring out some strange characters. Mr. Plowman of Cheskin recalls a woman who showed up at a focus group with a mastiff and insisted that the giant dog accompany her in the study.[12]

> **focus group moderator**
> Person hired by the client to lead the focus group; this person should have a background in psychology or sociology or, at least, marketing.

Moderator   Having qualified respondents and a good focus group moderator are the keys to a successful focus group. A **focus group moderator** needs two sets of skills. First, the moderator must be able to conduct a group properly. Second, he or she must have good business skills in order to effectively interact with the client. Key attributes for conducting a focus group include the following:

1. Genuine interest in people, their behavior, emotions, lifestyles, passions, and opinions.
2. Acceptance and appreciation for the differences in people, especially those whose lives vary greatly from your own.
3. Good listening skills: the ability both to hear what is being said and to identify what is not being said.
4. Good observation skills: the ability to see in detail what is happening or not happening and to interpret body language.
5. Interest in a wide range of topics and the ability to immerse yourself in the topic and learn the necessary knowledge and language quickly.
6. Good oral and written communication skills: the ability to clearly express yourself and to do so confidently in groups of all types and sizes.
7. Objectivity: the ability to set your personal ideas and feelings aside and remain open to the ideas and feelings of others.
8. Sound knowledge of the basic principles, foundations, and applications of research, marketing, and advertising.
9. Flexibility, ability to live with uncertainty, make fast decisions, and think on your feet (or the part of your anatomy that is seated in the moderator's chair).
10. Good attention to detail and organizational ability.[13]

Rapport is the medium that makes research work. A moderator develops a free and easy sense of discourse about anything with respondents. These strangers meet and are helped to a common ground through the ease of rapport. In a comfortable, nonthreatening, lively place, they can talk about anything at all—about sausage, insurance, tires, baked goods, magazines. In research the moderator is the bridge builder, and rapport is the bridge between people's everyday lives and the client's business interest.

Jeff Eschrich, president of Catalyst Qualitative Research, offers a few techniques for building rapport:

1. Ask personal questions during warm-up. Get to know them as people first, then as consumers. Ask about their kids, applaud their anniversaries or birthdays. Inquire about the schools they attend, the courses they're taking. Get personal.
2. By the same token, it helps for the moderator to include personal information in the first round of introductions. If you expect revelations from them, you should reveal a bit about yourself. I usually say where I'm from, that I'm married for 10 years, and that I have two girls aged eight and four and reside in Kansas City.
3. Don't be afraid to ask respondents for assistance in the process of the research. It helps rapport if they're up and moving around and feel comfortable in the space. Ask them to pass out stimulus, keep time, pin things to the wall, or take notes. This small involvement opens the two-way involvement in the relationship.

Dilbert

DILBERT reprinted by permission of United Features Syndicate, Inc.

4. Lighten things up with humor. Laughter is energy. It goes a long way to helping break the ice and pick up the pace. Encourage humor from others and enjoy yourself as well. Self-deprecating humor can be more successful than focusing on any of the respondents.[14]

In addition to the above, a moderator needs the following client-focused skills:

1. An ability to understand the client's business in more than just a cursory fashion, to become an integral part of the project team, and to have credibility with senior management.

2. The ability to provide the strategic leadership in both the planning and the execution phases of a project in order to improve the overall research design and provide more relevant information on which to base decisions.

3. The ability to provide feedback to and be a sounding board for the client at every stage of the research process, including before, during, and after the groups. This includes being able to turn the research findings into strategically sound implications for the client at the end of the project.

4. Reliability, responsiveness, trustworthiness, independence, and a dogged determination to remove obstacles in order to get the job done.

5. A personal style that is a comfortable match with the client.[15]

In the past few years, there has been an increase in the number of formal moderator training courses offered by advertising agencies, research firms, and manufacturers with large marketing research departments. Most programs are strictly for employees, but a few are open to anyone. Also, there is the Qualitative Research Consultants Association that promotes professionalism in a qualitative research. The association has a quarterly publication, *QRCAViews*, that features ideas and tools for qualitative research. In addition, the organization holds an annual conference dedicated to improving qualitative research. You can learn more at *www.qrca.org*.

Discussion Guide   Regardless of how well trained and personable the moderator is, a successful focus group requires a well-planned discussion guide. A **discussion guide** is a written outline of the topics to be covered during the session. Usually the guide is generated by the moderator based on the research objectives and client information needs. It

> **discussion guide**
> Written outline of topics to be covered during a focus group discussion.

I. Warm-Up Explanation of Focus Group/Rules (10–12 minutes)

A. Explain focus groups.
B. No correct answers—only your opinions. You are speaking for many other people like yourself.
C. Need to hear from everyone.
D. Some of my associates are watching behind mirror. They are very interested in your opinions.
E. Audiotapes—because I want to concentrate on what you have to say—so I don't have to take notes. Video, too.
F. Please—only one person talking at a time. No side discussions—I'm afraid I'll miss some important comments.
G. Don't ask me questions because what I know and what I think are not important—it's what you think and how you feel that are important. That's why we're here.
H. Don't feel bad if you don't know much about some of the things we'll be talking about—that's okay and important for us to know. If your view is different from that of others in the group, that's important for us to know. Don't be afraid to be different. We're not looking for everyone to agree on something unless they really do.
I. We need to cover a series of topics, so I'll need to move the discussion along at times. Please don't be offended.
J. *Any questions?*

II. Credit Card History (15 minutes)

First of all, I am interested in your attitudes toward, and usage of, credit cards.
A. How many have a major credit card? Which credit card/cards do you have? When did you acquire these cards?
B. Why/how did you get that credit card/cards?
C. Which credit card do you use most often? Why do you use that credit card most often? For what purpose/purposes do you use your credit card/cards most often?
D. Is it difficult for college students to get credit cards? Are some cards easier to get? Which ones? Is it difficult for college students to get a "good" or "desirable" credit card?
E. What is your current attitude toward credit cards and their use? Have your attitudes toward credit cards changed since you got one? How have they changed?

III. Tabletop Concepts (15 minutes)

Now I am going to show you several concepts for tabletop displays for credit cards that might be set up on campus in places where students congregate, such as student union and student activities buildings. Each display would be one of several displays for different products and services. I am interested in your reactions to the different displays. After I show you each display, I would like for you to write down your initial reactions on this form (*show and pass out form*). I am interested in your initial reactions. After we take a minute for you to write down your reactions, we will discuss each concept in more detail.
A. SHOW FIRST CONCEPT.
   1. HAVE THEM WRITE FIRST REACTION.
   2. DISCUSSION.
      a. What was your first reaction to this tabletop display? What, if anything, do you particularly *like* about this display?
      b. Would you stop to find out more? Are you drawn to this display? Why? Why not? What, if anything, is interesting about it?
      c. What is your reaction to ENVIRONMENTAL/EDUCATION/MUSIC OFFER? Likes/dislikes?
B. REPEAT FOR SECOND CONCEPT.
C. REPEAT FOR THIRD CONCEPT.
D. SHOW ALL THREE CONCEPTS.
   1. Which of these concepts, if any, would be *most likely* to attract your attention? Get you to stop for more information? Why?
   2. Which one would be *least likely* to attract your attention? Get you to stop for more information? Why?

IV. Brochures and Offers (25 minutes)

Now I would like for you to see the credit card offers that might go with each of the displays we just discussed. First of all, I will show you a sample brochure and offer. Next, I would like for you to indicate your first reaction to the offer on the sheet provided. Finally, we will discuss your reactions to each offer.

   A. SHOW FIRST BROCHURE AND OFFER.
      1. ASK THEM TO RECORD THEIR FIRST REACTION.
      2. DISCUSSION.
         a. What was your first reaction to this offer?
         b. What, if anything, do you particularly *like* about this offer? What, if anything, do you particularly *dislike* about this offer?
         c. Do you understand the offer?
         d. Do you feel it is an important benefit?
         e. Would you sign up for this offer? Why?
         f. Would this card displace an existing card?
         g. Would this be your card of choice?
         h. Would you continue to use this product after college?
         i. How does this card, described in this offer, compare with the card you use most frequently?
         j. How likely would you be to apply for this card? Why/why not? Would you plan to actually use this card, or just have it? Would you plan to keep it after college?
   B. REPEAT FOR SECOND BROCHURE AND OFFER.
   C. REPEAT FOR THIRD BROCHURE AND OFFER.
   D. SHOW ALL THREE BROCHURES AND OFFERS.
      1. Which of these is the best offer? Why do you say that?
      2. Which, if any, of the cards described in these offers would you apply for? Why?

V. Designs (10 minutes)

Finally, I would like for you to see three alternative designs for the credit card that would go with the environmental offer. As with the two previous sections of the discussion, I will show each design, ask for you to write down your initial reaction to the design, and then we will discuss each design. Please use the form provided earlier to write down your initial reactions.

   A. SHOW FIRST DESIGN.
      1. ASK THEM TO WRITE DOWN FIRST REACTION.
      2. DISCUSSION.
         a. What is your first reaction to this design? Is there anything you particularly *like* about this design? *Dislike* about it?
         b. Is there anything about this design that would make you uncomfortable about using it while you are in college? How about after you get out of college?
   B. REPEAT FOR SECOND DESIGN.
   C. REPEAT FOR THIRD DESIGN.
   D. SHOW ALL THREE DESIGNS.
      1. Which, if any, of these cards would you use? Prefer?
      2. Are there any of these cards you would not use? Why?

Thanks for your participation.

---

serves as a checklist to ensure that all salient topics are covered and in the proper sequence. For example, an outline might begin with attitudes and feelings toward eating out, then move to fast foods, and conclude with a discussion of the food and decor of a particular chain. It is important to get the research director and other client observers, such as a brand manager, to agree that the topics listed in the guide are the most important ones to be covered. It is not uncommon for a team approach to be used in generating a discussion guide.

The guide tends to lead the discussion through three stages. In the first stage, rapport is established, the rules of group interactions are explained, and objectives are given.

In the second stage, the moderator attempts to provoke intensive discussion. The final stage is used for summarizing significant conclusions and testing the limits of belief and commitment.

Exhibit 5.5 shows an actual discussion guide (more detailed than most) used by a moderator to explore the credit card usage of college students, their reactions to different concepts for tabletop displays that might be used in student unions to entice students to sign up for cards, their reactions to different product concepts for credit cards, and, finally, their reactions to different designs for credit cards. The displays and offers are built around three concepts:

1. *CDs.* When a student signs up, he or she chooses a free CD from a list. Students can earn points toward more free CDs via card usage.

2. *Environment.* The card issuer donates money to plant a certain number of trees based on card usage. The money is given to an internationally recognized environmental organization.

3. *Credit education.* Educational material on credit use and abuse is provided periodically. Credit reports are provided free of charge once per year. A gold card is provided after graduation if the user's credit history is good.

The groups were conducted in several areas of the country, with students from a variety of universities and colleges. In general, students did not find the education approach to be attractive. Participants were split in their preference for a free CD and contributions toward environmental causes. However, none of the concepts tested particularly well.

Dr. Murray Simon, president of D/R/S HealthCare Consultants, offers several tips in developing a discussion guide in the following Practicing Marketing Research box.

PRACTICING MARKETING RESEARCH

Dr. Murray Simon offers several guidelines to consider in developing a discussion guide:

☐ Stay true to the objectives of the study: prioritize questions and distill out the nice-to-know from the need-to-know.

☐ Resist the temptation to put two or three market research projects into a one-project bucket.

☐ Encourage your moderator to play an active/aggressive role in developing and formatting the discussion guide.

☐ If the guide seems too long, it probably is. Seek out and eliminate redundancies.

☐ Run a pretest to develop concise questioning and eliminate timing issues.

☐ Create an "if time permits" section at the end of the discussion guide for those questions that are somewhat less then essential but might add to the depth and richness of understanding.

☐ A critical component of any qualitative study for the moderator is to understand the objectives of the study and stay on course with those objectives throughout the project. The same holds true, of course, for the client.[16]

EXHIBIT 5.6	Response Time per Question per Respondent		
	Focus Group Length		
Number of Questions	75 min.	90 min.	120 min.
15	:30	:36	:48
20	:23	:27	:36
25	:18	:22	:29
30	:15	:18	:24
35	:13	:15	:21
40	:11	:14	:18

Note: The analysis assumes a group comprising 10 respondents.

Source: Dennis Rook, "Out of Focus Groups," *Marketing Research* (Summer 2003), p. 13.

Focus Group Length   Many managers today prefer shorter (around an hour) focus groups. Yet the average group today is still about 90 minutes. Although shorter groups may be the trend, there is much to be said for longer focus groups. By a longer group we mean 2 hours or longer. A long group helps managers get more things done in a single session, and it also allows the respondents to get more involved, participate in more time-consuming tasks, and interact more extensively.

The group length issue is not an isolated one; rather, it is intertwined with a second key factor: the number of questions in the discussion guide. One of the biggest problems with focus groups today, in our opinion, is the tendency to prepare discussion guides that pose far too many questions, which virtually precludes any depth of coverage or any significant group interactions. Managers want to get their money's worth, so it makes sense for them to ask every possible question. The "focus group" turns into a group interrogation or survey but without the controls and statistical power of scientific surveys.

In order to think more explicitly and logically about the number of questions to ask, managers should examine the interactions between the length of the focus group and the size of the discussion guide. As illustrated in Exhibit 5.6, more questions and less time combine to create a research environment that elicits responses that are mere survey-like sound bites. Also, moderators who have to plow through 40 questions in 90 minutes are likely to feel rushed, unable to probe interesting responses, and inclined to be abrupt with long-winded or slow individuals. As we move up and to the right in the table, these pressures and constraints diminish. With fewer questions and more time, respondents can elaborate their answers, moderators can probe more effectively, and the pace becomes more relaxed, natural, and humanistic.[17]

Focus Group Report   Typically, after the final group in a series is completed, there will be a moderator debriefing, sometimes called **instant analysis**. This tradition has both pros and cons. Arguments for instant analysis include the idea that it serves as a forum for combining the knowledge of the marketing specialists who viewed the group with that of the moderator. It gives the client an opportunity to hear and react to the moderator's initial perceptions, and it harnesses the heightened awareness and excitement of the moment to generate new ideas and implications in a brainstorming environment.

> **instant analysis**
> Moderator debriefing, offering a forum for brainstorming by the moderator and client observers.

The shortcomings include the possibility of biasing future analysis on the part of the moderator with this "hip-shooting commentary," conducted without the benefit of time to reflect on what transpired. Instant analysis will be influenced by recency, selective recall, and other factors associated with limited memory capabilities; it does not allow the moderator to hear all that was said in a less than highly involved and anxious state. There is nothing wrong with a moderator debriefing as long as the moderator explicitly reserves the right to change her or his opinion after reviewing the tapes.

PRACTICING MARKETING RESEARCH

Early in the analysis and reporting process, I decide what to report to clients as "value added." I talk with the client ahead of the report submission and determine which of these approaches is the best match for client needs:

1. A straight summary of what respondents said with no conclusions.

2. Conclusions that interpret what the data means.

3. Recommendations that let the client know what to consider doing next.

4. Moderator insights that recommend the client to xyz next (if the moderator thinks additional research should be conducted before major decisions are made).

Sometimes the client gets a blend (e.g., summary and conclusions or conclusions and recommendations). The decision is based on study purpose and client needs.[18]

Today, a formal focus group report is typically a PowerPoint presentation. The written report is nothing more than a copy of the PowerPoint slides.

Naomi Henderson, CEO of RIVA Marketing Research, has conducted over 5,000 focus groups. Her insights on preparing focus group reports are offered in the Practicing Marketing Research box above.

Benefits and Drawbacks of Focus Groups

The benefits and drawbacks of qualitative research in general also apply to focus groups. But focus groups have some unique pros and cons that deserve mention.

Advantages of Focus Groups

The interactions among respondents can stimulate new ideas and thoughts that might not arise during one-on-one interviews. And group pressure can help challenge respondents to keep their thinking realistic. Energetic interactions among respondents also make it likely that observation of a group will provide firsthand consumer information to client observers in a shorter amount of time and in a more interesting way than will individual interviews.

Another advantage focus groups offer is the opportunity to observe customers or prospects from behind a one-way mirror. In fact, there is growing use of focus groups to expose a broader range of employees to customer comments and views. "We have found that the only way to get people to really understand what customers want is to let them see customers, but there are few people who actually come in contact with customers," says Bonnie Keith, corporate market research manager at Hewlett-Packard. "Right now, we are getting people from our manufacturing and engineering operations to attend and observe focus groups."

Another advantage of focus groups is that they can be executed more quickly than many other research techniques. In addition, findings from groups tend to be easier to understand and to have a compelling immediacy and excitement. "I can get up and show a client all the charts and graphs in the world, but it has nowhere near the impact of showing 8 or 10 customers sitting around a table and saying that the company's service isn't good," says Jean-Anne Mutter, director of marketing research at Ketchum Advertising.[19]

Disadvantages of Focus Groups Unfortunately, some of the strengths of focus groups also can become disadvantages. For example, the immediacy and apparent understandability of focus group findings can cause managers to be misled instead of informed. Mutter says, "Even though you're only getting a very small slice, a focus group gives you a sense that you really understand the situation." She adds that focus groups can strongly appeal to "people's desire for quick, simple answers to problems, and I see a decreasing willingness to go with complexity and to put forth the effort needed to really think through the complex data that will be yielded by a quantitative study."[20]

This sentiment is echoed by Gary Willets, director of marketing research for NCR Corporation. He notes, "What can happen is that you will do the focus group, and you will find out all of these details, and someone will say, 'OK, we've found out all that we need to know.' The problem is that what is said in a focus group may not be all that typical. What you really want to do is do a qualitative study on the front end and follow it up with a quantitative study."[21] Focus groups, like qualitative research in general, are essentially inductive in approach. The research is data-driven, with findings and conclusions being drawn directly from the information provided. In contrast, quantitative studies generally follow a deductive approach, in which formulated ideas and hypotheses are tested with data collected specifically for that purpose.

Other disadvantages relate to the focus group process itself. For example, focus group recruiting may be a problem if the type of person recruited responds differently to the issues being discussed than do other target segments. White middle-class individuals, for example, participate in qualitative research in numbers disproportionate to their presence in the marketplace. Also, some focus group facilities create an impersonal feeling, making honest conversation unlikely. Corporate or formal settings with large boardroom tables and unattractive or plain decor may make it difficult for respondents to relax and share their feelings.

The greatest potential for distortion is during the group interview itself. As a participant in the social interaction, the moderator must take care not to behave in ways that prejudice responses. The moderator's style may contribute to bias. For example, an aggressive, confronting style may lead respondents to say whatever they think the moderator wants them to say, to avoid attack. Or "playing dumb" may create the perception that the moderator is insincere or phony and cause respondents to withdraw.

Respondents also can be a problem. Some individuals are simply introverted and do not like to speak out in group settings. Other people may attempt to dominate the discussion. These are people who know it all—or think they do—and answer every question first, without giving others a chance to speak. A dominating participant may succeed in swaying other group members. If a moderator is abrupt with a respondent, it can send the wrong message to other group members—"You'd better be cautious, or I will do the same thing to you." Fortunately, a good moderator can stifle a dominant group member and not the rest of the group. Simple techniques used by moderators include avoiding eye contact with a dominant person; reminding the group that "we want to give everyone a chance to talk"; saying "Let's have someone else go first"; or if someone else is speaking and the dominant person interrupts, looking at the initial speaker and saying, "Sorry, I cannot hear you."

Conducting focus groups in an international setting raises a number of other issues, as the Global Research feature on China explains.

Online Focus Groups

Perhaps the hottest area in qualitative research today is **online focus groups**. Many marketing researchers, such as Greenfield Online, NFO Interactive, and Harris Black International, believe that Internet focus groups can replace face-to-face focus groups, although

> **online focus groups**
> Focus groups conducted via the Internet.

they acknowledge that online research has limitations. Others that are moving aggressively into online marketing research, such as Millward Brown International and Digital Marketing Services (DMS), were slower to use online focus groups.

Advantages of Online Focus Groups   Marketers who have used online focus groups, and the marketing researchers conducting them, say that benefits far outweigh limitations. Those benefits include lack of geographic barriers, much lower costs (about half as much), faster turnaround time, and intangibles such as increased openness on the part of respondents when they do not have an interviewer staring them in the face.

"I think [the panelists] were more definite about things they didn't like than they'd be in front of a moderator," said Lisa Crane, vice president of sales and marketing for Universal Studios Online, which used an online focus group to test a redesigned site it's developing for Captain Morgan Original Spiced Rum, a brand of its parent company, Seagram Company. Rudy Nadilo, president and CEO of Greenfield Online, which conducted the online focus groups for Universal, said they are meant "to complement, not replace" traditional panels.[22]

Not only are the costs lower for online focus groups, but there are substantial travel savings for the client as well. Expenditures for round-trip airline tickets to distant cities, meals, hotels, and taxis are avoided. Clients merely log on in their own office, or even at home, to observe the research in progress.

Another advantage of online focus groups lies in access to the hard-to-reach target population. Online, it's possible to reach populations that are traditionally inaccessible because of time or professional constraints—groups such as physicians, lawyers, and senior business executives. Chances are higher that they will be available to participate, too, since they do not need to take time from their busy schedules to visit a focus group facility but, rather, can participate from the privacy of their own homes.

Another advantage claimed for online focus groups is efficient moderator–client interaction. During the traditional focus group, the client observes the discussion from behind a one-way glass; communication with the moderator is impossible without interfering with the discussion. An online focus group, however, offers a remarkable opportunity for two-way interaction between the moderator and the client. This direct interaction, while the moderator conducts the group, has become a necessity in operating a fully effective online focus group discussion. Rather than sneaking into the room with a note scribbled on a piece of paper, the client can address the moderator directly, clearly, and efficiently, without interrupting the group dynamic.

Traditional focus groups always include "natural talkers," who dominate the discussion, despite a good moderator's attempt to equalize participant contributions. Other participants will be less comfortable voicing opinions in a group; they may express themselves more freely when not face to face with their peers. The online focus group has a built-in leveling effect, in the sense that shy participants can express themselves as freely as more outgoing participants. One participant points out why he likes participating in online focus groups, explaining, "I can be honest without the face-to-face peer pressure of focus groups"; another offers, "I get to express my opinion without having to hear someone's reaction."[23] At least in terms of honesty and willingness to offer genuine ideas and opinions, respondents tend to feel more comfortable participating from the privacy of their own homes.

Disadvantages of Online Focus Groups   Critics say that the research community does itself an injustice by calling qualitative research sessions conducted over the Internet "focus groups." Their criticisms include the following:

- ▢ *Group dynamics.* One of the key reasons for using traditional focus groups is to view the interactions among the group participants, as they can provide excellent insights.

GLOBAL RESEARCH

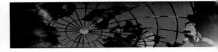

Tips for Conducting Focus Groups in China

China's total market size is over one billion. It is already the world's largest consumer of TVs, refrigerators, and mobile phones. China's middle class is leaping forward; it already stands at 100 million and is growing at 20 percent a year. Since a relatively low proportion of household income is currently spent on housing, there is lots of room for discretionary spending and accumulation of personal assets. Five to six million Chinese have a net worth in excess of $100,000. Ten thousand mainland citizens have assets over $1 million.

The challenge for Chinese researchers, however, is to acquire the value-added skills that will make them important assets in worldwide marketing efforts. They need to move from being responsible for just fieldwork on behalf of global companies to being strategic consultants on Chinese consumers. The success of the qualitative research industry in China will be based on its ability to offer clear insights into the psychological and cultural factors that motivate its customers.

Here are eight tips for doing focus groups in China:

1. Markets

Although most global marketers focus on the major cities of Beijing, Shanghai, and Guangzhou, it may be easier to encounter the "real" emerging Chinese consumer in secondary markets such as Chengdu, Chongqing, Tianjin, Wuhan, Hangzhou, and Xian.

2. Venues

Unlike the United States with its vast networks of independent focus group facilities, full-service market research companies tend to dominate fieldwork. Each has its own modern one-way mirror setup complete with audio, video, and translation equipment and an on-site staff to recruit prospective respondents.

3. Collaboration

It is essential to collaborate with a local Chinese partner in conducting any research in China to be alert to cultural differences as well as to government regulations. In multicity studies, expect that research companies will partner with each other in order to provide local one-way mirrors and on-site recruiting.

4. Specialization

Some market research companies in China are more specialized than others, having divisions for automotive, technology, or pharmaceutical research. If those are your categories, make sure you select a company that specializes in these areas in order to achieve the best context and expertise for your research.

5. Experience

Although perhaps 1,000 women and men are conducting qualitative research in China, only about 100 to 200 of them are reasonably experienced. When negotiating with a Chinese market research company for qualitative research, make sure you discuss moderator credentials and obtain a partner that is devoted to this specialty.

6. Language

Although there are eight major dialects and many more subdialects in the People's Republic of China, most of the mainland reads and writes Mandarin using characters simplified from the 1950s onward. Those in Guangdong province and Hong Kong speak Cantonese. Make sure your stimuli and all other written materials are

(Continued)

executed in Mandarin, which is the official national language.

7. B2B Populations

Busy business executives, physicians, and professors are very hard to recruit. Extra effort and investment will be required to obtain respondents who are not overused.

8. Politeness

Chinese citizens, like many Asians, are unfailingly polite. In order to break this "politeness trap," encourage the moderator to use deep elicitation and projective techniques. Make sure to listen carefully to the moderator's own interpretation of responses that may sound favorable but may be merely polite.[24]

In cyberspace, it is difficult, if not impossible, to create any real group dynamics, particularly when the participants are reading from computer screens rather than interacting verbally.

☐ *Nonverbal inputs.* Experienced moderators use nonverbal inputs from participants while moderating and analyzing sessions. It is not always possible to duplicate the nonverbal input in an online environment.

☐ *Client involvement.* Many organizations use the focus group methodology because it gives clients an opportunity to experience some direct interface with consumers in an objective environment. Nothing can replace the impact of watching focus groups from behind a one-way mirror, no matter how good the videotapes, remote broadcast facilities, or reports written by moderators.

☐ *Exposure to external stimuli.* A key use of focus groups is to present advertising copy, new product concepts, prototypes, or other stimuli to the participants in order to get their reactions. In an online chat situation, it is almost impossible to duplicate the kind of exposure to external stimuli that occurs in the live focus group environment. As a result, the value of the input received online is more questionable than that of input coming from a live environment.

☐ *Role and skill of the moderator.* Most marketing professionals agree that the most important factor in the quality of traditional focus group research is the skill of the moderator. Experienced moderators do more than simply ask questions of participants. A good moderator uses innovative techniques to draw out quiet or shy participants, energize a slow group, and delve a little deeper into the minds of the participants. The techniques available to a moderator sitting at a computer terminal are not the same as face-to-face involvements.

Exhibit 5.8 summarizes the advantages and disadvantages of traditional and online focus groups.

Using Channel M2 to Conduct Online Focus Groups
Channel M2 provides market researchers with user-friendly virtual interview rooms, recruiting and technical support for conducting virtual qualitative research efficiently and effectively. By using Channel M2, the moderator and client can see and hear every respondent. You can see a demo at *www.channelM2.com*.

Focus group recruiting at M2 uses a blend of e-mail recruitment (from a global panel with access to over 15 million online consumers) and telephone verification and confirmation. Specifically, e-mails elicit involvement and direct participants to an online qualification questionnaire to ensure that each meets screening criteria. Telephone follow-up confirms that respondents qualify. Prior to the interview, respondents know they must show photo ID on camera so as to verify identity. Specifically, respondents are directed to show their driver's license to their Web cam.

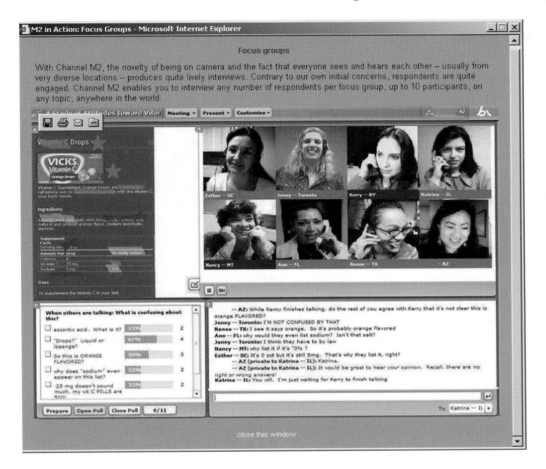

Exhibit 5.7

An M2 Online Focus Group Underway

Source: Channel M2.

Channel M2 focus groups begin by the participants logging onto a Web page where everyone sees and hears each other, and communicates in a group setting. Participants are recruited using traditional methods and then sent a Web camera so that both verbal and nonverbal reactions can be recorded. Installation of the Web cam is simple, aided by Channel M2 tech support 1 to 2 days prior to the interview.

Participants are then provided instructions via e-mail including a link to the Channel M2 interviewing room and a toll-free teleconference number to call. Upon clicking on the link, participants sign on and see the Channel M2 interview room, complete with live video of the other participants, text chat, screen or slide sharing, and whiteboard (see Exhibit 5.7).

Once the focus group is underway, questions and answers occur in "real time" in a lively setting. Participants comment spontaneously, both verbally or via text messaging, yet the moderator can provide direction exactly as they would in a traditional setting.[25]

Types of Online Focus Groups Decision Analyst, one of America's most progressive firms in applying Internet technology to marketing research, offers two types of online focus groups:

1. **Real-Time Online Focus Groups.** These are live, interactive sessions with four to six participants and a moderator in a chat room format. The typical session lasts no longer than 45 to 50 minutes. The technique is best for simple, straightforward issues

EXHIBIT 5.8	Advantages and Disadvantages of Traditional and Online Focus Groups	
	Traditional Focus Groups	**Online Focus Groups**
Basic costs	More expensive	Cheaper
Participants	Participants are locally based, because of travel time and expense.	Anyone in the world with a computer and modem can participate.
Time commitment	Approximately 3½-hour time commitment. Busy respondents are less likely to be available.	No driving to facility, approximately 60-minute time commitment. Busy respondents are more likely to be available.
Openness of respondents	Some respondents are intimidated and afraid to speak openly in a face-to-face group setting.	Lack of direct face-to-face contact may lead respondents to express true feelings in writing if no Web cam is available.
Group dynamics	What one person says and does (gestures and expressions) can lead others to react.	None, according to critics.
Nonverbal communication	Body language can be observed.	Body language can only be observed if Web cameras are used.
Transcripts	Transcript is time-consuming and expensive to obtain; often not in complete sentences or thoughts.	Word-for-word transcripts are available almost immediately; usually in complete sentences/ thoughts.
Respondent recruiting	Recruiting certain types of respondents (e.g., physicians, top managers) is difficult.	It is easier to obtain all types of respondents.
Client travel costs	Very expensive when client must go to several cities for one or two days each.	None.
Communication with moderator	Observers can send notes into focus group room.	Observers can communicate privately with moderator on a split screen.
Respondent security	Participants are accurately identified.	It is sometimes more difficult to ascertain who is participating.
Client involvement	Client can observe flesh-and-blood consumers interacting.	Client can observe via Web cameras.
Exposure to external stimuli	Package designs, advertising copy, and product prototypes with demonstrations can be shown to participants.	Ability to show stimuli is somewhat limited.

that can be covered in a limited time. The results tend to be superficial compared to in-person focus groups—but this is acceptable for certain types of projects. Typically, three to four groups are recommended as a minimum. Clients can view the chat room as the session unfolds and communicate with the moderator.

2. **Time-Extended Online Focus Groups.** These sessions follow a message board format and usually last 5 to 10 days. The 15 to 20 participants must comment at least 2 or 3 times per day, and spend 15 minutes a day logged in to the discussion. The moderator reviews respondents' comments several times per day (and night) and probes or redirects the discussion as needed. This technique provides 3 to 4 times as much content as the average in-person focus group. Time-extended online focus groups give participants time to reflect, time to talk to others, time to visit a store, or time to check the pantry. This extra time translates into richer content and deeper insights. Clients can view the online content as it is posted and may communicate with the moderator at any time.

FROM THE FRONT LINE

Secrets of Conducting Good Focus Groups and/or In-Depth Interviews

Richard Kagel, Ph.D., President, Kagel Research Associates, consultant to DSS Research

The biggest secret I have learned in conducting focus groups and in-depth interviews for nearly 25 years is to make myself as invisible as possible to the process. The best discussion or interview imaginable would be to get the conversation going and let the participants complete the discussion guide on their own without any intervention from me. This is of course an ideal, but it is what I have foremost in mind when I go into any focus group or interview—how can I not intervene and bias the respondents in any way?

This approach is completely against my nature. What a great opportunity to lead and control a discussion for 90 minutes. I am an emeritus university professor. I love to dominate everything and get my opinion out there. I want everyone to agree with me. I have important things to say. I am an expert. This is exactly the opposite of what you want to achieve in market research interviewing.

So how do you become transparent and unobtrusive to the process? You start by creating a safe environment for the discussion. I get to know each individual first by greeting them at the door and shaking their hand as they enter the room. Touching helps. Smiling helps. I let them introduce themselves by talking about their family, hobbies, job, and interests, and I may ask them a friendly question or two about their life. I sometimes add a little humor. I am friendly, open, and interested. I assure them that their opinions are welcome and that I will believe and accept everything they say. There is no wrong answer here. This is not a test of their knowledge or experience. I set myself up as a facilitator and nothing more, no credentials, no fluff.

I start the discussion with easy questions and offer body language to let them know that their comments are appreciated. I speak as little as possible throughout, but do all I can to keep them interested, motivated, and on track. I never, ever share my views. I say "okay" or "I see" but never more than that. I remain neutral. I don't participate. The idea is to create a good feeling and a safe, comfortable environment so that they can open up and tell me things they might not have otherwise said.

Other Qualitative Methodologies

Most of this chapter has been devoted to focus groups because of their pervasive use in marketing research. However, several other qualitative techniques are also used, albeit on a much more limited basis.

Individual Depth Interviews

Individual depth interviews (IDI) are relatively unstructured one-on-one interviews. The interviewer is thoroughly trained in the skill of probing and eliciting detailed answers to each question. Sometimes psychologists are used as depth interviewers: They may employ nondirective clinical techniques to uncover hidden motivations. IDIs are the second most popular form of qualitative research.

The direction of a depth interview is guided by the responses of the interviewee. As the interview unfolds, the interviewer thoroughly probes each answer and uses the replies

> **Individual depth interviews**
> One-on-one interviews that probe and elicit detailed answers to questions, often using nondirective techniques to uncover hidden motivations.

as a basis for further questioning. For example, a depth interview might begin with a discussion of snack foods. The interviewer might follow each answer with "Can you tell me more?" "Would you elaborate on that?" or "Is that all?" The interviewer might then move into the pros and cons of various ingredients, such as corn, wheat, and potatoes. The next phase could delve into the sociability of the snack food. Are Fritos, for example, more commonly eaten alone or in a crowd? Are Wheat Thins usually reserved for parties? When should you serve Ritz crackers?

The advantages of depth interviews over focus groups are as follows:

1. Group pressure is eliminated, so the respondent reveals more honest feelings, not necessarily those considered most acceptable among peers.

2. The personal one-on-one situation gives the respondent the feeling of being the focus of attention—that his or her thoughts and feelings are important and truly wanted.

3. The respondent attains a heightened state of awareness because he or she has constant interaction with the interviewer and there are no group members to hide behind.

4. The longer time devoted to individual respondents encourages the revelation of new information.

5. Respondents can be probed at length to reveal the feelings and motivations that underlie statements.

6. Without the restrictions of cultivating a group process, new directions of questioning can be improvised more easily. Individual interviews allow greater flexibility to explore casual remarks and tangential issues, which may provide critical insights into the main issue.

7. The closeness of the one-on-one relationship allows the interviewer to become more sensitive to nonverbal feedback.

8. A singular viewpoint can be obtained from a respondent without influence from others.

9. The interview can be conducted anywhere, in places other than a focus group facility.

10. Depth interviews may be the only viable technique for situations in which a group approach would require that competitors be placed in the same room. For example, it might be very difficult to do a focus group on systems for preventing bad checks with managers from competing department stores or restaurants.

The disadvantages of depth interviews relative to focus groups are as follows:

1. Depth interviews are much more expensive than focus groups, particularly when viewed on a per-interview basis.

2. Depth interviews do not generally get the same degree of client involvement as focus groups. It is difficult to convince most client personnel to sit through multiple hours of depth interviews so as to benefit firsthand from the information.

3. Because depth interviews are physically exhausting for the moderator, they do not cover as much ground in one day as do focus groups. Most moderators will not do more than four or five depth interviews in a day, whereas they can involve 20 people in a day in two focus groups.

4. Focus groups give the moderator an ability to leverage the dynamics of the group to obtain reactions that might not be generated in a one-on-one session.[26]

The success of any depth interview depends mainly on the skills of the interviewer. Good depth interviewers, whether psychologists or not, are hard to find and expensive.

A second factor that determines the success of depth research is proper interpretation. The unstructured nature of the interview and the clinical nature of the analysis increase the complexity of the task. Small sample sizes, the difficulty of making comparisons, the subjective nature of the researcher's interpretations, and high costs have all contributed to the lack of popularity of depth interviewing. Classic applications of depth interviews include:

☐ Communication checks (for example, review of print, radio, or TV advertisements or other written materials)

☐ Sensory evaluations (for example, reactions to varied formulations for deodorants or hand lotions, sniff tests for new perfumes, or taste tests for a new frosting)

☐ Exploratory research (for example, defining baseline understanding or a product, service, or idea)

☐ New product development, prototype stage

☐ Packaging or usage research (for example, when clients want to "mirror" personal experience and obtain key language descriptors)[27]

A variation of the depth interview is called customer care research (CCR). The basic idea is to use depth interviewing to understand the dynamics of the purchase process. The following seven questions are the basis for CCR:

1. What started you on the road to making this purchase?

2. Why did you make this purchase now?

3. What was the hardest part of this process? Was there any point where you got stuck?

4. When and how did you decide the price was acceptable?

5. Is there someone else with whom I should talk to get more of the story behind this purchase?

6. If you've purchased this product before, how does the story of your last purchase differ from this one?

7. At what point did you decide you trusted this organization and this person to work with in your best interests?[28]

Using Hermeneutics   Some IDI researchers use a technique called hermeneutic research to achieve their goals. **Hermaneutic research** focuses on interpretation as a basis of understanding the consumer. Interpretation comes about through "conversations" between the researcher and the participant. In hermaneutic research, the researcher answers the participant's questions and, as in the traditional method, the researcher only questions the respondent. There are no predetermined questions, but questions arise spontaneously as the conversation unfolds.

> **hermaneutic research**
> research that focuses on interpretation through conversations

For example, a researcher and consumer in conversation about why that individual purchased a high-end home theater system may discuss the reasons for making the purchase, such as holding movie parties, enjoying a stay-at-home luxury, or immersing oneself in sporting events. The researcher may interpret "holding movie parties" as a reason for purchase to mean that without the system, the consumer would not hold the parties at all, and so the researcher will return to the consumer for additional information. Upon reviewing the data and talking more, the researcher and consumer determine that why the item was purchased and why it is used (which may or may not be the same) are not as telling as how the product makes its owner feel. In this case, the owner may feel confident as an entertainer, more social, powerful, wealthy, relaxed, or rejuvenated. Talking and probing more about the use of the home theater, the researcher uncovers both new data and new issues to address or consider moving forward.[29]

Online Individual Depth Interviewing A few marketing research firms are experimenting with online IDIs. After respondents are recruited, each participant is given a private blog where they can create their online journal for the project. Over a period of days, the respondents are given a series of questions to ponder in their blogs. A second phase of the research may feature a telephone, e-mail, or bulletin-board in-depth discussion. The discussion topics are derived from the blogs.

Projective Tests

Projective techniques are sometimes incorporated into depth interviews. The origins of projective techniques lie in the field of clinical psychology. In essence, the objective of any **projective test** is to delve below surface responses to obtain true feelings, meanings, and motivations. The rationale behind projective tests comes from the knowledge that people are often reluctant or unable to reveal their deepest feelings. In some instances, they are unaware of those feelings because of psychological defense mechanisms.

Projective tests are techniques for penetrating a person's defense mechanisms to allow true feelings and attitudes to emerge. Generally, a respondent is presented with an unstructured and nebulous situation and asked to respond. Because the situation is ill-defined and has no true meaning, the respondent must impose her or his own frame of reference. In theory, the respondent "projects" personal feelings into the unstructured situation, bypassing defense mechanisms because the respondent is not referring directly to herself or himself. As the individual talks about something or someone else, her or his inner feelings are revealed.

Most projective tests are easy to administer and are tabulated like other open-ended questions. They are often used in conjunction with nonprojective open- and closed-ended questions. A projective test may gather "richer," and perhaps more revealing, data than do standard questioning techniques. Projective techniques are used often in image questionnaires and concept tests, and occasionally in advertising pretests. It is also common to apply several projective techniques during a depth interview.

The most common forms of projective techniques used in marketing research are word association tests, sentence and story completion tests, cartoon tests, photo sorts, consumer drawings, storytelling, and third-person techniques. Other techniques, such as psychodrama tests and the Thematic Apperception Test (TAT), have been popular in treating psychological disorders but of less help in marketing research.

Word Association Tests **Word association tests** are among the most practical and effective projective tools for marketing researchers. An interviewer reads a word to a respondent and asks him or her to mention the first thing that comes to mind. Usually, the individual will respond with a synonym or an antonym. The words are read in quick succession to avoid allowing time for defense mechanisms to come into play. If the respondent fails to answer within 3 seconds, some emotional involvement with the word is assumed.

Word association tests are used to select brand names, advertising campaign themes, and slogans. For example, a cosmetic manufacturer might ask consumers to respond to the following words as potential names for a new perfume: infinity, encounter, flame, desire, precious, erotic. One of these words or a synonym suggested by respondents might then be selected as the brand name.

Sentence and Story Completion Tests **Sentence and story completion tests** can be used in conjunction with word association tests. The respondent is furnished with an incomplete story or group of sentences and asked to complete it. A few examples of incomplete sentences follow:

1. Best Buy is . . .
2. The people who shop at Best Buy are . . .

> **projective test**
> Technique for tapping respondents' deepest feelings by having them project those feelings into an unstructured situation.

> **word association test**
> Projective test in which the interviewer says a word and the respondent must mention the first thing that comes to mind.

> **sentence and story completion tests**
> Projective tests in which respondents complete sentences or stories in their own words.

3. Best Buy should really . . .

4. I don't understand why Best Buy doesn't . . .

Here's an example of a story completion test:

Sally Jones just moved to Chicago from Los Angeles, where she had been a salesperson for IBM. She is now a district manager for the Chicago area. Her neighbor Rhonda Smith has just come over to Sally's apartment to welcome her to Chicago. A discussion of where to shop ensues. Sally notes, "You know, I've heard some things about Best Buy. . . ." What is Rhonda's reply?

As you can see, story completion tests provide a more structured and detailed scenario for the respondent. Again, the objective is for the interviewees to put themselves in the role of the imaginary person mentioned in the scenario.

Sentence and story completion tests have been considered by some researchers to be the most useful and reliable of all the projective tests. Decision Analyst is now offering both online sentence completion and online word association research to its clients.

Cartoon Tests   The typical **cartoon test** consists of two characters with balloons, similar to those seen in comic books; one balloon is filled with dialogue, and the other balloon is blank (see Exhibit 5.9). The respondent is asked to fill in the blank balloon. Note that the cartoon figures in Exhibit 5.9 are left vague and without expression so that the respondent is not given clues regarding a suggested type of response. The ambiguity is designed to make it easier for the respondent to project his or her feelings into the cartoon situation.

Cartoon tests are extremely versatile and highly projective. They can be used to obtain differential attitudes toward two types of establishments and the congruity or lack of congruity between these establishments and a particular product. They can also be used to measure the strength of an attitude toward a particular product or brand; or to ascertain what function is being performed by a given attitude.

Photo Sorts   With **photo sorts**, consumers express their feelings about brands by manipulating a specially developed photo deck depicting different types of people, from

> **cartoon test**
> Projective test in which the respondent fills in the dialogue of one of two characters in a cartoon.

> **photo sort**
> Projective technique in which a respondent sorts photos of different types of people, identifying those people who she or he feels would use the specified product or service.

Exhibit 5.9

Cartoon Test

Hey John, I finally saved up enough money to buy that new vehicle I've been wanting so badly. I'm thinking about buying a Jeep Grand Cherokee.

business executives to college students. Respondents connect the individuals in the photos with the brands they think they would use.

BBDO Worldwide, one of the country's largest advertising agencies, has developed a trademarked technique called Photosort. A Photosort conducted for General Electric found that consumers thought the brand attracted conservative, older, business types. To change that image, GE adopted the "Bring Good Things to Life" campaign. A Photosort for Visa found the credit card to have a wholesome, female, middle-of-the-road image in customers' minds. The "Everywhere You Want to Be" campaign was devised to interest more high-income men.

Another photo sort technique, entitled Pictured Aspirations Technique (PAT), was created by Grey Advertising, also a large New York advertising agency. The technique attempts to uncover how a product fits into a consumer's aspirations. Consumers sort a deck of photos according to how well the pictures describe their aspirations. In research done for Playtex's 18-hour bra, this technique revealed that the product was out of sync with the aspirations of potential customers. The respondents chose a set of pictures that depicted "the me they wanted to be" as very energetic, slim, youthful, and vigorous. But the pictures they used to express their sense of the product were a little more old-fashioned, a little stouter, and less vital and energetic looking. Out went the "Good News for Full-Figured Gals" campaign, with Jane Russell as spokesperson, and in came the sexier, more fashionable concept of "Great Curves Deserve 18 Hours."

Consumer Drawings   Researchers sometimes ask consumers to draw what they are feeling or how they perceive an object. **Consumer drawings** can unlock motivations or express perceptions. For example, McCann-Erickson advertising agency wanted to find out why Raid roach spray outsold Combat insecticide disks in certain markets. In interviews, most users agreed that Combat is a better product because it kills roaches without any effort on the user's part. So the agency asked the heaviest users of roach spray—low-income women from the southern United States—to draw pictures of their prey (see Exhibit 5.10). The goal was to get at their underlying feelings about this dirty job.

> **consumer drawings**
> Projective technique in which respondents draw what they are feeling or how they perceive an object.

All of the 100 women who participated in the agency's interviews portrayed roaches as men. "A lot of their feelings about the roach were very similar to the feelings that they had about the men in their lives," said Paula Drillman, executive vice president at McCann-Erickson. Many of the women were in common-law relationships. They said that the roach, like the man in their life, "only comes around when he wants food." The act of spraying roaches and seeing them die was satisfying to this frustrated, powerless group. Setting out Combat disks may have been less trouble, but it just didn't give them the same feeling. "These women wanted control," Drillman said. "They used the spray because it allowed them to participate in the kill."

> **storytelling**
> Projective technique in which respondents are required to tell stories about their experiences, with a company or product, for example; also known as the *metaphor technique.*

Storytelling   As the name implies, **storytelling** requires consumers to tell stories about their experiences. It is a search for subtle insights into consumer behavior.

Gerald Zaltman, a Harvard Business School professor, has created a metaphor laboratory to facilitate the storytelling process. (A metaphor is a description of one thing in terms that are usually used to describe another; it can be used to represent thoughts that are tacit, implicit, and unspoken.) Zaltman elicits metaphors from consumers by asking them to spend time over several weeks thinking about how they would visually represent their experiences with a company. To help them with the process, he asks them to cut out magazine pictures that somehow convey those experiences. Then, consumers come to his lab and spend several hours telling stories about all of the images they chose and the connections between the images and their experiences with the firm.

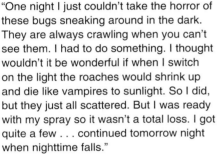

"One night I just couldn't take the horror of these bugs sneaking around in the dark. They are always crawling when you can't see them. I had to do something. I thought wouldn't it be wonderful if when I switch on the light the roaches would shrink up and die like vampires to sunlight. So I did, but they just all scattered. But I was ready with my spray so it wasn't a total loss. I got quite a few . . . continued tomorrow night when nighttime falls."

"A man likes a free meal you cook for him; as long as there is food he will stay."

"I tiptoed quietly into the kitchen, perhaps he wasn't around. I stretched my arm up to turn on the light. I hoped I'd be alone when the light went on. Perhaps he is sitting on the table I thought. You think that's impossible? Nothing is impossible with that guy. He might not even be alone. He'll run when the light goes on I thought. But what's worse is for him to slip out of sight. No, it would be better to confront him before he takes control and 'invites a companion'."

Exhibit 5.10

Consumer Drawings That Helped Identify Respondents' Need for Control

Source: Courtesy of McCann-Erickson, New York.

One metaphor study was conducted on pantyhose. "Women in focus groups have always said that they wear them because they have to, and they hate it," says Glenda Green, a marketing research manager at DuPont, which supplies the raw material for many pantyhose manufacturers. "We didn't think we had a completely accurate picture of their feelings, but we hadn't come up with a good way to test them."[30] DuPont turned to storytelling for better insights. Someone brought a picture of a spilled ice cream sundae, capturing the rage she feels when she spots a run in her hose. Another arrived with a picture of a beautiful woman with baskets of fruit. Other photos depicted a Mercedes and Queen Elizabeth. "As we kept probing into the emotions behind the choice of these photos, the women finally began admitting that hose made them feel sensual, sexy, and more attractive to men," says Green. "There's no way anyone would admit that in a focus group." Several stocking manufacturers used this information to alter their advertising and package design.

Third-Person Technique   Perhaps the easiest projective technique to apply, other than word association, is the **third-person technique**. Rather than directly asking respondents what they think, researchers couch the question in terms of "your neighbor," "most people," or some other third party. Rather than asking a mother why she typically does not fix a nutritionally balanced breakfast for her children, a researcher might ask, "Why don't many people provide their families nutritionally balanced breakfasts?" The third-person technique is often used to avoid questions that might be embarrassing or evoke hostility if posed directly to a respondent.

> **third-person technique**
> Projective technique in which the interviewer learns about respondents' feelings by asking them to answer for a third party, such as "your neighbor" or "most people."

Future of Qualitative Research

The rationale behind qualitative research tests is as follows:

1. The criteria employed and the evaluations made in most buying and usage decisions have emotional and subconscious content, which is an important determinant of buying and usage decisions.

2. Such content is adequately and accurately verbalized by the respondent only through *indirect* communicative techniques.

To the extent that these tenets remain true or even partially correct, the demand for qualitative applications in marketing research will continue to exist. But the problems of small sample sizes and subjective interpretation will continue to plague some forms of qualitative research. Inability to validate and replicate qualitative research will further deter its use.

On the positive side, the use of online focus groups will grow. Focus group research can provide data and insights not available through any other techniques. Low cost and ease of application will lend even greater impetus to use online focus groups. Finally, the qualitative–quantitative split will begin to close as adaptations and innovations allow researchers to enjoy the advantages of both approaches simultaneously.

SUMMARY

Qualitative research refers to research whose findings are not subject to quantification or quantitative analysis. It is often used to examine consumer attitudes, feelings, and motivations. Qualitative research, particularly the use of focus groups, continues to grow in popularity for three reasons. First, qualitative research is usually cheaper than quantitative studies. Second, it is an excellent means of understanding the in-depth motivations and feelings of consumers. Third, it can improve the efficiency of quantitative research.

Qualitative research is not without its disadvantages. Sometimes, qualitative research does not distinguish small differences in attitudes or opinions about a marketing mix as well as large-scale quantitative studies do. Also, respondents in qualitative studies are not necessarily representative of the population of interest to the researcher. And the quality of the research may be questionable, given the number of individuals who profess to be experts in the field, yet lack formal training.

Focus groups are the most popular type of qualitative research. A focus group typically consists of 8 to 12 paid participants who are led by a moderator in an in-depth discussion on a particular topic or concept. The goal of the focus group is to learn and understand what people have to say and why. The emphasis is on getting people to talk at length and in detail about the subject at hand. The interaction associated with group dynamics is essential to the success of focus group research. The idea is that a response from one person will become a stimulus for another person, thereby generating an interplay of responses that will yield more information than if the same number of people had contributed independently.

Most focus groups are held in a group facility, which is typically set up in a conference room, with a large one-way mirror built into one wall. Microphones are placed in unobtrusive locations to record the discussion. Behind the mirror is a viewing room. The moderator plays a critical role in the success or failure of the group and is aided in his or her efforts by a well-planned discussion guide. More and more focus groups are being conducted online because online focus groups are fast and cost effective; they also reach populations that are typically inaccessible. However, there are several problems associated with online focus groups.

A number of other qualitative research methodologies are used but on a much more infrequent basis. One such technique is depth interviews. Individual depth interviews are unstructured one-on-one interviews. The interviewer is thoroughly trained in the skill of probing and eliciting detailed answers to each question. He or she often uses nondirective clinical techniques to uncover hidden motivations. The use of projective techniques represents another form of qualitative research. The objective of any projective test is to delve below the surface responses to obtain true feelings, meanings, or motivations. Some common forms of projective techniques are word association tests, sentence and story completion tests, cartoon tests, photo sorts, consumer drawings, storytelling, and third-person techniques.

KEY TERMS & DEFINITIONS

qualitative research Research whose findings are not subject to quantification or quantitative analysis.

quantitative research Research that uses mathematical analysis.

focus group Group of 8 to 12 participants who are led by a moderator in an in-depth discussion on one particular topic or concept.

group dynamics Interaction among people in a group.

focus group facility Research facility consisting of a conference room or living room setting and a separate observation room with a one-way mirror or live audio-visual feed.

focus group moderator Person hired by the client to lead the focus group; this person should have a background in psychology or sociology or, at least, marketing.

discussion guide Written outline of topics to be covered during a focus group discussion.

instant analysis Moderator debriefing, offering a forum for brainstorming by the moderator and client observers.

online focus groups Focus groups conducted via the Internet.

individual depth interviews One-on-one interviews that probe and elicit detailed answers to questions, often using nondirective techniques to uncover hidden motivations.

hermeneutic research Research that focuses on interpretation through conversations.

projective test Technique for tapping respondents' deepest feelings by having them project those feelings into an unstructured situation.

word association test Projective test in which the interviewer says a word and the respondent must mention the first thing that comes to mind.

sentence and story completion tests Projective tests in which respondents complete sentences or stories in their own words.

cartoon test Projective test in which the respondent fills in the dialogue of one of two characters in a cartoon.

photo sort Projective technique in which a respondent sorts photos of different types of people, identifying those people who she or he feels would use the specified product or service.

consumer drawings Projective technique in which respondents draw what they are feeling or how they perceive an object.

storytelling Projective technique in which respondents are required to tell stories about their experiences, with a company or product, for example; also known as the *metaphor technique*.

third-person technique A projective technique in which the interviewer learns about respondents' feelings by asking them to answer for a third party, such as "your neighbor" or "most people."

QUESTIONS FOR REVIEW & CRITICAL THINKING

1. What are the major differences between quantitative and qualitative research?

2. What are some of the possible disadvantages of using focus groups?

3. Create a story completion test for downloading music from the Internet.

4. What can the client do to get more out of focus groups?

5. What is the purpose of a projective test? What major factors should be considered in using a projective technique?

Team Exercise

6. Divide the class into groups of four and eight. The groups of four will select a topic below (or one suggested by your instructor) and create a discussion guide. One of the four will then serve as the group moderator. One of the groups of eight will then serve as participants in the focus group. The groups should last at least 20 minutes and be observed by the remainder of the class. Suggested topics:
   a. New video games
   b. Buying a hybrid gasoline/electric car
   c. Student experiences at the student union
   d. The quality of existing frozen dinners and snacks and new items that would be desired by students
   e. How students spend their entertainment dollars and what additional entertainment opportunities they would like to see offered

7. What are some major issues in conducting international focus groups?

8. What are the advantages and disadvantages of online focus groups? Should they really be considered focus groups?

9. Take a consumer drawing test—draw a typical Pepsi drinker and a typical Coke drinker. What do the images suggest about your perceptions of Coke and Pepsi drinkers?

10. Use the metaphor technique to tell a story about going to the supermarket.

WORKING THE NET

Go to *http://www.researchconnections.com*. Under "Live Demos," look at the information available at Focus Connect. Report your findings to the class.

REAL-LIFE RESEARCH • 5.1

Fossil Watch, Inc.

Fossil, headquartered in Richardson, Texas, is a leader in the design and marketing of contemporary, high-quality watches, apparel, jewelry, and accessories that are predicated on both fashion and value. Fossil was founded in 1984 at a time when watches were created for function rather than fashion. The company sought to fill this void in the market and began designing watches to serve as a fashion accessory. Fossil incorporated a 1950s Americana design into the brand image in an attempt to target value-driven consumers. The concept paid off, and Fossil quickly emerged as the leader of a growing industry. Today Fossil produces over 300 different styles of watches in a line that continually changes.

Through constant study of the world's fashion trends, the company is able to continually bring the most unique products to the market. Because Fossil products can be found in department stores, in upscale retailing outlets, and in its own stores in more than 80 countries around the world, understanding the fashion tastes of potential Fossil customers across these countries is indispensable. To update their insights into preferences from around the globe, Fossil marketing managers decided to enlist the help of the University of Texas at Arlington's Master of Science in Marketing Research (MSMR) graduate class in qualitative research.

Seventeen MSMR students were asked to conduct qualitative interviews with international students attending their university. Four of the respondents were from India, two from France, two from Russia, two from Brazil, three from the United Kingdom, two from Kenya, and two from Australia. All were from major cities in these countries. Males and females were almost equally represented among the students from each country.

Each MSMR student conducted an individual depth interview (IDI) with an international student about brands and brand personality. These depth interviews were conducted at the College of Business's Behavioral Research Lab. As part of these depth interviews, both word associations and projective tasks (such as "If your watch manufacturer was a car, which one would it be?") were employed. In addition, two focus groups each including 12 persons rounded out the data collection effort for the project.

Results of the qualitative interviews disclosed several insights. Fossil was perceived as a quality brand available for a reasonable price. It was perceived as providing good style, variety, and value-for-money. The qualities that respondents agreed represented Fossil to a high degree were (1) masculine or unisex, (2) young and single, and (3) American. Along the line of masculine impression, Fossil was seen to have outdoorsy and almost rugged qualities. Fossil was not perceived to be the extreme daredevil or adventurer, but was regarded as quite active and sporty. As one respondent put it—"It's just kind of a solid brand that's right down in the middle." The respondents' classification of brands could be summarized as follows:[31]

Upper Range	Rolex	
Midrange	{ Fossil	Swatch Guess, Relics Seiko, Casio	Increasing perceived quality/price
Lower Range	Timex	

Questions

1. How suitable was the sample of respondents in representing globally minded, fashion-conscious consumers in their twenties from different corners of the globe?

2. In your estimation, how much time and effort would have to be expended by Fossil to obtain a better sample?

3. What other qualitative research techniques would complement the depth interviews and focus groups of this study?

4. What are the costs and benefits of including other qualitative research techniques in this study?

5. Was the qualitative research done here sufficient for management to make strategic decisions for Fossil? Tactical decisions?

REAL-LIFE RESEARCH•5.2

The Parenthood Project

KDA Research, San Francisco, decided it wanted to be a pioneer in online individual in-depth interviews. To test their methodology, the company created the Parenthood Project. It was a research effort that sought to learn how values and lives change when people become parents. The topic is deeply personal, so it was felt this would be a good test of the participants' willingness to share their emotions and viewpoints online. It also lent itself nicely to studying two perspectives on the same experience of parenthood. KDA gathered data separately from both new moms and new dads in the same family and then compared results.

For the Parenthood Project, KDA recruited four couples in each of three markets (New York, San Francisco, and Houston). Each couple had children between the ages of 1 and 4. Since one of the research goals was to see whether they could gather two different perspectives on the issue from within one family, they screened for participants within a family who were able to participate separately (at different e-mail addresses). KDA also screened for ownership of a digital camera, because they wanted to experiment with the use of images to provide the firm with more context about the lives of the participants.

During phase one, each participant was given a private blog where they could create their own online journals for the project. Over the course of five days, KDA presented participants with a set of images and a set of questions to engage their thinking on various aspects of their lives relating to parenthood. KDA then asked them to share their reactions to what was presented and to record their thoughts in their online journals. The firm also created a photo exercise in which participants took photos representing aspects of their lives before and after becoming parents and posted them in their online journals. The photo exercise added a visual window into participants' lives and thinking.

Phase two featured group discussion using a bulletin-board format with a facilitated discussion, which took place over two days immediately following the first phase. The discussion topics were fueled by KDA's analysis of the journaling exercises from phase one.

After the two research phases, the company conducted a post-project survey to learn about the experiences of the participants and to help the researchers assess the success of the system and method.

Participants shared intimate details of their lives regarding their relationships with their spouses and their children and about other aspects of their lives as parents. All of the participants said they enjoyed the experience. Many of them said that they appreciated the opportunity to reflect on the issues and that they had learned something from the experience.

The online format was popular with the participants. In the post-project survey, the participants told the researchers that they found it easy to use the online format.[32]

Questions

1. Were these really individual depth interviews? Why or why not?
2. The researchers claimed that they moved into phase two too quickly. The rich journals demanded more analytical time to properly determine what would be discussed in phase two. Do you think that waiting several weeks before moving to phase two might cause respondents to drop out or lose interest? Why?
3. Could all types of IDI be conducted in this manner?
4. What do you see as limitations of this technique?

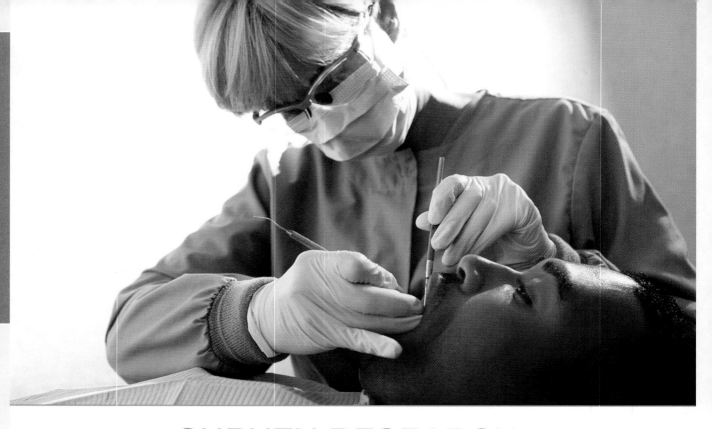

SURVEY RESEARCH:
THE PROFOUND IMPACT
OF THE INTERNET

LEARNING OBJECTIVES

1.	To understand the reasons for the popularity of survey research.
2.	To learn about the types of errors in survey research.
3.	To learn about the types of surveys.
4.	To understand the advantages and disadvantages of online surveys.
5.	To gain insight into the ways online surveys can be conducted.
6.	To learn about recruiting sources for online surveys.
7.	To recognize the special issues that arise in designing online questionnaires.
8.	To gain insight into the factors that determine the choice of particular survey methods.

According to the *Yankelovich Monitor Minute*, men have become more interested in personal health and wellness issues during the last few years, particularly those related to disease prevention and early detection. In some cases, men are taking action on these concerns and are even closing the gap with women in terms of some lifestyle attitudes and adjustments.

But there's still a gender gap, perhaps because men are less likely than women to believe they are knowledgeable about a number of personal health matters. Women are more likely to be "extremely" or "very" concerned about taking care of themselves (64 vs. 56 percent of men) and are more preoccupied with taking measures now to ensure good health when older (59 vs. 48 percent). However, a high degree of confusion about health information exists among both sexes today. So much contradictory material is being written about these issues that the majority of consumers (81 percent of men, 86 percent of women) say it's difficult to know what they should or shouldn't believe.

Compared to the women who were surveyed by Yankelovich, men are not as confident that they are well informed about how to eat healthy (56 percent say they are vs. 66 percent of women), choose the right doctor (42 vs. 51 percent), recognize the signs of depression and mental problems in oneself (41 vs. 52 percent), access fat content in foods (33 vs. 46 percent), and count calories (33 vs. 45 percent).

Men Who Care About. . . .

Maintaining a healthy weight	61%
Reducing stress levels	47%
Visiting dentist 2× a year	48%
Watching blood pressure	40%
Watching cholesterol	43%

Among Men Who Care about a Specific Health Issue, Those Who Are Doing the Following. . . .

Maintaining a healthy weight	75%
Reducing stress levels	71%
Visiting dentist 2× a year	80%
Watching blood pressure	84%
Watching cholesterol	72%[1]

Survey research, such as the men's healthcare survey, is the use of a questionnaire to gather facts, opinions, and attitudes; it is the most popular way to gather primary data. What are the various types of survey research? As noted previously, not everyone is willing to participate in a survey. What kinds of errors does that create? What are the other types of errors encountered in survey research? Why has Internet survey research become so popular, and what are its drawbacks? These questions are answered in this chapter.

Popularity of Survey Research

Some 126 million Americans have been interviewed at some point in their lives. Each year, about 70 million people are interviewed in the United States, which is the equivalent of over 15 minutes per adult per year. Surveys have a high rate of usage in marketing research compared to other means of collecting primary data, for some very good reasons.

- ☐ *The need to know why.* In marketing research, there is a critical need to have some idea about why people do or do not do something. For example, why did they buy or not buy a particular brand? What did they like or dislike about it? Who or what influenced them? We do not mean to imply that surveys can prove causation, only that they can be used to develop some idea of the causal forces at work.

- ☐ *The need to know how.* At the same time, the marketing researcher often finds it necessary to understand the process consumers go through before taking some action. How did they make the decision? What time period passed? What did they examine or consider? When and where was the decision made? What do they plan to do next?

- ☐ *The need to know who.* The marketing researcher also needs to know who the person is, from a demographic or lifestyle perspective. Information on age, income, occupation, marital status, stage in the family life cycle, education, and other factors is necessary for the identification and definition of market segments.

A new survey of marketing research professionals found that the most common source of market research information is survey data, used by 94 percent of companies surveyed. Other sources include: syndicated research (78 percent); focus groups (74 percent); company sales data (67 percent); and scanner data (16 percent). Also, 88 percent of corporations use online methods to conduct survey-based market research. Sixty-five percent of those surveyed agree that the speed of online research has helped accelerate the pace of their business. Half of all online research dollars are spent on projects transitioning from traditional (i.e., telephone, mail, mall) research methods.[2] We will discuss online research in detail later in the chapter.

Types of Errors in Survey Research

When assessing the quality of information obtained from survey research, the manager must determine the accuracy of those results. This requires careful consideration of the research methodology employed in relation to the various types of errors that might result (see Exhibit 6.1).

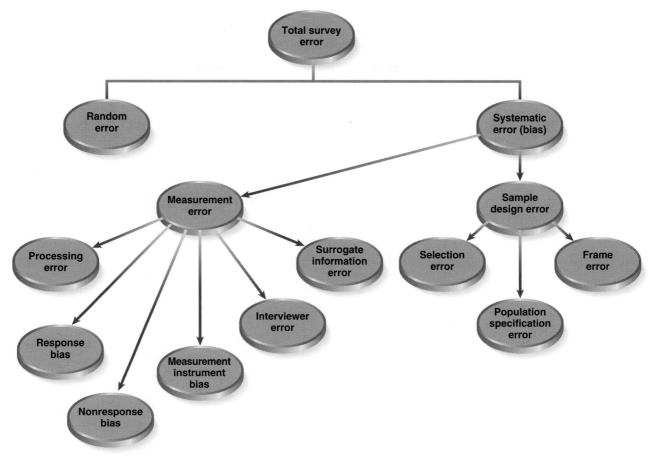

Exhibit 6.1

Types of Survey

Sampling Error

Two major types of errors may be encountered in connection with the sampling process. They are random error and systematic error, sometimes referred to as bias.

Surveys often attempt to obtain information from a representative cross section of a target population. The goal is to make inferences about the total population based on the responses given by respondents sampled. Even when all aspects of the sample are investigated properly, the results are still subject to a certain amount of **random error** (or **random sampling error**) because of chance variation. **Chance variation** is the difference between the sample value and the true value of the population mean. This error cannot be eliminated, but it can be reduced by increasing the sample size. It is possible to estimate the range of random error at a particular level of confidence. Random error and the procedures for estimating it are discussed in detail in Chapters 12 and 13.

Systematic Error

Systematic error, or **bias**, results from mistakes or problems in the research design or from flaws in the execution of the sample design. Systematic error exists in the results of a sample if those results show a consistent tendency to vary in one direction (consistently

> **random error,** or **random sampling error**
> Error that results from chance variation.

> **chance variation**
> The difference between the sample value and the true value of the population mean.

> **systematic error,** or **bias**
> Error that results from problems or flaws in the execution of the research design; sometimes called *nonsampling error*.

higher or consistently lower) from the true value of the population parameter. Systematic error includes all sources of error except those introduced by the random sampling process. Therefore, systematic errors are sometimes called *nonsampling errors*. The nonsampling errors that can systematically influence survey answers can be categorized as *sample design error* and *measurement error*.

Sample Design Error

Sample design error is a systematic error that results from a problem in the sample design or sampling procedures. Types of sample design errors include frame errors, population specification errors, and selection errors.

Frame Error. The **sampling frame** is the list of population elements or members from which units to be sampled are selected. **Frame error** results from using an incomplete or inaccurate sampling frame. The problem is that a sample drawn from a list that is subject to frame error may not be a true cross section of the target population. A common source of frame error in marketing research is the use of a published telephone directory as a sampling frame for a telephone survey. Many households are not listed in a current telephone book because they do not want to be listed or are not listed accurately because they have recently moved or changed their telephone number. Research has shown that those people who are listed in telephone directories are systematically different from those who are not listed in certain important ways, such as socioeconomic levels.[3] This means that if a study purporting to represent the opinions of all households in a particular area is based on listings in the current telephone directory, it will be subject to frame error.

Population Specification Error. **Population specification error** results from an incorrect definition of the population or universe from which the sample is to be selected. For example, suppose a researcher defined the population or universe for a study as people

sample design error
Systematic error that results from an error in the sample design or sampling procedures.

sampling frame
The list of population elements or members from which units to be sampled are selected.

frame error
Error resulting from an inaccurate or incomplete sampling frame.

population specification error
Error that results from incorrectly defining the population or universe from which a sample is chosen.

A population must be defined before research can begin. Errors can occur if a population is not defined correctly or if selection procedures are not followed properly.

over the age of 35. Later, it was determined that younger individuals should have been included and that the population should have been defined as people 20 years of age or older. If those younger people who were excluded are significantly different in regard to the variables of interest, then the sample results will be biased.

Selection Error.   Selection error can occur even when the analyst has a proper sampling frame and has defined the population correctly. **Selection error** occurs when sampling procedures are incomplete or improper or when appropriate selection procedures are not properly followed. For example, door-to-door interviewers might decide to avoid houses that do not look neat and tidy because they think the inhabitants will not be agreeable to doing a survey. If people who live in messy houses are systematically different from those who live in tidy houses, then selection error will be introduced into the results of the survey. Selection error is a serious problem in nonprobability samples, a subject discussed in Chapter 12.

selection error
Error that results from incomplete or improper sample selection procedures or not following appropriate procedures.

Measurement Error   Measurement error is often a much more serious threat to survey accuracy than is random error. When the results of public opinion polls are given in the media and in professional marketing research reports, an error figure is frequently reported (say, plus or minus 5 percent). The television viewer or the user of a marketing research study is left with the impression that this figure refers to total survey error. Unfortunately, this is not the case. This figure refers only to random sampling error. It does not include sample design error and speaks in no way to the measurement error that may exist in the research results. **Measurement error** occurs when there is variation between the information being sought (true value) and the information actually obtained by the measurement process. Our main concern in this text is with systematic measurement error. Various types of error may be caused by numerous deficiencies in the measurement process. These errors include surrogate information error, interviewer error, measurement instrument bias, processing error, nonresponse bias, and response bias.

measurement error
Systematic error that results from a variation between the information being sought and what is actually obtained by the measurement process.

Surrogate Information Error.   **Surrogate information error** occurs when there is a discrepancy between the information actually required to solve a problem and the information being sought by the researcher. It relates to general problems in the research design, particularly failure to properly define the problem. A few years ago, Kellogg spent millions developing a line of 17 breakfast cereals that featured ingredients that would help consumers cut down on their cholesterol. The product line was called Ensemble. It failed miserably in the marketplace. Yes, people want to lower their cholesterol, but the real question was whether they would purchase a line of breakfast cereals to accomplish this task. This question was never asked in the research. Also, the name "Ensemble" usually refers to either an orchestra or something you wear. Consumers didn't understand either the product line or the need to consume it.

surrogate information error
Error that results from a discrepancy between the information needed to solve a problem and that sought by the researcher.

Interviewer Error.   **Interviewer error**, or **interviewer bias**, results from the interviewer's influencing a respondent—consciously or unconsciously—to give untrue or inaccurate answers. The dress, age, gender, facial expressions, body language, or tone of voice of the interviewer may influence the answers given by some or all respondents. This type of error is caused by problems in the selection and training of interviewers or by the failure of interviewers to follow instructions. Interviewers must be properly trained and supervised to appear neutral at all times. Another type of interviewer error occurs when deliberate cheating takes place. This can be a particular problem in door-to-door interviewing, where interviewers may be tempted to falsify interviews and get paid for work

interviewer error, or **interviewer bias**
Error that results from the interviewer's influencing—consciously or unconsciously—the answers of the respondent.

they did not actually do. The procedures developed by the researcher must include safeguards to ensure that this problem will be detected (see Chapter 14).

Measurement Instrument Bias. **Measurement instrument bias** (sometimes called *questionnaire bias*) results from problems with the measurement instrument or questionnaire (see Chapter 9). Examples of such problems include leading questions or elements of the questionnaire design that make recording responses difficult and prone to recording errors (see Chapter 11). Problems of this type can be avoided by paying careful attention to detail in the questionnaire design phase and by using questionnaire pretests before field interviewing begins.

Processing Error. **Processing errors** are primarily due to mistakes that occur when information from survey documents is entered into the computer. For example, a document may be scanned incorrectly.

Nonresponse Bias. Ideally, if a sample of 400 people is selected from a particular population, all 400 of those individuals should be interviewed. As a practical matter, this will never happen. Response rates of 5 percent or less are common in mail surveys. The question is "Are those who did respond to the survey systematically different in some important way from those who did not respond?" Such differences lead to **nonresponse bias**. We recently examined the results of a study conducted among customers of a large savings and loan association. The response rate to the questionnaire, included in customer monthly statements, was slightly under 1 percent. Analysis of the occupations of those who responded revealed that the percentage of retired people among respondents was 20 times higher than in the local metropolitan area. This overrepresentation of retired individuals raised serious doubts about the accuracy of the results.

Obviously, the higher the response rate, the less the possible impact of nonresponse because nonrespondents then represent a smaller subset of the overall picture. If the decrease in bias associated with improved response rates is trivial, then allocating resources to obtain higher response rates might be wasteful in studies in which resources could be used for better purposes.

Nonresponse error occurs when the following happens:

- ☐ A person cannot be reached at a particular time.
- ☐ A potential respondent is reached but cannot or will not participate at that time (for example, the telephone request to participate in a survey comes just as the family is sitting down to dinner).
- ☐ A person is reached but refuses to participate in the survey. This is the most serious problem because it may be possible to achieve future participation in the first two circumstances.

The **refusal rate** is the percentage of persons contacted who refused to participate in a survey. Today, the overall refusal rate is approximately 60 percent—up from 52 percent in 1992, according to the Council for Marketing and Opinion Research (CMOR). Most refusals (68 percent) occur before the survey introduction (initial refusals); only one-quarter (26 percent) occur after the introduction is read (qualified refusals). Few (6 percent) terminate once the survey is under way. While most individuals (71 percent) express a willingness to participate in future surveys, this willingness is lukewarm (nearly three times as many are "fairly willing" compared to "very willing").[4] While these percentages are based on a study by the CMOR and are not necessarily reflective of the entire industry, they do reflect the significant increase in the refusal rate.

➤ measurement instrument bias
Error that results from the design of the questionnaire or measurement instrument; also known as *questionnaire bias.*

➤ processing error
Error that results from the incorrect transfer of information from a survey document to a computer.

➤ nonresponse bias
Error that results from a systematic difference between those who do and those who do not respond to a measurement instrument.

➤ refusal rate
Percentage of persons contacted who refused to participate in a survey.

EXHIBIT 6.2	Types of Errors and Strategies for Minimizing Errors

I. Random error — This error can be reduced only by increasing sample size.

II. Systematic error — This error can be reduced by minimizing sample design and measurement errors.

A. Sample design error

Frame error — This error can be minimized by getting the best sampling frame possible and doing preliminary quality control checks to evaluate the accuracy and completeness of the frame.

Population specification error — This error results from incorrect definition of the population of interest. It can be reduced or minimized only by more careful consideration and definition of the population of interest.

Selection error — This error results from using incomplete or improper sampling procedures or not following appropriate selection procedures. It can occur even with a good sampling frame and an appropriate specification of the population. It is minimized by developing selection procedures that will ensure randomness and by developing quality control checks to make sure that these procedures are followed in the field.

B. Measurement error

Surrogate information error — This error results from seeking and basing decisions on the wrong information. It results from poor design and can be minimized only by paying more careful attention to specification of the types of information required to fulfill the objectives of the research.

Interviewer error — This error occurs because of interactions between the interviewer and the respondent that affect the responses given. It is minimized by careful interviewer selection and training. In addition, quality control checks should involve unobtrusive monitoring of interviewers to ascertain whether they are following prescribed guidelines.

Measurement instrument bias — Also referred to as *questionnaire bias,* this error is minimized only by careful questionnaire design and pretesting.

Processing error — This error can occur in the process of transferring data from questionnaires to the computer. It is minimized by developing and following rigid quality control procedures for transferring data and supporting quality control checks.

Nonresponse bias — This error results from the fact that those people chosen for the sample who actually respond are systematically different from those who are chosen and do not respond. It is particularly serious in connection with mail surveys. It is minimized by doing everything possible (e.g., shortening the questionnaire, making the questionnaire more respondent friendly, doing callbacks, providing incentives, contacting people when they are most likely to be at home) to encourage those chosen for the sample to respond.

Response bias — This error occurs when something about a question leads people to answer it in a particular way. It can be minimized by paying special attention to questionnaire design. In particular, questions that are hard to answer, might make the respondent look uninformed, or deal with sensitive issues should be modified (see Chapter 11).

> **response bias**
> Error that results from the tendency of people to answer a question incorrectly through either deliberate falsification or unconscious misrepresentation.

Response Bias. If there is a tendency for people to answer a particular question in a certain way, then there is **response bias**. Response bias can result from deliberate falsification or unconscious misrepresentation.

Deliberate falsification occurs when people purposefully give untrue answers to questions. There are many reasons why people might knowingly misrepresent information in a survey. They may wish to appear intelligent, not reveal information that they feel is embarrassing, or conceal information that they consider to be personal.

For example, in a survey about fast-food buying behavior, the respondents may have a fairly good idea of how many times they visited a fast-food restaurant in the past month. However, they may not remember which fast-food restaurants they visited or how many times they visited each restaurant. Rather than answering "Don't know" in response to a question regarding which restaurants they visited, the respondents may simply guess.

Unconscious misrepresentation occurs when a respondent is legitimately trying to be truthful and accurate but gives an inaccurate response. This type of bias may occur because of question format, question content, or various other reasons.

Strategies for minimizing survey errors are summarized in Exhibit 6.2.

Types of Surveys

Asking people questions is the essence of the survey approach. But what type of survey is best for a given situation? The non-Internet survey alternatives discussed in this chapter are door-to-door interviews, executive interviews, mall-intercept interviews, telephone interviews, self-administered questionnaires, and mail surveys.

Door-to-Door Interviews

door-to-door interviews
Interviews conducted face to face with consumers in their homes.

Door-to-door interviews, in which consumers are interviewed in person in their homes, were at one time thought to be the best survey method. This conclusion was based on a number of factors. First, the door-to-door interview is a personal, face-to-face interaction with all the attendant advantages—immediate feedback from the respondent, the ability to explain complicated tasks, the ability to use special questionnaire techniques that require visual contact to speed up the interview or improve data quality, and the ability to show the respondent product concepts and other stimuli for evaluation. Second, the participant is at ease in a familiar, comfortable, secure environment.

Door-to-door interviews began a steep decline in the early 1970s and have now virtually disappeared altogether from the U.S. marketing research scene. The primary reason is the cost of paying an interviewer's travel time, mileage, and survey time as well as ever-rising refusal rates. Door-to-door interviewing, however, is still used in developing countries. Caterina Gerlotto, a research manager for Ipsos-United Kingdom, talks about conducting door-to-door interviewing in the Global Research box.

Executive Interviews

executive interviews
Industrial equivalent of door-to-door interviewing.

Executive interviews are used by marketing researchers as the industrial equivalent of door-to-door interviews. This type of survey involves interviewing businesspeople at their offices concerning industrial products or services. For example, if Hewlett-Packard wants information about user preferences for features that might be offered in a new line of office computer printers, it needs to interview prospective user-purchasers of the printers. It would thus be appropriate to locate and interview these people at their offices.

This type of interviewing is expensive. First, individuals involved in the purchasing decision for the product in question must be identified and located. Sometimes lists can be obtained from various sources, but more frequently screening must be conducted over the telephone. A particular company may indeed have individuals of the type being sought, but locating them within a large organization can be expensive and time-consuming. Once a qualified person is located, the next step is to get that person to agree to be interviewed

GLOBAL RESEARCH

In India, the latest figures show that less than 10 percent of citizens have a telephone at home. The only real option therefore is face to face, which is time-consuming. Would it be faster if the interviewer were armed with a laptop? Experience has shown that interviewers conducting door-to-door interviews in India, with such a piece of equipment, would need to be armed with a lot more than the laptop! The only feasible methodology is pen and paper. Therefore, extra time must be included for the collation of data if India is involved in the project.

Similarly, in a more developed market, say Norway, a country with an average annual income after tax of $34,050, the telephone is nearly always used, essentially for two reasons. First is the geographical distribution: a nationally representative sample from a face-to-face methodology would cost a small fortune. Second, Scandinavians in general are uncomfortable with allowing a stranger into their house.[5]

and to set a time for the interview. This is not usually as hard as it might seem because most professionals seem to enjoy talking about topics related to their work.

Finally, an interviewer must go to the particular place at the appointed time. Long waits are frequent; cancellations are common. This type of survey requires highly skilled interviewers because they are frequently interviewing on topics they know little about. Executive interviews have essentially the same advantages and disadvantages as door-to-door interviews. More and more executive interviews are moving online.

Mall-Intercept Interviews

Mall-intercept interviews are a popular survey method for conducting personal interviews. This survey approach is relatively simple. Shoppers are intercepted in public areas of shopping malls and either interviewed on the spot or asked to come to a permanent interviewing facility in the mall. Approximately 500 malls throughout the country have permanent survey facilities operated by marketing research firms. An equal or greater number of malls permit marketing researchers to interview on a daily basis. Many malls do not permit marketing research interviewing, however, because they view it as an unnecessary nuisance to shoppers.

Mall surveys are less expensive than door-to-door interviews because respondents come to the interviewer rather than the other way around. Interviewers spend more of their time actually interviewing and less of their time hunting for someone to interview. Also, mall interviewers do not have the substantial travel time and mileage expenses associated with door-to-door interviewing. In addition to low-cost, mall-intercept interviews have many of the advantages associated with door-to-door interviews in that respondents can try test products on the spot.

However, a number of serious disadvantages are associated with mall-intercept interviewing. First, it is virtually impossible to get a sample representative of a large metropolitan area from shoppers at a particular mall. Even though malls may be large, most of them draw shoppers from a relatively small local area. In addition, malls tend to attract certain types of people, based on the stores they contain. Studies also show that some people shop more frequently than others and therefore have a greater chance of being selected. Finally, many people refuse mall interviews. In summary, mall-intercept interviewing cannot produce

> **mall-intercept interviews**
> Interviews conducted by intercepting mall shoppers (or shoppers in other high-traffic locations) and interviewing them face to face.

a good or representative sample except in the rare case in which the population of interest is coincident with or is a subset of the population that shops at a particular mall.

Second, the mall environment is not always viewed as a comfortable place to conduct an interview. Respondents may be ill at ease, in a hurry, or preoccupied by various distractions outside the researcher's control. These factors may adversely affect the quality of the data obtained. Even with all its problems, the popularity of mall-intercept interviews has only slightly declined in recent years.

Rather than interview in the public areas of malls, some researchers are conducting surveys in stores at the point-of-purchase. Firms such as Marketing Research Services, Inc. (*www.mrsi.com*), specialize in in-store interviewing. The company notes:

When a consumer reaches for a product on a store shelf, the eye of market research should be wide open. This is the only time and place that consumers' purchase interest and motivations are well defined and readily expressed. The moment of purchase is the most critical point in the entire marketing cycle. It is the moment when shoppers best recall why they made the choice to put a particular item in their shopping cart.[6]

Various companies, including Procter & Gamble, General Mills, Starbucks, McDonald's, and Walgreens, currently conduct in-store studies.

Telephone Interviews

Until 1990, telephone interviewing was the most popular form of survey research. The advantages of telephone interviewing are compelling. First, telephoning is a relatively inexpensive way to collect survey data. Second, the telephone interview has the potential to produce a high-quality sample. Ninety-five percent of all Americans have a telephone. *Random-digit sampling*, or *random-digit dialing*, is a frequently used sampling approach (see Chapter 12). The basic idea is simple: Instead of drawing a sample from the phone book or other directory, researchers use telephone numbers generated via a random-number procedure. This approach ensures that people with unlisted numbers and those who have moved or otherwise changed their telephone numbers since the last published phone book are included in the sample in the correct proportion.

The telephone survey approach has several inherent disadvantages. First, respondents cannot be shown anything in a typical telephone interview. This shortcoming ordinarily eliminates the telephone survey as an alternative in situations that require respondents to comment on visual product concepts, advertisements, and the like.

Second, some critics have suggested that telephone interviewers are unable to make the various judgments and evaluations that can be made by in-home interviewers (for example, evaluations concerning income, based on what the respondent's home looks like and other outward signs of economic status). In reality, marketing research interviewers are almost never called on to make such judgments.

A third disadvantage of the telephone interview is that it limits the quantity and types of information that can be obtained. A respondent's patience wears thin more easily over the phone, and it is easy to hang up the phone. The telephone is also a poor vehicle for conducting a depth interview or a long interview with many open-ended questions.

A fourth disadvantage of telephone interviewing is associated with the increased use of screening devices. These include answering machines, do-not-call lists, call blocking, caller ID, and distinctive ringing. On the average, for every hour an interviewer spends on the phone, 30 minutes is spent just trying to find a person who will agree to be surveyed.[7] This, of course, drives up the cost of telephone surveys.

A fifth disadvantage is that research has shown the potential for personality bias in phone surveys. That is, persons who agree to participate in a telephone interview may be more outgoing, confident, conscientious, and agreeable than those who will not.[8]

PRACTICING MARKETING RESEARCH

Although online panels are often touted as a reliable way to reach a respondent group while maximizing research budgets, the same can be said of telephone panels. Similar to a Web-based database, telephone panels include a group of screened individuals who have agreed to participate in ongoing research. Incentives are arranged before joining, and survey participation is generally limited to avoid any bias. Using a panel as opposed to a random-digit dial method or company-provided customer list minimizes recruitment time and thereby reduces overall project costs.

Web-Phone Method

When possible, researchers should combine telephone and online fielding methods. This approach allows for increased response rates and broad respondent reach. Once finalized, the survey is programmed for both computer-assisted telephone interviewing (CATI) and Web completion. This dual programming accommodates both methodologies, and by providing for both techniques simultaneously, programming charges are not increased. Web-based and telephone data can also be compared to see if there are any substantial differences between the groups.

Mail-Telephone Method

Another hybrid fielding technique combines mail and telephone methods. This is an appropriate choice for studies where it is critical to view a tangible sample (i.e., photos or printer samples) to be critiqued in the research. Implementing this approach, respondents are recruited via phone, and once screened and having agreed to participate, are sent a packet including the samples. After reviewing the documents, respondents are re-contacted via phone to collect their feedback. By ensuring that respondents are prescreened and willing to participate, researchers minimize the large postage and printing expense typically associated with the vast number of pieces needed to field unsolicited mail surveys.[9]

Today, nearly all telephone interviews are central-location telephone interviews. In some cases, firms are further centralizing the process by conducting completely automated telephone surveys. Al Fitzgerald, president of Answers Research, talks about telephone panels and several combination methods of surveying in the Practicing Marketing Research box.

Central-Location Telephone Interviews **Central-location telephone interviews** are conducted from a facility set up for that purpose. The reason for the popularity of central-location phone interviews is fairly straightforward—in a single word, control. First, the interviewing process can be monitored; most central-location telephone interviewing facilities have unobtrusive monitoring equipment that permits supervisors to listen in on interviews as they are being conducted. Interviewers who are not doing the interview properly can be corrected, and those who are incapable of conducting a proper interview can be terminated. One supervisor can monitor from 10 to 20 interviewers. Ordinarily, each interviewer is monitored at least once per shift. Second, completed interviews are edited on the spot as a further quality control check. Interviewers can be immediately informed of any deficiencies in their work. Finally, interviewers' working hours are controlled.

> **central-location telephone interviews**
> Interviews conducted by calling respondents from a centrally located marketing research facility.

> **computer-assisted telephone interviews (CATI)** Central-location telephone interviews in which interviewers enter respondents' answers directly into a computer.

Most research firms have computerized the central-location telephone interviewing process. In **computer-assisted telephone interviews (CATI)**, each interviewer is seated in front of a computer terminal or a personal computer. When a qualified respondent gets on the line, the interviewer starts the interview by pressing a key or series of keys on the keyboard. The questions and multiple-choice answers appear on the screen one at a time. The interviewer reads the question and enters the response, and the computer skips ahead to the appropriate next question. For example, the interviewer might ask whether the respondent has a dog. If the answer is yes, there might be a series of questions regarding what type of dog food the person buys. If the answer is no, those questions would be inappropriate. The computer takes into account the answer to the dog ownership question and skips ahead to the next appropriate question.

In addition, the computer can help customize questionnaires. For example, in the early part of a long interview, a respondent is asked the years, makes, and models of all the cars he or she owns. Later in the interview, questions might be asked about each specific car owned. The question might come up on the interviewer's screen as follows: "You said you own a 2007 GMC truck. Which family member drives this vehicle most often?" Other questions about this vehicle and others owned would appear in similar fashion.

Another advantage of CATI is that computer tabulations can be run at any point in the study. This luxury is not available with a pencil-and-paper interview. Based on preliminary tabulations, certain questions might be dropped, saving time and money in subsequent interviewing. If, for example, 98.3 percent of those interviewed answer a particular question in the same manner, there is probably no need to continue asking the question. Tabulations may also suggest the need to add questions to the survey. If an unexpected pattern of product use is uncovered in the early stages of interviewing, questions can be added that delve further into this behavior. Finally, management may find the early reporting of survey results useful in preliminary planning and strategy development.

Kiosk-based computer interviewing is a relatively new and successful way of capturing data on consumers' recent experiences. Go to *www.intouchsurvey.com* to find out more about the kiosk-based offerings of In-Touch Survey Systems, Inc.

> **self-administered questionnaires** Questionnaires filled out by respondents with no interviewer present.

Gaining respondent cooperation is the key to a successful telephone interview. Amanda Durkee, senior project manager for Zanthus Research, Portland, Oregon, talks about the importance of a good first impression in the Practicing Marketing Research box.

Self-Administered Questionnaires

The self-administered and mail survey methods explained in this section have one thing in common. They differ from the other survey methods discussed in that no interviewer—human or computer—is involved. The major disadvantage of **self-administered questionnaires** is that no one is present to explain things to the respondent and clarify responses to open-ended questions. For example, if someone were asked via an open-ended question why he or she does not buy a particular brand of soft drink, a typical answer might be "because I don't like it." From a managerial perspective, this answer is useless. It provides no information that can be used to alter the marketing mix and thereby make the product more attractive. An interviewer conducting the survey, however, would "probe" for a response—after receiving and

PRACTICING MARKETING RESEARCH

Picture yourself sitting at work. Your phone rings. On the other end, a voice tentatively says, "Hi, this is Bob from Masterful Research. I'm conducting a survey today on widgets. Is this a good time for me to ask you a few questions?"

What would you do?

For many purchase decision makers at businesses, such as IT managers, this type of call is an everyday occurrence. Unless there's a compelling reason to participate from the very beginning, it's very likely that they'll pass on the opportunity. The following are some guidelines to increase the persuasiveness of your survey introduction.

- *Keep the intro short and natural.* Interviewers are trained to read introductions and questions verbatim, so keep the scripted introduction short and simple.

- *Make sure to say why you're calling.* Identifying the subject of the survey will not only help generate interest but also avoid confusion and result in more direct, informed responses.

- *Tell the respondent how much time you need.* If the survey is under 20 minutes, disclose the length up front. A survey conducted by the Marketing Research Association shows that cooperation rates drop off sharply after 20 minutes, so if your survey is longer you may want to consider shortening it!

- *Offer an incentive.* If the length is over 15 or 20 minutes and/or if the audience has a particularly low incidence among the population, it is very possible that you will need an incentive to gain participation.

- *Distinguish yourself from telemarketers in a non-salesy way.* An example introduction is, "We are very interested in the opinions of companies like yours so that manufacturers of [product] can continually improve the products and services they provide. Would you help me with my research?"

- *Identify the client, if possible.* Tell respondents who is conducting the survey, particularly if you or your client is a well-established, well-regarded brand and disclosing sponsorship won't bias answers.

- *Offer confidentiality and respect for respondents.* Last but certainly not least, remind respondents that their responses will be held in confidence, and that they will not be placed on any mailing lists or receive any sales solicitations as a result of their participation.

Remind them also that their opinions are valuable![10]

recording the useless response, the interviewer would ask the respondent what it was that he or she did not like about the product. The interviewee might then indicate a dislike for the taste. Next, the interviewer would ask what it was about the taste that the person did not like. Here the interviewer might finally get something useful, with the respondent indicating that the product in question was, for example, "too sweet." If many people give a similar response, management might elect to reduce the sweetness of the drink. The point is that, without probing, management would have only the useless first response.

Some have argued that the absence of an interviewer is an advantage in that it eliminates one source of bias. There is no interviewer whose appearance, dress, manner of speaking, or failure to follow instructions may influence respondents' answers to questions.

Exhibit 6.3

Self-Administered Questionnaire

Source: Courtesy of Accent Marketing & Research, Ltd., London.

GATWICK EXPRESS
Customer Survey

+ ☐☐☐☐☐☐☐☐☐☐ 0 1 2 3 4 5 6 7 8 R

Please complete this questionnaire by ticking the appropriate boxes or by writing in your answer in the space provided. A separate questionnaire should be completed by EACH member of your travelling party aged 14 and over.

Veuillez compléter le questionnaire suivant en cochant les cases appropriées ou en écrivant votre réponse dans l'espace prévu. Un questionnaire séparé devrait être complété par CHAQUE membre de votre groupe de voyage âgé de 14 ans et au-delà.

Bitte füllen Sie den nachfolgenden Fragebogen durch Ankreuzen der entsprechenenb Kästchen bzw. schriftlich an den vorgesehenen Stellen aus. JEDES Mitglied Ihrer Reisegruppe über 14 Jahren sollte einen separaten Fragebogen ausfüllen.

Q1 Are you sitting in Club (1st) class or Express (2nd) class on this train?
Etes vous assis en classe Club (1ère) ou Express (2ème) dans ce train?
Sitzen Sie in der Club-Klasse (1. Kl) oder in der Express-Klasse (2. Kl) dieses Zuges?
Club (1st) ☐
Express (2nd) ☐

Q2 Are you flying or have you flown today?
Est-ce vous partez en voyage ou avez-vous voyagé par avion aujourd'hui?
Fliegen Sie heute oder Sie heute schon geflogen?
I will fly /*Je vais voyager par avion /Ich fliege* ☐
I have flown / *J'ai voyagé par avion /Ich bin geflogen* ☐
I am not flying **(GO TO Q11)** ☐
Je ne voyage pas par avion /Ich fliege nicht (ALLEZ A /WEITER ZU Q11)

Q3a Please write in the origin and destination of your flight and the scheduled arrival and departure times.
Veuillez inscrire l'origine et la destination de votre vol ainsi que les heures prévues de départ et d'arrivée.
Bitte geben Sie Ihren Abflug- und Zielort und die planmäßige Abflug- und Ankunftszeit an.
From / *De /Von* ....
To / *A /Zu* ....
Departure time / *Départ /Abflugzeit* ....
Arrival time / *Arrivée /Ankunftzeit* ....

Q3b Do you know your flight number?
Connaissez-vous le numéro de votre vol?
Wissen Sie Ihre Flugnummer?
If yes **PLEASE WRITE IN** ....

Q3c Which airline will/did you fly with?
Avec quelle compagnie aérienne volerez-vous/avez-vous volé?
Mit welcher Fluggesellschaft fliegen Sie/sind Sie geflogen?

OFFICE USE ONLY
0 1 2 3 4 5 6 7 8 9
☐☐☐☐☐☐☐☐☐☐ 1000
☐☐☐☐☐☐☐☐☐☐ 100
☐☐☐☐☐☐☐☐☐☐ 10
☐☐☐☐☐☐☐☐☐☐ 1

0 1 2 3 4 5 6 7 8 9
☐☐☐☐☐☐☐☐☐☐ 100
☐☐☐☐☐☐☐☐☐☐ 10
☐☐☐☐☐☐☐☐☐☐ 1

Q4 Are/were you on the outward or return leg of your air journey?
Outward ☐   Return ☐
Single leg journey ☐

Q5a Is/was this flight a direct one or will/did you change planes en route?
Direct flight **(GO TO Q6)** ☐
Will/did change planes en route ☐

Q5b Please write in your ultimate origin and ultimate destination airports of this trip.
Origin ☐   Destination ☐

Q6 What flight ticket type do/did you have?
Economy Full Fare ☐   First Class ☐
Stand-by/Apex ☐   Business/Club ☐
Staff-Discount ☐   Don't know ☐
Other discount ☐   Other ☐

Q7 What is the UK origin/destination of your journey today?
Central London ☐   Outer London (North) ☐
Outer London (South) ☐   Other South East ☐
East Anglia ☐   South West ☐
Midlands ☐   Northern England ☐
Scotland ☐   Wales ☐
N.Ireland ☐   Other ☐
Don't know ☐

Q8 What is your usual country of residence?
Mainland UK ☐   Northern Ireland/Eire ☐
Channel Islands ☐   Other ☐

Q9 How many adults are in your party (including yourself)?
One adult ☐   Two adults ☐
Three adults ☐   More than three adults ☐

PLEASE TURN OVER

(continued)

Self-administered interviews are often used in malls or other central locations where the researcher has access to a captive audience. Airlines, for example, often have programs in which questionnaires are administered during the flight. Passengers are asked to rate various aspects of the airline's services, and the results are used to track passenger perceptions of service over time. Many hotels, restaurants, and other service businesses provide brief questionnaires to patrons to find out how they feel about the quality of service provided (see Exhibit 6.3).

A recent development in the area of direct computer interviewing is kiosk-based computer interviewing. Kiosks are developed with multimedia, touch-screen computers contained in freestanding cabinets. These computers can be programmed to administer complex surveys, show full-color scanned images (products, store layouts), and play

Exhibit 6.3

Self-Administered Questionnaire (continued)

Q10 How many **children** (aged 2-14) are in your party?

None ☐	
One child ☐	Two children ☐
Three children ☐	More than three ☐

Q11 What is/was the nature of your journey today?

Flying on business ☐
Flying for a conference/trade fair/exhibition ☐
Flying for a holiday (package) ☐
Flying for a holiday (arranged independently) ☐
Flying to visit friends/relatives ☐
Flying to/from work ☐
Flying for other purposes ☐

Meeting friends/relatives at the airport ☐
Business at the airport ☐
Travel to/from work at the airport ☐
Travel to/from work in London ☐
Other reason, but not flying ☐

Q12 How many times in the last 12 months have you travelled by air? (PLEASE INCLUDE ALL YOUR FLIGHTS TO/FROM ANY AIRPORT)

None ☐	Once only ☐
2-3 times ☐	4-5 times ☐
6-10 times ☐	11-40 times ☐
41-50 times ☐	More than 50 times ☐

Q13 Where did you hear about Gatwick Express?

In Britain ☐	Outside Britain ☐

Q14 How did you **first** hear about the Gatwick Express?　(TICK ONE BOX ONLY)

Advert in newspaper/magazine ☐
Poster/Leaflet ☐
Article in newspaper/magazine ☐
British Rail ☐
Word of mouth ☐
Signs at Gatwick Airport ☐
Signs at Victoria Station ☐
Travel guide ☐
Travel Agency information ☐
Airline leaflet or Airline Offices ☐
In-flight magazine ☐
In-flight announcement or flight staff ☐
Other ☐

Q15 Did you consider an alternative way of travelling between London and Gatwick Airport?

Yes ☐	No (GOTO Q17) ☐

Q16 Which alternative(s) did you consider? (YOU MAY TICK MORE THAN ONE BOX)

Taxi ☐	Car ☐
Coach ☐	South Central Trains ☐
Thameslink Trains ☐	Other ☐

Q17 What was the **main** reason you chose to travel **by rail** to/from Gatwick for your journey today? (TICK ONE BOX ONLY)

Speed ☐	Convenience ☐
Comfort ☐	Reliability ☐
Cost ☐	Other ☐

Q18 Why did you choose to travel **on the Gatwick Express** rather than any other train service between London and Gatwick Airport? (YOU MAY TICK MORE THAN ONE BOX)

Speed ☐	Convenience ☐
Comfort ☐	Reliability ☐
Frequency ☐	Cost ☐
Always a train ready to join ☐	
Didn't know about other train service ☐	
Other ☐	

Q19 What is your age?

Under 14 ☐	14-17 ☐
18-24 ☐	25-34 ☐
35-44 ☐	45-54 ☐
55-64 ☐	65 or over ☐

Q20 Are you male or female?

Male ☐	Female ☐

Q21 Do you have any other comments to make about the Gatwick Express service?

☐

THANK YOU FOR YOUR COOPERATION, PLEASE HAND THIS QUESTIONNAIRE TO THE INTERVIEWER WHEN THEY RETURN OR LEAVE IT ON YOUR SEAT WHEN YOU LEAVE THE TRAIN.
MERCI DE VOTRE COOPERATION, VEUILLEZ REMETTRE CE QUESTIONNAIRE A L'ENQUETEUR A SON RETOUR OU LE LAISSER SUR VOTRE SIEGE AVANT DE SORTIR DU TRAIN.
WIR DANKEN IHNEN FÜR IHRE FREUNDLICHE HILFE. BITTE HÄNDIGEN SIE DIESEN FRAGEBOGEN AN DEN INTERVIEWER ZURÜCK, WENN DIESE/R ZU IHREM ABTEIL ZURÜCKKEHRT ODER LASSEN SIE IHN AUF DEM SITZ LIEGEN, WENN SIE SIE DEN ZUG VERLASSEN.

sound and video clips. Kiosks have been used successfully at trade shows and conventions and are now being tested in retail environments, where they have many applications. From a research standpoint, kiosk-based interviewing can be used in place of exit interviews to capture data on recent experiences. Kiosks have other definite advantages: This form of interviewing tends to be less expensive, people tend to give more honest answers than they would to a human interviewer, and internal control is higher because the survey is preprogrammed.[11]

Mail Surveys

Two general types of mail surveys are used in marketing research: ad hoc mail surveys and mail panels. In **ad hoc mail surveys** (sometimes called *one-shot mail surveys*), the researcher selects a sample of names and addresses from an appropriate source and mails

> **ad hoc mail surveys**
> Questionnaires sent to selected names and addresses without prior contact by the researcher; sometimes called *one-shot mail surveys*.

> **mail panels**
> Precontacted and prescreened participants who are periodically sent questionnaires.

questionnaires to the people selected. Ordinarily, there is no prior contact, and the sample is used only for a single project. However, the same questionnaire may be sent to nonrespondents several times to increase the overall response rate. In contrast, **mail panels** operate in the following manner:

1. A sample group is precontacted by letter. In this initial contact, the purpose of the panel is explained, and people are usually offered a gratuity.

2. As part of the initial contact, consumers are asked to fill out a background questionnaire on the number of family members, their ages, education level, income, types of pets, types of vehicles and ages, types of appliances, and so forth.

3. After the initial contact, panel participants are sent questionnaires from time to time. The background data collected on initial contact enable researchers to send questionnaires only to appropriate households. For example, a survey about dog food usage and preferences would be sent only to dog owners.

> **longitudinal study**
> Study in which the same respondents are resampled over time.

A mail panel is a type of longitudinal study. A **longitudinal study** is one that questions the same respondents at different points in time. Several companies, including Market Facts, NPD Research, and National Family Opinion Research, operate large (more than 100,000 households) consumer mail panels.[12]

On first consideration, mail appears to be an attractive way to collect survey data. There are no interviewers to recruit, train, monitor, and pay. The entire study can be sent out and administered from a single location. Hard-to-reach respondents can be readily surveyed. Mail surveys appear to be convenient, efficient, and inexpensive.

Like self-administered questionnaires, mail surveys of both types encounter the problems associated with not having an interviewer present. In particular, no one is there to probe responses to open-ended questions, a real constraint on the types of information that can be sought. The number of questions—and, consequently, the quantity of obtainable information—is usually more limited in mail surveys than in surveys involving interviewers.

Ad hoc mail surveys suffer from a high rate of nonresponse and attendant systematic error. Nonresponse in mail surveys is not a problem as long as everyone has an

EXHIBIT 6.4	Tactics Employed to Increase Mail Survey Response Rates

☐ Advance postcard or telephone call alerting respondent to survey
☐ Follow-up postcard or phone call
☐ Monetary incentives (half-dollar, dollar)
☐ Premiums (pencil, pen, keychain, etc.)
☐ Postage stamps rather than metered envelopes
☐ Self-addressed, stamped return envelope
☐ Personalized address and well-written cover letter
☐ Promise of contribution to favorite charity
☐ Entry into drawings for prizes
☐ Emotional appeals
☐ Affiliation with universities or research institutions
☐ Personally signed cover letter
☐ Multiple mailings of the questionnaire
☐ Reminder that respondent participated in previous studies (for mail panel participants)

equal probability of not responding. However, numerous studies have shown that certain types of people—such as those with more education, those with high-level occupations, women, those less interested in the topic, and students—have a greater probability of not responding than other types.[15] Response rates in ad hoc mail surveys may run anywhere from less than 5 percent to more than 50 percent, depending on the length of the questionnaire, its content, the group surveyed, the incentives employed, and other factors.[16] Those who operate mail panels claim response rates in the vicinity of 70 percent.

Many strategies designed to enhance response rates have been developed. Some of the more common ones are summarized in Exhibit 6.4. The question must always be, "Is the cost of the particular strategy worth the increased response rate generated?" Unfortunately, there is no clear answer to this question that can be applied to all procedures in all situations.

Even with its shortcomings, mail surveying remains a popular data collection technique in commercial marketing research. In fact, more people participate in mail surveys than in any other type of traditional survey research.

Non-Internet survey alternatives discussed in this section are summarized in Exhibit 6.5.

EXHIBIT 6.5	Non-Internet Forms of Survey Research
Type of Interview	**Description**
Door-to-door interviews	Interviews are conducted in respondents' homes (rarely used today in the United States).
Executive interviews	Interviews of industrial product users (e.g., engineers, architects, doctors, executives) or decision makers are conducted at their place of business.
Mall-intercept interviews	Interviews with consumers are conducted in a shopping mall or other high-traffic location. Interviews may be done in a public area of the mall, or respondents may be taken to a private test area.
Central-location telephone interviews	Interviews are conducted from a telephone facility set up for that purpose. These facilities typically have equipment that permits supervisors to unobtrusively monitor the interviewing while it is taking place. Many of these facilities do national sampling from a single location. An increasing number have computer-assisted interviewing capabilities. At these locations, the interviewer sits in front of a computer terminal with a personal computer. The questionnaire is programmed into the computer, and the interviewer uses the keyboard to directly enter responses.
Self-administered questionnaires	Self-administered questionnaires are most frequently employed at high-traffic locations such as shopping malls or in captive audience situations such as classrooms and airplanes. Respondents are given general information on how to fill out the questionnaire and expected to fill it out on their own. Kiosk-based point-of-service touch screens provide a way to capture information from individuals in stores, health clinics, and other shopping or service environments.
Ad hoc (one-shot) mail surveys	Questionnaires are mailed to a sample of consumers or industrial users, without prior contact by the researcher. Instructions are included; respondents are asked to fill out the questionnaire and return it via mail. Sometimes a gift or monetary incentive is provided.
Mail panels	Questionnaires are mailed to a sample of individuals who have been precontacted. The panel concept has been explained to them, and they have agreed to participate for some period of time, in exchange for gratuities. Mail panels typically generate much higher response rates than do ad hoc mail surveys.

Survey Research on the Internet

The Internet has forever changed the way we conduct survey research. As noted earlier, a vast majority of all U.S. research firms (88 percent) are now conducting online research.[13]

In the United States, the online population is now closely tracking the U.S. population in most key demographic areas. In 2005, over 164 million Americans logged on each month to shop, e-mail, find information, visit in chat rooms, and so forth.[14] These Web users mirrored the United States except in the following areas: households earning over $200,000 annually, persons over 65 years old, and those with less than a high school education. In each case, this group was underrepresented online as compared with the total U.S. population.[15]

Moreover, the number of Internet users around the world continues to explode, as shown in Exhibit 6.6. As the number of users grows worldwide, characteristics of a country's population and Internet user characteristics tend to meld. The reason for the phenomenal growth of online research is straightforward. The advantages far outweigh the disadvantages.

Advantages of Online Surveys

Most companies today face shorter product life cycles, increased competition, and a rapidly changing business environment. Management decision makers are having to make complex, rapid-fire decisions, and Internet research can help by providing timely information. The specific advantages of online surveys include the following[16]:

☐ *Rapid deployment, real-time reporting.* Online surveys can be broadcast to thousands of potential respondents simultaneously. Respondents complete surveys, and the results are tabulated and posted for corporate clients to view as the returns arrive. Thus, Internet survey results can be in the decision maker's hands in significantly less time than traditional survey results.

☐ *Reduced costs.* The use of electronic survey methods can cut costs by 25 to 40 percent and provide results in half the time it takes to do traditional telephone surveys. Data collection costs account for a large proportion of any traditional marketing research budget. Telephone surveys are labor-intensive efforts incurring training, telecommunications, and management costs. Online surveys eliminate these costs

EXHIBIT 6.6	**Internet Users Worldwide, by Region, 2003–2007 (in millions)**	
Area	**803.4** Total Population Online **2003**	**1.353.7** Total Population Online **2007**
North America	192.8	247.3
Western Europe	177.0	265.5
Eastern Europe	46.6	94.6
Asia Pacific	303.0	562.8
Central/S. America	51.8	100.9
Middle East/Africa	32.1	82.6

almost completely. Although the costs of traditional survey techniques rise in proportion to the number of interviews desired, electronic solicitations can grow in volume with less increase in project costs.

☐ *Ready personalization.* Internet surveys can be highly personalized for greater relevance to each respondent's own situation, thus speeding up the response process. Respondents appreciate being asked only pertinent questions, being able to pause and then resume the survey as needed, and having the ability to see previous responses and correct inconsistencies.

☐ *High response rates.* Busy respondents may be growing increasingly intolerant of "snail mail" or telephone-based surveys. Online surveys take less time to complete than phone interviews do, can be accomplished at the respondent's convenience (after work hours), and are much more stimulating and engaging. Graphics, interactivity, links to incentive sites, and real-time summary reports make the interview more enjoyable. The result: much higher response rates.

☐ *Ability to contact the hard-to-reach.* Certain groups are among the most difficult to reach (doctors, high-income professionals, CIOs in Global 2000 firms). Many of these groups are well represented online. Internet surveys provide convenient anytime/anywhere access that makes it easy for busy professionals to participate.

☐ *Simplified and enhanced panel management.* Internet panels are electronic communities, linked via the Internet, that are committed to providing feedback and counsel to research firms and their clients. They may be large or small, syndicated or proprietary, and they may consist of customers, potential customers, partners, or employees. Internet panels can be built and maintained at less cost and time required for traditional panels. Once a panel is created and a questionnaire is finalized, surveys can be deployed, data are collected, and top-level results are reported within days.

   A sophisticated database tracks panelist profile data and survey responses, facilitating longitudinal studies and data mining to yield insights into attitudes and behaviors over time and across segments. Response rates are high, typically 20 to 60 percent, because respondents have agreed in advance to participate in the survey. These participants tend to provide more detailed and thoughtful answers than do those in traditional surveys, because they don't have to provide demographic and lifestyle information (it's already been captured) and because they become engaged in the panel community over time.

☐ *External Internet Panels Simplify Life for Research Suppliers.* The availability of huge Internet panels maintained by firms such as Harris Interactive, SSI, Greenfield Online, and Decision Analysts makes the sampling process much easier for research companies that utilize these panels. We will discuss these panels in detail later in the chapter. Moreover, the cost to use the panels has dropped as the number of panel suppliers has increased.

Disadvantages of Online Surveys

The most common complaint about the use of online surveys has been that Internet users are not representative of the population as a whole. One retort, of course, is that most managers aren't interested in the population as a whole. Over 55 percent of the U.S. population now uses the Internet at home, work, school, or other locations.

   Dennis Gonier, president of Digital Marketing Services (DMS), a subsidiary of America Online (AOL), made a comparison of U.S. Census data, AOL users, and the demographics of Opinion Place, an opt-in survey research site on AOL managed by DMS. AOL's profile is not that different from that of the U.S. Census. And Opinion Place is close and getting closer to both of them. More importantly, when DMS made an extensive comparability study between Opinion Place results and the same survey administered by mall-intercept or telephone interviews, the comparability study documented a consistent business direction finding.[17] In other words, the same business strategies were developed using data from mall-intercept and telephone surveys as using data from the Opinion Place. Similarly, Harris Interactive and DSS Research have conducted over 300 surveys using parallel modes (telephone and Internet) and found that the research produced similar results. In all of the studies, it was rare to find a statistically significant difference between the sampling modes.[18] DSS concluded that the Internet panel methodology offered the best alternative for market share measurement and competitive benchmarking objectives based on cost (half the cost of telephone), speed (can be completed in less than half the time of telephone), and accuracy of measurement.

Lee Smith, COO of Insight Express, conducted a side-by-side comparison of online research and mail surveys. He found that online research delivered data of the same quality as using mail surveys in one-eighth the time and at one-eighth the cost.[19] Other research has shown that in most countries where the Internet penetration rate exceeds 20 percent, online surveys tend to yield similar results to those found in traditional methods such as telephone or paper-and-pencil survey research.[20]

Raymond Pettit, president of ERP Associates, and Robert Monster, CEO of Global Market Insite, discuss how the Internet is helping globalize marketing research in the Global Research box.

A second complaint is security on the Internet. Users today are quite understandably worried about privacy issues. This fear has been fueled by sensational media accounts of cyberstalkers and con artists who prey on Internet users. A solution to the security issue already exists in the form of **SSL (secure socket layer) technology**. Most responsible organizations collecting sensitive information over the Internet use this technology. The major problem is that consumers do not understand that this type of 128-bit encryption provides an extremely high level of security for all their sensitive information. It is up to the industry to communicate this fact to potential users.

A third problem exists when an **unrestricted Internet sample** is set up on the Internet. This means anyone who wishes to complete the questionnaire can do so. It is fully self-selecting and probably representative of no one except Web surfers. The problem gets worse if the same Internet user can access the questionnaire over and over. For example, the first time *InfoWorld*, a computer user magazine, conducted its Readers' Choice survey on the Internet, the results were so skewed by repeat voting for one product that the entire survey was publicly abandoned and the editor had to ask for readers' help to avoid the problem again. All responsible organizations conducting surveys over the Internet easily guard against this problem by providing unique passwords to those individuals they invite to participate. These passwords permit one-time access to the survey.

A fourth problem is that the sample frame needed may not be available on the Internet. Assume that Guido's, a popular Italian restaurant in Dayton, Ohio, wanted to know how its customers perceived the food quality and service compared with that of the big chains, such as Olive Garden. A large Internet panel, such as Greenfield Online, is probably not going to have enough members in Dayton, Ohio, that patronize Guido's to give a representative sample. If Guido's doesn't have customer e-mail addresses, then an Internet sample isn't feasible.

Other problems include a lack of "callback" procedures to clarify open-end responses, potential for questionnaire programming errors, and a lack of bandwidth (some potential respondents can't complete the survey or download photos and video quickly). Some companies may view Internet research as fast and simple, and software to conduct basic surveys is readily available. However, some research companies don't have the technical expertise to conduct survey research properly.

SSL (secure socket layer) technology
Computer encryption system that secures sensitive information.

unrestricted Internet sample
Self-selected sample group consisting of anyone who wishes to complete an Internet survey.

GLOBAL RESEARCH

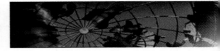

Globalization of Business Has Put New Demands on the Marketing Research Industry

The globalization of business is redefining what a client wants and expects from market research efforts. Challenges notwithstanding, at a fundamental level, global clients want:

- To be able to compare results between countries using consistent methods and assumptions
- To achieve enterprisewide understanding of geographically dispersed consumers
- To develop work processes that enable faster global innovation

The evolution of the market research industry, as driven by internal and external forces, continues to be played out on an emerging global landscape. Based on today's unique convergence of trends and pressures, it is possible to fast-forward to a market research industry that displays the following characteristics:

- Internet-based market research will be the standard for managing and deploying quantitative multicountry consumer research.
- The analysis of multicountry results will be conducted via Web-based applications rather than desktop PCs.
- Consumer research data will be closely integrated into global enterprise computing systems.
- Large portions of custom, omnibus, and tracking research, perhaps the majority, will be conducted using managed panels.

To illustrate the transformation in the architecture made possible by the Internet, consider the comparative case study shown in the accompanying chart of a global market research firm conducting a 10-country study requiring 1,000 fifteen-minute quantitative interviews in each country. The online research, with or without a panel, is significantly cheaper and faster.[21]

	CATI	Online with Lists	Online with Panel
Research Design			
Data collection	CATI from 6 call centers in 4 countries	Online self-administered interview	Online/Self-administered interview
Sampling method	RDD list	Purchased list of nonprofiled respondents	Profiled panel
Notification method	Telephone	Bulk email	Targeted e-mail
Incentive	None	Sweepstakes	Points program
Productivity			
Cooperation rate	24%	3%	50%
Percent of respondents eligible	30%	30%	95%
Required number of respondent contacts	138,889	1,111,111	17,544
Person-hours elapsed including call center and customer service	11,574	60	10
Data processing hours	170	10	5

	CATI	Online with Lists	Online with Panel
Budget[a]			
Data collection	$173,611	$35,000	$14,947
Data processing	$10,200	$600	$300
Telecom/IT costs	$34,722	$1,500	$600
Prerecruitment list	$4,166	$33,333	$15,790
Timeline			
Top-line results	8–10 weeks	2–5 days	2–4 days
Clean data	9–12 weeks	3–7 days	3–5 days
Respondent incentives	Negligible	$15,000	$67,544
Total research cost	$222,699	$85,433	$99,181
Methodology risk			
Representativeness	Low risk	Medium/High risk	Low risk
Interviewer bias	Moderate risk	None	None

[a]Data collection costs only. Analysis excludes project management and translation costs that are assumed to be roughly equivalent in each example.

Methods of Conducting Online Surveys

There are several basic methods for conducting online surveys: Web survey systems, survey design Web sites, and Web hosting. Each of these methods is briefly discussed.

Web Survey Systems Web survey systems are software systems specifically designed for Web questionnaire construction and delivery. They consist of an integrated questionnaire designer, Web server, database, and data delivery program, designed for use by nonprogrammers.

In a typical use, the questionnaire is constructed with an easy-to-use edit feature, using a visual interface, and then automatically transmitted to the Web server system. The Web server distributes the questionnaire and files responses in a database. The user can query the server at any time via the Web for completion statistics, descriptive statistics on responses, and graphical displays of data. Several popular online survey research software packages are SPSS Quanquest, Inquisite, Sawtooth CiW, Web Survent, Infopoll, SurveyMonkey, and SurveyPro.

Survey Design and Web Hosting Sites Several Web sites allow the researcher to design a survey online without loading design software. The survey is then administered on the design site's server. Some offer tabulation and analysis packages as well. Two popular sites that offer Web hosting are WebSurveyor and Perseus. Several of the other firms mentioned in the previous paragraph also offer Web hosting.

Internet Samples

Developing a good questionnaire is only half the battle in conducting online surveys. The researcher must also find respondents. We have already discussed unrestricted samples as a disadvantage of conducting surveys online.

Screened Internet Samples In **screened Internet samples**, the researcher adjusts for the unrepresentativeness of the self-selected respondents by imposing quotas based on some desired sample characteristics. These are often demographic characteristics,

> **screened Internet sample** Selected sample group in which quotas are imposed, based on some desired sample characteristics.

such as gender, income, or geographic region, or product-related criteria, such as past purchase behavior, job responsibilities, or current product use. The applications for screened samples are generally similar to those for unrestricted samples.

Screened sample questionnaires typically use a branching, or skip, pattern for asking screening questions to determine whether or not the full questionnaire should be presented to the respondent. Some Web survey systems can make immediate market segment calculations that assign a respondent to a particular segment based on screening questions, then select the appropriate questionnaire to match the respondent's segment.

Alternatively, some Internet research providers maintain Internet panels that recruit respondents, who fill out a preliminary classification questionnaire. This information is used to classify respondents into demographic segments. Clients specify the desired segments, and the respondents who match the desired demographics are permitted to fill out the questionnaires of all clients who specify that segment.

Recruited Internet Samples

Recruited Internet samples are used in surveys that require more control over the makeup of the sample. Recruited samples are ideal for applications in which there is already a database from which to recruit the sample. For example, a good application would be a survey that used a customer database to recruit respondents for a purchaser satisfaction study. So, Jeep might use its database of new Jeep purchasers to measure satisfaction with Jeep's service and warranty.

> **recruited Internet sample**
> Sample group recruited to ensure representativeness of a target population.

Respondents are recruited by telephone, mail, e-mail, or in person. After qualification, they are sent the questionnaire by e-mail or are directed to a Web site that contains a link to the questionnaire. At Web sites, passwords are normally used to restrict access to the questionnaire to only recruited sample members. Since the makeup of the sample is known, completions can be monitored, and, to improve the participation rate, follow-up messages can be sent to those who have not completed the questionnaire.

Sources of recruited Internet samples include recruited panels, opt-in list rentals, customer databases, opt-in panels, numerous Web-based incentive marketing programs (see Chapter 4), random intercepts of Web site visitors, and Web sites that have collected personal information about their visitors. The advantages and disadvantages of each are discussed below.

Recruited Panels. By far, the most popular form of Internet sampling is using a recruited panel. In the early days of Internet recruiting, panels were created by means of Web-based advertising, or posting, that offered compensation for participation in online studies. This method allowed research firms to build large pools of individuals who were available to respond quickly to the demands of online marketing research. Internet panels have grown rapidly and now account for over 40 percent of all custom research sampling in the United States.[22]

These specially constructed panels had certain drawbacks. There are expenses associated with advertising to recruit the panel and then collecting, storing, and updating the associated data. To keep the panel members satisfied, research firms must provide them with a certain number of studies, or else they are likely to drop out of the program. Many panels experienced rapid growth but also massive churn rates, as unmotivated prospective respondents moved on to other panels for compensation or changed e-mail addresses.

Research firms discovered that, to prevent panel members from becoming oversensitized, it was important to limit the number or frequency of studies, even if it resulted in higher attrition. Using contests with cash awards or prizes instead of paying for a completed study helped establish a fixed incentive cost for a study. However, it also reduced the number of people willing to participate, as respondents no longer received instant gratification for time invested. Therefore, some panels offer a cash payment.

Renting Internet Panels Very few marketing research companies build their own Internet panels because of the huge expense involved. Instead they rent a sample from an established panel provider. The largest and oldest sample provider in the nation is Survey Sampling, Inc. (SSI). SSI only provides samples; it does not conduct marketing research surveys. Therefore, it doesn't compete with marketing research firms. As with its other (non-Internet) panels, Survey Sampling offers subsets of its main panel, which is balanced demographically. In other words, its panel looks exactly like the U.S. population in terms of demographics, based on the 2000 U.S. Census. SSI purchased a European sampling company, Bloomerce, in 2005.

SSI Internet panels can target lifestyles, topics of interest, and demographics. Its three main offerings are: SurveySpot panel, eLITe, and Global eSamples Panel Management.

SurveySpot Panel SSI's Internet panel of respondents delivers high response rates and allows selection of members based on Census demographics. The SurveySpot panel is continuously growing and is updated weekly with over 5 million members. Panelists are also offered rewards with each survey invitation, increasing their likelihood of participation (see Exhibit 6.7).

Exhibit 6.7

SurveySpot Allows Precise Targeting

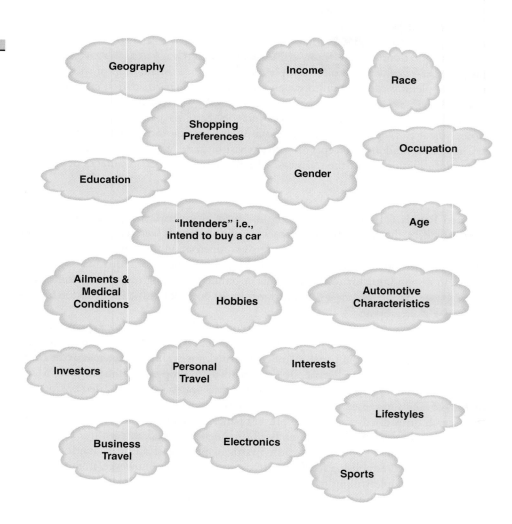

eLITe   SSI offers a large network of high-quality, low-incidence targeted e-mail addresses categorized by lifestyle—more than 3,500 topical lists and over 12 million names from which to choose.

Global eSamples   SSI/Bloomerce eSample offers access to a community of nearly 8 million household members, representing more than 3.2 million unique e-mail addresses worldwide. With a facility in Rotterdam, the Netherlands, SSI/Bloomerce understands the different European cultures.

Global eSamples can be targeted by a myriad of possible selection criteria, including, but not limited to, demographics such as age, presence of children, occupation, marital status, education level, Internet hours, and income. Global coverage is currently available in 30 countries.[23]

SSI Panel Management   Survey Sampling provided samples in 2005 for over 32 million completed interviews.[24] In order for samples to be drawn orderly and efficiently with the "right respondents," SSI must maintain excellent panel management. This means not oversurveying a given panel member, providing the necessary incentives to keep selected members motivated to respond, and removing inactive and/or unresponsive panel members (see Exhibit 6.8).

How DSS and SSI Work Together   Recall that one of your coauthors is president of DSS Research, one of the 30 largest research firms in America. DSS and SSI work together on many projects each year. The process is outlined in Exhibit 6.9. When DSS receives an RFP (Request for Proposal), it contacts SSI and builds into the research

Exhibit 6.8

How Survey Sampling Incorporated Monitors Inactive and Unresponsive Panel Members

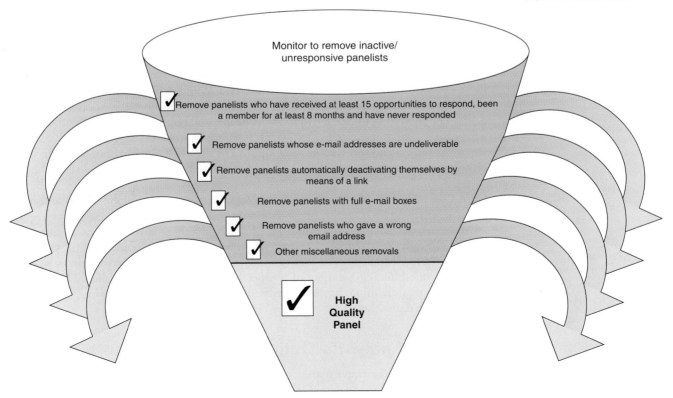

Monitor to remove inactive/
unresponsive panelists

✓ Remove panelists who have received at least 15 opportunities to respond, been a member for at least 8 months and have never responded

✓ Remove panelists whose e-mail addresses are undeliverable

✓ Remove panelists automatically deactivating themselves by means of a link

✓ Remove panelists with full e-mail boxes

✓ Remove panelists who gave a wrong email address

✓ Other miscellaneous removals

✓ **High Quality Panel**

DSS Research client has research need	DSS Research bids on project integrating panel sampling solution into proposal	DSS Research designs study, sets timeline, programs and hosts	SSI directs panelists, according to DSS's requirements, to DSS's website to take survey	DSS Research completes analysis and delivers to its client

Panel Allows Study Control

- Targeting respondents by personal characteristics, geography, etc.

- Scheduling initial invitations.

- Controlling access.

- Scheduling reminders.

Exhibit 6.9

Panel Research Process Flow

design a sampling plan from SSI. If DSS wins the bid, it designs the study, sets timelines, creates programs, and prepares to host the study on a DSS server. SSI then directs SurveySpot panel members to the DSS Web site to take the survey. DSS then completes the study and delivers it to the client.

Random Web Site Intercepts.   Another way to elicit research data from Internet users is the use of random intercept banners inviting Web site visitors to participate in surveys. These banners, which pop up in a preset random pattern, ask whether the visitor would like to participate in a short survey. A visitor who accepts is linked to a page where he or she fills out screening questions that can be used to identify and qualify potential respondents. The survey has to be short since most people will not be motivated to participate in a long survey without compensation. (One exception is when the individual feels strongly about the subject and wants to provide input.) For the most part, random Web site intercepts have not proven cost-effective and are rarely used by most professional researchers.

Data Capture of Visitors.   As company Web sites grow more sophisticated and more valuable, studying their visitors becomes increasingly important. These visitors can be organized and utilized to study a multitude of issues, including customer service, consumer needs, customer satisfaction, proposed site redesign and developments, and core customer concerns. Methods exist that can help a Web site better serve its visitors while at the same time building a variety of prospective panels for future studies. These panels will grow ever more important in contributing to companies' understanding of their customers in the digital age.

Decision Analyst's Online Household Panels

One of the most progressive marketing research firms in the development and use of online panels is Decision Analyst. Decision Analyst both rents its panels to other research firms and uses the panels for its own projects. Accordingly, we will use the company to illustrate online panel offerings. Decision Analyst was one of the first research firms to recognize the emerging potential of the Internet and began to convert its American Consumer Opinion mail panel into an Internet-based panel in early 1996. In rapid succession, Decision Analyst expanded its online consumer panel from domestic to international, and quickly followed with online business-to-business panels, as follows:[25]

American Consumer Opinion A global Internet panel of over 6 million members in over 150 different countries. Consumers can sign up to become a member in many different languages. Complete demographic profiles are maintained on each household, including family composition, income, gender, and ages of all household members.

Technology Advisory Board An Internet panel of over 100,000 information technology and information systems professionals, engineers, scientists, and other technology professionals. Personal and company profiles are maintained for each member. The Internet is an ideal way to reach these technology professionals, compared to the very costly and time-consuming alternative of telephone interviewing.

Executive Advisory Board An international online panel of over 100,000 managers, executives, and directors of companies large and small. Executives are very busy and difficult to reach by telephone, but with the Internet the busy executive can complete a survey whenever it's convenient, whether that's early in the morning or late at night. Information on the size of the company, type of industry, job function, and job title of the member is stored in the panel database.

Contract Advisory Boards An international online panel of general contractors, subcontractors, architects, engineers, and executives from all segments of the building and construction industry, including remodeling, retrofit, and new construction in residential, commercial, and industrial markets. The panel database includes information about each member's industry, company size, job function, and age.

Physicians Advisory Council An Internet panel of over 25,000 physicians and surgeons in the United States and western Europe, including both general practitioners and specialists. The Internet panel is ideal for doctors because they can respond to surveys whenever they have the time. Background data on each doctor and his or her practice are kept in the panel database.

Medical Advisory Board An online panel of over 30,000 nurses, dentists, pharmacists, dieticians, and other nonphysician medical workers, located primarily in the United States.

Decision Analyst uses these online panels as a strategic platform to provide proprietary research services to its clients:

☐ **CopyTrack** An advertising tracking system to monitor brand awareness, advertising awareness, message recall, trial, repeat purchase, and brand image through periodic online surveys. An advantage of the Internet, compared to telephone tracking, is that excerpts of ads can be shown to measure ad recognition.

☐ **CopyTest** An advertising pretesting system to determine the probable effectiveness of radio and television commercials and print advertisements. Commercials are video-streamed to respondents over the Internet, and panelists complete a questionnaire via the Internet to give feedback.

☐ **ConceptTest** An online concept testing system to gauge consumer reactions to new products. Concept boards are shown to panelists over the Internet, who then complete an online questionnaire to record their reactions. The results are fed into a mathematical model, along with inputs from the brand's marketing plan, to develop a volumetric sales forecast of the new product's retail sales during its initial year of introduction.

☐ **Optima** A product testing system. Respondents are screened and qualified over the Internet, and test products are shipped to the panel member to use in-home and provide feedback over the Internet. The results are fed into the **Pii** mathematical model to implicitly determine the product attributes that need to be modified to improve consumer acceptance of the product.

☐ **PromotionTest** An online promotion testing system. Promotion concepts and ads are shown to target respondents over the Internet, and consumer reactions to the promotion are recorded.

☐ **PackageTest** Proposed package graphic designs are shown to a sample of panelists over the Internet, and their responses are measured by a follow-up online survey.

☐ **NameScreen** An online system to screen up to 100 possible brand names to choose the best names for further evaluation. A multistage sorting process is used to simplify the consumer's decision process.

Creating Online Questionnaires

Questionnaire writing will be discussed in detail in Chapter 11. However, some issues unique to Internet questionnaires are more appropriately addressed here. The simplest way to create an Internet survey is to use a survey design Web site such as Perseus XP or Internet survey research software.

Surveys need to load quickly in order to achieve a good response. People won't wait; they'll move on to another Web site. Graphics increase the time required for a survey to load. Although it's tempting to make beautiful backgrounds, all those graphics can be a problem. What will the background and text look like on different browsers and at different font sizes? Whatever graphics are selected should look good and load quickly, no matter what kind of computer setup the respondent has.

"Our own reaction at the beginning was to design a fairly fancy questionnaire," says Bob Tortora, chief methodologist at The Gallup Organization. "You're much better off using a very plain questionnaire—something that looks like a mail questionnaire. When you start getting fancy, you start slowing down transmission times."[26]

The survey should be easy to respond to as well. It's a lot easier to click on a response than to type one in. The entry mechanism should be matched to the question—buttons or drop-down menus for a single response, check boxes for multiple answers. It's useful to include an option for "Other" responses, but few people will use it, so it should be considered supplemental, not part of the core response data.

Buttons are best when there are five or fewer answers to choose from; a drop-down menu is easier to use with more than five answers. For really lengthy lists with short identifiers, such as the 50 states, it's wise to allow respondents the option of typing in the two-letter abbreviation rather than forcing them to scroll through the list.

Researchers must be aware of any default answers (No Opinion, Don't Know, None of the Above). A common mistake among inexperienced Internet survey programmers is to unintentionally make the first response in a list the default answer; this can seriously skew the results. It isn't a problem if you use survey design software, as it avoids such errors automatically, but if you're doing the programming yourself, you'll need to check the default values when you're working on online surveys.

Interactive Marketing Research Organization

In 2001, a new organization called the **Interactive Marketing Research Organization (IMRO)** was formed. The first objective of IMRO is to be "a confederation of

> **Interactive Marketing Research Organization (IMRO)**
> Organization dedicated to the development, dissemination, and implementation of interactive marketing research concepts, practice, and information.

Why Isn't All Data Collection Moving to the Internet?

Elizabeth Anderson, Research Analyst, DSS Research

As discussed in the text, the Internet has proven to be an efficient and fast way to collect reliable data. The reliability and, to a lesser extent, the validity (which is harder to demonstrate) of the data produced by Internet surveys have been demonstrated in a number of studies.

Recently, we conducted a study involving 56,000 Internet surveys, and we completed it in about 10 days. The cost was approximately one-third of what it would have cost to do the survey by telephone, and it was completed in a fraction of the time a telephone study would have taken. Comparison of the results with previous waves of the same research conducted by telephone showed a high level of consistency and no apparent differences due to the change in mode of data collection.

So, given all these wonderful advantages, why don't we collect all our surveys by Internet? There are a number of reasons why this is not advisable or feasible:

- Generally, except in very special cases, the Internet does not work for customer satisfaction surveys because in the vast majority of instances clients do not have any e-mail addresses for customers; or, if they do, it is not a comprehensive list of customer e-mail addresses. This may change in the future, but it is not the case today and it will not be the case in the near future.

- The Internet does not work for many surveys of business decision makers, especially if we are looking at a narrow geography (i.e., metro area, region of a state with a smaller population). Yes, there are business-to-business panels out there, and they are often feasible for national studies of certain types of business decision makers. The problem comes when we are looking for individuals in organizations who make decisions to purchase certain specialized products or services. None of the panels has consistently accurate information on realms of decision making for different panelists. This means that we cannot specifically target them by e-mail invitation but must screen huge numbers of panelists to try to find them the old-fashioned way.

- Studies where you need to measure unaided awareness can be a problem. Questions such as "name all the makes and models of cars that you can think of" present problems because the list is likely to be long and requires a lot of typing by the respondent. In a telephone study, you would just name the cars and an interviewer would check them off of a list. In an Internet poll, however, it's unlikely a respondent will want to, or have the patience, to type out 40 to 50 different car makes and models, nor can you give them the list of cars because the goal is to check their unaided awareness and giving them the list directly aids them.

- Any study focusing on a narrow geography (smaller market or portion of a market) can be a problem because the Internet panel company you are using may not have enough panelists to produce the number of interviews you need.

- Low-incidence populations (e.g., people who have purchased MP3 players made by a certain manufacturer in the last two weeks) can also present a problem for Internet panels because they simply don't have enough people in their panel who meet the required qualifications. Combine low incidence with narrow geography and the problem is compounded. These types of studies can, of course, present problems for any interviewing method.

- Surveys with subpopulations, such as those over 65 years of age who are less likely to be Internet users, may be difficult to complete via Internet and may produce biased samples. These samples may be biased because those in the subpopulation who are online may be systematically different from those not online.

world leaders among firms involved in new technology marketing research, to lead in the development, dissemination, and implementation of interactive marketing research concepts, practice, and information."[27] Thirteen Internet marketing research suppliers, including Modalis Research Technologies, Greenfield Online, Market Facts, NPD Online, NFO Interactive, and Cyber Dialogue, along with eight client companies, including Dell Computer, IBM, Intel, and Time Warner, helped to found the organization.

IMRO's initial efforts focused on spam and the misuse of personal data. The organization hosts conferences, debates, and workshops and publishes a quarterly newsletter called *The Edge*. It also publishes the *Journal of Online Research* in conjunction with the Advertising Research Foundation.

Determination of the Survey Method

A number of factors may affect the choice of a survey method in a given situation. The researcher should choose the survey method that will provide data of the desired types, quality, and quantity at the lowest cost. The major considerations in the selection of a survey method are summarized in Exhibit 6.10.

Sampling Precision

The required level of sampling precision is an important factor in determining which survey method is appropriate in a given situation. Some projects by their very nature

EXHIBIT 6.10	Factors That Determine the Selection of a Particular Survey Method
Factor	**Comment**
Sampling precision	If the need for accuracy in the study results is not great, less rigorous and less expensive sampling procedures may be appropriate.
Budget	It is important to determine how much money is available for the survey portion of the study.
Need to expose respondent to various stimuli and have respondent perform specialized tasks	Taste tests and prototype usage tests usually require face-to-face contact. Card sorts, certain visual scaling methods, and the like require either face-to-face contact or the Internet.
Quality of data required	It is important to determine how accurate the results of the study need to be.
Length of questionnaire	Long questionnaires are difficult to do by mail, over the phone, or in a mall.
Incidence rate	Are you looking for people who make up 1 percent of the total population or 50 percent of the population? If you are looking for a needle in a haystack, you need an inexpensive way to find it. The Internet is probably the best source.
Degree of structure of questionnaire	Highly unstructured questionnaires may require data collection by personal interview.
Time available to complete survey	There may not be time to wait for responses via snail-mail. The Internet is the fastest way to go.

require a high level of sampling accuracy, whereas this may not be a critical consideration in other projects. If sampling accuracy were the only criterion, the appropriate data-collection technique would probably be central-location telephone interviewing, an online survey of a sample drawn from a huge Internet panel, or some other form of polling of a sample drawn from customer lists. The appropriate survey method for a project not requiring a high level of sampling accuracy might be the mail approach or some type of mall survey.

The trade-off between the central-location telephone survey, Internet panel, and the mail survey methods in regard to sampling precision is one of accuracy versus cost. A central-location telephone survey employing a random-digit dialing sampling procedure will probably produce a better sample than the mail survey method. However, the mail survey will most likely cost less. In some cases, Internet samples will provide both lower cost and greater accuracy.

Budget

The commercial marketing researcher frequently encounters situations in which the budget available for a study has a strong influence on the survey method used. For example, assume that for a particular study the budgetary constraint for interviewing is $10,000 and the sample size required for the necessary accuracy is 1,000. If the cost of administering the questionnaire using the mall-intercept method is $27.50 per interview and the cost of administering it via Internet survey is $.50 per interview, the choice is fairly clear—assuming that nothing about the survey absolutely requires face-to-face contact.

Taste tests are most often conducted in a controlled environment because of their unique requirements. Can you imagine conducting this type of research through a mail survey?

Requirements for Respondent Reactions

In some studies, the marketing researcher needs to get respondent reactions to various marketing stimuli—perhaps product prototype usage (a new style of PC keyboard) or a taste test. In these cases, the need to get respondent reactions to stimuli normally requires personal contact between interviewer and respondent.

Taste tests typically require food preparation. This preparation must be done under controlled conditions so that the researcher can be certain that each person interviewed is responding to the same stimulus. The only viable survey alternative for tests of this type is the mall-intercept approach or some variant. One variant, for example, is recruiting people to come to properly equipped central locations, such as community centers, to sample products and be interviewed.

Some surveys require face-to-face interviewing because of the need to use special measurement techniques or obtain specialized forms of information. The tasks are so complex that the interviewer must be available to explain the tasks and ascertain whether the respondents understand what is required of them.

Quality of Data

The quality of data required is an important determinant of the survey method. Data quality is measured in terms of validity and reliability. (These two concepts are discussed in detail in Chapter 9.) *Validity* refers to the degree to which a measure reflects the characteristic of interest. In other words, a valid measure provides an accurate reading of whatever the researcher is trying to measure. *Reliability* refers to the consistency with which a measure produces the same results with the same or comparable populations.

Many factors beyond the interviewing method affect data quality. Sampling methods, questionnaire design, specific scaling methods, and interviewer training are a few of them. However, each of the various interviewing methods has certain inherent strengths and weaknesses in terms of data quality. These strengths and weaknesses are summarized in Exhibit 6.11.

The important point here is that the issue of data quality may override other considerations such as cost. For example, although the least expensive way to get responses to a long questionnaire with many open-ended questions might be via a mall-intercept interview, the data obtained by this method might be so biased—because of respondent fatigue, distraction, and carelessness—that the results would be worthless at best and misleading at worst.

Length of the Questionnaire

The length of the questionnaire—the amount of time it takes the average respondent to complete the survey—is an important determinant of the appropriate survey method to use. If the questionnaire for a particular study takes an hour to complete, the choices of survey method are extremely limited. Telephone, mall-intercept, and most other types of surveys, with the exception of personal interviews, will not work. People shopping at a

EXHIBIT 6.11	Strengths and Weaknesses of Selected Data-Collection Methods in Terms of Quality of Data Produced	
Method	**Strengths**	**Weaknesses**
Mall-intercept interview	Interviewer can show, explain, and probe.	Many distractions are inherent in the mall environment; respondent may be in a hurry, not in proper frame of mind to answer survey questions; there is more chance for interviewer bias; nonprobability sampling problems arise.
Central-location telephone interview	Supervisor can monitor the interviewing process easily; excellent samples can be obtained; interviewer can explain and probe.	Respondent may be distracted by things going on at their location; problems arise in long interviews and interviews with many open-ended questions. Many refuse to participate.
Self-administered questionnaire	Interviewer and associated biases are eliminated; respondent can complete the questionnaire when convenient; respondent can look up information and work at own pace.	There is no interviewer to show, explain, or probe; sample may be poor because of nonresponse; who actually completes the questionnaire cannot be controlled.
Mail survey	Same strengths as for self-administered method.	Same weaknesses as for self-administered questionnaire; sample quality is better with mail panel.
Online survey	Administration is inexpensive; data can be gathered quickly; questions can be readily personalized; response rates are high, especially for the hard-to-reach; renting a panel can save time and money and reach narrow market segments.	Users may not be representative of whole population; privacy concerns may arise; in poorly managed panels, some respondents are over surveyed. Internet won't work for narrowly defined populations without email addresses (e.g. patrons of Joe's Hamburgers in Winslow, Arizona).

mall ordinarily do not have an hour to spend being interviewed. Terminations increase and tempers flare when interviewers must try to keep respondents on the phone for an hour. Response rates plummet when people receive through the mail questionnaires that take an hour or more to complete. The trick is to match the survey technique to the length of the questionnaire.

SurveySpot, SSI's huge Internet panel, asked its panel members what was the ideal survey length. The responses were as follows:[28]

☐	Less than 2 minutes	2%
☐	2 to 5 minutes	21%
☐	6 to 10 minutes	44%
☐	11 to 15 minutes	21%
☐	16 to 25 minutes	3%
☐	26 minutes or more	0%
☐	no ideal length	8%
☐	Not sure	1%

Incidence Rate

Recall that the incidence rate refers to the percentage of people, households, or businesses in the general population that would qualify as interviewees in a particular study. Search costs, which correlate with the time spent trying to locate qualified respondents, sometimes exceed the costs of interviewing. In situations where the researcher expects incidence rates to be low and search costs high, it is important to select the method or combination of methods that will provide the desired survey results at a reasonable cost.

Doing a low-incidence rate study in a mall would be very expensive. This approach should be taken only if there is some compelling reason for doing so—a long in-depth interview, for example. The lowest-cost survey alternative for the low-incidence study is probably the Internet panel, assuming that this approach meets the other data collection requirements of the study. One advantage of the Internet panel is that it can be pre-screened; people can be asked a number of questions, usually including some on product usage. For example, if panel members were asked during prescreening whether anyone in their household participated in downhill or alpine skiing, the Internet panel operator could—at very low cost—pull out only those households with one or more skiers for a survey of Alpine skiers.

Structure of the Questionnaire

In addition to the length of the questionnaire, the degree of structure required in the questionnaire may be a factor in determining which survey method is most appropriate for a given study. *Structure* refers to the extent to which the questionnaire follows a set sequence or order, has a predetermined wording of questions, and relies on closed-ended (multiple-choice) questions. A questionnaire that does all these things would be structured; one that deviates from these set patterns would be considered unstructured. A questionnaire with little structure is likely to require a face-to-face interview. Very brief, highly structured questionnaires do not require face-to-face contact between interviewer and respondent. Mail, telephone, self-administered, and online surveys are viable options for studies of this type.

Time Available to Complete the Survey

If the client needs to have survey results quickly, the Internet is the best choice. Generally, central-location telephone and mall-intercept interviews can also be completed in a timely manner.

Marketing Research Interviewer

No discussion of survey research in marketing would be complete without considering the person who actually does the interviewing. As noted in Chapter 2, most marketing research in-person interviewing is still done under the direct supervision of field service firms. The actual interviewing is conducted, to a large extent, by individuals who work part-time for relatively low wages. A new, totally inexperienced interviewer works at a rate somewhere between minimum wage and minimum wage plus 20 percent. It is unusual to find even the most experienced interviewers earning more than minimum wage plus 50 percent. The pay is not good, and fringe benefits are minimal. Ordinarily, an interviewer's involvement with an interviewing assignment begins when he or she is asked by a supervisor at a field service firm to work on a particular job. If the interviewer accepts the assignment, he or she will be given a date and time for a briefing about the job. At the briefing, the questionnaire for the study and all deadlines and requirements for the job are discussed.

Interviewers are typically the main interface with consumers and are, therefore, a vital link to consumer cooperation. Their skill level and pay level are areas of concern now being addressed by the Marketing Research Association, which has several suggestions for developing and strengthening interviewers' consumer interaction skills: good training programs that cover ways to establish consumer rapport and a basic understanding of "cooperation turning points," frequent monitoring of interviewers' interaction skills to evaluate their impact on consumer cooperation, and feedback to interviewers on monitoring results.

SUMMARY

Surveys are popular for several reasons. First, managers need to know why people do or do not do something. Second, managers need to know how decisions are made. Third, managers need to know what kind of person, from a demographic or lifestyle perspective, is making the decision to buy or not to buy a product.

There are two major categories of errors in survey research: random error and systematic error, or bias. Systematic error can be further broken down into measurement error and sample design error. Types of sample design error include selection, population specification, and frame errors. Frame error results from the use of an incomplete or inaccurate sampling frame. Population specification error results from an incorrect definition of the universe or population from which the sample is to be selected. Selection error results from adopting incomplete or improper sampling procedures or not properly following appropriate selection procedures.

The second major category of systematic error is measurement error. Measurement error occurs when there is a discrepancy between the information being sought (true value) and the information actually obtained by the measurement process. Measurement error can be created by a number of factors, including surrogate information error, interviewer error, measurement instrument bias, processing error, nonresponse bias, and response bias. Surrogate information error results from a discrepancy between the information actually required to solve a problem and the information sought by the researcher. Interviewer error occurs when an interviewer influences a respondent to give untrue or inaccurate answers. Measurement instrument bias is caused by problems within the questionnaire itself. Processing error results from mistakes in the transfer of information from survey documents to the computer. Nonresponse bias occurs when a particular individual in a sample cannot be reached or refuses to participate in the survey. Response bias arises when interviewees tend to answer questions in a particular way, whether out of deliberate falsification or unconscious misrepresentation.

There are several types of traditional surveys. Mall-intercept interviews are conducted with shoppers in public areas of shopping malls, either by interviewing them in the mall or by asking them to come to a permanent interviewing facility within the mall. Executive interviews are the industrial equivalent of door-to-door interviews; they involve interviewing professional people at their offices, typically concerning industrial products or services. Central-location telephone interviews are conducted from a facility set up for the specific purpose of doing telephone survey research. Computer-assisted telephone interviewing (CATI) is a form of central-location interviewing. Each interviewer is seated in front of a computer terminal or personal computer. The computer guides the interviewer and the interviewing process by exhibiting appropriate questions on the computer screen. The data are entered into the computer as the interview takes place. A self-administered questionnaire is filled out by the respondent. The big disadvantage of this approach is that probes cannot be used to clarify responses. Mail surveys can be divided into ad hoc, or one-shot, surveys and mail panels. In ad hoc mail surveys, questionnaires are mailed to potential respondents without prior contact. The sample is used for only a single survey project. In a mail panel, consumers are precontacted by letter and are offered an incentive for participating in the panel for a period of time. If they agree, they fill out a background questionnaire. Then, periodically, panel participants are sent questionnaires.

The Internet is beginning to dominate survey research. Internet surveys offer rapid deployment and real-time reporting, dramatically reduced costs, ready personalization, high response rates, the ability to reach low-incidence respondents, simplified and enhanced panel management, and profitability for survey research firms. The disadvantages are the potential nonrepresentativeness of Internet users, privacy and security concerns, a lack of callback procedures to clarify open-end responses, bandwidth problems, and the sample frame needed may not be available on the Internet.

The types of Internet samples are unrestricted, screened, and recruited. Online surveys can be conducted through Web survey systems and survey design Web sites. Sources for Internet surveys are recruited panels, rented Internet panels, random Web site intercepts, and data capture of Web site visitors.

Creating online questionnaires requires special attention to the number and type of graphics. Long downloads cause respondents to terminate surveys. Whether and how to use "buttons," drop-down menus, and default answers must also be considered.

The factors that determine which survey method to use include the degree of sampling precision required, budget size, whether respondents need to react to various stimuli or to perform specialized tasks, the quality of data required, the length of the questionnaire, the degree of structure of the questionnaire, and the time available to complete the survey.

KEY TERMS & DEFINITIONS

random error, or **random sampling error** Error that results from chance variation.

chance variation Difference between the sample value and the true value of the population mean.

systematic error, or **bias** Error that results from problems or flaws in the execution of the research design; sometimes called non-sampling error.

sample design error Systematic error that results from an error in the sample design or sampling procedures.

sampling frame List of population elements or members from which units to be sampled are selected.

frame error Error resulting from an inaccurate or incomplete sampling frame.

population specification error Error that results from incorrectly defining the population or universe from which a sample is chosen.

selection error Error that results from incomplete or improper sample selection procedures or not following appropriate procedures.

measurement error Systematic error that results from a variation between the information being sought and what is actually obtained by the measurement process.

surrogate information error Error that results from a discrepancy between the information needed to solve a problem and that sought by the researcher.

interviewer error, or **interviewer bias** Error that results from the interviewer's influencing—consciously or unconsciously—the respondent.

measurement instrument bias Error that results from the design of the questionnaire or measurement instrument; also known as questionnaire bias.

processing error Error that results from the incorrect transfer of information from a survey document to a computer.

nonresponse bias Error that results from a systematic difference between those who do and those who do not respond to a measurement instrument.

refusal rate Percentage of persons contacted who refused to participate in a survey.

response bias Error that results from the tendency of people to answer a question incorrectly through either deliberate falsification or unconscious misrepresentation.

door-to-door interviews Interviews conducted face to face with consumers in their homes.

executive interviews Industrial equivalent of door-to-door interviewing.

mall-intercept interviews Interviews conducted by intercepting mall shoppers (or shoppers in other high-traffic locations) and interviewing them face to face.

central-location telephone interviews Interviews conducted by calling respondents from a centrally located marketing research facility.

computer-assisted telephone interviews (CATI) Central-location telephone interviews in which interviewers enter respondents' answers directly into a computer.

self-administered questionnaires Questionnaires filled out by respondents with no interviewer present.

ad hoc mail surveys Questionnaires sent to selected names and addresses without prior contact by the researcher; sometimes called one-shot mail surveys.

mail panels Precontacted and prescreened participants who are periodically sent questionnaires.

longitudinal study Study in which the same respondents are resampled over time.

SSL (secure socket layer) technology Computer encryption system that secures sensitive information.

unrestricted Internet sample Self-selected sample group consisting of anyone who wishes to complete an Internet survey.

screened Internet sample Self-selected sample group in which quotas are imposed, based on some desired sample characteristics.

recruited Internet sample Sample group recruited to ensure representativeness of a target population.

Interactive Marketing Research Organization (IMRO) Organization dedicated to the development, dissemination, and implementation of interactive marketing research concepts, practice, and information.

QUESTIONS FOR REVIEW & CRITICAL THINKING

1. The owner of a hardware store in Eureka, California, is interested in determining the demographic characteristics of people who shop at his store versus those of people who shop at competing stores. He also wants to know what his image is relative to the competition. He would like to have the information within 3 weeks and is working on a limited budget. Which survey method would you recommend? Why?

2. Discuss this statement: "A mall-intercept interview is representative only of people who shop in that particular mall. Therefore, only surveys that relate to shopping patterns of consumers within that mall should be conducted in a mall-intercept interview."

3. A colleague is arguing that the best way to conduct a study of attitudes toward city government in your community is through a mail survey because it is the cheapest method. How would you respond to your colleague? If time were not a critical factor in your decision, would your response change? Why?

4. Discuss the various types of sample design errors and give examples of each.

5. Why is it important to consider measurement error in survey research? Why is this typically not discussed in professional marketing research reports?

6. What types of error might be associated with the following situations?
   a. Conducting a survey about attitudes toward city government, using the telephone directory as a sample frame.
   b. Interviewing respondents only between 8:00 A.M. and 5:00 P.M. on features they would like to see in a new condominium development.
   c. Asking people if they have visited the public library in the past 2 months.
   d. Asking people how many tubes of toothpaste they used in the past year.
   e. Telling interviewers they can probe using any particular example they wish to make up.

7. What are the advantages and disadvantages of conducting surveys on the Internet?

8. Explain the types of Internet samples, and discuss why a researcher might choose one over the others.

Team Exercise

9. Divide the class into teams. Each team should go to a different opt-in survey site on the Web and participate in an online survey. A spokesperson for each team should report the results to the class.

10. What are various ways to obtain respondents for online surveys?

11. Describe the advantages and disadvantages of online surveys.

WORKING THE NET

1. Go to *http://www.perseusdevelopment.com* and explain how the company's software allows users to distribute questionnaires over the Internet.

2. Go to American Consumer Opinion's Web site at *http://www.acop.com*. Describe the type of Internet samples being drawn and the types of surveys being conducted.

3. Participate in a survey at one of the following URLs and report on your experience to the class:
   a. Type A Personality test:
      www.queendom.com
   b. IQ test:
      www.iqtest.com
   c. Values and Lifestyles (VALS) test:
      www.sric-bi.com
   d. Various online surveys on topics such as politics and consumer trends:
      http://www.survey.net
   e. Spending Personality Assessment:
      www.healthy.net/library/articles/cash/assessment/assessment.htm
   f. Miscellaneous surveys:
      http://www.dssresearch.com/mainsite/surveys.htm

REAL-LIFE RESEARCH • 6.1

Dairy Management Inc.

Dairy Management Inc. (DMI) is the domestic and international planning and management organization responsible for increasing demand for U.S.-produced dairy products on behalf of America's dairy farmers.* DMI and state and regional organizations manage the programs of the American Dairy Association, the National Dairy Council, and the U.S. Dairy Export Council. The mission of DMI is to increase demand for dairy prod-

*http://www.dairycheckoff.com

ucts through the development and execution of an industrywide, market-driven business plan that invests resources in a strategic manner and provides the best possible economic advantage to dairy farmers.

Since 1997, DMI's national dairy marketing efforts have specifically targeted kids (6 to 12 years of age) and their moms. Four elements comprised these marketing efforts. First, "got milk?" ads on kids' favorite TV shows depicted milk as hip, cool, and fun. Second, the dairy promotions in retail stores have included a joint promotion with Kellogg's cereals that aims to involve kids in milk purchasing decisions and increase white gallon milk sales. The promotion is prominently featured on several Kellogg's brand cereals, with in-store displays and other point-of-sale materials. Third, national, state, and regional dairy promotion organizations have aggressively implemented programs to improve kid's milk-drinking experiences in schools. Cafeteria promotions use fun, hip posters that promote milk's many great-tasting flavors. Fourth, milk publicity and special events have taken the theme of making the "Great Soda Swap." In this way, nutrient-deficient soft drinks would be replaced with fun, nutrient-rich flavored milks.

Now, DMI managers would like to evaluate some of the effects of these marketing efforts. They are considering buying syndicated research on beverage consumption produced by the National Family Opinion (NFO) WorldGroup research agency. The NFO SIP (Share of Intake Panel) is a special panel of U.S. consumers who record their consumption of beverages in a diary for 2 weeks at a time. Typically, 12,000 consumers participate in the NFO SIP panel each year. NFO SIP reveals both at-home and away-from-home beverage consumption (excluding tap water) by household members during any 2-week period. This database has more than 20 years of data gathered from more than 12,000 respondents a year including kids, teens, and adults.

Upon contacting NFO WorldGroup's SIP team, DMI managers discovered that 90 percent of all kids (ages 6 to 12) drank at least one serving of milk as a beverage during an average 2-week period and that kids consumed 28 gallons of milk annually per capita.

Questions

1. If you were working for the DMI research team, what questions would you want to ask the NFO WorldGroup team about its data and the methods used in collecting this data in deciding whether to purchase a complete report from NFO World Group or to purchase part of the database?

2. What are the advantages and disadvantages of mail panel research? What other survey methods could have been used to gather the information? Why do you think NFO chose a mail panel?

Paramount Parks Where the Theme Is Fun

Mark Kupferman has an unfair advantage over a lot of his fellow marketing researchers. Although others have to subject their respondents to attribute scales on laundry detergents or foot powders, he gets to ask people about roller coasters and water parks. Kupferman is corporate director of research for Paramount Parks, the theme-park division of entertainment giant Viacom. With annual revenues of $500 million, Paramount Parks owns and operates theme parks around the globe.

Paramount Parks has an online consumer panel and also conducts a host of other online and offline projects throughout the year to measure guest satisfaction with the parks' rides, dining, shopping, games, and shows. The main vehicle for much of the company's online surveying is Inquisite, a software package from the Austin, Texas-based firm of the same name.

Now boasting about 14,000 participants, the online panel (which debuted in 2003) is always welcoming new members. "We don't require someone to take a minimum number of surveys. Depending on the survey, 30 to 40 percent will complete whatever we send them within one or two days," Kupferman says.

Paramount Parks is able to draw prospective respondents from a database of about 500,000 e-mail addresses of park visitors obtained from various sources, including those who have signed up to receive the company's online newsletter.

Kupferman notes that some of the rides they have put in are based almost entirely on what people told them, from the general theme of the ride all the way down to the details and what they told them they wanted from the experience. In one survey, respondents were given a list of Paramount movies and were asked what kind of rides the movies might make. "When you ask a question like that, you get a lot of very interesting ideas from people. We can then go back a few days later and ask that same group or a different group, 'All right, we are looking at doing a ride based on a brand like Star Trek, and we are going to make it a roller coaster. What do you see as being part of that experience?' And you can really delve into it."

Kupferman says that research is a key driver in developing new parks and redeveloping existing ones. He says, "At our park in Cincinnati, we put in a new water park, almost 100 percent as a result of feedback people gave us. We asked what did they like and not like about the existing water park. And they said, 'There is too much concrete.' 'The rides are great but there is no place to sit down, no shade.' Well, for our new product we redeveloped the entire water park, we put in trees, we put things closer together, we created what we called Water Park Resort."[29]

Questions

1. Why do you think that Paramount's online panel has such a high response rate? What other tactics could they use to obtain more panel members?

2. Can you think of research questions that might be better answered with an independent panel like SurveySpot as opposed to their customer panel?

3. Paramount also conducts a lot of in-park research. Why do you think they do this? What types of data might they be gathering? Would they also conduct an identical survey to one being given to their online panel? Why?

4. Kupferman is quite pleased with Inquisite survey software. Go to *www.inquisite.com* and learn about their product offerings. Explain how you can create a Web survey using Inquisite.

PRIMARY DATA COLLECTION: OBSERVATION

LEARNING OBJECTIVES

1.	To develop a basic understanding of observation research.
2.	To learn the approaches to observation research.
3.	To understand the advantages and disadvantages of observation research.
4.	To explore the types of human observation.
5.	To understand the types of machine observation and their advantages and disadvantages.
6.	To explore the tremendous impact of scanner-based research on the marketing research industry.
7.	To learn about observation research on the Internet

Stepping into a Gap store in Braintree, Massachusetts, at the South Shore Shopping Plaza, Laura Munro became a research statistic. Twelve feet above her, a device resembling a smoke detector, mounted on the ceiling and equipped with a hidden camera, took a picture of her head and shoulders. The image was fed to a computer and shipped to a database in Chicago, where ShopperTrak RCT Corporation, a consumer research firm, keeps count of shoppers nationwide using 40,000 cameras placed in stores and malls.

ShopperTrak is a leader in "video mining"—an emerging field in marketing research enabled by technology that can analyze video images without relying on human eyes. ShopperTrak says it doesn't take pictures of faces. The company worries that shoppers would perceive that as an invasion of privacy. But nearly all of its videotaping is done without the knowledge of the people being taped.

Using proprietary software to gauge the size of the images of people, a ShopperTrak computer determined that Ms. Munro was an adult, not a child, and thus a bona fide shopper. Weeding out youngsters is critical in accurately calculating one of the valuable bits of data ShopperTrak sells—the percentage of shoppers that buy and the percentage that only browses. It arrives at this data, including the so-called conversion rate, by comparing the number of people taped entering the store with the number of transactions.

Ms. Munro's visit was tallied up twice: once as a visitor to the Gap and once in a national count of shoppers. Gap Incorporated, of San Francisco, pays ShopperTrak for the tally of Gap shoppers. ShopperTrak sells the broader data—gleaned from 130 retail clients and 380 malls—to economists, bankers, and retailers. ShopperTrak takes into account how much shoppers spend, data that it gets from credit card companies and banks, and extrapolates outward to the entire retail landscape.[1] ■

The ShopperTrak story describes a form of observation research. What is observation research? What are its advantages and limitations? Are mechanical devices used in observation research? These are some of the questions we will consider in this chapter.

Nature of Observation Research

> **observation research**
> Systematic process of recording patterns of occurrences or behaviors without normally communicating with the people involved.

Instead of asking people questions, as a survey does, observation research depends on watching what people do. Specifically, **observation research** can be defined as the systematic process of recording patterns of occurrences or behaviors without normally questioning or communicating with the people involved. (Mystery shopping is an exception.) A marketing researcher using the observation technique witnesses and records events as they occur or compiles evidence from records of past events. The observation may involve watching people or watching phenomena, and it may be conducted by human observers or by machines. Exhibit 7.1 gives examples of these various observation situations.

Conditions for Using Observation

Three conditions must be met before observation can be successfully used as a data collection tool for marketing research:

1. The needed information must be either observable or inferable from behavior that is observable. For example, if a researcher wants to know why an individual purchased a new Jeep rather than an Explorer, observation research will not provide the answer.
2. The behavior of interest must be repetitive, frequent, or in some manner predictable. Otherwise, the costs of observation may make the approach prohibitively expensive.
3. The behavior of interest must be of relatively short duration. Observation of the entire decision-making process for purchasing a new home, which might take several weeks or months, is not feasible.

Approaches to Observation Research

Researchers have a variety of observation approaches to choose from. They are faced with the task of choosing the most effective approach for a particular research problem, from

EXHIBIT 7.1	**Observation Situations**
Situations	**Example**
People watching people	Observers stationed in supermarkets watch consumers select frozen Mexican dinners, with the purpose of seeing how much comparison shopping people do at the point of purchase.
People watching phenomena	Observers stationed at an intersection count vehicles moving in various directions to establish the need for a traffic light.
Machines watching people	Movie or video cameras record consumers selecting frozen Mexican dinners.
Machines watching phenomena	Traffic-counting machines monitor the flow of vehicles at an intersection.

the standpoint of cost and data quality. The dimensions along which observation approaches vary are (1) natural versus contrived situations, (2) open versus disguised observation, (3) human versus machine observers, and (4) direct versus indirect observation.

Natural versus Contrived Situations   Counting how many people use the drive-in window at a particular bank during certain hours is a good example of a completely natural situation. The observer plays no role in the behavior of interest. Those being observed should have no idea that they are under observation. At the other extreme is recruiting people to do their shopping in a simulated supermarket (rows of stocked shelves set up in a field service's mall facility) so that their behavior can be carefully observed. In this case, the recruited people must be given at least some idea that they are participating in a study. The participants might be given grocery carts and told to browse the shelves and pick out items that they might normally use. The researchers might use alternative point-of-purchase displays for several products under study. To test the effectiveness of the various displays, the observers would note how long the shopper paused in front of the test displays and how often the product was actually selected.

A contrived environment enables the researcher to better control extraneous variables that might have an impact on a person's behavior or the interpretation of that behavior. Use of such an environment also tends to speed up the data-gathering process. The researcher does not have to wait for natural events to occur but instead instructs the participants to perform certain actions. Because more observations can be collected in the same length of time, the result will be either a larger sample or faster collection of the targeted amount of data. The latter should lower the costs of the project.

The primary disadvantage of a contrived setting is that it is artificial, and thus the observed behavior may be different from what would occur in a real-world situation. The more natural the setting, the more likely it is that the behavior will be normal for the individual being observed.

Open versus Disguised Observation   Does the person being observed know that he or she is being observed? It is well known that the presence of an observer may have an influence on the phenomena being observed.[2] Two general mechanisms work to bias the data. First, if people know they are being observed (as in **open observation**), they may behave differently. Second, the appearance and behavior of the observer offers a potential for bias similar to that associated with the presence of an interviewer in survey research.

Disguised observation is the process of monitoring people who do not know they are being watched. A common form of disguised observation is observing behavior from behind a one-way mirror. For example, a product manager may observe respondent reactions to alternative package designs from behind a one-way mirror during a focus group discussion.

> **open observation**
> Process of monitoring people who know they are being watched.

> **disguised observation**
> Process of monitoring people who do not know they are being watched.

Human versus Machine Observers   In some situations, it is possible and even desirable to replace human observers with machines—when machines can do the job less expensively, more accurately, or more readily. Traffic-counting devices are probably more accurate, definitely cheaper, and certainly more willing than human observers. It would not be feasible, for example, for ACNielsen to have human observers in people's homes to record television viewing habits. Movie cameras and audio-visual equipment record behavior much more objectively and in greater detail than human observers ever could. Finally, the electronic scanners found in most retail stores provide more accurate and timely data on product movement than human observers ever could.

Direct versus Indirect Observation   Most of the observation carried out for marketing research is direct observation of current behavior. However, in some cases, past behavior must be observed. To do this, the researcher must turn to some record of

> **garbologists**
> Researchers who sort through people's garbage to analyze household consumption patterns.

the behavior. Archaeologists dig up sites of old settlements and attempt to determine the nature of life in early societies from the physical evidence they find. **Garbologists** sort through people's garbage to analyze household consumption patterns. Marketing research usually is much more mundane. In a product prototype test, it may be important to learn how much of the test product the consumer used. The most accurate way to find this out is to have the respondent return the unused product so that the researcher can see how much is left. If a study involved the in-home use of a laundry soil and stain remover, it would be important to know how much of the remover each respondent actually used. All of the respondents' answers to questions would be considered from this usage perspective.

Advantages of Observation Research

Watching what people actually do rather than depending on their reports of what they did has one very significant and obvious advantage: Firsthand information is not subject to many of the biasing factors associated with the survey approach. Specifically, the researcher avoids problems associated with the willingness and ability of respondents to answer questions. Also, some forms of data are gathered more quickly and accurately by observation. Letting a scanner record the items in a grocery bag is much more efficient than asking the shopper to enumerate them. Similarly, rather than asking young children which toys they like, major toy manufacturers prefer to invite target groups of children into a large playroom and observe via a one-way mirror which toys are chosen and how long each holds the child's attention.

Disadvantages of Observation Research

The primary disadvantage of observation research is that only behavior and physical personal characteristics usually can be examined. The researcher does not learn about motives, attitudes, intentions, or feelings. Also, only public behavior is observed; private behavior—such as dressing for work or committee decision making within a company—is beyond the scope of observation research. A second problem is that present observed behavior may not be projectable into the future. The fact that a consumer purchases a certain brand of milk after examining several alternatives does not mean that he or she will continue to do so in the future.

Observation research can be time-consuming and costly if the observed behavior occurs rather infrequently. For example, if observers in a supermarket are waiting to watch the purchase behavior of persons selecting Lava soap, they may have a long wait. And if the choice of consumers to be observed is biased (for example, shoppers who go grocery shopping after 5:00 P.M.), distorted data may be obtained.

Human Observation

As noted in Exhibit 7.1, people can be employed to watch other people or certain phenomena. For example, people can act as mystery shoppers, observers behind one-way mirrors, or recorders of shopper traffic and behavior patterns. Researchers also can conduct retail and wholesale audits, which are types of observation research.

> **ethnographic research**
> Study of human behavior in its natural context, involving observation of behavior and physical setting.

Ethnographic Research

Ethnographic research comes to marketing from the field of anthropology. The popularity of the technique in commercial marketing research is increasing. **Ethnographic research,** or the study of human behavior in its natural context, involves observation of behavior and physical settings. Ethnographers directly observe the population they are studying. As "participant observers," ethnographers can use their intimacy with the people they are studying to gain richer, deeper insights into culture and behavior—in short, what makes people do what they do. Approximately $100 million annually is spent on ethnographic research.[3] Today, corporations, such as Eastman Kodak and Microsoft, have their own in-house ethnographers. Ethnographic studies can cost anywhere from $5,000 to as much as $800,000, depending on how deeply a company wants to delve into its customers' lives.

The first step of the research is to find an informant. An informant is a participant who can introduce the researchers to a particular group of people and explain the meaning behind the rituals, language, and general goings on. After entering a social group, ethnographers keenly observe activities, listen to conversation, conduct ongoing informal interviews, and participate in meaningful activities. Interactions are also observed to ascertain the effects of social influence.

Data is recorded in the form of field notes, jotted down in a notebook whenever researchers get a chance. The researchers may also use photographs, audio, and video. There an attempt to build a collection of artifacts—items that represent particular meaning to the people being studied. A researcher's own experiences—reactions, feelings, thoughts—are also important data. There are some things researchers can't fully understand until they experience them themselves.

The next step is to analyze and interpret all of the data collected to find themes and patterns of meaning. This is no simple task. Hours and hours of audio and video must be transcribed and re-studied. Even for the well-trained and experienced ethnographer, the amount of data can at times be overwhelming. But through careful and thorough analysis of the data, themes and categories emerge and applicable findings become clear. Ethnographers usually create frameworks to help companies think about their consumers and understand what it all means.

Triangulation, the process of checking findings against what other people say and against similar research already conducted, is a way to verify the accuracy of collected data. While traditional ethnography stops with the description of the group studies, this is not sufficient for businesses. They need actionable guidelines, recommendations, and an outline of strategy. The findings must be presented in a fashion to enable companies to create innovative and successful solutions.[4]

For managers at Cambridge SoundWorks, it was a perplexing problem: in retail outlets across the country, men stood wide-eyed when sales reps showed off the company's hi-fi, "blow-your-hair-back" stereo speakers. So why didn't such unabashed enthusiasm for the product translate into larger—and bigger ticket—sales?

To find out, the Andover, Massachusetts, manufacturer and retailer of stereo equipment hired research firm Design Continuum, in West Newton, Massachusetts, to follow a dozen prospective customers over the course of 2 weeks. The researchers' conclusion: the high-end speaker market suffered from something referred to as "the spouse acceptance factor." While men adored the big black boxes, women hated their unsightly appearance. Concerned about the way the speakers would "look" in the living room, women would talk their husbands out of buying a cool but hideous and expensive piece of stereo equipment. Even those who had purchased the product had trouble showing it off: Men would attempt to display the loudspeakers as trophies in living rooms, while women would hide them behind plants, vases, and chairs. "Women would come into the store, look at the speakers and say, 'that thing is ugly,'" says Ellen Di Resta, principal at Design Continuum. "The men would lose the argument and leave the store without a stereo. The solution was to give the target market what men and women *both* wanted: a great sound system that looks like furniture so you don't have to hide it."

Armed with this knowledge, Cambridge SoundWorks unveiled a new line. The furniture-like Newton Series of speakers and home theater systems comes in an array of colors and finishes. The result: The Newton Series is the fastest growing and best-selling product line in the firm's 14-year history.[5]

Jim Stengel, Procter & Gamble's chief marketing officer, notes, "I'm a big observational guy." So he has urged the P&G marketers to spend lots of time with consumers in their homes, watching the ways they wash their clothes, clean their floors, and diaper their babies, and asking them about their habits and frustrations. Back in 2000, the typical brand marketer spent less than 4 hours a month with consumers. Says Stengel: "It's at least triple that now."[6]

Mystery Shoppers

mystery shoppers
People who pose as consumers and shop at a company's own stores or those of its competitors to collect data about customer–employee interactions and to gather observational data; they may also compare prices, displays, and the like.

Mystery shoppers are used to gather observational data about a store (for example, are the shelves neatly stocked?) and to collect data about customer–employee interactions. In the latter case, of course, there is communication between the mystery shopper and the employee. The mystery shopper may ask, "How much is this item?" "Do you have this in blue?" or "Can you deliver this by Friday?" The interaction is not an interview, and communication occurs only so that the mystery shopper can observe the actions and comments of the employee. Mystery shopping is, therefore, classified as an observational marketing research method, even though communication is often involved.

The mystery shopping concept has four basic levels, which differ in the depth and type of information collected:

- ☐ *Level 1*—The mystery shopper conducts a mystery telephone call. Here, the mystery shopper calls the client location and evaluates the level of service received over the phone, following a scripted conversation.

- ☐ *Level 2*—The mystery shopper visits an establishment and makes a quick purchase; little or no customer–employee interaction is required. For example, in a level 2 mystery shop, a mystery shopper purchases an item (for example, gas, a hamburger, or a lottery ticket) and evaluates the transaction and image of the facility.

- ☐ *Level 3*—The mystery shopper visits an establishment and, using a script or scenario, initiates a conversation with a service and/or sales representative. Level 3 mystery shopping usually does not involve an actual purchase. Examples include discussing different cellular telephone packages with a sales representative, reviewing services provided during an oil change, and so forth.

- ☐ *Level 4*—The mystery shopper performs a visit that requires excellent communication skills and knowledge of the product. Discussing a home loan, the process for purchasing a new car, or visiting apartment complexes serve as examples. The "HotelSpy" in the Practicing Market Research box is another example of Level 4 mystery shopping.

Mystery shopping can have any one of several objectives. These objectives include measuring employee training, preparing for new competition, monitoring the competition through comparison shopping, and recognizing good employees. For more information go to *www.mysteryshop.org*. Guidelines for conducting mystery shopping in Europe are explained in the Global Research box on page 213.

Ron Welty, president of Intell.Shop, a mystery shopping firm, discusses how technology has changed mystery shopping in the last few years in the following Practicing Marketing Research box.

one-way mirror observation
Practice of watching behaviors or activities from behind a one-way mirror.

One-Way Mirror Observations

The discussion of focus groups in Chapter 5 noted that focus group facilities almost always provide **one-way mirror observation**, which allows clients to observe the group

PRACTICING MARKETING RESEARCH

Integrated, total-customer-experience evaluations that measure what happens at every possible touchpoint. Automated, fast report distribution via e-mail. Web-based reporting. Digitally recorded phone call evaluations. Hidden-video captures. High-resolution digital photos, embedded directly in online reports. Reports, call recordings, and photos burned onto CDs. Rewards presented on-the-spot to client employees who perform well. Palm Pilots and laptop computers. Certified professional evaluators. Same-day report turnaround. Instantaneous, online summary capabilities presenting over 40 different formats, for true, real-time reporting. These are just some of the latest advances in mystery shopping.

Recently, an industrywide effort to help improve overall skills and assist members in improving the quality of reporting was undertaken by the Mystery Shopping Providers Association (MSPA), which began offering a certification process for interested mystery shoppers. Currently, two certifications are available: silver and gold.

Silver certification requires a shopper to attend an online educational program, followed by a comprehensive test about general mystery shopping skills. If they pass, they are awarded silver certification. Gold certification is open only to shoppers with silver certification and requires shoppers to attend a one-day seminar, held in approximately 25 locations annually throughout the United States. These seminars cover the issues shoppers are required to know and comply with in the course of their duties. In 2005, almost 22,000 shoppers were awarded silver certification, and more than 2,000 were awarded gold certification.[7]

discussion as it unfolds. New product development managers, for example, can note consumers' reactions to various package prototypes as they are demonstrated by the moderator. (One researcher spent 200 hours watching mothers change diapers to gather information for the redesign of disposable diapers.) In addition, the clients can observe the degree of emotion exhibited by the consumer as he or she speaks. One-way mirrors are also sometimes used by child psychologists and toy designers to observe children at play.

The lighting level in the observation room must be very dim relative to that in the focus group room. Otherwise, the focus group participants can see into the observation room. Several years ago, we (the authors) were conducting a focus group of orthopedic surgeons in St. Louis, Missouri. One physician arrived approximately 20 minutes early and was ushered into the group room. A young assistant product manager for the pharmaceutical manufacturer was already seated in the observation room. The physician, being alone in the group room, decided to take advantage of the large framed mirror on the wall for some last-minute grooming. He walked over to the mirror and began combing his hair. At the same time, the assistant product manager, sitting about a foot away on the other side of the mirror, decided to light a cigarette. As the doctor combed his hair, there was suddenly a bright flash of light, and another face appeared through the mirror. What happened next goes beyond the scope of this text. In recent years, the trend has been to inform participants of the one-way mirror and to explain who is in the other room watching and why.

Audits

Audits are another category of human observation research. An **audit** is the examination and verification of sales of a product. Audits generally fall into two categories: retail audits,

 audit
Examination and verification of the sales of a product.

PRACTICING MARKETING RESEARCH

Undercover with a Hotel Spy

J. C. Schaefer unscrews a light bulb from a bedside lamp in the posh Windsor Court Hotel in New Orleans and begins violently whacking it against the bedspread. He shakes the light bulb to make sure the filament inside is broken and then carefully screws it back into the lamp.

Mr. Schaefer isn't your average hotel guest. In fact, he isn't even J. C. Schaefer. His real name is David Richey, and he's a hotel spy who uses a variety of aliases to check out luxury hotels all over the world. Over two days, he'll employ an extensive bag of tricks to see if the Windsor Court—rated as the top hotel in the world in a *Condé Nast Traveler* magazine poll—is as good as its reputation. The "burnt-out light bulb" test is one of the toughest. Only 11 percent of hotels tested by Mr. Richey's Chevy Chase, Maryland, firm, Richey International, detect the burnt-out bulb on the housekeeping staff's first pass.

The Windsor Court is a member of Preferred Hotels & Resorts Worldwide, a group of 120 independent luxury hotels that share a common reservations system. Preferred requires that all its hotels meet at least 80 percent of its standards in a test conducted annually by Richey International.

After checking in, Mr. Richey heads off to lunch while his room is being prepared. The Windsor Court has a five-star dining room, but the mystery shopper decides to eat at the hotel bar, the Polo Club Lounge. Mr. Richey orders crab cakes from the menu, then orders french fries to see if the bar readily accommodates off-menu orders. It does.

The food is good, and the service is friendly. But the waiters get marked down for not making eye contact and for not busing away the ketchup after the meal is done. "They're nice guys," Mr. Richey says, "But they're not real polished."

A little after 2 P.M. Mr Richey walks into a sprawling $295-a-night suite at the Windsor Court. He pulls out a disposable camera and begins taking pictures. Overall, the room gets high marks for cleanliness and creature comforts. But Mr. Richey spots scuff marks on the baseboard and a snag in one of the curtains.

Then it's on to the bathroom. "Forty percent of hotels have hair in either the sink, the tub or on the floor," Mr. Richey announces as he begins his inspection. This room, it turns out, does not.

Before leaving for dinner, Mr. Richey sets up a test to see how well the housekeeping staff will pick up the room when they turn down the covers on the bed later that evening. He leaves some magazines askew in the magazine rack, puts a cup of pistachio shells on the table and disables the light bulb.

After dinner, Mr. Richey heads downstairs for another test. "I have changed my travel plans and will be going to New York tomorrow," Mr. Richey informs the concierge. "Can you make reservations for me?" "Unfortunately we can't do that," the concierge replies. "You either have to do it yourself or call a travel agent." Mr. Richey, as always, takes the news calmly. "That was awful," he says later. "I'm sure the general manager will be horrified."

Back in the room, Mr. Richey finds a neatly turned-down bed. However, the housekeeper hasn't done a very good job of tidying the room. And the defective light bulb hasn't been replaced. Mr. Richey takes copious photos. It's 10 P.M., but Mr. Richey will be up for another couple of hours preparing his report.[8]

GLOBAL RESEARCH

ESOMAR (formerly the European Society for Opinion and Marketing Research) has over 4,000 members in 100 countries. It recently created global guidelines for conducting mystery research.

ESOMAR Guidelines for Mystery Shopping

ESOMAR expects researchers to conform to the following requirements when carrying out mystery shopping research:

1. Mystery shopping studies must be designed and carried out in ways that avoid unreasonably wasting the time and money or abusing the goodwill of the organizations and individuals being researched. Researchers must take great care to minimize the risk of any disruption to the normal working of the organization being researched.

2. Individual staff members must not be identifiable in the report on a mystery shopping study (this issue is normally unlikely to arise in the case of "competitive" mystery shopping). Similarly, reporting should not be at individual outlet/branch level since in many cases this would implicitly identify specific individuals (e.g., because there is only one relevant staff member at a given location): data should be reported only at a higher, aggregated level.

3. The interviews must not be electronically recorded unless respondents have agreed to this in advance. Electronic recording of interviews is not permitted if it could endanger the anonymity of respondents.

4. If for any research purposes (e.g., for field work quality checking or further follow-up research) individuals or individual outlets/branches are to be identified, respondents must have agreed to this in advance. Any such agreement must be restricted to the use of individual information for research purposes only; any other use is not permissible. The identity of respondents must not be revealed to the client but to other researchers only.

5. For mystery shopping calls on the client's own organization: the client should be made aware of any time and other operational costs to the organization of the calls involved and agree to these in advance. In addition, in order to minimize any staff concerns about such research:

    a. It is good practice (and in some countries, a legislative requirement) to inform staff—and also any relevant staff association, works council, and so on—if the organization proposes to carry out mystery shopping studies (but not necessarily the timing or precise details of these). Staff should be told the objectives and general nature of such research and given reassurances that individuals and individual outlets/branches will not be identified in the reports (but see 5b below) and that no disciplinary or similar action will be taken vis-à-vis individuals as a result of the research.

    b. Where staff remuneration to any extent depends on commission or bonuses, consideration may be given to making good any losses of salary as a result of time spent in dealing with mystery shopping calls.

6. For mystery shopping calls on nonclient organizations: occasionally there will be agreement (not necessarily a formal one) within a given industry to accept "competitive" mystery shopping calls in the interests of general quality improvement. Where no such agreement exists, it is even more important that the time and other demands created by such calls are kept to a minimum (and generally acceptable) level. What this level is likely to be will vary with the nature

(Continued)

of the calls (e.g., the proportion of observation to interviewing time), by industry and possibly by country:

a. Simple observational checks of shopper/staff behavior are unlikely to create problems of this kind provided that there is no interference with the normal working of the organization (although it may be necessary to deal with possible management objections).

b. Similarly with calls where the interviewing of staff members lasts only 2 to 3 minutes in total, or calls where a purchase is made, the value of which is commensurate with the time taken up by the call.

c. In other cases the acceptable length of time spent with members of staff may be determined by local codes of practice. Where these do not exist, it is recommended that, unless there is some strong technical reason to the contrary, such time should normally not exceed (a) 10 minutes in manufacturing and re-

tail businesses (other than automotive) and (b) 15 to 20 minutes in other service industries and businesses.

d. If the project is one where part of the evaluation involves some follow-up paperwork by the organization called on (e.g., provision of a brochure, etc.), this must also be kept to a minimum.

e. If mystery shopping calls are made on self-employed or professional people, and so on, where time spent on an interview may literally cost them (lost) money, consideration should be given to reimbursing the individuals involved at an appropriate professional rate.

7. Where there would be difficulty in conforming to the preceding recommendations, the activity should not be regarded as a form of market research and should not be carried out by, or under the name of, a market research organization.

Copyright ESOMAR *www.esomar.nl.*

which measure sales to final consumers, and wholesale audits, which determine the amount of product movement from warehouses to retailers. Wholesalers and retailers allow auditors into their stores and stockrooms to examine the company's sales and order records in order to verify product flows. In turn, the retailers and wholesalers receive cash compensation and basic reports about their operations from the audit firms.

Because of the availability of scanner-based data (discussed later in this chapter), physical audits at the retail level may someday all but disappear. The largest nonscanner-based wholesale audit company, SAMI, has already gone out of business. Its client list was sold to Information Resources, Incorporated (IRI), a company that specializes in providing scanner-based data. ACNielsen, the largest retail audit organization, no longer uses auditors in grocery stores. The data are entirely scanner-based. Currently, ACNielsen uses both auditors and scanner-based data for some other types of retail outlets. However, the data probably will be scanner-based only in the near future.

Machine Observation

The observation methods discussed so far have involved people observing things or consumers. Now we turn our attention to observation by machines, including traffic counters, physiological measurement devices, opinion and behavior management devices, and scanners.

≥ traffic counters
Machines used to measure vehicular flow over a particular stretch of roadway.

Traffic Counters

Among the most common and popular machines in observation research are **traffic counters**. As the name implies, traffic counters measure vehicular flow over a particular stretch of roadway. Outdoor advertisers rely on traffic counts to determine number of

GLOBAL RESEARCH

Observation Research Is Used Sparingly in Many Countries

Observation research is used extensively in the United States and Japan, but less so in Europe. For example, little observation research is conducted in Ireland. Where it is used, it tends to be as a generalized technique to get a research idea or to help the researcher decide what aspects of the problem are worth researching. It may be used as a check on other research techniques. Many researchers avoid using the method due to its inability to observe such factors as attitudes, motivations, and plans.

There is a reluctance on the part of Irish business to allow the researcher to come on-site and observe behaviors over a period of time. Many Irish researchers would question the reliability of what they are observing. There is a tendency for many people to act differently than they would otherwise. Most of the observation that is used is of the natural, direct, and unobtrusive type.[9]

exposures per day to a specific billboard. Retailers use the information to ascertain where to locate a particular type of store. Convenience stores, for example, require a moderately high traffic volume to reach target levels of profitability.

Physiological Measurement Devices

When an individual is aroused or feels inner tension or alertness, his or her condition is referred to as *activation*. Activation is stimulated via a subcortical unit called the *reticular activation system (RAS)*, located in the human brain stem. The sight of a product or advertisement, for example, can activate the RAS. When the arousal processes in the RAS are directly provoked, the processing of information increases. Researchers have used a number of devices to measure the level of a person's activation.

Electroencephalograph An **electroencephalograph (EEG)** is a machine that measures electric pulses on the scalp and generates a record of electrical activity in the brain. Although electroencephalography probably is the most versatile and sensitive procedure for detecting arousal, it involves expensive equipment, a laboratory environment, and complex data analysis requiring special software programs. Using EEG technology developed by NASA to monitor astronauts' alertness levels, Capita Corporation has begun measuring respondents' reactions to advertisements. Capita uses a headset that reads electrical signals coming from a subject's scalp five times per second, as the person interacts with media such as a television program, a commercial, a Web page, or a banner ad. These brain waves are converted into a scrolling graph synchronized with the visual stimuli on the screen, giving the marketer a play-by-play view of which segments excite the viewer and which ones don't.

Recently, Capita, with the help of U.S. Interactive, an Internet services company that tracks Web ads, tested the system's reliability. Capita monitored the brain waves of 48 respondents as they confronted four banner ads with strong click-through rates and four ads with low rates. In three of four tests, Capita's measure correctly identified the "strong" banners.[11]

The ability to accurately translate the data is what troubles one cable network executive. "An ad might get someone to perspire or their eyes to dilate or their brain waves to

electroencephalograph (EEG)
Machine that measures electrical pulses on the scalp and generates a record of electrical activity in the brain.

peak, but the resounding issue is, what does that really tell you?" he says. "Just because the needles are moving does not mean that it will affect their behavior, get them to purchase something, or improve their brand awareness."[12]

Galvanic Skin Response **Galvanic skin response (GSR)**, also known as *electrodermal response*, is a change in the electric resistance of the skin associated with activation responses. A small electric current of constant intensity is sent into the skin through electrodes attached to the palmar side of the fingers. The changes in voltage observed between the electrodes indicate the level of stimulation. Because the equipment is portable and not expensive, measuring GSR is the most popular way to assess emotional reaction to a stimulus. GSR is used primarily to measure stimulus response to advertisements but is sometimes used in packaging research.

> **galvanic skin response (GSR)**
> Change in the electric resistance of the skin associated with activation responses; also called *electrodermal response*.

Inner Response, Incorporated uses GSR to evaluate commercials. In tests of an Eastman Kodak Company digital photo processing ad, Inner Response determined that viewers' interest levels built slowly in the opening scenes, rose when a snapshot of an attractive young woman was shown, but spiked highest when a picture appeared of a smiling, pigtailed girl. Knowing which scenes had the highest impact helped Kodak in making changes in the spot's content and cutting its length.

Pupilometer The **pupilometer** measures changes in pupil dilation as subjects view an advertisement, while brightness and distance from the screen are held constant. The basic assumption is that increased pupil size reflects positive attitudes, interest, and arousal. The pupilometer has fallen from favor among many researchers because pupil dilation appears to measure some combination of arousal, mental effort, processing load, and anxiety.[13] Arousal alone is much better measured by GSR.

> **pupilometer**
> Machine that measures changes in pupil dilation.

Voice Pitch Analysis **Voice pitch analysis** measures emotion by examining changes in the relative vibration frequency of the human voice. In voice pitch analysis, the normal, or baseline, pitch of an individual's speaking voice is charted by engaging the subject in an unemotional conversation. Then, the more pitch deviates from the baseline, the greater is said to be the emotional intensity of the person's reaction to a stimulus, such as a question. Voice pitch analysis has several advantages over other forms of physiological measurement:

> **voice pitch analysis**
> Studying changes in the relative vibration frequency of the human voice to measure emotion.

☐ One can record without physically connecting wires and sensors to the subject.
☐ The subject need not be aware of the recording and analysis.
☐ The nonlaboratory setting avoids the weaknesses of an artificial environment.
☐ It provides instantaneous evaluation of answers and comments.[14]

Voice pitch analysis has been used in package research to measure consumers' emotional responses to advertising, to predict consumer brand preference for dog food, and to determine which consumers from a target group would be most predisposed to try a new product. Validity of the studies to date has been subject to serious question.[15]

The devices just discussed are used to measure involuntary changes in an individual's physiological makeup. Arousal produces adrenaline, which enhances the activation process via a faster heart rate, increased blood flow, an increase in skin temperature, and perspiration, pupil dilation, and an increase in brain-wave frequency. Researchers often infer information about attitudes and feelings from these measures.

Facial Action Coding Service (FACS) Researchers at the University of California at San Francisco identified the 43 muscle movements responsible for all human facial expression (see Exhibit 7.2). They spent seven years categorizing roughly

Exhibit 7.2

Which One Is Blowing Smoke?

Dan Hill, president of Sensory Logic, says that some of the consumers who tell you they like what you're selling don't really mean it. Here he shows us how to tell who's being genuine and who's just making nice.

Which One Is Fake?
Is it ever really clear if consumers like what you're selling? Some might tell you they like your product even if they don't. Who's really interested and who's just being polite? Can you tell?
The areas around the eyes and around the mouth are the places to look for clues. A true smile will involve the eyes (a reaction of an involuntary nerve) as well as the mouth. Also, a true smile will curve the lips while a fake smile won't. In a fake smile, the corners of the mouth will move outward, not upward.

3,000 combinations of such movements and the emotions they convey—the "eyelid tightener" expresses anger, for instance, and the "nasolabial fold deepener" manifests sadness. The system has proved to be highly accurate; the FBI and CIA reportedly use the FACS method to determine the emotions of suspects during interrogations.[16]

Sensory Logic, a St. Paul, Minnesota, research firm, uses FACS to get to the "truth." The firm's clients include Target, Nextel, General Motors, and Eli Lilly, according to Don Hill, the firm's president (see *www.sensorylogic.com*). To measure initial gut reactions to a commercial or ad, Hill first attaches electrodes to the side of a subject's mouth (monitoring the zygomatic muscle, for smiles), above the eyebrow (corrugator muscle, for frowns), and on two fingers (for sweat). He says the facial muscle movements reflect appeal, whereas perspiration translates into what he calls "impact"—emotional power. After Hill takes initial readings, he removes the electrodes and he videotapes an interview with each subject. Later, his FACS-trained team reviews the video, second by second, cataloguing emotions.

Even some of Hill's happy customers say that face reading has limitations. For one thing, not everyone believes that pitches have to aim for the heart. "A lot of the advertising we do is a more rational sell," a General Motors researcher says, "so emotional research doesn't apply."[17]

Opinion and Behavior Measurement Devices

People Reader The PreTesting Company has invented a device called the **People Reader,** which looks like a lamp. When respondents sit in front of it, they are not aware that it is simultaneously recording both their reading material and the activity of their eyes. The self-contained unit is totally automatic and can record any respondent—with or without glasses—without the use of attachments, chin rests, helmets, or special optics. It allows respondents to read any size magazine or newspaper and lets them spend

People Reader
Machine that simultaneously records the respondent's reading material and eye reactions.

The People Reader, an opinion and behavior measurement device developed by the PreTesting Company, unobtrusively records reading material and readers' eye activity to determine readers' habits as well as the stopping power and brand-name recall associated with different-sized ads. Go to *http://www. pretesting.com* to learn about the products and services this company offers.

as much time as they want reading and rereading the publication. Through use of the People Reader and specially designed hidden cameras, the PreTesting Company has been able to document both reading habits and the results of different-sized ads in terms of stopping power and brand-name recall. The company's research has found the following:

☐ Nearly 40 percent of all readers either start from the back of a magazine or "fan" a magazine for interesting articles and ads. Fewer than half the readers start from the very first page of a magazine.

☐ Rarely does a double-page ad provide more than 15 percent additional top-of-mind awareness than a single-page ad. Usually, the benefits of a double-page spread are additional involvement and communication, not top-of-mind awareness.

☐ In the typical magazine, nearly 35 percent of each of the ads receive less than 2 seconds' worth of voluntary examination.

☐ The strongest involvement power recorded for ads has been three or more successive single-page ads on the right-hand side of a magazine.

☐ Because most ads "hide" the name of the advertisers and do not show a close-up view of the product package, brand-name confusion is greater than 50 percent on many products such as cosmetics and clothing.

☐ A strong ad that is above average in stopping power and communication will work regardless of which section in the magazine it is placed. It will also work well in any type of ad or editorial environment. However, an ad that is below average in stopping power and involvement will be seriously affected by the surrounding environment.[18]

The Portable People Meter and Project Apollo

For the past decade or so, watching television in America has been defined by the families recruited by Nielsen Media Research who have agreed to have an electronic meter attached to their televisions or to record in a diary what shows they watch. This approach may not last much longer because technology demands it. Bob Luff, the chief technology officer at Nielsen, views the modern American home as a digital zoo: radio is going on the Web, TV is going on cell phones, the Web is going on TV, and everything, it seems, is moving to video-on-demand (VOD) and (quite possibly) the iPod and the PlayStation Portable. "Television and media," Luff said over the noise of five sets tuned to five different channels, "will change more in the next 3 or 5 years than it's changed in the past 50."[19]

Arbitron has counted radio listeners—and, at various times, television viewers—since the late 1940s. It has harnessed new technology to measure audiences. Participants wear a black plastic box that looks like a pager, 3 inches by 2 inches by ½ inch, whose circuitry is roughly as complex as that of a cell phone. The device is called the **portable people meter**, or the PPM.

Participants clip the PPM to their belts, or to any other article of clothing, and wear it throughout their waking hours. Before going to bed, they dock the PPM in a cradle so that overnight it can automatically send its data to a computer center in Maryland, where marketing researchers can download and review the information. The PPM will tell Arbitron exactly what kind—and exactly how much—television and radio programming a person was exposed to during the day. Eventually, the PPM may also tell the researchers

➤ portable people meter
Device worn by people that measures the radio and TV programming to which the participant was exposed during the day.

at Arbitron a host of other things too, such as whether a PPM-wearer heard any Web streaming, or supermarket Muzak, or any electronic media with audible sound that someone might encounter on a typical day.

Project Apollo is a venture between ACNielsen and Arbitron in conjunction with Procter & Gamble. The idea can be thought of as "a day in the life of" thousands of consumers. The project uses Arbitron's personal people meters to learn about media habits and exposure; then it follows up with Nielsen's Homescan consumer panel. The panel uses scanner data to monitor participants' purchases of all scanned consumer goods. *Note:* We will describe Information Resources' scanner-based panel in detail later in the chapter. In addition, Project Apollo will conduct print (e.g., magazines and newspapers) readership studies and purchase behavior and attitude studies across a variety of industries and product categories. The object of Project Apollo is to accomplish marketing's holy grail. That is, how did the marketing mix influence the purchase of specific goods and services.[20]

Scanner-Based Research

Two electronic monitoring tools comprise the basic scanner-based research system: television meters and laser scanners, which "read" the UPC codes on products and produce instantaneous information on sales. Separately, each monitoring device provides marketers with current information on the advertising audience and on sales and inventories of products. Together, television meters and scanners measure the impact of marketing. Has scanner-based research been of much benefit to marketers? The top executive of one manufacturer estimates that one-third to one-half of its gains in profitability in the past several years can be attributed to scanner-based research.[21]

The marriage of scanners, database management, telecommunications, artificial intelligence, and computing gives hope for a "brave new world" of marketing.

The two major scanner-based research suppliers are Information Resources, Incorporated (IRI) and ACNielsen; each has about half the market. So that you can gain an appreciation of scanner-based research, we will discuss the product offerings of IRI in detail.[22]

BehaviorScan   IRI is the founder of scanner-based research and the developer of **BehaviorScan**, which has a household panel in each of five markets. The BehaviorScan markets are geographically dispersed cities: Pittsfield, Massachusetts; Eau Claire, Wisconsin; Cedar Rapids, Iowa; Grand Junction, Colorado; and Midland, Texas (see Exhibit 7.3). Panel members shop with an ID card, which is presented at check-outs in supermarkets, drugstores, and mass merchandisers. This card allows IRI to electronically track each household's purchases, item by item, over time. For nonparticipating retailers, panel members use a hand-held scanner at home to record their purchases. With such a measure of household purchasing, it is possible to analyze real changes in consumer buying behavior associated with manipulating marketing variables (such as TV advertising or consumer promotions) or introducing a new product.

For strategic tests of alternative marketing plans, the BehaviorScan household panels are split into two or more subgroups, balanced on past purchasing, demographics, and stores shopped. A test commercial can be broadcast over the cable network to one group of households, while the other group gets a control ad, without the consumer even realizing that the commercial is only a test ad. Alternatively, three different test ads per city can be used simultaneously to see which ad generates the greatest demand. This feature makes BehaviorScan a most effective means of evaluating changes in advertising. In each market, IRI maintains permanent warehouse facilities and staff to control distribution,

BehaviorScan
Scanner-based research system that can manipulate the marketing mix for household panels in geographically dispersed markets and then electronically track consumer purchases.

Exhibit 7.3

BehaviorScan Market Map

Source: www.infores.com.

BehaviorScan Market Map

Converter (Panel HH) Targetable TV

Checkerboard (Cable Zone) Targetable TV

price, and promotions. Competitive activity is monitored, and a record of pricing, displays, and features permits an assessment of the responsiveness to a brand promotion.

For testing consumer promotions such as coupons, product samples, and refund offers, balanced panel subsamples are again created within each market. Then, through direct mail or split newspaper-route targeting, a different treatment is delivered to each group. Both sales and profits are analyzed.

In-store variables may also be tested. Within the markets, split groups of stores are used to read the effect on sales of a change in packaging, shelf placement, or pricing. Tests are analyzed primarily on a store movement basis, but purchasing by panel shoppers in the test and control stores can also be analyzed. With the BehaviorScan system, it is possible to evaluate alternative advertising levels while simultaneously varying in-store prices or consumer promotions, thereby testing a completely integrated marketing plan.

In summary, BehaviorScan allows marketing managers to answer critical marketing questions such as the following:

- ☐ What is the impact of our new advertising program?
- ☐ How can we minimize incremental media costs?
- ☐ What happens to sales if we change the ad frequency or day part?
- ☐ How many units of our new product will we sell in a year?
- ☐ How many units will be cannibalized from existing products by the new product?
- ☐ What is the effectiveness of each marketing mix element in driving trial and repeat purchasing?
- ☐ What is the impact of an alternative marketing program on results?

Frito-Lay senior vice president Dwight Riskey said, "BehaviorScan is a critical component of Frito-Lay's go-to-market strategy for a couple of reasons. First, it gives us absolutely the most accurate read on the sales potential of a new product, and a well-rounded view of consumer response to all elements of the marketing mix. Second,

BehaviorScan TV ad testing enables us to significantly increase our return on our advertising investment. We definitely plan to continue using BehaviorScan."[23]

InfoScan **InfoScan Custom Store Tracking** provides the retail sales and causal information essential to developing, implementing, and evaluating marketing programs. InfoScan is based on all-store, census scanner data, which are collected weekly from more than 32,000 supermarkets, drugstores, and mass merchandiser outlets across the United States. InfoScan gives manufacturers and retailers access to detailed information on sales, share, distribution, pricing, and promotion for hundreds of product categories. InfoScan Custom Store Tracking can help marketing managers:

☐ Understand and track categories, products, and competitive factors for effective marketing and sales planning.

☐ Identify opportunities for new product development and marketing mix improvements for existing products.

☐ Monitor and evaluate promotions and new product launches and execute timely modifications to plans.

☐ Implement sales and broker compensation programs based on measurable objectives.

☐ Increase salesforce efficiency by allocating resources to critical sales drivers and local opportunities.

☐ Maximize return on trade promotion spending by evaluating compliance and response at the retail level.

☐ Strengthen manufacturer/retailer relationships by developing and implementing category management programs that maximize joint profitability.[24]

InfoScan Syndicated Store Tracking is a common source of retail scanner-based information for manufacturers, retailers, and brokers. In addition, financial analysts, trade publications, and the business media use InfoScan Syndicated Store Tracking to gain consumer packaged goods (CPG) industry understanding. InfoScan Syndicated Store Tracking provides the tools needed to develop targeted marketing strategies based on product performance, distribution, and promotion responsiveness across a wide range of geographical areas. InfoScan Syndicated Store Tracking provides:

☐ 266 InfoScan categories reflecting a standard view of the CPG industry.

☐ Product details including category, type (segment) parent company, manufacturer, brand, and UPC.

☐ Customized product groupings via IRI's software tools.

☐ Data on supermarkets, drugstores, mass merchandisers, and a three-outlet combination; 8 IRI regions per outlet; 64 supermarket outlet markets; census and sample key accounts; and drugstore census accounts.

☐ A comprehensive list of retail measures covering sales, share, distribution, pricing, and promotion activities.

☐ Annual, quarterly, monthly, and weekly time periods, many of which cover the last 5 calendar years. Year-ago comparisons are also available for many time periods.

☐ Monthly database updates.

☐ User access via IRI's timeshare environment using Oracle Sales Analyzer, the Internet via ReviewNet, or data delivery on CD-ROM, in spreadsheet format or on hard copy.

☐ Data available on a subscription or one-time basis.[25]

▷ **InfoScan Custom Store Tracking**
Scanner-based data system that collects information on consumer packaged goods.

Observation Research on the Internet

In Chapter 4, we discussed how the ability to track online surfers had enabled organizations to build huge databases on Internet surfing and online shopping behavior. Although privacy concerns are being raised by both consumer advocacy groups and members of Congress, new Internet tracking companies are being created on a regular basis.

Clickstream data represent the idiosyncratic steps and behaviors of consumers on their way to information and entertainment as well as online purchase decisions. Assume a firm has clickstream data from its current customers. Clickstream data initially are collected in Web logs. Different methods exist for collecting clickstream data (for example, cookies, proxy servers), and pulling and manipulating this online data is typically a large undertaking that is unique to every site. Depending on the Web site, a researcher can capture codes about clicks, rotating offers, banners, page sequences, duration, and product configuration.

In some cases clickstream data can be supplemented with other customer data, such as attitudes or offline (media) behavior. Most firms that operate in business-to-business markets also have end-user data in the form of an overlay database that they purchased typically from the American Business Institute (ABI), Dun & Bradstreet, and so forth. This overlay can be matched to customers and give additional (and very important) firmographic data: North American Industry Classification System Codes (NAICS), number of employees, sales revenue, information technology (IT) budget, length of time in business, metropolitan statistical area (MSA), and designated market area (DMA). The online end-user data also can be matched with attitudinal data.

Predictive Customer Intelligence

The clickstream data can be a vital foundation of a predictive customer intelligence system. Two components are needed to build a predictive customer intelligence system. The first required component involves the way the Web site is designed. Web site design should be matched up with the buying process (for example, need recognition, searching, comparing, purchasing, after-sales service), and the Web pages should be categorized accordingly.

The second required component involves the modeling of clickstream and other customer data. The first objective is to increase understanding of the online customer base and use this to customize the Web site and improve the Web site experience. A second objective of this modeling stage is to develop predictive models. This entails predicting who are the most likely purchasers and who will respond best to which marketing action. By relating purchasing data to the sequences of the clickstream, as well as to the additional information included on the customer, it's possible to derive models to help predict future visits and help predict what customers are most likely to do during these future visits. This also can help determine whether the clicker's path through the Web site indicates that the visit is a research visit, support-seeking visit, or a purchasing visit. If it is a purchasing visit, this data can indicate when, what, and how much the customer is likely to buy.

When a customer enters the Web site and starts with a particular click sequence, the predictive system will kick in. Rather than spending 40 minutes on the site and seeing 25 page views and ultimately purchasing a product, the clicker instead is offered the right product (with the "hot buttons" appropriately messaged) after, say, 10 minutes and 10 page views.[26]

DoubleClick DoubleClick is the largest company tracking clickstreams on the Internet. Clicks are only the most basic way to measure online marketing programs. The following are among the metrics sophisticated advertisers are now using to measure the effectiveness of their online campaigns:

- ☐ post-click conversions
- ☐ cost per conversion
- ☐ unique reach of ads delivered
- ☐ average frequency of exposures
- ☐ frequency-to-conversion ratio
- ☐ ad exposure time (rich media)
- ☐ ad interaction rate (rich media)
- ☐ brand impact lift versus control ad (including ad recall, brand awareness, message association, brand favorability, purchase intent)
- ☐ view-through rate (i.e., delayed visits to advertiser's site without a direct ad click-through)
- ☐ Web page eye tracking
- ☐ offline sales lift[27]

Two of the most important developments in online advertising in the past decade also play directly to the Internet's strength of measurability: rich media and search engine advertising.

The term *rich media* describes a variety of online advertising media experiences, including high-quality animation, streaming audio and video, and software-like features that can be embedded in relatively small ad files, such as games, registration forms, and detailed marketing information. A user can explore all of those features in the ad unit without ever leaving the content page on which the ad appears.

DoubleClick's Motif platform can report, for example, the total time the ad is displayed on the user's page, any interactions the reader makes with her mouse over the ad, and the total time she spends exploring features of the ad. Rich media has risen steadily in popularity with online advertisers, now accounting for over 35 percent of all ad impressions.[28]

In principle, search advertising is elegantly straightforward: advertisers bid on keywords to affect the rank positions of their text ads on search results pages, and they pay only when a person clicks on their ad. Today, over 40 percent of online advertising is being spent on search advertising.[29]

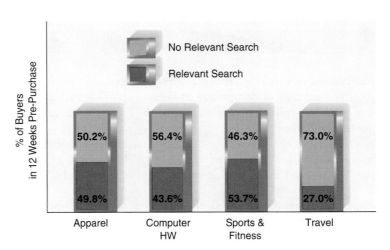

Exhibit 7.4

Roughly half of online buyers make a related search before their purchase

Source: DoubleClick Performics and comScore Networks, "Search Before the Purchase" report, 2005.

Search listings are prominent in the online ad mix primarily because consumers rely heavily on search to aid their online shopping behavior. DoubleClick demonstrated that conclusively in a study that its search marketing division Performics released in 2005 year with comScore Networks, titled "Search Before the Purchase." The study concluded that roughly half of the people examined in the study who made an online purchase first conducted a search related to the product sometime in the 12 weeks prior. In the case of the travel category, 73 percent of ticket buyers first researched their purchase on a search engine, as shown in Exhibit 7.4.

SUMMARY

Observation research is the systematic process of recording patterns of occurrences or behaviors without questioning or normally communicating with the people involved. For observation to be used successfully, the needed information must be observable and the behavior of interest must be repetitive, frequent, or in some manner predictable. The behavior of interest also should be of a relatively short duration. There are four dimensions along which observation approaches vary: (1) natural versus contrived situations, (2) open versus disguised observation, (3) human versus machine observers, and (4) direct versus indirect observation.

The biggest advantage of observation research is that researchers can see what people actually do rather than having to rely on what they say they did, thereby avoiding many biasing factors. Also, some forms of data are more quickly and accurately gathered by observation. The primary disadvantage of this type of research is that the researcher learns nothing about motives, attitudes, intentions, or feelings.

People watching people or objects can take the form of ethnographic research, mystery shopping, one-way mirror observations (for example, child psychologists might watch children play with toys), shopper pattern and behavior studies, and audits.

Machine observation may involve traffic counters, physiological measurement devices, opinion and behavior measurement devices, or scanners. The use of scanners in carefully controlled experimental settings enables the marketing researcher to accurately and objectively measure the direct causal relationship between different kinds of marketing efforts and actual sales. The leaders in scanner-based research are Information Resources, Incorporated and ACNielsen.

Observation research on the Internet consists largely of tracking the surfing patterns of Internet users.

KEY TERMS & DEFINITIONS

observation research Systematic process of recording patterns of occurrences or behaviors without normally communicating with the people involved.

open observation Process of monitoring people who know they are being watched.

disguised observation Process of monitoring people who do not know they are being watched.

garbologists Researchers who sort through people's garbage to analyze household consumption patterns.

ethnographic research Study of human behavior in its natural context, involving observation of behavior and physical setting.

mystery shoppers People who pose as consumers and shop at a company's own stores or those of its competitors to collect data about customer–employee interactions and to gather observational data; they may also compare prices, displays, and the like.

one-way mirror observation Practice of watching behaviors or activities from behind a one-way mirror.

audit Examination and verification of the sales of a product.

traffic counters Machines used to measure vehicular flow over a particular stretch of roadway.

electroencephalograph (EEG) Machine that measures electrical pulses on the scalp and generates a record of electrical activity in the brain.

galvanic skin response (GSR) Change in the electric resistance of the skin associated with activation responses; also called *electrodermal response.*

pupilometer Machine that measures changes in pupil dilation.

voice pitch analysis Studying changes in the relative vibration frequency of the human voice to measure emotion.

People Reader Machine that simultaneously records the respondent's reading material and eye reactions.

portable people meter Device worn by people that measures the radio and TV programming to which the participant was exposed during the day.

BehaviorScan Scanner-based research system that can manipulate the marketing mix for household panels in geographically dispersed markets and then electronically track consumer purchases.

InfoScan Custom Store Tracking Scanner-based data system that collects information on consumer packaged goods.

QUESTIONS FOR REVIEW & CRITICAL THINKING

1. You are charged with the responsibility of determining whether men are brand conscious when shopping for racquetball equipment. Outline an observation research procedure for making that determination.

2. Fisher-Price has asked you to develop a research procedure for determining which of its prototype toys is most appealing to 4- and 5-year-olds. Suggest a methodology for making this determination.

3. What are the biggest drawbacks of observation research?

4. Compare the advantages and disadvantages of observation research with those of survey research.

5. It has been said that "people buy things not for what they will do, but for what they mean." Discuss this statement in relation to observation research.

6. You are a manufacturer of a premium brand of ice cream. You want to know more about your market share, competitors' pricing, and the types of outlets where your product is selling best. What kind of observation research data would you purchase? Why?

7. How might a mystery shopper be valuable to the following organizations?
   a. Jetblue Airlines
   b. Macy' Department Store
   c. H&R Block

8. Use ethnographic research to evaluate the dining experience at your student center. What did you learn?

9. Why has Project Apollo been seen as "the ultimate answer" for marketing researchers? Do you see any disadvantages of this methodology?

10. Describe how clickstream research can benefit an online retailer.

(Team Exercise) 11. Divide the class into teams of five. Each team should select a different retailer (services are okay for mystery shopping). Two members of the team should prepare a list of 10 to 15 questions to be answered. A sample of questions for an Eye Care Clinic are shown below. The remaining three members of the team should become mystery shoppers with the goal of answering the questions created by the team. After the shopping is complete, the team should combine their findings and make a report to the class.

Sample Mystery Shopping Questions for an Eye Care Clinic

1. Was the phone answered within three rings?
2. How long did you have to wait for an appointment?
3. Were you given clear directions to the office?
4. Did you receive a new patient packet in the mail?
5. Were signs directing you to the office clear and visible?
6. Did the receptionist greet you when you entered the office?
7. How long did you wait before being taken into a room for the pre-exam?
8. Did all staff members have a name tag on?
9. Was the facility clean?
10. Were your eyes dilated before you saw the doctor?
11. Were exam procedures explained clearly?
12. Were you given an opportunity to ask the doctor questions?
13. Were your questions answered promptly and respectfully?
14. Were you directed to the optical shop after your exam?
15. Were your glasses/contacts ready when promised?

WORKING THE NET

1. Go to *http://acnielsen.com* and *http://www.infores.com* and determine what ACNielsen and IRI are saying on the Web about their latest scanner-based research technology.

2. Go to *www.doubleclick.com* and read its latest research findings. Make an oral presentation to your class.

REAL-LIFE RESEARCH • 7.1

Food Lion and Others Capitalize on Loyalty Cards

Just swipe the card at the checkout register and get a discount on tomatoes or toothpaste, or whatever the specials are. You save money, and the store builds a record that lets it know how to serve its best customers.

Loyalty cards have been around for a few years now, and supermarket and drugstore chains are beginning to reap the benefits. With a huge amount of data being collected on shoppers, from the types of soda they buy to whether they like to shop late at night, merchants are getting smarter at tracking consumer trends. And they're changing their merchandise, store layout, and advertising accordingly to keep their most loyal customers spending.

A few examples:

- CVS Corporation launched its loyalty card program and discovered that cosmetic buyers are its best customers. So beauty products have been put up front in a third of the stores, instead of being relegated to the back corners.

- Food Lion started offering loyalty cards a few years ago and now is stocking up on peppers, cactus leaves, and plantains in its Charlotte, North Carolina, stores to better serve Hispanic customers from the Caribbean.

- Winn-Dixie Stores, which began rolling out a loyalty card program in March 2002, can now measure the effectiveness of ads on top customers and knows the 25 items that attract the most loyal shoppers.

Retailers estimate that 20 percent of their shoppers account for 80 percent of store sales, so finding out what their best customers want is essential. By simply scanning purchases, stores track what's selling, but when that information is tied to loyalty cards, merchants obtain richer information on who is buying what. This is the prized asset of supermarkets' future.[30]

Questions

1. Why are loyalty cards the key to supermarkets' "prized asset to the future"?
2. What type of data would be best to get from customers when they apply for a loyalty card?
3. How could the above demographic/psychographic data be used in conjunction with shoppers purchase data?
4. What actions might supermarkets take based upon loyalty card data?

Continental Airlines Online Advertising

REAL-LIFE RESEARCH • 7.2

While click rates have become the de facto measurement of the direct effectiveness of online advertising, the debate has continued over the true value of the impact over time (or "in-direct response") of online advertisements. Current technology enables marketers to track consumers who saw an online ad and then also track user behavior in terms of actual online conversions on the marketer's Web site (sales, registrations, etc.). This postimpression conversion activity (users saw an ad, did not click on it, but ultimately performed the activity designated as a conversion) is referred to as a "view-through" and is typically measured for one month post the impression being viewed. View-through activity has been an available metric for quite some time, but there has been little investigation into its validity. If a consumer on the Internet sees an advertisement for a Web site but does not click on it, can the fact that this person visited that Web site later be directly attributed to seeing that ad? Certainly, other factors drive visitors to Web sites, including other forms of media, but what is the true impact over time of online advertising? Determined to discover what the real effect of this in-direct response is,

DoubleClick, along with Continental Airlines and its online media buying agency, Arc Worldwide (formerly Semaphore Partners), conducted a test to help evaluate view-through activity and response to online advertising over time.

Methodology

Individuals in the research were exposed to either test or control ads during the one-month period of Continental Airlines' online media campaign. Both sets of ads were running during the same time period. Impression levels and frequency were controlled for in both groups. View-through activity was tracked for sales and registrations occurring 1 hour, 1 day, 7 days, 14 days, and 30 days after exposure. The data were then analyzed for the control group to establish a baseline to determine the effectiveness of the test group results. The differences between the control and test group were analyzed at the campaign as well as creative level. There were 3,588,870 unique users in the study: 1,467,239 in the control and 2,121,631 in the exposed group.

Key Findings

Test results suggest independent effects of exposure to online creative ads on subsequent conversions. The test creative placements consistently performed better than the control placements:

- ☐ For this test campaign, 67.5 percent of the test group's view-through registrations and sales are attributable to online creative ads.
- ☐ The study shows significant impact of exposure to online creative ads for most of the above-defined time lag intervals after exposure.
- ☐ Impressions volume and site/placement are identified as significant factors in in-direct response to online advertising, with impressions being the most significant factor.

Online Advertising's Share of View-through Activity

Overall, for the Continental campaign, approximately 67.5 percent of conversions generated by online advertising are attributable to online marketing. The percentage of registrations attributable to online marketing is slightly higher than the percentage of attributable sales. This is most likely because Continental Airlines already has such a strong brand in the market that people are naturally likely to go to the Web site and purchase airline tickets regardless of online advertising.

Percentage of View-Through Conversions by Source

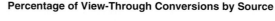

Naturally occurring   Attributable to online media

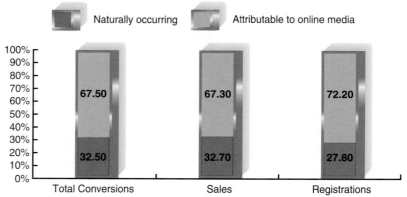

	Total Conversions	Sales	Registrations
Attributable to online media	67.50	67.30	72.20
Naturally occurring	32.50	32.70	27.80

In order to determine what share of activity actually comes from online advertising, the effective conversion rates (ECR) for both the control and test groups are calculated. The ECR for the control group is used as a baseline to discount the ECR of the test group and determine the share of conversion directly attributable to online creative. Although some activity counted as in-direct response occurred as a result of other factors, over time there is a significant impact of response to online advertising.

Impact of Time Lag on In-Direct Response

For almost every time period, there is a significant difference between the test and control groups. Although the volume of view-through e-mail registrations directly attributable to online advertising was higher than the corresponding activity for sales, the impact of online advertising on sales increased over time, while the opposite was true for registrations. Over the course of the 30-day period, the impact of delayed response on e-mail registrations decreased by 50 percent after one day, whereas the impact on sales transactions increased by 3 percent during the same period. The difference between these two events is most likely due to the fact that making airline ticket purchases involves a longer decision process. When you combine all the view-through activity for these two events, the impact of time mirrors that of the sales transactions, since sales accounted for 96 percent of the view-through conversions.

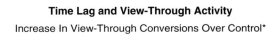

Time Lag and View-Through Activity

Increase In View-Through Conversions Over Control*

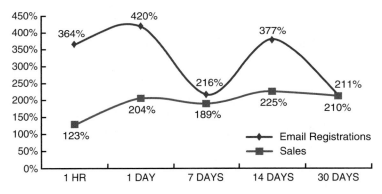

All results are significant at the 95 percent confidence level or higher; however, there was no statistically significant difference between the test and control groups for sales occurring within 1 hour.

Factors Influencing In-Direct Response
Subscriptions and Transactions

The test results showed that there was a strong correlation (0.94) between view-through e-mail registrations and sales, so they must be caused by the same factors. Three key factors were at the core of the increase in delayed response sales and, based on correlation analysis and regression, e-mail registrations:

☐ Exposure to campaign creative (as opposed to control)

☐ Increased volume of impressions, with some signs of diminishing returns

❑   Creative placements on specific regional sites related to Continental's "hub" city and homepage placements

Other variables, such as section content and ad size, were examined to measure their impact on sales and e-mail registrations, but either their impact was insignificant compared to other factors in this campaign or there was not enough data to make any conclusions at this time. Creative was one variable that was limited by the fact that not all of the ad sizes ran in multiple sites and placements.

The results from this test reinforce the importance of larger campaigns (impressions) as well as reaching consumers in the right places (sites/placements). The regression models show that increasing the volume of impressions has a positive effect on the in-direct response, but there is a point of limitation where diminishing returns start to play a factor. With the data available, it is not possible to determine exactly where diminishing returns start for this campaign. Nevertheless, the point of diminishing returns will most likely vary for different campaigns, and it should be addressed on a case-by-case basis. Similarly, although the aforementioned sites show positive influence on this campaign, these variables could vary for different campaigns, brands, and objectives.[31]

Glossary

In-Direct Response   The response to an online ad that occurs over time without the action of a click

Click-Through   The interaction with an online advertisement that redirects the user to a designated URL

Control Ad   Any non-Continental Airlines advertisement, including, but not limited to, media sites' house ads and DoubleClick ads

Control Group   Internet users who were never exposed to test ads over the course of the campaign and the following 30-day period

Effective Conversion Rate (ECR)   The total number of conversions (sales and/or e-mail registrations) per impression (conversions, impressions)

Test Ad   Any Continental Airlines advertisement

Test Group   Internet users who were exposed to test ads over the course of the campaign. *Note:* the test group could have been exposed to control ads during the test period

View-Through   A metric in the DoubleClick DART system that captures Web site activity that occurs when a user has been exposed to, but did not click on, an online advertisement, visits the Web site later on by typing in the URL or any other method, and performs an activity designated by the advertiser as a conversion.

Questions

1.   You are a promotion manager for Continental Airlines. What action might you take based on this research?

2.   Would you recommend that further industrywide studies be conducted? If so, what should they encompass?

3.   How could this type of data be meshed with Project Apollo (discussed in this chapter)?

4. Go through the key findings of the research and explain, in your own words, what each one means.

5. What role does the control group play in the effective conversion rates?

6. Explain the impact of time lag on in-direct response.

7. What key factors increased delayed response sales? Explain why each of the three factors may have had an impact.

PRIMARY DATA COLLECTION: EXPERIMENTATION AND TEST MARKETS

LEARNING OBJECTIVES

→	1.	To understand the nature of experiments.
→	2.	To gain insight into requirements for proving causation.
→	3.	To learn about the experimental setting.
→	4.	To examine experimental validity.
→	5.	To learn the limitations of experimentation in marketing research.
→	6.	To compare types of experimental designs.
→	7.	To gain insight into test marketing.

Researchers are often faced with the need to measure the effects of marketing mix variables such as price and advertising. Experimental designs are the way to address these issues.

Krista Weseman is new to her position as marketing research director for Healthco, a company that sells group health insurance to firms with 100 or more employees. She has been charged with evaluating the effectiveness of a new advertising campaign. In the past, Healthco, like other group health insurance companies, has made very limited use of advertising. However, changes in the group health insurance industry, including a movement toward consumerism and consolidation of regional health insurance firms into much larger national organizations, point to the need for image and brand development. In turn, this is going to require more extensive use of advertising than has been the case in the past. Healthco has decided to use Tampa, Florida, as a test market for its new advertising campaign developed by a major advertising agency in New York and designed to increase awareness and perceptions on key image dimensions for Healthco.

The initial thinking regarding the test is that it should measure certain key metrics such as unaided awareness, interest in Healthco, and a number of image dimensions that have been shown in other research to be related to actual sales. Furthermore, it has been decided to do a telephone survey of 400 individuals who would be decision makers for company health insurance benefits at the conclusion of the campaign. The survey would be designed to measure the metrics noted above. However, the vice president to whom Krista reports has raised questions about the proposed research design. His concern is that if they only have measures at the end of the campaign then they have no real idea of how the campaign has caused changes in key metrics. Krista has pointed out to him that they could use results from a national study covering these measures that was conducted by Healthco two years ago. Furthermore, the vice president has noted that certain things outside of their control such as competitor advertising during the course of their test might skew the results. Wouldn't it be useful to also measure the key metrics in a market where Healthco is not going to be conducting advertising that is similar to Tampa?

After you have completed this chapter, you should recognize that Krista's initial design is the weak *one-shot case study* design. The vice president's first suggestion anticipated a stronger one-group pretest–posttest design; his second suggestion is for a one-shot case study design and his third was for what is referred to as a before and after with control group design. ▪

What Is an Experiment?

experiment
Research approach in which one variable is manipulated and the effect on another variable is observed.

Research based on experimentation is fundamentally different from research based on surveys or observation.[1] In the case of both survey and observation research, the researcher is, in essence, a passive assembler of data. The researcher asks people questions or observes what they do. In experimental research, the situation is very different: the researcher becomes an active participant in the process.

In concept, an **experiment** is straightforward. The researcher changes or manipulates one thing (called an *experimental, treatment, independent,* or *explanatory variable*) to observe the effect on something else (referred to as a *dependent variable*). In marketing experiments, the dependent variable is frequently some measure of sales, such as total sales, market share, or the like; experimental variables are typically marketing mix variables, such as price, amount or type of advertising, and changes in product features.

Demonstrating Causation

causal research
Research designed to determine whether a change in one variable likely caused an observed change in another.

Experimental research is often referred to as **causal** (not casual) **research** because it is the only type of research that has the potential to demonstrate that a change in one variable *causes* some predictable change in another variable. To demonstrate causation (that *A* likely caused *B*), one must be able to show three things:

1. Concomitant variation (correlation)
2. Appropriate time order of occurrence
3. Elimination of other possible causal factors

Please note that we are using the terms *causation* and *causality* in the scientific sense.[2] The scientific view of causation is quite different from the popular view, which often implies that there is a single cause of an event. For example, when someone says in everyday conversation that *X* is the cause of some observed change in *Y*, he or she generally means that *X* is the only cause of the observed change in *Y*. But the scientific view holds that *X* is only one of a number of possible determining conditions that caused the observed change in *Y*.

In addition, the everyday view of causality implies a completely deterministic relationship, while the scientific view implies a probabilistic relationship. The popular view is that if *X* is the cause of *Y*, then *X* must always lead to *Y*. The scientific view holds that *X* can be a cause of *Y* if the presence of *X* makes the occurrence of *Y* more probable, or likely.

Finally, the scientific view holds that one can never definitively prove that *X* is a cause of *Y* but only infer that a relationship exists. In other words, causal relationships are always inferred and never demonstrated conclusively beyond a shadow of a doubt. Three types of evidence—concomitant variation, appropriate time order of occurrence, and elimination of other possible causal factors—are used to infer causal relationships.

Concomitant Variation

concomitant variation
Statistical relationship between two variables.

To provide evidence that a change in *A* caused a particular change in *B*, one must first show that there is **concomitant variation,** or correlation, between *A* and *B*; in other words, *A* and *B* must vary together in some predictable fashion. This might be a *positive* or an *inverse* relationship. Two variables that might be related in a positive manner are advertising and sales. They would be positively related if sales increased by some predictable amount when advertising increased by a certain amount. Two variables that might be related in an inverse manner are price and sales. They would be inversely (negatively) related if sales increased when price decreased and decreased when price increased. The researcher can test for the existence and direction of statistical relationships by means of a number of statistical procedures, including chi-square analysis, correlation analysis, regression analysis, and analysis of variance to mention a few. All of these statistical procedures are discussed later in the text (chi-square, correlation analysis, and regression analysis in Chapter 15, and analysis of variance in Chapter 16).

However, concomitant variation by itself does not prove causation. Simply because two variables happen to vary together in some predictable fashion does not prove that one causes the other. For example, suppose you found a high degree of correlation between sales of a product in the United States and the GDP (gross domestic product) of Germany. This might be true simply because both variables happened to be increasing at a similar rate. Further examination and consideration might show that there is no true link between the two variables. To infer causation, you must be able to show correlation—but correlation alone is not proof of causation.

Appropriate Time Order of Occurrence

The second requirement for demonstrating that a causal relationship likely exists between two variables is showing that there is an **appropriate time order of occurrence.** To demonstrate that A caused B, one must be able to show that A occurred before B occurred. For example, to demonstrate that a price change had an effect on sales, you must be able to show that the price change occurred before the change in sales was observed. However, showing that A and B vary concomitantly and that A occurred before B still does not provide evidence strong enough to permit one to conclude that A is the likely cause of an observed change in B.

> **appropriate time order of occurrence**
> Change in an independent variable occurred before an observed change in the dependent variable.

Elimination of Other Possible Causal Factors

The most difficult thing to demonstrate in marketing experiments is that the change in B was not caused by some factor other than A. For example, suppose a company increased its advertising expenditures and observed an increase in the sales of its product. Correlation and appropriate time order of occurrence are present. But has a likely causal relationship been demonstrated? The answer is "no." It is possible that the observed change in sales is due to some factor other than the increase in advertising. For example, at the same time advertising expenditures were increased, a major competitor may have decreased advertising expenditures, or increased price, or pulled out of the market. Even if the competitive environment did not change, one or a combination of other factors may have influenced sales. For example, the economy in the area might have received a major boost for some reason that has nothing to do with the experiment. For any of these reasons or many others, the observed increase in sales might have been caused by some factor or combination of factors other than or in addition to the increase in advertising expenditures. Much of the discussion in this chapter is related to designing experiments so as to eliminate or adjust for the effects of other possible causal factors.

Experimental Setting

Experiments can be conducted in a laboratory or a field setting.[3] Most experiments in the physical sciences are conducted in a laboratory setting; many marketing experiments are field experiments.

Laboratory Experiments

> **laboratory experiments**
> Experiments conducted in a controlled setting.

Laboratory experiments provide a number of important advantages.[4] The major advantage of conducting experiments in a laboratory is the ability to control extraneous causal factors—temperature, light, humidity, and so on—and focus on the effect of a change in *A* on *B*. In the lab, the researcher can effectively deal with the third element of proving causation (elimination of other possible causal factors) and focus on the first two elements (concomitant variation and appropriate time order of occurrence). This additional control strengthens the researcher's ability to infer that an observed change in the dependent variable was caused by a change in the experimental, or treatment, variable. As a result, laboratory experiments are viewed as having greater internal validity (discussed in greater detail in the next section). On the other hand, the controlled and possibly sterile environment of the laboratory may not be a good analog of the marketplace. For this reason, the findings of laboratory experiments sometimes do not hold up when transferred to the marketplace. Therefore, laboratory experiments are seen as having greater problems with external validity (see the next section). However, laboratory experiments are probably being used to a greater extent in marketing research today than in the past because of their many advantages.

Field Experiments

> **field experiments**
> Tests conducted outside the laboratory in an actual environment, such as a marketplace.

Field experiments are conducted outside the laboratory in an actual market environment. Test markets, discussed later in this chapter, are a frequently used type of field experiment. Field experiments solve the problem of the realism of the environment but open up a whole new set of problems. The major problem is that in the field the researcher cannot control all the spurious factors that might influence the dependent variable, such as the actions of competitors, the weather, the economy, societal trends, and the political climate. Therefore, field experiments have more problems related to internal validity, whereas lab experiments have more problems related to external validity.

Experimental Validity

Validity is defined as the degree to which an experiment actually measures what the researcher was trying to measure (see Chapter 9). The validity of a measure depends on the extent to which the measure is free from both systematic and random error. Two specific kinds of validity are relevant to experimentation: internal validity and external validity.

> **internal validity**
> Extent to which competing explanations for the experimental results observed can be ruled out.

Internal validity refers to the extent to which competing explanations for the experimental results observed can be ruled out. If the researcher can show that the experimental, or treatment, variable actually produced the differences observed in the dependent variable, then the experiment can be said to be internally valid. This kind of validity requires evidence demonstrating that variation in the dependent variable was caused by exposure to the treatment variable and not other possible causal factors.

> **external validity**
> Extent to which causal relationships measured in an experiment can be generalized to outside persons, settings, and times.

External validity refers to the extent to which the causal relationships measured in an experiment can be generalized to outside persons, settings, and times.[5] The issue here is how representative the subjects and the setting used in the experiment are of other populations and settings to which the researcher would like to project the results. As noted earlier, field experiments offer a higher degree of external validity and a lower degree of internal validity than do laboratory experiments. See Practicing Marketing Research on page 237.

PRACTICING MARKETING RESEARCH

Be Careful Who You Talk To

External validity requires that the sample of subjects in our test be comparable to the general population. This is not always as easy as it might seem.

Research conducted by Alistair Munro shows that if you are doing research on money and purchasing patterns, your results may vary widely depending on whether you get your measures from the man or the woman of the house. He polled couples who had lived together for as little as 12 months, those who had been married for 40 years or more, and everything in between. The sample was representative on other issues such as occupation, education, and income. The measures obtained covered financial matters as well as family and marital relationships.

Munro found that 60 percent of the couples queried did not agree on basic facts about their use of money or even the length of their relationship. Men were twice as likely to misrepresent family finances, saying they were jointly managed, while the women were more likely to report that the men managed the cash. About 75 percent said that they would take risks with money if it were their spouse's but would play it safe with their own. Newly married and unmarried couples tended to report their domestic arrangements the most accurately, with partners providing matching answers twice as often as longer-term married couples.

These results point to the need to be careful about whom we talk to when we are developing experimental designs that are intended to test the effects of marketing variables on household behavior and that need to have external validity (i.e., can be applied to the marketplace).

Experimental Notation

In our discussion of experiments, we will use a standard system of notation, described as follows:

- X is used to indicate the exposure of an individual or a group to an experimental treatment. The experimental treatment is the factor whose effects we want to measure and compare. Experimental treatments may be factors such as different prices, package designs, point-of-purchase displays, advertising approaches, or product forms.

- O (for observation) is used to refer to the process of taking measurements on the test units. *Test units* are individuals, groups of individuals, or entities whose response to the experimental treatments is being tested. Test units might include individual consumers, groups of consumers, retail stores, total markets, or other entities that might be the targets of a firm's marketing program.

- Different time periods are represented by the horizontal arrangement of the X's and O's. For example,

$$O_1 \qquad X \qquad O_2$$

would describe an experiment in which a preliminary measurement O_1 was taken of one or more test units, then one or more test units were exposed to the experimental variable X, and then a measurement O_2 of the test units was taken. The X's and O's can be arranged vertically to show simultaneous exposure and measurement of different test units. For example, the following design involves two different groups of test units:

$$X_1 \qquad O_1$$
$$X_2 \qquad O_2$$

The two groups of test units received different experimental treatments at the same time (X_1 and X_2), and then the two groups were measured simultaneously (O_1 and O_2).[6]

Extraneous Variables

In interpreting experimental results, the researcher would like to be able to conclude that the observed response is due to the effect of the experimental variable. However, many things stand in the way of the ability to reach this conclusion. In anticipation of possible problems in interpretation, the researcher needs to design the experiment so as to eliminate as many extraneous factors as possible as causes of the observed effect.

Examples of Extraneous Variables

Examples of extraneous factors or variables that pose a threat to experimental validity are history, maturation, instrument variation, selection bias, mortality, testing effects, and regression to the mean.[7]

History

history
Intervention, between the beginning and end of an experiment, of outside variables or events that might change the dependent variable.

History refers to the intervention, between the beginning and end of the experiment, of any variable or event—other than those manipulated by the researcher (experimental variables)—that might affect the value of the dependent variable. Early tests of Prego spaghetti sauce by the Campbell Soup Company provide an example of a possible problem with extraneous variables. Campbell executives claim that Ragu greatly increased its advertising levels and use of cents-off deals during their tests. They believe that this increased marketing activity was designed to get shoppers to stock up on Ragu and make it impossible for Campbell to get an accurate reading of potential sales for its Prego product.

Maturation

maturation
Changes in subjects occurring during the experiment that are not related to the experiment but which may affect subjects' response to the treatment factor.

Maturation refers to changes in subjects during the course of the experiment that are a function of time; it includes getting older, hungrier, more tired, and the like. Throughout the course of an experiment, the responses of people to a treatment variable may change because of these maturation factors and not because of the treatment variable. The likelihood that maturation will be a serious problem in a particular experiment depends on the length of the experiment. The longer the experiment runs, the more likely it is that maturation will present problems for interpreting the results.

Instrument Variation

instrument variation
Changes in measurement instruments (e.g., interviewers or observers) that might affect measurements.

Instrument variation refers to any changes in measurement instruments that might explain differences in the measurements taken. It is a serious problem in marketing experiments where people are used as interviewers or observers to measure the dependent variable. If measurements on the same subject are taken by different interviewers or observers at different points in time, differences between measurements may reflect variations in the way the interviewing or observation was done by different interviewers or observers. On the other hand, if the same interviewer or observer is used to take measurements on the same subject over time, differences may reflect the fact that the particular observer or interviewer has become less interested and is doing a sloppier job.

Selection Bias   The threat to validity posed by **selection bias** is encountered in situations where the experimental or test group is systematically different from the population to which the researcher would like to project the experimental results or from the control group. In projecting the results to a population that is systematically different from the test group, the researcher may get results very different from those we got in the test because of differences in the makeup of the two groups. Similarly, an observed difference between a test group and an untreated control group (not exposed to the experimental variable) may be due to differences between the two groups and not to the effect of the experimental variable. Researchers can ensure equality of groups through either randomization or matching. *Randomization* involves assigning subjects to test groups and control groups at random. *Matching* involves what the name suggests—making sure that there is a one-to-one match between people or other units in the test and control groups in regard to key characteristics (e.g., age). Specific matching procedures are discussed later in this chapter.

selection bias
Systematic differences between the test group and the control group due to a biased selection process.

Mortality   **Mortality** refers to the loss of test units during the course of an experiment. It is a problem because there is no easy way to know whether the lost units would have responded to the treatment variable in the same way as those units that remained throughout the entire experiment. An experimental group that was representative of the population or that matched a control group may become nonrepresentative because of the systematic loss of subjects with certain characteristics. For example, in a study of music preferences of the population, if nearly all the subjects under the age of 25 were lost during the course of the experiment, then the researcher would likely get a biased picture of music preferences at the end of the experiment. In this case, the results would lack external validity.

mortality
Loss of test units or subjects during the course of an experiment, which may result in a nonrepresentativeness.

Testing Effects   **Testing effects** result from the fact that the process of experimentation may produce its own effect on the responses observed. For example, measuring attitude toward a product before exposing subjects to an ad may act as a treatment variable, influencing perception of the ad. Testing effects come in two forms:

testing effect
Effect that is a by-product of the research process itself.

- ☐ *Main testing effects* are the possible effects of earlier observations on later observations. For example, students taking the GMAT for the second time tend to do better than those taking the test for the first time, even though the students have no information about the items they actually missed on the first test. This effect also can be reactive in the sense that responses to the first administration of an attitude test have some actual effect on subjects' attitudes that is reflected in subsequent applications of the same test.

- ☐ *Interactive testing effect* is the effect of a prior measurement on a subject's response to a later measurement. For example, if subjects are asked about their awareness of advertising for various products (pre-exposure measurement) and then exposed to advertising for one or more of these products (treatment variable), postmeasurements would likely reflect the joint effect of the pre-exposure and the treatment condition.

Regression to the Mean   **Regression to the mean** refers to the observed tendency of subjects with extreme behavior to move toward the average for that behavior during the course of an experiment. Test units may exhibit extreme behavior because of chance, or they may have been specifically chosen because of their extreme behavior. The researcher might, for example, have chosen people for an experimental group because they were extremely heavy users of a particular product or service. In such situations, their tendency to move toward the average behavior may be interpreted as having been caused by the treatment variable when in fact it has nothing to do with the treatment variable.

regression to the mean
Tendency of subjects with extreme behavior to move toward the average for that behavior during the course of an experiment.

Controlling Extraneous Variables

> **randomization**
> Random assignment of subjects to treatment conditions to ensure equal representation of subject characteristics.

> **physical control**
> Holding constant the value or level of extraneous variables throughout the course of an experiment.

> **design control**
> Use of the experimental design to control extraneous causal factors.

> **statistical control**
> Adjusting for the effects of confounded variables by statistically adjusting the value of the dependent variable for each treatment condition.

Causal factors that threaten validity must be controlled in some manner to establish a clear picture of the effect of the manipulated variable on the dependent variable. Extraneous causal factors are ordinarily referred to as *confounding variables* because they confound the treatment condition, making it impossible to determine whether changes in the dependent variable are due solely to the treatment conditions.

Four basic approaches are used to control extraneous factors: randomization, physical control, design control, and statistical control.

Randomization is carried out by randomly assigning subjects to treatment conditions so that extraneous causal factors related to subject characteristics can reasonably be assumed to be represented equally in each treatment condition, thus canceling out extraneous effects.

Physical control of extraneous causal factors may involve somehow holding constant the value or level of the extraneous variable throughout the experiment. Another approach to physical control is matching respondents in regard to important personal characteristics (e.g., age, income, lifestyle) before assigning them to different treatment conditions. The goal is to make sure there are no important differences between characteristics of respondents in the test and control groups.

Design control is the control of extraneous factors by means of specific types of experimental designs developed for this purpose. Such designs are discussed later in this chapter.

Finally, **statistical control** can be used to account for extraneous causal factors if these factors can be identified and measured throughout the course of the experiment. Procedures such as analysis of covariance can adjust for the effects of a confounded variable on the dependent variable by statistically adjusting the value of the dependent variable for each treatment condition.

Experimental Design, Treatment, and Effects

> **experimental design**
> Test in which the researcher has control over and manipulates one or more independent variables.

In an **experimental design**, the researcher has control over and manipulates one or more independent variables. In the experiments we discuss, typically only one independent variable is manipulated. Nonexperimental designs, which involve no manipulation, are often referred to as ex post facto (after the fact) research—an effect is observed, and then some attempt is made to attribute this effect to some causal factor.

An experimental design includes four factors:

1. The *treatment,* or experimental, *variable* (independent variable) that is manipulated
2. The *subjects* who participate in the experiment
3. A *dependent variable* that is measured
4. Some *plan or procedure* for dealing with extraneous causal factors

> **treatment variable**
> Independent variable that is manipulated in an experiment.

The **treatment variable** is the independent variable that is manipulated. *Manipulation* refers to a process in which the researcher sets the levels of the independent variable to test a particular causal relationship. To test the relationship between price (independent variable) and sales of a product (dependent variable), a researcher might expose subjects to three different levels of price and record the level of purchases at each price level. As the variable that is manipulated, price is the single treatment variable, with three treatment conditions or levels.

An experiment may include a test, or treatment, group and a control group. A *control group* is a group in which the independent variable is not changed during the course of the experiment. A *test group* is a group that is exposed to manipulation (change) of the independent variable.

The term **experimental effect** refers to the effect of the treatment variable on the dependent variable. The goal is to determine the effect of each treatment condition (level of treatment variable) on the dependent variable. For example, suppose that three different markets are selected to test three different prices, or treatment conditions. Each price is tested in each market for 3 months. In market 1, a price 2 percent lower than existing prices for the product is tested; in market 2, a price 4 percent lower is tested; and in market 3, a price 6 percent lower is tested. At the end of the 3-month test, sales in market 1 are observed to have increased by less than 1 percent over sales for the preceding 3-month period. In market 2, sales increased by 3 percent; and in market 3, sales increased by 5 percent. The change in sales observed in each market is the experimental effect.

 **experimental effect**
Effect of the treatment variable on the dependent variable.

Limitations of Experimental Research

As the preceding discussion shows, experiments are an extremely powerful form of research—the only type of research that can truly explore the existence and nature of causal relationships between variables of interest. Given these obvious advantages over other research designs for primary data collection, you might ask why experimental research is not used more often. There are many reasons, including the cost of experiments, the issue of security, and problems associated with implementing experiments.

High Cost of Experiments

To some degree, when making comparisons of the costs of experiments with the costs of surveys or observation-based research, we are comparing apples to oranges. Experiments can be very costly in both money and time. In many cases, managers may anticipate that the costs of doing an experiment would exceed the value of the information gained. Consider, for example, the costs of testing three alternative advertising campaigns in three different geographic areas. Three different campaigns must be produced; airtime must be purchased in all three markets; the timing in all three markets must be carefully coordinated; some system must be put into place to measure sales before, during, and after the test campaigns have run; measurements of other extraneous variables must be made; extensive analysis of the results must be performed; and a variety of other tasks must be completed in order to execute the experiment. All of this will cost a bare minimum of $1 million for a low-profile product and as much as tens of millions for a high-profile brand.

Security Issues

Conducting a field experiment in a test market involves exposing a marketing plan or some key element of a marketing plan in the actual marketplace. Undoubtedly, competitors will find out what is being considered well in advance of full-scale market introduction. This advance notice gives competitors an opportunity to decide whether and how to respond. In any case, the element of surprise is lost. In some instances, competitors have actually "stolen" concepts that were being tested in the marketplace and gone into national distribution before the company testing the product or strategy element completed the test marketing.

Implementation Problems

Problems that may hamper the implementation of an experiment include difficulty gaining cooperation within the organization, contamination problems, differences between test markets and the total population, and the lack of an appropriate group of people or geographic area for a control group.

It can be extremely difficult to obtain cooperation within the organization to execute certain types of experiments. For example, a regional marketing manager might be very reluctant to permit her market area to be used as a test market for a reduced level of advertising or a higher price. Quite naturally, her concern would be that the experiment might lower sales for the area.

Contamination occurs when buyers from outside the test area come into the area to purchase the product being tested, thereby distorting the results of the experiment. Outside buyers might live on the fringes of the test market area and receive TV advertisements—intended only for those in the test area—that offer a lower price, a special rebate, or some other incentive to buy a product. Their purchases will indicate that the particular sales-stimulating factor being tested is more effective than actually is the case.

In some cases, test markets may be so different, and the behavior of consumers in those markets so different, that a relatively small experimental effect is difficult to detect. This problem can be dealt with by careful matching of test markets and other similar strategies designed to ensure a high degree of equivalency of test units.

Finally, in some situations, no appropriate geographic area or group of people may be available to serve as a control group. This may be the case in a test of industrial products, whose very small number of purchasers are concentrated geographically. An attempt to test a new product among a subset of such purchasers would almost certainly be doomed to failure.

> **contamination**
> Inclusion in a test of a group of respondents who are not normally there—for example, buyers from outside the test market who see an advertisement intended only for those in the test area and enter the area to purchase the product being tested.

Selected Experimental Designs

This section presents examples of pre-experimental, true experimental, and quasi-experimental designs.[8] In outlining these experimental designs, we will use the system of notation introduced earlier.

Pre-Experimental Designs

> **pre-experimental designs**
> Designs that offer little or no control over extraneous factors.

Studies using **pre-experimental designs** generally are difficult to interpret because such designs offer little or no control over the influence of extraneous factors. As a result, these studies often are not much better than descriptive studies when it comes to making causal inferences. With these designs, the researcher has little control over aspects of exposure to the treatment variable (such as to whom and when) and measurements. However, these designs frequently are used in commercial test marketing because they are simple and inexpensive. They are useful for suggesting new hypotheses but do not offer strong tests of existing hypotheses. The reasons for this will be clear after you review the discussion of pre-experimental designs that follows.

> **one-shot case study design**
> Pre-experimental design with no pretest observations, no control group, and an after measurement only.

One-Shot Case Study Design

The **one-shot case study design** involves exposing test units (people or test markets) to the treatment variable for some period of time and then taking a measurement of the dependent variable. Symbolically, the design is shown as follows:

$$X \quad O_1$$

There are two basic weaknesses in this design. No pretest observations are made of the test units that will receive the treatment, and no control group of test units that did not receive the treatment is observed. As a result of these deficiencies, the design does not deal with the effects of any of the extraneous variables discussed previously. Therefore, the design lacks internal validity and, most likely, external validity as well. This design is useful for suggesting causal hypotheses but does not provide a strong test of such hypotheses. Many test markets for new products (not previously on the market) are based on this design.

One-Group Pretest–Posttest Design   The **one-group pretest–posttest design** is the design employed most frequently for testing changes in established products or marketing strategies. The fact that the product was on the market before the change provides the basis for the pretest measurement (O_1). The design is shown symbolically as follows:

$$O_1 \qquad X \qquad O_2$$

Pretest observations are made of a single group of subjects or a single test unit (O_1) that then receives the treatment. Finally, a posttest observation is made (O_2). The treatment effect is estimated by $O_2 - O_1$.

History is a threat to the internal validity of this design because an observed change in the dependent variable might be caused by an event that took place outside the experiment between the pretest and posttest measurements. In laboratory experiments, this threat can be controlled by insulating respondents from outside influences. Unfortunately, this type of control is impossible in field experiments.

Maturation is another threat to this type of design. An observed effect might be caused by the fact that subjects have grown older, smarter, more experienced, or the like between the pretest and the posttest.

This design has only one pretest observation. As a result, the researcher knows nothing of the pretest trend in the dependent variable. The posttest score may be higher because of an increasing trend of the dependent variable in a situation where this effect is not the treatment of interest.

True Experimental Designs

In a **true experimental design,** the experimenter randomly assigns treatments to randomly selected test units. In our notation system, the random assignment of test units to treatments is denoted by (R). Randomization is an important mechanism that makes the results of true experimental designs more valid than the results of pre-experimental designs. True experimental designs are superior because randomization takes care of many extraneous variables. The principal reason for choosing randomized experiments over other types of research designs is that they clarify causal inference.[9] Two true experimental designs are discussed in this section: before and after with control group design and after-only with control group design.

Before and After with Control Group Design   The **before and after with control group design** can be presented symbolically as follows:

$$\begin{array}{llccc}
\text{Experimental Group:} & (R) & O_1 & X & O_2 \\
\text{Control Group:} & (R) & O_3 & & O_4
\end{array}$$

Because the test units in this design are randomly assigned to the experimental and control groups, the two groups can be considered equivalent. Therefore, they are likely to be subject to the same extraneous causal factors, except for the treatment of interest in the experimental group. For this reason, the difference between the pre- and postmeasurements

one-group pretest–posttest design
Pre-experimental design with pre- and postmeasurements but no control group.

true experimental design
Research using an experimental group and a control group, to which test units are randomly assigned.

before and after with control group design
True experimental design that involves random assignment of subjects or test units to experimental and control groups and pre- and postmeasurements of both groups.

of the control group ($O_4 - O_3$) should provide a good estimate of the effect of all the extraneous influences experienced by each group. The true impact of the treatment variable X can be known only when the extraneous influences are removed from the difference between the pre- and postmeasurements of the experimental group. Thus, the true impact of X is estimated by ($O_2 - O_1$) − ($O_4 - O_3$). This design generally controls for all but two major threats to validity: mortality and history.

Mortality is a problem if units drop out during the study and these units differ systematically from the ones that remain. This results in a selection bias because the experimental and control groups are composed of different subjects at the posttest than at the pretest. History will be a problem in those situations where factors other than the treatment variable affect the experimental group but not the control group, or vice versa. Examples of this design and the after-only with control group design are provided in Exhibit 8.1.

> **after-only with control group design**
> True experimental design that involves random assignment of subjects or test units to experimental and control groups, but no premeasurement of the dependent variable.

After-Only with Control Group Design The **after-only with control group design** differs from the static-group comparison design (the pre-experimental design with nonequivalent groups) in regard to the assignment of the test units. In the static-group comparison design, test units are not randomly assigned to treatment groups. As a result, it is possible for the groups to differ in regard to the dependent variable before

EXHIBIT 8.1	Examples of True Experimental Designs

Situation: California Tan wants to measure the sales effect of a point-of-purchase display. The firm is considering two true experimental designs.

After-Only with Control Group Design	Before and After with Control Group Design

After-Only with Control Group Design

Basic design:
  Experimental Group: (R)   X O_1
  Control Group: (R) O_2

Sample: Random sample of stores that sell their products. Stores are randomly assigned to test and control groups. Groups can be considered equivalent.

Treatment (X): Placing the point-of-purchase display in stores in the experimental group for 1 month.

Measurements (O_1, O_2): Actual sales of company's brand during the period that the point-of-purchase displays are in test stores.

Comments:
Because of random assignment of stores to groups, the test group and control group can be considered equivalent. Measure of the treatment effect of X is $O_1 - O_2$. If $O_1 = 125,000$ units and $O_2 = 113,000$ units, then treatment effect = 12,000 units.

Before and After with Control Group Design

Basic design:
  Experimental Group: (R) O_1 X O_2
  Control Group: (R) O_3 O_4

Sample: Same as after-only design.
Treatment (X): Same as after-only design.
Measurements (O_1 to O_4):
  O_1 and O_2 are pre- and postmeasurements for the experimental group;
  O_3 and O_4 are the same for the control group.

Results:
  $O_1 = 113,000$ units
  $O_2 = 125,000$ units
  $O_3 = 111,000$ units
  $O_4 = 118,000$ units

Comments:
Random assignment to groups means that the groups can be considered equivalent.

Because groups are equivalent, it is reasonable to assume that they will be equally affected by the same extraneous factors.

The difference between pre- and postmeasurements for the control group ($O_4 - O_3$) provides a good estimate of the effects of all extraneous factors on both groups. Based on these results, $O_4 - O_3 = 7,000$ units. The estimated treatment effect is ($O_2 - O_1$) − ($O_4 - O_3$) = (125,000 − 113,000) − (118,000 − 111,000) = 5,000 units.

presentation of the treatment. The after-only with control group design deals with this shortcoming; it can be shown symbolically as follows:

$$\text{Experimental Group: } (R) \quad X \quad O_1$$
$$\text{Control Group: } \quad (R) \quad \quad O_2$$

Notice that the test units are randomly (R) assigned to experimental and control groups. This random assignment should produce experimental and control groups that are approximately equal in regard to the dependent variable before presentation of the treatment to the experimental group. It can reasonably be assumed that test unit mortality (one of the threats to internal validity) will affect each group in the same way.

Considering this design in the context of the sun tan lotion example described in Exhibit 8.1, we see a number of problems. Events other than the treatment variable may have occurred during the experimental period in one or a few stores in the experimental group. If a particular store in the experimental group ran a sale on certain other products and, as a result, had a larger than average number of customers in the store, sun tan lotion sales might have increased because of the heavier traffic. Events such as these, which are store-specific (history), may distort the overall treatment effect. Also, there is a possibility that a few stores may drop out during the experiment (mortality threat), resulting in selection bias because the stores in the experimental group will be different at the posttest.

Quasi-Experiments

When designing a true experiment, the researcher often must create artificial environments to control independent and extraneous variables. Because of this artificiality, questions are raised about the external validity of the experimental findings. Quasi-experimental designs have been developed to deal with this problem. They generally are more feasible in field settings than are true experiments.

In **quasi-experiments,** the researcher lacks complete control over the scheduling of treatments or must assign respondents to treatments in a *nonrandom* fashion. These designs frequently are used in marketing research studies because cost and field constraints often do not permit the researcher to exert direct control over the scheduling of treatments and the randomization of respondents. Examples of quasi-experiments are interrupted time-series designs and multiple time-series designs.

> **quasi-experiments**
> Studies in which the researcher lacks complete control over the scheduling of treatments or must assign respondents to treatments in a nonrandom manner.

Interrupted Time-Series Designs **Interrupted time-series designs** involve repeated measurement of an effect both before and after a treatment is introduced that "interrupts" previous data patterns. Interrupted time-series experimental designs can be shown symbolically as follows:

$$O_1 \quad O_2 \quad O_3 \quad O_4 \quad X \quad O_5 \quad O_6 \quad O_7 \quad O_8$$

> **interrupted time-series design**
> Research in which repeated measurement of an effect "interrupts" previous data patterns.

A common example of this type of design in marketing research involves the use of consumer purchase panels. A researcher might use such a panel to make periodic measurements of consumer purchase activity (the O's), introducing a new promotional campaign (the X) and examining the panel data for an effect. The researcher has control over the timing of the promotional campaign but cannot be sure when the panel members were exposed to the campaign or whether they were exposed at all.

This design is very similar to the one-group pretest–posttest design

$$O_1 \quad X \quad O_2$$

However, time-series experimental designs have greater interpretability than the one-group pretest–posttest design because the many measurements allow more understanding of extraneous variables. If, for example, sales of a product were on the rise and a new promotional campaign were introduced, the true effect of this campaign could not be estimated if a pretest–posttest design were used. However, the rising trend in sales would be obvious if a number of pretest and posttest observations had been made. Time-series designs help determine the underlying trend of the dependent variable and provide better interpretability in regard to the treatment effect.

The interrupted time-series design has two fundamental weaknesses. The primary weakness is the experimenter's inability to control history. Although maintaining a careful log of all possibly relevant external happenings can reduce this problem, the researcher has no way of determining the appropriate number and timing of pretest and posttest observations.

The other weakness of this design comes from the possibility of interactive effects of testing and evaluation apprehension resulting from the repeated measurements taken on test units. For example, panel members may become "expert" shoppers or simply become more conscious of their shopping habits. Under these circumstances, it may be inappropriate to make generalizations to other populations.

Multiple Time-Series Designs   If a control group can be added to an interrupted time-series design, then researchers can be more certain in their interpretation of the treatment effect. This design, called the **multiple time-series design**, can be shown symbolically as follows:

> **multiple time-series design**
> Interrupted time-series design with a control group.

Experimental Group: $O_1 \quad O_2 \quad O_3 \quad X \quad O_4 \quad O_5 \quad O_6$

Control Group: $\quad\quad O_1 \quad O_2 \quad O_3 \quad\quad O_4 \quad O_5 \quad O_6$

The researcher must take care in selecting the control group. For example, if an advertiser were testing a new advertising campaign in a test city, that city would constitute the experimental group and another city that was not exposed to the new campaign would be chosen as the control group. It is important that the test and control cities be roughly equivalent in regard to characteristics related to the sale of the product (e.g., competitive brands available).

Test Markets

> **test market**
> Testing of a new product or some element of the marketing mix using an experimental or quasi-experimental design.

A common form of experimentation used by marketing researchers is the test market. The term **test market** is used rather loosely to refer to any research that involves testing a new product or change in an existing marketing strategy (e.g., product, price, place promotion) in a single market, group of markets, or region of the country through the use of experimental or quasi-experimental designs.[10]

New product introductions play a key role in a firm's financial success or failure. The conventional wisdom in the corporate world is that new products will have to be more profitable in the future than they were in the past because of higher levels of competition and a faster pace of change. Estimates of new product failure rates vary all over the place and range to more than 90 percent.

As you probably already recognize, test market studies have the goal of helping marketing managers make better decisions about new products and additions or changes to existing products or marketing strategies. A test market study does this by providing a real-world test for evaluating products and marketing programs. Marketing managers use test markets to evaluate proposed national programs with many separate elements on a smaller, less costly scale. The basic idea is to determine whether the estimated profits from rolling the product out on a national basis justify the potential risks. Test market studies are designed to provide information in regard to the following issues:

- ☐ Estimates of market share and volume.

- ☐ The effects that the new product will have on sales of similar products (if any) already marketed by the company. This is referred to as the *cannibalization rate*.

- ☐ Characteristics of consumers who buy the product. Demographic data will almost surely be collected, and lifestyle, psychographic, and other types of classification data may also be collected. This information is useful in helping the firm refine the marketing strategy for the product. For example, knowing the demographic characteristics of likely purchasers will help in developing a media plan that will effectively and efficiently reach target customers. Knowing the psychographic and lifestyle characteristics of target customers will provide valuable insights into how to position the product and the types of promotional messages that will appeal to them.

- ☐ The behavior of competitors during the test. This may provide some indication of what competitors will do if the product is introduced nationally.

Lifestyle data are often collected to find out about the characteristics of possible consumers. This information helps a firm refine the marketing strategy for its product. What might lifestyle data reveal about consumers who would purchase this ring?

Types of Test Markets

The vast majority of test markets can be categorized into four types—traditional, scanner or electronic, controlled, and simulated.[11] The *traditional or standard test market* involves testing the product and other elements of the marketing mix through a firm's regular channels of distribution. Traditional test markets take a relatively long time (six months or more), are costly, and immediately tip one's hand to the competition. Some have argued that the traditional test market provides the best read on how a product and the associated marketing mix will actually do if introduced because it provides the best analog of the real marketplace. However, some of the other options, discussed below, may provide very good estimates at a fraction of the cost, more quickly and without giving the competition advance warning regarding what a company is planning to do.

Scanner or electronic test markets are markets where scanner panel research firms have panels of consumers who carry scannable cards for use in buying particular products, especially those sold through grocery stores. These panels permit us to analyze the characteristics of those consumers who buy and those who don't buy the test products. Purchase/nonpurchase by individual panel participants can be related to their detailed demographic data, past purchase history, and, in some cases, media viewing habits. Firms offering scanner panels include ACNielsen and Information Resources. This approach offers speed, lower cost, and some degree of security regarding the marketing strategy or changes in strategy we are considering. The major criticism of this approach to test marketing relates to what some argue is its unrepresentative sampling: those who agree to participate in these panels may not be representative of the broader populations of consumers in these markets and other markets.

Controlled test markets are managed by research suppliers who ensure that the product is distributed through the agreed upon types and numbers of distributors. Research suppliers who offer controlled test markets, such as ACNielsen, pay distributors to provide the required amount of shelf space for test products. Research suppliers carefully monitor sales of the product in these controlled test markets. They enable companies to get their products into test more quickly, often supply more realistic levels of distribution, and provide better monitoring of product movement.

STMs (simulated test markets) are just what the name implies—simulations of the types of test markets noted above. As such, they can normally be conducted more quickly than the other two approaches, at a lower cost, and produce results that are, in most cases, highly predictive of what will actually happen. In these simulated test markets, a more limited amount of information is used in conjunction with mathematical models that include estimates of the effects of different marketing variables that can be adjusted to fit the situation. A number of different companies, including ACNielsen (Bases), Harris Interactive (Litmus), and Synovate (MarkeTest), offer these services, and each one has special features. However, they all share the following elements:

☐ A sample of consumers is selected based on the expected or known characteristics of the target consumer for the test product.

☐ Consumers sampled are recruited to come to a central location testing facility to view commercials for the test product and competitive products.

☐ Consumers are then given the opportunity to purchase the test product in the actual marketplace or in a simulated store environment.

☐ Purchasers are contacted after they have had time to use the product. They are asked how likely they are to repurchase and for their evaluations of the product.

☐ The above information is used with the proprietary model of the STM company to generate estimates of sales volume, market share, and other key market metrics.[12]

Costs of Test Marketing

Test marketing is expensive. A simple two-market test can cost a bare minimum of $1 million and probably much more. A long-running, more complex test can cost in the tens of millions of dollars. These estimates refer only to direct costs, which may include the following:

☐ Production of commercials
☐ Payments to an advertising agency for services
☐ Media time, charged at a higher rate because of low volume
☐ Syndicated research information
☐ Customized research information and associated data analysis
☐ Point-of-purchase materials
☐ Coupons and sampling
☐ Higher trade allowances to obtain distribution[13]

Many *indirect costs* are also associated with test marketing, including the following:

☐ Cost of management time spent on the test market
☐ Diversion of sales activity from existing products
☐ Possible negative impact of a test market failure on other products with the same family brand
☐ Possible negative trade reactions to products if the firm develops a reputation for not doing well
☐ Cost of letting competitors know what the firm is doing, thereby allowing them to develop a better strategy or beat the firm to the national market[14]

Test markets are expensive, and, as a result, they should be used only as the last step in a research process that has shown the new product or strategy has potential. In some situations, it may be cheaper to go ahead and launch the product, even if it fails.

Decision to Conduct Test Marketing

From the preceding discussion, you can see that test markets offer at least two important benefits to the firm conducting the test.[15]

☐ First and foremost, the test market provides a vehicle by which the firm can obtain a good estimate of a product's sales potential under realistic market conditions. A researcher can develop estimates of the product's national market share on the basis of these test results and use this figure to develop estimates of future financial performance for the product.

☐ Second, the test should identify weaknesses of the product and the proposed marketing strategy for the product and give management an opportunity to correct any weaknesses. It is much easier and less expensive to correct these problems at the test market stage than after the product has gone into national distribution.

These benefits must be weighed against a number of costs and other negatives associated with test markets.[16] The financial costs of test markets are not insignificant. And test markets give competitors an early indication of what the firm is planning to do. They thus share the opportunity to make adjustments in their marketing strategy; or, if the idea is simple and not legally protected, they may be able to copy the idea and move into national distribution faster than the original firm can.

Four major factors should be taken into account in determining whether to conduct a test market:

1. Weigh the cost and risk of failure against the probability of success and associated profits. If estimated costs are high and you are uncertain about the likelihood of success, then you should lean toward doing a test market. On the other hand, if both expected costs and the risk of product failure are low, then an immediate national rollout without a test market may be the appropriate strategy.

2. Consider the likelihood and speed with which competitors can copy your product and introduce it on a national basis. If the product can be easily copied, then it may be appropriate to introduce the product without a test market.

3. Consider the investment required to produce the product for the test market versus the investment required to produce the product in the quantities necessary for a national rollout. In cases where the difference in investment required is very small, it may make sense to introduce the product nationally without a test market. However, in cases where a very large difference exists between the investment required to produce the product for test market and that required for a national rollout, conducting a test market before making a decision to introduce the product nationally makes good sense.

4. Consider how much damage an unsuccessful new product launch would inflict on the firm's reputation. Failure may hurt the firm's reputation with other members of the channel of distribution (retailers) and impede the firm's ability to gain their cooperation in future product launches.

Steps in a Test Market Study

Once the decision has been made to conduct test marketing, a number of steps must be carried out if we are to achieve a satisfactory result.

Step One: Define the Objective   As always with these kinds of lists, the first step in the process is to define the objectives of the test. Typical test market objectives include the following:

☐ Develop share and volume estimates.

☐ Determine the characteristics of people who are purchasing the product.

- ☐ Determine frequency and purpose of purchase.
- ☐ Determine where (retail outlets) purchases are made.
- ☐ Measure the effect of sales of the new product on sales of similar existing products in the line.

Step Two: Select a Basic Approach   After specifying the objectives of the test market exercise, the next step is to decide on the appropriate type of test market, given the stated objectives.

Earlier in the chapter, we discussed the characteristics, advantages, and disadvantages of four types of test markets:

- ☐ Traditional or standard test market
- ☐ Scanner or electronic test market
- ☐ Controlled test market
- ☐ Simulated test market (STM) (See Practicing Marketing Research on page 255 for more discussion of STMs.)

The decision regarding which type of test market to use in a given situation depends on how much time you have, how much budget you have, and how important it is to keep the competition in the dark about what you are planning to do.

Selecting markets for a test is an important decision. Significant regional differences should be considered in choosing cities as test markets. To find some readily apparent regional differences between Seattle and Miami, visit *http://www.ci.seattle.wa.us* and *http://www.miami.com*.

Step Three: Develop Detailed Test Procedures   After the objectives and a basic approach for the test have been developed, the researcher must develop a detailed plan for conducting the test. Manufacturing and distribution decisions must be made to ensure that adequate product is available and that it is available in most stores of the type that sell that particular product class. In addition, the detailed marketing plan to be used for the test must be specified. The basic positioning approach must be selected, the actual commercials must be developed, a pricing strategy must be chosen, a media plan must be developed, and various promotional activities must be specified.

Step Four: Select Test Markets   The selection of markets for the test is an important decision. A number of factors must be taken into account in making this decision. First there are the overall standards[17]:

☐   There should be a minimum of two test markets, in addition to a control market, for an existing national brand or a minimum of three markets for testing a new brand.

☐   The markets selected should be geographically dispersed; if the brand is a regional brand, the markets should cover several dispersed markets within that region.

☐   Markets should be demographically representative of the United States, unless, for instance, a pronounced ethnic skew is desirable for a specific brand.

☐   Depending on the product purchase cycle, the test should be run for at least 6 months, up to 12 months, before the results can be considered reliably projectable. If the product is purchased infrequently, it is advisable to run the test for even longer than a year.

☐   The market must have a variety of media outlets, including at least four television stations, cable penetration no more than 10 percent above or below the U.S. average, at least four radio stations, a dominant local newspaper with daily and Sunday editions, a Sunday supplement with a syndicated edition, or a local supplement of similar quality.

☐   There should be a dominant newspaper in the market or a dominant newspaper in each city the market encompasses.

☐   The market should be as reflective as possible of the U.S. population or regional population if that is more appropriate for the particular test.

See Practicing Marketing Research on page 252 for discussion of what makes a good test market.

Step Five: Execute the Plan   Once the plan is in place, the researcher can begin execution. At this point, a key decision has to be made: how long should the test run? The average test runs for 6 to 12 months. However, shorter and longer tests are not uncommon. The test must run long enough for an adequate number of repeat purchase cycles to be observed in order to provide a measure of the "staying power" of a new product or marketing program. The shorter the average period is, the shorter the test needs to be. Cigarettes, soft drinks, and packaged goods are purchased every few days, whereas such products as shaving cream and toothpaste are purchased only every few months. The latter products would require a longer test. Whatever the product type, the test must be continued until the repeat purchase rate stabilizes. The percentage of people making repeat purchases tends to drop for some period of time before reaching a relatively constant level. Repeat purchase rate is critical to the process of estimating ultimate sales of the product. If the test is ended too soon, sales will be overestimated.

PRACTICING MARKETING RESEARCH

Magic City?

What makes the ideal test market? It depends, of course, on the product. Here are four recent examples of test markets selected by firms, based on either how they match the demographics of the United States as a whole or how their specific features ideally suit the product.

Galveston County in Texas is the nation's best test market, reports *American City Business Journals*. They analyzed 3,141 U.S. counties and independent cities, comparing their characteristics to the national averages for 20 statistical indicators. These included population densities for whites, blacks, Hispanics, and Asians; population age distribution (five categories); length of residency in one's current home, homeownership, value, and size; median household income; type of job and educational level; and commuting distance.

The young adult population (ages 25–44) of Galveston County exactly matches the national average at 30.2 percent, as does the percentage of homes occupied by their owners (66.2 percent) and very nearly does the percentage of adults with high school diplomas (80.9 percent for Galveston vs. 80.4 percent nationally).

On a 100-point scale, Galveston County scored 89.24 in matching these 20 indicators and national demographics. The top 10 counties, in order, were Camden County, New Jersey; Hillsborough County, Florida; Jackson County, Missouri; Greenville County, South Carolina; Jefferson County, Kentucky; Forsyth County, North Carolina; Montgomery County, Ohio; Winnebago County, Illinois; and Hampden County, Massachusetts.[18]

On the basis of different selection criteria compiled by the advertising agency Dancer, Fitzgerald & Sample, South Bend, Indiana, made the list of the eight best test markets in the United States. More precisely, it was South Bend ADI (meaning Area of Dominant Influence), a 10-countywide population

and market base. Market researchers know that a given market is a demographic match if it is less than 5 percent different from the national average; the South Bend ADI was 4.2 percent different from the national average. The other seven top test markets were Erie, Pennsylvania; Fort Wayne, Indiana; Grand Rapids, Michigan; Spokane, Washington; Syracuse, New York; Albuquerque, New Mexico; and Lexington, Kentucky.[19]

McDonald's Corporation targets specific cities to test its new products. The company used its 78 outlets in Hawaii to test market a new breakfast offering made of egg, rice, and Spam (processed pork). McDonald's called it Spam musubi (cooked Spam on rice, wrapped in a seaweed sushi-like girdle) because both the name and taste matched the culinary favorites of Hawaiians. McDonald's found that most Baby Boomer consumers (roughly those aged 40 to 56) on the mainland United States scorn Spam, but that Hawaiians love it, provided it's cooked. Indeed, Hawaiians have the highest per capita Spam consumption of all 50 states.[20]

Indiana is a preferred test market for new tobacco products. Vector Tobacco selected Indiana, along with New York, New Jersey, Pennsylvania, Illinois, and Michigan, as the ideal test market for its new Quest cigarettes. The innovation involved here was the smokers' ability to choose their nicotine content from three varieties, all starting out with reduced nicotine. Their Quest One brand had 17 percent less nicotine than the typical cigarette; Quest Two 58 percent less; and Quest Three almost no nicotine.[21]

Brown & Williamson Tobacco in Louisville, Kentucky, the country's third largest tobacco products manufacturer, also targeted Indiana. It selected Indiana's capital city, Indianapolis, to test market Advance Lights, a new cigarette the company claimed significantly reduced toxins ordinarily found in cigarette smoke by way of a special filter and improved tobacco-curing process.[22]

Two other considerations in determining the length of the test relate to the expected speed of competitor reaction and the costs of running the test. If there is reason to expect that competitors will react quickly to the test marketing (introduce their own versions of the new product), then the test should be as short as possible. Minimizing the length of the test reduces the amount of time competitors have to react. Finally, the value of additional information to be gained from the test must be balanced against the cost of continuing to run the test. At some point, the value of additional information will be outweighed by its cost.

Step Six: Analyze the Test Results   The data produced by an experiment should be evaluated throughout the test period. However, after completion of the experiment, a more careful and thorough evaluation of the data must be performed. This analysis will focus on four areas:

☐   *Purchase data.* The purchase data are often the most important data produced by an experiment. The levels of initial purchase (trial) throughout the course of the experiment provide an indication of how well the advertising and promotion program worked. The repeat rate (percentage of initial triers who made second and subsequent purchases) provides an indication of how well the product met the expectations created through advertising and promotion. Of course, the trial and repeat purchase results provide the basis for estimating sales and market share if the product was distributed nationally.

☐   *Awareness data.* How effective were the media expenditures and media plan in creating awareness of the product? Do consumers know how much the product costs? Do they know its key features?

☐   *Competitive response.* Ideally, the responses of competitors should be monitored during the period of the test market. For example, competitors may try to distort test results by offering special promotions, price deals, and quantity discounts. Their actions may provide some indication of what they will do if the product moves into national distribution and some basis for estimating the effect of these actions on their part.

☐   *Source of sales.* If the product is a new entry in an existing product category, it is important to determine where sales are coming from. In other words, which brands did the people who purchased the test product previously purchase? This information

General Mills used the "rolling rollout" when it introduced MultiGrain Cheerios to the public. Visit *http://www.generalmills.com* to find out what new products the company may be introducing.

GLOBAL RESEARCH

Hot Test Marketing in the South of India

If you want to roll out flavored foods and sweetened beverages in India and aren't sure how they'll be received, try Chennai and Bangalore. Indian marketing researchers report that the south of India is the most suitable test market area in the entire country, a market, incidentally, that tops one billion consumers.

What's so special about southern India? Distribution and transport systems as well as wholesale markets are much better organized there; its per capita consumption of many product categories is higher than in other parts of India; cable and satellite penetration is stronger; and at the same time the media reach is insular, so that marketers know their viewers demographically and what they're watching with more certainty than elsewhere. Furthermore, local channel advertising in southern India is cost-effective, making this area media-friendly for new product introductions.

Raghavan Srinivasan is executive director of the research agency TNS Mode in India. In his view, "marketers use the south to test their operational efficiencies." Srinivasan states that test marketing used to be very expensive, but now marketers have premarket tools that provide simulated test market data.

The big cash-rich food companies are heeding the word of the south. Dabur Foods test marketed *papads* and pickles in four flavors in Chennai for a year, and based on the poor response, it canceled its planned all-India rollout. Pepsi India marketers know that the south is a strong flavor-based market and that the southern consumer, especially in Chennai, has a strong affinity for fruit drinks. Pepsi India was planning to introduce Dole, a fruit-based drink, but when Indian consumers south of the Vindhyas said no, Pepsi India switched to Tropicana.

Hindustan Lever brought its hard-boiled candies to the northern markets only after they had been well tested and well received in the reliable Chennai marketplace first. Chennai consumers have also seen Cadbury and Nestle compete for their market approval with their new, nonrefrigerated chocolate products.

Coca-Cola India road-tested its carbonated soft drink line with new offerings in green apple and watermelon flavors in Chennai and Bangalore. The reason? The previous year sales of its Fanta Orange drink grew by 30 percent in the Tamil Nadu market. In 2001, Coca-Cola India released Sunfill, a powdered soft drink, in Hyderabad and extended the test to Tamil Nadu. These are the other two hot test market states in southern India.[23]

provides a true indication of real competitors. If the firm has an existing brand in the market, it also indicates to what extent the new product will take business from existing brands and from the competition.

Based on the evaluation, a decision will be made to improve the marketing program or the product, drop the product, or move the product into national or regional distribution.

Other Types of Product Tests

In addition to traditional test marketing and STMs, there are other means by which companies can gauge a product's potential. One alternative is a *rolling rollout*, which usually follows a pretest. A product is launched in a certain region rather than in one or two cities. Within a matter of days, scanner data can provide information on how the product

PRACTICING MARKETING RESEARCH

When in Rome . . .

Simulated test markets (STMs) are frequently used to predict success for product introductions in global markets, but interpretation of the data from different countries is tricky and can have a big impact on the reliability of the forecasts. Normally, STM researchers figure an accuracy margin of ±20 percent; an erroneous interpretation of the data could increase that to anywhere from 57 to 354 percent, a new study shows.

According to Jim Miller, senior vice president of ACNielsen BASES, the intelligent design of multicountry research using STMs must address three crucial considerations. First, as a market researcher, should you believe what consumers say about their future buying behavior? Yes, but not fully, says Miller. His research shows that consumers in a given country will not follow their own predicted behavior to the letter but only approximately. Thus, beware of the gap between claimed intentions and actual behaviors.

Second, does this gap differ from country to country? Yes, Miller says, and it's a function of demographics, particularly education. He found that consumers with more education had less of a tendency to overstate their future purchasing behaviors than did those with less education.

Further complicating the picture is the fact that overstatement levels vary by country, so it is necessary to assess what overstatement level is representative of a given country before drawing any reliable marketing conclusions from STM results.

Third, given the cultural differences in overstatement tendencies, will this consideration materially affect volume forecast based on STM research? Yes. The differences are big enough "to have enormous impact on forecasting volume," explains Miller. He uses the following case study to make his point.

Miller's firm was testing receptivity to a confection concept and product for a major consumer packaged goods manufacturer and wanted to try it out in Argentina, Mexico, Canada, and the United States. Miller's company conducted a full test in each country and used this test to generate a multicountry forecast. Unadjusted consumer scores led to the conclusion that Mexicans liked the product concept the best, far more than Americans did. Yet once Miller adjusted the data to accommodate each country's "unique level of overstatement," he found that consumer interest in Mexico was about equal to that of the United States.

(Continued)

Graph 1	

Consumers consistently overstate their purchase behavior . . .

Visions—Global Research: Evaluating new products globally; Using consumer research to predict success

Consumers "Claimed Intentions" vs. "Actual Behaviors"

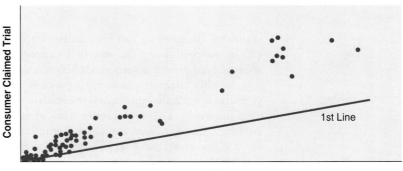

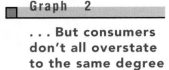

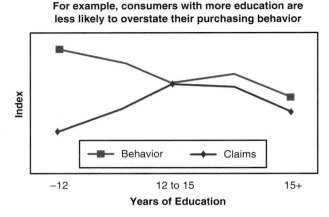

This same process of adjusting the data to remove country overstatement bias yielded another valuable set of data. When you identify and remove the different degrees of cultural overstatement, then you can see genuine differences in consumer interest in each country under study. Initially, the research showed that the level of consumer interest in the products in Argentina and Mexico, both before and after product use, was similar. After adjustment for overstatement, however, interest in Argentina was far stronger than that in Mexico.

Miller adjusted the data in the other countries so that individual country forecasts could be combined to make a four-country regional forecast. He cautions that if he had not made these adjustments for overstatement, the product sales volume estimates would have ranged, erroneously, from 57 to 354 percent. If you don't take the overstatement issue into consideration, compounded by the inherent ±20 percent inaccuracy of STM data, your market estimates based on lead-country forecasts could end up being "essentially meaningless."

As for which approach—country-specific versus lead-country—is the most accurate, the country-specific may be the most accurate but it generally costs too much, whereas the lead-country can produce very misleading results. The solution, Miller proposes, is to conduct the full test in the true lead country (or countries) combined with a reduced-base testing in the other targeted countries. This research design saves money and increases accuracy, and it captures important cultural differences in consumer responses, with only a small degree of forecasting variance within the accepted ±20 percent range of error.[24]

is doing. The product can then be launched in additional regions; ads and promotions can be adjusted along the way to a national introduction. General Mills has used this approach for products such as MultiGrain Cheerios.

Another alternative is to try a product out in a foreign market before rolling it out globally. Specifically, one or a few countries can serve as a test market for a continent or even the world. This *lead country strategy* has been used by Colgate-Palmolive Company. In 1991, the company launched Palmolive Optims shampoo and conditioner in the Philippines, Australia, Mexico, and Hong Kong. Later, the products were rolled out in Europe, Asia, Latin America, and Africa.

Some marketers think that classic test marketing will make a comeback. It may be that for totally new products, more thorough testing will be necessary, whereas for other types of product introductions, such as line extensions, an alternative approach is more appropriate.

SUMMARY

Experimental research provides evidence of whether a change in an independent variable causes some predictable change in a dependent variable. To show that a change in A likely caused an observed change in B, one must show three things: concomitant variation, appropriate time order of occurrence, and the elimination of other possible causal factors. Experiments can be conducted in a laboratory or a field setting. The major advantage of conducting experiments in a laboratory is that the researcher can control extraneous factors. However, in marketing research, laboratory settings often do not appropriately replicate the marketplace. Experiments conducted in the actual marketplace are called field experiments. The major difficulty with field experiments is that the researcher cannot control all the other factors that might influence the dependent variable.

In experimentation, we are concerned with internal and external validity. Internal validity refers to the extent to which competing explanations of the experimental results observed can be ruled out. External validity refers to the extent to which causal relationships measured in an experiment can be generalized to other settings. Extraneous variables are other independent variables that may affect the dependent variable and thus stand in the way of the ability to conclude that an observed change in the dependent variable was due to the effect of the experimental, or treatment, variable. Extraneous factors include history, maturation, instrument variation, selection bias, mortality, testing effects, and regression to the mean. Four basic approaches are used to control extraneous factors: randomization, physical control, design control, and statistical control.

In an experimental design, the researcher has control over and manipulates one or more independent variables. Nonexperimental designs, which involve no manipulation, are referred to as ex post facto research. An experimental design includes four elements: the treatment, subjects, a dependent variable that is measured, and a plan or procedure for dealing with extraneous causal factors. An experimental effect is the effect of the treatment variable on the dependent variable.

Experiments have an obvious advantage in that they are the only type of research that can demonstrate the existence and nature of causal relationships between variables of interest. Yet the amount of actual experimentation done in marketing research is limited because of the high cost of experiments, security issues, and implementation problems. There is evidence to suggest that the use of experiments in marketing research is growing.

Pre-experimental designs offer little or no control over the influence of extraneous factors and are thus generally difficult to interpret. Examples include the one-shot case study design, the one-group pretest–posttest design, and the static-group comparison design. In a true experimental design, the researcher is able to eliminate all extraneous variables as competitive hypotheses to the treatment. Examples of true experimental designs are the before and after with control group design and the after-only with control group design.

In quasi-experiments, the researcher has control over data collection procedures but lacks complete control over the scheduling of treatments. The treatment groups in a quasi-experiment normally are formed by assigning respondents to treatments in a non-random fashion. Examples of quasi-experimental designs are the interrupted time-series design and the multiple time-series design.

Test marketing involves testing a new product or some element of the marketing mix by using experimental or quasi-experimental designs. Test markets are field experiments, and they are extremely expensive to conduct. The steps in conducting a test market study include defining the objectives for the study, selecting a basic approach to be used, developing detailed procedures for the test, selecting markets for the test, executing the plan, and analyzing the test results.

KEY TERMS & DEFINITIONS

experiment Research approach in which one variable is manipulated and the effect on another variable is observed.

causal research Research designed to determine whether a change in one variable likely caused an observed change in another.

concomitant variation Statistical relationship between two variables.

appropriate time order of occurrence Change in an independent variable occurring before an observed change in the dependent variable.

laboratory experiments Experiments conducted in a controlled setting.

field experiments Tests conducted outside the laboratory in an actual environment, such as a marketplace.

internal validity Extent to which competing explanations for the experimental results observed can be ruled out.

external validity Extent to which causal relationships measured in an experiment can be generalized to outside persons, settings, and times.

history Intervention, between the beginning and end of an experiment, of outside variables or events that might change the dependent variable.

maturation Changes in subjects occurring during the experiment that are not related to the experiment but that may affect subjects' response to the treatment factor.

instrument variation Changes in measurement instruments (e.g., interviewers or observers) that might affect measurements.

selection bias Systematic differences between the test group and the control group due to a biased selection process.

mortality Loss of test units or subjects during the course of an experiment, which may result in a nonrepresentativeness.

testing effect Effect that is a by-product of the research process itself.

regression to the mean Tendency of subjects with extreme behavior to move toward the average for that behavior during the course of an experiment.

randomization Random assignment of subjects to treatment conditions to ensure equal representation of subject characteristics.

physical control Holding constant the value or level of extraneous variables throughout the course of an experiment.

design control Use of the experimental design to control extraneous causal factors.

statistical control Adjusting for the effects of confounded variables by statistically adjusting the value of the dependent variable for each treatment condition.

experimental design Test in which the researcher has control over and manipulates one or more independent variables.

treatment variable Independent variable that is manipulated in an experiment.

experimental effect Effect of the treatment variable on the dependent variable.

contamination Inclusion in a test of a group of respondents who are not normally there—for example, buyers from outside the test market who see an advertisement intended only for those in the test area and who enter the area to purchase the product being tested.

pre-experimental designs Designs that offer little or no control over extraneous factors.

one-shot case study design Pre-experimental design with no pretest observations, no control group, and an after measurement only.

one-group pretest–posttest design Pre-experimental design with pre- and postmeasurements but no control group.

true experimental design Research using an experimental group and a control group, to which test units are randomly assigned.

before and after with control group design True experimental design that involves random assignment of subjects or test units to experimental and control groups and pre- and postmeasurements of both groups.

after-only with control group design True experimental design that involves random assignment of subjects or test units to experimental and control groups, but no premeasurement of the dependent variable.

quasi-experiments Studies in which the researcher lacks complete control over the scheduling of treatments or must assign respondents to treatments in a nonrandom manner.

interrupted time-series design Research in which repeated measurements of an effect "interrupts" previous data patterns.

multiple time-series design An interrupted time-series design with a control group.

test market Testing of a new product or some element of the marketing mix using an experimental or quasi-experimental design.

(Team Exercise) 1. Divide the class into as many as six groups, as appropriate. Each group will have the task of recommending a test market design and addressing the associated questions for one of the following scenarios.

☐ Design a test of a new pricing strategy for orange juice concentrate. The brand is an established brand, and we are only interested in testing the effect of a 5 percent price increase and a 5 percent decrease. All other elements of the marketing mix will remain the same.

QUESTIONS FOR REVIEW & CRITICAL THINKING

☐ A soft drink company has determined in taste tests that consumers prefer the taste of their diet product when sweetened with Splenda® in comparison to Equal®. Now they are interested in determining how the new sweetener will play in the marketplace. Design a test market that will achieve this goal.

☐ A national pizza chain wants to test the effect on sales of four different discount coupons. Design a test that will do this in a way that gives a clear read. Your focus should be on the effect on sales volume. Financial analysis after the test results are in will address the revenue and profit impact.

☐ A national value-priced hotel chain needs to understand the business impact of including a free buffet style breakfast to guests. Design and justify a test that will do this.

☐ A credit card company needs to test its strategy for attracting college students to its card. It is going to continue using booths in student unions and other high-traffic campus locations. It has been offering free CDs from a list to those who sign up for its card, but since other card companies are using this approach, the company wants to try some alternatives. It is considering free MP3 downloads from iTunes and t-shirts featuring popular music groups. Design a test that will tell the company which option to choose if its goal is to increase signups by the largest amount.

2. Tico Taco, a national chain of Mexican fast-food restaurants, has developed the "Super Sonic Taco," which is the largest taco in the market and sells for $1.19. Tico Taco has identified its target customers for this new product as men under 30 who are not concerned about health issues, such as fat content or calories. It wants to test the product in at least four regional markets before making a decision to introduce it nationally. What criteria would you use to select test cities for this new product? Which cities would you recommend using? Why would you recommend those cities?

3. Of the primary data-collection techniques available to the researcher (survey, observation, experiment), why is the experiment the only one that can provide conclusive evidence of causal relationships? Of the various types of experiments, which type or types provide the best evidence of causation or noncausation?

4. What are some important independent variables that must be dealt with in an experiment to test consumer reactions to a pilot for a new TV series? Explain why those variables are important.

5. Managers of the student center at your university or college are considering three alternative brands of frozen pizza to be offered on the menu. They want to offer only one of the three and want to find out which brand students prefer. Design an experiment to determine which brand of pizza the students prefer.

6. Night students at the university or college are much older than day students. Introduce an explicit control for day versus night students in the preceding experiment.

7. Why are quasi-experiments much more popular in marketing research than true experiments?

8. How does history differ from maturation? What specific actions might you take to deal with each in an experiment?

9. A manufacturer of microwave ovens has designed an improved model that will reduce energy costs and cook food evenly throughout. However, this new model will increase the product's price by 30 percent because of extra components and

engineering design changes. The company wants to determine what effect the new model will have on sales of its microwave ovens. Propose an appropriate experimental design that can provide the desired information for management. Why did you select this design?

10. Discuss various methods by which extraneous causal factors can be controlled.

11. Discuss the alternatives to traditional test marketing. Explain their advantages and disadvantages.

Market Analysts and Promotional Specialists, Incorporated

Market Analysts and Promotional Specialists, Incorporated (M.A.P.S.) is a marketing consulting firm that specializes in the development of promotional campaigns. The firm was formed 5 years ago by two young marketing graduate students, David Roth and Lisa Ryan, who soon overcame their initial lack of experience and have since become known for their innovativeness and creativity. Their clients include industrial wholesalers, retail product manufacturers, food brokers, and distributors, as well as retail outlets.

In 1994, Dixie Brewing Company enlisted M.A.P.S. to develop a new promotional campaign for its line of beers. At the time, Dixie was the last of the microbreweries in New Orleans and distributed its products within a 200-mile radius of the city. The company had enjoyed a good reputation for a number of years, but its image had recently been tarnished by the accidental distribution of a shipment of bad beer. Dixie also was losing market share because of increased competition from national brewers. Miller High Life had purchased Cresent Distributors, a large liquor distributor in the New Orleans area, and was beginning to implement aggressive promotional tactics in the local market.

Dixie was concerned primarily with its retail merchandising methods. David and Lisa immediately began to study Dixie's product line and its present shelf space allocations in various stores throughout the market area. M.A.P.S.'s previous work with food brokers helped them realize that proper shelf placement was extremely important in supermarket merchandising.

The company's product line consisted of two beers, Dixie and Dixie Light. Both beers were sold in 32-ounce glass bottles, 12-ounce glass-bottle six-packs, and 12-ounce can six-packs.

In New Orleans, beer may be purchased in supermarkets and convenience stores. Also, in most stores, beer can be purchased either warm or cold. In studying the refrigerated closets holding beverages, David and Lisa noticed that most were small—8 to 12 feet in length—and had glass doors on the front. Because of the relatively small size of the entire cold beer display, they believed that the typical consumer would view the case from left to right; therefore, they believed Dixie should place its products on the extreme left side of all cold beer cases.

Warm beer was displayed in a much different manner. Most stores displayed beverage products in bulk and usually devoted an entire aisle to such displays. David and Lisa reasoned that the normal consumer could not view all the brands at once and thus would have to "shop," or walk into the aisle. For this reason, they recommended that Dixie place its beer in the middle of the other brands.

Because Dixie Light was produced in response to Miller Lite, David and Lisa recommended that it be placed to the left of Miller Lite in both warm and cold beer displays. Traditionally, Dixie Light had been placed next to its standard beer brand. Dixie had noticed a significant decrease in its regular brand's market share after the introduction of Dixie Light.

To test their theories, David and Lisa selected a convenience store, located in a suburb of New Orleans, that contained both warm and cold beer displays. This store was then used in an experiment to measure the effect of shelf placement on beer sales. One treatment consisted of setting up the displays as they were currently being used in stores across town. The second treatment arranged the displays according to the new M.A.P.S. plan. All other factors, such as price and number of bottles, were held constant throughout the experiment. The first version of the setup was used for the first 2 weeks in April, and the second treatment was run for the last 2 weeks of the month.

The following data show the percentage of beer purchased by brand for each treatment:

	Treatment 1 (%)	Treatment 2 (%)
Dixie	18	23
Miller	18	15
Bud	19	18
Coors	13	13
Dixie Light	10	8
Miller Lite	13	14
Coors Light	9	9

Questions

1. Critique the research design with respect to internal and external validity considerations.

2. Discuss the advantages and disadvantages of using the convenience store in this experiment.

3. Based on the information given, what conclusions can be reached regarding the M.A.P.S. plan?

4. Recommend a research design that would produce more interpretable results.

REAL-LIFE RESEARCH • 8.2

Healthco

Review the opening vignette for this chapter. Now that you have read the chapter, comment on the three designs suggested in the vignette: one-shot case study, one-group pretest–posttest, and before and after with control group design.

Questions

1. Comment on the advantages and disadvantages of each design.

2. What measures of the effect of the experimental variable are provided by the different designs? Which one offers the clearest picture? Why?

3. Which design provides a measure of the effects of variables not included in the experiment? Explain how it accomplishes this.

CHAPTER 9

THE CONCEPT OF
MEASUREMENT

LEARNING OBJECTIVES

1. To understand the concept of measurement.

2. To learn about the measurement process and how to develop a good measurement scale.

3. To understand the four levels of scales and their typical usage.

4. To explore the concepts of reliability and validity.

More consumers than ever before are patronizing different stores when shopping for items ranging from household cleaning supplies to pet food. Factors such as everyday low pricing and good customer service matter more than special deals and promotions, selection, and convenient location, according to a study of consumers nationwide conducted by Meyers Research Center, New York.

The online poll of more than 400 consumers asked shoppers to rate factors most important to them in choosing locations to purchase a wide variety of products. Factors ranged from pricing to customer service and convenient store locations, the influence of special promotions, offering quality brands, and being among the first to offer new products.

"Shoppers overall told us that everyday low pricing, good customer service, products that are in-stock, and stores that are well-organized and easy to shop are their favorites," says Jeff Friedlaender, vice president of Meyers Research Center. "Those factors outweigh such considerations as special promotions and being first on the block to offer new products."

Consumers rated dollar stores, today's fastest-growing retail format, as the best place to find everyday low pricing and convenience stores as the worst place for good pricing. But in some cases, a good deal on price has its own price to pay: good customer service. Dollar stores were rated the worst for customer service, whereas supermarkets and office supply stores gained high marks. Dollar stores also scored low on the rest of the top five factors that drive consumers to a particular channel: in-stock products and stores being easy to shop. Supermarkets were rated highest on both of those attributes.

Price never drops out of the equation of top factors, regardless of consumer need when shopping, whether it be stocking up for the household or getting one or two desperately needed items or wanted/rewarded items.

Sixty-nine percent of consumers surveyed said there was a specific retailer they "could not live without." Among those consumers who expressed an opinion, Wal-Mart led the pack as the number one retailer they could not live without (31 percent), followed by club store Costco (17 percent) and Target (13 percent). Warehouse club BJ's (11 percent) was fourth, and supermarkets Kroger and Albertson's tied for the fifth spot (9 percent). Trailing the pack of 14 retailers cited by consumers were mass merchant Kmart and drug store Rite Aid, each with 2 percent.

Consumers interviewed cited Wal-Mart's wide variety, low pricing, and the convenience of multiple categories at one location as factors in their number one ranking. Consumers who selected Target and Costco as their favorites said the stores were fun to shop; cited were in-store food samples at Costco and good organization and sense of fashion at Target.[1]

The retail shopping study is all about understanding the construct of shopper loyalty. No single definition of customer loyalty applies to all companies and industries. To an investment banking firm, for example, loyal customers might be businesses that use their investment banking firm exclusively and plan to continue doing so, while a soft drink company might consider loyal customers to be consumers who are more likely to choose their soft drink over any other, even if they also buy other soft drinks. The definition of a loyal customer can encompass a wide variety of attitudes and behaviors, and the best definition to use depends on the specific situation. Elements of customer loyalty may include:

- ☐ **Psychological commitment.** Does the customer feel any emotional connection to the product or company?
- ☐ **Referenceability.** Does the customer consider himself a positive reference for the product or company?
- ☐ **Purchase history.** Has the customer purchased the product (or from the company) consistently in the past?

❑ **Repurchase intentions.** Does the customer plan to buy the product (or buy from the company) again in the future?

❑ **Future purchase levels.** Does the customer plan to spend more, less, or maintain current spending levels in the future?

❑ **Perception of competitive advantage.** Does the customer feel that the company's products provide a competitive advantage?

❑ **Satisfaction.** How satisfied is the customer with the product or company?

The best approaches to measuring loyalty are directly related to desirable customer behaviors or attitudes as well as the surrounding context (the presence or absence of competitors, barriers to entering and exiting the relationship).[2]

As you can see, the construct of shopper loyalty may encompass many dimensions. What may seem like a simple notion on the surface, shopper loyalty, requires a rigorous process in order to be properly measured. What is a construct, and how can it be measured? How does one determine the reliability and validity of the information? These are some of the issues we will explore in this chapter. ■

Measurement Process

> **measurement**
> Process of assigning numbers or labels to persons, objects, or events in accordance with specific rules for representing quantities or qualities of attributes.

> **rule**
> Guide, method, or command that tells a researcher what to do.

Measurement is the process of assigning numbers or labels to persons, objects, or events in accordance with specific rules for representing quantities or qualities of attributes. Measurement, then, is a procedure used to assign numbers that reflect the amount of an attribute possessed by a person, object, or event. Note that it is not the person, object, or event that is being measured, but rather its attributes. A researcher, for example, does not measure a consumer per se but rather measures that consumer's attitudes, income, brand loyalty, age, and other relevant factors.

The concept of rules is key to measurement. A **rule** is a guide, a method, or a command that tells a researcher what to do. For example, a rule of measurement might state, "Assign the numbers 1 through 5 to people according to their disposition to do household chores. If they are extremely willing to do any and all household chores, assign them a 1. If they are not willing to do any household chores, assign them a 5." The numbers 2, 3, and 4 would be assigned based on the *degree* of their willingness to do chores, as it relates to the absolute end points of 1 and 5.

A problem often encountered with rules is a lack of clarity or specificity. Some things are easy to measure because rules are easy to create and follow. The measurement of gender, for example, is quite simple, as the researcher has concrete criteria to apply in assigning a 1 for a male and a 2 for a female. Unfortunately, many characteristics of interest to a marketing researcher—such as brand loyalty, purchase intent, and total family income—are much harder to measure because of the difficulty of devising rules to assess the true value of these consumer attributes. The steps a researcher should take to measure a phenomenon appear in Exhibit 9.1.

Step One: Identify the Concept of Interest

The measurement process begins with identification of the concept of interest. A *concept* is an abstract idea generalized from particular facts. It is a category of thought used to group sense data together "as if they were all the same." All perceptions regarding a stop light at the intersection of South and Main Streets form a category of thought, though a relatively narrow one. Perceptions of all stoplights, regardless of location, would be a broader concept, or category of thought.

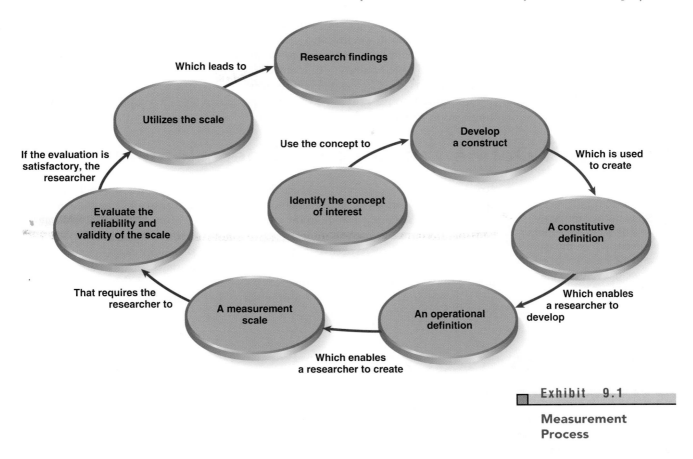

Exhibit 9.1

Measurement
Process

Step Two: Develop a Construct

Constructs are specific types of concepts that exist at higher levels of abstraction than do everyday concepts. Constructs are invented for theoretical use and thus are likely to cut across various preexisting categories of thought. The value of specific constructs depends on how useful they are in explaining, predicting, and controlling phenomena, just as the value of everyday concepts depends on how helpful they are in everyday affairs. Generally, constructs are not directly observable. Instead, they are inferred by some indirect method from results such as findings on a questionnaire. Examples of marketing constructs include brand loyalty, high-involvement purchasing, social class, personality, and channel power. Constructs aid researchers by simplifying and integrating the complex phenomena found in the marketing environment.[3]

> **constructs**
> Specific types of concepts that exist at higher levels of abstraction.

Step Three: Define the Concept Constitutively

The third step in the measurement process is to define the concept constitutively. A **constitutive** (or *theoretical*, or *conceptual*) **definition** is a statement of the meaning of the central idea or concept under study, establishing its boundaries. Constructs of a scientific theory are defined constitutively. Thus, all constructs, to be capable of being used in theories, must possess constitutive meaning. Like a dictionary definition, a constitutive definition should fully distinguish the concept under investigation from all other concepts, making the study concept readily discernible from very similar but

> **constitutive definition**
> Statement of the meaning of the central idea or concept under study, establishing its boundaries; also known as *theoretical*, or *conceptual*, *definition*.

different concepts. A vague constitutive definition can cause an incorrect research question to be addressed. For instance, to say that researchers are interested in studying marital roles would be so general as to be meaningless. To say that they want to examine the marital roles of newlyweds (married less than 12 months) from 24 to 28 years of age with 4 years of college may not even suffice. While one researcher may be interested in communication patterns as partners assume certain roles, a second researcher may be interested in parenting roles.

Step Four: Define the Concept Operationally

> **operational definition**
> Statement of precisely which observable characteristics will be measured and the process for assigning a value to the concept.

A precise constitutive definition makes the operational definition task much easier. An **operational definition** specifies which observable characteristics will be measured and the process for assigning a value to the concept. In other words, it assigns meaning to a construct in terms of the operations necessary to measure it in any concrete situation.

Because it is overly restrictive in marketing to insist that all variables be operationally defined in directly measurable terms, many variables are stated in more abstract terms and measured indirectly, based on theoretical assumptions about their nature. For example, it is impossible to measure an attitude directly, because an attitude is an abstract concept that refers to things inside a person's mind. It is possible, nonetheless, to give a

EXHIBIT 9.2	Constitutive and Operational Definitions of Role Ambiguity
Constitutive Definition	Role ambiguity is a direct function of the discrepancy between the information available to the person and that which is required for adequate performance of a role. It is the difference between a person's actual state of knowledge and the knowledge that provides adequate satisfaction of that person's personal needs and values.
Operational Definition	Role ambiguity is the amount of uncertainty (ranging from very uncertain to very certain on a five-point scale) an individual feels regarding job role responsibilities and expectations from other employees and customers.
Measurement Scale	The measurement scale consists of 45 items, with each item assessed by a five-point scale with category labels 1 = very certain, 2 = certain, 3 = neutral, 4 = uncertain, 5 = very uncertain. Samples of the 45 items follow: ☐ How much freedom of action I am expected to have ☐ How I am expected to handle nonroutine activities on the job ☐ The sheer amount of work I am expected to do ☐ To what extent my boss is open to hearing my point of view ☐ How satisfied my boss is with me ☐ How managers in other departments expect me to interact with them ☐ What managers in other departments think about the job I perform ☐ How I am expected to interact with my customers ☐ How I should behave (with customers) while on the job ☐ If I am expected to lie a little to win customer confidence ☐ If I am expected to hide my company's foul-ups from my customers ☐ About how much time my family feels I should spend on the job ☐ To what extent my family expects me to share my job-related problems ☐ How my co-workers expect me to behave while on the job ☐ How much information my co-workers expect me to convey to my boss

Source: Adapted from Jagdip Singh and Gary K. Rhoads, "Boundary Role Ambiguity in Marketing-Oriented Positions: A Multidimensional, Multi-faceted Operationalization," *Journal of Marketing Research*, Vol. 28 (August 1991), pp. 328–338. Reprinted by permission of the American Marketing Association.

clear theoretical definition of an attitude as an enduring organization of motivational, emotional, perceptual, and cognitive processes with respect to some aspect of the environment. On the basis of this definition, instruments have been developed for measuring attitudes indirectly, by asking questions about how a person feels, what the person believes, and how the person intends to behave.

In summary, an operational definition serves as a bridge between a theoretical concept and real-world events or factors. Constructs such as "attitude" and "high-involvement purchasing" are abstractions that cannot be observed. Operational definitions transform such constructs into observable events. In other words, they define or give meaning to a construct by spelling out what the researcher must do to measure it. There are many different potential operational definitions for any single concept, regardless of how exact the constitutive definition may be. The researcher must choose the operational definition that fits most appropriately with the objectives of the research.

An example of a constitutive definition, a corresponding operational definition, and a resultant measurement scale are shown in Exhibit 9.2. The operational definition of role ambiguity was developed by two marketing professors for use with salespeople and customer service personnel. The theoretical notion is that role ambiguity leads to job stress and impedes a worker's ability to improve performance and obtain job-based rewards, leading to job dissatisfaction.

Construct equivalence deals with how people see, understand, and develop measurements of a particular phenomenon. The problem confronting the global marketing researcher is that, because of sociocultural, economic, and political differences, construct perspectives may be neither identical nor equivalent. The examples provided in the Global Research feature highlight the construct equivalence problem faced by global marketing researchers.

Step Five: Develop a Measurement Scale

Exhibit 9.2 includes a scale that ranges from "very certain" to "very uncertain." A **scale** is a set of symbols or numbers so constructed that the symbols or numbers can be assigned by a rule to the individuals (or their behaviors or attitudes) to whom the scale is applied. The assignment on the scale is indicated by the individual's possession of whatever the scale is supposed to measure. Thus, a salesperson who feels he knows exactly how he is supposed to interact with customers would mark *very certain* for that item on the scale in Exhibit 9.2.

Creating a measurement scale begins with determining the level of measurement desirable or possible. Exhibit 9.3 describes the four basic levels of measurement: nominal, ordinal, interval, and ratio.

> **scale**
> Set of symbols or numbers so constructed that the symbols or numbers can be assigned by a rule to the individuals (or their behaviors or attitudes) to whom the scale is applied.

Nominal Level of Measurement

Nominal scales are among those most commonly used in marketing research. A nominal scale partitions data into categories that are mutually exclusive and collectively exhaustive, implying that every bit of data will fit into one and only one category and that all data will fit somewhere on the scale. The term *nominal* means "name-like," indicating that the numbers assigned to objects or phenomena are naming or classifying them but have no true number value; that is, the numbers cannot be ordered, added, or divided. The numbers are simply labels or identification numbers and nothing else. Examples of two nominal scales follow:

> **nominal scales**
> Scales that partition data into mutually exclusive and collectively exhaustive categories.

Gender: (1) Male   (2) Female

Geographic area: (1) Urban   (2) Rural   (3) Suburban

EXHIBIT 9.3	The Four Basic Levels of Measurement			
Level	**Basic Empirical Description***	**Operations**	**Typical Descriptive Typical Usage**	**Statistics**
Nominal	Uses numerals to identify objects, individuals, events, or groups	Determination of equality/inequality	Classification (male/female; buyer/nonbuyer)	Frequency counts, percentages/modes
Ordinal	In addition to identification, provides information about the relative amount of some characteristic possessed by an event, object, etc.	Determination of greater or lesser	Rankings/ratings (preferences for hotels, banks, etc.; social class; ratings of foods based on fat content, cholesterol)	Median (mean and variance metric)
Interval	Possesses all the properties of nominal and ordinal scales plus equal intervals between consecutive points	Determination of equality of intervals	Preferred measure of complex concepts/constructs (temperature scale, air pressure scale, level of knowledge about brands)	Mean/variance
Ratio	Incorporates all the properties of nominal, ordinal, and interval scales plus an absolute zero point	Determination of equality of ratios	Preferred measure when precision instruments are available (sales, number of on-time arrivals, age)	Geometric mean/harmonic mean

*Because higher levels of measurement contain all the properties of lower levels, higher level scales can be converted into lower level ones (i.e., ratio to interval or ordinal or nominal, or interval to ordinal or nominal, or ordinal to nominal).
Source: Adapted from S. S. Stevens, "On the Theory of Scales of Measurement," *Science*, Vol. 103 (June 7, 1946), pp. 677–680.

The only quantifications in numerical scales are the number and percentage of objects in each category—for example, 50 males (48.5 percent) and 53 females (51.5 percent). Computing a mean of 2.4 for geographic area would be meaningless; only the mode, the value that appears most often, would be appropriate.

Ordinal Level of Measurement

> **ordinal scales**
> Scales that maintain the labeling characteristics of nominal scales and have the ability to order data.

Ordinal scales have the labeling characteristics of nominal scales plus an ability to order data. Ordinal measurement is possible when the transitivity postulate can be applied. (A *postulate* is an assumption that is an essential prerequisite to carrying out an operation or line of thinking.) The *transitivity postulate* is described by the notion that "if *a* is greater than *b*, and *b* is greater than *c*, then *a* is greater than *c*." Other terms that can be substituted for *is greater than* are *is preferred to*, *is stronger than*, and *precedes*. An example of an ordinal scale follows:

Please rank the following online dating services from 1 to 5, with 1 being the most preferred and 5 the least preferred.

www.AmericanSingles.com   _____
www.eharmony.com   _____
www.yahoopersonals.com   _____
www.greatexpectations.com   _____
www.friendfinder.com   _____

Ordinal numbers are used strictly to indicate rank order. The numbers do not indicate absolute quantities, nor do they imply that the intervals between the numbers are

GLOBAL RESEARCH

Construct Equivalence Problems Often Occur in Global Marketing Research

Construct equivalence problems in global marketing research may relate to functional equivalence, conceptual equivalence, or definitional equivalence. Some examples of each type of problem follow.

Functional Equivalence. In England, Germany, and Scandinavia, beer is generally perceived as an alcoholic beverage. In Mediterranean lands, however, beer is considered akin to soft drinks. Therefore, a study of the competitive status of beer in northern Europe would have to build in questions on wine and liquor. In Italy, Spain, or Greece, the comparison would have to be with soft drinks.

In Italy, it's common for children to have a bar of chocolate between two slices of bread as a snack. In France, bar chocolate is often used in cooking. But a German housewife would be revolted by either practice.

Conceptual Equivalence. A researcher using the concepts "out-group" and "in-group" would be dealing with very different groups in the United States and Greece. In the United States, the in-group includes people from one's own country, and the out-group includes foreigners. In Greece, the out-group includes countrymen with whom one is not closely associated. (When Athenians were asked to help fellow Greeks and foreigners mail letters, the Greeks received worse treatment than did the foreigners.)

Personality traits such as aggressiveness or assertiveness may not be relevant in all countries or cultures. The concept may be absent from the culture and language, or it may have an entirely different meaning.

As a final example, Japanese and Western concepts of decision making differ considerably. Whereas the Westerner sees decision making as a discrete event, the Japanese cannot make that distinction.

Definitional Equivalence. In France, fragrance is measured on a hot–cold continuum. In the United States and the United Kingdom, hot and cold are not attributes assigned to fragrances. That is, an attribute used to categorize product classes may vary from one country or culture to another.

Perceptions of beer, as cited under functional equivalence, also provide an example of problems in achieving definitional equivalence. In the United Kingdom, beer would be classified as an alcoholic drink. In Mediterranean cultures, it would be classified as a soft drink.[4]

---

equal. For example, a person ranking fax machines might like Toshiba only slightly more than Savin and view Ricoh as totally unacceptable. Such information would not be obtained from an ordinal scale.

Because ranking is the objective of an ordinal scale, any rule prescribing a series of numbers that preserves the ordered relationship is satisfactory. In other words, AmericanSingles could have been assigned a value of 30; eharmony, 40; YahooPersonals, 27; GreatExpectations, 32; and FriendFinder, 42. Or any other series of numbers could have been used, as long as the basic ordering was preserved. In the case just cited, FriendFinder is 1; eHarmony 2; GreatExpectations 3; AmericanSingles 4; and YahooPersonals 5. Common arithmetical operations such as addition and multiplication cannot be used with ordinal scales. The appropriate measure of central tendency is the mode or the median. A percentile or quartile measure is used for measuring dispersion.

A controversial (yet rather common) use of ordinal scales is to rate various characteristics. In this case, the researcher assigns numbers to reflect the relative ratings of a series of statements, then uses these numbers to interpret relative distance. Recall that the

Commonly used temperature scales are based on equal intervals and an arbitrary zero point. Marketing researchers often prefer interval scales because they can measure how much more of a trait one consumer has than another.

▷ interval scales
Scales that have the characteristics of ordinal scales, plus equal intervals between points to show relative amounts; they may include an arbitrary zero point.

▷ ratio scales
Scales that have the characteristics of interval scales, plus a meaningful zero point so that magnitudes can be compared arithmetically.

marketing researchers examining role ambiguity used a scale ranging from *very certain* to *very uncertain.* The following values were assigned:

(1)	(2)	(3)	(4)	(5)
Very Certain	**Certain**	**Neutral**	**Uncertain**	**Very Uncertain**

If a researcher can justify the assumption that the intervals are equal within the scale, then the more powerful parametric statistical tests can be applied. (Parametric statistical tests will be discussed in Chapters 15 and 16.) Indeed, some measurement scholars argue that equal intervals should be normally assumed.

The best procedure would seem to be to treat ordinal measurements as though they were interval measurements but to be constantly alert to the possibility of gross inequality of intervals. As much as possible about the characteristics of the measuring tools should be learned. Much useful information has been obtained by this approach, with resulting scientific advances in psychology, sociology, and education. In short, it is unlikely that researchers will be led seriously astray by heeding this advice, if they are careful in applying it.[5]

Interval Level of Measurement

Interval scales contain all the features of ordinal scales with the added dimension that the intervals between the points on the scale are equal. The concept of temperature is based on equal intervals. Marketing researchers often prefer interval scales over ordinal scales because they can measure how much of a trait one consumer has (or does not have) over another. An interval scale enables a researcher to discuss differences separating two objects. The scale possesses properties of order and difference but with an arbitrary zero point. Examples are the Fahrenheit and Celsius scales; the freezing point of water is zero on one scale and 32 degrees on the other.

The arbitrary zero point of interval scales restricts the statements that a researcher can make about the scale points. One can say that 80°F is hotter than 32°F or that 64°F is 16° cooler than 80°F. However, one cannot say that 64°F is twice as warm as 32°F. Why? Because the zero point on the Fahrenheit scale is arbitrary. To understand this point, consider the transformation of the two Fahrenheit temperatures to Celsius using the formula Celsius = $(F-32)(5/9)$; 32°F equals 0°C, and 64°F equals 17.8°C. The statement we made about the Fahrenheit temperatures (64° is twice as warm as 32°) does not hold for Celsius. The same would be true of rankings of online dating services on an interval scale. If YahooPersonals had received a 20 and GreatExpectations a 10, we cannot say that YahooPersonals is liked twice as much as GreatExpectations, because a point defining the absence of liking has not been identified and assigned a value of zero on the scale.

Interval scales are amenable to computation of an arithmetic mean, standard deviation, and correlation coefficients. The more powerful parametric statistical tests such as t tests and F tests can be applied. In addition, researchers can take a more conservative approach and use nonparametric tests if they have concern about the equal intervals assumption.

Ratio Level of Measurement

Ratio scales have all the characteristics of those scales previously discussed as well as a meaningful absolute zero or origin. Because there is universal agreement as to the location of the zero point, comparisons among the magnitudes of ratio-scaled values are acceptable. Thus, a ratio scale reflects the actual amount of a variable. Physical characteristics of a respondent such as age, weight, and height are examples of ratio-scaled variables. Other ratio scales are based on area, distance, money values, return rates, population counts, and lapsed periods of time.

Because some objects have none of the property being measured, a ratio scale originates at a zero point with absolute empirical meaning. For example, an investment (albeit a poor one) can have no rate of return, or a census tract in New Mexico could be devoid of any persons. An absolute zero implies that all arithmetic operations are possible, including multiplication and division. Numbers on the scale indicate the actual amounts of the property being measured. A large bag of McDonald's french fries weighs 8 ounces and a regular bag at Burger King weighs 4 ounces; thus, a large McDonald's bag of fries weighs twice as much as a regular Burger King bag of fries.

FROM THE FRONT LINE

Tips on Making Sure You Have the Right Level of Scaling

Krista White, Research Analyst, DSS Research

Though seemingly arcane, the level of scaling—nominal, ordinal, interval, or ratio—is a critical consideration. Normally, we simplify the four categories into two, with the nominal and ordinal scales referred to as nonmetric and the interval and ratio scales as metric. We must make sure that when we move toward the end of a project we have the kind of data we need to conduct the types of analyses required to meet the project objectives.

If we only need cross tabulations, they can be produced with any level of scaling. However, if more powerful multivariate procedures, such as regression analysis, are required, then we need metric data (interval or ratio). For example, if we need to have respondents indicate the importance of different product or service characteristics and we need to use the results as predictor variables in a regression analysis, then we need metric data. Furthermore, this means that if we are weighing the possibility of having respondents rate or rank each item, then we should go the rating route.

Ranking data are nonmetric and cannot be used in most multivariate procedures such as regression analysis. Rating data are generally considered to be metric (there is some debate on this point) and are appropriate for regression analysis. Going one step further, we would use at least a 5-point scale for the rating task and possibly a 7-point scale to provide a reasonable range for our measures.

The point is this: when you are deciding on the kinds of measures you are going to generate, think ahead to the analysis you need to do later so that you will have what you need when you get to the analysis phase.

Step Six: Evaluate the Reliability and Validity of the Measurement

An ideal marketing research study would provide information that is accurate, precise, lucid, and timely. Accurate data imply accurate measurement, or $M = A$, where M refers to measurement and A stands for complete accuracy. In marketing research, this ideal is rarely, if ever, achieved. Instead,

$$M = A + E$$

where E = errors

Errors can be either random or systematic, as noted in Chapter 6. Systematic error results in a constant bias in the measurements, caused by faults in the measurement instrument or process. For example, if a faulty ruler (on which one inch is actually one and a half inches) is used in Pillsbury's test kitchens to measure the height of chocolate cakes baked with alternative recipes, all cakes will be recorded at less than their actual height. *Random error* also influences the measurements but not systematically. Thus, random error is transient in nature. A person may not answer a question truthfully because he is in a bad mood that day.

Two scores on a measurement scale can differ for a number of reasons.[6] Only the first of the following eight reasons does not involve error. A researcher must determine whether any of the remaining seven sources of measurement differences are producing random or systematic error.

Two scores on a measurement scale can differ for a number of reasons. McDonald's may score higher on one person's survey than on another person's because of real differences in perceptions of the service or because of a variety of random or systematic errors. The reliability and validity of the type of measurement should always be checked.

1. *A true difference in the characteristic being measured.* A perfect measurement difference is solely the result of actual differences. For example, John rates McDonald's service as 1 (excellent) and Sandy rates its service as 4 (average), and the variation is due only to actual attitude differences.

2. *Differences due to stable characteristics of individual respondents,* such as personality, values, and intelligence. Sandy has an aggressive, rather critical personality, and she gives no one and nothing the benefit of the doubt. She actually was quite pleased with the service she received at McDonald's, but she expects such service and so gave it an average rating.

3. *Differences due to short-term personal factors,* such as temporary mood swings, health problems, time constraints, or fatigue. Earlier on the day of the study, John had won $400 in a "Name That Tune" contest on a local radio station. He stopped by McDonald's for a burger after he picked up his winning check. His reply on the service quality questionnaire might have been quite different if he had been interviewed the previous day.

4. *Differences caused by situational factors,* such as distractions or others present in the interview situation. Sandy was giving her replies while trying to watch her 4-year-old nephew, who was running amok on the McDonald's playground; John had his new fiancée along when he was interviewed. Replies of both people might have been different if they had been interviewed at home while no other friend or relative was present.

5. *Differences resulting from variations in administering the survey.* Interviewers can ask questions with different voice inflections, causing response variation. And because of such factors as rapport with the interviewee, manner of dress, sex, or race, different interviewers can cause responses to vary. Interviewer bias can be as subtle as a nodding of the head. One interviewer who tended to nod unconsciously was found to bias some respondents. They thought that the interviewer was agreeing with them when he was, in fact, saying, "Okay, I'm recording what you say—tell me more."

6. *Differences due to the sampling of items included in the questionnaire.* When researchers attempt to measure the quality of service at McDonald's, the scales and other questions used represent only a portion of the items that could have been used. The scales created by the researchers reflect their interpretation of the construct (service quality) and the way it is measured. If the researchers had used different words or if items had been added or removed, the scale values reported by John and Sandy might have been different.

7. *Differences due to a lack of clarity in the measurement instrument.* A question may be ambiguous, complex, or incorrectly interpreted. A survey that asked "How far do you live from McDonald's?" and then gave choices "(1) less than 5 minutes, (2) 5 to 10 minutes," and so forth, would be ambiguous; someone walking would undoubtedly take longer to get to the restaurant than a person driving a car or riding a bike. This topic is covered in much greater detail in Chapter 10.

8. *Differences due to mechanical or instrument factors.* Blurred questionnaires, lack of space to fully record answers, missing pages in a questionnaire, incorrect computer keystrokes, or a balky pen can result in differences in responses.

Martin Weinberger, executive vice president of Oxtoby-Smith, Incorporated, offers his perspectives on measurement in the Practicing Marketing Research feature.

Reliability

A measurement scale that provides consistent results over time is reliable. If a ruler consistently measures a chocolate cake as 9 inches high, then the ruler is said to be reliable. Reliable scales, gauges, and other measurement devices can be used with confidence and with the knowledge that transient and situational factors are not interfering with the measurement process. Reliable instruments provide stable measures at different times under different conditions. A key question regarding reliability is "If we measure some phenomenon over and over again with the same measurement device, will we get the same or highly similar results?" An affirmative answer means that the device is reliable.

Thus, **reliability** is the degree to which measures are free from random error and, therefore, provide consistent data. The less error there is, the more reliable the observation is, so a measurement that is free of error is a correct measure. A reliable measurement, then, does not change when the concept being measured remains constant in value. However, if the concept being measured does change in value, the reliable measure will indicate that change. How can a measuring instrument be unreliable? If your weight stays constant at 150 pounds but repeated measurements on your bathroom scale show your weight to fluctuate, the scale's lack of reliability may be due to a weak spring.

There are three ways to assess reliability: test–retest, the use of equivalent forms, and internal consistency.

Test–Retest Reliability
Test–retest reliability is obtained by repeating the measurement with the same instrument, approximating the original conditions as closely as possible. The theory behind test–retest is that if random variations are present, they will be revealed by differences in the scores between the two tests. **Stability** means that very few differences in scores are found between the first and second administrations of the test; the measuring instrument is said to be stable. For example, assume that a 30-item department store image measurement scale was administered to the same group of shoppers at two different times. If the correlation between the two measurements was high, the reliability would be assumed to be high.

There are several problems with test–retest reliability. First, it may be very difficult to locate and gain the cooperation of respondents for a second testing. Second, the first measurement may alter a person's response on the second measurement. Third, environmental or personal factors may change, causing the second measurement to change.

Equivalent Form Reliability
The difficulties encountered with the test–retest approach can be avoided by creating equivalent forms of a measurement instrument. For example, assume that the researcher is interested in identifying inner-directed versus

> **reliability**
> Degree to which measures are free from random error and, therefore, provide consistent data.

> **test–retest reliability**
> Ability of the same instrument to produce consistent results when used a second time under conditions as similar as possible to the original conditions.

> **stability**
> Lack of change in results from test to retest.

Truth about What Respondents Say

Martin Weinberger is executive vice president of Oxtoby-Smith, Incorporated, New York, one of America's largest and oldest marketing research companies. His 25 years of experience in the research industry has led him to develop certain perspectives regarding measurement in consumer research. Several of those perspectives are described below.

1. Sometimes Consumers Don't Tell the Truth; Sometimes They Are Willing to Reveal It. Several years ago, a major catalogue company was having trouble with its boys' slacks—it was getting an unusually large number of returns. Consumers were writing that the reason for the return was that the slacks did not fit properly. On the basis of that information, the catalogue sales company believed something must be wrong with the diagrams and instructions it provided to consumers for ordering the right size slacks. Oxtoby-Smith was asked to find out what was wrong with the diagrams or the instructions so that the client could fix them. We were given the names of consumers who had returned the boys' slacks.

We sent our interviewers into the field, carrying the heavy catalogue, with the diagrams and the instructions. What we found was not what we had expected to find. The consumers told us the slacks had fit perfectly well. The mothers had ordered three or four pairs of slacks for their teenage sons in the hope that the son would find *one* pair he would be willing to wear. Then the mother had to face returning the other two or three pairs. The mothers felt uncomfortable giving any explanation for the return of the slacks other than "poor fit." This finding indicated that the diagrams were not the problem. The instructions were not the problem. The catalogue company had to learn to live with the returns in the same way the mothers had to live with the habits of their teenage sons.

2. Sometimes Consumers Claim More Than They Know; Sometimes They Are Just Confused. It has been well established that consumers sometimes claim awareness of brands that do not exist. That is why it is important to include fictitious brand names in studies of brand awareness to see how much claiming is going on. In fact, I have done a study in which a fictitious brand name had *more* brand awareness than the client's brand and the client considered changing the name of its brand to the fictitious brand name!

3. Sometimes Consumers Don't Know Why They Buy the Brands They Buy. This section could be subtitled, "Why you should not ask why." I have conducted a large number of studies asking consumers, at the client's request, *why* they buy the products they buy, and I have looked at their answers to that question. At the same time, I have looked at their answers to other questions. I have found that consumers often do not really *know* why they buy the brands they buy.

A simple case in point is a food or beverage product. Ask consumers why they buy a brand, and they usually will tell you "because it tastes good." If you give a consumer a blind product test, you may find out that this individual cannot differentiate between his or her preferred Brand X and Brand Y. If you use a double-blind paired comparison, in one paired blind test a consumer will prefer X and in another paired blind test the same individual will prefer Y.

4. Consumers Not Only Have Opinions, They Have Passions. Generally, consumers are very cooperative. They will answer almost any questions you ask them. But my experience teaches me that you need to know more than just their opinions; you need to know their passions.

For example, a manufacturer of toilet paper that is thinking of introducing a scented version might ask us to find out which of a series of scents is preferred by consumers. We could test the scents and tell them scent A is more widely preferred than scent B. However, we would be remiss in our job if we failed to find out whether consumers would be disposed toward toilet paper *with any scent at all* and what the scent preferences are of those who *like* the idea of scented toilet paper. Possibly those who are interested in toilet paper with scents prefer scent B over scent A, whereas scent A appeals to those who, in the marketplace, would be buying *unscented* paper.[7]

EXHIBIT 9.4	Statements Used to Measure Inner-Directed Lifestyles

I often don't get the credit I deserve for things I do well.
I try to get my own way regardless of others.
My greatest achievements are ahead of me.
I have a number of ideas that someday I would like to put into a book.
I am quick to accept new ideas.
I often think about how I look and what impression I am making on others.
I am a competitive person.
I feel upset when I hear that people are criticizing or blaming me.
I'd like to be a celebrity.
I get a real thrill out of doing dangerous things.
I feel that almost nothing in life can substitute for great achievement.
It's important for me to be noticed.
I keep in close touch with my friends.
I spend a good deal of time trying to decide how I feel about things.
I often think I can feel my way into the innermost being of another person.
I feel that ideals are powerful motivating forces in people.
I think someone can be a good person without believing in God.
The Eastern religions are more appealing to me than Christianity.
I feel satisfied with my life.
I enjoy getting involved in new and unusual situations.
Overall, I'd say I'm happy.
I feel I understand where my life is going.
I like to think I'm different from other people.
I adopt a commonsense attitude toward life.

outer-directed lifestyles. Two questionnaires can be created containing measures of inner-directed behavior (see Exhibit 9.4) and measures of outer-directed behavior. These measures should receive about the same emphasis on each questionnaire. Thus, although the questions used to ascertain the lifestyles are different on the two questionnaires, the number of questions used to measure each lifestyle should be approximately equal. The recommended interval for administering the second equivalent form is 2 weeks, although in some cases the two forms are given one after the other or simultaneously. **Equivalent form reliability** is determined by measuring the correlation of the scores on the two instruments.

> **equivalent form reliability**
> Ability of two very similar forms of an instrument to produce closely correlated results.

There are two problems with equivalent forms that should be noted. First, it is very difficult, and perhaps impossible, to create two totally equivalent forms. Second, if equivalence can be achieved, it may not be worth the time, trouble, and expense involved. The theory behind the equivalent forms approach to reliability assessment is the same as that of the test–retest. The primary difference between the test–retest and the equivalent forms methods is the testing instrument itself. Test–retest uses the same instrument, whereas the equivalent forms approach uses a different, but highly similar, measuring instrument.

Internal Consistency Reliability **Internal consistency reliability** assesses the ability to produce similar results when different samples are used to measure a phenomenon during the same time period. The theory of internal consistency rests on the concept of equivalence. *Equivalence* is concerned with how much error may be introduced by using different samples of items to measure a phenomenon; it focuses on variations at one point in time among samples of items. A researcher can test for item equivalence

> **internal consistency reliability**
> Ability of an instrument to produce similar results when used on different samples during the same time period to measure a phenomenon.

split-half technique
Method of assessing the reliability of a scale by dividing the total set of measurement items in half and correlating the results.

by assessing the homogeneity of a set of items. The total set of items used to measure a phenomenon, such as inner-directed lifestyles, is divided into two halves; the total scores of the two halves are then correlated. Use of the **split-half technique** typically calls for scale items to be randomly assigned to one half or the other. The problem with this method is that the estimate of the coefficient of reliability is totally dependent on how the items were split. Different splits result in different correlations when, ideally, they should not.

To overcome this problem, many researchers now use the *Cronbach alpha technique*, which involves computing mean reliability coefficient estimates for all possible ways of splitting a set of items in half. A lack of correlation of an item with other items in the scale is evidence that the item does not belong in the scale and should be omitted. One limitation of the Cronbach alpha is that the scale items require equal intervals. If this criterion cannot be met, another test called the KR-20 can be used. The *KR-20 technique* is applicable for all dichotomous or nominally scaled items.

Validity

validity
The degree to which what the researcher was trying to measure was actually measured.

Recall that the second characteristic of a good measurement device is validity. **Validity** addresses the issue of whether what the researcher was trying to measure was actually measured. When Pontiac brought out the Aztek, research told them that the car would sell between 50,000 and 70,000 units annually despite the controversial styling. After selling only 27,000 cars per year, the model was discontinued in 2005. Unfortunately, the research measuring instrument was not valid. The validity of a measure refers to the extent to which the measurement instrument and procedure are free from both systematic and random error. Thus, a measuring device is valid only if differences in scores reflect true differences on the characteristic being measured rather than systematic or random error. You should recognize that a necessary precondition for validity is that the measuring instrument be reliable. An instrument that is not reliable will not yield consistent results when measuring the same phenomenon over time.

A scale or other measuring device is basically worthless to a researcher if it lacks validity because it is not measuring what it is supposed to. On the surface, this seems like a rather simple notion, yet validity often is based on subtle distinctions. Assume that your teacher gives an exam that he has constructed to measure marketing research knowledge, and the test consists strictly of applying a number of formulas to simple case problems. A friend receives a low score on the test and protests to the teacher that she "really understands marketing research." Her position, in essence, is that the test was not valid. She maintains that, rather than measuring knowledge of marketing research, the test measured memorization of formulas and the ability to use simple math to find solutions. The teacher could repeat the exam only to find that student scores still fell in the same order. Does this mean that the protesting student was incorrect? Not necessarily; the teacher may be systematically measuring the ability to memorize rather than a true understanding of marketing research.

Unlike the teacher attempting to measure marketing research knowledge, a brand manager is interested in successful prediction. The manager, for example, wants to know if a purchase intent scale successfully predicts trial purchase of a new product. Thus, validity can be examined from a number of different perspectives, including face, content, criterion-related, and construct validity (see Exhibit 9.5).

face validity
Degree to which a measurement seems to measure what it is supposed to measure.

Face Validity   **Face validity** is the weakest form of validity. It is concerned with the degree to which a measurement seems to measure what it is supposed to. It is a judgment call by the researcher, made as the questions are designed. Thus, as each question is

PRACTICING MARKETING RESEARCH

The Anonymity Gradient

Bill MacElroy, president of Socratic Technologies, San Francisco, discusses the concept of the importance of anonymous responses to respondents:

We feel that the privacy of the interviewee's environment may play a key role in the types of answers given because the change in the characteristics of answers doesn't stop when no specific interviewer is present. Even within self-administered interviewing situations, the degree to which the respondent feels "secure and alone" appears to produce more candor. We have called this observed phenomenon the anonymity gradient.

Over the past three years, we have had several opportunities to run side-by-side studies in which the same questions were asked using different modes of field methodology (e.g., one-on-one interviewing, CATI telephone, paper and pencil, disk-by-mail, and Web-based interviewing). As we examined the answers to identically worded questions, a curious pattern began to emerge. Increased human presence had the distinctive effect of producing kinder, less frank answers. This difference was also noted between paper and pencil surveys conducted with and without other people in the area.

The most candid answers (based on the degree to which people reported known problems, complained about service that was known to be a concern, and gave in-depth responses when probed for areas that needed improvement)

came from people using their own personal computers. Researchers have reported that when people use computers, they tend to enter a "cool and immersive, womb-like environment" in which the level of engagement can produce exaggerated levels of perceived privacy. The anonymity gradient can be thought of as a pattern of candor that changes with the perceived level of privacy.

By itself, the anonymity gradient might be an interesting anomaly but without much practical value. We have, however, found some distinctive characteristics that may be helpful to people as they are planning conversions from certain forms of research to others. This is particularly important if your company has been tracking satisfaction, performance, problem resolution, and other similar topics using telephone, paper and pencil, or one-on-one interviewing techniques. There can be an unpleasant shock to the system when, after many periods of hearing from your customers that they are completely satisfied with no problems to report, you suddenly find out that they are less satisfied and have a whole list of demands for improvement. You may encounter this when converting traditional methodologies to newer technologies.

For example, most data related to purchase interest tends to be overstated when actual purchases are tallied. Although we haven't had the benefit of tracking actual results, we suspect that some data related to purchase interest collected using a more anonymous technology may be closer to what will really happen when the product actually ships.[8]

---

scrutinized, there is an implicit assessment of its face validity. Revisions enhance the face validity of the question until it passes the researcher's subjective evaluation. Alternatively, *face validity* can refer to the subjective agreement of researchers, experts, or people familiar with the market, product, or industry that a scale logically appears to be accurately reflecting what it is supposed to measure.[9] A straightforward question such as "What is your age?" followed by a series of age categories generally is agreed to have face validity. Most scales used in marketing research attempt to measure attitudes or behavioral intentions, which are much more elusive.

EXHIBIT 9.5	Assessing the Validity of a Measurement Instrument
Face validity	The degree to which a measurement instrument seems to measure what it is supposed to, as judged by researchers.
Content validity	The degree to which measurement items represent the universe of the concept under study.
Criterion-related validity	The degree to which a measurement instrument can predict a variable that is designated a criterion.
	a. Predictive validity: The extent to which a future level of a criterion variable can be predicted by a current measurement on a scale.
	b. Concurrent validity: The extent to which a criterion variable measured at the same point in time as the variable of interest can be predicted by the measurement instrument.
Construct validity	The degree to which a measurement instrument confirms a hypothesis created from a theory based on the concepts under study.
	a. Convergent validity: The degree of association among different measurement instruments that purport to measure the same concept.
	b. Discriminant validity: A measure of the lack of association among constructs that are supposed to be different.

content validity
Representativeness, or sampling adequacy, of the content of the measurement instrument.

Content Validity

Content validity is the representativeness, or sampling adequacy, of the content of the measurement instrument. In other words, does the scale provide adequate coverage of the topic under study? Say that McDonald's has hired you to measure its image among adults 18 to 30 years of age who eat fast-food hamburgers at least once a month. You devise the following scale:

Modern building	1	2	3	4	5	Old-fashioned building
Beautiful landscaping	1	2	3	4	5	Poor landscaping
Clean parking lots	1	2	3	4	5	Dirty parking lots
Attractive signs	1	2	3	4	5	Unattractive signs

A McDonald's executive would quickly take issue with this scale, claiming that a person could evaluate McDonald's on this scale and never have eaten a McDonald's hamburger. In fact, the evaluation could be made simply by driving past a McDonald's. The executive could further argue that the scale lacks content validity because many important components of image—such as the quality of the food, cleanliness of the eating area and restrooms, and promptness and courtesy of service—were omitted.

The determination of content validity is not always a simple matter. It is very difficult, and perhaps impossible, to identify all the facets of McDonald's image. Content validity ultimately becomes a judgmental matter. One could approach content validity by first carefully defining precisely what is to be measured. Second, an exhaustive literature search and focus groups could be conducted to identify all possible items for inclusion on the scale. Third, a panel of experts could be asked their opinions on whether an item should be included. Finally, the scale could be pretested and an open-ended question asked that might identify other items to be included. For example, after a more refined image scale for McDonald's has been administered, a follow-up question could be "Do you have any other thoughts about McDonald's that you would like to express?" Answers to this pretest question might provide clues for other image dimensions not previously considered.

criterion-related validity
Degree to which a measurement instrument can predict a variable that is designated a criterion.

Criterion-Related Validity

Criterion-related validity examines the ability of a measuring instrument to predict a variable that is designated a criterion. Suppose that we wish to devise a test to identify marketing researchers who are exceptional at moderating

A politician is interested in what issues those likely to vote perceive as important. The predictive validity of the politician's measures may determine whether or not he or she is elected.

focus groups. We begin by having impartial marketing research experts identify from a directory of researchers those they judge to be best at moderating focus groups. We then construct 300 items to which all the group moderators are asked to reply yes or no, such as "I believe it is important to compel shy group participants to speak out" and "I like to interact with small groups of people." We then go through the responses and select the items that the "best" focus group moderators answered one way and the rest of the moderators answered the other way. Assume that this process produces 84 items, which we put together to form what we shall call the Test of Effectiveness in Focus Group Moderating (TEFGM). We feel that this test will identify good focus group moderators. The criterion of interest here is the ability to conduct a good focus group. We might explore further the criterion-related validity of TEFGM by administering it to another group of moderators, each of whom has been designated as either "best" or "not as good." Then we could determine how well the test identifies the section to which each marketing researcher is assigned. Thus, criterion-related validity is concerned with detecting the presence or absence of one or more criteria considered to represent constructs of interest.

Two subcategories of criterion-related validity are predictive validity and concurrent validity. **Predictive validity** is the extent to which a future level of a criterion variable can be predicted by a current measurement on a scale. A voter-motivation scale, for example, is used to predict the likelihood that a person will vote in the next election. A savvy politician is not interested in what the community as a whole perceives as important problems but only in what persons who are likely to vote perceive as important problems. These are the issues that the politician would address in speeches and advertising. Another example of predictive validity is the extent to which a purchase intent scale for a new Pepperidge Farm pastry predicts actual trial of the product.

Concurrent validity is concerned with the relationship between the predictor variable and the criterion variable, both of which are assessed at the same point in time—for example, the ability of a home pregnancy test to accurately determine whether a woman

> **predictive validity**
> Degree to which a future level of a criterion variable can be forecast by a current measurement scale.

> **concurrent validity**
> Degree to which another variable, measured at the same point in time as the variable of interest, can be predicted by the measurement instrument.

is pregnant right now. Such a test with low concurrent validity could cause a lot of undue stress.

Construct Validity Construct validity, though not often consciously addressed by many marketing researchers on a day-to-day basis, is extremely important to marketing scientists. Assessing construct validity involves understanding the theoretical foundations underlying the obtained measurements. A measure has **construct validity** if it behaves according to the theory behind the prediction. Purchase behavior can be observed directly; someone either buys product A or does not. Yet scientists have developed constructs on lifestyle, involvement, attitude, and personality that help explain why someone does or does not purchase something. These constructs are largely unobservable. Researchers can observe behavior related to the constructs—that is, the purchase of a product. However, they cannot observe the constructs themselves—such as an attitude. Constructs help scientists communicate and build theories to explain phenomena.[10]

Two statistical measures of construct validity are convergent and discriminant validity. **Convergent validity** reflects the degree of correlation among different measures that purport to measure the same construct. **Discriminant validity** reveals the lack of—or low—correlation among constructs that are supposed to be different. Assume that we develop a multi-item scale that measures the propensity to shop at discount stores. Our theory suggests that this propensity is caused by four personality variables: high level of self-confidence, low need for status, low need for distinctiveness, and high level of adaptability. Furthermore, our theory suggests that propensity to shop at discount stores is not related to brand loyalty or high-level aggressiveness.

Evidence of construct validity exists if our scale does the following:

☐ Correlates highly with other measures of propensity to shop at discount stores, such as reported stores patronized and social class (convergent validity)

☐ Has a low correlation with the unrelated constructs of brand loyalty and a high level of aggressiveness (discriminant validity)

All the types of validity discussed here are somewhat interrelated in both theory and practice. Predictive validity is obviously very important on a scale to predict whether a person will shop at a discount store. A researcher developing a discount store patronage scale probably would first attempt to understand the constructs that provide the basis for prediction. The researcher would put forth a theory about discount store patronage—that, of course, is the foundation of construct validity. Next, the researcher would be concerned with which specific items to include on the discount store patronage scale and whether these items relate to the full range of the construct. Thus, the researcher would ascertain the degree of content validity. The issue of criterion-related validity could be addressed in a pretest by measuring scores on the discount store patronage scale and actual store patronage. Read more about measurement tips in the Practicing Marketing Research box on page 283.

Reliability and Validity—A Concluding Comment

The concepts of reliability and validity are illustrated in Exhibit 9.6. Situation 1 shows holes all over the target, which could be caused by the use of an old rifle, being a poor shot, or many other factors. This complete lack of consistency means there is no reliability. Because the instrument lacks reliability, thus creating huge errors, it cannot be valid. Measurement reliability is a necessary condition for validity.

---

construct validity
Degree to which a measurement instrument represents and logically connects, via the underlying theory, the observed phenomenon to the construct.

convergent validity
Degree of correlation among different measurement instruments that purport to measure the same construct.

discriminant validity
Measure of the lack of association among constructs that are supposed to be different.

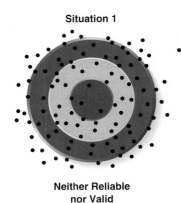

Situation 1

Neither Reliable
nor Valid

Situation 2

Highly Reliable
but Not Valid

Situation 3

Highly Reliable
and Valid

Exhibit 9.6

Illustrations of Possible Reliability and Validity Situations in Measurement

PRACTICING MARKETING RESEARCH

Tips for Managers on Putting Measurement to Work

Craig Bailey, president of Customer Centricity, Inc., was formerly manager of a customer care organization. The organization had been routinely sending out customer satisfaction surveys. One day, when signing "thank you" letters to send to survey participants, he decided that something needed to change. He describes the situation, in his own words:

The reality was that the organization was investing resources in a process to perform customer satisfaction surveys and not getting the maximum value possible. And, worse, we were wasting our customers' time.

At such a juncture, you have two choices: stop the survey process (save your money and your customers' time) and throw the thank-you letters in the trash, or leverage the customer satisfaction survey results as a catalyst for continuous improvement. We selected option No. 2.

In order to make the customer survey information meaningful, we started at the beginning and examined what, for our purposes, we were

measuring. We adopted the following principles to get the most out of customer surveys:

☐ *Any measurement that does not hold an individual responsible is not an effective metric. While many companies adhere to one element of the first measurement principle (that of "measuring" customer satisfaction), managing it requires that an individual be held responsible for the customer satisfaction metrics. For example, a customer satisfaction survey program may be designed to produce feedback on customer service, account management, billing, and provisioning, for example. At the end of the day, the managers of these organizations are responsible for the customer satisfaction levels of their respective areas. As such, they should be fully engaged in your customer satisfaction survey program.*

☐ *No one should ever be held responsible for a measurement that they cannot influence. Too often, employees who deal with customers know that the firm is performing customer satisfaction surveys, but they don't know what the customers are saying in the results. This causes tremendous frustration, because front-line personnel want* to know what they can do to improve customer satisfaction. Your program should be designed to include communications to them, so they know what they can do to improve customer satisfaction.

☐ *The importance of a measurement is determined by how high in an organization it is consistently reviewed.* Make no mistake, business is about numbers. In my opinion, there are two sets of numbers that every company must track and manage: the financials and customer satisfaction levels. If executives of a corporation only care about the financial indicators, the company will lose sight of their source of revenue—the customer. To be truly successful, companies must include customer satisfaction results on their list of key performance indicators that are reviewed by executive leadership on a monthly basis.

☐ *Every measurement must have clear and rational goals.* After establishing a baseline for its customer satisfaction levels, a company must set measureable and achievable goals in terms of where it wants to be. Many firms initially find that customers are totally satisfied in some areas of performance, while not satisfied in others. Often, companies focus their efforts only on areas of dissatisfaction, which is an appropriate step upon establishing a baseline. However, the customer satisfaction survey program needs to pay attention to all areas, because customer expectations are continuously changing. As such, areas in which customers are satisfied today may turn into areas of dissatisfaction, if a company doesn't remain progressive.

☐ *If a "carrot and stick" is not clear, measurement will fall into disuse.* Building upon each of the above principles, it is not good enough to simply measure, manage, influence, promote visibility and set goals for customer satisfaction results. Those personnel that can influence customer satisfaction, directly or indirectly, must benefit from reaching, and be affected by missing, customer satisfaction goals. To accomplish this, management must ensure the organization's compensation model is tied to customer satisfaction levels. This could be in the form of annual performance reviews in which merit increases would reflect the goals that were achieved, or missed. Alternatively, this could occur through a bonus program that is administered on a monthly, quarterly, or annual basis.[11]

Situation 2 denotes a very tight pattern (consistency), but the pattern is far removed from the bull's-eye. This illustrates that an instrument can have a high level of reliability (little variance) but lack validity. The instrument is consistent, but it does not measure what it is supposed to measure. The shooter has a steady eye, but the sights are not adjusted properly. Situation 3 shows the reliability and validity that researchers strive to achieve in a measurement instrument; it is on target with what the researcher is attempting to measure.

SUMMARY

Measurement consists of using rules to assign numbers or labels to objects in such a way as to represent quantities or qualities of attributes. A measurement rule is a guide, a method, or a command that tells a researcher what to do. Accurate measurement requires rules that are both clear and specific.

The measurement process comprises the following steps: (1) identify the concept of interest, (2) develop a construct, (3) define the concept constitutively, (4) define the concept operationally, (5) develop a measurement scale, and (6) evaluate the reliability and validity of the scale. A constitutive definition is a statement of the meaning of the central concept under study, establishing its boundaries. An operational definition specifies which observable characteristics will be measured and the process for assigning a value to the concept.

There are four basic levels of measurement: nominal, ordinal, interval, and ratio. A nominal scale partitions data into categories that are mutually exclusive and collectively exhaustive. The numbers assigned to objects or phenomena have no true numerical meaning; they are simply labels. Ordinal scales have the labeling characteristics of nominal scales plus an ability to order data. Interval scales contain all the features of ordinal scales with the added dimension that the intervals between the points on the scale are equal. Interval scales enable the researcher to discuss differences separating two objects. They are amenable to computation of an arithmetic mean, standard deviation, and correlation coefficients. Ratio scales have all the characteristics of previously discussed scales as well as a meaningful absolute zero or origin, thus permitting comparison of the absolute magnitude of the numbers and reflecting the actual amount of the variable.

Measurement data consist of accurate information and errors. Systematic error results in a constant bias in the measurements. Random error also influences the measurements but is not systematic; it is transient in nature. Reliability is the degree to which measures are free from random error and therefore provide consistent data. There are three ways to assess reliability: test–retest, internal consistency, and use of equivalent forms. Validity addresses whether the attempt at measurement was successful. The validity of a measure refers to the extent to which the measurement device or process is free from both systematic and random error. Types of validity include face, content, criterion-related, and construct validity.

KEY TERMS & DEFINITIONS

measurement Process of assigning numbers or labels to persons, objects, or events in accordance with specific rules for representing quantities or qualities of attributes.

rule Guide, method, or command that tells a researcher what to do.

constructs Specific types of concepts that exist at higher levels of abstraction.

constitutive definition Statement of the meaning of the central idea or concept under study, establishing its boundaries; also known as *theoretical,* or *conceptual, definition.*

operational definition Statement of precisely which observable characteristics will be measured and the process for assigning a value to the concept.

scale Set of symbols or numbers so constructed that the symbols or numbers can be assigned by a rule to the individuals (or their behaviors or attitudes) to whom the scale is applied.

nominal scales Scales that partition data into mutually exclusive and collectively exhaustive categories.

ordinal scales Scales that maintain the labeling characteristics of nominal scales and have the ability to order data.

interval scales Scales that have the characteristics of ordinal scales, plus equal intervals between points to show relative amounts; they may include an arbitrary zero point.

ratio scales Scales that have the characteristics of interval scales, plus a meaningful zero point so that magnitudes can be compared arithmetically.

reliability Degree to which measures are free from random error and, therefore, provide consistent data.

test–retest reliability Ability of the same instrument to produce consistent results when used a second time under conditions as similar as possible to the original conditions.

stability Lack of change in results from test to retest.

equivalent form reliability Ability of two very similar forms of an instrument to produce closely correlated results.

internal consistency reliability Ability of an instrument to produce similar results when used on different samples during the same time period to measure a phenomenon.

split-half technique Method of assessing the reliability of a scale by dividing the total set of measurement items in half and correlating the results.

validity Degree to which what the researcher was trying to measure was actually measured.

face validity Degree to which a measurement seems to measure what it is supposed to measure.

content validity Representativeness, or sampling adequacy, of the content of the measurement instrument.

criterion-related validity Degree to which a measurement instrument can predict a variable that is designated a criterion.

predictive validity Degree to which a future level of a criterion variable can be forecast by a current measurement scale.

concurrent validity Degree to which another variable, measured at the same point in time as the variable of interest, can be predicted by the measurement instrument.

construct validity Degree to which a measurement instrument represents and logically connects, via the underlying theory, the observed phenomenon to the construct.

convergent validity Degree of correlation among different measurement instruments that purport to measure the same construct.

discriminant validity Measure of the lack of association among constructs that are supposed to be different.

QUESTIONS FOR REVIEW & CRITICAL THINKING

1. What is measurement?
2. Differentiate among the four types of measurement scales, and discuss the types of information obtained from each.
3. How does reliability differ from validity? Give examples of each.
4. Give an example of a scale that would be reliable but not valid. Also give an example of a scale that would be valid but not reliable.
5. What are three methods of assessing reliability?
6. What are three methods of assessing validity?

(Team Activity) 7. Divide the class into teams of four or five. Each team should go to the Internet and find the results of a survey with data. Each team should then determine the face validity and content validity of the research. Also, each team should suggest a method for assessing reliability of the survey.

WORKING THE NET

Go to a Web search engine and look up "validity and reliability." Describe to the class the new insights you gain into these important concepts.

It's True—Not All Men or All Women Are Alike!

REAL-LIFE RESEARCH • 9.1

Distinguishing biological sex has always been a useful way to classify consumers. Men and women buy different goods and different services, read different magazines, watch different television programs, and respond differently to every option open to brand managers. As a dichotomy, however, sex has a major limitation. When consumers are coded male or female, all men are identical and identically different from all women. This practice overlooks within-sex differences.

The dichotomous nature of biological sex is especially limiting when sex is a surrogate for gender. Unlike sex, gender is continuous. There are degrees of masculinity and femininity. Thus, the goal of the researchers was to create a useful supplement to the traditional male/female classification system used in marketing research.

The researchers began with an item pool that included 206 activity, interest, and opinion items from a national survey conducted yearly by DDB Worldwide Communications Group Inc., an international marketing communications agency. The DDB items were developed for use in consumer research and as such offer several advantages. They were culled and edited for more than 20 years to isolate items that correlate with consumer behavior, and they were administered to large samples of respondents who represent the U.S. consumer population. The following items made the final cut:

- I enjoy looking through fashion magazines.
- I like to bake.
- In our family, I take care of the checkbook and pay the bills.
- I am concerned about getting enough calcium in my diet.
- I am good at fixing mechanical things.
- I would do better than average in a fistfight.
- I shop a lot for specials.
- Before going shopping, I sit down and make out a complete shopping list.
- I enjoy getting dressed up.
- The kitchen is my favorite room.

The correlation between the 10-item gender scale and biological sex was .63. This means that the gender scale and biological sex are positively and significantly ($p < .01$) correlated, but are far from interchangeable.

Market researchers will continue to use biological sex as a primary discriminator. When that is the case, the question becomes: does the gender scale provide useful information after biological sex has been taken into consideration? To answer that question, the researchers separated male respondents from female respondents and compared the highest (most feminine) scoring males with the lowest (most masculine) scoring males, and the highest (most feminine) scoring females with the lowest (most masculine) scoring females.

They labeled the most feminine (highest quartile) males "nontraditional males" (NTM), and the most masculine (lowest quartile) males "traditional males" (TM). Correspondingly, they labeled the most feminine (highest quartile) females "traditional females" (TF), and the most masculine (lowest quartile) females "nontraditional females" (NTF). The activities, interests, opinions, and consumption practices of these four segments affirm the logic of these designations.

TMs differed from NTMs, and TFs differed from NTFs in many ways. The purpose was to demonstrate the scale's discriminating power, not to be comprehensive. They therefore focused on the most interesting comparisons. All the within-sex differences reported here are statistically significant ($p < .01$), and all replicate across at least two independent surveys.

Demographic Findings

Exhibit 1 summarizes demographic differences among traditional and nontraditional males and females. Compared with NTMs, TMs are significantly more likely to own their homes, live in multiple-person households, and have annual incomes of more than $60,000. NTMs are more likely than TMs to be single, age 35 or older, and college

EXHIBIT 1	Demographic and Personality Differences			
	Traditional		**Non-Traditional**	
	Male	**Female**	**Male**	**Female**
	(387)	**(535)**	**(388)**	**(516)**
Demographics	**%**	**%**	**%**	**%**
Single, never married	4	7	30	14
More than one person living in the household	97	79	71	80
Household income $60,000+	40	24	26	32
Under 35	25	15	23	27
Over 55	22	45	37	26
Graduated high/trade school only	33	36	24	32
Graduated college	12	15	19	15
Some postgraduate	11	9	19	16
Own home	80	78	68	78
Personality Characteristics				
Likes to be seen as:				
Stylish	33	69	60	49
Sophisticated	43	61	64	48
Trendsetter	27	44	48	31
Up to date	66	82	84	66
Sensitive	76	94	89	89
Spiritual	58	85	76	72
Affectionate	78	95	89	89
Organized	81	94	90	91
Outdoorsy	76	57	65	60
Thrifty	67	87	74	71
Fun loving	87	96	92	89

EXHIBIT 2	Activity Differences			
	Traditional		**Non-Traditional**	
%Variable	Male (387) %	Female (535) %	Male (388) %	Female (516) %
Sent a greeting card	8	66	33	50
Dusted or vacuumed the house	75	98	92	96
Bought paper towels	21	50	34	44
Purchased plastic "zipper-close" bags	8	21	15	16
Bought paper napkins	9	28	15	22
Worked on a do-it-yourself project around the house	27	11	13	13
Shopped at a hardware store	35	14	20	15
Did small repair jobs around the house	96	76	90	82
Cooked outdoors	53	36	31	36
Visited a fast-food restaurant	70	54	52	64
Shopped at an automotive supply store	22	5	8	5
Attended church or other place of worship	31	58	39	41
Explored an interest or hobby	26	19	24	29
Bought food at a fast-food or other restaurant to eat at home	40	30	31	39
Had some type of meal delivered to the home (pizza, chicken, Mexican, Oriental, etc.)	28	14	18	23
Sent e-mail	36	28	36	42
Used the Internet	29	21	33	36
(% service done to vehicle in past year)				
Replaced brakes, battery, muffler, shocks, alternator, or starter myself	46	14	26	13
Changed oil, brake/transmission fluid, windshield wipers, or installed filters myself	65	20	42	24

graduates. Compared with NTFs, TFs are less well-educated and older. These demographic differences underlie some, but not all, of the psychological and behavioral differences that follow.

Personality Traits

Exhibit 1 also shows some of the personality differences among traditional and nontraditional males and females.

Household Activities

Another section of the DDB questionnaire asked about common household activities (see Exhibit 2). Marketing-relevant differences among traditional and nontraditional males and females emerged in five important areas: do-it-yourself projects around the home, housecleaning and meal preparation, use of greeting cards, use of the Internet, and religious participation. These differences correspond with some of the demographic and self-image differences shown in Exhibit 1.[12]

Questions

1. What is the construct in the research? Give a constitutive definition.
2. What level(s) of measurement are the researchers using? Why did they not use a higher or lower level of measurement?
3. What could the researchers have used to measure reliability?
4. How did the researchers approach the measurement of validity?
5. Would you say that the research demonstrated a high level of construct validity? Why or why not?
6. Do you see this scale as having value to marketing researchers? Why?

REAL-LIFE RESEARCH • 9.2

Evaluating Service Quality

The service industry accounts for 70 percent of the gross national product, absorbs approximately 72 percent of the total workforce, and is responsible for more than one-half of all consumer spending. *The Atlanta Journal* and *The Atlanta Constitution* invited their readers to fill out a questionnaire printed in the newspapers regarding service quality. A total of 610 readers filled out and mailed the questionnaire. The results are in the following table.

Responses to a Questionnaire on Survey Quality

| Industry | Atlanta readers believe service is... | | |
	Good (%)	Bad (%)	No Response (%)
Airlines	55.7	16.2	28.0
Auto dealers	15.6	52.1	32.3
Auto service	8.7	71.5	19.8
Banks	44.6	36.4	19.0
Brokerage firms	20.3	13.8	65.9
Car rentals	27.2	16.2	56.4
Department stores	29.3	46.2	24.4
Discount brokers	18.0	50.5	31.3
Doctor/dentist	47.9	26.6	25.6
Dry cleaning	47.9	15.9	36.2
Electric hookup	23.9	12.6	63.4
Fast food	35.1	36.1	28.9
Grocery stores	45.4	25.6	29.0
Hospitals	27.1	34.4	38.5
Insurance companies	19.8	44.3	35.9
Local governments	9.0	59.3	31.5
Motels/hotels	44.4	16.7	38.9
Newspapers	49.7	20.0	30.3
Restaurants	35.9	27.2	36.9
Small appliance repair	9.2	29.7	61.2
Telephone hookup	26.1	30.0	43.9

Questions

1. What are the constructs? What are the constitutive definitions in this case? Are they sufficient? If not, what are the implications?
2. What kind of scale was probably used? What is the highest level of scaling that could have been used? Give an example.
3. Describe four possible sources of error in the data.
4. Do you think the scale is reliable? Why or why not? What could be done to test for reliability?
5. Is the scale valid in your opinion? Why? How might you determine validity?

CHAPTER 10

USING MEASUREMENT SCALES TO BUILD MARKETING EFFECTIVENESS

LEARNING OBJECTIVES

1.	To understand the linkage among attitudes, behavior, and marketing effectiveness.
2.	To become familiar with the concept of scaling.
3.	To learn about the various types of attitude scales.
4.	To examine some basic considerations in selecting a type of scale.
5.	To realize the importance of attitude measurement scales in management decision making.

Journalists, political activists, and many others routinely use political labels to describe politicians and policies as conservative or liberal, right-wing or left-wing. A Harris Poll measured what a cross section of U.S. adults understand by these and other labels. Most people, it appears, understand these labels in pretty much the same way political pundits do. Large majorities believe that conservatives favor moral values and cutting taxes, and oppose same-sex marriage, gay rights, and abortion rights. Majorities believe liberals favor abortion rights, gay rights, same-sex marriages, and affirmative action. But substantial numbers of people do not know where conservatives and liberals stand on those and other issues. Some people even seem to completely misunderstand these labels. These are the results of a Harris Poll of 2,209 U.S. adults surveyed online by Harris Interactive, Rochester, New York.

Although most people gave the expected answers, substantial minorities think that conservatives oppose cutting taxes (19 percent) or are not sure (11 percent) whether they favor or oppose cutting taxes. In other words, 30 percent of all adults do not give the expected response that conservatives favor cutting taxes. Similarly, 50 percent believe or are not sure that conservatives support gun control; 46 percent think or are not sure that conservatives support affirmative action; 23 percent think or are not sure that conservatives support abortion rights; 19 percent think or are not sure that conservatives support gay rights; 15 percent believe or are not sure that conservatives support same-sex marriage.

Large majorities believe liberals favor abortion rights, gay rights, and same-sex marriage, but substantial minorities give more surprising responses. Fully 39 percent believe liberals favor cutting taxes, and 17 percent are not sure. Thirty-seven percent believe that liberals either oppose gun control (24 percent) or are not sure (13 percent). Significant but smaller numbers do not believe or are not sure whether liberals support gun control (37 percent), affirmative action (26 percent), same-sex marriage (22 percent), gay rights (17 percent), or abortion rights (16 percent).

Unsurprisingly, perceptions of moderates and independents fall between those of conservatives and liberals and between right- and left-wingers. But there are some interesting, possibly surprising findings. Moderates, for example, are seen by many people to resemble conservatives in supporting moral values and tax cuts but to resemble liberals in supporting abortion rights, gun control, and gay rights. Smaller numbers, but still pluralities, believe that independents favor tax cuts, abortion rights, affirmative action, gay rights, gun control, and same-sex marriage. Overall, therefore, people are more likely to see moderates and independents as resembling liberals than resembling conservatives. For more information, visit *www.harrisinteractive.com.*

Understanding political labels such as left-wing or conservative is based on the concept of measurement. Measuring attitudes toward liberal issues, taxes, gun control, and a host of other important, but emotional, issues typically requires attitude scales. What are the various ways to measure attitude? Why is it useful to measure attitudes? What factors should be considered in selecting an attitude scale? These questions will be answered in this chapter.[1] ■

Attitudes, Behavior, and Marketing Effectiveness

An attitude is a psychological construct, a way of conceptualizing an intangible. Attitudes cannot be observed or measured directly; their existence is inferred from their consequences. An **attitude** is an enduring organization of motivational, emotional, perceptual, and cognitive processes with respect to some aspect of a person's environment. In marketing research, it is a learned predisposition to respond in a consistently favorable or unfavorable manner toward an object or concept. Attitudes tend to be long lasting and consist of clusters of interrelated beliefs. They encompass a person's value system, which represents her or his standards of good and bad, right and wrong, and so forth. Thus, an individual may have a specific attitude toward Disney World, based on beliefs about need for entertainment, cartoon characters, fantasy, crowds of people, waiting in lines, and many other things. Disney World also may be highly valued as good, clean, wholesome fun.

> **attitude**
> Enduring organization of motivational, emotional, perceptual, and cognitive processes with respect to some aspect of a person's environment.

Link between Attitudes and Behavior

The link between attitudes and behavior is complex. Predictions of future behavior for a group of consumers tend to be more accurate than those for a single consumer. Specifically, researchers have identified the following links:

1. The more favorable the attitude of consumers, the higher the incidence of product usage; the less favorable the attitude, the lower the incidence of product usage.

2. The less favorable people's attitudes toward a product, the more likely they are to stop using it.

3. The attitudes of people who have never tried a product tend to be distributed around the mean in the shape of a normal distribution.[2]

4. When attitudes are based on actually trying and experiencing a product, attitudes predict behavior quite well. Conversely, when attitudes are based on advertising, attitude–behavior consistency is significantly reduced.[3]

Some marketing researchers have become rather pessimistic about the ability of attitude research to predict behavior.[4] The present view of most researchers, however, is that one must learn to recognize the factors that influence the extent to which measured attitudes accurately predict behavior. Six factors should be considered in assessing whether attitude research findings will predict behavior:[5]

Attitude measurement must be reliable, valid, and specific to the particular behavior. If the behavior is contributing to the American Cancer Society, the questions asked should refer only to that charity. Go to *http://www.cancer.org* to find out what information is available to help in framing such questions.

1. *Involvement of the consumer.* Attitudes are likely to predict purchase behavior only under conditions of high involvement.

2. *Attitude measurement.* The measure of attitude has to be reliable, valid, and at the same level of abstraction as the measure of behavior. For example, if the behavior involves contributing to a specific charity, such as the American Cancer Society, the attitude measure cannot ask less specific (i.e., more abstract) questions about consumers' attitudes toward charities in general. A similar consistency must be applied to the variable of time. If the behavior involves buying a new Porsche within the next 6 months, the measure should include a time parameter. The longer the time between attitude measurement and the behavior, the weaker the relationship is.

3. *Effects of other people.* The feelings of other people toward the purchase and the consumer's motivation to comply with these feelings influence the extent to which attitudes predict behavior.

4. *Situational factors.* If situational factors, such as holidays, time pressures, or sickness, intervene, measured attitudes may fail to predict behavior well.

5. *Effects of other brands.* Even though a consumer's attitude toward a brand may be quite favorable, if that consumer's attitude toward another brand is even more favorable, the other brand will probably be purchased. One reason the "attitude toward the object" model is often unable to accurately predict behavior is that it fails to include measures of attitudes toward other objects.

6. *Attitude strength.* For an attitude to influence behavior, it must be held with sufficient strength and conviction to be activated in memory.[6] The degree of association between an attitude and an object varies across a continuum. At one end of the continuum is the nonattitude: the consumer has neither positive nor negative feelings about a particular brand. At the other end of the continuum is the extreme attitude: The consumer feels very strongly about the brand.

Enhancing Marketing Effectiveness

Attitudes are truly the essence of the "human change agent" that all marketers strive to influence. Marketing managers realize that there is not a perfect correlation between attitudes and behavior. Yet in designing or modifying a marketing mix, managers know that attitude measures are often the best tool available for finding an effective mix. When Chrysler is trying to decide which of three potential new grille designs will sell the most Jeeps, it relies on attitude research. The implicit assumption is the grille most preferred in attitude research testing will sell the most Jeeps, all other things being equal. Thus, marketing managers measure attitudes in an attempt to predict behavior; correct predictions will enable managers to bring the "right" new product to the marketplace. This new product will be accompanied by the "right" marketing mix, again usually based to some extent on attitude research. Demographic data and past purchase patterns also are important data sources in deciding on a new marketing mix.

Scaling Defined

The term **scaling** refers to procedures for attempting to determine quantitative measures of subjective and sometimes abstract concepts. It is defined as a procedure for assigning numbers (or other symbols) to properties of an object in order to impart some numerical characteristics to the properties in question. Actually, numbers are assigned to *indicants* of the properties of objects. The rise and fall of mercury in a glass tube (a thermometer) is an indicant of temperature variations.

A scale is a measurement tool. Scales are either unidimensional or multidimensional. **Unidimensional scales** are designed to measure only one attribute of a concept, respondent, or object. Thus, a unidimensional scale measuring consumers' price sensitivity might include several items to measure price sensitivity, but combined into a single measure; all interviewees' attitudes are then placed along a linear continuum, called *degree of price sensitivity*. **Multidimensional scales** are based on the premise that a concept, respondent, or object might be better described using several dimensions. For example, target customers for Jaguar automobiles may be defined in three dimensions: level of wealth, degree of price sensitivity, and appreciation of fine motor cars.

Advice on what makes a good scale is given in the Practicing Marketing Research box.

scaling
Procedures for assigning numbers (or other symbols) to properties of an object in order to impart some numerical characteristics to the properties in question.

unidimensional scales
Scales designed to measure only one attribute of a concept, respondent, or object.

multidimensional scales
Scales designed to measure several dimensions of a concept, respondent, or object.

PRACTICING MARKETING RESEARCH

What Makes a Good Scale?

Kunal Gupta, Jamie Baker-Prewitt, and Jeff Miller, all of Burke Marketing Research, discuss the popularity of itemized rating scales and the properties of any good scale.

The prevalent use of itemized rating scales is not surprising because . . .

☐ They are fairly easy to construct.

☐ Marketing research studies that have used such scales abound, and scales from such studies can be easily duplicated or adapted for new research.

☐ They enable respondents to express their attitudes and opinions in common and simple words, or through the use of numerical values.

Properties of a Good Scale

While there is no single, itemized scale that works well under all situations, it is important to recognize that the chosen scale must meet certain overall criteria. These criteria help to ensure that responses are being measured and reported in a reliable and valid manner. In particular, good scales should:

☐ Be easy to understand by respondents.

☐ Discriminate well between respondent perceptions.

☐ Be easy to interpret.

☐ Have minimal response bias.

☐ Be easy to administer.

☐ Be credible and useful.

Thus, marketing researchers should strive to design scales that perform well against the maximum number of these criteria rather than search for a universally applicable, one-size-fits-all scale.[7]

Attitude Measurement Scales

Measurement of attitudes relies on less precise scales than those found in the physical sciences and hence is much more difficult. Because an attitude is a construct that exists in the mind of the consumer, it is not directly observable—unlike, for example, weight in the physical sciences. In many cases, attitudes are measured at the nominal or ordinal level. Some more sophisticated scales enable the marketing researcher to measure at the interval level. One must be careful not to attribute the more powerful properties of an interval scale to the lower-level nominal or ordinal scales.

Graphic Rating Scales

> **graphic rating scales**
> Measurement scales that include a graphic continuum, anchored by two extremes.

Graphic rating scales offer respondents a graphic continuum, typically anchored by two extremes. Exhibit 10.1 depicts three types of graphic rating scales that might be used to evaluate La-Z-Boy recliners. Scale A represents the simplest form of a graphic scale. Respondents are instructed to mark their response on the continuum. After respondents have done so, scores are ascertained by dividing the line into as many categories as desired and assigning a score based on the category into which the mark has been placed. For example, if the line were 6 inches long, every inch might represent a category. Scale B offers the respondent slightly more structure by assigning numbers along the scale.

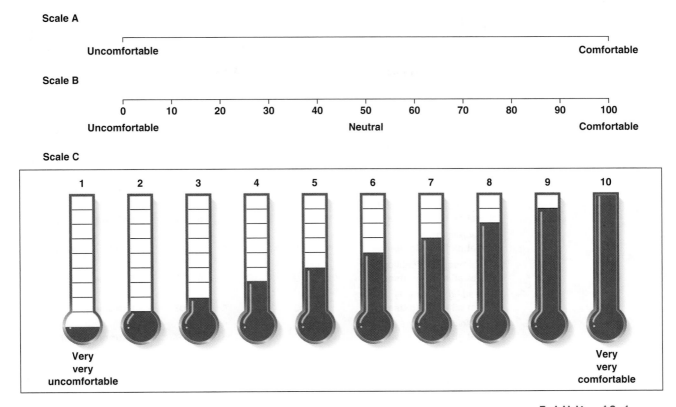

Exhibit 10.1

Three Types of Graphic Rating Scales

Responses to graphic rating scales are not limited to simply placing a mark on a continuum, as scale C illustrates. Scale C has been used successfully by many researchers to speed up self-administered interviews. Respondents are asked to touch the thermometer on the computer screen that best depicts their feelings.

Graphic rating scales can be constructed easily and are simple to use. They enable a researcher to discern fine distinctions, assuming that the rater has adequate discriminatory abilities. Numerical data obtained from the scales are typically treated as interval data.

One disadvantage of graphic rating scales is that overly extreme anchors tend to force respondents toward the middle of the scale. Also, some research has suggested that such scales are not as reliable as itemized rating scales.

Itemized Rating Scales

Itemized rating scales are similar to graphic rating scales, except that respondents must select from a limited number of ordered categories rather than placing a mark on a continuous scale. (Purists would argue that scale C in Exhibit 10.1 is an itemized rating scale.) Exhibit 10.2 shows some examples of itemized rating scales taken from nationwide marketing research surveys. Starting items are rotated on each questionnaire to eliminate the order bias that might arise from starting with the same item each time.

Scale A was used by a dot-com company in determining what features and services it should add to its Web site. Scale B was used in measuring satisfaction with an online travel site. Scale C was used by an e-commerce music retailer to better understand how people select a music Web site. Scale D was also an Internet survey, conducted by a producer of customer relationship management software. Examples of other itemized rating scales are shown in Exhibit 10.3.

itemized rating scales Measurement scales in which the respondent selects an answer from a limited number of ordered categories.

■ **Exhibit 10.2**

Itemized Rating Scales Used in Internet and Mall Surveys

If offered, how likely would you be to use the following areas on this site?

Scale A

a. Auctions
Not at all likely to use   ○1 ○2 ○3 ○4 ○5 ○6 ○7   **Extremely likely to use**

b. Fee-based education tools
Not at all likely to use   ○1 ○2 ○3 ○4 ○5 ○6 ○7   **Extremely likely to use**

c. Event registration
Not at all likely to use   ○1 ○2 ○3 ○4 ○5 ○6 ○7   **Extremely likely to use**

d. Online shopping markets
Not at all likely to use   ○1 ○2 ○3 ○4 ○5 ○6 ○7   **Extremely likely to use**

e. Recruiting
Not at all likely to use   ○1 ○2 ○3 ○4 ○5 ○6 ○7   **Extremely likely to use**

f. Research subscription
Not at all likely to use   ○1 ○2 ○3 ○4 ○5 ○6 ○7   **Extremely likely to use**

g. Trading community
Not at all likely to use   ○1 ○2 ○3 ○4 ○5 ○6 ○7   **Extremely likely to use**

h. Training/seminars
Not at all likely to use   ○1 ○2 ○3 ○4 ○5 ○6 ○7   **Extremely likely to use**

Scale B

Submitting a Request for a Hotel Reservation

We'd like to get your feedback regarding your experience in submitting a request for a hotel reservation at our Web site today. Please rate your satisfaction with each of the following aspects of *fasthotels.com* based on **your experience this visit**.

	Very Satisfied				**Very Dissatisfied**
	1	2	3	4	5
Ability to access the offer page	○	○	○	○	○
Ability to locate hotel information	○	○	○	○	○
Ability to locate city information	○	○	○	○	○
Clarity of how the bonus program works	○	○	○	○	○
Clarity of the purchase agreement	○	○	○	○	○

Please rate the extent to which you are satisfied that *Fasthotels.com* **has communicated** each of the following to you during this visit:

	Very Satisfied				**Very Dissatisfied**
	1	2	3	4	5
Your hotel reservation is/will be nonchangeable	○	○	○	○	○
Your hotel reservation is/will be nonrefundable	○	○	○	○	○

How **satisfied** would you say you were with **this visit** to *Fasthotels.com*?
○ Very satisfied
○ Satisfied
○ Somewhat satisfied
○ Neither satisfied nor dissatisfied
○ Somewhat dissatisfied
○ Dissatisfied
○ Very dissatisfied

Exhibit 10.2

Itemized Rating Scales Used in Internet and Mall Surveys—continued

Scale C

What factors influence your choice of music Web sites? (Rate the importance of each item.)

	Not at All Important				Very Important
Customer benefits or rewards for shopping	○	○	○	○	○
Customer service or delivery options	○	○	○	○	○
Ease of use of Web site	○	○	○	○	○
Low prices	○	○	○	○	○
Real-time audio sampling of CDs	○	○	○	○	○
Reviews and artist information	○	○	○	○	○

Scale D

How interested would you be in obtaining additional information about this customer relationship management solution for your business?

○ Extremely interested   ○ Somewhat interested   ○ Not at all interested

○ Very interested   ○ Not very interested

How likely is it that your business will invest in this type of customer relationship management solution within the next 12 months?

○ Extremely likely   ○ Somewhat likely   ○ Not at all likely

○ Very likely   ○ Not very likely

EXHIBIT 10.3	Selected Itemized Rating Scales

Characteristic of Interest	Rating Choices				
Purchase Intent	Definitely will buy	Probably will buy	Probably will not buy	Definitely will not buy	
Level of Agreement	Strongly agree	Somewhat agree	Neither agree nor disagree	Somewhat disagree	Strongly disagree
Quality	Very good	Good	Neither good nor bad	Fair	Poor
Dependability	Completely dependable	Somewhat dependable	Not very dependable	Not dependable at all	
Style	Very stylish	Somewhat stylish	Not very stylish	Completely unstylish	
Satisfaction	Completely satisfied	Somewhat satisfied	Neither satisfied nor dissatisfied	Somewhat dissatisfied	Completely dissatisfied
Cost	Extremely expensive	Expensive	Neither expensive nor inexpensive	Slightly inexpensive	Very inexpensive
Ease of Use	Very easy to use	Somewhat easy to use	Not very easy to use	Difficult to use	
Color Brightness	Extremely bright	Very bright	Somewhat bright	Slightly bright	Not bright at all
Modernity	Very modern	Somewhat modern	Neither modern nor old-fashioned	Somewhat old-fashioned	Very old-fashioned

Although itemized rating scales do not allow for the fine distinctions that can be achieved in a graphic rating scale, they are easy to construct and administer. And the definitive categories found in itemized rating scales usually produce more reliable ratings.

Advice for analyzing rating scales is given in the Practicing Marketing Research box below.

PRACTICING MARKETING RESEARCH

Thomas Sernon, an independent marketing research consultant, warns us to be careful when averaging scale data.

A mean is an index, a reductionist device to compress a set of data into a single number. Inevitably, some of the information is lost in the reduction process. Aside from the information loss inherent in any index, using the mean to reflect a set of scale ratings requires great faith in the universal validity of arithmetic—a faith that is misplaced in this instance.

Arithmetic works on real numbers. Abraham Lincoln supposedly once asked, "If you call a horse's tail a leg, how many legs does a horse have?" He answered his own question, correctly: "Four. Calling the tail a leg doesn't make it one."

Similarly, labeling the positions on a scale with numbers like "5, 4, 3, 2, 1" does not endow those positions with the properties of real numbers. Successive real numbers always differ by the same amount: one. All arithmetic processes are dependent on that fact, which does not apply to the value of scale ratings in most cases. Generally, the difference between the top rating and the one just below it is far more important than the difference between the bottom rating and the one just above it. Averaging the ratings treats them as equivalent differences.

Here are imaginary results, based on five-point rating scales for products A and B:

Ratings	A (%)	B (%)
5	10	20
4	48	41
3	31	21
2	9	10
1	2	8
"Mean"	3.55	3.55

Presenting the results in terms of means indicates no difference between A and B.

That wrong conclusion is due both to the index's loss-of-information feature and the inappropriate arithmetical process used. The averaging process assumes not only that the differences between successive positions are constant, but also that a reduction in low ratings offsets a similar increase in high ratings. In arithmetic, a double negative is equivalent to a positive; in real life (including marketing), that is usually not true. The increase in positive ratings is more valuable than a similar decrease in negative ratings.

Aside from its reliance on inappropriate arithmetic, the mean has a practical, conceptual flaw: it is an aggregate measure. Marketing depends on the decisions of individual household or business consumers. It is convenient for analysts and strategies to think of markets in terms of totals or segments, but these are ex post facto summaries, not operating realities. A market segment may be identified as a high-potential group, but the segment itself never buys anything; buying is done by the individual units in it. For that reason, disaggregate information, such as the *incidence* of high ratings, is a more valid type of information than aggregates.[8]

Rank-Order Scales

Itemized and graphic scales are considered to be **noncomparative scales** because the respondent makes a judgment without reference to another object, concept, or person. **Rank-order scales**, on the other hand, are **comparative scales** because the respondent is asked to compare two or more items and rank each item. Rank-order scales are widely used in marketing research for several reasons. They are easy to use and give ordinal measurements of the items evaluated. Instructions are easy to understand, and the process typically moves at a steady pace. Some researchers claim that rank-order scales force respondents to evaluate concepts in a realistic manner. Exhibit 10.4(A) illustrates a series of rank-order scales taken from a study on eye shadows. Exhibit 10.4(B) shows an online scale on automobile resale value percentage.

Rank-order scales possess several disadvantages. If all of the alternatives in a respondent's choice set are not included, the results could be misleading. For example, a

> **noncomparative scales**
> Measurement scales in which judgment is made without reference to another object, concept, or person.

> **rank-order scales**
> Measurement scales in which the respondent compares two or more items and ranks them.

> **comparative scales**
> Measurement scales in which one object, concept, or person is compared with another on a scale.

Exhibit 10.4(A)

Series of Rank-Order Scales Used to Evaluate Eye Shadows and Car Resale Values

Eye Shadow Scales

Please rank the following eye shadows, with 1 being the brand that best meets the characteristic being evaluated and 6 the worst brand on the characteristic being evaluated. The six brands are listed on card C. (HAND RESPONDENT CARD C.) Let's begin with the idea of having high-quality compacts or containers. Which brand would rank as having the highest quality compacts or containers? Which is second? (RECORD BELOW.)

	Q.48. Having High-Quality Container	Q.49. Having High-Quality Applicator	Q.50. Having High-Quality Eye Shadow
Avon	_____	_____	_____
Cover Girl	_____	_____	_____
Estee Lauder	_____	_____	_____
L'Oreal	_____	_____	_____
Natural Wonder	_____	_____	_____
Revlon	_____	_____	_____

Card C		
Avon	Cover Girl	Estee Lauder
L'Oreal	Natural Wonder	Revlon

Car Resale Value Scale

Based on your personal experience or what you have seen, heard or read, please rank the following car brands according to the resale value percentage—that is, the brand that enables you to recover the largest dollar amount (percentage) of your original purchase price of the vehicle.

Place a "1" next to the brand that has the highest resale value percentage, a "2" next to the brand that has the next highest resale value percentage, and so forth. Remember, no two cars can have the same ranking.

_____ Chevrolet
_____ Toyota
_____ BMW
_____ Ford

respondent's first choice on all dimensions in the eye shadow study might have been Wet'n'Wild, which was not included. A second problem is that the concept being ranked may be completely outside a person's choice set, thus producing meaningless data. Perhaps a respondent doesn't use eye shadow and feels that the product isn't appropriate for any woman. Another limitation is that the scale gives the researcher only ordinal data. Nothing is learned about how far apart the items stand or how intensely the respondent feels about the ranking of an item. Finally, the researcher does not know why the respondent ranked the items as he or she did.

Q-Sorting

> **Q-sorting**
> Measurement scale employing a sophisticated form of rank ordering using card sorts.

Q-sorting is basically a sophisticated form of rank ordering. A respondent is given cards listing a set of objects—such as verbal statements, slogans, product features, or potential customer services—and asked to sort them into piles according to specified rating categories. For example, the cards might each describe a feature that could be incorporated into a new automobile design, and the respondent might be asked to sort the cards according to how well he or she likes the potential feature. Q-sorts usually contain a large number of cards—from 60 to 120 cards. For statistical convenience, the respondent is instructed to put varying numbers of cards in several piles, the whole making up a normal statistical distribution.

Here is a Q-sort distribution of 90 items:

Excellent Feature										Poor Feature
3	4	7	10	13	16	13	10	7	4	3
10	9	8	7	6	5	4	3	2	1	0

This is a rank-order continuum from Excellent Feature (10) to Poor Feature (0), with varying degrees of approval and disapproval between the extremes.

The numbers 3, 4, 7, . . . , 7, 4, 3 are the numbers of cards to be placed in each pile. The numbers below the line are the values assigned to the cards in each pile. That is, the three cards on the left (Excellent Feature) are each assigned 10, the four cards in the next pile are assigned 9, and so on through the distribution, to the three cards on the extreme right (Poor Feature), which are assigned 0. The center pile, containing 16 cards, is a neutral pile. The respondent is told to put into the neutral pile cards that are left over after other choices have been made; these include cards that seem ambiguous or about which he or she cannot make a decision. In brief, this Q-sort will contain 11 piles of varying numbers of cards, and the cards in each pile will be assigned a value from 0 through 10. A Q-sort can be used to determine the relative ranking of items by individuals and to identify clusters of individuals who exhibit the same preferences. These clusters may then be analyzed as a potential basis for market segmentation. (Factor analysis, discussed in Chapter 17, is used to identify clusters of individuals.) Thus, Q-sorts have a much different objective than other types of scaling—the goal is to uncover groups of individuals who possess similar attitudes.

> **paired comparison scales**
> Measurement scales that ask the respondent to pick one of two objects in a set, based on some stated criteria.

Paired Comparisons

Paired comparison scales ask a respondent to pick one of two objects from a set, based on some stated criteria. The respondent, therefore, makes a series of paired judgments between objects. Exhibit 10.5 shows a paired comparison scale used in a national study

Exhibit 10.5

Paired Comparison Scale for Sun Care Products

Here are some characteristics used to describe sun care products in general. Please tell me which characteristic in each pair is more important to you when selecting a sun care product.

a. Tans evenly	**b.** Tans without burning
a. Prevents burning	**b.** Protects against burning and tanning
a. Good value for the money	**b.** Goes on evenly
a. Not greasy	**b.** Does not stain clothing
a. Tans without burning	**b.** Prevents burning
a. Protects against burning and tanning	**b.** Good value for the money
a. Goes on evenly	**b.** Tans evenly
a. Prevents burning	**b.** Not greasy

for sun care products. Only part of the scale is shown; the data collection procedure typically requires the respondent to compare all possible pairs of objects.

Paired comparisons overcome several problems of traditional rank-order scales. First, it is easier for people to select one item from a set of two than to rank a large set of data. Second, the problem of order bias is overcome; there is no pattern in the ordering of items or questions to create a source of bias. On the negative side, because all possible pairs are evaluated, the number of paired comparisons increases geometrically as the number of objects to be evaluated increases arithmetically. Thus, the number of objects to be evaluated should remain fairly small to prevent interviewee fatigue.

Constant Sum Scales

To avoid long lists of paired items, marketing researchers use **constant sum scales** more often than paired comparisons. Constant sum scales require the respondent to divide a given number of points, typically 100, among two or more attributes based on their importance to him or her. Respondents must value each item relative to all other items. The number of points allocated to each alternative indicates the ranking assigned to it by the respondent, as well as the relative magnitude of each alternative as perceived by the respondent. A constant sum scale used in a national study of tennis sportswear is shown in Exhibit 10.6. Another advantage of the constant sum scale over a rank-order or paired comparison scale is that if the respondent perceives two characteristics to have equal value, he or she can so indicate.

A major disadvantage of this scale is that the respondent may have difficulty allocating the points to total 100 if there are a lot of characteristics or items. Most researchers feel that 10 items is the upper limit on a constant sum scale.

> **constant sum scales**
> Measurement scales that ask the respondent to divide a given number of points, typically 100, among two or more attributes, based on their importance to him or her.

Semantic Differential Scales

The semantic differential was developed by Charles Osgood, George Suci, and Percy Tannenbaum.[9] The focus of their original research was on the measurement of meaning of an object to a person. The object might be a savings and loan association, and the meaning its image among a certain group of people.

The construction of a **semantic differential scale** begins with determination of a concept to be rated, such as the image of a company, brand, or store. The researcher selects dichotomous (opposite) pairs of words or phrases that could be used to describe the concept. Respondents then rate the concept on a scale (usually 1 to 7). The mean of the responses for each pair of adjectives is computed, and the means are plotted as a profile, or image.

> **semantic differential scales**
> Measurement scales that examine the strengths and weaknesses of a concept by having the respondent rank it between dichotomous pairs of words or phrases that could be used to describe it; the means of the responses are then plotted as a profile, or image.

Exhibit 10.6

Constant Sum Scale Used in Tennis Sportswear Study

Below are seven characteristics of women's tennis sportswear. Please allocate 100 points among the characteristics such that the allocation represents the importance of each characteristic to you. The more points that you assign to a characteristic, the more important it is. If the characteristic is totally unimportant, you should not allocate any points to it. When you've finished, please double-check to make sure that your total adds to 100.

Characteristics of Tennis Sportswear	Number of Points
Is comfortable to wear	_____
Is durable	_____
Is made by well-known brand or sports manufacturers	_____
Is made in the United States	_____
Has up-to-date styling	_____
Gives freedom of movement	_____
Is a good value for the money	_____
	100 points

Exhibit 10.7 is an actual profile of an Arizona savings and loan association as perceived by noncustomers with family incomes of $80,000 and above. A quick glance shows that the firm is viewed as somewhat old-fashioned, with rather plain facilities. It is viewed as well-established, reliable, successful, and probably very nice to deal with. The institution has parking problems and perhaps entry and egress difficulties. Its advertising is viewed as dismal.

The semantic differential is a quick and efficient means of examining the strengths and weaknesses of a product or company image versus those of the competition. More

Exhibit 10.7

Semantic Differential Profile of an Arizona Savings and Loan Association

Adjective 1	Mean of Each Adjective Pair	Adjective 2
	1 2 3 4 5 6 7	
Modern		Old-fashioned
Aggressive		Defensive
Friendly		Unfriendly
Well-established		Not well-established
Attractive exterior		Unattractive exterior
Reliable		Unreliable
Appeals to small companies		Appeals to big companies
Makes you feel at home		Makes you feel uneasy
Helpful services		Indifferent to customers
Nice to deal with		Hard to deal with
No parking or transportation problems		Parking or transportation problems
My kind of people		Not my kind of people
Successful		Unsuccessful
Ads attract a lot of attention		Haven't noticed ads
Interesting ads		Uninteresting ads
Influential ads		Not influential

GLOBAL RESEARCH

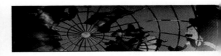

Be Cautious in Interpreting Scales Used in Global Research

Sabra Brock, vice president of Citicorp, notes that devising scales and other types of questions requires careful planning when conducting marketing research in Asia. In Asia, many countries have the capability of conducting some kinds of Western-style marketing research. Japan, Hong Kong, Singapore, and the Philippines have fairly advanced research industries. Other countries in Asia such as China, South Korea, Indonesia, and India have research capabilities, but they are so underdeveloped as to require special supervision. Asia also has fewer research and marketing firms that can act as data "translators," people who can transform computer tables and research results into specific marketing directions.

Attitudes toward research vary from country to country in Asia, as do reactions to pricing, distribution, and promotion strategies. Most Asians respond differently to being interviewed than Americans. They frequently have less patience with the abstract and rational phrasing commonly used in questionnaires, particularly where literacy rates are low.

The interpretation of research tools like scales is different among educated Asians. The Japanese desire not to contradict, for example, makes for more yea-saying and upward scale bias than in a Western culture.

Apart from the varying reactions to research, there also are design implications to the distinct pricing and distribution strategies employed in Asia. For example, when querying Asians about pricing, the researcher must realize that they are especially prone to equating high price with high quality. In countries where imports are restricted or highly taxed, like South Korea and the Philippines, "imported" and especially "made in USA" are strong product claims.

Among the Chinese countries in Asia, many distinct dialects are spoken. A Hong Kong native speaks the Cantonese dialect and must study Mandarin to communicate easily in Taiwan. These language dissimilarities are critical in questionnaire development. In Hong Kong, written and oral Cantonese are different enough to necessitate rewriting a questionnaire when the methodology changes from self-administered to interviewer-read.[12]

importantly, however, the semantic differential has been shown to be sufficiently reliable and valid for decision making and prediction in marketing and the behavioral sciences.[10] Also, the semantic differential has proved to be statistically robust (generalizable from one group of subjects to another) when applied to corporate image research.[11] This makes possible the measurement and comparison of images held by interviewees with diverse backgrounds.

Although these advantages have led many researchers to use the semantic differential as an image measurement tool, it is not without disadvantages. First, the semantic differential suffers from a lack of standardization. It is a highly generalized technique that must be adapted for each research problem. There is no single set of standard scales, and hence the development of customized scales becomes an integral part of the research.

The number of divisions on the semantic differential scale also presents a problem. If too few divisions are used, the scale is crude and lacks meaning; if too many are used, the scale goes beyond the ability of most people to discriminate. Researchers have found the seven-point scale to be the most satisfactory.

Another disadvantage of the semantic differential is the *halo effect*. The rating of a specific image component may be dominated by the interviewee's overall impression of the concept being rated. Bias may be significant if the image is hazy in the respondent's mind. To partially counteract the halo effect, the researcher should randomly reverse scale adjectives so that all the "good" ones are not placed on one side of the scale and the "bad" ones on the other. This forces the interviewee to evaluate the adjectives before responding. After the data have been gathered, all the positive adjectives are placed on one side and the negative ones on the other to facilitate analysis.

In analysis of a seven-point semantic differential scale, care must be taken in interpreting a score of 4. A response of 4 indicates one of two things—the respondent either is unable to relate the given pair of adjectives to the concept or is simply neutral or indifferent. Image studies frequently contain a large number of 4 responses. This phenomenon tends to pull the profiles toward the neutral position. Thus, the profiles lack clarity, and little distinction appears.

Stapel Scales

> **Stapel scales**
> Measurement scales that require the respondent to rate, on a scale ranging from +5 to −5, how closely and in what direction a descriptor adjective fits a given concept.

The **Stapel scale** is a modification of the semantic differential. A single adjective is placed in the center of the scale, which typically is a 10-point scale ranging from +5 to −5. The technique is designed to measure both the direction and the intensity of attitudes simultaneously. (The semantic differential, on the other hand, reflects how closely the descriptor adjective fits the concept being evaluated.) An example of a Stapel scale is shown in Exhibit 10.8.

The primary advantage of the Stapel scale is that it enables the researcher to avoid the arduous task of creating bipolar adjective pairs. The scale may also permit finer discrimination in measuring attitudes. A drawback is that descriptor adjectives can be phrased in a positive, neutral, or negative vein, and the choice of phrasing has been shown to affect the scale results and the person's ability to respond.[13] The Stapel scale has never had much popularity in commercial research and is used less frequently than the semantic differential.

Exhibit 10.8

Stapel Scale Used to Measure a Retailer's Web Site

+5	+5
+4	+4
+3	+3
+2	+2
+1	+1
Cheap Prices	Easy to Navigate
−1	−1
−2	−2
−3	−3
−4	−4
−5	−5

Select a "plus" number for words you think describe the Web site accurately. The more accurately you think the word describes the Web site, the larger the "plus" number you should choose. Select a "minus" number for words you think do not describe the Web site accurately. The less accurately you think the word describes the Web site, the larger the "minus" number you should choose. Therefore, you can select any number from +5 for words you think are very accurate all the way to −5 for words you think are very inaccurate.

Likert Scales

The **Likert scale** is another scale that avoids the problem of developing pairs of dichotomous adjectives. The scale consists of a series of statements expressing either a favorable or an unfavorable attitude toward the concept under study. The respondent is asked to indicate the level of her or his agreement or disagreement with each statement by assigning it a numerical score. The scores are then totaled to measure the respondent's attitude.

Exhibit 10.9 shows two Likert scales for an Internet game site targeted toward teenagers. Scale A measures attitudes toward the registration process; scale B evaluates users' attitudes toward advertising on the Web site.

With the Likert scale, the respondent is required to consider only one statement at a time, with the scale running from one extreme to the other. A series of statements (attitudes) can be examined, yet there is only a single set of uniform replies for the respondent to choose from.

Rensis Likert created this scale to measure a person's attitude toward concepts (e.g., unions), activities (e.g., swimming), and so forth. He recommended the following steps in building the scale:

1. The researcher identifies the concept or activity to be scaled.

2. The researcher assembles a large number of statements (75 to 100) concerning the public's sentiments toward the concept or activity.

3. Each test item is classified by the researcher as generally "favorable" or "unfavorable" with regard to the attitude under study. No attempt is made to scale the items;

> **Likert scales**
> Measurement scales in which the respondent specifies a level of agreement or disagreement with statements expressing either a favorable or an unfavorable attitude toward the concept under study.

People's attitudes toward activities like skiing can be measured using Likert scales.

Exhibit 10.9

Likert Scales Used by an Internet Game Site

Scale A

How did you feel about the registration process when you became a new user?

	Strongly disagree	Somewhat disagree	Neutral	Somewhat agree	Strongly agree
The registration was simple.	○	○	○	○	○
The registration questions were "nonthreatening."	○	○	○	○	○
Registration here will protect my privacy.	○	○	○	○	○
The registration did not take a long time to complete.	○	○	○	○	○
The registration informed me about the site.	○	○	○	○	○

Scale B

How do you feel about the following statements?

	Strongly disagree	Somewhat Disagree	Neutral	Somewhat agree	Strongly agree
Allowing companies to advertise on the Internet allows me to access free services.	○	○	○	○	○
I do not support advertising on this site even though it provides me with free entertainment.	○	○	○	○	○
There is extremely too much advertising on the Internet.	○	○	○	○	○
There is extremely too much advertising on this site.	○	○	○	○	○
It's easy for me to ignore the advertising on this site and just play the game.	○	○	○	○	○

however, a pretest is conducted that involves the full set of statements and a limited sample of respondents.

4. In the pretest, the respondent indicates agreement (or not) with *every* item, checking one of the following direction-intensity descriptors:
   a. Strongly agree
   b. Agree

c. Undecided
d. Disagree
e. Strongly disagree

5. Each response is given a numerical weight (e.g., 5, 4, 3, 2, 1).

6. The individual's *total attitude score* is represented by the algebraic summation of weights associated with the items checked. In the scoring process, weights are assigned so that the direction of attitude—favorable to unfavorable—is consistent over items. For example, if 5 were assigned to "strongly agree" for favorable items, 5 should be assigned to "strongly disagree" for unfavorable items.

7. After seeing the results of the pretest, the researcher selects only those items that appear to discriminate well between high and low *total* scorers. This may be done by first finding the highest and lowest quartiles of subjects on the basis of *total* score and then comparing the mean differences on each *specific* item for these high and low groups (excluding the middle 50 percent of subjects).

8. The 20 to 25 items finally selected are those that have discriminated "best" (i.e., exhibited the greatest differences in mean values) between high and low total scorers in the pretest.

9. Steps 3 through 5 are then repeated in the main study.

Likert created the scale so that a researcher could look at a summed score and tell whether a person's attitude toward a concept was positive or negative. For example, the maximum favorable score on a 20-item scale would be 100; therefore, a person scoring 92 would be presumed to have a favorable attitude. Of course, two people could both score 92 and yet have rated various statements differently. Thus, specific components of their overall attitude could differ markedly. For example, if respondent A strongly agreed (5) that a particular bank had good parking and strongly disagreed (1) that its loan programs were the best in town and respondent B had the exact opposite attitude, both would have summed scores of 6.

In the world of marketing research, Likert-like scales are very popular. They are quick and easy to construct and can be administered by telephone or via the Internet. Commercial researchers rarely follow the textbook-like process just outlined. Instead, the scale usually is developed jointly by a client project manager and a researcher. Many times, the scale is created following a focus group.

Developing and administering scales in the real world of marketing research sometimes presents problems not emphasized in textbooks. In the Practicing Marketing Research feature, Diane Schmalensee, president of Schmalensee Partners, discusses several dos and don'ts she has learned in many years of building marketing research scales.

Purchase Intent Scales

Perhaps the single scale used most often in marketing research is the **purchase intent scale**. The ultimate issue for marketing managers is, Will they buy the product or not? If so, what percentage of the market can I expect to obtain? The purchase intent question normally is asked for all new products and services and product and service modifications, by manufacturers, retailers, and even nonprofit organizations.[15]

During new product development, the purchase intent question is first asked during concept testing to get a rough idea of demand. The manager wants to quickly eliminate potential turkeys, take a careful look at those products for which purchase intent is moderate, and push forward the products that seem to have star potential. At this stage, investment is minimal and product modification or concept repositioning is an easy task. As the product moves through development, the product itself, promotion

> **purchase intent scales**
> Scales used to measure a respondent's intention to buy or not buy a product.

PRACTICING MARKETING RESEARCH

Diane Schmalensee, president of Schmalensee Partners, offers a few dos and don'ts on creating scales.

Rule 1: Use scale wording that motivates action. Scale wording should be meaningful to decision makers and to their employees who will act on the results of the research. There are two aspects to this: (1) full labeling of the scales versus end-point labeling only and (2) choosing words that motivate versus words that merely describe.

Let's start by considering a scale that is fully labeled versus one that is labeled only at the end points in the following table. The respondents' answers are identical numerically but very different in their impact on decision makers and goal setting.

With the fully labeled scale, decision makers can set meaningful and motivational goals that specify how much they need to increase the excellent or very good ratings (say from 50 to 70 percent) and decrease the fair or poor ratings (say from 20 to 10 percent).

With the end-point labeled scale, results are commonly reported as averages rather than percentages. These averages are difficult to use to motivate employees and often increase by such small-seeming amounts as to discourage employee effort. For example, employees are far less likely to be motivated to increase the average rating from 3.4 to 3.75 than by the statistical equivalent of increasing excellent/very good ratings from 50 to 70 percent and decreasing the poor/fair ratings from 20 to 10 percent.

Now consider the motivation of using value-neutral scales (such as agree/disagree) versus more value-laden scales (such as excellent/poor).

Employees are far more likely to be motivated by a goal of increasing excellent ratings than by a goal of increasing agree ratings.

Rule 2: Allow "don't know" responses. It is important to offer the respondents a "don't know" choice. Not uncommonly, some respondents in satisfaction surveys are unaware of some of the issues raised in the survey. Some may not have experienced a certain service or event and may be unable to rate the survey sponsor. Respondents often terminate in frustration if they aren't permitted to say they don't know because they don't want to randomly pick a misleading rating answer.

Rule 3: Use parallel or matching wording in scales and questions. A final no-no is mismatched scales or wording. One scale I saw recently (I am not making this up) was 7 = I would definitely buy versus 1 = wouldn't recommend. The end points dealt with different concepts and didn't match, which made answering and interpretation (I'm sure) very difficult. I've also seen (especially in employee satisfaction surveys) questions with wording that was not equivalent.

For example, statements in a battery might range from the trivial "the lunch room is clean" to the overarching "this is the best place I've ever worked" or from the clearly desirable "my boss treats me with respect" to the desirability-unclear "my firm advertises a lot in the help wanted ads." In these cases, the mismatched wording makes answering and interpretation very difficult.

What is the bottom line? There is an art to scale wording. Wording does matter—just as much or more than the number of points in the scale.[14]

Fully Labeled Scale	% of Respondents Rating Firm. . . .	End-Point Labeled Scale	% of Respondents Rating Firm. . . .
5-Excellent	20	5-Excellent	20
4-Very Good	30	4	30
3-Good	30	3	30
2-Fair	10	2	10
1-Poor	10	1-Poor	10
	3.4 Avg.		3.4 Avg.

strategy, price levels, and distribution channels become more concrete and focused. Purchase intent is evaluated at each stage of development, and demand estimates are refined. The crucial go–no go decision for national or regional rollout typically comes after test marketing. Immediately before test marketing, commercial researchers have another critical stage of evaluation. Here, the final or near-final version of the product is placed in consumers' homes in test cities around the country. After a period of in-home use (usually 2 to 6 weeks), a follow-up survey is conducted among participants to find out their likes and dislikes, how the product compares with what they use now, and what they would pay for it. The critical question near the end of the questionnaire is purchase intent.

Question 21 in Exhibit 10.10 is a purchase intent question taken from a follow-up study on in-home placement of a fly trap. The trap consisted of two 3-inch disks held about one-quarter inch apart by three plastic pillars; it looked somewhat like a large, thin yo-yo. The trap contained a pheromone to attract the flies and a glue that would remain sticky for 6 months. Supposedly, the flies flew in but never out. Centered on the back side of one of the disks was an adhesive tab so that the disk could be attached to a kitchen window. The concept was to eliminate flies in the kitchen area without resorting to a pesticide. Question 22 was designed to aid in positioning the product, and question 23 traditionally was used by the manufacturer as a double check on purchase intent. If 60 percent of the respondents claimed that they definitely would buy the product and 90 percent said they definitely would not recommend the product to their friends, the researcher would question the validity of the purchase intent. A recent article in the *Harvard Business Review* argued that willingness to recommend the product is the best predictor of future purchasing.[16]

The purchase intent scale has been found to be a good predictor of consumer choice of frequently purchased and durable consumer products.[17] The scale is very easy

---

Exhibit 10.10

Purchase Intent Scale and Related Questions for In-Home Product Placement of Fly Traps

---

21. If a set of three traps sold for approximately $3.00 and was available in the stores where you normally shop, would you:

	(51)
definitely buy the set of traps	1
probably buy	2
probably not buy	3
definitely not buy	4

22. Would you use the traps (a) instead of or (b) in addition to existing products?

	(52)
instead of	1
in addition to	2

23. Would you recommend this product to your friends?

	(53)
definitely	1
probably	2
probably not	3
definitely not	4

to construct, and consumers are simply asked to make a subjective judgment of their likelihood of buying a new product. From past experience in the product category, a marketing manager can translate consumer responses on the scale to estimates of purchase probability. Obviously, everyone who "definitely will buy" the product will not do so; in fact, a few who state that they definitely will not buy actually will buy the product. The manufacturer of the fly trap is a major producer of both pesticide and nonpesticide pest control products. Assume that, based on historical follow-up studies, the manufacturer has learned the following about purchase intent of nonpesticide home-use pest-control products:

- ☐ 63 percent of the "definitely will buy" actually purchase within 12 months.
- ☐ 28 percent of the "probably will buy" actually purchase within 12 months.
- ☐ 12 percent of the "probably will not buy" actually purchase within 12 months.
- ☐ 3 percent of the "definitely will not buy" actually purchase within 12 months.

Suppose that the fly trap study resulted in the following:

- ☐ 40 percent—definitely will buy
- ☐ 20 percent—probably will buy
- ☐ 30 percent—probably will not buy
- ☐ 10 percent—definitely will not buy

Assuming that the sample is representative of the target market,

$$(0.4)(63\%) + (0.2)(28\%) + (0.3)(12\%) + (0.1)(3\%)$$
$$= 35.7\% \text{ market share}$$

Most marketing managers would be deliriously happy about such a high market share prediction for a new product. Unfortunately, because of consumer confusion, the product was killed after the in-home placement despite the high prediction.

It is not uncommon for marketing research firms to conduct studies containing a purchase intent scale in cases where the client does not have historical data to use as a basis for weighing the results. A reasonable but conservative estimate would be 70 percent of the "definitely will buy," 35 percent of the "probably will buy," 10 percent of the "probably will not buy," and zero of the "definitely will not buy."[18] Higher weights are common in the industrial market.

Some companies use the purchase intent scale to make go–no go decisions in product development without reference to market share. Typically, managers simply add the "definitely will buy" and "probably will buy" percentages and compare that total to a predetermined go–no go threshold. One consumer goods manufacturer, for example, requires a combined score of 80 percent or higher at the concept testing stage and 65 percent for a product to move from in-home placement tests to test marketing.

Considerations in Selecting a Scale

Most nonimage studies include a purchase intent scale. But many other questions arise in selecting a scale. Considerations include the nature of the construct being measured, type of scale, balanced versus nonbalanced scale, number of scale categories, and forced versus nonforced choice.

The Nature of the Construct Being Measured

A basic check of the appropriateness of a scale is confirmation that it is drawn directly from the overall objective of the research study. The scope of the research objectives has a fundamental effect on the manner in which scales are used for survey measurement. For instance, when crafting the satisfaction survey item for an ongoing tracking program, the researcher must first identify the scope of the satisfaction measurement objective for the program, that is, measuring satisfaction at the transactional level, or measuring satisfaction at the relational or cumulative level. Transactional measurement is normally designed to measure the perceptions of a recent interaction with the company or company representatives. An appropriate itemized rating scale for such a measurement objective would be: "Based on your most recent visit to this restaurant at this location, how would you rate your satisfaction? Would you say you are . . ." On the other hand, relational or cumulative satisfaction is usually intended to gauge the generalized satisfaction of customers beyond their perceptions of one or a few transactions. Accordingly, an appropriate scale would be "Overall, how satisfied are you with this restaurant?"

Aside from the transactional versus relational consideration, the scope of the research objectives also involves, particularly for customer satisfaction research, determining whether the focus is on satisfaction with the product, the service, the organization, the sales representative, or other "touch points" with the customer. While the satisfaction scores with each of these components are likely to be correlated, they are not necessarily so; a good product might be delivered with lousy service.[19]

Type of Scale

Most commercial researchers lean toward scales that can be administered over the telephone or via the Internet, to save interviewing expense. Ease of administration and development also are important considerations. For example, a rank-order scale can be quickly created, whereas developing a semantic differential (rating) scale is often a long and tedious process. The client's decision-making needs are always of paramount importance. Can the decision be made using ordinal data, or must the researcher provide interval information? Researchers also must consider the respondents, who usually prefer nominal and ordinal scales because of their simplicity. Ultimately, the choice of which type of scale to use will depend on the problem at hand and the questions that must be answered. It is not uncommon to find several types of scales in one research study. For example, an image study for a grocery chain might have a ranking scale of competing chains and a semantic differential to examine components of the chain's image.

Marketing researchers sometimes borrow scales directly from other studies or Internet sites. Many online survey sites have libraries of scales available. (See *surveymonkey.com*; *custominsight.com*; *surveysystem.com*; and *express.perseus.com*). There are also several scale handbooks that facilitate the appropriate measures and encourage researchers to standardize on previously developed and validated measures.[20] This makes the research stream more cumulative. Marketing researchers often find that these borrowed scales work just fine. Sometimes, however, they don't work very well.

A marketing researcher should fully understand the nature of the construct that was measured, the scope of the measurement, and the content and phrasing of the scale items for relevance to a new population before borrowing a scale. In sum, the caveat is "borrow with caution."[21]

Past research has indicated that the YMCA has an overall positive image. This means that a nonbalanced scale with more positive gradients than negative can be used in future research about the YMCA. Go to *http://www.ymca.com* to see how the YMCA is using research to reach new customers.

Balanced versus Nonbalanced Scale

> **balanced scales**
> Measurement scales that have the same number of positive and negative categories.

A **balanced scale** has the same number of positive and negative categories; a **nonbalanced scale** is weighted toward one end or the other. If the researcher expects a wide range of opinions, then a balanced scale probably is in order. If past research or a preliminary study has determined that most opinions are positive, then using a scale with more positive gradients than negative ones will enable the researcher to ascertain the degree of positiveness toward the concept being researched. We have conducted a series of studies for the YMCA and know that its overall image is positive. Thus, we used the following categories to track the YMCA's image: (1) outstanding, (2) very good, (3) good, (4) fair, (5) poor.

> **nonbalanced scales**
> Measurement scales that are weighted toward one end or the other of the scale.

Number of Scale Categories

The number of categories to be included in a scale is another issue that must be resolved by the marketing researcher. If the number of categories is too small—for example, good, fair, poor—the scale is crude and lacks richness. A 3-category scale does not reveal the intensity of feeling that, say, a 10-category scale offers. Yet, a 10-category scale may go beyond a person's ability to accurately discriminate among categories. Research has shown that rating scales with either 5 or 7 points are the most reliable.[22]

With an even number of scale categories, there is no neutral point. Without a neutral point, respondents are forced to indicate some degree of positive or negative feelings on an issue. Persons who are truly neutral are not allowed to express their neutrality. On the other hand, some marketing researchers say that putting a neutral point on a scale gives the respondent an easy way out, allowing the person with no really strong opinion to avoid concentrating on his or her actual feelings. Of course, it is rather unusual for any individual to be highly emotional about a new flavor of salad dressing, a package design, or a test commercial for a pickup truck!

Keith Chrzan and Joey Michaud, both of Maritz Research in St. Louis, discuss balanced and unbalanced scales, midpoints, and number of scale categories in the accompanying Practicing Marketing Research feature.

Forced versus Nonforced Choice

As mentioned in the discussion of semantic differential scales, if a neutral category is included, it typically will attract those who are neutral and those who lack adequate knowledge to answer the question. Some researchers have resolved this issue by adding a "Don't know" response as an additional category. For example, a semantic differential might be set up as follows:

Friendly	1	2	3	4	5	6	7	**Unfriendly**	Don't Know
Unexciting	1	2	3	4	5	6	7	**Exciting**	Don't Know

A "Don't know" option, however, can be an easy out for the lazy respondent.

If it has a neutral point, a scale without a "Don't know" option does not force a respondent to give a positive or negative opinion. A scale without a neutral point or a "Don't know" option forces even those persons with no information about an object to state an opinion. The argument for forced choice is that the respondent has to concentrate on his or her feelings. The arguments against forced choice are that inaccurate data are recorded and that some respondents may refuse to answer the question. A questionnaire that continues to require respondents to provide an opinion when, in fact, they lack the necessary information to do so can create ill will and result in early termination of the interview.

PRACTICING MARKETING RESEARCH

Scale Balance

Balanced scales have equal numbers of positive and negative points: completely satisfied; mostly satisfied; mostly dissatisfied; completely dissatisfied. Although there are exceptions, a best practice with respect to balanced scales is that the use of modifiers should be symmetrical on the positive and negative ends of the scale.

Unbalanced scales attempt to get greater discrimination on one side of the scale than on the other. If past experience suggested that most respondents are satisfied with a certain product or service, a researcher might want to "stretch out" the positive side of the scale, as in this extreme example (five positives and only two negatives): completely satisfied; very satisfied; mostly satisfied; somewhat satisfied; barely satisfied; mostly dissatisfied; completely dissatisfied.

Whether a scale should be balanced or unbalanced usually depends on whether we're measuring a unipolar or a bipolar concept of satisfaction. A unipolar satisfaction scale might range from "not satisfied" to "completely satisfied" (i.e., it doesn't measure any more extreme dissatisfaction at all). In contrast, a bipolar scale would range from "completely dissatisfied" to "completely satisfied" (i.e., it measures extremes of both satisfaction and dissatisfaction).

When we don't know ahead of time whether most respondents will tend to be satisfied or dissatisfied, or if we expect high levels of dissatisfaction, a balanced bipolar scale is appropriate. If we know from past experience to expect low levels of dissatisfaction, an unbalanced unipolar scale will be better. In our firm's experience, most studies show low levels of dissatisfaction, so our most frequent scale recommendation is for an unbalanced satisfaction scale.

Some people think that satisfaction and dissatisfaction should be measured separately and are different entities. Although Maritz Research has observed that satisfaction and dissatisfaction may sometimes have different drivers, and there may be nonlinear relationships between satisfaction and other variables, we have seen no compelling reason to measure them separately.

Midpoints

A midpoint communicates neutrality on a balanced scale. "Neither satisfied nor dissatisfied" serves as the midpoint in this balanced bipolar scale: completely satisfied; mostly satisfied; neither satisfied nor dissatisfied; mostly dissatisfied; completely dissatisfied.

There seems to be no difference in quality between scales that have a midpoint and those that do not. For bipolar scales, however, Maritz Research advises to "include the middle category unless there are persuasive reasons not to do so."

Number of Scale Points

Despite the strong opinions of some scale enthusiasts, there just isn't powerful empirical evidence that a single number of scale points is always the best. A literature review summarizes the consensus regarding self-administered surveys: "Seven, plus or minus two, appears to be a reasonable range for the optimal number of response alternatives." Internal research at Maritz has not indicated a consistent difference in quality between 5- and 10-point scales. Maritz's experience with mail studies has shown that 5-point scales provide better dispersion of responses (and are, therefore, more discriminating) than other scales. We expect these results to generalize to other visual survey modes (e.g., PC or Web-based).

The findings about the superiority of 5-point scales apply specifically to visually perceived scales and may or may not generalize to questions that respondents hear rather than see.

In summary, Maritz prefers a 5-point fully word-anchored unbalanced response scale for measuring overall satisfaction. The preferred scale works well in both hearing and visual survey modes (see example below). We also recommend that it be presented without associated numbers. [23]

Preferred Scale—Visual mode (paper, PC or Web-based, personal with "show card")

Overall, how satisfied were you with _____? Please check only one box

Not at All Satisfied	Slightly Satisfied	Somewhat Satisfied	Very Satisfied	Completely Satisfied
☐	☐	☐	☐	☐

Preferred Scale—Telephone or Mail Mode

Overall, how satisfied were you with _____? Would you say that you were not at all satisfied, slightly satisfied, somewhat satisfied, very satisfied, or completely satisfied? [RECORD ONE ANSWER.]

Attitude Measures and Management Decision Making

▷ determinant attitudes
Those consumer attitudes most closely related to preferences or to actual purchase decisions.

So far in this chapter we have discussed the nature of attitudes, various types of measurement scales, and some considerations in creating a scale. We now turn our attention to making attitude research more valuable for management decision making.

In the wide spectrum of features of a product or brand, there are some that predispose consumers to action (that is, to preference for the product, to actual purchase, to making recommendations to friends, and so on) and others that do not. Attitudes that are most closely related to preference or to actual purchase decisions are said to be **determinant attitudes**. Other attitudes—no matter how favorable—are not determinant. Obviously, marketers need to know which features lead to attitudes that "determine" buying behavior, for these are the features around which marketing strategy must be built.[24]

With reference to determinant attitudes, Nelson Foote, manager of the consumer and public relations research program for General Electric, commented: "In the electrical appliance business, we have been impressed over and over by the way in which certain characteristics of products come to be taken for granted by consumers, especially those concerned with basic functional performance or with values like safety."

"If these values are missing in a product, the user is extremely offended," he said. "But if they are present, the maker or seller gets no special credit or preference because, quite logically, every other maker and seller is assumed to be offering equivalent values. In other words, the values that are salient in decision making are the values that are problematic— that are important, to be sure, but also those which differentiate one offering from another."

In proprietary studies evaluating such automobile attributes as power, comfort, economy, appearance, and safety, for example, consumers often rank safety as first in importance. However, these same consumers do not see various makes of cars as differing widely with respect to safety; therefore, safety is not a determinant feature in the actual purchase decision. This fact should rightly lead the company to concentrate on raising its performance in features other than safety. However, if safety is totally ignored, the brand may soon be

PRACTICING MARKETING RESEARCH

What Is the Scale Really Telling You?

Tim Glowa, president of North Country Research–Calgary, Canada, measured airline customer satisfaction with flight attendants in four different ways. Depending on how the question was asked, satisfaction levels varied. The survey was conducted with 1,000 residents across Canada. The results are as follows:

☐ *Standard scale—excellent to poor.* The question was asked, "Please rate the courtesy and professionalism of the flight attendants on your most recent journey." The response categories were: excellent, very good, good, fair, and poor. Seventy percent gave the airline either excellent or very good marks. The first observation relating to this scale is that it is not balanced; there are three "good" measures compared to only two "not so good" measures.

☐ *Completely satisfied to completely unsatisfied.* An alternative six-point balanced scale with only the two end points defined was also used to measure satisfaction. In response to the question "Using a scale of 1 to 6, where 6 is completely satisfied and 1 is completely unsatisfied, how satisfied were you with the courtesy and professionalism of the flight

attendants?" Eighty-two percent selected the top two boxes. This scale is attractive because of the definitiveness of the two end points; if a customer is completely satisfied, it is not possible to improve satisfaction.

☐ *Asking respondents directly.* The third scale tested in this study simply asked the respondents if they were satisfied. In response to the question "Overall, were you satisfied with the courtesy and professionalism of the flight attendants?" 95 percent of the respondents replied "yes." This approach is certainly the most direct; the researcher gains a very clear understanding of how a customer feels about the service.

Propositional Descriptive

The final scale tested is the propositional descriptive scale. This scale not only provides an assessment of the degree of satisfaction with a given product, but also quantifies what steps are needed to make an improvement. This scale requires respondents to select the appropriate descriptor corresponding to their level of satisfaction. In response to the question "Please rate the courtesy and professionalism of the flight attendants towards serving you. Were they. . . . ," customers selected from a series of statements. These statements, with the percentage of passengers who selected each, appear in the following chart:

Statement	Percent Responding to
Made you feel that they were genuinely pleased to serve you and happily provided assistance	47
Were pleased to serve you and provided assistance when required	41
Made you feel like they were just doing their jobs when serving you	12

Although the previously described scales all provide, to some measure, an assessment of how satisfied customers are at a particular point in time, they are difficult to act on strate-

gically. The propositional descriptive scale goes beyond these traditional scales by providing a quantifiable, nonsubjective measure of satisfaction that can easily be understood and made actionable, if desired, by senior management.

Unlike a scale that measures flight attendant satisfaction as "good" or "very good," this scale provides both a very clear measurement of performance and a ruler against which future satisfaction can be measured. The vice president of in-flight operations for the airline might struggle with how to improve satisfaction beyond "good" to "very good" or "excellent." Conversely, if the same vice president is provided a customer satisfaction report using the propositional descriptive scale, and wanted to improve satisfaction among passengers, he has a greater understanding of the problem.[25]

perceived as being so unsafe that it loses some of its share of the market. At this point, safety would achieve determinance, a quality it would hold until concentration on safety by the "unsafe" company brought its product back into line with those of other companies.

To identify determinant attitudes and discern their relative degree of determinance, researchers must go beyond the scaling of respondents' attitudes. The study design must include a methodology for measuring determinance, for it will not naturally develop in the course of scaling. There are three major approaches to identifying determinant attitudes: (1) direct questioning, (2) indirect questioning, and (3) observation.

Direct Questioning

The most obvious way to approach determinant attitudes is to ask consumers directly what factors they consider important in a purchasing decision. Through direct questioning, respondents may be asked to explain their reasons for preferring one product or brand over another. Or they may be asked to rate their "ideal brand" for a given product in terms of several product attributes so that a model profile can be constructed (see the discussion of semantic differential scales).

This approach has the appeal of seeming to get directly to the issue of "Why do you buy?" Unfortunately, it rests on two very questionable assumptions: (1) respondents know why they buy or prefer one product over another, and (2) they will willingly explain what these reasons are.

Another direct questioning approach is "dual questioning," which involves asking two questions concerning each product attribute that might be determinant. Consumers are first asked what factors they consider important in a purchasing decision and then asked how they perceive these factors as differing among the various products or brands.

Exhibits 10.11 and 10.12 illustrate this approach through ratings of attitudes toward savings and loan associations, given during a survey of the general public in the Los Angeles area. (The various benefits or claims are ranked in descending order in each exhibit so that comparisons between the exhibits can be made more easily.) Notice that some items are high in rated importance but are not thought to differ much among the various savings and loan associations (for example, safety of money, interest rate earned). Thus, while safety of money is ranked first in importance, about half of all respondents feel there is no difference among savings and loan associations in terms of safety; therefore, safety of funds is probably not a determinant feature. Conversely, some items show big differences among the various associations but are considered to be of relatively little importance in determining the choice of a savings and loan (for example, years in business, parking convenience).

On the other hand, "interest rate earned" has a very high importance ranking, and far fewer respondents feel there is no difference among the various associations relative to interest rate. Financial strength is rated somewhat lower in importance but is second highest in terms of the difference between associations. Therefore, financial strength appears to be

EXHIBIT 10.11	Importance Ratings of Savings and Loan Characteristics

Benefit or Claim	Average Ratings*
Safety of money	1.4
Interest rate earned	1.6
Government insurance	1.6
Financial strength	2.0
Ease of withdrawing money	2.0
Management ability	2.0
Attitude of personnel	2.1
Speed/efficiency of service	2.2
Compounding frequency	2.2
Branch location convenience	2.3
Time required to earn interest	2.3
Parking convenience	2.4
Years in business	2.5
Other services offered	3.1
Building/office attractiveness	3.4
Premiums offered	4.0

*1—extremely important; 2—very important; 3—fairly important; 4—slightly important, etc.
Source: James Myers and Mark Alpert, "Determinant Buying Attitudes: Meaning and Measurement," *Marketing Management* (Summer 1997), p. 52. Reprinted by permission of the American Marketing Association.

EXHIBIT 10.12	Difference Ratings of Savings and Loan Characteristics

Benefit or Claim	Big Difference	Small Difference	No Difference	Don't Know
Years in business	53%	31%	10%	6%
Financial strength	40	32	22	6
Parking convenience	37	35	22	6
Safety of money	36	15	47	2
Management ability	35	26	27	12
Government insurance	35	11	51	3
Branch location convenience	34	36	28	2
Attitude of personnel	34	28	33	5
Interest rate earned	33	30	35	2
Speed/efficiency of service	32	28	35	5
Ease of withdrawing money	29	18	48	5
Compounding frequency	28	36	31	5
Time required to earn interest	26	34	33	7
Building/office attractiveness	24	44	30	2
Other services offered	21	34	29	16
Premiums offered	15	36	38	11

Source: James Myers and Mark Alpert, "Determinant Buying Attitudes: Meaning and Measurement," *Marketing Management* (Summer 1997), p. 53. Reprinted by permission of the American Marketing Association.

PRACTICING
MARKETING RESEARCH

Is Satisfaction Measurement Helping the Bottom Line?

Tim Glowa and Sean Lawson of North Country Research point out that measuring satisfaction per se is often an end goal. This, they believe, is wrong.

How satisfied do you want them to be? Management must answer this question. However, in order to answer it, management will need to know what drives client satisfaction and how a company can affect satisfaction ratings. Once the satisfaction level of a group is clearly understood

in terms of its determinants, then management can decide whether the efforts (and costs) required to increase satisfaction are worth it.

If management is ultimately concerned with the bottom line, then increasing satisfaction in a group should increase the client's market share enough to justify the resources required to achieve the higher rating. If this is not the case, then higher satisfaction ratings, for that client, have become counterproductive. The research into satisfaction must be tied to the costs of achieving higher satisfaction and whether there will be an offsetting increase in demand to justify the expenditure.[27]

---

relatively determinant of attitudes. Similarly, the researcher can proceed through the rest of the ratings to identify those attitudes that seem to influence the choice among various savings and loans most strongly and thus, presumably, are determinant attitudes.

Indirect Questioning

Another approach to identifying determinant attitudes is indirect questioning, of which there are many forms. Recall from Chapter 5 that indirect questioning is any interviewing approach that does not directly ask respondents to indicate the reasons why they bought a product or service or which features or attributes are most important in determining choice.

Observation

A third technique for identifying buying motives is observation research (see Chapter 7). For example, in one study, supermarket shoppers were observed, and detailed reports were recorded of their movements and statements while interacting with certain products on display in several different stores. The authors drew conclusions concerning who does the shopping, the influence of children and adult males on purchasing decisions, the effect of pricing, where brand choices seem to be made, and how much package study is involved. One of the findings of this study was that shoppers seemed to reject certain candy packaging in favor of other packaging. This finding suggests that package design might be a determinant feature, though by no means the only one.[26] (The disadvantages of observation research were discussed in Chapter 7.)

Choosing a Method for Identifying Determinant Attitudes

Direct questioning, indirect questioning, and observation each have some limitations in identifying determinant attitudes. Therefore, the marketing researcher should use two or more of the techniques. Convergent findings will offer greater assurance that the attitudes identified are indeed determinant attitudes. Several statistical tools can aid the researcher in this process; they will be discussed in Chapters 14 to 17.

SUMMARY

An attitude is an enduring organization of motivational, emotional, perceptual, and cognitive processes with respect to some aspect of a person's environment. In marketing research, it is a learned predisposition to respond in a consistently favorable or unfavorable manner toward an object or concept.

The term *scaling* refers to procedures for attempting to determine quantitative measures of subjective and sometimes abstract concepts. It is defined as a procedure for assigning numbers or other symbols to properties of an object in order to impart some numerical characteristics to the properties in question. Scales are either unidimensional or multidimensional. A unidimensional scale is designed to measure only one attribute of a concept, respondent, or object. Multidimensional scaling is based on the premise that a concept, respondent, or object might be better described using several dimensions.

One type of scale is called a graphic rating scale. Respondents are presented with a graphic continuum, typically anchored by two extremes. Itemized rating scales are similar to graphic rating scales except that respondents must select from a limited number of categories rather than placing a mark on a continuous scale. A rank-order scale is a comparative scale because respondents are asked to compare two or more items with each other. Q-sorting is a sophisticated form of rank ordering. Respondents are asked to sort a large number of cards into piles of predetermined size according to specified rating categories. Paired comparison scales ask the respondent to pick one of two objects from a set, based on some stated criteria. Constant sum scales require the respondent to divide a given number of points, typically 100, among two or more attributes, based on their importance to him or her. Respondents must value each item relative to all other items. The number of points allocated to each alternative indicates the ranking assigned to it by the respondent.

The semantic differential was developed to measure the meaning of an object to a person. The construction of a semantic differential scale begins with determination of a concept to be rated, such as a brand image; then the researcher selects dichotomous pairs of words or phrases that could be used to describe the concept. Respondents then rate the concept on a scale, usually 1 to 7. The mean of the responses is computed for each pair of adjectives, and the means are plotted as a profile, or image. In the Stapel scale, a single adjective is placed in the center of the scale. Typically, a Stapel scale is designed to simultaneously measure both the direction and the intensity of attitudes. The Likert scale is another scale that avoids the problem of developing pairs of dichotomous adjectives. The scale consists of a series of statements expressing either a favorable or an unfavorable attitude toward the concept under study. The respondent is asked to indicate the level of his or her agreement or disagreement with each statement by assigning it a numerical score. Scores are then totaled to measure the respondent's attitude.

The scale that is used most often and perhaps is most important to marketing researchers is the purchase intent scale. This scale is used to measure a respondent's intention to buy or not buy a product. The purchase intent question usually asks a person to state whether he would definitely buy, probably buy, probably not buy, or definitely not buy the product under study. The purchase intent scale has been found to be a good predictor of consumer choice of frequently purchased consumer durable goods.

Several factors should be considered in selecting a particular scale for a study. The first is the type of scale to use: rating, ranking, sorting, or purchase intent. Next, consideration must be given to the use of a balanced scale versus a nonbalanced scale. The number of categories also must be determined. A related factor is whether to use an odd or even number of categories. Finally, the researcher must consider whether to use forced or nonforced choice sets.

Attitudes that predispose consumers to action are called determinant attitudes. Marketing researchers need to identify which attitudes, of all those measured, are determinant. This can be accomplished by direct questioning, indirect questioning, and observation research.

KEY TERMS & DEFINITIONS

attitude Enduring organization of motivational, emotional, perceptual, and cognitive processes with respect to some aspect of a person's environment.

scaling Procedures for assigning numbers (or other symbols) to properties of an object in order to impart some numerical characteristics to the properties in question.

unidimensional scales Scales designed to measure only one attribute of a concept, respondent, or object.

multidimensional scales Scales designed to measure several dimensions of a concept, respondent, or object.

graphic rating scales Measurement scales that include a graphic continuum, anchored by two extremes.

itemized rating scales Measurement scales in which the respondent selects an answer from a limited number of ordered categories.

noncomparative scales Measurement scales in which judgment is made without reference to another object, concept, or person.

rank-order scales Measurement scales in which the respondent compares two or more items and ranks them.

comparative scales Measurement scales in which one object, concept, or person is compared with another on a scale.

Q-sorting A measurement scale employing a sophisticated form of rank ordering using card sorts.

paired comparison scales Measurement scales that ask the respondent to pick one of two objects in a set, based on some stated criteria.

constant sum scales Measurement scales that ask the respondent to divide a given number of points, typically 100, among two or more attributes, based on their importance to him or her.

semantic differential scales Measurement scales that examine the strengths and weaknesses of a concept by having the respondent rank it between dichotomous pairs of words or phrases that could be used to describe it; the means of the responses are then plotted as a profile, or image.

Stapel scales Measurement scales that require the respondent to rate, on a scale ranging from $+5$ to -5, how closely and in what direction a descriptor adjective fits a given concept.

Likert scales Measurement scales in which the respondent specifies a level of agreement or disagreement with statements expressing either a favorable or an unfavorable attitude toward the concept under study.

purchase intent scales Scales used to measure a respondent's intention to buy or not buy a product.

balanced scales Measurement scales that have the same number of positive and negative categories.

nonbalanced scales Measurement scales that are weighted toward one end or the other of the scale.

determinant attitudes Those consumer attitudes most closely related to preferences or to actual purchase decisions.

1. Discuss some of the considerations in selecting a rating, ranking, or purchase intent scale.

2. What are some of the arguments for and against having a neutral point on a scale?

3. Compare and contrast the semantic differential scale, Stapel scale, and Likert scale. Under what conditions would a researcher use each one?

4. The local department store in your home town has been besieged by competition from the large national chains. What are some ways that target customers' attitudes toward the store could be changed?

5. Develop a Likert scale to evaluate the parks and recreation department in your city.

6. Develop a purchase intent scale for students eating at the university's cafeteria. How might the reliability and validity of this scale be measured? Why do you think purchase intent scales are so popular in commercial marketing research?

7. When might a researcher use a graphic rating scale rather than an itemized rating scale?

8. What is the difference between a rating and a ranking? Which is best for attitude measurement? Why?

9. Develop a rank-order scale for soda preferences of college students. What are the advantages and disadvantages of this type of scale?

10. What are determinant attitudes, and why are they important?

11. Discuss the relationship between customer satisfaction and profits.

12. Divide the class into teams. Each team should create five adjective pairs of phrases *(Team Exercise)* that could be used in a semantic differential to measure the image of your college or university. The instructor will then aggregate the suggestions into a single semantic differential. Each team member should then conduct five interviews with students not in the class. The data can then be analyzed later in the term when statistical analysis is covered.

SRIC-BI (Stanford Research Institute Consulting-Business Intelligence) is a spinoff of the Stanford Research Institute. One of its most popular products is called VALS (Values and Life Style Survey). SRIC-BI uses VALS to segment the marketplace on the basis of personality traits that drive consumer behavior. VALS is used in all phases of the marketing mix. The survey categorizes consumers into one of eight personality types. GEOVALS applies the power of VALS to local marketing efforts by identifying the concentration of the VALS consumer group residing within a specific block group or zip code.

Go to *www.sric-bi.com*, then click on the VALS SURVEY link. Next, click on "Take the survey."

1. Explain the theory behind the creation of VALS.

2. Do you agree with your VALS classification? Learn more by going to "The VALS Types" link.

3. What kind of scale was used in the survey? Could other types of scales have been used?

4. Explain how a marketer could use GEOVALS.

Digital Insight's Online Customer Feedback Program Continues to Improve Service Quality

Headquartered in Calabasas, California, Digital Insight was founded in 1995 and grew rapidly to become a leading provider of Internet-based banking services for commercial banks and credit unions. The company's range of secure, hosted services includes retail and commercial Internet banking and electronic bill payment.

In the summer of 2000, Lois Koch, the then new vice president of customer service and client relations, was given an ambitious directive from the company's CEO: raise the quality of Digital Insight's customer service and client relations to a world-class level. By mid-2000, it had become clear that Digital Insight's rapid growth had strained the existing customer service and client relations infrastructure and was impacting the company's reputation. At that time, fewer than 30 percent of Digital Insight's financial institution clients were willing to serve as references to potential new clients, causing sales to be lost to competitors. Koch and her staff determined that improving Digital Insight's service quality was their top priority.

The team evaluated several strategies and technologies to measure and report on client satisfaction and loyalty. Because DI was itself an online service provider, the team recognized the importance of using online technology as a means for obtaining timely, accurate feedback that could be readily disseminated throughout the organization. DI chose to partner with CustomerSat, Inc., a Mountain View, California, research firm.

Digital Insight now uses online client feedback to drive action through a combination of processes, practices, and technology. Client feedback generates alerts to the appropriate individuals in the Digital Insight organization, notifying them immediately if clients are dissatisfied. Interactive dashboards allow managers and supervisors to pinpoint problems and opportunities. Push reports deliver up-to-the-minute statistics, trend lines, charts, and graphs of survey results directly to the e-mail boxes of Digital Insight managers.

Digital Insight managers use these services to recognize and address client concerns; reward and recognize Digital Insight customer service staff for outstanding performance; and provide targeted training and coaching, including issue-focused cross-departmental training.

As a result of findings from the first survey, four key issues were identified as drivers of customer dissatisfaction with the current level of customer service:

1. Lack of standards for answering and returning calls.
2. Inadequate product knowledge of the service staff.
3. Lack of customer service skills.
4. Inadequate follow-up and resolution of issues.

In response to customer feedback, Digital Insight took a wide range of actions from late 2000 through 2002. As a result of these actions, Digital Insight enjoyed improved results:

- Customer assessments of service (level of satisfaction on a 10-point scale) improved from 6.5 at Q4 2000 to 8.0 in Q2 2002.
- Customer assessments of account management (level of satisfaction on a 10-point scale) improved from 6.4 in Q4 2000 to 7.7 in Q2 2002.

- Referenceable client percentage improved from less than 30 percent at year-end (YE) 2000 to 75 percent by YE 2001 and to 85 percent by YE 2002.

In addition to these overall results:

- Improved service times meant that 97 percent of service calls were handled before customers abandoned the call, up from 84 percent previously.
- The abandon rate for calls dropped from 12 percent to 3 percent.
- The average queue time dropped from 2 minutes to 20 seconds.
- The average number of days to resolve an incident dropped by 50 percent.
- The average incidents outstanding dropped by 100 percent.

  Scores and performance have continued to improve since 2002.[28]

Questions

1. Suggest three different types of scales that could be used in the DI service quality surveys.
2. If DI decides to implement its service quality program in Mexico, what measurement problems might they encounter?
3. What is the ultimate goal of service quality research? Explain the linkage to the ultimate objective of DI.
4. Why might DI want to measure the ROI of customer feedback?
5. Go to *www.digitalinsights.com*. Create a 10-question form that DI could use to evaluate the quality of its Web site.

Frigidaire Refrigerators

Frigidaire Refrigerators was interested in comparing its image with those of a number of other appliance corporations. Some of the questions used on the questionnaire follow.

Q.1 We are interested in your overall opinion of five companies that manufacture refrigerators. Please rank them from 1 to 5, with 1 being the best and 5 the worst. (READ LIST. WRITE IN NUMBER GIVEN FOR *EACH* COMPANY LISTED. BE SURE *ONE* ANSWER IS RECORDED FOR EACH COMPANY.)

Companies	Rank
General Electric	_____
Westinghouse	_____
Frigidaire	_____
Sears	_____
Whirlpool	_____

Q.2 Now, I would like to have your opinion on a few statements that could be used to describe Frigidaire and the refrigerators it makes.

For each statement I read, please tell me how much you *agree* or *disagree* with the statement about Frigidaire. If you *agree completely* with the statement made, you should give it a *10* rating. If you *disagree completely* with the statement made, you should give it a *0* rating. Or, you can use any number in between which best expresses your opinion on each statement about Frigidaire. (READ

LIST. BEGIN WITH STATEMENT CHECKED AND WRITE IN NUMBER GIVEN FOR *EACH* STATEMENT LISTED. BE SURE *ONE* ANSWER IS RECORDED FOR EACH.)

Statements	Rating
( ) They are a modern, up-to-date company.	_____
( ) Their refrigerators offer better value than those made by other companies.	_____
( ) Their refrigerators last longer than those made by other companies.	_____
( ) They are a company that stands behind their products.	_____
(√) Their refrigerators have more special features than those made by other companies.	_____
( ) They are a well-established, reliable company.	_____
( ) Their refrigerators are more dependable than those made by other companies.	_____
( ) Their refrigerators offer higher-quality construction than those made by other companies.	_____
( ) Their refrigerators have a better guarantee or warranty than those made by other companies.	_____

Q.3 If you were buying a (READ APPLIANCE) today, what make would be your first choice? Your second choice? Your third choice? (DO *NOT* READ LIST. CIRCLE NUMBER BELOW APPROPRIATE APPLIANCE. *BEGIN WITH APPLIANCE CHECKED.*)

Brands	( ) Refrigerator			(√) Electric Range		
	First Choice	Second Choice	Third Choice	First Choice	Second Choice	Third Choice
General Electric	1	1	1	1	1	1
Westinghouse	2	2	2	2	2	2
Frigidaire	3	3	3	3	3	3
Sears	4	4	4	4	4	4
Whirlpool	5	5	5	5	5	5
Other (SPECIFY)						

Q.4 If you were in the market for a refrigerator today, how interested would you be in having the Frigidaire refrigerator that was described in the commercial in your home? Would you say you would be . . . (READ LIST)

	Very interested	1
(CIRCLE	Somewhat interested	2
ONE	Neither interested or disinterested	3
NUMBER)	Somewhat disinterested, or	4
	Very disinterested	5

Q.5 Why do you feel that way? (PROBE FOR COMPLETE AND MEANINGFUL ANSWERS.)

_____

_____

_____

_____

_____

Q.6 Now, I would like to ask you a few questions for statistical purposes only:

(A) Do you currently own any major appliances made by Frigidaire?

(CIRCLE ONE NUMBER)	Yes	1
	No	2

(B) Is the head of household male or female?

(CIRCLE ONE NUMBER)	Male	1
	Female	2

(C) Which letter on this card corresponds to your age group?

	A. Under 25	1
(CIRCLE	B. 25 to 34	2
ONE	C. 35 to 44	3
NUMBER)	D. 45 to 54	4
	E. 55 and over	5

Questions

1. What types of scales are represented in the questionnaire? What is the purpose of each scale? What other scales could have been substituted to obtain the same data?

2. Could a semantic differential scale have been used in this questionnaire? If so, what are some of the adjective pairs that might have been used?

3. Do you think the managers of Frigidaire have the necessary information now to evaluate the company's competitive position as perceived by consumers? If not, what additional questions should be asked?

CHAPTER 11

QUESTIONNAIRE DESIGN

LEARNING OBJECTIVES

1.	To understand the role of the questionnaire in the data-collection process.
2.	To become familiar with the criteria for a good questionnaire.
3.	To learn the process for questionnaire design.
4.	To become knowledgeable about the three basic forms of questions.
5.	To learn the necessary procedures for successful implementation of a survey.
6.	To understand how software and the Internet are influencing questionnaire design.
7.	To understand the impact of the questionnaire on data-collection costs.

Cathi Flaherty had never heard of a "weekend bag" before she was given one for Mother's Day this year. Over the summer, the 50-year-old first-grade teacher in Winchester, Massachusetts, found herself so enamored of the hot pink Coach bag that she began choosing outfits to show it off better.

Ms. Flaherty used to carry the same purse all year. Now she's planning to retire the weekend bag in preference for a black leather Coach model that better suits the cool fall weather. "You're matching your bag to your jewelry, shoes, and to the season in the air," she says.

Behind Ms. Flaherty's shopping plans is a New York company that has become a fashion and retail star by shrewdly helping engineer a big shift in women's buying behavior. For generations, it was established fashion wisdom that American women would buy about two purses a year—one for everyday use and another for dressy occasions. But in recent years, Coach Inc. has pushed to make handbags the shoes of the 21st century: a way to frequently update wardrobes with different styles without shelling out for new clothes.

Coach was known for decades as a sturdy purveyor of conservative, long-lasting handbags. Following a late-1990s strategic overhaul, it has successfully convinced women to buy weekend bags, evening bags, backpacks, satchels, clutches, totes, briefcases, diaper bags, coin purses, duffels, and a mini handbag that doubles as a bag-within-a-bag called a wristlet.

Its strategy is simple: even in the absence of any obvious need, Coach creates and markets new kinds of bags to fill what it calls "usage voids," activities that range from weekend getaways to dancing at nightclubs to trips to the grocery store. The company updates collections nearly every month with new colors, fabrics, and sizes. It prices bags lower than luxury designers but high enough for women to buy as a special treat.

Coach used marketing research to understand "usage voids." The company spends about $3 million on research and interviews more than 14,000 shoppers about everything from Coach's brand image to its strap lengths.

Marketing research revealed that Coach customers either enjoyed or aspired to "a relaxed-but-sophisticated lifestyle." Research further showed that women were interested in nonleather bags as well as leather ones. Using the data, Coach created "The Weekend Collection" made of a durable, water-resistant material and an easily foldable shape. Since it was introduced, the collection has sold over 200,000 bags.[1] ■

The cornerstone of all of Coach's marketing research was the questionnaire. What are the objectives of questionnaire design? What makes for a good questionnaire? What steps are involved in questionnaire development? What impact does the Internet have on questionnaires? We will explore these and other issues in this chapter.

Role of a Questionnaire

> **questionnaire**
>
> Set of questions designed to generate the data necessary to accomplish the objectives of the research project; also called an *interview schedule* or *survey instrument*.

Every form of survey research relies on the use of a questionnaire, the common thread in almost all data-collection methods. A **questionnaire** is a set of questions designed to generate the data necessary to accomplish the objectives of the research project; it is a formalized schedule for collecting information from respondents. You have most likely seen or even filled out a questionnaire recently. Creating a good questionnaire requires both hard work and imagination.

A questionnaire standardizes the wording and sequencing of questions and imposes uniformity on the data-gathering process. Every respondent sees or hears the same words; every interviewer asks identical questions. Without such standardization, interviewers could ask whatever they wanted, and researchers would be left wondering whether respondents' answers were a consequence of interviewer influence or interpretation; a valid basis for comparing respondents' answers would not exist. The jumbled mass of data would be unmanageable from a tabulation standpoint. In a very real sense, then, the questionnaire is a control device, but it is a unique one, as you will see.

The questionnaire (sometimes referred to as an *interview schedule* or *survey instrument*) plays a critical role in the data-collection process. An elaborate sampling plan, well-trained interviewers, proper statistical analysis techniques, and good editing and coding are all for naught if the questionnaire is poorly designed. Improper design can lead to incomplete information, inaccurate data, and, of course, higher costs. The questionnaire is the production line of marketing research. It is here that the product, be it good or bad, is created. The questionnaire is the tool that creates the basic product (respondent information).

Exhibit 11.1 illustrates the pivotal role of the questionnaire. It is positioned between survey objectives (drawn from the manager's problem) and respondent information. In this position, it must translate the objectives into specific questions to solicit the required information from respondents.

Assume that Swatch is considering the development of a child's wristwatch. The timepiece would have a plastic casing with printed circuits inside. Swatch's engineering staff believes that it can come up with a watch that will withstand the potential abuse from the normal activities of a child between 8 and 13 years old. Preliminary marketing research is called for to determine the acceptability of the watch to the target market. One objective is to determine children's

Exhibit 11.1

Questionnaire's Pivotal Role in the Research Process

(flowchart: Survey objectives → Questionnaire ← Respondent information; Questionnaire → Data analysis → Findings → Recommendations → Managerial action)

reactions to the watch. The marketing researchers must translate the objectives into language understandable to child respondents, as a child of eight probably won't be able to respond to questions that use such terms as *acceptability, efficiency*, and *likelihood of purchase*.

This example illustrates the pivotal role of the questionnaire: It must translate the survey objectives into a form understandable to respondents and "pull" the requisite information from them. At the same time, it must recover their responses in a form that can be easily tabulated and translated into findings and recommendations that will satisfy a manager's information requirements. Questionnaires also play a key role in survey costs, which will be discussed in detail later in the chapter.

Criteria for a Good Questionnaire

To design a good questionnaire, the researchers must consider a number of issues: does it provide the necessary decision-making information for management? Does it consider the respondent? Does it meet editing, coding, and data processing requirements?

Does It Provide the Necessary Decision-Making Information?

The primary role of any questionnaire is to provide the information required for management decision making. Any questionnaire that fails to provide important insights for management or decision-making information should be discarded or revised. Therefore, the managers who will be using the data should always approve the questionnaire. By signing off on the questionnaire, the manager is saying, "Yes, this instrument will supply the data I need to reach a decision." If the manager does not sign off, then the marketing researcher must continue to revise the questionnaire.

A questionnaire should always fit the respondent. Though parents typically purchase cereal, children often make the decision about what kind to buy. A taste test questionnaire for children should be worded in language they can understand.

Does It Consider the Respondent?

As companies have recognized the importance of marketing research, the number of surveys taken annually has mushroomed. Poorly designed, confusing, and lengthy surveys have literally turned off thousands of potential respondents. It is estimated that more than 60 percent of all persons contacted refuse to participate in surveys.

The researcher designing a questionnaire must consider not only the topic and the type of respondent, but the interviewing environment and questionnaire length as well. Respondents will answer somewhat longer questionnaires when they are interested in the topic and when they perceive that they will have little difficulty in responding to the questions.

A questionnaire should be designed explicitly for the intended respondents. For example, although a parent typically is the purchaser of cold cereals, the child, either directly or indirectly, often makes the decision as to which brand. Thus, a taste test questionnaire about cold cereals should be formulated in children's language. On the other hand, a survey about *purchasing* cold cereals should be worded in language suitable for adult interviewees. One of the most important tasks of questionnaire design is to fit the questions to the prospective respondent. The questionnaire designer must strip away any marketing jargon and business terminology that may be misunderstood by the respondent. In fact, it is best to use simple, everyday language, as long as the result is not insulting or demeaning to the respondent.

Does It Meet Editing and Coding Requirements?

Once the information has been gathered, it will have to be edited and then coded for data processing. A questionnaire should be designed with these later processes in mind.

Editing refers to going through each questionnaire to make certain that skip patterns were followed and required questions were filled out. The **skip pattern** is the sequence in which questions are asked, based on a respondent's answer. Exhibit 11.2 shows a clearly defined skip pattern from question 4a to question 5a for persons who answer "No" to question 4a.

Most marketing research data analysis software automatically catches coding errors. Computer-aided telephone interviewing (CATI) and Internet software programs take care of skip patterns automatically. Flexibility is programmed into a questionnaire in two ways:

☐ Branching takes the participant to a different set of questions based on the answer that is given to a prior question. This could be a "simple skip," in which questions are skipped because they would not be relevant to the respondent, or could be "dynamic branching," in which one of many possible sets of questions is presented to the participant depending on the way that he or she responded to a question.

☐ Piping integrates responses from a question into later questions. A participant could be asked to type an answer to an open-ended question, and the text of that answer could be incorporated into the wording of the next question.

In mall and telephone interviews, replies to all open-ended questions (which ask respondents to answer in their own words) are recorded verbatim by the interviewer (see later discussion). Sometimes the responses are then **coded** by listing the answers from a number of randomly selected completed questionnaires; however, if at all possible, responses to open-ended questions should be precoded. Those responses occurring with the greatest frequency are listed on a coding sheet (such as the one in Exhibit 11.3), which the

editing
Going through each questionnaire to ensure that skip patterns were followed and the required questions filled out.

skip pattern
Sequence in which questions are asked, based on a respondent's answer.

coding
The process of grouping and assigning numeric codes to the various responses to a question.

■ Exhibit 11.2

Example of a Questionnaire Skip Pattern

4a. Do you usually use a cream rinse or a hair conditioner on your child's hair?
(1) ( ) No (SKIP to 5a)   (2) ( ) Yes (ASK Q. 4b)

4b. Is that a cream rinse that you pour on or a cream rinse that you spray on?
(1) ( ) Cream rinse that you pour on
(2) ( ) Cream rinse that you spray on

4c. About how often do you use a cream rinse or a hair conditioner on your child's hair? Would you say less than once a week, once a week, or more than once a week?
(1) ( ) Less than once a week
(2) ( ) Once a week
(3) ( ) More than once a week

5a. Thinking of the texture of your child's hair, is it. . . . (READ LIST)
(1) ( ) Fine   (2) ( ) Coarse   (3) ( ) Regular

5b. What is the length of your child's hair? (READ LIST)
(1) ( ) Long   (2) ( ) Medium   (3) ( ) Short

EXHIBIT 11.3	Coding Sheet for the Question "What Is Your Occupation?"
Category	**Code**
Professional/technical	1
Manager/official/self-employed	2
Clerical/sales	3
Skilled worker	4
Service worker	5
Unskilled laborer	6
Farm operator or rancher	7
Unemployed or student	8
Retired	9

editor uses to code all other responses to the open-ended question. Today, sophisticated neural network systems software is decreasing the necessity for manually coding responses to open-ended questions.

Stephen Hellebusch, president of Hellebusch Research and Consulting, discusses coding in the following Practicing Marketing Research feature.

PRACTICING MARKETING RESEARCH

Suppose we are conducting an interview about air fresheners. The respondent is asked, "What do you like about it?" A random selection of verbatims from the question are examined, and code numbers are assigned based on the similarity of various statements. For example, one person says, "I like the smell because it is sweet." Another says, "I like the sweet smell and the color." Both would get a "sweet smell" code, and the second one would also receive a "like the color" code. These coded responses are then assigned to categories. In this example, the "sweet smell" comments may be assigned to a Smell/Odor category, and the color comment would likely be assigned to a category called Appearance.

One person can make two comments that fall into one category. Say what? For example, if a respondent said, "I like the smell because it is sweet and subtle," the code for "sweet smell" would be assigned, as would a code for "subtle smell." Since we want to count people, not comments, the category net is created that tells us how many people made a Smell/Odor comment.

The person who said "I like the smell because it is sweet and subtle" would be counted once in "sweet smell," once in "subtle smell," and only once in the category net line because it counts people, not comments. The net line will always be equal to or less than the sum of the number making the comments in the category. For example, the two comments, as shown below, add to 35 percent but were given by 26 percent of the 250 respondents. If the net is not less than or equal to the sum of the comments, something is wrong.

Comments	Total Respondents	
Base: Total (250)	#	%
Smell/Odor (Net)	*65*	*26*
Sweet smell	55	22
Subtle smell	32	13

One challenge, handled in different ways by different researchers, is a comment that logically fits into two different categories. Suppose, with our air freshener, someone says they like it because "The size makes the placement easier." There is a Placement net, which includes comments such as "would place in family room" or "would put in bedroom." There is also an Ease of Use category that includes codes such as "easy to remove from package" and "just plug it in."

Comments	Double-coded Total Respondents	
Base: total (250)	#	%
East of Use (Net)	*63*	*25*
Just plug it in	25	10
Size makes placement easier	20	8
Easy to remove from package	18	7
Placement (Net)	*60*	*24*
Put in family room	25	10
Size makes placement easier	20	8
Put in bathroom	12	5
Put in bedroom	11	4

Some coders double-code—that is, put the comment in both places. The 20 people who said "Size makes placement easier" are the same 20 people in both the Ease of Use and the Placement categories.

Others will single-code—that is, only include the comment once, in the category judged to be the best fit. In this case, the comment fits better in Ease of Use, since the size is what is making things easier, and all of the Placement comments are referring to a place.

So, what percent made Placement comments? It depends. If you double-code, you

Comments	Single-coded Total Respondents	
Base: total (250)	#	%
Ease of Use (Net)	*63*	*25*
Just plug it in	25	10
Size makes placement easier	20	8
Easy to remove from package	18	7
Placement (Net)	*40*	*16*
Put in family room	25	10
Put in bathroom	12	5
Put in bedroom	11	4

would say 24 percent; if you single-code, you would say 16 percent. Technically, neither is right and neither is wrong. If many comments are double-coded, results will look very different than if only single-coding is used.

If the research user is thinking of the categories as mutually exclusive with respect to the comments (usually an implicit assumption), then that user will take an incorrect understanding from the double-coded question. This will likely occur when the user is given a presentation that summarizes the research where only the category net lines from the open ends are shown. There is no way to know from just the net lines that the same comment is in two category nets.

If you like to understand what you are looking at, it may be helpful to learn whether the open-end responses are double-coded, triple-coded, or (perhaps) single-coded. It may make a big difference in how results from an open-ended question are understood.[2]

In summary, a questionnaire serves many masters. First, it must accommodate all the research objectives in sufficient depth and breadth to satisfy the information requirements of the manager. Next, it must "speak" to the respondent in understandable language and at the appropriate intellectual level. Furthermore, it must be convenient for the interviewer to administer, and it must allow the interviewer to quickly record the respondent's answers. At the same time, the questionnaire must be easy to edit and check for completeness. It also should facilitate coding. Finally, the questionnaire must be translatable into findings that respond to the manager's original questions.

Kyle Langley, managing partner of Multicultural Insights, discusses how important it is to ask the right questions in the following Practicing Marketing Research box.

PRACTICING MARKETING RESEARCH

Many sets of eyes need to review a questionnaire prior to field. Everyone from the client to the chief analyst should review the questionnaire to determine that the necessary inputs are there and that the inputs are worded correctly. The client must ensure that all questions are entered to deliver desired outcomes, whereas the analyst has to ensure that necessary questions are included to get at all of the requested analysis.

Here are a few things to avoid in questionnaire design:

☐ *Either/or Questions*
The Either/or query is just that. It asks respondents to identify some aspect of a question by giving them an either/or opportunity. Although this may sound fine, it often is not. For example and simplicity, asking a respondent if his favorite color is blue or green is not helpful and can skew data because the execution was biased from the start. His favorite color may, in fact, be red.

☐ *Future Intent/Usage Questions*
Some future intent questions are workable, such as "What is the likelihood you will purchase a new car in the next 12 months?" But often, companies seeking more precise measures of profit potential seek to answer questions that can skew data and make it unbelievable. For example, a question that may be a stretch is, "How much do you think you will spend on men's underwear in the next 12 months?" Does anyone really know the answer to this question? In our experience, even among those who think they know, big differences exist among cultural segments, with some tending to exaggerate on future purchase intent.

☐ *Hypothetical Questions*
Hypothetical questions are just that: hypothetical. Although these questions are often used in research, using their results to build business models and make business decisions can be problematic. Why? Attitudes do not always match behavior. An example would be to ask respondents, "If car maker X offered a six-door pickup truck would you be likely to buy one?" Even lacking information on the vehicle's appearance or cost, if the respondent is a fan of car maker X or a pickup truck owner she may say yes, but would never have any intent to purchase the vehicle in question once she saw it.

☐ *Negatively Phrased/Double-Negative Questions*
One might be surprised that so many negatively worded questions are included in questionnaires. "Would it not be fair to say this is untrue?" If you had to stop and think about that question, imagine being on the phone and having to think something like that through. Imagine how such questions can take up valuable time in questionnaire completion.[3]

Questionnaire Design Process

Designing a questionnaire involves a series of logical steps, as shown in Exhibit 11.4. The steps may vary slightly when performed by different researchers, but all researchers tend to follow the same general sequence. Committees and lines of authority can complicate the process, so it is wise to clear each step with the individual who has the ultimate authority for the project. This is particularly true for the first step: determining survey objectives, resources, and constraints. Many work hours have been wasted because a researcher developed a questionnaire to answer one type of question and the "real" decision maker wanted something entirely different. It also should be noted that the design process itself—specifically, question wording and format—can

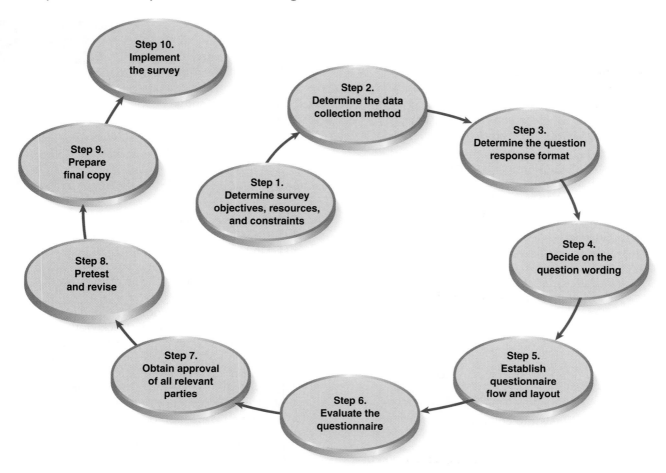

Exhibit 11.4

Questionnaire Design Process

raise additional issues or unanswered questions. This, in turn, can send the researcher back to step one for a clearer description of the information sought. Things to avoid in questionnaire design are discussed in the Practicing Marketing Research box on page 335.

Step One: Determine Survey Objectives, Resources, and Constraints

The research process often begins when a marketing manager, brand manager, or new product development specialist has a need for decision-making information that is not available. In some firms, it is the manager's responsibility to evaluate all secondary sources to make certain that the needed information has not already been gathered. In other companies, the manager leaves all research activities, primary and secondary, to the research department. The discussion of uses of marketing research in Chapter 2 covers this issue in more detail.

Although a brand manager may initiate the research request, everyone affected by the project—including the assistant brand manager, the group product manager, and even the marketing manager—should provide input into exactly what data are needed. **Survey objectives** (outlining the decision-making information required) should be spelled out as clearly and precisely as possible. If this step is completed carefully and thoroughly, the rest of the process will follow more smoothly and efficiently.

survey objectives
Outline of the decision-making information sought through the questionnaire.

Step Two: Determine the Data-Collection Method

Given the variety of ways in which survey data can be gathered, such as via the Internet, telephone, mail, or self-administration, the research method will have an impact on questionnaire design. An in-person interview in a mall will have constraints (such as a time limitation) not encountered with an Internet questionnaire. A self-administered questionnaire must be explicit and is usually rather short; because no interviewer will be present, respondents will not have the opportunity to clarify a question. A telephone interview may require a rich verbal description of a concept to make certain the respondent understands the idea being discussed. In contrast, an Internet survey can show the respondent a picture or video or demonstrate a concept.

Step Three: Determine the Question Response Format

Once the data-collection method has been determined, a decision must be made regarding the types of questions to be used in the survey. Three major types of questions are used in marketing research: open-ended, closed-ended, and scale-response questions.

Open-Ended Questions

Open-ended questions are those to which the respondent replies in her or his own words. In other words, the researcher does not limit the response choices.

Often, open-ended questions require probes from the interviewer. In a *probe,* the interviewer encourages the respondent to elaborate or continue the discussion. The interviewer may say, "Is there anything else?" or "Would you elaborate on that?" in order to clarify the respondent's interests, attitudes, and feelings. Computers are playing an increasingly important role in analyzing and recording probes to open-ended questions.

Open-ended questions offer several advantages to the researcher. They enable respondents to give their general reactions to questions like the following:

1. What advantages, if any, do you think ordering from an e-retailer company offers compared with buying from local retail outlets? (*Probe:* What else?)

2. Why do you have one or more of your rugs or carpets professionally cleaned rather than cleaning them yourself or having someone else in the household clean them?

3. What do you think is most in need of improvement here at the airport?

4. What is there about the color of _____ [product] that makes you like it the best? (*Probe:* What color is that?)

5. Why do you say that brand [the one you use most often] is better?

Each of the preceding questions was taken from a different nationwide survey covering five products and services. Note that open-ended questions 2 and 4 are part of a skip pattern. Before being asked question 2, the respondent has already indicated that he or she uses a professional carpet cleaning service and does not depend on members of the household.

Open-ended responses have the advantage of providing the researcher with a rich array of information. The respondent's answers are based on his or her personal frame of reference and described in real-world terminology rather than laboratory or marketing jargon. Often, this is helpful in designing promotion themes and campaigns; it enables copywriters to use the consumer's language. This rich array of information can now be captured even in computer-assisted interviews and Internet surveys.

The inspection of open-ended responses also can serve as a means of interpreting closed-ended questions. Analysis often sheds additional light on the motivations or

> **open-ended questions**
> Questions to which the respondent replies in her or his own words.

attitudes behind closed-ended response patterns. It is one thing to know that color ranks second in importance out of five product attributes—but it might be much more valuable to know why color is important. For example, a recent study of mobile home park residents identified a great deal of dissatisfaction with the trash pick-up service, but further inspection of the open-ended responses uncovered the reason: neighbors' dogs were allowed to run free and were overturning the receptacles.

Similarly, open-ended questions may suggest additional alternatives not listed in a closed-ended response format. For example, a previously unrecognized advantage of using an e-retail company might be uncovered in responses to question 1. A closed-ended question on the same subject would not have this advantage.

One manufacturer for which we consult always ends product placement questionnaires with the following: "Is there anything else that you would like to tell us about the product that you have tried during the past three weeks?" This probe seeks any final tidbit of information that might provide additional insight for the researcher.

Alexa Smith, president of Research Department in New York City, suggests several open-ended questions that can be asked for greater insights in the accompanying Practicing Marketing Research box.

Open-ended questions are not without their problems. Editing and coding can consume great amounts of time and money if done manually. Editing open-ended responses requires collapsing the many response alternatives into some reasonable number. If too many categories are used, data patterns and response frequencies may be difficult to interpret. Even if a proper number of categories is used, editors may still have to interpret what the interviewer has recorded and force the data into a category. If the categories are too broad, the data may be too general and important meaning may be lost.

A related problem of open-ended questions is the potential for interviewer bias. Although training sessions continually stress the importance of verbatim recording of open-ended questions, interviewers in the field often take shortcuts. Also, slow writers may unintentionally miss important comments. Good probes that ask "Can you tell me a little more?" or "Is there anything else?" are helpful in dealing with this problem.

If a food study on tacos asked "What, if anything besides meat, do you normally add to a taco you have prepared at home?" coding categories would need to be determined to categorize answers to this open-ended question.

PRACTICING
MARKETING RESEARCH

Here are some open-ended questions, often overlooked, that lead to greater insight:

☐ **What would it take to get you to use or buy a product or service?** Such a question is useful at the end of a focus group or in-depth interview. At minimum, it can provide a handy summation of the findings that have gone before. It can also serve as a forum for problems and issues that have not yet surfaced. In a study about children's magazines developed in Europe, for example, the respondents said the text would need to be simplified and the illustrations improved for the magazines to be acceptable for children in the United States.

☐ **What is the best thing about the product, service, or promotion?** This question yields far more than the typical "What do you like about it?" question and can be useful as an addition to the traditional "likes" question. A food company had developed a frozen breakfast item that did not seem to be winning any awards for quality and taste. But asking what respondents liked about the food item yielded little because respondents were dissatisfied with the product. By asking what the *best* thing about it was, however, the company found it was "the idea." Many of the participants in the study were working mothers and longed for a quick and convenient hot breakfast item they could provide for their family. Based on answers to a question on simple likes, the whole idea might have been thrown out, but based on "the best thing," the client knew the company was on to something and that the product just needed taste and quality improvements.

☐ **What is the worst thing about the product, service, or promotion?** The corollary to "the best thing," this question also often yields surprising answers. Respondents who talked about going to the dentist responded rationally to what they disliked, including pain, expense, and insecurity about

their personal experience. When asked, "What is the worst thing that can happen when you go to the dentist?" many said, "You could die!" Dying in the dentist's chair is a rare occurrence, but the response taught the study's sponsor something about the level of fear people were dealing with.

☐ **Main idea registration.** At the least, the researcher needs to know if respondents have the correct understanding of an idea. Asking for main idea registration is often a good shortcut to identifying communications problems with a concept that would otherwise impede acceptance of an idea. Sometimes the executional elements of a concept can provide a sticking point that can be distracting. A quick fix may be either to verbally correct the misunderstanding or to rewrite the concepts in-between focus groups or interviews. If respondents do not understand the intended message, they often find it difficult to answer a question about whether anything is confusing or hard to understand.

☐ **How would friends and close associates relate to this idea?** Sometimes an idea or a concept can be so blatant that it causes a consumer backlash. This can happen when a company tries to create an upscale, status-conscious image for its product or service. In this case, consumers will indicate something to the effect that they would never be so snobbish as to relate to the idea. When this happens, the merit of the strategy can become apparent if the question is moved into the third person, such as "Do you know friends and associates who would relate to this idea?" If respondents say "yes," then the researcher can determine what friends and associates would like about the idea. In telling how their friends and associates would relate to the idea, consumers are really talking about themselves in a more socially sanctioned way. A surprising number of clients are not aware of this and tend to pass the moderator admonishing notes about just wanting to know what respondents themselves think.

☐ **What do you do just before you use a product or service?** Elderly women were asked this question in the context of reading their favorite magazine and how special the experience was when they explained that they take their shoes off, put on their favorite slippers, change into comfortable clothes, and go off by themselves to read the magazine. Reading the magazine was something they did entirely for themselves, and the publisher learned that the magazine was truly a valued companion to these women.[4]

Precoding open-ended questions can partially overcome these problems. Assume that this question was to be asked in a food study: "What, if anything, do you normally add to a taco that you have prepared at home, besides meat?" Coding categories for this open-ended question might be as follows:

Response	Code
Avocado	1
Cheese (Monterey Jack, cheddar)	2
Guacamole	3
Lettuce	4
Mexican hot sauce	5
Olives (black or green)	6
Onions (red or white)	7
Peppers (red or green)	8
Pimento	9
Sour cream	0
Other	X

These answers would be listed on the questionnaire, and a space would be provided to write in any nonconforming reply in the "Other" category. In a telephone interview, the question would still qualify as open-ended because the respondents would not see the categories and the interviewer would be instructed not to divulge them. Precoding necessitates that the researcher have sufficient familiarity with previous studies of a similar nature to anticipate respondents' answers. Otherwise, a pretest with a fairly large sample is needed.

Open-ended questions may be biased toward the articulate interviewee. A person with elaborate opinions and the ability to express them may have much greater input than a shy, inarticulate, or withdrawn respondent. Yet, both might be equally likely prospective consumers of a product.

Suppose an editor confronted the following responses to the taco question: "I usually add a green, avocado-tasting hot sauce." "I cut up a mixture of lettuce and spinach." "I'm a vegetarian; I don't use meat at all. My taco is filled only with guacamole." How should the editor code these?

A basic problem with open-ended questions lies in the interpretation-processing area. A two-phase judgment must be made. First, the researcher must decide on an appropriate set of categories, and then each response must be evaluated to determine into which category it falls.

A final difficulty with open-ended questions is their inappropriateness on some self-administered questionnaires. With no interviewer there to probe, respondents may give a shallow, incomplete, or unclear answer. On a self-administered questionnaire without precoded choices, answers to the taco question might read "I use a little bit of everything" or "I use the same things they use in restaurants." These answers would have virtually no value to a researcher.

Closed-Ended Questions

A **closed-ended question** requires the respondent to make a selection from a list of responses. The primary advantage of closed-ended questions is simply the avoidance of many of the problems associated with open-ended questions. Reading response alternatives may jog a person's memory and generate a more realistic response. Interviewer bias is eliminated because the interviewer is simply clicking a box, circling a category, recording a number, or punching a key. Because the option of expounding on a topic is not given to a respondent, there is no bias toward the articulate. Finally, coding and data entry can be done automatically with questionnaire software programs.

It is important to realize the difference between a precoded open-ended question and a multiple-choice question. A precoded open-ended question allows the respondent to answer in a freewheeling format; the interviewer simply checks coded answers as they are given. Probing is used, but a list is never read. If the answer given is not one of the precoded ones, it is written verbatim in the "Other" column. In contrast, a closed-ended question requires that a list of alternatives be read by the respondent or interviewer.

Traditionally, marketing researchers have separated closed-ended questions into two types: **dichotomous questions**, with a two-item response option, **multiple-choice (or multichotomous) questions**, with a multi-item response option.

Dichotomous Questions. In a dichotomous question, the two response categories are sometimes implicit. For instance, the implicit response options to the question "Did you buy gasoline for your automobile in the last week?" are "Yes" and "No." Even if the respondent says, "I rented a car last week, and they filled it up for me. Does that count?" the question would still be classified as dichotomous. A few examples of dichotomous questions follow:

1. Did you heat the Danish roll before serving it?
   Yes   1
   No   2

2. The federal government doesn't care what people like me think.
   Agree   1
   Disagree   2

3. Do you think that inflation will be greater or less than it was last year?
   Greater than   1
   Less than   2

Because the respondent is limited to two fixed alternatives, dichotomous questions are easy to administer and tabulate and usually evoke a rapid response. Many times, a neutral response option is added to dichotomous questions; if it is omitted, interviewers may jot down "DK" for "Don't know" or "NR" for "No response."

The "don't know" response has raised some concerns as telephone surveys have migrated to the Internet. Randall Thomas, a senior research scientist at Harris Interactive, discusses the dilemma in the accompanying Practicing Marketing Research box.

Dichotomous questions are prone to a large amount of measurement error. Because alternatives are polarized, the wide range of possible choices between the poles is omitted. Thus, appropriate wording is critical to obtaining accurate responses. Questions phrased in a positive form may well result in opposite answers from questions expressed in a negative form. For example, responses may depend on whether "Greater than" or "Less

----

closed-ended questions
Questions that require the respondent to choose from a list of answers.

dichotomous questions
Closed-ended questions that ask the respondents to choose between two answers.

multiple-choice questions
Closed-ended questions that ask the respondent to choose among several answers; also called *multichotomous questions*.

PRACTICING
MARKETING RESEARCH

A common purpose of a customer tracking survey, such as customer satisfaction, is to gauge a population's opinions, (i.e., all customers of *Amazon.com*) based on a sample of that population and to track changes in that group's attitudes, interests, and behaviors. Many factors affect the researcher's ability to generalize findings from a specific sample to the larger population of interest (all Amazon customers) to the client. One factor that threatens generalizability is survey nonresponse.

One aspect of item nonresponse involves how to handle "not sure" or "don't know" (NS/DK) responses. Typically, telephone-based approaches do not explicitly offer the option "not sure" or "don't know" but will generally accept such a response if volunteered by a respondent (with some amount of effort often expended by the interviewer to minimize item nonresponse). Since Web-based interviews are self-administered, the NS/DK option is either offered explicitly or it is not. One concern that has been often voiced about the explicit presentation of NS/DK responses is that it will decrease comparability to telephone data. Clients often wish to retain historical data when they are transitioning from a telephone-based approach to a Web-based approach. In other words, if a client is tracking customer satisfaction each quarter and is transitioning

the survey to the Internet, the client wants to make certain that the satisfaction scores compare "apples to apples." Some researchers believe that including these NS/DK responses would improve data quality by reducing the pressure to provide opinions when no true opinions exist.

Harris Interactive conducted a series of experiments to determine the effects of including a NS/DK response to opinion questions so that we could better understand the effects of item nonresponse on data comparability across types of surveys such as telephone versus the Internet. The research had two experimental conditions in the online survey. The NS Present condition presented a series of questions with "not sure" provided as a response option, while the NS Absent condition received the same series of questions with "not sure" absent. We randomly assigned 1,044 respondents to the NS Present condition and 1,054 respondents to the NS Absent condition. Each respondent answered eight rating questions using a four-category rating scale (poor, only fair, pretty good, excellent).

The experiment shows that the presentation of a "not sure" or "don't know" category for opinion questions presented online is more likely to yield data comparable to that found by way of telephone data. So don't leave NS/DK off of your online surveys![5]

than" is listed first. These problems can be overcome by using a split ballot technique: one-half of the questionnaires have "Greater than" listed first, and the other half have "Less than" first. This procedure helps reduce potential order bias.

Another problem with the dichotomous question is that responses frequently fail to communicate any intensity of feeling on the part of the respondent. In some cases, like the gasoline purchasing example, the matter of intensity does not apply. But in some instances, strong feelings about an issue may be lost in the dichotomous response form. If the gasoline purchasing interview continued with the question "Would you purchase gasoline priced $1.00 per gallon above current prices if you were guaranteed twice the miles per gallon?" responses would likely range in intensity from "No; absolutely not" to "You bet!"

Multiple-Choice Questions. With multiple-choice questions, replies do not have to be coded as they do with open-ended questions, but the amount of information provided is more limited. The respondent is asked to give one alternative that correctly expresses his or her opinion or, in some instances, to indicate all alternatives that apply. Some examples of multiple-choice questions follow:

1. I'd like you to think back to the last footwear of any kind that you bought. I'll read you a list of descriptions and would like for you to tell me into which category it falls. (READ LIST AND CHECK THE PROPER CATEGORY)

Dress and/or formal	1	Specialized athletic shoes	4
Casual	2	Boots	5
Canvas-trainer-gym shoes	3		

2. (HAND RESPONDENT CARD) Please look at this card and tell me the letter that indicates the age group to which you belong.

A.	Under 17	1	D.	35–49 years	4
B.	17–24 years	2	E.	50–64 years	5
C.	25–34 years	3	F.	65 and over	6

3. In the last three months, have you used Noxzema Skin Cream . . . (CHECK ALL THAT APPLY)

as a facial wash?	1
for moisturizing the skin?	2
for treating blemishes?	3
for cleansing the skin?	4
for treating dry skin?	5
for softening skin?	6
for sunburn?	7
for making the facial skin smooth?	8

Question 1 from a mall intercept interview, may not cover all possible alternatives and, thus, may not capture a true response. Where, for example, would an interviewer record work shoes? The same thing can be said for question 3. Not only are all possible alternatives not included, but respondents cannot elaborate or qualify their answers. The problem could be easily overcome by adding an "Any other use?" alternative to the question.

The multiple-choice question has two additional disadvantages. First, the researcher must spend time generating the list of possible responses. This phase may require brainstorming or intensive analysis of focus group tapes or secondary data. Second, the researcher must settle on a range of possible answers. If the list is too long, the respondent may become confused or lose interest. A related problem with any list is *position bias*. Respondents typically will choose either the first or the last alternative, all other things being equal. When Internet questionnaire software and CATI systems are used, however, position bias is eliminated by automatically rotating response order.

Scaled-Response Questions

Scaled-Response Questions The last response format to be considered is **scaled-response questions**, which are closed-ended questions where the response choices are designed to capture intensity of feeling. Consider the following questions.

1. Now that you have used the product, would you say that you would buy it or not? (CHECK ONE)
    Yes, would buy it
    No, would not buy it

2. Now that you have used the product, would you say that you . . . (CHECK ONE)
    definitely would buy it?
    probably would buy it?
    might or might not buy it?

> **scaled-response questions**
> Closed-ended questions in which the response choices are designed to capture the intensity of the respondent's feeling.

probably would not buy it?

definitely would not buy it?

The first question fails to capture intensity. It determines the direction ("Yes" versus "No"), but it cannot compare with the second question in completeness or sensitivity of response. The latter also has the advantage of being ordinal in nature.

A primary advantage of using scaled-response questions is that scaling permits measurement of the intensity of respondents' answers. Also, many scaled-response forms incorporate numbers that can be used directly as codes. Finally, the marketing researcher can use much more powerful statistical tools with some scaled-response questions (see Chapter 16).

The most significant problems with scaled-response questions arise from respondent misunderstanding. Scaled questions sometimes tax respondents' abilities to remember and answer. First, the questionnaire must explain the response category options; then, the respondent must translate these options into his or her own frame of reference. Interviewers usually are provided with a detailed description of the response categories allowed and often are instructed to have the respondent state that he or she understands the scale before they ask any questions. Take a look at Exhibit 11.5 for

Exhibit 11.5

Sample Telephone Interviewer's Instructions for a Scaled-Response Question Form

---

Example 1

I have some statements that I will read to you. For each one, please indicate whether you "strongly agree," "agree," "disagree," "strongly disagree," or have no opinion. I will read the statement, and you indicate *your* opinion as accurately as possible. Are the instructions clear?

(IF THE RESPONDENT DOES NOT UNDERSTAND, REPEAT RESPONSE CATEGORIES. THEN GO ON TO READ STATEMENTS AND RECORD RESPONSES. CIRCLE RESPONDENT'S OPINION IN EACH CASE.)

Example 2

Now I'm going to read you a list of statements that may or may not be important to you in deciding where to shop for computer equipment. Let's use your telephone keypad as a scale. Number 1 would mean "definitely disagree," and number 6 would mean "definitely agree." Or you can pick any number in between that best expresses your feelings.

Let's begin. To what extent do you agree or disagree that (INSERT STATEMENT) is an important aspect when deciding where to shop for computer equipment?

Example 3

Now I shall read a list of statements about automotive servicing that may or may not be important to you when servicing your car.

Let's use your telephone dial as a scale. . . .

Number 1 would mean you *disagree completely* with the statement.

Number 2 would mean you *disagree* with the statement.

Number 3 would mean you *somewhat disagree* with the statement.

Number 4 would mean you *somewhat agree* with the statement.

Number 5 would mean you *agree* with the statement.

Number 6 would mean you *agree completely* with the statement.

Do you have any questions about the scale?

1. To what extent do you agree or disagree that (INSERT STATEMENT) is a feature you consider when selecting a place to have your car serviced?

---

examples of a telephone interviewer's instructions to respondents. In the case of self-administered questionnaires or Internet surveys, the researcher often presents the respondent with an example of how to respond to a scale as part of the instructions.

Step Four: Decide on the Question Wording

Once the marketing researcher has decided on the specific types of questions and the response formats, the next task is the actual writing of the questions. Wording specific questions can require a significant investment of the researcher's time unless questionnaire software or a survey Web site like Perseus is used. Four general guidelines about the wording of questions are useful to bear in mind: (1) The wording must be clear, (2) the wording must not bias the respondent, (3) the respondent must be able to answer the questions, and (4) the respondent must be willing to answer the questions.

Make Sure the Wording Is Clear   Once the researcher has decided that a question is absolutely necessary, the question must be stated so that it means the same thing to all respondents. Ambiguous terminology—for example, "Do you live within five minutes of here?" or "Where do you usually shop for clothes?"—should be avoided. The respondent's answer to the first question will depend on such factors as mode of transportation (maybe the respondent walks), driving speed, and perceptions of elapsed time. (The interviewer would do better to display a map with certain areas delineated and ask whether the respondent lives within the area outlined.) The second question depends on the type of clothing being purchased and the meaning of the word "Where."

Clarity also calls for the use of reasonable terminology. A questionnaire is not a vocabulary test. Jargon should be avoided, and verbiage should be geared to the target audience. The question "What is the level of efficacy of your preponderant dishwashing liquid?" probably would be greeted by a lot of blank stares. It would be much simpler to ask "Are you (1) very satisfied, (2) somewhat satisfied, or (3) not satisfied with your current brand of dishwashing liquid?" Words with precise meanings, universal usage, and minimal connotative confusion should be selected. When respondents are uncertain about what a question means, the incidence of "No response" answers increases.

A further complication in wording questions is the need to tailor the language to the target respondent group, whether it is lawyers or construction laborers. This advice may seem painfully obvious, but there are instances in which failure to relate to respondents' frames of reference has been disastrous. A case in point is the use of the word *bottles* (or *cans*) in this question: "How many bottles of beer do you drink in a normal week?" Because in some southern states beer is sold in 32-, 12-, 8-, 7-, 6-, and even 4-ounce bottles, a "heavy" drinker (defined as someone who consumes eight bottles of beer per week) may drink as little as 32 ounces while a "light" drinker (defined as someone who consumes up to three bottles) may actually drink as much as 96 ounces.

Clarity can be improved by stating the purpose of the survey at the beginning of the interview. To put the questions in the proper perspective, the respondent needs to understand the nature of the study and what is expected of him or her but not necessarily who is sponsoring the project.

To achieve clarity in wording, the researcher should avoid asking two questions in one, sometimes called a *double-barreled question*. For example, "How did you like the taste and texture of the coffee cake?" should be broken into two questions, one concerning taste and the other texture. Each question should address only one aspect of evaluation.

Avoid Biasing the Respondent   Questions such as "Do you often shop at lower-class stores like Super Shop?" and "Have you purchased any high-quality Black & Decker tools in the past six months?" show an obvious bias. Leading questions, such as "Weren't you pleased with the good service you received last night at the Holiday Inn?" is also quite obviously biased. However, bias may be much more subtle than that illustrated in these examples.

Sponsor identification early in the interviewing process can distort answers. An opening statement such as "We are conducting a study on the quality of banking for Northeast National Bank and would like to ask you a few questions" should be avoided. Similarly, it will not take long, for example, for a person to recognize that the survey is being conducted for Miller beer if, after the third question, every question is related to this product.

Consider the Respondent's Ability to Answer the Questions   In some cases, a respondent may never have acquired the information needed to answer the question. For example, a husband may not know which brand of sewing thread is preferred by his wife, and respondents will know nothing about a brand or store that they have never encountered. A question worded so as to imply that the respondent should be able to answer it will often elicit a reply that is nothing more than a wild guess. This creates measurement error, since uninformed opinions are being recorded.

Another problem is forgetfulness. For example, you probably cannot remember the answers to all these questions: What was the name of the last movie you saw in a theater? Who were the stars? Did you have popcorn? How many ounces were in the container? What price did you pay for the popcorn? Did you purchase any other snack items? Why or why not? The same is true for the typical respondent. Yet a brand manager for Mars, Incorporated wants to know what brand of candy you purchased last, what alternative brands you considered, and what factors led you to the brand selected. Because brand managers want answers to these questions, market researchers ask them. This, in turn, creates measurement error. Often respondents will give the name of a well-known brand, like Milky Way or Hershey. In other cases, respondents will mention a brand that they often purchase, but it may not be the last brand purchased.

To avoid the problem of a respondent's inability to recall, the researcher should keep the referenced time periods relatively short. For example, if the respondent says "Yes" to the question "Did you purchase a candy bar within the past seven days?" then brand and purchase motivation questions can be asked. A poor question like "How many movies have you rented in the past year to view at home on your DVD?" might be replaced with the following:

a.   How many movies have you rented in the past month to view on your DVD?

b.   Would you say that, in the last month, you rented more movies, fewer movies, or about the average number of movies you rent per month? (IF "MORE" or "LESS," ASK THE FOLLOWING QUESTION)

c.   What would you say is the typical number of movies you rent per month?

Here are two questions from actual marketing research studies. The first is from a mail survey and the second from a telephone survey. Question one: In the past three months, how much have you spent on movies you saw advertised in the newspaper? Most people haven't a clue as to how much they have spent on movies in the last three months unless it is "nothing." And they certainly don't recall which of the movies were advertised where. Also, what if the respondent bought tickets for the whole family? Question two: Of your last ten drinks of scotch, how many were at home? At a friend's? At a restaurant? At a bar or tavern? A light scotch drinker may have consumed ten drinks over a period of not less than two years! Maybe he carries around a scotch intake logbook, but it's doubtful.

The above questions are bad, but the questions below, from a real mail panel survey, were written by either a careless questionnaire designer or one who lives quite differently from most of us. Question: How many times in an average day do you apply your usual underarm product? One to two times per day? Three to four times per day? Five to six times per day? More than six times per day? Question: How many times in an average day do you shower/bathe? One time per day? Two times per day? Three times per day? Four times per day? Five or more times per day? Good grooming is important, but perhaps these questions are over the line.

Consider the Respondent's Willingness to Answer the Question   A respondent may have a very good memory, yet not be willing to give a truthful reply. If an event is perceived as embarrassing, sensitive in nature, threatening, or divergent from the respondent's self-image, it is likely either not to be reported at all or to be distorted in a socially desirable direction.

Embarrassing questions that deal with topics such as borrowing money, personal hygiene, sexual activities, and criminal records must be phrased carefully to minimize measurement error. One technique is to ask the question in the third person—for example, "Do you think that most people charge more on their credit cards than they should? Why?" By generalizing the question to "most people," the researcher may be able to learn more about individual respondents' attitudes toward credit and debt.

Another method for soliciting embarrassing information is for the interviewer to state, prior to asking the question, that the behavior or attitude is not unusual—for example, "Millions of Americans suffer from hemorrhoids; do you or any member of your family suffer from this problem?" This technique, called *using counterbiasing statements*, makes embarrassing topics less intimidating for respondents to discuss.

Step Five: Establish Questionnaire Flow and Layout

After the questions have been properly formulated, the next step is to sequence them and develop a layout for the questionnaire. Questionnaires are not constructed haphazardly; there is a logic to the positioning of each section (see Exhibit 11.6). Experienced marketing researchers are well aware that good questionnaire development is the key to obtaining a completed interview. A well-organized questionnaire usually elicits answers that are more carefully thought out and detailed. Researcher wisdom has led to the following general guidelines concerning questionnaire flow.

Use Screening Questions to Identify Qualified Respondents   Most marketing research employs some type of quota sampling. Only qualified respondents are interviewed, and specific minimum numbers (quotas) of various types of qualified respondents may be sought. For example, a food products study generally has quotas of users of specific brands, a magazine study screens for readers, and a cosmetic study screens for brand awareness.

Screeners (screening questions) may appear on the questionnaire, or a screening questionnaire may be filled out for everyone who is interviewed. Any demographics obtained provide a basis against which to compare persons who qualify for the full study. A long screening questionnaire can significantly increase the cost of the study, as more information must be obtained from every contact with a respondent. But it may provide important data on the nature of nonusers, nontriers, and persons unaware of the product or service being researched. Short screening questionnaires, such as the one in

screeners
Questions used to identify appropriate respondents.

EXHIBIT 11.6	How a Questionnaire Should Be Organized		
Location	**Type**	**Examples**	**Rationale**
Screeners	Qualifying questions	"Have you been snow skiing in the past 12 months?" "Do you own a pair of skis?"	The goal is to identify target respondents.
First few questions	Warm-ups	"What brand of skis do you own?" "How many years have you owned them?"	Easy-to-answer questions show the respondent that the survey is simple.
First third of questions	Transitions	"What features do you like best about the skis?"	Questions related to research objectives require slightly more effort.
Second third	Difficult and complicated questions	"Following are 10 characteristics of snow skis. Please rate your skis on each characteristic, using the scale below."	The respondent has committed to completing the questionnaire.
Last third	Classifing and demographic questions	"What is the highest level of education you have attained?"	The respondent may leave some "personal" questions blank, but they are at the end of the survey.

Exhibit 11.7, quickly eliminate unqualified persons and enable the interviewer to move immediately to the next potential respondent.

Most importantly, screeners provide a basis for estimating the costs of a survey. A survey in which all persons are qualified to be interviewed is going to be much cheaper to conduct than one with a 5 percent incidence rate. Many surveys are placed with field

Exhibit 11.7

Screening Questionnaire That Seeks Men 15 Years of Age and Older Who Shave at Least Three Times a Week with a Blade Razor

Hello. I'm from Data Facts Research. We are conducting a survey among men, and I'd like to ask you a few questions.

1. Do you or does any member of your family work for an advertising agency, a marketing research firm, or a company that manufactures or sells shaving products?

   (TERMINATE)   Yes ( )
   (CONTINUE WITH Q. 2)   No ( )

2. How old are you? Are you . . . (READ LIST)

   (TERMINATE)   Under 15 yrs. old? ( )

   (CHECK QUOTA CONTROL FORM—IF QUOTA GROUP FOR   15 to 34 yrs. old? ( )
   WHICH THE RESPONDENT QUALIFIES *IS NOT* FILLED,
   CONTINUE, IF QUOTA GROUP *IS* FILLED, THEN TERMINATE.)   Over 34 yrs. old? ( )

3. The last time you shaved, did you use an electric razor or a razor that uses blades?

   (TERMINATE)   Electric Razor ( )

   (CONTINUE WITH Q. 4)   Blade Razor ( )

4. How many times have you shaved in the past seven days?
   (IF LESS THAN THREE TIMES, TERMINATE. IF THREE OR MORE
   TIMES, CONTINUE WITH THE MAIN QUESTIONNAIRE.)

services at a flat rate per completed questionnaire. The rate is based on a stated average interview time and incidence rate. Screeners are used to determine whether, in fact, the incidence rate holds true in a particular city. If it does not, the flat rate is adjusted accordingly.

Tips on writing good screeners can be found in the Practicing Marketing Research box below.

PRACTICING MARKETING RESEARCH

Some Problems and Potential Solutions with Screening Questions

Based on the recommended methods for screening, a researcher who has the unfortunate task of conducting a phone survey of bus commuters who earn over $50,000 a year and live in ZIP Code 23456 might start the survey by asking if the person on the phone earns over $50,000 a year, lives in zip code 23456, and has commuted to work by bus in the past week. Such a method might be used despite the fact that researchers usually ask about income at the end of the survey, after some rapport has been established.

While having to screen for three characteristics may be an extreme example for a phone survey, needing to screen for multiple characteristics is very common when recruiting for focus groups. In fact, a review of 68 recent focus group screeners used by clients of Continental Research found an income screener on the first page of over 70 percent of them.

Sometimes researchers can reduce the number of screening questions or eliminate them altogether by narrowing the initial sample frame. In the above example, the need to ask for zip code could be eliminated by using a sampling frame that contains only households in the desired zip code. Similarly, if the researcher purchased a list of people living in that zip code who earned over $50,000 a year, then two of the "screeners" could be asked at the end of the survey as confirmation questions (anticipating a very high incidence). While only one screening question, bus ridership, would be necessary, one does have to weigh any possible biases caused by the list source.

Some problem screeners and solutions created by Continental Research of Norfolk, Virginia, are as follows.

Career Choice Survey

The purpose of this telephone survey was to learn more about how women between ages 20 and 29 made certain career decisions. To minimize costs, the questionnaire started with:

Hello, I'm with Acme Research in (city). We're doing a survey this evening with women in their twenties.

IF MALE SAY: *Does anyone in your home fit this description? (Get female, repeat introduction)*

IF FEMALE SAY: *May I ask your age?*

At the close of the first evening of interviewing, we found a female in the age group in only 23 (12.8 percent) of 180 households contacted. Researchers began to suspect that some people were using the screening criteria to politely end the interview. The survey was revised by placing three opinion questions after a brief introduction. The newly revised survey read:

Hello, I'm with Acme Research in (city). We're doing a brief opinion survey this evening.

IF MALE SAY: *We alternate who we ask for in our surveys; may I speak with an adult female?*

IF FEMALE SAY: *Do you think that employees should be allowed to smoke in ALL workplaces, SOME, or in NO workplaces?*

(THEN, TWO OTHER OPINION ITEMS WERE ASKED BEFORE THE AGE QUESTION.)

Using this survey format, we found that the improved incidence rate was 26.6 percent. The difference was found to be statistically significant.

Pet Product Survey

A client who was considering creating an infomercial for a pet product had identified his target market as dog and/or cat owners who held a major credit card. He wanted these prospects to evaluate various features of his new product. To minimize cost, the questionnaire started with:

1. *Hello, I'm with (company). We're doing a survey this evening with pet owners, do you have a dog or cat?*
2. *And do you have a major credit card such as MasterCard or VISA?*

Based on other research done previously, the client said that we should expect an incidence rate of between 30 and 40 pecent. Unfortunately, the incidence rate we found when using this survey format was only 8.9 percent.

To help account for the lower-than-expected incidence rate, we split the sample frame and reworded some surveys as follows:

1. *Hello, I'm with (company). We're doing a brief lifestyle survey tonight and we'd like to know how many refrigerators and televisions you have in your home.*
2. *Do you have a DVD?*
3. *Do you have a dog or cat?*
4. *Do you have more than one car?*
5. *Do you have a major credit card?*

By the end of the project, the incidence rate was 11.4 percent using the first, more direct questioning method and 31.8 percent using the second, more indirect technique. The difference between these two percentages was found to be statistically significant.[6]

Begin with a Question That Gets the Respondent's Interest   After introductory comments and screens to find a qualified respondent, the initial questions should be simple, interesting, and nonthreatening. To open a questionnaire with an income or age question could be disastrous. These are often considered threatening and immediately put the respondent on the defensive. The initial question should be easy to answer without much forethought.

Ask General Questions First   Once the interview progresses beyond the opening warm-up questions, the questionnaire should proceed in a logical fashion. First, general questions are asked to get the person thinking about a concept, company, or type of product; then the questionnaire moves to the specifics. For example, a questionnaire on shampoo might begin with "Have you purchased a hair spray, hair conditioner, or hair shampoo within the past 6 weeks?" Then it would ask about the frequency of shampooing, brands purchased in the past 3 months, satisfaction and dissatisfaction with brands purchased, repurchase intent, characteristics of an "ideal" shampoo, respondent's hair characteristics, and finally demographics.

Ask Questions That Require "Work" in the Middle   Initially, the respondent will be only vaguely interested in and understanding of the nature of the survey. As the interest-building questions transpire, momentum and commitment to the interview will build. When the interview shifts to questions with scaled-response formats, the respondent must be motivated to understand the response categories and options. Alternatively, questions might necessitate some recall or opinion formation on the part of the respondent. Established interest and commitment must sustain the respondent in this part of the interview.

Insert "Prompters" at Strategic Points   Good interviewers can sense when a respondent's interest and motivation sag and will attempt to build them back up. However, it is always worthwhile for the questionnaire designer to insert short encouragements at strategic locations in the questionnaire. These may be simple statements such as "There are only a few more questions to go" or "This next section will be easier." Encouraging words may also be inserted as part of an introduction to a section: "Now that you have helped us with those comments, we would like to ask a few more questions."

Position Sensitive, Threatening, and Demographic Questions at the End   As mentioned earlier, the objectives of a study sometimes necessitate questions on topics about which respondents may feel uneasy. These topics should be covered near the end of the questionnaire to ensure that most of the questions are answered before the respondent becomes defensive or breaks off the interview. Another argument for placing sensitive questions toward the end is that by the time these questions are asked, interviewees have been conditioned to respond. In other words, the respondent has settled into a pattern of seeing or hearing a question and giving an answer.

Allow Plenty of Space for Open-Ended Responses   An open-ended question that allows half a line for a reply usually will receive a reply of that length and nothing more. Generally speaking, three to five lines of blank space are deemed sufficient for open-ended replies. The researcher must judge how much detail is desirable in an open-ended reply. "Which department store did you visit most recently?" requires much less answer space than the follow-up question "What factors were most important in your decision to go to [name of department store]?"

Put Instructions in Capital Letters   To avoid confusion and to clarify what is a question and what is an instruction, all instructions should be in capital letters—for example, "IF 'YES' TO QUESTION 13, SKIP TO QUESTION 17." Capitalizing helps bring the instructions to the interviewer's or respondent's attention.

Use a Proper Introduction and Closing   Every questionnaire must have an introduction and closing. The Council for Marketing and Opinion Research (CMOR) has developed a model survey introduction and closing based on research findings from a number of different studies. CMOR recommends the following:[7]

Model Introduction/Opening

- ☐ In order to gain the trust of the respondent, the interviewer should provide his or her first name or agreed upon contact name. Providing a last name is optional but is recommended for business-to-business studies or surveys involving professionals such as those in the medical field.

- ☐ Provide the name of the company that the interviewer represents and the name of the client/sponsor of the research whenever possible.

- ☐ Explain the nature of the study topic/subject matter in general terms.

- ☐ State, as early in the interview as possible, that no selling will be involved as a result of the call.

- ☐ The respondent should be told in the introduction the approximate length of the survey.

- ☐ It is recommended as standard practice to obtain two-party consent to monitoring/recording; that is, both the respondent and the interviewer should be informed that the call might be monitored/recorded for quality control purposes.

- ☐ Reinforce the fact that the respondent's time is appreciated/valued.

- ☐ Invite the respondent to participate in the survey, determine if the interview time is convenient, and, if not, offer an alternative callback time and date to complete the survey.

Hello, my name is _____ and I'm calling from (company). Today/Tonight we are calling to gather opinions regarding (general subject), and are not selling anything. This study will take approximately (length) and may be monitored (and recorded) for quality purposes. We would appreciate your time. May I include your opinions?

Model Closing

- ☐ At the conclusion of the survey, thank the respondent for his or her time.
- ☐ Express the desired intention that the respondent had a positive survey experience and will be willing to participate in future market research projects.
- ☐ Remind the respondent that his or her opinions do count.

Thank you for your time and cooperation. I hope this experience was a pleasant one and you will participate in other marketing research projects in the future. Please remember that your opinion counts! Have a good day/evening.

Alternative: Participate in collecting respondent satisfaction data to improve survey quality.

Thank you very much for taking part in this survey. Because consumers like you are such a valued part of what we do, I'd like you to think about the survey you just participated in. On a scale from 1 to 10 where 10 means "it was a good use of my time," and 1 means "it was not a good use of my time," which number between 1 and 10 best describes how you feel about your experience today? That's all the questions I have. Please remember that your opinion counts! Have a good day/evening!

Step Six: Evaluate the Questionnaire

Once a rough draft of the questionnaire has been designed, the marketing researcher is obligated to take a step back and critically evaluate it. This phase may seem redundant, given the careful thought that went into each question. But recall the crucial role played by the questionnaire. At this point in the questionnaire development, the following issues should be considered: (1) Is the question necessary? (2) Is the questionnaire too long? (3) Will the questions provide the information needed to accomplish the research objectives?

Is the Question Necessary?   Perhaps the most important criterion for this phase of questionnaire development is the necessity for a given question. Sometimes researchers and brand managers want to ask questions because "they were on the last survey we did like this" or because "it would be nice to know." Excessive numbers of demographic questions are very common. Asking for education data, numbers of children in multiple age categories, and extensive demographics on the spouse simply is not warranted by the nature of many studies.

Each question must serve a purpose. Unless it is a screener, an interest generator, or a required transition, it must be directly and explicitly related to the stated objectives of the particular survey. Any question that fails to satisfy at least one of these criteria should be omitted.

Is the Questionnaire Too Long?   At this point, the researcher should role-play the survey, with volunteers acting as respondents. Although there is no magic number of interactions, the length of time it takes to complete the questionnaire should be averaged over a minimum of five trials. Any questionnaire to be administered in a mall or over the telephone should be a candidate for cutting if it averages longer than 20 minutes. Sometimes mall-intercept interviews can run slightly longer if an incentive is provided to the respondent. Most Internet surveys should take less than 15 minutes to complete.

Common incentives are movie tickets, pen and pencil sets, and cash or checks. The use of incentives often actually lowers survey costs because response rates increase and terminations during the interview decrease. If checks are given out instead of cash, the canceled checks can be used to create a list of survey participants for follow-up purposes.

A technique that can reduce the length of questionnaires is called a split-questionnaire design. It can be used when the questionnaire is long and the sample size is large. The questionnaire is split into one core component (such as demographics, usage patterns, and psychographics) and a number of subcomponents. Respondents complete the core component plus a randomly assigned subcomponent.

Will the Questions Provide the Information Needed to Accomplish the Research Objectives? The researcher must make certain that sufficient numbers and types of questions are contained within the questionnaire to meet the decision-making needs of management. A suggested procedure is to carefully review the written objectives for the research project and then write each question number next to the objective that the particular question will address. For example, question 1 applies to objective 3, question 2 to objective 2, and so forth. If a question cannot be tied to an objective, the researcher should determine whether the list of objectives is complete. If the list is complete, the question should be omitted. If the researcher finds an objective with no questions listed beside it, appropriate questions should be added. Lynn Newman, vice president of Maritz Marketing Research, discusses the difficulties of writing a good questionnaire in the following Practicing Marketing Research feature.

Step Seven: Obtain Approval of All Relevant Parties

After the first draft of the questionnaire has been completed, copies should be distributed to all parties who have direct authority over the project. Practically speaking, managers may step in at any time in the design process with new information, requests, or concerns. When this happens, revisions are often necessary. It is still important to get final approval of the first draft even if managers have already intervened in the development process.

Managerial approval commits management to obtaining a body of information via a specific instrument (questionnaire). If the question is not asked, the data will not be gathered. Thus, questionnaire approval tacitly reaffirms what decision-making information is needed and how it will be obtained. For example, assume that a new product questionnaire asks about shape, material, end use, and packaging. By approving the form, the new product development manager is implying, "I know what color the product will be" or "It is not important to determine color at this time."

Step Eight: Pretest and Revise

When final managerial approval has been obtained, the questionnaire must be pretested. No survey should be conducted without a pretest. Moreover, a pretest does not mean that one researcher is administering the questionnaire to another researcher. Ideally, a pretest is done by the best interviewers who will ultimately be working on the job and is administered to target respondents for the study. In a **pretest**, researchers look for misinterpretations by respondents, lack of continuity, poor skip patterns, additional alternatives for precoded and closed-ended questions, and general respondent reaction to the interview. The pretest should be conducted in the same mode as the final interview—that is, if the study is to be an Internet survey, then the pretest should be too.

pretest
Trial run of a questionnaire.

PRACTICING MARKETING RESEARCH

Tips for Writing a Good Questionnaire

If you have ever sent what you thought was a "final" questionnaire to a marketing research supplier, only to have it returned to you full of wording changes, deletions, and other editorial comments, you're not alone. Writing a questionnaire does not, at first glance, appear to be a very difficult task: just figure out what you want to know, and write questions to obtain that information. But although writing questions is easy, writing good questions is not. Here are some do's and don'ts when writing questions.

1. *Avoid abbreviations, slang, or uncommon words that your audience might not understand.* For example: What is your opinion of PPOs? It is quite possible that not everyone knows that PPO stands for Preferred Provider Organization. If the question targets the general public, the researcher might run into problems. On the other hand, if the question is for physicians or hospital administrators, then the acronym PPO is probably acceptable.

2. *Be specific.* The problem with vague questions is that they generate vague answers. For example: What is your household income? As respondents come up with numerous interpretations to this question, they will give all kinds of answers—income before taxes, income after taxes, and so on. Another example: How often did you attend sporting events during the past year? (1) Never, (2) Rarely, (3) Occasionally, (4) Regularly. Again, this question is open for interpretation. People will interpret "sporting event" and the answer list differently—does "regularly" mean weekly, monthly, or what?

3. *On the other hand, don't overdo it.* When questions are too precise, people cannot answer them. They will either refuse or guess. For example: How many books did you read [last year]? You need to give them

some ranges: (1) None, (2) 1–10, (3) 11–25, (4) 26–50, (5) More than 50.

4. *Make sure your questions are easy to answer.* Questions that are too demanding will also lead to refusals or guesses. For example: Please rank the following 20 items in order of importance to you when you are shopping for a new car. You're asking respondents to do a fair amount of calculating. Don't ask people to rank 20 items; have them pick the top 5.

5. *Don't assume too much.* This is a fairly common error, in which the question writer infers something about people's knowledge, attitudes, or behavior. For example: Do you tend to agree or disagree with the president's position on gun control? This question assumes that the respondent is aware that the president has a position on gun control and knows what that position is. To avoid this error, the writer must be prepared to do some educating. For example: "The president has recently stated his position on gun control. Are you aware that he has taken a stand on this issue?" If the answer is yes, then continue with: "Please describe in your own words what you understand his position on gun control to be." And, finally, "Do you tend to agree or disagree with his stand?"

6. *Watch out for double questions and questions with double negatives.* Combining questions or using a double negative leads to ambiguous questions and answers. For example: "Do you favor the legalization of marijuana for use in private homes but not in public places?" If this question precisely describes the respondent's position, then a "yes" answer is easily interpreted. But a "no" could mean the respondent favors use in public places but not in private homes, or opposes both, or favors both. Similarly, here is an example of a question with a double negative: "Should the police chief not be directly responsible to the mayor?" The question is

Questionnaire Design Process | 355

ambiguous; almost any answer will be even more so.

7. *Check for bias.* A biased question can influence people to respond in a manner that does not accurately reflect their positions. There are several ways in which questions can be prejudiced. One is to imply that respondents should have engaged in a certain behavior. For example: "The movie, *XYZ*, was seen by more people than any other movie this year. Have you seen this movie?" So as not to appear "different," respondents may say yes even though they haven't seen the movie. The question should be: "Have you seen the movie, *XYZ*?" Another way to bias a question is to have unbalanced answer choices. For example: "Currently our country spends XX billion dollars a year on foreign aid. Do you feel this amount should be (1) increased, (2) stay the same, (3) decreased a little, (4) decreased somewhat, (5) decreased a great deal?" This set of responses encourages respondents to select a "decrease" option, since there are three of these and only one increase option.

Pretesting: The Survey Before the Survey

All the rewriting and editing in the world won't guarantee success. However, pretesting is the least expensive way to make sure your questionnaire research project is a success. The primary purpose of a pretest is to make certain that the questionnaire gives the respondent clear, understandable questions that will evoke clear, understandable answers.[8]

After completion of the pretest, any necessary changes should be made. Managerial approval should then be re-obtained before going forward. If the original pretest results in extensive design and question alterations, a second pretest is in order.

Step Nine: Prepare Final Questionnaire Copy

Even the final copy phase does not allow the researcher to relax. Precise instructions for skip patterns, numbering, and precoding must be set up, and the results proofread. In a mail survey, compliance and subsequent response rates may be affected positively by a professional-looking questionnaire. For telephone interviews, the copy is typically read from a computer screen. Survey software for online interviews often lets the designer choose backgrounds, formats, and so forth.

Step Ten: Implement the Survey

Completion of the questionnaire establishes the basis for obtaining the desired decision-making information from the marketplace. As discussed in Chapter 2, most mall and telephone research interviewing is conducted by field service firms. It is the firm's job to complete the interviews and send them back to the researcher. In essence, field services are the in-person interviewers, the production line of the marketing research industry. A series of forms and procedures must be issued with the questionnaire to make certain that the field service firm gathers the data correctly, efficiently, and at a reasonable cost. Depending on the data collection method, these may include supervisor's instructions, interviewer's instructions, screeners, call record sheets, and visual aids.

Supervisor's Instructions As mentioned above, mall, focus group, and some other types of research are handled by field services. This necessitates supervisor's instructions. **Supervisor's instructions** inform the field services firm of the nature of the study, start and completion dates, quotas, reporting times, equipment and facility requirements,

supervisor's instructions
Written directions to the field service firm on how to conduct the survey.

sampling instructions, number of interviewers required, and validation procedures. In addition, detailed instructions are required for any taste test that involves food preparation. Quantities typically are measured and cooked using rigorous measurement techniques and devices.

A vital part of any study handled by a field service, supervisor's instructions establish the parameters for conducting the research. Without clear instructions, the interview may be conducted 10 different ways in 10 cities. A sample page from a set of supervisor's instructions is shown in Exhibit 11.8.

Exhibit 11.8

Sample Page of Supervisor's Instructions for a Diet Soft Drink Taste Test

Purpose	To determine from diet soft drink users their ability to discriminate among three samples of Diet Dr Pepper and give opinions and preferences between two of the samples
Staff	3–4 experienced interviewers per shift
Location	One busy shopping center in a middle to upper-middle socioeconomic area. The center's busiest hours are to be worked by a double shift of interviewers.
	In the center, 3–4 private interviewing stations are to be set up and a refrigerator and good counterspace made available for product storage and preparation.
Quota	192 completed interviews broken down as follows:
	A minimum of 70 Diet Dr Pepper users
	A maximum of 122 other diet brand users
Project materials	For this study, you are supplied the following:
	250 Screening Questionnaires
	192 Study Questionnaires
	4 Card A's
Product/preparation	For this study, our client shipped to your refrigerated facility 26 cases of soft drink product. Each case contains 24 10-oz. bottles—312 coded with an *F* on the cap, 312 with an *S*.
	Each day, you are to obtain from the refrigerated facility approximately 2–4 cases of product—1–2 of each code. Product must be transported in coolers and kept refrigerated at the location. It should remain at approximately 42°F.
	In the center, you are to take one-half of the product coded *F* and place the #23 stickers on the bottles. The other half of the *F* product should receive #46 stickers.
	The same should be done for product *S*—one-half should be coded #34, the other half #68. A supervisor should do this task before interviewing begins. Interviewers will select product by *code number*. Code number stickers are enclosed for this effort.
	Each respondent will be initially testing three product samples as designated on the questionnaire. Interviewers will come to the kitchen, select the three designated bottles, open and pour 4 oz. of each product into its corresponding coded cup. The interviewer should cap and *refrigerate* leftover product when finished pouring and take only the three *cups* of product on a tray to respondent.

Field Management Companies

Conducting fieldwork is much easier today than it was in years past. The stereotypical "kitchen table" field service firm is passing into history. In its place are companies that specialize in field management. **Field management companies**, such as QFact, On-Line Communications, and Direct Resource, generally provide questionnaire formatting, screener writing, development of instructional and peripheral materials, shipping services, field auditing, and all coordination of data collection, coding, and tab services required for the project. On completion of a study, they typically submit a single, comprehensive invoice for the project. Generally lean on staff, these companies provide the services clients need without attempting to compete with the design and analytical capabilities of full-service companies and ad agency research staffs.

> **field management companies**
> Firms that provide such support services as questionnaire formatting, screener writing, and coordination of data collection.

A number of full-service companies and qualitative professionals have discovered that using field management companies can be cost-effective; it can increase productivity by allowing them to take on more projects while using fewer of their internal resources. One example of this trend is the business relationship between Heakin Research and MARC, which hired Heakin to handle field management on particular types of studies. Likewise, several qualitative researchers have developed ongoing relationships with field management companies, whose personnel function as extensions of the consultant's staff, setting up projects and freeing up the researcher to conduct groups, write reports, and consult with clients.

Of course, like any other segment of the research industry, field management has its limitations. By definition, field management companies generally do not have design and analytical capabilities. This means that their clients may, on occasion, need to seek other providers to meet their full-service needs. In addition, because this is a relatively new segment of the industry, experience, services, and standards vary tremendously from firm to firm. It's advisable to carefully screen prospective companies and check references. These limitations notwithstanding, field management companies provide a way for researchers to increase their productivity in a cost-effective manner, while maintaining the quality of the information on which their company's decisions and commitments are based.

Impact of the Internet on Questionnaire Development

As with most other aspects of marketing research, the Internet has affected questionnaire development and use in several ways. For example, a marketing research company can now create a questionnaire and send it as an e-mail attachment to management for comments and approval; once approved, it can be placed on the client's server to be used as an Internet survey. Or researchers can simply use an Internet company like Perseus, Inquisite, Web Surveyor, SSI Web, or many others to create a survey on the Internet.

Perseus, for example, is a leading Internet self-service questionnaire-building site. It allows marketing researchers to create online surveys quickly and then view real-time results anytime and anywhere, using remote access. The advantage is that the marketing research client has no questionnaire software to install, and no programming or administration is required. All operations are automated and performed through the Perseus Web site. This includes survey design, respondent invitation, data collection, analysis, and results reporting.

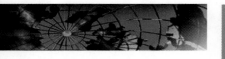

FROM THE FRONT LINE

Six Secrets of Good Questionnaire Design

Suzanne Wagner, Project Manager,
DSS Research

I began my career in market research as an interviewer in the phone room of DSS Research, a national full-service market research firm in North Texas. I believe that my experience "on the front lines" has helped me immensely in designing a good questionnaire. I've found that the key to successful questionnaire design lies in thinking about how the respondent and the interviewer will react to the survey instrument. Technical aspects aside, it is of the utmost importance that a survey instrument be logical and easy to understand for interviewer and respondent.

- **Secret 1—Use index cards in the initial survey design.** I learned this from an account executive who had been in the business for many years. When designing a survey from scratch, write out one question per index card; then you can shuffle questions around into the order that makes the most sense. It seems old-fashioned, but it helps organize your thoughts and gets you thinking about skip patterns.
- **Secret 2—Make language appropriate to the population surveyed.** It's fine to use technical jargon if you are interviewing doctors, lawyers, or engineers, but not so much with the general public. Keep concepts and language as simple and as specific as possible, and avoid slang, acronyms (without spelling them out), and abbreviations.
- **Secret 3—Remember that length matters.** We're in the lightning-fast 21st century now, and our attention span is getting shorter.

Respondent fatigue is an issue these days, and surveys need to be as short as possible to prevent this problem. Avoid redundancy. Group similar questions into a logical order. Use headings to be read by interviewers before a question series so that respondents know what's coming and stay interested (e.g., "Now I'd like to ask you a few questions about XYZ"). Have clear interviewer instructions as to when and how often to read scales.

- **Secret 4—Pretest and monitor, monitor, monitor.** Running a pretest and monitoring the first few days of interviewing will give you information about how the survey instrument flows and if respondents are struggling with any questions. It will give you information about timing and other technical aspects of the survey that you cannot get firsthand any other way.
- **Secret 5—Know your interviewers.** Get involved with the phone room and get to know the best interviewers on the floor. They will tell you what's working and what's not in your survey but ought to be. Interviewers are your allies, and having a rapport with them will help them feel a part of the process and keep them doing the best research possible for you. If you use outsource vendors instead of an in-house call center, first have an in-depth briefing by phone or Internet with them and later keep them interested and informed about the project.
- **Secret 6—Don't expect rocket science.** Survey design can be challenging, and it is the key to a successful research project, but it's an art as much as it is a science. Use simple language, logical question flow, and concise wording, and keep respondents interested (your interviewers are critical here)—these are the keys to creating a solid, useful survey instrument.

Software for Questionnaire Development

Sawtooth Software offers some of the most widely used analytical and questionnaire development software in the world. The systems are both powerful and easy to use. SSI's online interviewing product is called SSI Web. Exhibit 11.9 illustrates the kinds of questions that can be used with SSI Web. Some of the capabilities of SSI Web are:

☐ **Easy-to-use, template-based authoring on the researcher's own PC**

☐ **Randomization of pages, questions, and response options**

☐ **Data piping**

☐ **Constructed (dynamic) lists**:
One of the most powerful aspects of SSI Web is the ability to create custom lists of response options. These lists are defined by rules you specify and are customized to each respondent, based on the respondent's answers. The following example demonstrates how a constructed list might be used.

Which cities have you visited?		**Out of all the cities that you visited, which is your favorite?**
☒ Seattle		○ Seattle
☐ Portland	⟶	○ San Diego
☒ San Diego		○ Denver
☒ Denver		
☐ Dallas		

☐ **Automatic question response verification.**
Questions must be answered before moving to the next question.

☐ **Powerful skip logic**
SSI Web makes it easy to add skip logic (branching) within your survey. Skips can be executed with the page loads (pre-skips) or after it has been submitted (post-skips). That means respondents can receive pages that only include the subset of questions that apply to them, and respondents can skip pages that are not relevant.

In the global market of today, a product may be tested in many countries at the same time. The need for questionnaires in several different languages has grown considerably in the last decade.

Exhibit 11.9

Types of Questions That Can Be Used with SSI Web

Single Select Response (radio) question type

If you had the opportunity to visit one of the following cities, which one would you choose?

○ Seattle
○ Hong Kong
○ Miami
○ Paris

Multiple Select Response (checkbox)—question

Please select all of the activities you enjoy:

☐ Shopping   ☐ Walking
☐ Bowling   ☐ Skiing
☐ Swimming   ☐ Golfing
☐ Kayaking   ☐ Other (please specify)
☐ Bird Watching   ☐ None of these

Single Select Response (combo box) question type

Which is your favorite holiday?

(Holidays are listed in drop-down box)

The Numeric question type. A response from 0 to 100 is required.

How old are you? ☐

Open-end (multiple-line) question type

In the box below tell us about where you grew up.

Grid question type. This grid has select questions (radio buttons)
specified for the rows.

Please tell us how likely you are to participate in each activity over the next 3 months.

	Not Likely		Somewhat Likely		Very Likely
Shopping	○	○	○	○	○
Bowling	○	○	○	○	○
Swimming	○	○	○	○	○
Kayaking	○	○	○	○	○
Bird Watching	○	○	○	○	○

Grid question type. This example shows the flexibility in grids by
demonstrating how different question types can be
set for each row.

Please answer the following questions about the electronic products displayed below.

Which items do you own?	☐	☐	☐	☐
Which is your favorite:	○	○	○	○
How much would you pay for each?	$	$	$	$

Ranking question type

Please rank the top three activities that you enjoy.
☐ Shopping
☐ Bowling
☐ Swimming
☐ Kayaking
☐ Bird Watching

Constant Sum question type

Given a budget of $3,000, please specify how much you would spend for each holiday.
☐ Easter
☐ 4th of July
☐ Halloween
☐ Thanksgiving
☐ Christmas
☐ New Years
☐ Total (Total is automatically computed each time numbers are entered into a holiday box.)

Free Format question type. The Free Format question type allows researchers to specify their own HTML to create custom questions.

Personal Information

First Name: _____

Last Name: _____

Street Address: _____

_____

City: _____ **State:** _____ **Zip:** _____ - _____

Gender: ○ Male ○ Female

Interests: ☐ **Walking**
☐ **Running**
☐ **Hiking**
☐ **Swimming**
☐ **Eating**

Source: Sawtooth Software, Inc.

☐ **Quota control**
☐ **Foreign language character support**
☐ **Questionnaire preview and testing on local PC**
☐ **Ability to create your own custom questions with HTML and "Free Format" question type**
☐ **Power users may insert HTML, JavaScript, or Perl**
☐ **Respondent restart (without cookies)**
☐ **Similar look across different browsers, including Mac and legacy browsers**
☐ **Automatic respondent password generation, or import from text file**
☐ **Link to/from other online interviewing systems and Web sites**
☐ **Online administrative module for real-time reports, download, and data management**
☐ **Exports to common formats (including Excel, SPSS), with label[9]**

GLOBAL RESEARCH

Consistency Is the Key in Global Research

When collecting and processing data for international research, consistency is paramount. If the data are not collected and processed consistently, then the results cannot be compared regionally, and eventually project cost and turnaround time will increase. Attention to details and their standardization is imperative.

Specialized software packages for survey design can be tremendously helpful, allowing a library of standard questions, responses, and even routing logic to be compiled. They can be easily retrieved and used to create the different versions of the survey, to achieve consistency in the wording of questions and responses.

Some of these software packages also interface to, or contain, translation utilities. Using these utilities, a researcher can create a database of commonly used phrases, translated into different languages and easily retrieved and used.[10]

Today's global marketers offer a variety of products to their customers throughout the world. Many times, a new product concept is tested simultaneously in a number of different countries, requiring questionnaires in a variety of languages. Fortunately, new software programs ease the "language problem," as the Global Research feature explains.

Costs, Profitability, and Questionnaires

A discussion of questionnaires would not be complete without mentioning their impact on costs and profitability. Marketing research suppliers typically bid against one another for a client's project. A supplier who overestimates costs will usually lose the job to a lower-cost competitor. In all survey research, the questionnaire and incidence rate (see Chapter 6) are the core determinants of a project's estimated costs. When one of America's largest research suppliers examined costs and bids for all of its projects conducted by central-location telephone interviewing, it found that it had overestimated project costs 44 percent of the time during a recent 18-month period. The resulting overbidding had translated into millions of dollars of lost sales opportunities.

To avoid overbidding, managers must better understand questionnaire costs. In one central-location telephone study with a 50 percent incidence rate and calls lasting an average of 15 minutes, MARC, a large international marketing research firm, found that only 30 percent of the data-collection costs involved asking the questions. Seventy percent of the data-collection costs were incurred trying to reach a qualified respondent.[11]

Exhibit 11.10 depicts the numerous roadblocks an interviewer can encounter trying to get a completed interview. Each roadblock adds to the costs. MARC, for example, has found that simply adding a security screener to a questionnaire can increase the cost of interviewing by as much as 7 percent.

Another major source of extra cost in survey research is premature termination of interviews. People terminate interviews for four major reasons: the subject matter, redundant or difficult-to-understand questions, questionnaire length, and changing the subject during an interview. People like to talk about some subjects and not others. For example, the subject of gum is no problem, but bringing up mouthwash results in many

EXHIBIT 11.10	Difficulties in Finding a Qualified Respondent in a Central-Location Telephone Interview

1. **Failed Attempts**
   - Busy
   - No answer
   - Answering machine
   - Business number
   - Phone/language problem
   - Discontinued line

2. **Cooperation Problems**
   - Respondent not at home
   - Respondent refused to be interviewed

3. **Screener Determines Respondent Not Eligible**
   - Failed security test (works for marketing research firm, advertising agency, or the client)
   - Doesn't use the product
   - Demographic disqualification (wrong gender, age, etc.)
   - Quota filled (For example, survey has a quota of 500 users of Tide and 500 users of other clothes washing powders. Interviewer already has 500 Tide users; the current respondent uses Tide.)

4. **Respondent terminated during Interview**

terminations. Exhibit 11.11 reveals that a 20+-minute interview on gum results in few terminations (actual data). However, many people terminate a mouthwash interview within 3 minutes or in the 19- to 22-minute range. Terminations of a leisure travel interview don't become a serious problem until the interview reaches 20 minutes in length. Terminations usually mean that the interview must be redone and all the time

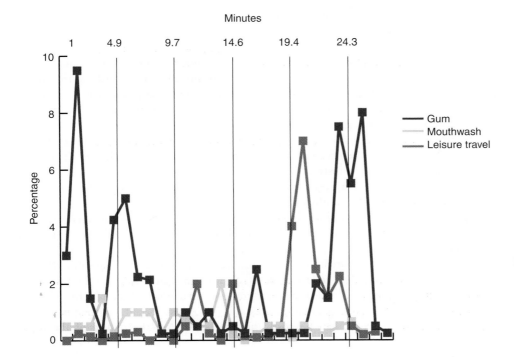

Exhibit 11.11

Actual Respondent Termination Patterns for Interviews in Three Different Product Categories

spent interviewing the respondent was wasted. However, preliminary research has found that callbacks on terminated interviews can sometimes result in a completed interview.[12] (The same research on callbacks to persons who originally refused to be surveyed was not productive.)

Once managers understand the actual costs of data collection, they should be in a better position to bid on jobs with a high degree of cost accuracy. Better information should result in less overbidding and therefore more contracts.

SUMMARY

The questionnaire plays a critical role in the data-collection process. The criteria for a good questionnaire may be categorized as follows: (1) providing the necessary decision-making information, (2) fitting the respondent, and (3) meeting editing, coding, and data processing requirements.

The process of developing a questionnaire is a sequential one:

Step One. Determine survey objectives, resources, and constraints.

Step Two. Determine the data-collection method.

Step Three. Determine the question response format.

Step Four. Decide on the question wording.

Step Five. Establish questionnaire flow and layout.

Step Six. Evaluate the questionnaire.

Step Seven. Obtain approval of all relevant parties.

Step Eight. Pretest and revise.

Step Nine. Prepare final questionnaire copy.

Step Ten. Implement the survey.

The three different types of questions—open-ended, closed-ended, and scaled-response questions—each have advantages and disadvantages. In establishing the wording and positioning of questions within the questionnaire, the researcher must try to ensure that the wording is clear and does not bias the respondent and that the respondent will be able and willing to answer the questions.

During the implementation of survey research, procedures must be followed to ensure that the data are gathered correctly, efficiently, and at a reasonable cost. These include preparing supervisor's instructions, interviewer's instructions, screeners, call record sheets, and visual aids. Many research organizations are now turning to field management companies to actually conduct the interviews.

Questionnaire software and the Internet are having a major impact on survey design. Perseus Web surveyor, SSI Web, and others enable researchers to go to the Web site and create online surveys.

The role of the questionnaire in survey research costs can be a decisive one. If a research firm overestimates data-collection costs, chances are that it will lose the project to another supplier. Most data-collection costs are associated not with conducting the actual interview, but with finding a qualified respondent. A respondent's propensity to terminate an interview, which can be costly, is often based on the nature of the topic discussed.

questionnaire Set of questions designed to generate the data necessary to accomplish the objectives of the research project; also called an *interview schedule* or *survey instrument*.

editing Going through each questionnaire to ensure that skip patterns were followed and the required questions were filled out.

skip pattern Sequence in which questions are asked, based on a respondent's answer.

coding Process of grouping and assigning numeric codes to the various responses to a question.

survey objectives Outline of the decision-making information sought through the questionnaire.

open-ended questions Questions to which the respondent replies in her or his own words.

closed-ended questions Questions that require the respondent to choose from a list of answers.

dichotomous questions Closed-ended questions that ask the respondent to choose between two answers.

multiple-choice questions Closed-ended questions that ask the respondent to choose among several answers; also called *multichotomous questions*.

scaled-response questions Closed-ended questions in which the response choices are designed to capture the intensity of the respondent's feeling.

screeners Questions used to identify appropriate respondents.

pretest Trial run of a questionnaire

supervisor's instructions Written directions to the field service firm on how to conduct the survey.

field management companies Firms that provide such support services as questionnaire formatting, screener writing, and coordination of data collection.

1. Explain the role of the questionnaire in the research process.
2. How do respondents influence the design of a questionnaire? Give some examples (e.g., questionnaires designed for engineers, baseball players, army generals, migrant farmworkers).
3. Discuss the advantages and disadvantages of open-ended questions and closed-ended questions.
4. Assume that you are developing a questionnaire about a new sandwich for McDonald's. Use this situation to outline the procedure for designing a questionnaire.
5. Give examples of poor questionnaire wording, and explain what is wrong with each question.
6. Once a questionnaire has been developed, what other factors need to be considered before the questionnaire is put into the hands of interviewers?
7. Why is pretesting a questionnaire important? Are there some situations in which pretesting is not necessary?

8. Design three open-ended and three closed-ended questions to measure consumers' attitudes toward BMW automobiles.

9. What's wrong with the following questions?
   a. How do you like the flavor of this high-quality Maxwell House coffee?
   b. What do you think of the taste and texture of this Sara Lee coffee cake?
   c. We are conducting a study for Bulova watches. What do you think of the quality of Bulova watches?

10. What do you see as the major advantages of using a field management company? What are the drawbacks?

11. Discuss the advantages and disadvantages of Web-based questionnaires.

(Team Activity) 12. Divide the class into groups of four or five. Next, match the groups evenly into supplier and client teams. The instructor will then pair a client team with a supplier team. Each client team should pick some aspect of the university such as student housing, student transportation, sports, sororities, fraternities, food on campus, or some other aspect of student life. Next, the client team should create four management objectives for their topic and construct a questionnaire to meet the management objectives. In addition, the questionnaire should include the following demographics: age, gender, major, and others determined by your instructor. Once the client team approves the questionnaire, both the client and supplier team members should complete 10 interviews each. The results should then be presented to the class. *Note:* this data can be formatted into SPSS for more detailed analysis later in the text.

WORKING THE NET

1. How might the Internet affect questionnaire design in the future?

2. Using Dogpile or another search engine, type in "questionnaire design." Report to the class on two questionnaire design software programs you find on the Internet.

3. Go to *www.sawtoothsoftware.com* and describe the capabilities of SSI Web. Compare this to the offerings of *www.websurveyor.com*.

REAL-LIFE RESEARCH • 11.1

Understanding Buyer Behavior

Yes, what you see below is an actual questionnaire (with very minimal modifications). It was a student-designed questionnaire (not from a business school) intended to understand shopping behavior in a midwestern city. It violates numerous principles of questionnaire design. See how many you can find as you read through the instrument.

Survey Instrument

1. How old are you? _____
2. How old is your husband/wife? _____

3. How long have you been married? _____
4. What is the highest level of education you or your husband/wife have achieved?
   a. No formal education
   b. Primary education
   c. Secondary education
   d. College
   e. Two-year college
   f. Four-year college
   g. Graduate college
5. What is the highest level of education your partner has achieved?
   a. No formal education
   b. Primary education
   c. Secondary education
   d. College
   e. Two-year college
   f. Four-year college
   g. Graduate college
6. Are you currently employed or engaged in an income-generating business?
   a. Yes
   b. No
7. (IF ANSWER IS YES, PROCEED WITH QUESTION #8. OTHERWISE, SKIP TO QUESTION #9.) How much do you make per month from your employment and/or business?
   a. _____ Enter amount in dollars.
8. Is your husband/wife currently employed or engaged in an income-generating business?
   a. Yes
   b. No
9. (IF ANSWER IS YES, PROCEED WITH QUESTION #10. OTHERWISE, SKIP TO QUESTION #11.) How much does your husband/wife make per month from his employment and/or business?
   a. _____ Enter amount in dollars.
10. Do you and your husband have any children?
    a. Yes
    b. No
11. (IF ANSWER IS YES, PROCEED WITH QUESTION #12. OTHERWISE, SKIP TO QUESTION #14.) How many children do you have?
    a. _____ Enter exact number.
12. What are the ages of your children? _____
13. Do they go to school? Where? _____
14. Between you and your husband, who is the dominant decision maker concerning general family issues such as where to live, when to go on vacations, what furniture to buy, etc.?
    a. I am
    b. My husband
    c. Neither or both
15. Are there any other adult family members living with you and your husband?
    a. Yes
    b. No
    c. Sometimes. Who? _____
16. Where do you shop? _____

17. Why there and not at another place? _____

_____

_____

18. How would you describe what they sell?
    a. Very good
    b. Quite good
    c. Not very good
    d. Poor
19. How did you learn about this store?
    a. On TV
    b. On the Internet
    c. Through friends
    d. Advertisement
    e. Newspaper
    f. I just happened to be passing by.
20. I think my friends would enjoy shopping at this store.
    a. Very strongly agree
    b. Somewhat agree
    c. Agree
    d. Don't really agree
    e. Strongly disagree

21. What do you like best? _____

    _____

    _____

22. What could be improved? _____

    _____

    _____

Questions

1. Critique each question and explain how it could be improved.
2. Suggest some questions that could be used to understand shopping behavior, for both goods and services, in a midwestern city.
3. How should the revised questionnaire be reordered?

REAL-LIFE RESEARCH • 11.2

S. T. Arrow

S. T. Arrow owned a chain of dry cleaners in Portland, Oregon. Competition from One-Hour Martinizing and a regional chain had lowered Arrow's market share from 14 to 12 percent. Moreover, his overall profits had fallen 11 percent from the previous year. Arrow decided that an aggressive marketing strategy was in order. Before establishing such a strategy, he felt that a thorough study of the dry cleaning market was needed. The following questionnaire was created by Arrow and given to each customer as the customer left one of Arrow's stores.

Dry Cleaning Questionnaire

Name_____

Address _____

Phone number_____

Where do you take your dry cleaning and laundry? _____

How much do you spend on dry cleaning/laundry?_____

Sex: Male _____   Female _____

Age Group: Under 30 _____ 30–40 _____ 40–50 _____ 50–60 _____ Over 60 _____

Marital Status: Single _____ Married _____

Income: Under $20,000 _____ $20,000–40,000 _____ $41,000–80,000 _____

     Over $80,000 _____

Number living in home: Alone _____ 2 people _____ 3 people _____

4 people _____ 5 people or more _____

Home: Rent _____ Own _____ What type of housing? _____

Education: High school _____ Associate degree _____

     Bachelor's degree _____ Master's degree _____ More _____

1. How long have you been using your dry cleaner? _____

2. How would you rate it? Great _____ Good _____ OK _____

Not too good _____ Bad _____

3. The dry cleaning establishment

	I now use offers	I would like to use if would offer
Convenience		
—All work done on premises	_____	_____
—Wash'n'wear cleaning services	_____	_____
—Pressing while you wait	_____	_____
—Washing while you wait	_____	_____
—A drive-through window	_____	_____
—Computerized receipts and organization	_____	_____
—Shirt laundry service	_____	_____
—An outlet for drop off/pick up	_____	_____
—Machines to pick up/drop off after hours	_____	_____
—A special for people moving into a new location where the cleaners pick up, clean, and deliver rugs and drapes for new home	_____	_____

	I now use offers	I would like to use if would offer
4. Services		
—Shoe repair	_____	_____
—Shoe shining	_____	_____
—Mending	_____	_____
—Altering and tailoring	_____	_____
—Hand pressing	_____	_____
—Dyeing	_____	_____
—Summer/winter clothing storage	_____	_____
—Hand laundering	_____	_____
—Sponged and pressed	_____	_____
—Fur storage	_____	_____
5. For Sale		
—Ties and other accessories	_____	_____
—Spot removers, lint brushes, etc.	_____	_____
—Buttons, thread, zippers, etc.	_____	_____
—Woolite	_____	_____
6. Who in your home drops off/picks up the dry cleaning/laundry?		
—Wife/mother/self	_____	_____
—Husband/father/self	_____	_____
—Each decides their own clothing is ready	_____	_____
—We take turns	_____	_____

7. Who within the household decides that the clothing is in need of dry cleaning?
—Wife/mother/self _____ _____
—Husband/father/self _____ _____
—Each decides their own clothing is ready _____ _____
—Other family member/self _____ _____

8. Please check one for each topic.

	A) I am this type	**B) I would like to remain as this type**
—I hate housework. I just hate having to do it.	_____	_____
—I'd rather pay more to enjoy more. It's easier to pay someone to clean my home and clothes so that I'm free to do what I want to do.	_____	_____
—I enjoy being at home. I was brought up believing a woman's place is in the home and that's where I'm happy.	_____	_____
—I like cleaning my home. It gives me a good feeling.	_____	_____
—Since I have small children, I'm at home, so I clean. But if I were working, it would be easier to have someone come in.	_____	_____
—I don't feel right having someone else cleaning up after me. I find myself cleaning before they come and after they leave. They don't clean the way I do.	_____	_____

9. Check the phrase in each group that best describes
(Check one for each column)

	Your present dry cleaner	**The way you would like your dry cleaner to be or remain**
a. Makes me feel like an intruder.	_____	_____
Keeps me waiting.	_____	_____
Is businesslike.	_____	_____
Always has a friendly word.	_____	_____
b. Gives the feeling he's too busy for me.	_____	_____
Forgets my name when they're crowded.	_____	_____
Always says hello even when they're busy.	_____	_____
Takes the time to treat me individually no matter what.	_____	_____
c. There's a chemical odor, and the posters are outdated and curled at the ends.	_____	_____
There's nothing noticeable about the shop good or bad.	_____	_____
The shop smells clean, the clothes are scientifically racked, and the posters are helpful.	_____	_____
d. Standardized service	_____	_____
Efficient but distant	_____	_____
Interested in personal requirements	_____	_____
Go out of their way to please.	_____	_____
e. The shop leaves an unkempt impression.	_____	_____
Store is neat but cluttered.	_____	_____
There is space to move around.	_____	_____
Shop has a warm, cared-for look.	_____	_____
f. The store could use a thorough cleaning.	_____	_____
The shop is acceptably clean.	_____	_____
The store is assuringly sanitary.	_____	_____

g. There's never an answer to questions.   _____   _____
   I must point out spots, belts, loose buttons.   _____   _____
   We discuss whether it can be cleaned.   _____   _____
   The dry cleaner explains particular
      processes and new chemicals.   _____   _____

Questions

1. Critique S. T. Arrow's questionnaire.
2. What additional topics should have been covered?
3. Discuss the sampling procedure.
4. Did S. T. Arrow develop his questionnaire in a scientific manner?

BASIC SAMPLING ISSUES

LEARNING OBJECTIVES

1.	To understand the concept of sampling.
2.	To learn the steps in developing a sampling plan.
3.	To understand the concepts of sampling error and nonsampling error.
4.	To understand the differences between probability samples and nonprobability samples.
5.	To understand sampling implications of surveying over the Internet.

Elizabeth Dodd, director of marketing research for Texas Power (TXP), is in the process of reviewing the results of a survey just completed over the Internet. The survey targeted household decision makers for energy needs in the state of Texas. Dodd conducted the Internet survey at the urging of her boss, the senior marketing officer for TXP, who was concerned about the increasing cost of marketing research studies and the length of time it took to complete them. Because the electric power industry in Texas is deregulated, energy producers like TXP feel pressured to develop strategies to hold on to current residential electric customers in their traditional service areas and to begin to market to potential customers outside of their regulated market area. The need to develop new strategies and make decisions for the postregulation era has necessitated spending large sums of money on marketing research—much more than TXP was accustomed to spending. A research firm marketing the Internet approach for data collection has convinced Dodd's boss that the Internet approach offered a solution to the cost and time problems.

For this first study, the research firm had obtained 12,435 completed surveys at a cost of just under $100,000 in less than 4 days. The survey was hosted on the research firm's Web site, and TXP was not identified as its sponsor. No comprehensive list of e-mail addresses for Texas homeowners was available, so the research firm placed banner ads on the sites of AOL, Yahoo!, Northern Light, and Excite. They argued that these banner ads were seen by millions of people every day and that therefore the resulting sample would be representative of the population of all Texas household decision makers for energy needs. The banner ads made it clear that the survey was for Texas homeowners only and that a prize drawing would be held from among those who responded. Top prizes were five high-definition televisions and five DVD players.

Looking at the survey results, Dodd is concerned that the sample may not be totally representative of the target population and that the results may therefore be misleading. First of all, the survey questions provide no means of determining whether individual respondents are Texas homeowners. They may not be from Texas, and, if they are from Texas, then they may not be homeowners. Dodd has compared the demographic characteristics of the Internet sample to those of random telephone samples from prior studies, and the Internet sample appears to be significantly younger, better educated, more affluent, and more male. She is concerned that some demographic groups have been excluded or, at least, undersampled and that the opinions of these groups are not adequately reflected in the sample. She wants to discuss these issues with her boss, but given his current excitement about the new survey medium, she knows that she must be well prepared to argue her case. In addition, the cost savings are dramatic. A telephone survey with a similar sample size would have cost over $200,000. Consider what she should say to her boss to make her point regarding the potential unrepresentativeness of the Internet sample. ■

The material in this chapter will put you in a position to make a decision like the one she is facing.

Concept of Sampling

> **sampling**
> Process of obtaining infor-
> mation from a subset of a
> larger group.

Sampling refers to the process of obtaining information from a subset (a sample) of a larger group (the universe or population). A user of marketing research then takes the results from the sample and makes estimates of the characteristics of the larger group. The motivation for sampling is to be able to make these estimates more quickly and at a lower cost than would be possible by any other means. It has been shown time and again that sampling a small percentage of a population can result in very accurate estimates. An example that you are probably familiar with is polling in connection with a presidential election. Most major polls use samples of 1,000 to 1,500 people to make predictions regarding the voting behavior of tens of millions of people, and their predictions have proven to be remarkably accurate.

The key to making accurate predictions about the characteristics or behavior of a large population on the basis of a relatively small sample lies in the way in which individuals are selected for the sample. It is critical that they be selected in a scientific manner, which ensures that the sample is representative—that it is a true miniature of the population. All of the major types of people who make up the population of interest should be represented in the sample in the same proportions in which they are found in the larger population. This sounds simple, and as a concept, it is simple. However, achieving this goal in sampling from a human population is not easy.

Population

> **population**
> Entire group of people
> about whom information
> is needed; also called
> *universe* or *population of
> interest*.

In discussions of sampling, the terms *population* and *universe* are often used interchangeably.[1] In this textbook, we will use the term *population*. The **population**, or *population of interest*, is the entire group of people about whom the researcher needs to obtain information. One of the first steps in the sampling process is defining the population of interest. This often involves defining the target market for the product or service in question.

Consider a product concept test for a new nonprescription cold symptom–relief product, such as Contac. You might take the position that the population of interest includes everyone, because everyone suffers from colds from time to time. Although this is true, not everyone buys a nonprescription cold symptom-relief product when he or she gets a cold. In this case, the first task in the screening process would be to determine whether people have purchased or used one or more of a number of competing brands during some time period. Only those who had purchased or used one of these brands would be included in the population of interest.

Defining the population of interest is a key step in the sampling process. There are no specific rules to follow in defining the population of interest. What the researcher must do is apply logic and judgment in addressing the basic issue: Whose opinions are needed in order to satisfy the objectives of the research? Often, the definition of the population is based on the characteristics of current or target customers.

Sample versus Census

> **census**
> Collection of data ob-
> tained from or about
> every member of the pop-
> ulation of interest.

In a **census**, data are obtained from or about every member of the population of interest. Censuses are seldom employed in marketing research, as populations of interest to marketers normally include many thousands or even millions of individuals. The cost and time required to collect data from a population of this magnitude are so great that censuses are usually out of the question. It has been demonstrated repeatedly that a relatively small but carefully chosen sample can very accurately reflect the characteristics of the

PRACTICING
MARKETING RESEARCH

Why the Result of a Sample Can Be More Accurate Than the Result of a Census

That a sample result can be more accurate than a census result is not intuitively obvious. After all, a census result is subject only to measurement errors, whereas a sample result is subject to both measurement errors and sampling errors—that is, errors also occur because only a portion of the population is being studied in the sample. To see why a sample result can be more accurate than a census result, consider the 10 percent of the housing units of, say, a county who do not respond to the initial census enumeration. A census enumeration of the nonresponding housing units will be subject to a variety of measurement errors—some respondents will be entirely missed, information for others from secondary sources will be incorrect, and so forth.

Should a more effective enumeration method be available, although at a higher cost per respondent, a sample using this more effective enumeration method may be selected at the same total cost, or at a lower total cost, as

for the standard enumeration of the 10 percent of the population remaining. It may then be found that the reduction in measurement errors achieved with the more effective enumeration method may more than compensate for the presence of sampling errors when a sample of the 10 percent of the population remaining is utilized. If funding were available, it might be preferable to employ this more effective enumeration method for the entire population, but realistically it would be employed only where it is most needed.

The achievement of greater accuracy depends on how much more accurate the refined enumeration procedure is than the standard procedure and how much greater is its cost.[2] These factors need to be evaluated for each specific case to determine the comparative accuracy of census and sample results. It should also be noted that more refined enumeration methods can sometimes only be employed with smaller-scale (that is, sample) studies. Reasons for this include the need for highly trained enumerators who are available only in limited numbers and the use of burdensome questionnaires that can be employed only with a small sample.

---

population from which it is drawn. A **sample** is a subset of all the members of a population. Information is obtained from or about a sample and used to make estimates about various characteristics of the total population. Ideally, the sample from or about which information is obtained is a representative cross section of the total population.

Although censuses are used infrequently in marketing research, there are instances in which they are appropriate and feasible. For example, a census may be useful to an industrial products firm that has only a small number of customers for some highly specialized product it sells. In such a situation, it may be possible to obtain information from the entire population of customers.

Note that the popular belief that a census provides more accurate results than a sample is not necessarily true. In a census of a human population, there are many impediments to actually obtaining information from every member of the population. The researcher may not be able to obtain a complete and accurate list of the entire population, or certain members of the population may refuse to provide information. Because of these barriers, the ideal census is seldom attainable, even with very small populations. See Practicing Marketing Research above for more discussion of barriers. You may have read or heard about these types of problems in connection with the 1990 and 2000 U.S. Census.[3]

> **sample**
> Subset of all the members of a population of interest.

Developing a Sampling Plan

The process of developing an operational sampling plan can be summarized by the seven steps shown in Exhibit 12.1. These steps are defining the population, choosing a data-collection method, identifying a sampling frame, selecting a sampling method, determining sample size, developing operational procedures, and executing the sampling plan.

Step One: Define the Population of Interest

The basic issue in developing a sampling plan is to specify the characteristics of those individuals or things (for example, customers, companies, stores) from whom or about whom information is needed to meet the research objectives. The population of interest is often specified in terms of geographic area, demographic characteristics, product or service usage characteristics, and/or awareness measures (see Exhibit 12.2). In surveys, the question of whether a particular individual does or does not belong to the population of interest is often dealt with by means of screening questions. Even with a list of the population and a sample from that list, researchers still need screening questions to qualify potential respondents. Exhibit 12.3 provides a sample sequence of screening questions.

In addition to defining who will be included in the population of interest, researchers should also define the characteristics of individuals who should be excluded. For example, most commercial marketing research surveys exclude some individuals for so-called security reasons. Very frequently, one of the first questions on a survey asks whether the respondent or anyone in the respondent's immediate family works in marketing research, advertising, or the product or service area at issue in the survey (see, for example, question 5 in Exhibit 12.3). If the individual answers "Yes" to this question, the interview is terminated. This type of question is called a *security question* because those who work in the industries in question are viewed as security risks. They may be competitors or work for competitors, and managers do not want to give them any indication of what their company may be planning to do.

There may be reasons to exclude individuals for other reasons. For example, the Dr Pepper Company might wish to do a survey among individuals who drink five or more

Exhibit 12.1

Developing a Sampling Plan

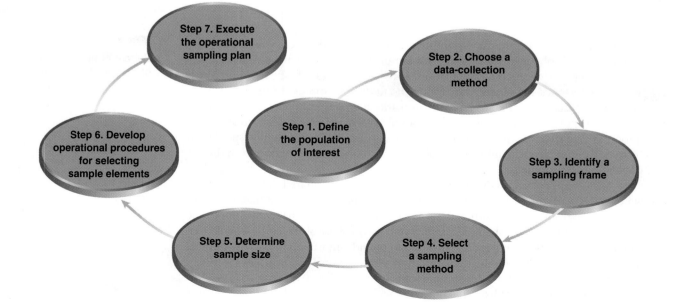

EXHIBIT 12.2	Some Bases for Defining the Population of Interest
Geographic Area	What geographic area is to be sampled? This is usually a question of the client's scope of operation. The area could be a city, a county, a metropolitan area, a state, a group of states, the entire United States, or a number of countries.
Demographics	Given the objectives of the research and the target market for the product, whose opinions, reactions, and so on are relevant? For example, does the sampling plan require information from women over 18, women 18–34, or women 18–34 with household incomes over $35,000 per year who work and who have preschool children?
Usage	In addition to geographic area and/or demographics, the population of interest frequently is defined in terms of some product or service use requirement. This is usually stated in terms of use versus nonuse or use of some quantity of the product or service over a specified period of time. The following examples of use screening questions illustrate the point: ■ Do you drink five or more cans, bottles, or glasses of diet soft drinks in a typical week? ■ Have you traveled to Europe for vacation or business purposes in the past two years? ■ Have you or has anyone in your immediate family been in a hospital for an overnight or extended stay in the past two years?
Awareness	The researcher may be interested in surveying those individuals who are aware of the company's advertising, to explore what the advertising communicated about the characteristics of the product or service.

cans, bottles, or glasses of soft drink in a typical week but do not drink Dr Pepper, because the company is interested in developing a better understanding of heavy soft drink users who do not drink its product. Therefore, researchers would exclude those who drank one or more cans, bottles, or glasses of Dr Pepper in the past week.

Step Two: Choose a Data-Collection Method

The selection of a data-collection method has implications for the sampling process. As noted in the vignette, for example, both telephone interviews and Internet surveys have certain inherent disadvantages in regard to sampling.

Step Three: Identify a Sampling Frame

The third step in the process is to identify the **sampling frame**, which is a list of the members or elements of the population from which units to be sampled are to be selected. Identifying the sampling frame may simply mean specifying a procedure for generating such a list. In the ideal situation, the list of population members is complete and accurate. Unfortunately, there usually is no such list. For example, the population for a study may be defined as those individuals who have spent two or more hours on the Internet in the past week; there can be no complete listing of these individuals. In such instances, the sampling frame specifies a procedure that will produce a representative sample with the desired characteristics. Thus, there seldom is a perfect correspondence between the sampling frame and the population of interest.

> **sampling frame**
> List of population elements from which units to be sampled can be selected or a specified procedure for generating such a list.

For example, a telephone book might be used as the sample frame for a telephone survey sample in which the population of interest was all households in a particular city. However, the telephone book does not include households that do not have telephones and those with unlisted numbers. It is well established that those with listed telephone numbers are significantly different from those with unlisted numbers in regard to a number of important characteristics. Subscribers who voluntarily unlist their phone numbers

---

Exhibit 12.3

Example of Screening Question Sequence to Determine Population Membership

---

Hello. I'm _____ with _____ Research. We're conducting a survey about products used in the home. May I ask you a few questions?

1. Have you been interviewed about any products or advertising in the past 3 months?

Yes	(TERMINATE AND TALLY)
No	(CONTINUE)

2. Which of the following hair care products, if any, have you used in the past month? (HAND PRODUCT CARD TO RESPONDENT; CIRCLE ALL MENTIONS)

1 Regular shampoo

2 Dandruff shampoo

3 Creme rinse/instant conditioner

4 "Intensive" conditioner

(INSTRUCTIONS: IF "4" IS CIRCLED—SKIP TO Q. 4 AND CONTINUE FOR "INTENSIVE" QUOTA; IF "3" IS CIRCLED BUT NOT "4"—ASK Q. 3 AND CONTINUE FOR "INSTANT" QUOTA)

3. You said that you have used a creme rinse/instant conditioner in the past month. Have you used either a creme rinse or an instant conditioner in the past week?

Yes (used in the past week)	(CONTINUE FOR "INSTANT" QUOTA)
No (not used in past week)	(TERMINATE AND TALLY)

4. Into which of the following groups does your age fall? (READ LIST, CIRCLE AGE)

X	Under 18	(CHECK AGE QUOTAS)
1	18–24	
2	25–34	
3	35–44	
X	45 or over	

5. Previous surveys have shown that people who work in certain jobs may have different reactions to certain products. Now, do you or does any member of your immediate family work for an advertising agency, a marketing research firm, a public relations firm, or a company that manufactures or sells personal care products?

Yes	(TERMINATE AND TALLY)
No	(CONTINUE)

(IF RESPONDENT QUALIFIES, INVITE HIM OR HER TO PARTICIPATE AND COMPLETE NAME GRID BELOW)

---

are more likely to be renters, live in the central city, have recently moved, have larger families, have younger children, and have lower incomes than their counterparts with listed numbers.[5] There are also significant differences between the two groups in terms of purchase, ownership, and use of certain products.

Unlisted numbers are more prevalent in the western United States, in metropolitan areas, among nonwhites, and among those in the 18 to 34 age group. These findings have been confirmed in a number of studies.[6] The extent of the problem is suggested by the data in Exhibit 12.4. The implications are clear: if representative samples are to be obtained in telephone surveys, researchers should use procedures that will produce samples including appropriate proportions of households with unlisted numbers.

PRACTICING MARKETING RESEARCH

Don't Call Us, We Won't Call You Either—New Problems in Telephone Sampling

The establishment of the national Do-Not-Call (DNC) Registry in October 2003 may have been a boon to the 60 million directory-listed American households (as of May 2004) that entered their home telephone number on the list to stop telemarketers from calling them, but it created serious problems for market researchers. The exclusion of this many households could have a deep impact on the accuracy of any future telephone-based survey sampling.

Initially, it seemed that the DNC exempted registered households from all unsolicited telemarketing calls. Then a court case in Colorado challenged this, and the new ruling by the 10th Circuit Court of Appeals was that while DNC could rightfully stop commercial sales calls, described as "core commercial speech," marketing survey calls were still permissible. Even so, these 60 million households had already indicated that they preferred to not be called by anyone.

The trouble was that their exclusion would create "significant coverage bias" when including U.S. telephone households in any marketing survey, concluded Survey Sampling International (SSI) of Fairfield, Connecticut. SSI is a major survey sampling resource for marketing researchers. SSI was fairly certain about the typical demographics of DNC-listed households, and it wanted them back in the survey mix. DNC types tended to be older, nonminority, and of a higher income and education level than the average American.

To leave out this many people who occupied so clear a demographic slice would jeopardize any telephone survey's accuracy. Furthermore, the exclusion of the DNC-listed households from telephone surveys would increase the "not a working phone" rates for Random Digit Dial samples, thus hobbling the methodology.

Interestingly, a Harris Poll of 3,378 U.S. adults in January 2004 showed that 68 percent did not know if survey research firms and pollsters were still allowed to call them if they were DNC-registered; 41 percent said they had been polled at least once since signing up their telephone number. The Harris Poll also indicated that 57 percent of U.S. adults had joined the DNC list.

As for a solution, SSI knew that to flag the DNC households for special treatment, a popular idea for a while, would be technically illegal. Maybe they could simply call the DNC households as if they were not DNC-listed. SSI's research showed that DNC households will cooperate with market survey calls only slightly less than non-DNC numbers, in the neighborhood of 50 percent.[4]

One possibility is **random-digit dialing**, which generates lists of telephone numbers at random. This procedure can become fairly complex. Fortunately, companies such as Survey Sampling offer random-digit samples at a very attractive price. Details on the way such companies draw their samples can be found at *http://www.ssisamples.com/random_digit.html*. Developing an appropriate sampling frame is often one of the most challenging problems facing the researcher.[7]

> **random-digit dialing**
> Method of generating lists of telephone numbers at random.

Step Four: Select a Sampling Method

The fourth step in developing a sampling plan is selection of a sampling method, which will depend on the objectives of the study, the financial resources available, time limitations, and the nature of the problem under investigation. The major alternative sampling methods can

| EXHIBIT 12.4 | Household Phone Statistics by State in 2004 |

STATE	Population 1-Jan-04	Households 1-Jan-04	Estimated Telephone Households	% With Phone	RDD Listed Households	% Listed
Alabama	4,517,136	1,822,088	1,748,531	96%	1,259,537	72%
Alaska	655,899	234,433	227,749	97%	151,271	66%
Arizona	5,719,160	2,167,325	2,097,004	97%	1,013,547	48%
Arkansas	2,741,511	1,093,223	1,036,476	95%	717,435	69%
California	35,979,311	12,227,339	12,059,310	99%	5,570,852	46%
Colorado	4,625,293	1,797,550	1,774,673	99%	992,864	56%
Connecticut	3,507,246	1,357,133	1,342,738	99%	952,701	71%
Delaware	827,856	323,359	319,312	99%	211,755	66%
Washington DC	560,725	256,560	250,276	98%	141,585	57%
Florida	17,342,822	7,255,877	7,115,986	98%	4,741,206	67%
Georgia	8,836,255	3,380,788	3,284,648	97%	2,146,325	65%
Hawaii	1,272,696	429,724	421,464	98%	229,768	55%
Idaho	1,388,573	507,623	498,526	98%	324,410	65%
Illinois	12,725,117	4,736,295	4,597,367	97%	2,540,032	55%
Indiana	6,230,346	2,465,349	2,396,774	97%	1,550,538	65%
Iowa	2,949,245	1,174,389	1,154,652	98%	796,270	69%
Kansas	2,733,795	1,074,016	1,044,740	97%	688,755	66%
Kentucky	4,140,891	1,704,528	1,629,916	96%	1,065,731	65%
Louisiana	4,505,373	1,755,361	1,685,873	96%	1,199,469	71%
Maine	1,315,211	550,163	543,327	99%	421,225	78%
Maryland	5,574,702	2,117,321	2,085,320	98%	1,314,780	63%
Massachusetts	6,457,204	2,519,388	2,496,407	99%	1,676,116	67%
Michigan	10,121,382	3,984,102	3,884,355	97%	2,536,569	65%
Minnesota	5,101,284	2,027,904	2,006,263	99%	1,398,406	70%
Mississippi	2,892,228	1,103,166	1,034,634	94%	737,337	71%
Missouri	5,737,314	2,318,958	2,254,844	97%	1,490,840	66%
Montana	922,368	373,148	363,002	97%	240,299	66%
Nebraska	1,748,000	693,868	681,030	98%	432,229	63%
Nevada	2,315,504	880,502	863,425	98%	377,145	44%
New Hampshire	1,303,425	508,725	503,462	99%	369,832	73%
New Jersey	8,707,156	3,199,381	3,143,179	98%	1,956,163	62%
New Mexico	1,892,304	724,405	685,442	95%	380,692	56%
New York	19,254,372	7,204,879	7,072,175	98%	4,685,488	66%
North Carolina	8,517,110	3,462,050	3,367,113	97%	2,161,991	64%
North Dakota	631,440	259,937	255,318	98%	178,358	70%
Ohio	11,459,952	4,663,484	4,565,767	98%	2,648,643	58%
Oklahoma	3,530,711	1,411,715	1,349,700	96%	874,190	65%
Oregon	3,602,559	1,418,021	1,396,212	98%	763,708	55%
Pennsylvania	12,392,109	4,937,535	4,871,855	99%	2,986,805	61%
Rhode Island	1,084,664	429,549	423,612	99%	263,950	62%
South Carolina	4,188,493	1,663,078	1,599,303	96%	1,072,268	67%
South Dakota	767,184	301,193	292,737	97%	205,286	70%
Tennessee	5,888,107	2,394,744	2,328,315	97%	1,550,987	67%
Texas	22,508,240	8,216,915	7,982,006	97%	5,064,309	63%
Utah	2,387,580	770,119	759,317	99%	457,713	60%
Vermont	622,165	252,576	248,941	99%	202,284	81%
Virginia	7,480,156	2,955,415	2,897,759	98%	1,883,563	65%
Washington	6,204,912	2,416,587	2,385,477	99%	1,293,432	54%
West Virginia	1,811,363	761,032	726,246	95%	496,642	68%
Wisconsin	5,505,083	2,222,958	2,188,750	98%	1,620,450	74%
Wyoming	503,630	202,957	196,722	97%	126,481	64%
USA	293,687,162	112,708,735	110,138,030	98%	68,162,232	62%

Source: Survey Sampling, Inc., July 2005

be grouped under two headings: probability sampling methods and nonprobability sampling methods.

Probability samples are selected in such a way that every element of the population has a known, nonzero likelihood of selection.[8] Simple random sampling is the best known and most widely used probability sampling method. With probability sampling, the researcher must closely adhere to precise selection procedures that avoid arbitrary or biased selection of sample elements. When these procedures are followed strictly, the laws of probability hold, allowing calculation of the extent to which a sample value can be expected to differ from a population value. This difference is referred to as *sampling error.*

Nonprobability samples are those in which specific elements from the population have been selected in a nonrandom manner. *Nonrandomness* results when population elements are selected on the basis of convenience—because they are easy or inexpensive to reach. *Purposeful nonrandomness* occurs when a sampling plan systematically excludes or overrepresents certain subsets of the population. For example, if a sample designed to solicit the opinions of all women over the age of 18 were based on a telephone survey conducted during the day on weekdays, it would systematically exclude working women. See Practicing Marketing Research on page 382.

Probability samples offer several advantages over nonprobability samples, including the following:

☐ The researcher can be sure of obtaining information from a representative cross section of the population of interest.

☐ Sampling error can be computed.

☐ The survey results can be projected to the total population. For example, if 5 percent of the individuals in a probability sample give a particular response, the researcher can project this percentage, plus or minus the sampling error, to the total population.

On the other hand, probability samples have a number of disadvantages, the most important of which is that they are usually more expensive than nonprobability samples of the same size. The rules for selection increase interviewing costs and professional time spent in signing and executing the sample design.[9]

The disadvantages of nonprobability samples are essentially the reverse of the advantages of probability samples:

☐ The researcher does not know the degree to which the sample is representative of the population from which it was drawn.

☐ Sampling error cannot be computed.

☐ The results cannot and should not be projected to the total population.

Given the disadvantages of nonprobability samples, you may wonder why they are used so frequently by marketing researchers. The reasons for their use relate to their inherent advantages, which include the following:

☐ Nonprobability samples cost less than probability samples. Lower costs have considerable appeal in those situations where accuracy is not of critical importance. Exploratory research is an example of such a situation.

The population for a study must be defined. For example, a population for a study may be defined as those individuals who have spent two or more hours on the Internet in the past week.

▷ **probability samples**
Samples in which every element of the population has a known, nonzero likelihood of selection.

▷ **nonprobability samples**
Samples in which specific elements from the population have been selected in a nonrandom manner.

PRACTICING MARKETING RESEARCH

Why This Online Sample Was Not a Probability Sample

Harris Interactive, world-renowned for its Harris Polls, published the results of its 2005 Telecommunications Report in June 2005. The study had been conducted online in April 2005 using a sample of 1,088 adults (18 and older). Its results showed that 10 percent of U.S. adults now use wireless or cellular phones exclusively and have abandoned their connection to traditional phones.

In their methodology discussion, Harris Interactive researchers noted that they had weighted the demographics of their sampling pool, in terms of gender, race or ethnicity, educational level, religious affiliation, income, and sexual orientation, to match that of the total U.S. population. They further weighted the data, using propensity score weighting, to adjust for the respondents' propensity to be online.

Harris Interactive researchers explained that theoretically, using a probability sample of this size, they could be 95 percent certain their sampling error was ±3 percent. But some skepticism is in order, they added, because the sampling error for people saying they have disconnected their conventional phone systems (420 respondents) is ±3 percent.

Complicating the picture is that the additional sources of error involved in polls such as this ultimately are more problematic for the accuracy of the final data than anything a theoretical calculation of sampling error would indicate. Specifically, these sources of error include nonresponse (a respondent refusing to be interviewed), the way a question is worded or the order in which questions are presented, and the style, even the fact, of weighting. "It is impossible to quantify the errors that may result from these factors," the researchers said.[10]

☐ Nonprobability samples ordinarily can be gathered more quickly than probability samples can.

☐ Nonprobability samples of the population are reasonably representative if collected in a careful, thorough manner.[11]

In addition to choosing between probability and nonprobability sampling methods, the researcher must choose among sampling procedures. These choices are summarized in Exhibit 12.5 and discussed in greater detail later in the chapter.

Step Five: Determine Sample Size

Once a sampling method has been chosen, the next step is to determine the appropriate sample size. (The issue of sample size determination is covered in detail in Chapter 13.) In the case of nonprobability samples, researchers tend to rely on such factors as available budget, rules of thumb, and number of subgroups to be analyzed in their determination of sample size. However, with probability samples, researchers use formulas to calculate the sample size required, given target levels of *acceptable error* (the difference between sample result and population value) and *levels of confidence* (the likelihood that the confidence interval—sample result plus or minus the acceptable error—will take in the true population value). As noted earlier, the ability to make statistical inferences about population values based on sample results is the major advantage of probability samples.

PRACTICING MARKETING RESEARCH

Minimizing Sampling Error in an RDD (Random Digit Dialing) Survey of Hispanic Online Users

In July 2005, a new AOL-Roper study was published documenting new Web industry trends. This was the third annual AOL/Roper Hispanic Cyberstudy, and this year's results showed that 52 percent of online Hispanics access the Internet through a broadband connection at home and that the number of new Hispanic online users (14 percent in the first six months of 2005) was double that of the general at home new-to-the-Web population.

Of even greater interest to marketing researchers is how the AOL/Roper methodology adjusted its final data knowing it had drawn "disproportionate" samples from among five groups of American homes based on the density of their Hispanic population. Had the study compilers not adjusted their data for the disproportional sampling, the sampling error would have been high. Instead, based on a sample of 603 Hispanic home-based online users (polled by way of Random Digit Dialing, or RDD), the final sampling error was only ±4 percent. This approach resulted in a reduced sampling error over a comparable 2004 sample of 301 home Internet users drawn from the general (not specifically Hispanic) U.S. population. In that study, the sampling error was ±6 percent.

To compensate for the disproportionate sample drawn from densely populated Hispanic population centers, the AOL/Roper researchers then took larger proportions for their sample from higher density areas than if they had merely been sampling the general public. Next they weighted the data to accommodate this disproportional sampling. "While the technique greatly increases the incidence of Hispanic households, the result after weighting is a sample that is representative of all American Hispanics," researchers said. They added that these samples were comparable to those derived from a pure RDD.[12]

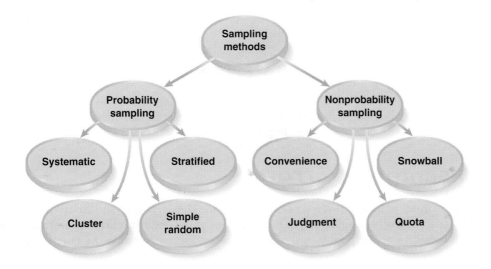

Exhibit 12.5

Classification of Sampling Methods

PRACTICING MARKETING RESEARCH

Random Error or Bias in Florida?

The results of the 2000 presidential election in Florida provide an interesting example of the results of random and systematic error in sampling. A random error affects all votes with equal probability and, therefore, does not affect the outcome. This is because random errors will affect both candidates equally. If all voters voted in exactly the same manner, say the old punch card system, all voter punch cards were handled in the same way and to the same degree, and all votes were counted in the same machine or in the same type of machine, there would still be errors in the counting, but those errors would be randomly distributed across the two candidates. The winning candidate would be extremely likely to reflect the will of the people who voted.

But if there are differences in the way the voters voted (punch cards versus optical scanner) or the way the votes are counted (machine versus hand), then the errors are no longer random and equally distributed. These errors could favor one candidate over the other. For example, if Bush supporters more often voted using procedures yielding fewer nonvotes than procedures that Gore voters used, then there could be an error favoring Bush. Under this scenario, Bush could win the election, but not reflect the true choice of the people who voted.[14]

Step Six: Develop Operational Procedures for Selecting Sample Elements

The operational procedures to be used in selecting sample elements in the data-collection phase of a project should be developed and specified, whether a probability or a nonprobability sample is being used.[13] However, the procedures are much more critical to the successful execution of a probability sample, in which case they should be detailed, clear, and unambiguous and should eliminate any interviewer discretion regarding the selection of specific sample elements. Failure to develop a proper operational plan for selecting sample elements can jeopardize the entire sampling process. Exhibit 12.6 provides an example of an operational sampling plan.

Step Seven: Execute the Operational Sampling Plan

The final step in the sampling process is execution of the operational sampling plan. This step requires adequate checking to ensure that specified procedures are followed.

Sampling and Nonsampling Errors

Consider a situation in which the goal is to determine the average gross income of the members of a particular population.[15] If the researcher could obtain accurate information about all members of the population, he or she could simply compute the population

Exhibit 12.6

Example of Operational Sampling Plan

In the instructions that follow, refers a segment of land surrounded by roads. In cities, this will be a city block. In rural areas, a your route, proceed down the opposite side of the street, road, or ction. Continue making right turns, where possible, calling at every s made to follow your route around a block. In cities, this will a segment of land surrounded by roads.

1. If you come to a dead e alley, traveling in the a block and return to the starting address without completing four third occupied d one homes, attempt an interview at the starting address. (This should v.)

2. If you go all e block and do not complete the required interviews, proceed to the dwelling on interview of the street (or rural route) that is *nearest* the starting address. Treat it as the se on your Area Location Sheet and interview that house only if the address appears ne on your sheet. If it does not, continue your interviewing to the left of that address. w the right turn rule.

no dwellings on the street or road opposite the starting address for an area, circle the site the starting address, following the right turn rule. (This means that you will circle the ing a clockwise direction.) Attempt interviews at every third dwelling along this route. ling the adjacent block opposite the starting address, you do not complete the nterviews, take the next block found, *following a clockwise direction*. block does not yield the dwellings necessary to complete your assignment, proceed to ocks as necessary to find the required dwellings; follow a clockwise path around the ck.

om "Belden Associates Interviewer Guide," reprinted by permission. The complete guide is over 30 ng and contains maps and other aids for the interviewer.

parameter average gross income. A *population parameter* is a value that defines a true characteristic of a total population. Assume that μ (the population parameter, average gross income) is $42,300. As already noted, it is almost always impossible to measure an entire population (take a census). Instead, the researcher selects a sample and makes inferences about population parameters from sample results. In this case, the researcher might take a sample of 400 from a population of 250,000. An estimate of the average age of the members of the population $(\overline{X})$ would be calculated from the sample values. Assume that the average gross income of the sample members is $41,100. A second random sample of 400 might be drawn from the same population, and the average again computed. In the second case, the average might be $43,400. Additional samples might be chosen, and a mean calculated for each sample. The researcher would find that the means computed for the various samples would be fairly close but not identical to the true population value in most cases.

The accuracy of sample results is affected by two general types of error: sampling error and nonsampling (measurement) error. The following formula represents the effects of these two types of error on estimating a population mean:

$$\overline{X} = \mu \pm \epsilon_s \pm \epsilon_{ns}$$

where $\overline{X}$ = sample mean

μ = true population mean

ϵ_s = sampling error

ϵ_{ns} = nonsampling, or measurement, error

FROM THE FRONT LINE

Secrets of Sample Management

Doug Zook, Operations Manager, DSS Research

#1 Understand what your client's analysis needs are up front. It is important to know if the analysis for a project will require information from a client's database. For instance, a study to gauge physician satisfaction with a health plan may need to include the physicians' specialties in the analysis. Trying to append this information after the study has fielded can introduce error and will hold up analysis while the data are being updated.

#2 Use the right tool for the job. Clients differ in their technical abilities to supply data to you. Some will send data in advanced database formats such as Microsoft SQL server or Oracle, whereas others will only be able to provide an MS Excel file to you, at best. Investing in a good data conversion utility will save a lot of work and headache. Be careful with file types that are not intended for database usage such as MS Excel and Word. Truncated and mismatched data are only a couple of the problems that can arise from using these file types.

#3 Communicate with the programmer of the study. It is very important to communicate effectively with the person programming the study. Many questionnaires include logic that uses information from the ... the programmer and the sam... need to agree on how the data ...ta. Both tured and on the codes to be inclu... the questionnaire will function correctly will fielding.

#4 Keep the original data. When it is ... essary to edit sample data, such as consoli... ing a group of codes into a single group ... stratification purposes, never overwrite the origi... nal data. Instead, make edits in a new location... It is important to be able to reference the origi... nal data later in case questions about the sample composition arise during analysis.

#5 Randomize correctly. When processing data, there are many ways to randomize it, not all of which are truly random. When drawing the random sample from the sample frame, be sure the method chosen is truly random. Failure to do so can result in a skewed sample and introduce bias to the study.

#6 Provide feedback to the client. While processing sample data, mistakes can occur in many technical areas. Clients may have specific requirements about complex stratification schemes or about how the data are to be de-duplicated, for instance. De-duplication refers to removing customers who were interviewed for other studies conducted for the client over the past year for example. It is important to send summary counts of the data to the client before pulling the final random sample. This simple step can help avoid many pitfalls and will give your client more assurance about the process.

> **sampling error**
> Error that occurs because the sample selected is not perfectly representative of the population.

> **nonsampling error**
> All error other than sampling error; also called *measurement error*.

Sampling error results when the sample selected is not perfectly representative of the population. There are two types of sampling error: administrative and random. *Administrative error* relates to the problems in the execution of the sample—that is, flaws in the design or execution of the sample that cause it to not be representative of the population. These types of error can be avoided or minimized by careful attention to the design and execution of the sample. *Random sampling error* is due to chance and cannot be avoided. This type of error can be reduced, but never totally eliminated, by increasing the sample size. **Nonsampling**, or measurement **error**, includes all factors other than sampling error that may cause inaccuracy and bias in the survey results. For an example see Practicing Marketing Research on page 383.

Probability Sampling Methods

As discussed earlier, every element of the population has a known and equal likelihood of being selected for a probability sample. There are four types of probability sampling methods: simple random sampling, systematic sampling, stratified sampling, and cluster sampling.

Simple Random Sampling

Simple random sampling is the purest form of probability sampling. For a simple random sample, the known and equal probability is computed as follows:

$$\text{Probability of selection} = \frac{\text{Sample size}}{\text{Population size}}$$

For example, if the population size is 10,000 and the sample size is 400, the probability of selection is 4 percent:

$$.04 = \frac{400}{10,000}$$

If a sampling frame (listing of all the elements of the population) is available, the researcher can select a **simple random sample** as follows:

1. Assign a number to each element of the population. A population of 10,000 elements would be numbered from 1 to 10,000.
2. Using a table of random numbers (such as Table 1 in Appendix 2, "Statistical Tables"), begin at some arbitrary point and move up, down, or across until 400 (sample size) five-digit numbers between 1 and 10,000 have been chosen. The numbers selected from the table identify specific population elements to be included in the sample.

Simple random sampling is appealing because it seems easy and meets all the necessary requirements of a probability sample. It guarantees that every member of the population has a known and equal chance of being selected for the sample. Simple random sampling begins with a current and complete listing of the population. Such listings, however, are extremely difficult, if not impossible, to obtain. Simple random samples can be obtained in telephone surveys through the use of random digit dialing. They can also be generated from computer files such as customer lists; software programs are available or can be readily written to select random samples that meet all necessary requirements.

> **simple random sample**
> Probability sample selected by assigning a number to every element of the population and then using a table of random numbers to select specific elements for inclusion in the sample.

Systematic Sampling

Because of its simplicity, **systematic sampling** is often used as a substitute for simple random sampling. It produces samples that are almost identical to those generated via simple random sampling.

To obtain a systematic sample, the researcher first numbers the entire population, as in simple random sampling. Then the researcher determines a *skip interval* and selects

> **systematic sampling**
> Probability sampling in which the entire population is numbered and elements are selected using a skip interval.

names based on this interval. The skip interval can be computed very simply through use of the following formula:

$$\text{Skip interval} = \frac{\text{Population size}}{\text{Sample size}}$$

For example, if you were using a local telephone directory and had computed a skip interval of 100, every 100th name would be selected for the sample. The use of this formula would ensure that the entire list was covered.

A random starting point should be used in systematic sampling. For example, if you were using a telephone directory, you would need to draw a random number to determine the page on which to start—say, page 53. You would draw another random number to determine the column to use on that page—for example, the third column. You would draw a final random number to determine the actual starting element in that column—say, the 17th name. From that beginning point, you would employ the skip interval until the desired sample size had been reached.

The main advantage of systematic sampling over simple random sampling is economy. Systematic sampling is often simpler, less time-consuming, and less expensive to use than simple random sampling. The greatest danger lies in the possibility that hidden patterns within the population list may inadvertently be pulled into the sample. However, this danger is remote when alphabetical listings are used.

Stratified Sampling

> **stratified sample**
> Probability sample that is forced to be more representative through simple random sampling of mutually exclusive and exhaustive subsets.

Stratified samples are probability samples that are distinguished by the following procedural steps:

1. The original, or parent, population is divided into two or more mutually exclusive and exhaustive subsets (for example, male and female).

2. Simple random samples of elements from the two or more subsets are chosen independently of each other.

Although the requirements for a stratified sample do not specify the basis on which the original or parent population should be separated into subsets, common sense dictates that the population be divided on the basis of factors related to the characteristic of interest in the population. For example, if you are conducting a political poll to predict the outcome of an election and can show that there is a significant difference in the way men and women are likely to vote, then gender is an appropriate basis for stratification. If you do not do stratified sampling in this manner, then you do not get the benefits of stratification, and you have expended additional time, effort, and resources for no benefit. With gender as the basis for stratification, one stratum, then, would be made up of men and one of women. These strata are mutually exclusive and exhaustive in that every population element can be assigned to one and only one (male or female) and no population elements are unassignable. The second stage in the selection of a stratified sample involves drawing simple random samples independently from each stratum.

Researchers prefer stratified samples over simple random samples because of their potential for greater statistical efficiency.[16] That is, if two samples are drawn from the same population—one a properly stratified sample and the other a simple random sample—the stratified sample will have a smaller sampling error. Also, reduction of a sampling error to a certain target level can be achieved with a smaller stratified sample. Stratified samples are statistically more efficient because one source of variation has been eliminated.

If stratified samples are statistically more efficient, why are they not used all the time? There are two reasons. First, the information necessary to properly stratify the sample frequently may not be available. For example, little may be known about the demographic characteristics of consumers of a particular product. To properly stratify the sample and to get the benefits of stratification, the researcher must choose bases for stratification that yield significant differences between the strata in regard to the measurement of interest. When such differences are not identifiable, the sample cannot be properly stratified. Second, even if the necessary information is available, the potential value of the information may not warrant the time and costs associated with stratification.

In the case of a simple random sample, the researcher depends entirely on the laws of probability to generate a representative sample of the population. With stratified sampling, the researcher, to some degree, forces the sample to be representative by making sure that important dimensions of the population are represented in the sample in their true population proportions. For example, the researcher may know that although men and women are equally likely to be users of a particular product, women are much more likely to be heavy users. In a study designed to analyze consumption patterns of the product, failure to properly represent women in the sample would result in a biased view of consumption patterns. Assume that women make up 60 percent of the population of interest and men account for 40 percent. Because of sampling fluctuations, a properly executed simple random sampling procedure might produce a sample made up of 55 percent women and 45 percent men. This is the same kind of error you would obtain if you flipped a coin 10 times. The ideal result of 10 coin tosses would be five heads and five tails, but more than half the time you would get a different result. In similar fashion, a properly drawn and executed simple random sample from a population made up of 60 percent women and 40 percent men is not likely to consist of exactly 60 percent women and 40 percent men. However, the researcher can force a stratified sample to have 60 percent women and 40 percent men.

A stratified sample may be appropriate in certain cases. For example, if a political poll is being done to predict who will win an election, a difference in the way men and women are likely to vote would make gender an appropriate basis for stratification.

Three steps are involved in implementing a properly stratified sample:

1. *Identify salient (important) demographic or classification factors*—factors that are correlated with the behavior of interest. For example, there may be reason to believe that men and women have different average consumption rates of a particular product. To use gender as a basis for meaningful stratification, the researcher must be able to show with actual data that there are significant differences in the consumption levels of men and women. In this manner, various salient factors are identified. Research indicates that, as a general rule, after the six most important factors have been identified, the identification of additional salient factors adds little in the way of increased sampling efficiency.[17]

2. *Determine what proportions of the population fall into the various subgroups under each stratum* (for example, if gender has been determined to be a salient factor, determine what proportion of the population is male and what proportion is female). Using these proportions, the researcher can determine how many respondents are required from each subgroup. However, before a final determination is made, a decision must be made as to whether to use proportional allocation or disproportional, or optimal, allocation.

Under **proportional allocation**, the number of elements selected from a stratum is directly proportional to the size of the stratum in relation to the size of the population. With proportional allocation, the proportion of elements to be taken from each stratum

> **proportional allocation**
Sampling in which the number of elements selected from a stratum is directly proportional to the size of the stratum relative to the size of the population.

is given by the formula n/N, where $n =$ the size of the stratum and $N =$ the size of the population.

Disproportional, or **optimal**, **allocation** produces the most efficient samples and provides the most precise or reliable estimates for a given sample size. This approach requires a double weighting scheme. Under this scheme, the number of sample elements to be taken from a given stratum is proportional to the relative size of the stratum and the standard deviation of the distribution of the characteristic under consideration for all elements in the stratum. This scheme is used for two reasons. First, the size of a stratum is important because those strata with greater numbers of elements are more important in determining the population mean. Therefore, such strata should have more weight in deriving estimates of population parameters. Second, it makes sense that relatively more elements should be drawn from those strata having larger standard deviations (more variation) and relatively fewer elements should be drawn from those strata having smaller standard deviations. Allocating relatively more of the sample to those strata where the potential for sampling error is greatest (largest standard deviation) is cost-effective and improves the overall accuracy of the estimates. There is no difference between proportional allocation and disproportional allocation if the distributions of the characteristic under consideration have the same standard deviation from stratum to stratum.[18]

3. *Select separate simple random samples from each stratum.* This process is implemented somewhat differently than traditional simple random sampling. Assume that the stratified sampling plan requires that 240 women and 160 men be interviewed. The researcher will sample from the total population and keep track of the number of men and women interviewed. At some point in the process, when 240 women and 127 men have been interviewed, the researcher will interview only men until the target of 160 men is reached. In this manner, the process generates a sample in which the proportion of men and women conforms to the allocation scheme derived in step 2.

Stratified samples are not used as often as one might expect in marketing research. The reason is that the information necessary to properly stratify the sample is usually not available in advance. Stratification cannot be based on guesses or hunches but must be based on hard data regarding the characteristics of the population and the relationship between these characteristics and the behavior under investigation. Stratified samples are frequently used in political polling and media audience research. In those areas, the researcher is more likely to have the information necessary to implement the stratification process.

Cluster Sampling

The types of samples discussed so far have all been single unit samples, in which each sampling unit is selected separately. In the case of **cluster samples,** the sampling units are selected in groups.[19] There are two basic steps in cluster sampling:

1. The population of interest is divided into mutually exclusive and exhaustive subsets.

2. A random sample of the subsets is selected.

If the sample consists of all the elements in the selected subsets, it is called a *one-stage cluster sample.* However, if the sample of elements is chosen in some probabilistic manner from the selected subsets, the sample is a *two-stage cluster sample.*

Both stratified and cluster sampling involve dividing the population into mutually exclusive and exhaustive subgroups. However, in stratified samples the researcher selects a sample of elements from each subgroup, while in cluster samples, the researcher selects a sample of subgroups and then collects data either from all the elements in the subgroup (one-stage cluster sample) or from a sample of the elements (two-stage cluster sample).

> **disproportional, or optimal, allocation**
> Sampling in which the number of elements taken from a given stratum is proportional to the relative size of the stratum and the standard deviation of the characteristic under consideration.

> **cluster sample**
> Probability sample in which the sampling units are selected from a number of small geographic areas to reduce data collection costs.

All the probability sampling methods discussed to this point require sampling frames that list or provide some organized breakdown of all the elements in the target population. Under cluster sampling, the researcher develops sampling frames that specify groups or clusters of elements of the population without actually listing individual elements. Sampling is then executed by taking a sample of the clusters in the frame and generating lists or other breakdowns for only those clusters that have been selected for the sample. Finally, a sample is chosen from the elements of the selected clusters

The most popular type of cluster sample is the area sample, in which the clusters are units of geography (for example, city blocks). A researcher, conducting a door-to-door survey in a particular metropolitan area, might randomly choose a sample of city blocks from the metropolitan area, select a sample of clusters, and then interview a sample of consumers from each cluster. All interviews would be conducted in the clusters selected, dramatically reducing interviewers' travel time and expenses. Cluster sampling is considered to be a probability sampling technique because of the random selection of clusters and the random selection of elements within the selected clusters.

> The most popular type of cluster sample is the area sample in which the clusters are units of geography (for example, city blocks). Cluster sampling is considered to be a probability sampling technique because of the random selection of clusters and the random selection of elements within the selected clusters.

Cluster sampling assumes that the elements in a cluster are as heterogeneous as those in the total population. If the characteristics of the elements in a cluster are very similar, then that assumption is violated and the researcher has a problem. In the city-block sampling just described, there may be little heterogeneity within clusters because the residents of a cluster are very similar to each other and different from those of other clusters. Typically, this potential problem is dealt with in the sample design by selecting a large number of clusters and sampling a relatively small number of elements from each cluster.

Another possibility is *multistage area sampling*, or *multistage area probability sampling*, which involves three or more steps. Samples of this type are used for national surveys or surveys that cover large regional areas. Here, the researcher randomly selects geographic areas in progressively smaller units. For example, a statewide door-to-door survey might include the following steps:

1. Choose counties within the state to make sure that different areas are represented in the sample. Counties should be selected with a probability proportional to the number of sampling units (households) within the county. Counties with a larger number of households would have a higher probability of selection than would counties with a smaller number of households.

2. Select residential blocks within those counties.

3. Select households within those residential blocks.

From the standpoint of statistical efficiency, cluster samples are generally less efficient than other types of probability samples. In other words, a cluster sample of a certain size will have a larger sampling error than a simple random sample or a stratified sample of the same size. To see the greater cost efficiency and lower statistical efficiency of a cluster sample, consider the following example. A researcher needs to select a sample of 200 households in a particular city for in-home interviews. If she selects these 200 households via simple random sampling, they will be scattered across the city. Cluster sampling might be implemented in this situation by selecting 20 residential blocks in the city and randomly choosing 10 households on each block to interview. It is easy to see that interviewing costs will be dramatically reduced under the cluster sampling approach. Interviewers do not have to spend as much time traveling and their mileage is dramatically reduced. In regard to sampling error, however, you can see that simple random sampling has the advantage. Interviewing 200 households scattered across the city increases the chance of getting a representative cross section of respondents. If all interviewing is conducted in 20 randomly selected blocks within the city, certain ethnic, social, or economic groups might be missed or over- or underrepresented.

As noted previously, cluster samples are, in nearly all cases, statistically less efficient than simple random samples. It is possible to view a simple random sample as a special type of cluster sample, in which the number of clusters is equal to the total sample size, with one sample element selected per cluster. At this point, the statistical efficiency of the cluster sample and that of the simple random sample are equal. From this point on, as the researcher decreases the number of clusters and increases the number of sample elements per cluster, the statistical efficiency of the cluster sample declines. At the other extreme, the researcher might choose a single cluster and select all the sample elements from that cluster. For example, he or she might select one relatively small geographic area in the city where you live and interview 200 people from that area. How comfortable would you be that a sample selected in this manner would be representative of the entire metropolitan area where you live?

Nonprobability Sampling Methods

In a general sense, any sample that does not meet the requirements of a probability sample is, by definition, a nonprobability sample. We have already noted that a major disadvantage of nonprobability samples is the inability to calculate sampling error for them. This suggests the even greater difficulty of evaluating the overall quality of nonprobability samples. How far do they deviate from the standard required of probability samples? The user of data from a nonprobability sample must make this assessment, which should be based on a careful evaluation of the methodology used to generate the nonprobability sample. Is it likely that the methodology employed will generate a cross section of individuals from the target population? Or is the sample hopelessly biased in some particular direction? These are the questions that must be answered. Four types of nonprobability samples are frequently used: convenience, judgment, quota, and snowball samples.

Convenience Samples

> **convenience samples**
> Nonprobability samples based on using people who are easily accessible.

Convenience samples are primarily used, as their name implies, for reasons of convenience. Companies such as Frito-Lay often use their own employees for preliminary tests of new product formulations developed by their R&D departments. At first, this may seem to be a highly biased approach. However, these companies are not asking employees to evaluate existing products or to compare their products with a competitor's products. They are asking employees only to provide gross sensory evaluations of new product formulations (for example, saltiness, crispness, greasiness). In such situations, convenience sampling may represent an efficient and effective means of obtaining the required information. This is particularly true in an exploratory situation, where there is a pressing need to get an inexpensive approximation of true value.

Some believe that the use of convenience sampling is growing at a faster rate than the growth in the use of probability sampling.[20] The reason, as suggested in the Practicing Marketing Research feature on SSI-LITe, is the growing availability of databases of consumers in low-incidence and hard-to-find categories. For example, suppose a company has developed a new athlete's foot remedy and needs to conduct a survey among those who suffer from the malady. Because these individuals make up only 4 percent of

PRACTICING MARKETING RESEARCH

SSI Provides Useful Convenience Samples

Survey Sampling, Incorporated (SSI) currently offers over 3,000 low-incidence consumer and business lists. SSI-LITe is a form of convenience sampling, which the research industry can use to assist in screening for low-incidence segments of the population. To the degree that SSI's sampling services act as a barometer of research activity, SSI-LITe sales suggest that the use of convenience samples is growing at a faster rate than the use of probability samples.

Probability sampling in the strictest sense allows each potential respondent an opportunity to be selected for a study. The probabilities of selection can be controlled and calculated as a result of sample selection. Research results can serve both enumerative and analytical purposes. This is not the case when a subjective selection of respondents is used, as with SSI-LITe and other nonprobability samples. Yet the practical constraints of time and budgets clearly make a case for the use of nonprobability samples.

When less than 1 percent of U.S. households purchase a certain brand, research options may become quite limited, and targeted samples, such as SSI-LITe, provide researchers with the opportunity to gain an understanding of attitudes and behaviors that they could not otherwise gain. The problem occurs when the researcher or research user attempts to project the findings to the total population, which can lead to costly wrong decisions. The researcher must understand the limitations of a research design that employs anything other than a probability sample.

---

the population, researchers conducting a telephone survey would have to talk with 25 people to find 1 individual who suffered from the problem. Purchasing a list of individuals known to suffer from the problem can dramatically reduce the cost of the survey and the time necessary to complete it. Although such a list might be made up of individuals who used coupons when purchasing the product or sent in for manufacturers' rebates, companies are increasingly willing to make the trade-off of lower cost and faster turnaround for a lower-quality sample. Exhibit 12.7 provides some examples of the more than 3,000 lists available from Survey Sampling, Incorporated.

Judgment Samples

The term **judgment sample** is applied to any sample in which the selection criteria are based on the researcher's judgment about what constitutes a representative sample. Most test markets and many product tests conducted in shopping malls are essentially judgment sampling. In the case of test markets, one or a few markets are selected based on the judgment that they are representative of the population as a whole. Malls are selected for product taste tests based on the researcher's judgment that the particular malls attract a reasonable cross section of consumers who fall into the target group for the product being tested.

> **judgment samples**
> Nonprobability samples in which the selection criteria are based on the researcher's personal judgment about representativeness of the population under study.

Quota Samples

Quota samples are typically selected in such a way that demographic characteristics of interest to the researcher are represented in the sample in target proportions. Thus, many people confuse quota samples and stratified samples. There are, however, two key differences

> **quota samples**
> Nonprobability samples in which quotas, based on demographic or classification factors selected by the researcher, are established for population subgroups.

Exhibit 12.7

Examples from the Activities List of Survey Sampling, Incorporated

Sports/Boating/Fishing/Outdoor Activities

Bicycling	Outdoor Enthusiast
Boating: Power	Outdoor Recreation
Boating: Sailing	Outdoor Sports Lover
Bow Hunting	Physical Fitness
Camping	Running/Jogging
Cycling	Sailing
Environmental Concerns	Scuba Diving
Exercise Equipment	Snow Boarding
Fishing	Snow Skiing
Fly Fishing	Soccer
Golf	Sports
Hiking	Sports Cards
Horseback Riding	Sports Equipment
Hunting/Shooting	Sports Items
Motorcycles, Interest in	Tennis
Motorcycling, Participation in	Walking for Health
NASCAR Enthusiast	Watching Sports on TV

between a quota sample and a stratified sample. First, respondents for a quota sample are not selected randomly, as they must be for a stratified sample. Second, the classification factors used for a stratified sample are selected based on the existence of a correlation between the factor and the behavior of interest. There is no such requirement in the case of a quota sample. The demographic or classification factors of interest in a quota sample are selected on the basis of researcher judgment.

Snowball Samples

 **snowball samples**
Nonprobability samples in which additional respondents are selected based on referrals from initial respondents.

In **snowball samples**, sampling procedures are used to select additional respondents on the basis of referrals from initial respondents. This procedure is used to sample from low-incidence or rare populations—that is, populations that make up a very small percentage of the total population.[21] The costs of finding members of these rare populations may be so great that the researcher is forced to use a technique such as snowball sampling. For example, suppose an insurance company needed to obtain a national sample of individuals who have switched from the indemnity form of healthcare coverage to a health maintenance organization in the past 6 months. It would be necessary to sample a very large number of consumers to identify 1,000 that fall into this population. It would be far more economical to obtain an initial sample of 200 people from the population of interest and have each of them provide the names of an average of 4 other people to complete the sample of 1,000.

The main advantage of snowball sampling is a dramatic reduction in search costs. However, this advantage comes at the expense of sample quality. The total sample is likely to be biased because the individuals whose names were obtained from those sampled in the initial phase are likely to be very similar to those initially sampled. As a result, the sample may not be a good cross section of the total population. There is general agreement that some limits should be placed on the number of respondents obtained through referrals, although there are no specific rules regarding what these limits should be. This approach may also be hampered by the fact that respondents may be reluctant to give referrals.

Internet Sampling

The advantages of Internet interviewing are compelling:

☐ *Target respondents can complete the survey at their convenience*—late at night, over the weekend, and at any other convenient time.

☐ *Data collection is inexpensive.* Once basic overhead and other fixed costs are covered, interviewing is essentially volume-insensitive. Thousands of interviews can be conducted at an actual data collection cost of less than $1 per survey. This low cost may, to some extent, be offset by the need to use incentives to encourage responses. By comparison, a 10-minute telephone interview targeting people who make up 50 percent of the population may cost $15 or more per survey. Data entry and data processing costs are dramatically reduced because respondents essentially do the data entry for the researcher.

☐ *The interview can be administered under software control,* which allows the survey to follow skip patterns and do other "smart" things.

☐ *The survey can be completed quickly.* Hundreds or thousands of surveys can be completed in a day or less.[22]

Unfortunately, there is no large body of scientific research regarding the representativeness of Internet samples, as there is for other data-collection approaches. Those who have carefully evaluated Internet surveying are most concerned that the pool of people available in cyberspace does not correctly represent the general population. The group of Internet respondents tend to be richer, whiter, more male, and more tech-savvy.[23] The biases are becoming less pronounced over time as the percentage of the population connected to the Internet increases.[24] However, the nonrepresentativeness of Internet respondents will exist for some time into the future. This general problem is compounded by the fact that no comprehensive and reliable source of e-mail addresses exists.

Companies such as Survey Sampling, Incorporated are busily building e-mail databases, but the problems are great. For example, although SSI claims to have 7 million e-mail addresses in its database, this number is small in relation to the total U.S. population. The problem is compounded by the fact that e-mail addresses are easily and frequently changed as people switch jobs, change Internet service providers, and open or close accounts at Yahoo!, Hotmail, and other e-mail providers. This means that any list of e-mail addresses will be constantly changing. For the foreseeable future, it will be virtually impossible to get an inclusive sampling frame of e-mail addresses for almost any generalized population, such as new car buyers, new home buyers, people with cable TV service, or fast-food users.

In some cases, researchers recruit samples of consumers via Internet bulletin board postings or banner advertising on search engines (Yahoo!, Google, Hotbot, and others). Once again, the biases are obvious. Those who do not use the Internet have no chance of being included in the sample, even though they might be part of the target population. Among Internet users, consumers who do not visit the sites in question or who do not visit those sites during the time that the banner ads are running have no chance of being included in the sample. In addition, those who visit the sites infrequently have less chance of being included than those who visit them frequently.

Finally, research firms such as Harris Black and Greenfield Online tout the fact that they have developed large panels of individuals who have responded to their solicitations and have agreed to accept and complete e-mail surveys.[26] Again, the biases are fairly obvious, and the lack of representativeness of their panels can be clearly seen. These firms counter criticism by claiming that they weight survey results to make them representative. For example, suppose a population is known to be 60 percent female and 40 percent

GLOBAL RESEARCH

Online Quantitative Research—Not Enough of the World Is Online Yet to Make a Representative Sample

Increasingly, market researchers are looking to the Internet as the means to conduct effective, quantitative global research for potential international markets. But how accurate and cost efficient is online research today? Is world use of the Internet up to the level that would assure dependable survey samples? Not quite, say researchers, and there are three reasons: penetration, cost, and cultural differences and customary ways of doing things.

First, in regard to penetration, Internet availability and use varies markedly among the countries. Brazil, as of 2003, could boast only 7 percent Internet penetration in its population. South Korea had a much higher access rate: an estimated 70 percent of its households had personal computers hooked up to the Internet in 2001. South Korea has this high rate of Internet access because the government made the provision of broadband access for its citizens a national priority.

"In Asia, Internet penetration is not growing as fast as wireless, and so this is an obvious route for marketing research companies to use in their online research," said Arno Hummerston of the London office of Taylor Nelson Sofres. He noted that China has the world's largest cellular use with an estimated 200 million subscribers, far higher than the United States.

However, recent data out of Beijing suggests that Chinese Internet use is rapidly accelerating, even in the space of one year. As of July 2005, the number of Chinese Internet users was placed at 103 million, second only to the United States. In 2005 alone, 9 million more Chinese went online, an 18.4 percent growth over 2004. And there is tremendous room for growth in China: while about 67 percent of Americans (135 million people) have Internet access, only 7.9 percent of Chinese and about 45.6 million computers are connected to the Internet. Given the rapid growth of Internet use in China, this 7.9 percent figure is likely to keep growing, making quantitative online research in China far more feasible very soon.

Growth in the Internet user base in China will certainly start to reduce the recruiting costs, which tend to account for 35 to 40 percent of online research and present a financial obstacle to low-cost online polling in many countries.

The second major problem for global market research relates to cost. Many countries lack the technical infrastructure of servers, hardware, and software, which is well established in the United States and Europe where Internet research is relatively inexpensive. The lack of this infrastructure, on the other hand, makes Internet research difficult and expensive in many countries outside Europe and the United States.

The third problem relates to cultural differences, prevailing research practices, and ways of doing things. Many people prefer live focus groups where they can physically mingle with other people and enjoy the social interaction. Online focus group participation is seen by these people as too abstract, too sterile. But there are nuances on this issue across countries. On the one hand, in some Asian countries where conformity is valued if not expected, Internet polling offers people the chance to respond against convention but anonymously. On the other hand, in Latin America the feeling that no real people are involved takes away the pleasure of social interaction. Here a combination of telephone and online interviews (facilitated by broadband) re-personalizes the process. In certain countries, such as China, where the government seeks to control information flow, researchers may get a strong "No!" when they ask the government permission to poll its citizens online asking all sorts of questions.[25]

male. If an Internet survey produces a sample that is 70 percent male and 30 percent female, the results can be weighted to align them with the known population proportions. However, this approach fails to recognize that other biases may lurk below the surface and only be distorted by such weighting.

There are cases where Internet surveys, with all their other inherent advantages, may produce excellent samples. Those cases involve situations where the client organization or the researcher has e-mail addresses for all members of a particular population. For example, high-technology firms such as Texas Instruments may have lists of essentially all individuals who make decisions regarding the purchase of their products for incorporation in other products. These industrial buyers are probably fairly heavy users of the Internet, both at home and at work. Selecting a true random sample of all members of such a population is relatively easy. At minimal cost, all the individuals can be sent invitations to participate and reminders to complete the survey. Response rates in excess of 70 percent are not uncommon for surveys of this type, especially if incentives are offered to encourage responses. Internet surveys are an emerging form of data collection that will probably become dominant at some point in the future. Their advantages are numerous and compelling. However, until the sampling issues discussed in this chapter can be resolved, the results of Internet surveys will be suspect because of lack of survey representativeness.

SUMMARY

The population, or universe, is the total group of people in whose opinions one is interested. A census involves collecting desired information from every member of the population of interest. A sample is simply a subset of a population. The steps in developing a sampling plan are as follows: define the population of interest, choose the data-collection method, identify the sampling frame, select the sampling method, determine sample size, develop and specify an operational plan for selecting sampling elements, and execute the operational sampling plan. The sampling frame is a list of the elements of the population from which the sample will be drawn or a specified procedure for generating the list.

In probability sampling methods, samples are selected in such a way that every element of the population has a known, nonzero likelihood of selection. Nonprobability sampling methods select specific elements from the population in a nonrandom manner. Probability samples have several advantages over nonprobability samples, including reasonable certainty that information will be obtained from a representative cross section of the population, a sampling error that can be computed, and survey results that can be projected to the total population. However, probability samples are more expensive than nonprobability samples and usually take more time to design and execute.

The accuracy of sample results is determined by both sampling and nonsampling error. Sampling error occurs because the sample selected is not perfectly representative of the population. There are two types of sampling error: random sampling error and administrative error. Random sampling error is due to chance and cannot be avoided; it can only be reduced by increasing sample size.

Probability samples include simple random samples, systematic samples, stratified samples, and cluster samples. Nonprobability samples include convenience samples, judgment samples, quota samples, and snowball samples. At the present time, Internet samples tend to be convenience samples. That may change in the future as better e-mail sampling frames become available.

KEY TERMS & DEFINITIONS

sampling Process of obtaining information from a subset of a larger group.

population Entire group of people about whom information is needed; also called *universe* or *population of interest.*

census Collection of data obtained from or about every member of the population of interest.

sample Subset of all the members of a population of interest.

sampling frame List of population elements from which units to be sampled can be selected or a specified procedure for generating such a list.

random-digit dialing Method of generating lists of telephone numbers at random.

probability samples Samples in which every element of the population has a known, nonzero likelihood of selection.

nonprobability samples Samples in which specific elements from the population have been selected in a nonrandom manner.

sampling error Error that occurs because the sample selected is not perfectly representative of the population.

nonsampling error All error other than sampling error; also called *measurement error.*

simple random sample Probability sample selected by assigning a number to every element of the population and then using a table of random numbers to select specific elements for inclusion in the sample.

systematic sampling Probability sampling in which the entire population is num-

bered and elements are selected using a skip interval.

stratified sample Probability sample that is forced to be more representative though simple random sampling of mutually exclusive and exhaustive subsets.

proportional allocation Sampling in which the number of elements selected from a stratum is directly proportional to the size of the stratum relative to the size of the population.

disproportional, or optimal, allocation Sampling in which the number of elements taken from a given stratum is proportional to the relative size of the stratum and the standard deviation of the characteristic under consideration.

cluster sample Probability sample in which the sampling units are selected from a number of small geographic areas to reduce data collection costs.

convenience samples Nonprobability samples based on using people who are easily accessible.

judgment samples Nonprobability samples in which the selection criteria are based on the researcher's personal judgment about representativeness of the population under study.

quota samples Nonprobability samples in which quotas, based on demographic or classification factors selected by the researcher, are established for population subgroups.

snowball samples Nonprobability samples in which additional respondents are selected based on referrals from initial respondents.

1. What are some situations in which a census would be better than a sample? Why are samples usually employed rather than censuses?

2. Develop a sampling plan for examining undergraduate business students' attitudes toward Internet advertising.

3. Give an example of a perfect sampling frame. Why is a telephone directory usually not an acceptable sampling frame?

4. Distinguish between probability and nonprobability samples. What are the advantages and disadvantages of each? Why are nonprobability samples so popular in marketing research?

5. Distinguish among a systematic sample, a cluster sample, and a stratified sample. Give examples of each.

6. What is the difference between a stratified sample and a quota sample?

7. American National Bank has 1,000 customers. The manager wishes to draw a sample of 100 customers. How could this be done using systematic sampling? What would be the impact on the technique, if any, if the list were ordered by average size of deposit?

8. Do you see any problem with drawing a systematic sample from a telephone book, assuming that the telephone book is an acceptable sample frame for the study in question?

9. Describe snowball sampling. Give an example of a situation in which you might use this type of sample. What are the dangers associated with this type of sample?

10. Name some possible sampling frames for the following:
    a. Patrons of sushi bars
    b. Smokers of high-priced cigars
    c. Snowboarders
    d. Owners of DVD players
    e. People who have visited one or more countries in Europe in the last year
    f. People who emigrated to the United States within the last 2 years
    g. People with allergies

11. Identify the following sample designs:
    a. The names of 200 patrons of a casino are drawn from a list of visitors for the last month, and a questionnaire is administered to them.
    b. A radio talk show host invites listeners to call in and vote yes or no on whether handguns should be banned.
    c. A dog food manufacturer wants to test a new dog food. It decides to select 100 dog owners who feed their dogs canned food, 100 who feed their dogs dry food, and 100 who feed their dogs semimoist food.
    d. A poll surveys men who play golf to predict the outcome of a presidential election.

WORKING THE NET

1. Go to the Survey Sampling site at *www.surveysampling.com/products/targeted/litecatalog.pdf.* Find the information on its LITe samples. What lists does it offer for "Families"? What lists does it have under the category "Electronics"?

2. Go to Survey Sampling at *www.surveysampling.com.* What does it offer in the way of random-digit telephone samples? When would you use samples of this type? What does SSI offer in regard to samples by country? Provide examples of two situations in which you might use its samples for Germany and Japan.

REAL-LIFE RESEARCH • 12.1

The Research Group

The Research Group has been hired by the National Internet Service Providers Association to determine the following:

☐ What specific factors motivate people to choose a particular Internet service provider (ISP)?

☐ How do these factors differ between choosing an ISP for home use and choosing an ISP for business use?

☐ Why do people choose one ISP over the others?

☐ How many have switched ISPs in the past year?

☐ Why did they switch ISPs?

☐ How satisfied are they with their current ISP?

☐ Do consumers know or care whether an ISP is a member of the National Internet Service Providers Association?

☐ What value-added services do consumers want from ISPs (for example, telephone support for questions and problems)?

The Research Group underbid three other research companies to get the contract. In fact, its bid was more than 25 percent lower than the next lowest bid. The primary way in which The Research Group was able to provide the lowest bid related to its sampling methodology. In its proposal, The Research Group specified that college students would be used to gather the survey data. Its plan called for randomly selecting 20 colleges from across the country, contacting the chairperson of the marketing department, and asking her or him to submit a list of 10 students who would be interested in earning extra money. Finally, The Research Group would contact the students individually with the goal of identifying five students at each school who would ultimately be asked to get 10 completed interviews. Students would be paid $10 for each completed survey. The only requirement imposed in regard to selecting potential respondents was that they had to be ISP subscribers at the time of the survey. The Research Group proposal suggested that the easiest way to do this would be for the student interviewers to go to the student union or student center during the lunch hour and ask those at each table whether they might be interested in participating in the survey.

Questions

1. How would you describe this sampling methodology?
2. What problems do you see arising from this technique?
3. Suggest an alternative sampling method that might give the National Internet Service Providers Association a better picture of the information it desired.

New Mexico National Bank

Florida National Bank (FNB) operates branches in 23 cities and towns throughout the state of New Mexico. The bank offers a complete range of financial services, including Visa and MasterCard credit cards. New Mexico National Bank (NMNB) has 53,400 people in the state using its credit cards. Based on their original applications, the bank has certain information about these individuals, including name, address, zip code, telephone number, income, education, and assets. NMNB is interested in determining whether a relationship exists between the volume of purchases charged on credit cards and the demographic characteristics of the individual cardholders. For example, are individuals in certain parts of the state more or less likely to be heavy users of the card? Is there a relationship between a person's income and his or her level of care usage? Is there a relationship between the person's level of education and card usage? The data can be used to more effectively target offerings sent through the mail if significant relationships are found. Paul Bruney, research director for NMNB, is in the process of developing a design for the research. If you were Paul Bruney, how would you answer the following questions?

Questions

1. How would you define the population of interest for the study?
2. What sampling frame(s) might you use for the project?
3. What procedure would you use to select a simple random sample from the sampling frame you chose above.
4. Would it make sense to use a stratified sample in the situation? Why or why not? How would you approach the process of developing a stratified sample from the sampling frame you chose?
5. Could you use the sampling frame to draw a cluster sample? How would you go about it? Would it make any sense to do this?
6. Which of the three probability sampling methods just mentioned would you choose for this study? Why would you choose that option?

SAMPLE SIZE

DETERMINATION

LEARNING OBJECTIVES

1.	To learn the financial and statistical issues in the determination of sample size.
2.	To discover methods for determining sample size.
3.	To gain an appreciation of a normal distribution.
4.	To understand population, sample, and sampling distributions.
5.	To distinguish between point and interval estimates.
6.	To recognize problems involving sampling means and proportions.

Bill Jackson, marketing director for SanTex Cable, has just finished reviewing a proposal from Data Dimensions, a research firm he has worked with in the past. He had invited Data Dimensions to submit a proposal on conducting a customer satisfaction survey with current SanTex customers in San Antonio. Jackson had stressed the fact that he had a limited budget for the research and had asked his account rep at Data Dimensions to come up with a solid research design at a "value" price.

The research firm proposes to employ a telephone survey, with all interviews conducted from its central-location telephone interviewing facility. It recommends that a random sample of 384 customers, selected from SanTex's current list of customers, be surveyed. In the proposal, Data Dimensions indicates that a random sample of 384 will produce estimates that are within ± 5 percent of true population values, with 95 percent confidence.

Jackson has several basic questions regarding the sample design. First, given that SanTex has 37,500 customers in San Antonio, the recommended sample size seems relatively small. Second, he is wondering whether the stated error range and confidence level will apply to results for different subgroups. In particular, analysis of complaints received from customers shows that SanTex gets a disproportionately large number of complaints from customers over the age of 50. Approximately half of all its customers are over 50, and approximately half are 50 or younger. Jackson believes that it is important to have estimates for each group that are within ± 5 percent of the true value group, with 95 percent confidence. On the one hand, he wonders whether 384 respondents are enough. On the other hand, if a larger sample size is required, he is concerned about the adequacy of his budget.

Finally, Jackson is interested in the procedures that Data Dimensions will use to get a representative sample of his customers. Its proposal says that it will employ a simple random sample. Jackson would like some additional explanation of how a random sample will ensure representativeness.[1] ■

Determining Sample Size for Probability Samples

The process of determining sample size for probability samples involves financial, statistical, and managerial issues. As a general rule, the larger the sample is, the smaller the sampling error. However, larger samples cost more money, and the resources available for a project are always limited. Although the cost of increasing sample size tends to rise on a linear basis (double the sample size, almost double the cost), sampling error decreases at a rate equal to the square root of the relative increase in sample size. If sample size is quadrupled, data-collection cost is almost quadrupled, but the level of sampling error is reduced by only 50 percent.

Managerial issues must be reflected in sample size calculations. How accurate do estimates need to be, and how confident must managers be that true population values are included in the chosen confidence interval? Some cases require high levels of precision (small sampling error) and confidence that population values fall in the small range of sampling error (the confidence interval). Other cases may not require the same level of precision or confidence. Examples of thinking behind sample size determination are provided in the Practicing Marketing Research feature on page 405.

Budget Available

The sample size for a project is often determined, at least indirectly, by the budget available. Thus, it is frequently the last project factor determined. A brand manager may have $50,000 available in the budget for a new product test. After deduction of other project costs (e.g., research design, questionnaire development, data processing), the amount remaining determines the size of the sample that can be surveyed. Of course, if the dollars available will not produce an adequate sample size, then management must make a decision: either additional funds must be found, or the project should be canceled.

Although this approach may seem highly unscientific and arbitrary, it is a fact of life in a corporate environment. Financial constraints challenge the researcher to develop research designs that will generate data of adequate quality for decision-making purposes at low cost. This "budget available" approach forces the researcher to explore alternative data-collection approaches and to carefully consider the value of information in relation to its cost. The Practicing Marketing Research feature on page 406 explains why you can't be too stingy on sample size.

Rule of Thumb

Potential clients may specify in the RFP (request for proposal) that they want a sample of 200, 400, 500, or some other size. Sometimes, this number is based on desired sampling error. In other cases, it is based on nothing more than past experience. The justification for the specified sample size may boil down to a "gut feeling" that a particular sample size is necessary or appropriate.

If the researcher determines that the sample size requested is not adequate to support the objectives of the proposed research, then she or he has a professional responsibility to present arguments for a larger sample size to the client and let the client make the final decision. If the client rejects arguments for a larger sample size, then the researcher may decline to submit a proposal based on the belief that an inadequate sample size will produce results with so much error that they may be misleading.[2]

Number of Subgroups Analyzed

In any sample size determination problem, consideration must be given to the number and anticipated size of various subgroups of the total sample that must be analyzed and about

PRACTICING MARKETING RESEARCH

Determining the Appropriate Sample Size for Your Market Study

The trick in determining the best sample size for your marketing survey is to reach a balance between cost and accuracy, and to do this, three essential questions must be addressed. First, will your data analysis be based on the entire sample? Second, and alternatively, do you plan to examine the subgroups? Third, what's your comfort level with resulting accuracy—how precise do you want it?

For example, say your study focuses on teenage use of MP3 players. Do you want to sample for the differences among gender users or just the entire market? Your choice here will affect the cost of the study.

As for accuracy, the norm among researchers tends to be a maximum error range of ±5 percent at a 95 percent confidence level, although some set it between ±5 and ±10 percent. At ±5 percent, if you repeated your study 100 times, in 95 cases the results would not vary more than 5 percent from the results of the original study. This accuracy level corresponds to a sample size of about 400. If you settle for ±10 percent accuracy, then your sample size can be as low as 100.

Often the differences among subgroups in the total sample can provide more valuable data than is possible from examining the total sample. Thus, how you define your subgroup size can be crucial, often even more so than sample size. Jason Ball, methodology director for Bardsley & Neidhart, a marketing research firm in Portland, Oregon, recommends a minimum of 100 respondents if you want to examine in depth a subgroup or subsample. If you're conducting comparisons across various subsamples, then you can get by with only 30 respondents.

How about determining the original total sample size? P:SNAP (Pathfinders Study of the Nation's Attitudes and Psychographics), based in New Delhi, India, and a division of Lintas India, went big on their sample size. They polled 21,300 consumers from 28 cities and in 247 categories for their 2005 study. According to Srinivasan Raman, Pathfinders' president: "Such a large sample size will allow analyzing the data at drilled down subsegments like unmarried women, the elderly market, CWE (chief wage-earner), housewives/decision makers, and people living in joint family and others." The large sample size also allowed for "greater sampling efficiency through a sharper focus" as well as a tighter segmentation of town classes, Raman explained.

A July 2005 poll conducted at Dallas-Fort Worth International Airport in Texas also went massive in their sample size. Using terminal intercept surveys, pollsters queried 2,714 passengers between July 2 and July 5 (the July 4th holiday-travel weekend, guaranteeing a huge raw sample base) if they preferred having Southwest Airlines fly out of DFW. "We wanted this very large sample size to make sure we accurately reflected the feelings of our passengers," said Joe Lopano, DFW executive vice president of marketing and terminal management. Their study's margin of error was only ±2 percent with a 95 percent confidence level.[3]

which statistical inferences must be made. For example, a researcher might decide that a sample of 400 is quite adequate overall. However, if male and female respondents must be analyzed separately and the sample is expected to be 50 percent male and 50 percent female, then the expected sample size for each subgroup is only 200. Is this number adequate for making the desired statistical inferences about the characteristics of the two groups? If the results are to be analyzed by both sex and age, then the problem gets even more complicated.

PRACTICING MARKETING RESEARCH

Sample Costs versus the Costs of an Invalid Survey

Marketers, all too often, try to save a few bucks on sample size and risk millions in opportunity loss. This is according to Thomas Semon, expert columnist for *Marketing News*. He noted that an ad agency that he once worked for bragged about using samples of 120 for copy research. Samples of this size can be adequate in some cases but not in others. There is not a one-size-fits-all sample size for any type of research. The really critical factor is the size of the expected difference or change to be measured—the smaller that is, the larger the sample must be, squared.

In testing two versions of an ad, a current or control version and a new version, we might adopt the rule that the new version will be adopted if it scores significantly higher than the current or control version. "Significance" might be set at either the 90 percent or 95 percent confidence level.

This type of decision criterion protects against the risk that random sampling error results in an overestimate of the favorable response and leads to the false conclusion that the new version should be adopted. However, the opposite problem (underestimate of the favorable response, leading to the false conclusion that the new version should be rejected) is just as likely, and the decision criterion specified does not protect against this possibility. In this example, a sample size of 120 does not have the statistical power to protect against the opportunity loss that may result from failure to recognize superiority of the new version.

When the effect size, the needed or expected difference, is large (e.g., more than 10 percentage points), then statistical power is typically not a problem. However, very small effect sizes (e.g., 2 percentage points) may require such large sample sizes as to be impractical from a cost perspective.[5]

Assume that it is important to analyze four subgroups of the total sample: men under 35, men 35 and over, women under 35, and women 35 and over. If each group is expected to make up about 25 percent of the total sample, a sample of 400 will include only 100 respondents in each subgroup. The problem is that as sample size gets smaller, sampling error gets larger, and it becomes more difficult to tell whether an observed difference between two groups is a real difference or simply a reflection of sampling error.

Other things being equal, the larger the number of subgroups to be analyzed, the larger the required total sample size. It has been suggested that a sample should provide, at a minimum, 100 or more respondents in each major subgroup and 20 to 50 respondents in each of the less important subgroups.[4]

Traditional Statistical Methods

You probably have been exposed in other classes to traditional approaches for determining sample size for simple random samples. These approaches are reviewed in this chapter. Three pieces of information are required to make the necessary calculations for a sample result:

☐ An estimate of the population standard deviation

☐ The acceptable level of sampling error

☐ The desired level of confidence that the sample result will fall within a certain range (result ± sampling error) of true population values

With these three pieces of information, the researcher can calculate the size of the simple random sample required.[6] See Practicing Marketing Research on page 405 for more discussion of the issues.

Normal Distribution

General Properties

The normal distribution is crucial to classical statistical inference. There are several reasons for its importance. First, many variables encountered by marketers have probability distributions that are close to the normal distribution. Examples include the number of cans, bottles, or glasses of soft drink consumed by soft drink users, the number of times that people who eat at fast-food restaurants go to such restaurants in an average month, and the average hours per week spent viewing television. Second, the normal distribution is useful for a number of theoretical reasons; one of the more important of these relates to the central limit theorem. According to the **central limit theorem**, for any population, regardless of its distribution, the distribution of sample means or sample proportions approaches a normal distribution as sample size increases. The importance of this tendency will become clear later in the chapter. Third, the normal distribution is a useful approximation of many other discrete probability distributions. If, for example, a researcher measured the heights of a large sample of men in the United States and plotted those values on a graph, a distribution similar to the one shown in Exhibit 13.1 would result. This distribution is a **normal distribution**, and it has a number of important characteristics, including the following:

1. The normal distribution is bell-shaped and has only one mode. The mode is a measure of central tendency and is the particular value that occurs most frequently. (A bimodal, or two-mode, distribution would have two peaks or humps.)

2. The normal distribution is symmetric about its mean. This is another way of saying that it is not skewed and that the three measures of central tendency (mean, median, and mode) are all equal.

3. A particular normal distribution is uniquely defined by its mean and standard deviation.

> **central limit theorem**
> Idea that a distribution of a large number of sample means or sample proportions will approximate a normal distribution, regardless of the distribution of the population from which they were drawn.

> **normal distribution**
> Continuous distribution that is bell-shaped and symmetric about the mean; the mean, median, and mode are equal.

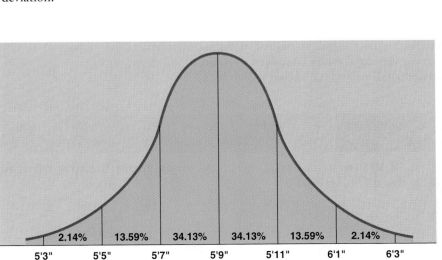

2.14% 13.59% 34.13% 34.13% 13.59% 2.14%

5'3"   5'5"   5'7"   5'9"   5'11"   6'1"   6'3"

Exhibit 13.1

Normal Distribution for Heights of Men

4. The total area under a normal curve is equal to one, meaning that it takes in all observations.

5. The area of a region under the normal distribution curve between any two values of a variable equals the probability of observing a value in that range when an observation is randomly selected from the distribution. For example, on a single draw, there is a 34.13 percent chance of selecting from the distribution shown in Exhibit 13.1 a man between 5′7″ and 5′9″ in height.

6. The area between the mean and a given number of standard deviations from the mean is the same for all normal distributions. The area between the mean and plus or minus one standard deviation takes in 68.26 percent of the area under the curve, or 68.26 percent of the observations. This **proportional property of the normal distribution** provides the basis for the statistical inferences we will discuss in this chapter.

> **proportional property of the normal distribution**
> Feature that the number of observations falling between the mean and a given number of standard deviations from the mean is the same for all normal distributions.

Standard Normal Distribution

Any normal distribution can be transformed into what is known as a standard normal distribution. The **standard normal distribution** has the same features as any normal distribution. However, the mean of the standard normal distribution is always equal to zero, and the standard deviation is always equal to one. The probabilities provided in Table 2 in Appendix 2 are based on a standard normal distribution. A simple transformation formula, based on the proportional property of the normal distribution, is used to transform any value X from any normal distribution to its equivalent value Z from a standard normal distribution:

> **standard normal distribution**
> Normal distribution with a mean of zero and a standard deviation of one.

$$Z = \frac{\text{Value of the variable} - \text{Mean of the variable}}{\text{Standard deviation of the variable}}$$

Symbolically, the formula can be stated as follows:

$$Z = \frac{X - \mu}{\sigma}$$

where $X =$ value of the variable

   $\mu =$ mean of the variable

   $\sigma =$ standard deviation of the variable

The areas under a standard normal distribution (reflecting the percent of all observations) for various Z values (**standard deviations**) are shown in Exhibit 13.2. The standard normal distribution is shown in Exhibit 13.3.

> **standard deviation**
> Measure of dispersion calculated by subtracting the mean of the series from each value in a series, squaring each result, summing the results, dividing the sum by the number of items minus 1, and taking the square root of this value.

EXHIBIT 13.2	Area under Standard Normal Curve for Z Values (Standard Deviations) of 1, 2, and 3
Z Values (Standard Deviation)	**Area under Standard Normal Curve (%)**
1	68.26
2	95.44
3	99.74

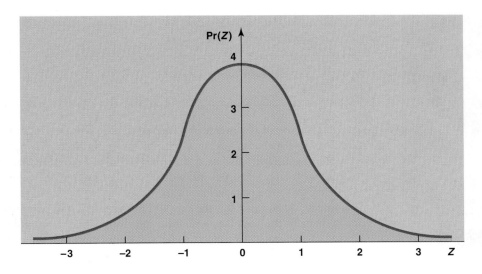

Exhibit 13.3

Standard Normal Distribution

Note: The term Pr(Z) is read "the probability of Z."

Population and Sample Distributions

The purpose of conducting a survey based on a sample is to make inferences about the population, not to describe the sample. The population, as defined earlier, includes all possible individuals or objects from whom or about which information is needed to meet the objectives of the research. A sample is a subset of the total population.

A **population distribution** is a frequency distribution of all the elements of the population. It has a mean, usually represented by the Greek letter μ, and a standard deviation, usually represented by the Greek letter σ.

A **sample distribution** is a frequency distribution of all the elements of an individual (single) sample. In a sample distribution, the mean is usually represented by $\bar{X}$ and the standard deviation is usually represented by S.

> **population distribution**
> Frequency distribution of all the elements of a population.

> **sample distribution**
> Frequency distribution of all the elements of an individual sample.

Sampling Distribution of the Mean

At this point, it is necessary to introduce a third distribution, the sampling distribution of the sample mean. Understanding this distribution is crucial to understanding the basis for our ability to compute sampling error for simple random samples. The **sampling distribution of the mean** is a conceptual and theoretical probability distribution of the means of all possible samples of a given size drawn from a given population. Although this distribution is seldom calculated, its known properties have tremendous practical significance. Actually deriving a distribution of sample means involves drawing a large number of simple random samples (for example, 25,000) of a certain size from a particular population. Then, the means for the samples are computed and arranged in a frequency distribution. Because each sample is composed of a different subset of sample elements, all the sample means will not be exactly the same. If the samples are sufficiently large and random, then the resulting distribution of sample means will approximate a normal distribution. This assertion is based on the central limit theorem, which states that as sample size increases, the distribution of the means of a large number of random samples taken from virtually any population approaches a normal distribution with a

> **sampling distribution of the mean**
> Theoretical frequency distribution of the means of all possible samples of a given size drawn from a particular population; it is normally distributed.

mean equal to μ and a standard deviation (referred to as *standard error*) $S_{\bar{x}}$, where n = sample size and

$$S_{\bar{x}} = \frac{\sigma}{\sqrt{n}}$$

The **standard error of the mean** ($S_{\bar{x}}$) is computed in this way because the variance, or dispersion, within a particular distribution of sample means will be smaller if it is based on larger samples. Common sense tells us that with larger samples individual sample means will, on the average, be closer to the population mean.

It is important to note that the central limit theorem holds regardless of the shape of the population distribution from which the samples are selected. This means that, regardless of the population distribution, the sample means selected from the population distribution will tend to be normally distributed.

The notation ordinarily used to refer to the means and standard deviations of population and sample distributions and sampling distribution of the mean is summarized in Exhibit 13.4. The relationships among the population distribution, sample distribution, and sampling distribution of the mean are shown graphically in Exhibit 13.5.

The results of a simple random sample of fast-food restaurant patrons could be used to compute the mean number of visits for the period of one month for each of the 1,000 samples.

➤ **standard error of the mean**
Standard deviation of a distribution of sample means.

Basic Concepts

Consider a case in which a researcher takes 1,000 simple random samples of size 200 from the population of all consumers who have eaten at a fast-food restaurant at least once in the past 30 days. The purpose is to estimate the average number of times these individuals eat at a fast-food restaurant in an average month.

If the researcher computes the mean number of visits for each of the 1,000 samples and sorts them into intervals based on their relative values, the frequency distribution shown in Exhibit 13.6 might result. Exhibit 13.7 graphically illustrates these frequencies in a histogram, on which a normal curve has been superimposed. As you can see, the histogram closely approximates the shape of a normal curve. If the researcher draws a large enough number of samples of size 200, computes the mean of each sample, and plots these means, the resulting distribution will be a normal distribution. The normal curve shown in Exhibit 13.7 is the sampling distribution

EXHIBIT 13.4	Notation for Means and Standard Deviations of Various Distributions	
Distribution	**Mean**	**Standard Deviation**
Population	μ	σ
Sample	$\bar{X}$	S
Sampling	$\mu_{\bar{x}} = \mu$	$S_{\bar{x}}$

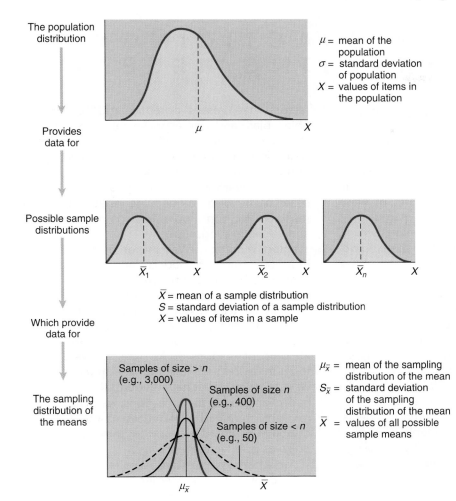

μ = mean of the population
σ = standard deviation of population
X = values of items in the population

$\bar{X}$ = mean of a sample distribution
S = standard deviation of a sample distribution
X = values of items in a sample

$\mu_{\bar{x}}$ = mean of the sampling distribution of the mean
$S_{\bar{x}}$ = standard deviation of the sampling distribution of the mean
$\bar{X}$ = values of all possible sample means

Exhibit 13.5

Relationships of the Three Basic Types of Distribution

Source: Adapted from *Statistics, A Fresh Approach*, 4th ed., by D. H. Sanders et al. © 1990 McGraw-Hill, Inc. Reprinted with permission of the McGraw-Hill Companies.

of the mean for this particular problem. The sampling distribution of the mean for simple random samples that are large (30 or more observations) has the following characteristics:

☐   The distribution is a normal distribution.

☐   The distribution has a mean equal to the population mean.

☐   The distribution has a standard deviation (the standard error of the mean) equal to the population standard deviation divided by the square root of the sample size:

$$\sigma_{\bar{x}} = \frac{\sigma}{\sqrt{n}}$$

This statistic is referred to as the standard error of the mean (instead of the standard deviation) to indicate that it applies to a distribution of sample means rather than to the standard deviation of a sample or a population. Keep in mind that this calculation applies *only* to a simple random sample. Other types of probability samples (for example, stratified samples and cluster samples) require more complex formulas for computing standard error.

PRACTICING MARKETING RESEARCH

Dealing with the Inherent Sample Bias in Nonresponse

Although random sampling is designed to avoid sampling bias, the nonresponse factor within random samples itself is a major form of bias. The calculation of sampling error, required sample size, and related issues are meaningless unless a sample is truly random and there is no systematic exclusion or inclusion of certain types of respondents.

It's almost a conundrum, but a random sample of the intended target population is not a truly random and thus representative slice because inevitably some people refused to take part in the poll. That means it's a random sample only of "that part of the population that was accessible and willing to be interviewed," notes Thomas T. Semon, a marketing research consultant.

Nonresponse bias, Semon contends, affects all survey research. It's an "unavoidable problem" present even in random or probability sampling, which usually presents itself as embodying scientifically drawn data. Maybe it doesn't.

Market researchers infer that the science is operative in the sample actually interviewed, but in fact far more often it refers only to the proportion of respondents interviewed. "If that is not a high percentage," Semon says, "it would throw a lot of cold water on the random-sample puffery." A more accurate reporting would involve the percentage of those responding (not polled), and it would be a more reliable indicator than the standard error ranges put forward.[7]

Wim F. de Heer and Ger Moritz of Statistic Netherlands emphasize that nonresponse is a "severe problem" in social statistics and survey research, making the estimates of surveys "questionable." Nonresponse is a "largely unknown factor" that creates potential and "unmeasurable" bias, and nonresponse rates are increasing. Even more troubling is the fact that weighting techniques will not completely reduce nonresponse bias in a sample.[8]

The question that intrigues market researchers revolves around the reasons for nonresponse. Do nonrespondents constitute a viable, and valuable, subgroup?

Joni Montez of Washington State University in a 2003 study concluded that the characteristics of nonrespondents "may somehow differ" from those of respondents. If so, this could potentially limit the external validity of the survey results. In Montez's 2003 study, the researcher actually polled the nonrespondents and got a 25 percent response. Five reasons were given for nonresponding: the nonrespondents didn't want to; they didn't have enough time; their job had changed so the questions were no longer relevant; they had preferences as to what kind of poll they would respond to; they thought the poll was poorly designed.[9]

In a comparable study, also from 2003, conducted by Craig A. Mertler of Bowling Green State University, 48 percent of nonrespondents gave as their reason a lack of interest in taking the time to respond; 20 percent said they had technological limitations in accessing the online survey; 15 percent reported the poll was too long; and 6 percent stated that the survey subject did not interest them.[10]

These two studies would suggest that nonrespondents are not a clearly defined subgroup but are simply people who had difficulties with or strong opinions about the poll or its mechanics (computers, online access). The studies also suggest that some of these people could be expected to be included in the respondents category the second time.

EXHIBIT 13.6	Frequency Distribution of 1,000 Sample Means: Average Number of Times Respondent Ate at a Fast-Food Restaurant in the Past 30 Days
Number of Times	Frequency of Occurrence
2.6–3.5	8
3.6–4.5	15
4.6–5.5	29
5.6–6.5	44
6.6–7.5	64
7.6–8.5	79
8.6–9.5	89
9.6–10.5	108
10.6–11.5	115
11.6–12.5	110
12.6–13.5	90
13.6–14.5	81
14.6–15.5	66
15.6–16.5	45
16.6–17.5	32
17.6–18.5	16
18.6–19.5	9
Total	1000

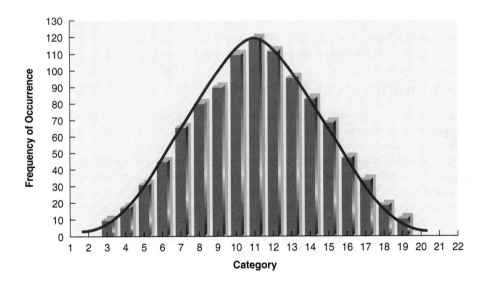

Exhibit 13.7

Actual Sampling Distribution of Means for Number of Times Respondent Ate at Fast-Food Restaurant in Past 30 Days

Making Inferences on the Basis of a Single Sample

In practice, there is no call for taking all possible random samples from a particular population and generating a frequency distribution and histogram like those shown in Exhibits 13.6 and 13.7. Instead, the researcher wants to take one simple random sample and make statistical inferences about the population from which it was drawn. The question is, what is the probability that any one simple random sample of a particular size

The sampling distribution of the proportion is used to estimate the percentage of the population that watches a particular television program.

will produce an estimate of the population mean that is within one standard error (plus or minus) of the true population mean? The answer, based on the information provided in Exhibit 13.2, is that there is a 68.26 percent probability that any one sample from a particular population will produce an estimate of the population mean that is within plus or minus one standard error of the true value, because 68.26 percent of all sample means fall in this range. There is a 95.44 percent probability that any one simple random sample of a particular size from a given population will produce a value that is within plus or minus two standard errors of the true population mean, and a 99.74 percent probability that such a sample will produce an estimate of the mean that is within plus or minus three standard errors of the population mean.

Point and Interval Estimates

The results of a sample can be used to generate two kinds of estimates of a population mean: point and interval estimates. The sample mean is the best **point estimate** of the population mean. Inspection of the sampling distribution of the mean shown in Exhibit 13.7 suggests that a particular sample result is likely to produce a mean that is relatively close to the population mean. However, the mean of a particular sample could be any one of the sample means shown in the distribution. A small percentage of these sample means are a considerable distance from the true population mean. The distance between the sample mean and the true population mean is the sampling error.

Given that point estimates based on sample results are exactly correct in only a small percentage of all possible cases, interval estimates generally are preferred. An **interval estimate** is a particular interval or range of values within which the true population value is estimated to fall. In addition to stating the size of the interval, the researcher usually states the probability that the interval will include the true value of the population mean. This probability is referred to as the **confidence level**, *confidence coefficient*, and the interval is called the **confidence interval**.

Interval estimates of the mean are derived by first drawing a random sample of a given size from the population of interest and calculating the mean of that sample. This sample mean is known to lie somewhere within the sampling distribution of all possible sample means, but exactly where this particular mean falls in that distribution is not known. There is a 68.26 percent probability that this particular sample mean lies within

> **point estimate**
> Particular estimate of a population value.

> **interval estimate**
> Interval or range of values within which the true population value is estimated to fall.

> **confidence level**
> Probability that a particular interval will include the true population value; also called *confidence coefficient*.

> **confidence interval**
> Interval that, at the specified confidence level, includes the true population value.

one standard error (plus or minus) of the true population mean. Based on this information, the researcher states that he or she is 68.26 percent confident that the true population value is equal to the sample value plus or minus one standard error. This statement can be shown symbolically, as follows:

$$\overline{X} - 1\sigma_{\bar{x}} \leq \mu \leq \overline{X} + 1\sigma_{\bar{x}}$$

By the same logic, the researcher can be 95.44 percent confident that the true population value is equal to the sample estimate ± 2 (technically 1.96) standard errors, and 99.74 percent confident that the true population value falls within the interval defined by the sample value ± 3 standard errors.

These statements assume that the standard deviation of the population is known. However, in most situations, this is not the case. If the standard deviation of the population were known, by definition the mean of the population would also be known, and there would be no need to take a sample in the first place. Because information on the standard deviation of the population is lacking, its value is estimated based on the standard deviation of the sample.

Sampling Distribution of the Proportion

Marketing researchers frequently are interested in estimating proportions or percentages rather than or in addition to estimating means. Common examples include estimating the following:

☐ The percentage of the population that is aware of a particular ad
☐ The percentage of the population that accesses the Internet one or more times in an average week
☐ The percentage of the population that has visited a fast-food restaurant four or more times in the past 30 days
☐ The percentage of the population that watches a particular television program

In situations in which a population proportion or percentage is of interest, the sampling distribution of the proportion is used.

The **sampling distribution of the proportion** is a relative frequency distribution of the sample proportions of a large number of random samples of a given size drawn from a particular population. The sampling distribution of a proportion has the following characteristics:

☐ It approximates a normal distribution.
☐ The mean proportion for all possible samples is equal to the population proportion.
☐ The standard error of a sampling distribution of the proportion can be computed with the following formula:

> **sampling distribution of the proportion**
> Relative frequency distribution of the sample proportions of many random samples of a given size drawn from a particular population; it is normally distributed.

$$S_p = \sqrt{\frac{P(1 - P)}{n}}$$

where S_p = standard error of sampling distribution of proportion
          P = estimate of population proportion
          n = sample size

Consider the task of estimating the percentage of all adults who have purchased something over the Internet in the past 90 days. As in generating a sampling distribution of the mean, the researcher might select 1,000 random samples of size 200 from the population of all adults and compute the proportion of all adults who have purchased something over the Internet in the past 90 days for all 1,000 samples. These values could then be plotted in a frequency distribution, and this frequency distribution would approximate a normal distribution. The estimated standard error of the proportion for this distribution can be computed using the formula provided earlier.

For reasons that will be clear to you after you read the next section, marketing researchers have a tendency to prefer dealing with sample size problems as problems of estimating proportions rather than means.

Determining Sample Size

Problems Involving Means

Consider once again the task of estimating how many times the average fast-food restaurant user visits a fast-food restaurant in an average month. Management needs an estimate of the average number of visits to make a decision regarding a new promotional campaign that is being developed. To make this estimate, the marketing research manager for the organization intends to survey a simple random sample of all fast-food users. The question is, what information is necessary to determine the appropriate sample size for the project? The formula for calculating the required sample size for problems that involve the estimation of a mean is as follows[11]:

$$n = \frac{Z^2 \sigma^2}{E^2}$$

where
Z = level of confidence expressed in standard errors
σ = population standard deviation
E = acceptable amount of sampling error

Three pieces of information are needed to compute the sample size required:

1. The acceptable or allowable level of sampling error E.
2. The acceptable level of confidence Z. In other words, how confident does the researcher want to be that the specified confidence interval includes the population mean?
3. An estimate of the population standard deviation σ.

> ➤ **allowable sampling error**
> Amount of sampling error the researcher is willing to accept.

The level of confidence Z and **allowable sampling error** E for this calculation must be set by the researcher in consultation with his or her client. As noted earlier, the level of confidence and the amount of error are based not only on statistical criteria, but also on financial and managerial criteria. In an ideal world, the level of confidence would always be very high and the amount of error very low. However, because this is a business decision, cost must be considered. An acceptable trade-off among accuracy, level of confidence, and cost must be developed. High levels of precision and confidence may be less important in some situations than in others. For example, in an exploratory study, you may be interested in developing a basic sense of whether attitudes toward your product are generally positive or negative. Precision may not be critical. However, in a product concept test, you would need a much more precise estimate of sales for a new product before making the potentially costly and risky decision to introduce that product in the marketplace.

Making an estimate of the **population standard deviation** presents a more serious problem. As noted earlier, if the population standard deviation were known, the population mean also would be known (the population mean is needed to compute the population standard deviation), and there would be no need to draw a sample. How can the researcher estimate the population standard deviation before selecting the sample? One or some combination of the following four methods might be used to deal with this problem:

> **population standard deviation**
> Standard deviation of a variable for the entire population.

1. *Use results from a prior survey.* In many cases, the firm may have conducted a prior survey dealing with the same or a similar issue. In this situation, a possible solution to the problem is to use the results of the prior survey as an estimate of the population standard deviation.

2. *Conduct a pilot survey.* If this is to be a large-scale project, it may be possible to devote some time and some resources to a small-scale pilot survey of the population. The results of this pilot survey can be used to develop an estimate of the population standard deviation that can be used in the sample size determination formula.

3. *Use secondary data.* In some cases, secondary data can be used to develop an estimate of the population standard deviation.

4. *Use judgment.* If all else fails, an estimate of the population standard deviation can be developed based solely on judgment. Judgments might be sought from a variety of managers in a position to make educated guesses about the required population parameters.

It should be noted that after the survey has been conducted and the sample mean and sample standard deviation have been calculated, the researcher can assess the accuracy of the estimate of the population standard deviation used to calculate the required sample size. At this time, if appropriate; adjustments can be made in the initial estimates of sampling error.[12]

Let's return to the problem of estimating the average number of fast-food visits made in an average month by users of fast-food restaurants:

☐ After consultation with managers in the company, the marketing research manager determines that an estimate is needed of the average number of times that fast-food consumers visit fast-food restaurants. She further determines that managers believe that a high degree of accuracy is needed, which she takes to mean that the estimate should be within .10 (one-tenth) of a visit of the true population value. This value (.10) should be substituted into the formula for the value of E.

☐ In addition, the marketing research manager decides that, all things considered, she needs to be 95.44 percent confident that the true population mean falls in the interval defined by the sample mean plus or minus E (as just defined). Two (technically, 1.96) standard errors are required to take in 95.44 percent of the area under a normal curve. Therefore, a value of 2 should be substituted into the equation for Z.

☐ Finally, there is the question of what value to insert into the formula for σ. Fortunately, the company conducted a similar study one year ago. The standard deviation in that study for the variable—the average number of times a fast-food restaurant was visited in the past 30 days—was 1.39. This is the best estimate of σ available. Therefore, a value of 1.39 should be substituted into the formula for the value of σ. The calculation follows:

$$n = \frac{Z^2\sigma^2}{E^2}$$

$$= \frac{2^2(1.39)^2}{(.10)^2}$$

$$= \frac{4(1.93)}{.01}$$

$$= \frac{7.72}{.01}$$

$$= 772$$

Based on this calculation, a simple random sample of 772 is necessary to meet the requirements outlined.

PRACTICING MARKETING RESEARCH

Can We Trust the Results of Call-in Polls and Infotainment Polls?

We can't overemphasize the importance of having true random samples. The following examples illustrate this point.

Say a newscaster on an evening news program invites viewers to phone in their opinions on a charged subject, for example, the U.S. president's performance on the economy. Many people phone in, and the next day the station announces that 41 percent of their viewers approve of the president's performance. Other viewers hear this result and assume it accurately represents the state of things.

Does it? The consensus among market researchers is no. Such polls are regarded as pseudo-polls, as inherently and deeply unscientific, as possessing entertainment or infotainment interest at best, but otherwise misleading and erroneous. For example, the same person can call in many times and express views; people who hold strong opinions on the particular subject are probably more motivated to respond than others, further skewing the sample accuracy.

"The unscientific call-in poll does not even try to be representative of the viewing populations," comments Stephen J. Hellebusch, president of Hellebusch Research & Consulting of Cincinnati, Ohio. The sample poll is almost entirely self-selected (people who felt moved to respond), drawn from the already specialized demographics of the given media's viewing base, and the results "represent nothing" and should not be heeded, Hellebusch adds.

How skewed call-in polls might be from the results of a scientifically conducted poll were made vividly clear by a CBS News study. Following the State of the Union address on January 28, 1992, newscasters on a CBS one-hour post-address commentary show invited viewers to phone in their views. They received 317,500 calls, and estimates placed the number of attempted call-ins at 24.6 million. The sheer quantity of viewer-call-ins delighted CBS executives.

But at the same time CBS put the question to a random sample of 1,241 adults who had been recruited earlier, on a scientific basis, to watch the show. The panel had been weighted to correct for possible biases due to selection, demographics, and nonresponse—everything the call-in "sample" had not.

On the question of whether one's financial situation was better now (1992) than in 1988, 54 percent of the call-ins said things were worse compared to 32 percent of the weighted sample. On whether people were worried about losing a job, 64 percent of the call-ins said yes, compared to 48 percent of the dedicated panel.

Based on the CBS News data, results from call-in polls can be expected to vary (that is, be inherently inaccurate) by as much as ±27 percent from results obtained through a scientific poll conducted according to the best marketing research standards.[13]

Financial situation now v. four years ago

	Random sample	Call-in poll	Difference
Same	44%	17%	−27
Worse	32%	54%	+22
Better	24%	29%	+5

Worried about you/family member losing a job

	Random sample	Call-in poll	Difference
Yes	48%	64%	+16
No	52%	36%	−16

Whether media exaggerates economic conditions

	Random sample	Call-in poll	Difference
Yes	35%	39%	+4
No	65%	61%	−4

Source: CBS News.

Problems Involving Proportions

Now let's consider the problem of estimating the proportion or percentage of all adults who have purchased something via the Internet in the past 90 days. The goal is to take a simple random sample from the population of all adults to estimate this proportion.[14]

☐ As in the problem involving fast-food users, the first task in estimating the population mean on the basis of sample results is to decide on an acceptable value for E. If, for example, an error level of ± 4 percent is acceptable, a value of .04 should be substituted into the formula for E.

☐ Next, assume that the researcher has determined a need to be 95.44 percent confident that the sample estimate is within ± 4 percent of the true population proportion. As in the previous example, a value of 2 should be substituted into the equation for Z.

☐ Finally, in a study of the same issue conducted one year ago, 5 percent of all respondents indicated they had purchased something over the Internet in the past 90 days. Thus, a value of .05 should be substituted into the equation for P.

The resulting calculations are as follows:

$$
\begin{aligned}
n &= \frac{Z^2[P(1 - P)]}{E^2} \\
&= \frac{2^2[.05(1 - .05)]}{.04^2} \\
&= \frac{4(.0475)}{.0016} \\
&= \frac{.19}{.0016} \\
&= 119
\end{aligned}
$$

Given the requirements, a random sample of 475 respondents is required. It should be noted that, in one respect, the process of determining the sample size necessary to estimate a proportion is easier than the process of determining the sample size necessary to estimate a mean: If there is no basis for estimating P, the researcher can make what is sometimes referred to as the most pessimistic, or worst-case, assumption regarding the value of P. Given the values of Z and E, what value of P will require the largest possible sample? A value of .50 will make the value of the expression $P(1 - P)$ larger than any possible value of P. There is no corresponding most pessimistic assumption that the researcher can make regarding the value of σ in problems that involve determining the sample size necessary to estimate a mean with given levels of Z and E.

Determining Sample Size for Stratified and Cluster Samples

The formulas for sample size determination presented in this chapter apply only to simple random samples. There also are formulas for determining required sample size and sampling error for other types of probability samples such as stratified and cluster samples. Although many of the general concepts presented in this chapter apply to these other types of probability samples, the specific formulas are much more complicated.[15] In addition, these formulas require information that frequently is not available or is difficult to obtain. For these reasons, sample size determination for other types of probability samples is beyond the scope of this introductory text. Those interested in pursuing the question of sample size determination for stratified and cluster samples are referred to advanced texts on the topic of sampling.

Population Size and Sample Size

You may have noticed that none of the formulas for determining sample size takes into account the size of the population in any way. Students (and managers) frequently find this troubling. It seems to make sense that one should take a larger sample from a larger population. But this is not the case. Normally, there is no direct relationship between the size of the population and the size of the sample required to estimate a particular population parameter with a particular level of error and a particular level of confidence. In fact, the size of the population may have an effect only in those situations where the size of the sample is large in relation to the size of the population. One rule of thumb is that an adjustment should be made in the sample size if the sample size is more than 5 percent of the size of the total population. The normal presumption is that sample elements are drawn independently of one another (*independence assumption*). This assumption is justified when the sample is small relative to the population. However, it is not appropriate when the sample is a relatively large (5 percent or more) proportion of the population. As a result, the researcher must adjust the results obtained with the standard formulas. For example, the formula for the standard error of the mean, presented earlier, is as follows:

$$\sigma_{\bar{x}} = \frac{\sigma}{\sqrt{n}}$$

For a sample that is 5 percent or more of the population, the independence assumption is dropped, producing the following formula:

$$\sigma_{\bar{x}} = \frac{\sigma}{\sqrt{n}} \sqrt{\frac{N - n}{N - 1}}$$

The factor $(N - n)/(N - 1)$ is referred to as the **finite population correction factor (FPC)**.

In those situations in which the sample is large (5 percent or more) in relation to the population, the researcher can appropriately reduce the required sample size using the FPC. This calculation is made using the following formula:

$$n' = \frac{nN}{N + n - 1}$$

where

n' = revised sample size

n = original sample size

N = population size

> **finite population correction factor (FPC)**
> An adjustment to the required sample size that is made in cases where the sample is expected to be equal to 5 percent or more of the total population.

If the population has 2,000 elements and the original sample size is 400, then

$$n' = \frac{400(2000)}{2000 + 400 - 1} = \frac{800,000}{2399}$$

$$= 333$$

With the FPC adjustment, a sample of only 333 is needed, rather than the original 400.

The key is not the size of the sample in relation to the size of the population, but whether the sample selected is truly representative of the population. Empirical evidence shows that relatively small but carefully chosen samples can quite accurately reflect characteristics of the population. Many well-known national surveys and opinion polls, such as the Gallup Poll and the Harris Poll, are based on samples of fewer than 2,000. These polls have shown that the behavior of tens of millions of people can be predicted quite accurately using samples that are minuscule in relation to the size of the population.

Determining How Many Sample Units Are Needed

Regardless of how the target sample size is determined, the researcher is confronted with the practical problem of figuring out how many sampling units (telephone numbers, addresses, and so on) will be required to complete the assignment. For example, if the target final sample size is 400, then obviously more than 400 telephone numbers will be needed to complete a telephone survey.

Some of the numbers on the list will be disconnected, some people will not qualify for the survey because they do not meet the requirements for inclusion in the population, and some will refuse to complete the survey. These factors affect the final estimate of the number of phone numbers, which may be used to place an order with a sample provider, such as Survey Sampling, Incorporated, or to ask the client for customer names and phone numbers for a satisfaction survey. This estimate must be reasonably accurate because the researcher wants to avoid paying for more numbers than are needed; on the other hand, the researcher doesn't want to run out of numbers during the survey and have to wait for more.

The Practicing Marketing Research feature provides a practical approach to developing these important estimates.

PRACTICING MARKETING RESEARCH

Estimating with Precision How Many Phone Numbers Are Needed

Calculating how many phone numbers are needed for a project may seem like a difficult task, but following a few basic rules can make it simple. The formula used by SSI to calculate sample size involves four factors: (1) the number of completed interviews needed, (2) the working phone (or "reachable") rate, (3) the incidence rate, and (4) the contact/completion rate.

Completed Interviews

The number of completed interviews is based on the sample size calculation formula for simple random samples. It is the final sample size you want to achieve.

Working Phone Rate

The working phone rate varies with the sampling methodology used. An SSI RDD sample yields a 60 percent working phone rate. That is a good number to use in the formula for estimation purposes.

Incidence Rate

The incidence rate is the percentage of contacts that will qualify for the interview. Or put another way, what percentage of people who answer the phone (or reply to your mail questionnaire) will pass your screening questions? Accurate incidence data are critical to determining proper sample size. An incidence figure that is too high will leave you short of sample once your study is in the field.

Contact/Completion Rate

The last factor is the contact/completion rate. SSI defines this rate as the percentage of people

who, once they qualify for your study, will agree to cooperate by completing the interview. There are several important elements you should consider when trying to reasonably estimate the completion rate:

- ☐ Contact rate
- ☐ Length of interview
- ☐ Sensitivity of topic
- ☐ Time of year
- ☐ Number of attempts/callbacks
- ☐ Length of time in the field

Provided that the interview is short (less than 10 minutes) and nonsensitive in nature, sufficient callbacks are scheduled, and the study will be in the field for an adequate period of time, SSI estimates a 30 percent completion rate. The completion rate should be adjusted according to the specifications of each study. If the subject matter is sensitive or the interview is long, the completion rate should be reduced. If the length of time in the field is less than one week, SSI recommends increasing the sample size by at least 20 percent.

An Example

Suppose you wish to complete 300 interviews in the United Kingdom. Using a random-digit sample, you can expect a working phone rate of 60 percent. Start by dividing the number of completed interviews you need (300) by the working phone rate (.60), to yield 500. You need to reach heavy soft drink users (17 percent of adults), and you estimate that 30 percent of the people contacted will complete the interview. Divide 500 by the incidence rate for the group under study (.17) and then by the completion rate (.30). This calculation shows you need 9,804 phone numbers to complete this survey.[16]

If you wish to complete 300 interviews in the United Kingdom, you need to determine the contact/completion rate in order to figure out how many calls will actually have to be made to complete the survey.

Statistical Power

Although it is standard practice in marketing research to use the formulas presented in this chapter to calculate sample size, these formulas all focus on *type I error*, or the error of concluding that there is a difference when there is not a difference. They do not explicitly deal with *type II error*, or the error of saying that there is no difference when there is a difference. The probability of not making a type II error is called **statistical power**.[17] The standard formulas for calculating sample size implicitly assume a power of 50 percent. For example, suppose a researcher is trying to determine which of two product concepts has stronger appeal to target customers and wants to be able to detect a 5 percent difference in the percentages of target customers who say that they are very likely to buy the products. The standard sample size formulas indicate that a sample size of approximately 400 is needed for each product test. By using this calculation, the researcher implicitly accepts the fact that there is a 50 percent chance of incorrectly concluding that the two products have equal appeal.

Exhibit 13.8 shows the sample sizes required, at an alpha (probability of incorrectly rejecting the null hypothesis) of .05, for specific levels of power and specific levels of differences between two independent proportions. Formulas are available to permit power calculations for any level of confidence; however, they are somewhat complex and will not help you

> **statistical power**
> Probability of not making a type II error.

EXHIBIT 13.8	Sample Size Required to Detect Differences between Proportions from Independent Samples at Different Levels of Power and an Alpha of .05					
Difference to Detect	**Power**					
	50%	**60%**	**70%**	**75%**	**80%**	**90%**
0.01	19,205	24,491	30,857	34,697	39,239	52,530
0.05	766	977	1,231	1,384	1,568	2,094
0.10	190	242	305	343	389	518
0.15	83	106	133	150	169	226

understand the basic concept of power. Programs available on the Internet can be used to make these calculations. To reproduce the numbers in Exhibit 13.8, go to *http://www.dssre-search. com/SampleSize/default.asp* and do the following:

☐ Click on the Two-Sample Using Percentage Values option under Sample Size.

☐ Enter the Sample 1 Percentage and the Sample 2 Percentage in the boxes so that the figures entered reflect the differences you want to be able to detect and the values are in the expected range. These figures are set at the 50 percent level (value of *p* in the standard sample size formula).

☐ Below those boxes, enter the Alpha and Beta Error Levels. Alpha is the value you would use for *E* in the standard sample size formula, and beta is the probability of incorrectly failing to reject the null hypothesis of no difference when a real difference exists. Power is equal to 1 − beta.

☐ Click on the Calculate Sample Size button at the bottom of the screen for the answer.

SUMMARY

Determining sample size for probability samples involves financial, statistical, and managerial considerations. Other things being equal, the larger the sample is, the smaller the sampling error. In turn, the cost of the research grows with the size of the sample.

There are several methods for determining sample size. One is to base the decision on the funds available. In essence, sample size is determined by the budget. Although seemingly unscientific, this approach is often a very realistic one in the world of corporate marketing research. The second technique is the so-called rule of thumb approach, which essentially involves determining the sample size based on a gut feeling or common practice. Samples of 300, 400, or 500 are often listed by the client in a request for proposal. A third technique for determining sample size is based on the number of subgroups to be analyzed. Generally speaking, the more subgroups that need to be analyzed, the larger is the required total sample size.

In addition to these methods, there are a number of traditional statistical techniques for determining sample size. Three pieces of data are required to make sample size calculations: an estimate of the population standard deviation, the level of sampling error that the researcher or client is willing to accept, and the desired level of confidence that the sample result will fall within a certain range of the true population value.

Crucial to statistical sampling theory is the concept of the normal distribution. The normal distribution is bell-shaped and has only one mode. It also is symmetric about its mean. The standard normal distribution has the features of a normal distribution; however, the mean of the standard normal distribution is always equal to zero, and the standard deviation is always equal to one. The transformation formula is used to transform any value X from any normal distribution to its equivalent value Z from a standard normal distribution. The central limit theorem states that the distribution of the means of a large number of random samples taken from virtually any population approaches a normal distribution with a mean equal to μ and a standard deviation equal to $S_{\bar{x}}$, where

$$S_{\bar{x}} = \frac{\sigma}{\sqrt{n}}$$

The standard deviation of a distribution of sample means is called the standard error of the mean.

When the results of a sample are used to estimate a population mean, two kinds of estimates can be generated: point and interval estimates. The sample mean is the best point estimate of the population mean. An interval estimate is a certain interval or range of values within which the true population value is estimated to fall. Along with the magnitude of the interval, the researcher usually states the probability that the interval will include the true value of the population mean—that is, the confidence level. The interval is called the confidence interval.

The researcher who is interested in estimating proportions or percentages rather than or in addition to means uses the sampling distribution of the proportion. The sampling distribution of the proportion is a relative frequency distribution of the sample proportions of a large number of random samples of a given size drawn from a particular population. The standard error of a sampling distribution of proportion is computed as follows:

$$S_p = \sqrt{\frac{P(1 - P)}{n}}$$

The following are required to calculate sample size: the acceptable level of sampling error E, the acceptable level of confidence Z, and an estimate of the population standard deviation σ. The formula for calculating the required sample size for situations that involve the estimation of a mean is as follows:

$$n = \frac{Z^2 \sigma^2}{E^2}$$

The following formula is used to calculate the required sample size for problems involving proportions:

$$n = \frac{Z^2[P(1 - P)]}{E^2}$$

Finally, statistical power is the probability of not making a type II error. A type II error is the mistake of saying that there is not a difference when there is a difference. The standard sample size formula implicitly assumes a power of 50 percent. It may be important to use different levels of power depending on the nature of the decision in question.

KEY TERMS & DEFINITIONS

central limit theorem Idea that a distribution of a large number of sample means or sample proportions will approximate a normal distribution, regardless of the distribution of the population from which they were drawn.

normal distribution Continuous distribution that is bell-shaped and symmetric about the mean; the mean, median, and mode are equal.

proportional property of the normal distribution Feature that the number of observations falling between the mean and a given number of standard deviations from the mean is the same for all normal distributions.

standard normal distribution Normal distribution with a mean of zero and a standard deviation of one.

standard deviation Measure of dispersion calculated by subtracting the mean of the series from each value in a series, squaring each result, summing the results, dividing the sum by the number of items minus 1, and taking the square root of this value.

population distribution Frequency distribution of all the elements of a population.

sample distribution Frequency distribution of all the elements of an individual sample.

sampling distribution of the mean Theoretical frequency distribution of the means of all possible samples of a given size drawn from a particular population; it is normally distributed.

standard error of the mean Standard deviation of a distribution of sample means.

point estimate Particular estimate of a population value.

interval estimate Interval or range of values within which the true population value is estimated to fall.

confidence level Probability that a particular interval will include the true population value; also called *confidence coefficient*.

confidence interval Interval that, at the specified confidence level, includes the true population value.

sampling distribution of the proportion Relative frequency distribution of the sample proportions of many random samples of a given size drawn from a particular population; it is normally distributed.

allowable sampling error Amount of sampling error the researcher is willing to accept.

population standard deviation Standard deviation of a variable for the entire population.

finite population correction factor (FPC) Adjustment to the required sample size that is made in cases where the sample is expected to be equal to 5 percent or more of the total population.

statistical power Probability of not making a type II error.

QUESTIONS FOR REVIEW & CRITICAL THINKING

1. Explain how the determination of sample size is a financial, statistical, and managerial issue.
2. Discuss and give examples of three methods that are used in marketing research for determining sample size.
3. A marketing researcher analyzing the fast-food industry noticed the following: The average amount spent at a fast-food restaurant in California was $3.30, with a standard deviation of $0.40. Yet in Georgia, the average amount spent at a fast-food restaurant was $3.25, with a standard deviation of $0.10. What do these statistics tell you about fast-food consumption patterns in these two states?
4. Distinguish among population, sample, and sampling distributions. Why is it important to distinguish among these concepts?
5. What is the finite population correction factor? Why is it used? When should it be used?
6. Assume that previous fast-food research has shown that 80 percent of the consumers like curly french fries. The researcher wishes to have a standard error of 6 percent or less and be 95 percent confident of an estimate to be made about curly french fry consumption from a survey. What sample size should be used for a simple random sample?
7. You are in charge of planning a chili cook-off. You must make sure that there are plenty of samples for the patrons of the cook-off. The following standards have been set: a confidence level of 99 percent and an error of less than 4 ounces per cooking team. Last year's cook-off had a standard deviation in amount of chili cooked of 3 ounces. What is the necessary sample size?

8. Based on a client's requirements of a confidence interval of 99.74 percent and acceptable sampling error of 2 percent, a sample size of 500 is calculated. The cost to the client is estimated at $20,000. The client replies that the budget for this project is $17,000. What are the alternatives?

9. A marketing researcher must determine how many telephone numbers she needs to order from a sample provider to complete a survey of ATM users. The goal is to complete 400 interviews with ATM users. From past experience, she estimates that 60 percent of the phone numbers provided will be working phone numbers. The estimated incidence rate (percentage of people contacted who are ATM users) is 43 percent. Finally, she estimates from previous surveys that 35 percent of the people contacted will agree to complete the survey. How many telephone numbers should she order?

WORKING THE NET

What size samples are needed for a statistical power of 70 percent in detecting a difference of 5 percent between the estimated percentages of recent CD buyers in two independent samples? Assume an expected percentage in the range of 50 percent and an alpha error of 5 percent. Use the sample size calculator at *http://www.dssresearch.com/SampleSize/default.asp* to get your answer.

REAL-LIFE RESEARCH • 13.1

Millennium Telecom

Millennium Telecom is an emerging provider of bundled communications services for residential users. It offers local telephone service, long-distance telephone service, digital cable, Internet service, and monitored home security service. Millennium is in the process of building awareness of its brand in selected areas of Texas, New Mexico, and Colorado. Now in its second year, the company plans to spend $4.2 million to promote awareness and brand image of its bundled communications services in the target area. Brand image and awareness are important to Millennium because it is competing with a number of much larger and better financed competitors, including AT&T, Southwestern Bell, and TCI Cable.

In the first year of the brand image campaign, Millennium spent $3 million pursuing the same goals of increasing awareness and brand image. In order to see if the campaign was successful, the company conducted tracking research by telephone. It conducted a pretest before the campaign began and a posttest at the end of the year. The surveys were designed to measure awareness and image of Millennium. Changes in either measure from the pretest to the posttest were to be attributed to the effects of the ad campaign. No other elements of the marketing strategy were changed during the course of the campaign.

Unaided, or top-of-mind, awareness ("What companies come to mind when you think of companies that provide residential communication services?") increased from 21 percent in the pretest to 25 percent in the posttest. In the pretest, 42 percent reported having a positive image of Millennium. This figure increased to 44 percent in the posttest. Although both key measures increased, the sample sizes for the two tests were relatively small. Random samples of 100 consumers were used for both tests. Sampling error for the measure of awareness at 95.44 percent confidence is ±8.7 percent. The comparable figure for the image measure is ±9.9 percent. The value used for P in the formula is the posttest result. With these relatively large sampling errors and the relatively small changes in awareness and image, Millennium could only say with 95.44 percent confidence that awareness in the posttest was 25 ± 8.7 percent, or in the range of 16.3 to 33.7 percent. In regard to the image measure, it could only say with 95.44 percent confidence that the percentage of consumers with a positive image of Millennium in the posttest was 44 ± 9.9 percent, or in the range of 34.1 to 53.9 percent. Based on the relatively small changes in awareness and image and the relatively large errors associated with these measures, Millennium could not conclude with any confidence that either measure had actually changed.

The CEO of Millennium is concerned about the amount of money being spent on advertising and wants to know whether the advertising is actually achieving what it is supposed to achieve. She wants a more sensitive test so that a definitive conclusion can be reached regarding the effect of the advertising.

Questions

1. Show how the sampling errors for the posttest measures were calculated.
2. If the CEO wants to have 95.44 percent confidence that the estimates of awareness and positive image are within ± 2 percent of the true value, what is the required sample size?
3. What is the required sample size if the CEO wants to be 99.74 percent confident?
4. If the current budget for conducting the telephone interviews is $20,000 and the cost per interview is $19, can Millennium reach the goal specified in question 3? With the $20,000 budget, what error levels can it reach for both measures? What is the budget required to reach the goal set in question 3?

REAL-LIFE RESEARCH• 13.2

Sky Meals

Sky Meals is the second largest airline caterer in the United States, providing nearly all the meals for passengers of the three largest airlines and several smaller commuter airlines. As part of a Total Quality Management (TQM) program, one of its clients, Continental Airlines, has recently met with representatives of Sky Meals to discuss a customer satisfaction program it is planning to implement.

Continental plans to interview a sample of its customers four times a year. In the survey, it intends to ask customers to rate the quality of meals provided on a 1-to-10 scale, where 1 means poor and 10 means excellent. It has just completed a benchmark study of 1,000 customers. In that study, meals received an average rating of 8.7 on the 10-point scale, with a standard deviation of 1.65. Continental has indicated that it wants Sky Meals to guarantee a level of satisfaction of 8.5 in the first quarterly survey, to be conducted in 3 months. For its quarterly surveys, Continental plans to use a sample size of 500. In the new contract with Sky Meals, Continental wants to include a clause that will penalize Sky Meals $25,000 for each one-tenth of a point it falls below an average of 8.5 on the next satisfaction survey.

Questions

1. What is the 95.44 percent confidence interval for the estimated satisfaction level in the benchmark survey? What is the 99.74 percent confidence interval?
2. Assume that the upcoming first-quarter satisfaction survey shows an average rating of 8.4 on satisfaction with meals. Compute the 95.44 percent confidence interval and the 99.74 confidence interval.
3. If you were negotiating for Sky Meals, how would you respond to Continental regarding the penalty clause?

surveysolutions XP ● **SPSS EXERCISES FOR CHAPTER 13**

Exercise #1: Sample Size Determination Using the Sample Means Method SPSS-H1

1. Go to the Wiley Web site at *www.wiley.com/college/mcdaniel* and download the *Segmenting the College Student Market for Movie Attendance* database to SPSS windows. Using the *Segmenting the College Student Market for Movie Attendance* database, <u>assume that the most important items in the survey are in question #5,</u> which has 9 movie items in which respondents rate their relative importance (download a copy of the *Segmenting the College Student Market for Movie Attendance* questionnaire). Notice the computer coding for each of the variables, which is the same as that in the *variable view* option on the SPSS Data Editor.

2. The Sample Means method of sample size determination consists of:
   i. required confidence level (z)
   ii. level of tolerable error (e)
   iii. estimated population variance (o)
   iv. estimated sample size (n)
   v. *Formula:* $n = (z^2 * o^2)/e^2$

3. Of the various methods of deriving sample size, estimated population standard deviation can be estimated based on prior studies, expert judgment, or by conducting a pilot sample. For this problem, we are going to estimate population standard deviation using a ***pilot sample***. To do this you will use only the first 200 cases in the *Segmenting the College Student Market for Movie Attendance* database. Invoke the *data/select cases* sequence to select the first 200 cases in the database. We are assuming that these are responses to a pilot sample, and we will use them to estimate the needed sample size.

4. Use the *analyze/descriptive statistics/descriptive* sequence to compute the standard deviation for variables Q5a–Q5i. We are assuming that each of the 9 variables is equally important with respect to the research objective.

5. From your knowledge of sample size determination, you should know that the variable to select for sample size determination is the one with <u>the largest standard deviation.</u> Select that variable.

Answer the following questions:

1. Which of the 9 movie theatre items had the largest standard deviation?

   _____

2. Invoke the sample means method of sample size determination to make the necessary computations for each of the following:
   a. Compute sample size given the following:
      i. required confidence level (Z) is 95.44%.
      ii. tolerable error (e) is .1 or 1/10 of a response point.
      iii. standard deviation (o) = _____
      iv. sample size (n) = _____

surveysolutions XP

b. Compute sample size given the following:
   i. required confidence level (Z) is 99.72%.
   ii. tolerable level (e) is .1 or 1/10 of a response point.
   iii. standard deviation (o) = _____
   iv. sample size (n) = _____

3. How do your computed sample sizes in the problems above compare to the total number of cases in the *Segmenting the College Student Market for Movie Attendance* database?
   _____

4. We are going to assume that the objective of our research concerning students attendance at movies can be expressed as a dichotomy (greater or lesser, etc.); for example, it doesn't matter how much one group attends movies over another group, but just *who* attends the most. To accomplish this we can use the much less complicated *sample proportions* formula. We are going to assume that we have no prior studies, hence, in the sample proportions formula P = .5 and (1 − P) = .5. **You will not need SPSS to assist you with this computation**.
   a. Compute sample size given the following:
      i. required confidence level (Z) is 95.44%.
      ii. tolerable error (e) is .05 or accuracy within 5% of the true population mean.
      iii. standard deviation P = .5 and (1 − P) = .5
      iv. sample size (n) = _____
   c. Compute sample size given the following:
      i. required confidence level (Z) is 99.72%.
      ii. tolerable error (e) is .03 or accuracy within 3% of the true population mean.
      iii. standard deviation P = .5 and (1 − P) = .5
      iv. sample size (n) = _____

Exercise #2: Determining the Reliability/Confidence of Sample Results

1. In the subsequent exercise the objective will not be to determine the needed sample size, but to evaluate the confidence level of results derived from the entire *Segmenting the College Student Market for Movie Attendance* database. To evaluate this type of confidence, using the sample means formula, solve for Z instead of n. Hence, use the formula $Z^2 = n * e^2/o^2$. Then take the square root of Z^2. Go to the normal distribution table in the appendix of your text to determine the confidence level associated with the database. For the sample proportions formula, solve for Z using the formula $Z^2 = (n * e^2)/[P(1 − P)]$, then take the square root of Z^2.

2. For this problem again assume that question #5 has the most important questions in the questionnaire, with respect to the research objectives. Using the *analyze/descriptive statistics/descriptives* sequence, compute the standard deviation for variables Q5a–Q5i. We are assuming that each of the 9 variables are equally important with respect to the research objective. Again, choose the variable with the largest standard deviation to input into the analysis.

3. Given the preceding, compute the confidence level associated with the *Segmenting the College Student Market for Movie Attendance* database, given the following:
   1. a. tolerable error is .1 or 1/10 of a response point
      b. sample size = 500
      c. standard deviation _____

2. Confidence Level = _____ %

3. How do the results in 2, above compare to the results in 2, of the sample size determination problem?

   _____

4. <u>Sample Proportions Formula</u>: Given the information below, compute the confidence level associated with the *Segmenting the College Student Marketing for Movie Attendance* database. ***You will not need SPSS to make this computation***.

   a. tolerable error is .05 or 5%

   b. sample size = 500

   c. standard deviation P = .5 and (1 − P) = .5

   1. Confidence Level = _____ %

   2. How do the results in this problem compare to the confidence level in #2 of (3)?

   _____

DATA PROCESSING
AND FUNDAMENTAL
DATA ANALYSIS

LEARNING OBJECTIVES

1.	To get an overview of the data analysis procedure.
2.	To develop an understanding of the importance and nature of quality control checks.
3.	To understand the data entry process and data entry alternatives.
4.	To learn how surveys are tabulated.
5.	To learn how to set up and interpret crosstabulations.
6.	To comprehend the basic techniques of statistical analysis.

Stephanie Benson, of Technology Decisions, is the firm's account executive for Dell Computer. She recently submitted a proposal to Dell for a project involving the processing of 20,000 to 25,000 questionnaires to be collected by Dell personnel from attendees at a series of high-tech trade shows over the next 6 months. On this project, she will be working directly with the manager from the sales group responsible for Dell's trade show activities, Jill Jackson. Benson did not take this into account when she wrote her proposal. Normally, she worked with marketing research department staff, who would interface between her and the managers for whom the research was being done. Knowing that these marketing researchers were well acquainted with editing, coding, data entry, and tabulation procedures, she did not cover those topics in any depth in her proposal.

She has just received a lengthy e-mail from Jackson who says she likes the price quoted and the sample report included in the proposal. However, Benson can see that Jackson is a process-oriented person who wants lots of details regarding how various things will be done. Jill Jackson's questions, taken from her e-mail, follow:

- ☐ Will the questionnaires be checked for logical consistency, accuracy, and completeness before they are entered into electronic files? How will this be done? What quality checks are built into this process?

- ☐ I'm assuming that no data entry will be done until questionnaires have been checked as suggested above. Is that assumption correct?

- ☐ As you know from the sample questionnaire, the survey has seven open-ended questions. This information is very important to us. We intend to use feedback from the trade show attendees—they are either customers or people we would like to have as customers—to guide us in developing a number of sales and marketing initiatives. Therefore, it is important that we get an accurate and complete summarization of these comments. Obviously, there are far too many questionnaires for us to read and somehow summarize ourselves. In your proposal, you refer to the "coding" of open-ended questions. I have only a very general idea of what that means. What does it mean to "code" open-ended questions? How do you go about it? Outline the process. What quality control checks are built into the process? Finally, can we [management] have some input in shaping how comments are coded?

- ☐ In your proposal, you say you will enter data from the paper questionnaires after completion of the coding process. I'm assuming that you're talking about transferring the data from the paper questionnaire to an electronic file. How will this be done? What quality control procedures are built into this process so that I can be assured that the data in the electronic file accurately reflect the original responses on the paper questionnaires?

- ☐ You refer to cross tabulations in your proposal. What are cross tabulations, and how are they produced? I know they are tables of some sort. Can we have input into the design of those tables?

- ☐ Finally, is there some way that we could have access to our data over the Internet? Having access to the tables would be okay, but we really would like to be able to have access to the data and a tool that would permit us to generate any tables that we might want to produce. Is this possible?

This chapter will offer answers to Jackson's questions by providing all of the background and tools needed to perform these important tasks. The seemingly mechanical data processing activities are a critical bridge between the data-collection and data analysis phases of a project. ■

You should be able to give her the answers after you read this chapter.

Overview of the Data Analysis Procedure

Once data collection has been completed and questionnaires have been returned, the researcher may be facing anywhere from a few hundred to several thousand interviews, each ranging from a few pages to 20 or more pages. We recently completed a study involving 1,300 questionnaires of 10 pages each. The 13,000 pages amounted to a stack of paper nearly 3 feet high. How should a researcher transform all the information contained on 13,000 pages of completed questionnaires into a format that will permit the summarization necessary for detailed analysis? At one extreme, the researcher could read all the interviews, make notes while reading them, and draw some conclusions from this review of the questionnaires. The folly of this approach is fairly obvious. Instead of this haphazard and inefficient approach, professional researchers follow a five-step procedure for data analysis:

Step One.	Validation and editing (quality control)
Step Two.	Coding
Step Three.	Data entry
Step Four.	Machine cleaning of data
Step Five.	Tabulation and statistical analysis

Step One: Validation and Editing

The purpose of the first step is twofold. The researcher wants to make sure that all the interviews actually were conducted as specified (validation) and that the questionnaires have been filled out properly and completely (editing).

Validation

First, the researcher must determine, to the extent possible, that each of the questionnaires to be processed represents a valid interview. Here, we are using the term *valid* in a different sense than in Chapter 9. In Chapter 9, *validity* was defined as the extent to which what was being measured was actually measured. In this chapter, **validation** is defined as the process of ascertaining that interviews were conducted as specified. In this context, no assessment is made regarding the validity of the measurement. The goal of validation is solely to detect interviewer fraud or failure to follow key instructions. You may have noticed that the various questionnaires presented throughout the text almost always have a place to record the respondent's name, address, and telephone number. This information is seldom used in any way in the analysis of the data; it is collected only to provide a basis for validation.

Professional researchers know that interviewer cheating does happen. Various studies have documented the existence and prevalence of interviewer falsification of several types. For this reason, validation is an integral and necessary step in the data processing stage of a marketing research project. See the Practicing Marketing Research feature on page 435 for some ways to address this problem.

After all the interviews have been completed, the research firm recontacts a certain percentage of the respondents surveyed by each interviewer. Typically, this percentage ranges from 10 to 20 percent. If a particular interviewer surveyed 50 people and the research firm

> **validation**
> Process of ascertaining that interviews actually were conducted as specified.

PRACTICING MARKETING RESEARCH

New Data Quality Procedures to Identify Interviewer Falsification

Interviewer falsification or cheating is a serious concern when it comes to data quality control. It introduces bias into survey responses, and it tends to increase when interviewers are working under terms of monetary incentives. The National Survey on Drug Use and Health (NSDUH), a federally sponsored annual survey on substance use and abuse that polls 150,000 households and 67,500 people, came up with innovative and effective new measures to catch interviewer falsification-generated responses before they enter the final data.

For example, in their reviews of interview data, NSDUH researchers focused on four interviewers whose work included 760 screenings and 464 interviews. NSDUH targeted these four because a preliminary inspection of their responses showed they had entered their own or another interviewer's telephone number for initial verification. Inspectors determined that only 38 percent (287) of screening cases and 29 percent (134) of interview cases were valid; 473 screenings and 330 interviews were falsified and thus rejected.

The NSDUH's solution was to rigorously examine timing data in the context of interview response and question level. Given an interviewer's caseload, the responses collected by an interviewer could be evaluated in terms of whether they seemed likely in the given time frame, which was generally set at anything less than 30 minutes or longer than 60. Timestamp data was collected from the interviewers' computer terminals each day; any cases falling outside this margin were entered on a weekly Interview Length Report. Then technical staff examined the timing data against any explanation the interviewers offered.

"If a problematic pattern emerges, the interviewer's cases may be forced into verification and examined for shortcutting or fraudulent behavior," explains Joe Murphy (and colleagues) of RTI International, who reported on NSDUH's methods at the American Association for Public Opinion Research's 59th Annual Conference in May 2004. Murphy notes that virtually the only way to beat this new falsification detection system would be for interviewers to have advanced detailed understanding of the prevalence and correlates of substance use so that they could concoct likely responses; this level of subject sophistication is unlikely.

Other methods in NSDUH's data quality monitoring system include response deviation score (falsification is suspected if the interviewer's response deviation score, based on prevalence rates, is five times higher than the average); rare response combinations (falsification is suspected if the interviewer's responses show at least two examples or 5 percent of the total); and total interview seconds per question (examiners look for shorter or longer than average interview duration times).[1]

---

normally validates at a 10 percent rate, 5 respondents surveyed by that interviewer would be recontacted by telephone. Telephone validation typically answers four questions:

1. Was the person actually interviewed?

2. Did the person who was interviewed qualify to be interviewed according to the screening questions on the survey? For example, the interview may have required that the person being interviewed come from a family with an annual household income of $25,000 or more. On validation, the respondent would again be asked whether the annual household income for his or her family was $25,000 or more per year.

A mall survey should be conducted in the designated mall. An important part of data analysis is validating that the data were gathered as specified.

3. Was the interview conducted in the required manner? For example, a mall survey should have been conducted in the designated mall. Was this particular respondent interviewed in the mall, or was she or he interviewed at some other place, such as a restaurant or someone's home?

4. Did the interviewer cover the entire survey? Sometimes interviewers recognize that a potential respondent is in a hurry and may not have time to complete the entire survey. If respondents for that particular survey are difficult to find, the interviewer may be motivated to ask the respondent a few questions at the beginning and a few questions at the end and then fill out the rest of the survey without the respondent's input. Validation for this particular problem would involve asking respondents whether they were asked various questions from different points in the interview.

Validation also usually involves checking for other problems. For example: Was the interviewer courteous? Did the interviewer speculate about the client's identity or the purpose of the survey? Does the respondent have any other comments about the interviewer or the interview experience?

The purpose of the validation process, as noted earlier, is to ensure that interviews were administered properly and completely. Researchers must be sure that the research results on which they are basing their recommendations reflect the legitimate responses of target individuals.

Editing

Whereas validation involves checking for interviewer cheating and failure to follow instructions, **editing** involves checking for interviewer and respondent mistakes. Paper questionnaires usually are edited at least twice before being submitted for data entry. First, they may be edited by the field service firm that conducted the interviews, and then they are edited by the marketing research firm that hired the field service firm to do the interviewing. CATI, Internet, and other software-driven surveys have built-in logical checking. The editing process for paper surveys involves manual checking for a number of problems, including the following:

> **editing**
> Process of ascertaining that questionnaires were filled out properly and completely.

1. *Whether the interviewer failed to ask certain questions or record answers for certain questions.* In the questionnaire shown in Exhibit 14.1, no answer was recorded for question 19. According to the structure of the questionnaire, this question should have been asked of all respondents. Also, the respondent's name does not give a clear indication of gender. The purpose of the first edit—the field edit—is to identify these types of problems when there is still time to recontact the respondent and determine the appropriate answer to questions that were not asked. This may also be done at the second edit (by the marketing research firm), but in many instances there is not time to recontact the respondent and the interview has to be discarded.

> **skip pattern**
> Sequence in which later questions are asked, based on a respondent's answer to an earlier question or questions.

2. *Whether skip patterns were followed.* According to the **skip pattern** in question 2 in Exhibit 14.1, if the answer to this question is "Very unlikely" or "Don't know," the interviewer should skip to question 16. The editor needs to make sure that the interviewer followed instructions. Sometimes, particularly during the first few interviews in a particular study, interviewers get mixed up and skip when they should not or fail to skip when they should.

3. *Whether the interviewer paraphrased respondents' answers to open-ended questions.* Marketing researchers and their clients usually are very interested in the responses to

Exhibit 14.1

Sample Questionnaire

Consumer Survey
Cellular Telephone Survey Questionnaire

Long Branch—Asbury, N.J.

Date ___1-05-01___

(01-03) _001_

Respondent Telephone Number _____201-555-2322_____

Hello. My name is ___Sally___ with POST Research. May I please speak with the male or female head of the household?

(IF INDIVIDUAL NOT AVAILABLE, RECORD NAME AND CALLBACK INFORMATION ON SAMPLING FORM.)

(WHEN MALE/FEMALE HEAD OF HOUSEHOLD COMES TO PHONE): Hello, my name is _____,
with POST Research. Your number was randomly selected, and I am not trying to sell you anything. I simply want to ask you a few
questions about a new type of telephone service.

1. First, how many telephone calls do you make during a typical day?

(04)

0–2	.1
3–5	.2
6–10	③
11–15	.4
16–20	.5
More than 20	.6
Don't know	.7

Now, let me tell you about a new service called cellular mobile telephone service, which is completely wireless. You can get either a
portable model that may be carried in your coat pocket or a model mounted in any vehicle. You will be able to receive calls and make
calls, no matter where you are. Although cellular phones are wireless, the voice quality is similar to your present phone service. This is
expected to be a time-saving convenience for household use.

This new cellular mobile phone service may soon be widely available in your area.

2. Now, let me explain to you the cost of this wireless service. Calls will cost 26 cents a minute plus normal toll charges. In addition, the
monthly minimum charge for using the service will be $7.50 and rental of a cellular phone will be about $40. Of course, you can buy the
equipment instead of leasing it. At this price, do you think you would be very likely, somewhat likely, somewhat unlikely, or very unlikely
to subscribe to the new phone service?

(05)

Very likely	.1
Somewhat likely	②
Somewhat unlikely	.3
Very unlikely ......(GO TO QUESTION 16)	.4
Don't know ....(GO TO QUESTION 16)	.5

INTERVIEWER—IF "VERY UNLIKELY" OR "DON'T KNOW," GO TO QUESTION 16.

3. Do you think it is likely that your employer would furnish you with one of these phones for your job?

(06)

No ....(GO TO QUESTION 5)	.1
Don't know ....(GO TO QUESTION 5)	.2
Yes ....(CONTINUE)	③

INTERVIEWER—IF "NO" OR "DON'T KNOW," GO TO QUESTION 5; OTHERWISE CONTINUE.

4. If your employer did furnish you with a wireless phone, would you also purchase one for household use?

(07)

Yes ....(CONTINUE)	①
No ....(GO TO QUESTION 16)	.2
Don't know ....(GO TO QUESTION 16)	.3

5. Please give me your best estimate of the number of mobile phones your household would use (write in "DK" for "Don't know").

Number of Units _____ _01_ _____ (08–09)

Exhibit 14.1 (*continued*)

6. Given that cellular calls made or received will cost 26 cents a minute plus normal toll charges during weekdays, how many calls on the average would you expect to make in a typical weekday?

RECORD NUMBER _____ *06* _____ (10–11)

7. About how many minutes would your average cellular call last during the week?

RECORD NUMBER _____ *05* _____ (12–13)

8. Weekend cellular calls made or received will cost 8 cents per minute plus normal toll charges. Given this, about how many cellular calls on the average would you expect to make in a typical Saturday or Sunday?

RECORD NUMBER _____ *00* _____ (14–15)

9. About how many minutes would your average cellular call last on Saturday or Sunday?

RECORD NUMBER _____ (16–17)

10. You may recall from my previous description that two types of cellular phone units will be available. The vehicle phone may be installed in any vehicle. The portable phone will be totally portable—it can be carried in a briefcase, purse, or coat pocket. The totally portable phones may cost about 25 percent more and may have a more limited transmitting range in some areas than the vehicle phone. Do you think you would prefer portable or vehicle phones if you were able to subscribe to this service?

(18)
Portable 1
Vehicle . . . . .②
Both 3
Don't know 4

11. Would you please tell me whether you, on the average, would use a mobile phone about once a week, less than once a week, or more than once a week from the following geographic locations.

	Less Than Once a Week	Once a Week	More Than Once a Week	Never	
Monmouth County	1	2	③	4	(19)
(IF "NEVER," SKIP TO QUESTION 16)					
Sandy Hook	1	2	3	④	(20)
Keansburg	1	2	3	④	(21)
Atlantic Highlands	1	2	③	4	(22)
Matawan-Middletown	①	2	3	4	(23)
Red Bank	①	2	3	4	(24)
Holmdel	1	2	③	4	(25)
Eatontown	1	②	3	4	(26)
Long Branch	1	2	3	④	(27)
Freehold	1	2	3	④	(28)
Manalapan	1	2	3	④	(29)
Cream Ridge	1	2	3	④	(30)
Belmar	1	2	3	④	(31)
Point Pleasant	1	2	③	4	(32)

I'm going to describe to you a list of possible extra features of the proposed cellular service. Each option I'll describe will cost not more than $3.00 a month per phone. Would you please tell me if you would be very interested, interested, or uninterested in each feature:

	Very Interested	Interested	Uninterested
12. Call forwarding (the ability to transfer any call coming in to your mobile phone to any other phone).	①	2	3 (33)
13. No answer transfer (service that redirects calls to another number if your phone is unanswered).	1	2	③ (34)

Exhibit 14.1 (*continued*)

	Very Interested	Interested	Uninterested	
14. Call waiting (a signal that another person is trying to call you while you are using your phone).	1	②	3	(35)
15. Voice mailbox (a recording machine that will take the caller's message and relay it to you at a later time. This service will be provided at $5.00 per month).	1	2	③	(36)

16. What is your age group? (READ BELOW)

(37)

Under 25 1
25–44 . . . . .②
45–64 3
65 and over 4
Refused, no answer, or don't know 5

17. What is your occupation?

(38)

Manager, official, or proprietor . . . . .①
Professional (doctors, lawyers, etc.) 2
Technical (engineers, computer programmers, draftsmen, etc.) 3
Office worker/clerical 4
Sales 5
Skilled worker or foreman 6
Unskilled worker 7
Teacher 8
Homemaker, student, retired 9
Not now employed X
Refused . . . . .Y

18. Into which category did your total family income fall in 2002? (READ BELOW)

(39)

Under $15,000 1
$15,000-$24,999 2
$25,000-$49,999 3
$50,000-$74,999 4
$75,000 and over . . . . .⑤
Refused, no answer, don't know 6

19. (INTERVIEWER—RECORD SEX OF RESPONDENT):

(40)

Male 1
Female 2

20. May I have your name? My office calls about 10 percent of the people I talk with to verify that I have conducted the interview.

Gave name . . . . .①
Refused 2

Jordan Beasley
Name

Thank you for your time. Have a good day.

open-ended questions. The quality of the responses, or at least what was recorded, is an excellent indicator of the competence of the interviewer who recorded them. Interviewers are trained to record responses verbatim and not to paraphrase or insert their own language. They also are instructed to probe the initial response. The first part of Exhibit 14.2 shows an example of an interviewer's paraphrasing and interpretation of a response to an open-ended question. The second part of Exhibit 14.2

Exhibit 14.2

Recording of Open-Ended Questions

A. Example of Improper Interviewer Recording of Response to an Open-Ended Question

Question: Why do you go to Burger King most often among fast food/quick service restaurants? (PROBE)

Response recorded:
The consumer seemed to think Burger King had better tasting food and better quality ingredients.

B. Example of Interviewer Failure to Probe a Response

Question: Same as Part A.

Only response recorded:
Because I like it.

C. Example of Proper Recording and Probing

Question: Same as Part A.

Response recorded:
Because I like it. (P)* I like it, and I go there most often because it is the closest place to where I work. (AE)** No.

*(P) is an interviewer mark indicating he or she has probed a response.

**(AE) is interviewer shorthand for "Anything else?" This gives the respondent an opportunity to expand on the original answer.

---

shows the result of interviewer failure to probe a response. The response is useless from a decision-making perspective. It comes as no surprise that the respondent goes to Burger King most often because he likes it. The third part of Exhibit 14.2 shows how an initial meaningless response can be expanded to a useful response by means of proper probing. A proper probe to the answer "Because I like it" would be "Why do you like it?" or "What do you like about it?" The respondent then indicates that he goes there most often because it is the fast-food restaurant most convenient to his place of work.

The person doing the editing must make judgment calls in regard to substandard responses to open-ended questions. She or he must decide at what point particular answers are so limited as to be useless and whether respondents should be recontacted.

The editing process is extremely tedious and time-consuming. (Imagine for a moment reading through 13,000 pages of interviews!) However, it is a very important step in the processing of survey responses.

Step Two: Coding

 coding

Process of grouping and assigning numeric codes to the various responses to a question.

As discussed in Chapter 11, **coding** refers to the process of grouping and assigning numeric codes to the various responses to a particular question. Most questions on surveys are closed-ended and precoded, meaning that numeric codes have been assigned to the various responses on the questionnaire. All answers to closed-ended questions should be precoded, as they are in question 1 on the questionnaire in Exhibit 14.1. Note that each answer has a numeric code to its right; the answer "0–2" has the code 1, the answer "3–5" has the code 2, and so on. The interviewer can record the response by circling the numeric code next to the answer given by the respondent. In this case, the respondent's answer was seven calls per day. The code 3 next to the category "6–10" (calls per day) is circled.

Open-ended questions create a coding dilemma. They were phrased in an open-ended manner because the researcher either had no idea what answers to expect or wanted a richer response than is possible with a closed-ended question. As with editing, the process of coding responses to open-ended questions is tedious and time-consuming. In addition, the procedure is to some degree subjective.[2] For these reasons, researchers tend to avoid open-ended questions unless they are absolutely necessary.

Coding Process

The process of coding responses to open-ended questions includes the following steps:

1. *List responses.* Coders at the research firm prepare lists of the actual responses given to each open-ended question on a particular survey. In studies of a few hundred respondents, all responses may be listed. With larger samples, responses given by a sample of respondents are listed. The listing of responses may be done as part of the editing process or as a separate step, often by the same individuals who edited the questionnaires.

2. *Consolidate responses.* A sample list of responses to an open-ended question is provided in Exhibit 14.3. Examination of this list indicates that a number of the responses can be interpreted to mean essentially the same thing; therefore, they can be appropriately consolidated into a single category. This process of consolidation might yield the list shown in Exhibit 14.4. Consolidating requires a number of subjective decisions—for example, does response number 4 in Exhibit 14.3 belong in category 1 or should it have its own category? These decisions typically are made by a qualified research analyst and may involve client input.

3. *Set codes.* A numeric code is assigned to each of the categories on the final consolidated list of responses. Code assignments for the sample beer study question are shown in Exhibit 14.4.

EXHIBIT 14.3	Sample of Responses to Open-Ended Question

Question: Why do you drink that brand of beer? (BRAND MENTIONED IN ANSWER TO PREVIOUS QUESTION)

Sample responses:
1. Because it tastes better.
2. It has the best taste.
3. I like the way it tastes.
4. I don't like the heavy taste of other beers.
5. It is the cheapest.
6. I buy whatever beer is on sale. It is on sale most of the time.
7. It doesn't upset my stomach the way other brands do.
8. Other brands give me headaches. This one doesn't.
9. It has always been my brand.
10. I have been drinking it for over 20 years.
11. It is the brand that most of the guys at work drink.
12. All my friends drink it.
13. It is the brand my wife buys at the grocery store.
14. It is my wife's/husband's favorite brand.
15. I have no idea.
16. Don't know.
17. No particular reason.

EXHIBIT 14.4	Consolidated Response Categories and Codes for Open-Ended Responses from Beer Study	
Response Category Descriptor	Response Items from Exhibit 14.1 Included	Assigned Numeric Code
Tastes better/like taste/tastes better than others	1, 2, 3, 4	1
Low/lower price	5, 6	2
Does not cause headache, stomach problems	7, 8	3
Long-term use, habit	9, 10	4
Friends drink it/influence of friends	11, 12	5
Wife/husband drinks/buys it	13, 14	6

EXHIBIT 14.5	Example Questionnaire Setup for Open-Ended Questions

37. Why do you drink that brand of beer? (BRAND MENTIONED IN PREVIOUS QUESTION)?

(48) ___2___

Because it's cheaper. (P) Nothing. (AE) Nothing.

4. *Enter codes*. After responses have been listed and consolidated and codes set, the last step is the actual entry of codes. This involves several substeps:
   a. Read responses to individual open-ended questions on questionnaires.
   b. Match individual responses with the consolidated list of response categories, and determine the appropriate numeric code for each response.
   c. Write the numeric code in the appropriate place on the questionnaire for the response to the particular question (see Exhibit 14.5) or enter the appropriate code in the database electronically.[3]

Here's an example of the process, using the listing of responses shown in Exhibit 14.3 and the consolidation and setting of codes shown in Exhibit 14.4.

☐ You turn to the first questionnaire and read this response to the question "Why do you drink that brand of beer?": "Because it's cheaper."

☐ You compare this response with the consolidated response categories and decide that it best fits into the "Low/lower price" category. The numeric code associated with this category is 2 (see Exhibit 14.4).

☐ You enter the code in the appropriate place on the questionnaire (see Exhibit 14.5).

Automated Coding Systems

With CATI and Internet surveys, data entry and coding are completely eliminated for closed-ended questions. However, when the text of open-ended questions is electronically captured, a coding process is still required. A number of developments are making it likely that the tedious coding process for open-ended questions will soon be replaced with computer-based systems requiring limited high-level human intervention and decision making.[4] The Practicing Marketing Research feature on page 443 provides an example of an automated coding system.

PRACTICING MARKETING RESEARCH

Text Analytics Software Streamlines Coding Open-Ended Responses

As market researchers well know, the major shortcoming of open-ended questions in a survey is the postinterview coding. Opinion-based answers do not easily lend themselves to simple numerical coding. It is very expensive, in terms of time and effort, to categorize individualized responses, and it tends to limit survey size so as to avoid this complication during data processing.

Keyword-based search software helps the human analysis of open-ended responses, but typically this kind of software cannot deal with the variety of unstructured responses. Each answer must be interpreted by an analyst at an average cost of $2.00 to $5.00 question.

A new Text Analytics software program called Content Analyst™ now offers an automated way to code open-ended responses and cut costs (and processing time) by about 50 percent. This now makes it feasible to conduct in-depth surveys of 100,000, for example, asking many open-ended questions without concern for the prohibitive postinterview cost of coding. The software automates the laborious analysis of conceptual information and the processing and interpretation of large volumes of open-ended data. The product is made by Content Analyst Company, LLC, of Reston, Virginia (*www.contentanalyst.com*).

"It's taking us in the direction of concept-based coding rather than keyword coding, and that's a significant advance," comments Justin Greeves of Worthlin Worldwide, an opinion research company based in MacLean, Virginia, that uses the software. The approach, Greeves adds, takes us one step closer to the "automation of human-level analysis." The software also shifts the focus from coding answers to a higher-value interpretation of results. "The open-ends reveal the voice of the customer," so that their different and unstructured answers are no longer a problem but a source of greater, more valuable market information.[5]

The TextSmart module of SPSS is one example of the new breed of automated coding systems. Algorithms based on semiotics[4] are at the heart of these systems and show great promise for speeding up the coding process, reducing its cost, and increasing its objectivity. Basically, these algorithms use the power of computers to search for patterns in open-ended responses and in group responses, based on certain keywords and phrases.

Step Three: Data Entry

Once the questionnaires have been validated, edited, and coded, it's time for the next step in the process—data entry. We use the term **data entry** here to refer to the process of converting information to a form that can be read by a computer. This process requires a data entry device, such as a computer terminal or a personal computer, and a storage medium, such as magnetic tape, a floppy disk, or a hard (magnetic) disk.

> **data entry**
> Process of converting information to an electronic format.

Intelligent Entry Systems

Most data entry is done by means of intelligent entry systems. With **intelligent data entry**, the information entered is checked for internal logic. Intelligent entry systems can

> **intelligent data entry**
> Form of data entry in which the information being entered into the data entry device is checked for internal logic.

be programmed to avoid certain types of errors at the point of data entry, such as invalid or wild codes and violation of skip patterns.

Consider question 2 on the questionnaire in Exhibit 14.1. The five valid answers have the associated numeric codes 1 through 5. An intelligent data entry system programmed for valid codes would permit the data entry operator to enter only one of these codes in the field reserved for the response to this question. If the operator attempts to enter a code other than those defined as valid, the device will inform the data entry operator in some manner that there is a problem. The data entry device, for example, might beep and display a message on the screen that the entered code is invalid. It will not advance to the next appropriate field until the code has been corrected. Of course, it is still possible to incorrectly enter a 3 rather than the correct answer 2. Referring again to question 2, note that if the answer to the question is "Very unlikely" or "Don't know," then the data entry operator should skip to question 16. An intelligent data entry device will make this skip automatically.

The Data Entry Process

The validated, edited, and coded questionnaires have been given to a data entry operator seated in front of a personal computer. The data entry software system has been programmed for intelligent entry. The actual data entry process is ready to begin. Usually, the data are entered directly from the questionnaires, because experience has shown that a large number of errors are introduced when questionnaire data are transposed manually to coding sheets. Going directly from the questionnaire to the data entry device and associated storage medium is much more accurate and efficient. To better understand the mechanics of the process, look again at Exhibit 14.1.

- ☐ In the upper right-hand corner of the questionnaire, the number 001 is written. This number uniquely identifies the particular questionnaire, which should be the first questionnaire in the stack that the data entry operator is preparing to enter. This number is an important point of reference because it permits the data entry staff to refer back to the original document if any errors are identified in connection with the data input.

- ☐ To the left of the handwritten number 001 is (01–03). This tells the data entry operator that 001 should be entered into fields 01–03 of the data record. Throughout the questionnaire, the numbers in parentheses indicate the proper location on the data record for the circled code for the answer to each question. Question 1 has (04) associated with the codes for the answers to the question. Thus, the answer to this question would be entered in field 04 of the data record. Now, take a look at the open-ended question in Exhibit 14.5. As with closed-ended questions, the number in parentheses refers to the field on the data record where the code or codes for the response to this question should be entered. Note the number 2 written in to the right of (48); a 2 should be entered in field 48 of the data record associated with this questionnaire.

Exhibit 14.1 clearly illustrates the relationship between the layout of the questionnaire, in terms of codes (numbers associated with different answers to questions) and fields (places on the data record where the code is entered), and the layout of the data record.

Scanning

As all students know, the scanning of documents (test scoring sheets) has been around for decades. It has been widely used in schools and universities as an efficient way to capture and score responses to multiple-choice questions. However, until more recently, its use in marketing research has been limited. This limited use can be attributed to two factors: setup costs and the need to record all responses with a No. 2 pencil. Setup costs include the cost of special paper, special ink in the printing process, and very precise placement of the bubbles for recording responses. The break-even point, at which the savings in data entry costs exceeded the setup costs, was in the 10,000 to 12,000 survey range. Therefore, for most surveys, scanning was not feasible.

However, changes in **scanning technology** and the advent of personal computers have changed this equation. Today, questionnaires prepared with any one of a number of Windows word-processing software packages and printed on a laser printer or by a standard printing process can be readily scanned, using the appropriate software and a scanner attached to a personal computer. In addition, the latest technology permits respondents to fill out the survey using almost any type of writing implement (any type of pencil, ballpoint pen, or ink pen). This eliminates the need to provide respondents with a No. 2 pencil and greatly simplifies the process of mailing surveys. Finally, the latest technology does not require respondents to carefully shade the entire circle or square next to their response choices; they can put shading, a check mark, an X, or any other type of mark in the circle or square provided for the response choice.[6]

As a result of these developments, the use of scannable surveys is growing dramatically. An analyst who expects more than 400 to 500 surveys to be completed will find scannable surveys to be cost-effective.

Though no reliable volume figures are available, it is an accepted fact that the amount of survey data being captured electronically is increasing. For example, electronic data capture is used in computer-assisted telephone interviewing, Internet surveys, disks-by-mail surveys, and TouchScreen kiosk surveys.

> **scanning technology**
> Form of data entry in which responses on questionnaires are read in automatically by the data entry device.

Step Four: Machine Cleaning of Data

At this point, the data from all questionnaires have been entered and stored in the computer that will be used to process them. It is time to do final error checking before proceeding to the tabulation and statistical analysis of the survey results. Many colleges have one or more statistical software packages available for the tabulation and statistical analysis of data, including SAS (Statistical Analysis System) and SPSS (Statistical Package for the Social Sciences), which have proven to be the most popular mainframe computer statistical packages. Most colleges have personal computer versions of SPSS and SAS, in addition to other PC statistical packages. The number of other PC packages is large and growing.

Regardless of which computer package is used, it is important to do a final computerized error check of the data, or what is sometimes referred to as **machine cleaning of data**. This may be done through error checking routines and/or marginal reports.

Some computer programs permit the user to write **error checking routines**. These routines include a number of statements to check for various conditions. For example, if a particular field on the data records for a study should be coded with only a 1 or a 2, a logical statement can be written to check for the presence of any other code in that field. Some of the more sophisticated packages generate reports indicating how many times a particular condition was violated and the data records on which it was violated. With this list, the user can refer to the original questionnaires and determine the appropriate values.

Exhibit 14.6 illustrates the **marginal report**, another approach to machine cleaning often used for error checking. The first row of this report lists the fields of the data record. The columns show the frequency with which each possible value was encountered in each field. For example, the second row in Exhibit 14.6 shows that in field 111 of the data records for this study there are 100 "1" punches, 100 "2" punches, 1 "3" punch, and 99 "10" punches. This report permits the user to determine whether inappropriate codes were entered and whether skip patterns were properly followed. If all the numbers are consistent, there is no need for further cleaning. However, if logical errors (violated skip patterns and impossible codes) are detected, then the appropriate original questionnaires must be located and the corrections made in the computer data file. Note that these

> **machine cleaning of data**
> Final computerized error check of data.

> **error checking routines**
> Computer programs that accept instructions from the user to check for logical errors in the data.

> **marginal report**
> Computer-generated table of the frequencies of the responses to each question, used to monitor entry of valid codes and correct use of skip patterns.

EXHIBIT 14.6	Sample Marginal Report (Marginal Counts of 300 Records)													
FIELD	1	2	3	4	5	6	7	8	9	10	11	12	BL	TOT
111	100	100	1	0	0	0	0	0	0	99	0	0	0	300
112	30	30	30	30	30	30	30	30	30	0	0	0	0	300
113	30	30	30	30	30	30	30	30	30	30	0	0	0	300
114	67	233	0	0	0	0	0	0	0	0	0	0	0	300
115	192	108	0	0	0	0	0	0	0	0	0	0	0	300
116	108	190	0	0	0	0	0	0	0	0	0	2	0	300
117	13	35	8	0	2	136	95	7	2	0	0	0	2	298
118	0	0	0	0	0	0	0	0	0	0	0	2	298	2
119	29	43	12	1	2	48	50	6	4	1	0	0	104	196
1111	6	16	6	1	1	10	18	4	2	0	0	0	236	64
1113	3	4	1	1	0	1	2	0	1	0	0	0	288	12
1115	0	0	0	1	1	0	0	2	0	0	0	0	296	4
1117	24	2	22	0	1	239	9	2	0	0	0	0	1	299
1118	0	0	0	0	0	0	0	0	0	0	0	0	299	1
1119	4	49	6	0	0	81	117	5	2	0	0	0	36	264
1120	0	0	0	0	0	0	0	0	0	0	0	36	264	36
1121	5	60	6	0	0	84	116	4	3	1	0	0	21	279
1122	0	0	0	0	0	0	0	0	0	0	0	21	279	21
1123	118	182	0	0	0	0	0	0	0	0	0	0	0	300
1124	112	187	0	0	0	0	0	0	0	0	0	0	1	299
1125	47	252	0	0	0	0	0	0	0	0	0	1	0	300
1126	102	198	0	0	0	0	0	0	0	0	0	0	0	300
1127	5	31	5	1	0	33	31	9	1	0	0	0	184	116
1128	0	0	0	0	0	0	0	0	0	0	0	2	298	2
1129	0	3	1	0	0	4	8	2	1	0	0	0	281	19
1131	7	16	3	0	2	60	21	3	0	0	0	0	188	112
1133	1	3	1	0	0	2	3	1	0	0	0	0	289	11

procedures cannot identify situations in which an interviewer or data entry operator incorrectly entered a 2 for a "no" response instead of a 1 for a "yes" response.

This is the final error check in the process. When this step is completed, the computer data file should be ready for tabulation and statistical analysis. Exhibit 14.7 shows the data for the first 50 respondents (out of a total of 400) for the study associated with the questionnaire shown in Exhibit 14.1. Note that the apparent gaps in the data are a result of the skip called for in question 4. Also note that the gender data (noted as missing earlier) for respondent 001 has been filled in with a 2 for female based on information obtained by recontacting the respondent.

Step Five: Tabulation and Statistical Analysis

The survey results have been stored in a computer file and are free of logical data entry and interviewer recording errors. The next step is to tabulate the survey results.

one-way frequency table
Table showing the number of respondents choosing each answer to a survey question.

One-Way Frequency Tables

The most basic tabulation is the **one-way frequency table**, which shows the number of respondents who gave each possible answer to each question. An example of this type of table appears in Exhibit 14.8. This table shows that 144 consumers (48 percent) said they

| EXHIBIT 14.7 | Printout of Data for the First 50 Respondents for Cellular Telephone Survey |

```
001323101060500    2344311324444443132321521
00224                                 23412
00334                                 49622
00414                                 36221
00524                                 33312
00634                                 22612
00714                                 21321
008221  020405031033423244443444222229321
00925                                 36311
01044                                 23311
0116131024005033013423444443443322330321
012622  014007200733444444444444132330511
013221  010603060323131233332322123216211
01424                                 29321
01514                                 40121
01624                                 22612
01774                                 20622
01854                                 34621
01924                                 25212
02024                                 23622
02114                                 16611
02214                                 36211
02314                                 15611
024131      00101004102213444444444442229611
02524                                 26621
026131  010103020312422142224441422322611
02724                                 10122
02814                                 59622
02924                                 39622
03024                                 49611
03134                                 53621
03234                                 32622
03321       01      1244444444444444211220211
03424                                 32622
035311  0410300430133131131113131211220121
0362323030105020133441443334424232320622
03724                                 37622
03814                                 40121
03934                                 30121
04024                                 16121
04124                                 26311
04264                                 26411
04324                                 20321
04414                                 26311
04524                                 19321
04634                                 19222
04724                                 29621
04824                                 31422
04924                                 33121
05014                                 21311
```

EXHIBIT 14.8	One-Way Frequency Table

Q.30 If you or a member of your family were to require hospitalization in the future, and the procedure could be performed in Minneapolis or St. Paul, where would you choose to go?

	Total
Total	300
	100%
To a hospital in St. Paul	144
	48.0%
To a hospital in Minneapolis	146
	48.7%
Don't know/no response	10
	3.3%

would choose a hospital in St. Paul, 146 (48.7 percent) said they would choose a hospital in Minneapolis, and 10 (3.3 percent) said they didn't know which location they would choose. A printout is generated with a one-way frequency table for every question on the survey. In most instances, a one-way frequency table is the first summary of survey results seen by the research analyst. In addition to frequencies, these tables typically indicate the percentage of those responding who gave each possible response to a question.

An issue that must be dealt with when one-way frequency tables are generated is what base to use for the percentages for each table. There are three options for a base:

1. *Total respondents.* If 300 people are interviewed in a particular study and the decision is to use total respondents as the base for calculating percentages, then the percentages in each one-way frequency table will be based on 300 respondents.

2. *Number of people asked the particular question.* Because most questionnaires have skip patterns, not all respondents are asked all questions. For example, suppose question 4 on a particular survey asked whether the person owned any dogs and 200 respondents indicated they were dog owners. Since questions 5 and 6 on the same survey were to be asked only of those individuals who owned a dog, questions 5 and 6 should have been asked of only 200 respondents. In most instances, it would be appropriate to use 200 as the base for percentages associated with the one-way frequency tables for questions 5 and 6.

3. *Number of people answering the question.* Another alternative base for computing percentages in one-way frequency tables is the number of people who actually answered a particular question. Under this approach, if 300 people were asked a particular question but 28 indicated "Don't know" or gave no response, then the base for the percentages would be 272.

Ordinarily, the number of people who were asked a particular question is used as the base for all percentages throughout the tabulations, but there may be special cases in which other bases are judged appropriate. Exhibit 14.9 is a one-way frequency table in which three different bases are used for calculating percentages.

Some questions, by their nature, solicit more than one response from respondents. For example, consumers might be asked to name all brands of vacuum cleaners that come to mind. Most people will be able to name more than one brand. Therefore, when these answers are tabulated, there will be more responses than respondents. If 200 consumers are surveyed and the average consumer names three brands, then there will

The base for each percentage must be determined before one-way frequency tables are run. If a survey question asks whether the person has a dog and 200 respondents indicate that they do, further questions designated for dog owners should have only 200 respondents.

be 200 respondents and 600 answers. The question is, should percentages in frequency tables showing the results for these questions be based on the number of respondents or the number of responses? Exhibit 14.10 shows percentages calculated using both bases. Most commonly, marketing researchers compute percentages for multiple-response

EXHIBIT 14.9	One-Way Frequency Table Using Three Different Bases for Calculating Percentages		

Q.35 Why would you not consider going to St. Paul for hospitalization?

	Total* Respondents	Total Asked	Total Answering
Total	300	64	56
	100%	100%	100%
They aren't good/service poor	18	18	18
	6%	28%	32%
St. Paul doesn't have the services/equipment that Minneapolis does	17	17	17
	6%	27%	30%
St. Paul is too small	6	6	6
	2%	9%	11%
Bad publicity	4	4	4
	1%	6%	7%
Other	11	11	11
	4%	17%	20%
Don't know/no response	8	8	
	3%	13%	

*A total of 300 respondents were surveyed. Only 64 were asked this question because in the previous question those respondents said they would not consider going to St. Paul for hospitalization. Only 56 respondents gave an answer other than "Don't know."

EXHIBIT 14.10	Percentages for a Multiple-Response Question Calculated on the Bases of Total Respondents and Total Responses

Q.34 To which of the following towns and cities would you consider going for hospitalization?

	Total Respondents	Total Responses
Total	300	818
	100%	100%
Minneapolis	265	265
	88.3%	32.4%
St. Paul	240	240
	80.0%	29.3%
Bloomington	112	112
	37.3%	13.7%
Rochester	92	92
	30.7%	11.2%
Minnetonka	63	63
	21.0%	7.7%
Eagan	46	46
	15.3%	5.6%

questions on the basis of the number of respondents, reasoning that the client is primarily interested in the proportion of people who gave a particular answer.

Cross Tabulations

cross tabulation
Examination of the responses to one question relative to the responses to one or more other questions.

Cross tabulations are likely to be the next step in analysis. They represent a simple-to-understand, yet powerful, analytical tool. Many marketing research studies go no further than cross tabulations in terms of analysis. The idea is to look at the responses to one question in relation to the responses to one or more other questions. Exhibit 14.11

EXHIBIT 14.11	Sample Cross tabulation

Q.30 If you or a member of your family were to require hospitalization in the future, and the procedure could be performed in Minneapolis or St. Paul, where would you choose to go?

	Total	Age			
		18–34	35–54	55–64	65 or Over
Total	300	65	83	51	100
	100%	100%	100%	100%	100%
To a hospital in St. Paul	144	21	40	25	57
	48.0%	32.3%	48.2%	49.0%	57.0%
To a hospital in Minneapolis	146	43	40	23	40
	48.7%	66.2%	48.2%	45.1%	40.0%
Don't know/no response	10	1	3	3	3
	3.3%	1.5%	3.6%	5.9%	3.0%

PRACTICING MARKETING RESEARCH

Six Practical Tips for Easier Cross Tabulations

Cross tabulation is a valuable method of mining further data and significance and teasing out unsuspected relationships from your basic survey data. Here are six practical tips to improve your cross tabulation gleanings from Custom Insight, a provider of Web-based survey software located in Carson City, Nevada (*www.custominsight.com*).

1. **Make Hypotheses.** Probably you already have one or two hunches about what the data might yield in cross tabulation. Articulate your initial hypotheses and use them as a starting point for cross tabulation.

2. **Look for What Is Not There.** After you observe what the data manifestly shows, examine it for what it doesn't show, that is, relationships that you may have assumed to be real or substantive. For example, if your hypothesis postulates that people with higher incomes plan to make more purchases, the data may actually refute that and thus reveal a new set of data—that affluent people are not planning to spend.

3. **Scrutinize for the Obvious.** Some relationships among the data may be obvious (e.g., age and student status). Finding these evident connections early on will validate your results and inspire greater confidence that your survey interviewers did a competent job.

4. **Keep Your Mind Open.** Don't be tied to your hypotheses and assumptions. You may see data relationships that you hadn't expected and that are not congruent with your hypotheses. Think about the data from this new angle and formulate new hypotheses to account for them.

5. **Trust the Data.** If your results don't match your initial expectations, maybe they're wrong, not the data. Study the data for new relationships even if they contradict your starting hypotheses.

6. **Watch the "n."** Small totals should raise suspicions, and if you have few respondents in a given category, do not trust the data or look for stronger trends first before drawing final conclusions. For example, your study shows that 38 percent of people under age 15 want a particular product, except that only 8 people comprise that 38 percent. Better is the fact that 88 percent of people under 15 are students. Even though the number of respondents is minimal, the relationship exhibited by the data (88 percent) is much stronger and can be trusted.[7]

---

shows a simple cross tabulation that examines the relationship between cities consumers are willing to consider for hospitalization and their age. This cross tabulation includes frequencies and percentages, with the percentages based on column totals. This table shows an interesting relationship between age and likelihood of choosing Minneapolis or St. Paul for hospitalization. Consumers in successively older age groups are increasingly likely to choose St. Paul and increasingly less likely to choose Minneapolis.

Following are a number of considerations regarding the setup of cross tabulation tables and the determination of percentages within them:

☐ The previous discussion regarding the selection of the appropriate base for percentages applies to cross tabulation tables as well.

☐ Three different percentages may be calculated for each cell in a cross tabulation table: column, row, and total percentages. Column percentages are based on the column total, row percentages are based on the row total, and total percentages are

EXHIBIT 14.12	Cross tabulation Table with Column, Row, and Total Percentages*

Q.34 To which of the following towns and cities would you consider going for hospitalization?

	Total	Male	Female
Total	300	67	233
	100.0%	100.0%	100.0%
	100.0%	22.3%	77.7%
	100.0%	22.3%	77.7%
St. Paul	265	63	202
	88.3%	94.0%	86.7%
	100.0%	23.6%	76.2%
	88.3%	21.0%	67.3%
Minneapolis	240	53	187
	80.0%	79.1%	80.3%
	100.0%	22.1%	77.9%
	80.0%	17.7%	62.3%
Bloomington	112	22	90
	37.3%	32.8%	38.6%
	100.0%	19.6%	80.4%
	37.3%	7.3%	30.0%

*Percentages listed are column, row, and total percentages, respectively.

based on the table total. Exhibit 14.12 shows a cross tabulation table in which the frequency and all three of the percentages are shown for each cell in the table.

☐ A common way of setting up cross tabulation tables is to use columns to represent factors such as demographics and lifestyle characteristics, which are expected to be

EXHIBIT 14.13	A Stub and Banner Table

North Community College—Anywhere, U.S.A.
Q.1c. Are you single, married, or formerly married?

	Total	Zones			Gender		Age		
		1	2	3	M	F	18–34	35–54	55 and Over
Total	300	142	103	55	169	131	48	122	130
	100%	100%	100%	100%	100%	100%	100%	100%	100%
Married	228	105	87	36	131	97	36	97	95
	76%	74%	84%	65%	78%	74%	75%	80%	73%
Single	5	1	2	2	4	1	2	1	2
	2%	1%	2%	4%	2%	1%	4%	1%	2%
Formerly married	24	11	10	3	12	12	3	9	12
	8%	8%	10%	5%	7%	9%	6%	7%	9%
Refused to answer	43	25	4	14	22	21	7	15	21
	14%	18%	4%	25%	13%	16%	15%	12%	16%

predictors of the state of mind, behavior, or intentions data shown as rows of the table. In such tables, percentages usually are calculated on the basis of column totals. This approach permits easy comparisons of the relationship between, say, lifestyle characteristics and expected predictors such as sex or age. For example, in Exhibit 14.11, this approach facilitates examination of how people in different age groups differ in regard to the particular factor under examination.

Cross tabulations provide a powerful and easily understood approach to the summarization and analysis of survey research results. However, it is easy to become swamped by the sheer volume of computer printouts if a careful tabulation plan has not been developed. The cross tabulation plan should be created with the research objectives and hypotheses in mind. Because the results of a particular survey might be cross tabulated in an almost endless number of ways, it is important for the analyst to exercise judgment and select from all the possibilities only those cross tabulations that are truly responsive to the research objectives of the project. Spreadsheet programs such as Excel and nearly all statistics packages (SAS, SPSS, SYSTAT, STATISTICA) can generate cross tabulations. Chapter 15 discusses the chi-square test, which can be used to determine whether the results in a particular cross tabulation table are significantly different from what would be expected based on chance. In other words, confronted with the question of whether the response patterns of men differ significantly from those of women, the analyst can use this statistical procedure to determine whether the differences between the two groups likely occurred because of chance or likely reflect real differences.

A complex cross tabulation, generated using the UNCLE software package, is shown in Exhibit 14.13. UNCLE was designed with the special needs of marketing researchers in mind and is widely used in the marketing research industry. As indicated, this more complex table is sometimes referred to as a *stub and banner table*. The column headings are the banner and the row titles are the stub. In this single table, the relationship between marital status and each of seven other variables is explored. Cross tabulation can be produced in Excel, as described in the Practicing Marketing Research feature on page 455, but it is a cumbersome process.

| | Race | | | Family Profile | | Vote History | | Registered Voter | |
	White	Black	Other	Child <18 years	Child >18 years	2–3 Times	4 Times or More	Yes	No
	268	28	4	101	53	104	196	72	228
	100%	100%	100%	100%	100%	100%	100%	100%	100%
	207	18	3	82	39	80	148	58	170
	77%	64%	75%	81%	74%	77%	76%	81%	75%
	5	—	—	—	—	2	3	1	4
	2%	—	—	—	—	2%	2%	1%	2%
	18	6	—	5	6	10	14	3	21
	7%	21%	—	5%	11%	10%	7%	4%	9%
	38	4	1	14	8	12	31	10	33
	14%	14%	25%	14%	15%	12%	16%	14%	14%

FROM THE FRONT LINE

Secrets of Developing a Good Set of Tables

Suzanne Simpson, Director of Data Processing, DSS Research

A solid and error-free set of cross tabulation tables is critical to the analysis and report preparation phase of any project. Developing a good set of tables goes well beyond the technical proficiency needed to complete the task. A keen eye for errors in the tables (e.g., tables that don't add up, skip patterns that have inconsistent numbers, incorrect labeling), a strong desire for consistency, and curiosity make the difference between creating clean, professional tables and tables that may not be passable.

Tables are only as good as the data used to create them. Clean data are the result of careful planning and meticulous checking. Familiarity with the data is a natural outcome of the cleaning process. A skilled programmer uses this familiarity to hunt for and find any inconsistencies that result from data entry or programming (CATI or Internet) problems. Here are some possible inconsistencies to look for: Were all the responses to rating scale questions entered in ascending order (lowest rating is lowest number, highest rating is highest number) with the exception of two or three questions? Did an unusual number of respondents fail to answer only one particular open-ended question? Any discrepancies or errors in data processing are easily identifiable and will be addressed at this stage. Remember, inconsistency is the breeding ground of tabulation error.

Pouring over a clean set of tables is like reading a well-written news article. Everything adds up, everything makes sense. The who, what, when, where, why, and how of your research objective will be answered. If even one of those six questions remains unanswered, it's not yet a finished set of tables. You might want to add another cut to the banner or columns in certain tables (see discussion of banner in this chapter) or perhaps filter some of the tables down to a smaller subset and keep looking. The answers are there waiting to be discovered.

Graphic Representations of Data

You have probably heard the saying "One picture is worth a thousand words." Graphic representations of data use pictures rather than tables to present research results. Results—particularly key results—can be presented most powerfully and efficiently through graphs. Some approaches to the display of statistical data are provided in the Practicing Marketing Research feature on page 456.

Marketing researchers have always known that important findings identified by cross tabulation and statistical analysis could be best presented graphically. However, in the early years of marketing research, the preparation of graphs was tedious, difficult, and time-consuming. The advent of personal computers, coupled with graphics software and laser printers, has changed all of this. Spreadsheet programs such as Excel have extensive graphics capabilities, particularly in their Windows versions. In addition, programs designed for creating presentations, such as PowerPoint, permit the user to generate a wide variety of high-quality graphics with ease. With these programs, it is possible to do the following:

☐ Quickly produce graphs.

☐ Display those graphs on the computer screen.

PRACTICING MARKETING RESEARCH

Doing Frequency and Cross Tabulation Tables in Excel

If you have your data in an Excel spreadsheet or if you can import them into an Excel spreadsheet, then you can use the Pivot Table feature in Excel to produce one-way frequency tables and cross tabulations. The spreadsheet should be prepared so that the columns represent numeric codes for responses to various survey questions and the rows represent responses given by each person surveyed.

To create a one-way frequency table, do the following:

☐ Select the Data sheet in the Pivot Table template and click on a cell containing data.

☐ Select the command Pivot Table Report under the Data menu.

☐ A dialog box will appear. Make sure the Excel list or database is selected. Click the Next button.

☐ In the Range box, enter the range that contains the database. Click the Next button.

☐ Another dialog box will appear. It is fairly detailed, with a number of different options. On the right side of the dialog box, you will see a list of all the fields in the database. In this case, they should be survey questions. The different answers to a question should appear as rows in the table. If, for example, you had the label Q1 at the top of the column that includes the responses to Q1 for all respondents, then you would drag the Q1 button into the area labeled ROW and drop it there.

☐ The button should read Sum of Q1. However, we want a count or frequency for Q1. Double-click on the Sum of Q1 button. In the dialog box that appears, select Count in the list and press the OK button. Count of Q1 should now appear in the DATA area.

☐ Click the Finish button. The tabulation you requested will appear on a separate sheet.[8]

☐ Make desired changes and redisplay.

☐ Print final copies on a laser, inkjet, or dot matrix printer.

All of the graphs shown in this section were produced using a personal computer, a laser printer, and a graphics software package.

Line Charts

Line charts are perhaps the simplest form of graphs. They are particularly useful for presenting a given measurement taken at several points over time. Exhibit 14.14 shows monthly sales data for Just Add Water, a retailer of women's swimwear. The results reveal similar sales patterns for 2001 and 2002, with peaks in June and generally low sales in January through March and September through December. Just Add Water is evaluating the sales data to identify product lines that it might add to improve sales during those periods.

Pie Charts

Pie charts are another type of graph that is frequently used. They are appropriate for displaying marketing research results in a wide range of situations. Exhibit 14.15 shows

PRACTICING MARKETING RESEARCH

Professional Pointers for the Best Graphic Design of Statistical Data

The graphical presentation of statistical data is a powerful information conveying tool, provided it's done right, and clearly, and effectively. Here are some practical tips from Carl James Schwarz, statistics professor at Simon Fraser University in Burnaby, British Columbia, in Canada, on how to do it:

1. Make sure your graph or chart is complete and self-explanatory, with a title and all axes labeled, so that it presents all the necessary information.

2. Graphing scale is fluid, so any scale will work fine provided the values don't get crowded into a corner or diffused across the page.

3. Typically, the axes of graphs intersect at zero, but you don't have to do it this way provided you clearly mark the starting point.

4. Multiple curves or lines are permissible on a single graph to emphasize comparisons. Try differentiating the different lines in color or with dotted or broken lines. Data values can be distinguished with symbols, such as m = males and f = females.

Professor Schwarz also describes seven common graphical errors:

1. Labels and titles are omitted, or axes aren't labeled or units specified.

2. Scales are used incorrectly or their increments change across the graph. Plot your data knowing that most people read a scale left to right.

3. The zero point is misplaced. Readers assume it's at the bottom of the graph, so if it's somewhere else, it can present a misleading impression of the amount of change depicted in the data.

4. The wrong chart type was used. Avoid pie charts. Line charts are preferable (over bar charts) if your horizontal axis represents time.

5. Grid lines were made too dark, left out, or are irrelevant. Good graph paper already has faint grey but serviceable background grid lines.

6. Shading and 3-D effects can often distort a graph rather than enliven it.

7. Dollar amounts were not adjusted for inflation, making comparisons misleading.[9]

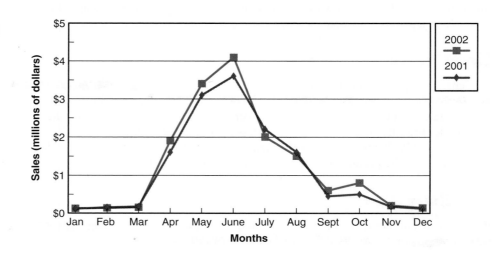

Exhibit 14.14

Line Chart for Sales of Women's Swimwear

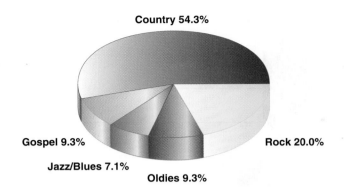

Exhibit 14.15

Three-Dimensional Pie Chart for Types of Music Listened to Most Often

radio music preferences gleaned from a survey of residents of several Gulf Coast metropolitan areas in Louisiana, Mississippi, and Alabama. Note the three-dimensional effect produced by the software.

Bar Charts

Bar charts may be the most flexible of the three types of graphs discussed in this section. Anything that can be shown in a line graph or a pie chart also can be shown in a bar chart. In addition, many things that cannot be shown—or effectively shown—in other types of graphs can be readily illustrated in bar charts. Four types of bar charts are discussed here.

1. *Plain bar chart.* As the name suggests, plain bar charts are the simplest form of bar chart. The same information displayed in the pie chart in Exhibit 14.15 is shown in the bar chart in Exhibit 14.16. Draw your own conclusions regarding whether the pie chart or the bar chart is the more effective way to present this information. Exhibit 14.16 is a traditional two-dimensional chart. Many of the software packages available today can take the same information and present it with a three-dimensional effect, as shown in Exhibit 14.17. Again, decide for yourself which approach is visually more appealing and interesting.

2. *Clustered bar chart.* The clustered bar chart is one of three types of bar charts useful for showing the results of cross tabulations. The radio music preference results are

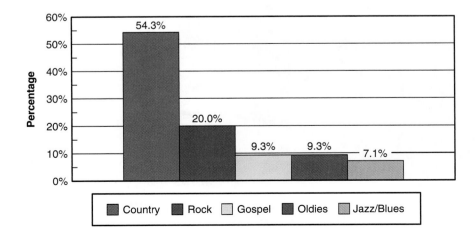

Exhibit 14.16

Simple Two-Dimensional Bar Chart for Types of Music Listened to Most Often

Exhibit 14.17

Simple Three-Dimensional Bar Chart for Types of Music Listened to Most Often

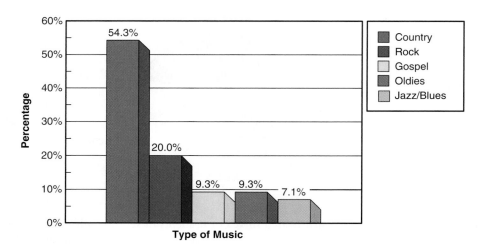

PRACTICING MARKETING RESEARCH

Learning from the Worst and the Best of Graphic Design for Statistics

Bad Design: The three-dimensional effects make reading the bars difficult, and where do you look? The front of the bars, the sides, or the back? The scale, which is nonhorizontal, artificially increases the values for the lower-income

Income levels

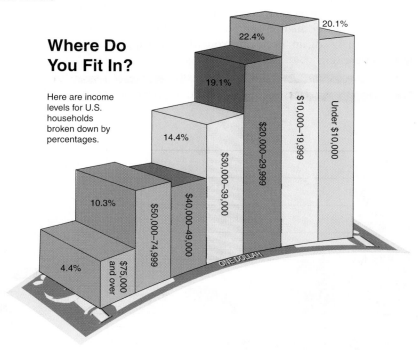

Where Do You Fit In?

Here are income levels for U.S. households broken down by percentages.

Cost of Living

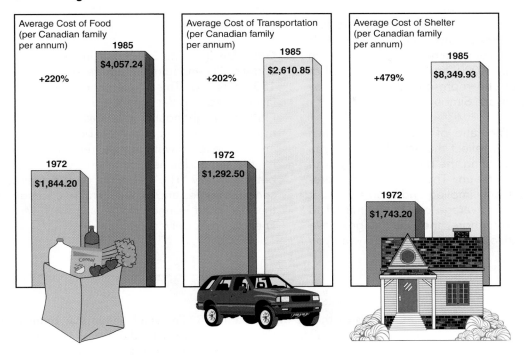

Average Cost of Food
(per Canadian family
per annum)

1985
$4,057.24

+220%

1972
$1,844.20

Average Cost of Transportation
(per Canadian family
per annum)

1985
$2,610.85

+202%

1972
$1,292.50

Average Cost of Shelter
(per Canadian family
per annum)

1985
$8,349.93

+479%

1972
$1,743.20

htttp://www.math.sfu.ca/~cschwartz/Stat-301/Handouts/node09.html

Causes of Mortality in the Army in the East April 1854 to March 1855

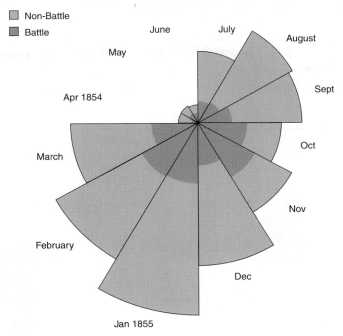

Non-Battle
Battle

May June July August

Apr 1854 Sept

March Oct

February Nov

Jan 1855 Dec

htttp://www.math.yorku.ca/SCS/Gallery/images/boxcomb.gif

bars in comparison to those for upper incomes. At least one bar doesn't have a percentage amount; another is misplaced and hard to find at first glance. Finally, the sizes of the intervals change: first it uses increments of 10,000, then 9,999, then only 9,000, and then 24,999, all of which confuses the representation (analysis by Carl James Schwarz, Simon Fraser University).[10]

Bad Design: The ratio of bar heights in each grouping doesn't reflect the actual ratio, as you can see by comparing the bars for housing with food or transportation. The graphs seem precise, but this is only implied and is unrealistic; it is unlikely that an average can be estimated to the penny. Furthermore, the percentages have been figured incorrectly; for example, when you double the costs, this represents only a 100 percent increase (analysis by Carl James Schwarz, Simon Fraser University).[11]

Good Design: This is a classic in clear, effective, and visually engaging design, even if it is nearly 150 years old. This coxcomb graphical design (also called a polar-area diagram, invented by Florence Nightingale, who was not only a famous nurse but passionate about statistics) is impressive for how it displays frequency by area. It's the same idea as a pie chart but is executed better visually. The coxcomb design maintains constant angles and varies its radius, something the pie chart cannot do (analysis by Michael Friendly, York University).[12]

cross tabulated by age in Exhibit 14.18. The graph shows that country music is mentioned most often as the preferred format by those over 35 and those 35 or under. The graph also shows that rock music is a close second for those 35 or under and is least frequently mentioned by those over 35. The results suggest that if the target audience is those in the 35 or under age group, then a mix of country and rock music is appropriate. A focus on country music probably would be the most efficient approach for those over 35.

3. *Stacked bar chart.* Like clustered bar charts, stacked bar charts are helpful in graphically representing cross tabulation results. The same music preference data shown in Exhibit 14.18 are presented as a stacked bar chart in Exhibit 14.19.

4. *Multiple-row, three-dimensional bar chart.* This type of bar chart provides what we believe to be the most visually appealing way of presenting cross tabulation information. The same music preference data displayed in Exhibits 14.18 and 14.19 are presented in a multiple-row, three-dimensional bar chart in Exhibit 14.20.

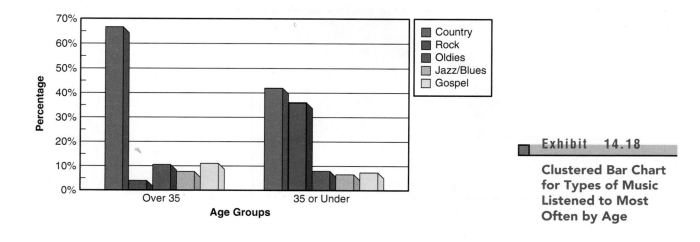

Exhibit 14.18

Clustered Bar Chart for Types of Music Listened to Most Often by Age

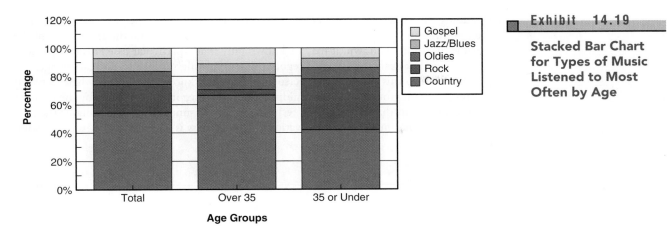

Exhibit 14.19

Stacked Bar Chart for Types of Music Listened to Most Often by Age

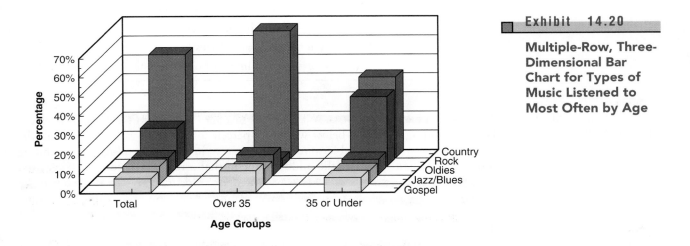

Exhibit 14.20

Multiple-Row, Three-Dimensional Bar Chart for Types of Music Listened to Most Often by Age

Descriptive Statistics

Descriptive statistics are the most efficient means of summarizing the characteristics of large sets of data. In a statistical analysis, the analyst calculates one number or a few numbers that reveal something about the characteristics of large sets of data.

Measures of Central Tendency

Before beginning this section, you should review the types of data scales presented in Chapter 9. Recall that there are four basic types of measurement scales: nominal, ordinal, interval, and ratio. Nominal and ordinal scales are sometimes referred to as nonmetric scales, whereas interval and ratio scales are called metric scales. Many of the statistical procedures discussed in this section and in following sections require metric scales, whereas others are designed for nonmetric scales.

The three measures of central tendency are the arithmetic mean, median, and mode. The **mean** is properly computed only from interval or ratio (metric) data. It is computed

> **mean**
> Sum of the values for all observations of a variable divided by the number of observations.

by adding the values for all observations for a particular variable, such as age, and dividing the resulting sum by the number of observations. With survey data, the exact value of the variable may not be known; it may be known only that a particular case falls in a particular category. For example, an age category on a survey might be 18 to 34 years of age. If a person falls into this category, the person's exact age is known to be somewhere between 18 and 34. With grouped data, the midpoint of each category is multiplied by the number of observations in that category, the resulting totals are summed, and the total is then divided by the total number of observations. This process is summarized in the following formula:

$$\overline{X} = \frac{\sum_{i=1}^{h} f_i X_i}{n}$$

where
f_i = frequency of the ith class
X_i = midpoint of that class
h = number of classes
n = total number of observations

> **median**
> Value below which 50 percent of the observations fall.

The **median** can be computed for all types of data except nominal data. It is calculated by finding the value below which 50 percent of the observations fall. If all the values for a particular variable were put in an array in either ascending or descending order, the median would be the middle value in that array. The median is often used to summarize variables such as income when the researcher is concerned that the arithmetic mean will be affected by a small number of extreme values and, therefore, will not accurately reflect the predominant central tendency of that variable for that group.

> **mode**
> Value that occurs most frequently.

The **mode** can be computed for any type of data (nominal, ordinal, interval, or ratio). It is determined by finding the value that occurs most frequently. In a frequency distribution, the mode is the value that has the highest frequency. One problem with using the mode is that a particular data set may have more than one mode. If three different values occur with the same level of frequency and that frequency is higher than the frequency for any other value, then the data set has three modes. The mean, median, and mode for sample data on beer consumption are shown in Exhibit 14.21.

Measures of Dispersion

Frequently used measures of dispersion include standard deviation, variance, and range. Whereas measures of central tendency indicate typical values for a particular variable, measures of dispersion indicate how spread out the data are. The dangers associated with relying only on measures of central tendency are suggested by the example shown in Exhibit 14.22. Note that average beer consumption is the same in both markets—3 cans/bottles/glasses. However, the standard deviation is greater in market two, indicating more dispersion in the data. Whereas the mean suggests that the two markets are the same, the added information provided by the standard deviation indicates that they are different.

EXHIBIT 14.21	Mean, Median, and Mode for Beer Consumption Data

A total of 10 beer drinkers (drink one or more cans, bottles, or glasses of beer per day on the average) were interviewed in a mall-intercept study. They were asked how many cans, bottles, or glasses of beer they drink in an average day.

Respondent	Number of Cans/Bottles/Glasses Per Day
1	2
2	2
3	3
4	2
5	5
6	1
7	2
8	2
9	10
10	1

Mode = 2 cans/bottles/glasses
Median = 2 cans/bottles/glasses
Mean = 3 cans/bottles/glasses

EXHIBIT 14.22	Measures of Dispersion and Measures of Central Tendency

Consider the beer consumption data presented in Exhibit 14.21. Assume that interviewing was conducted in two markets. The results for both markets are shown.

Respondent	Number of Cans/Bottles/Glasses Market One	Number of Cans/Bottles/Glasses Market Two
1	2	1
2	2	1
3	3	1
4	2	1
5	5	1
6	1	1
7	2	1
8	2	3
9	10	10
10	1	10
Mean	3	3
Standard deviation	2.7	3.7

The formula for computing the standard deviation for a sample of observations is as follows:

$$S = \sqrt{\frac{\sum\limits_{i=1}^{n} (X_i - \overline{X})^2}{n-1}}$$

where

S = sample standard deviation
X_i = value of the ith observation
$\overline{X}$ = sample mean
n = sample size

Occupation is an example of a categorical variable. The only results that can be reported for a variable of this type are the frequency and the relative percentage with which each category was encountered.

The variance is calculated by using the formula for standard deviation with the square root sign removed. That is, the sum of the squared deviations from the mean is divided by the number of observations minus 1. Finally, the range is equal to the maximum value for a particular variable minus the minimum value for that variable.

Percentages and Statistical Tests

In performing basic data analysis, the research analyst is faced with the decision of whether to use measures of central tendency (mean, median, mode) or percentages (one-way frequency tables, cross tabulations). Responses to questions either are categorical or take the form of continuous variables. Categorical variables such as "Occupation" (coded 1 for professional/managerial, 2 for clerical, etc.) limit the analyst to reporting the frequency and relative percentage with which each category was encountered. Variables such as age can be continuous or categorical, depending on how the information was obtained. For example, an interviewer can ask people their actual age or ask them which category (under 35, 35 or older) includes their age. If actual age data are available, mean age can be readily computed. If categories are used, one-way frequency tables and cross tabulations are the most obvious choices for analysis. However, continuous data can be put into categories, and means can be estimated for categorical data by using the formula for computing a mean for grouped data (presented earlier).

Finally, statistical tests are available that can indicate whether two means—for example, average expenditures by men and average expenditures by women at fast-food restaurants—or two percentages differ to a greater extent than would be expected by chance (sampling error) or whether there is a significant relationship between two variables in a cross-tabulation table. These tests are discussed in Chapter 15.

SUMMARY

Once the questionnaires have been returned from the field, a five-step process takes place. These steps are (1) validation and editing, which are quality control checks, (2) coding, (3) data entry, (4) machine cleaning of data, and (5) tabulation and statistical analysis. The first step in the process, making sure that the data have integrity, is critical. Otherwise, the age-old adage is true: "Garbage in, garbage out." Validation involves determining with as much certainty as possible that each questionnaire is, in fact, a valid interview. A valid interview in this sense is one that was conducted in an appropriate manner. The objective of validation is to detect interviewer fraud or failure to follow key instructions. Validation is accomplished by recontacting a certain percentage of the respondents surveyed by each interviewer. Any surveys found to be fraudulent are eliminated from the database. After the validation process is completed, editing begins. Editing involves checking for interviewer and respondent mistakes—making certain that all required questions were answered, that skip patterns were followed properly, and that responses to open-ended questions were accurately recorded.

Upon completion of the editing, the next step is to code the data. Most questions on surveys are closed-ended and precoded, which means that numeric codes already have been assigned to the various responses on the questionnaire. With open-ended questions, the researcher has no idea in advance what the responses will be. Therefore, the coder must establish numeric codes for response categories by listing actual responses to open-ended questions and then consolidating those responses and assigning numeric codes to the consolidated categories. Once a coding sheet has been created, all questionnaires are coded using the coding sheet categories.

The next step is data entry. Today, most data entry is done by means of intelligent entry systems that check the internal logic of the data. The data typically are entered directly from the questionnaires. New developments in scanning technology have made a more automated approach to data entry cost-effective for smaller projects.

Machine cleaning of data is a final, computerized error check of the data, performed through the use of error checking routines and/or marginal reports. Error checking routines indicate whether or not certain conditions have been met. A marginal report is a type of frequency table that helps the user determine whether inappropriate codes were entered and whether skip patterns were properly followed.

The final step in the data analysis process is tabulation of the data. The most basic tabulation involves a one-way frequency table, which indicates the number of respondents who gave each possible answer to each question. Generating one-way frequency tables requires the analyst to determine a basis for percentages. For example, are the percentages to be calculated based on total respondents, number of people asked a particular question, or number answering a particular question? Tabulation of data is often followed by cross tabulation—examination of the responses to one question in relation to the responses to one or more other questions. Cross tabulation is a powerful and easily understood approach to the analysis of survey research results.

Statistical measures provide an even more powerful way to analyze data sets. The most commonly used statistical measures are those of central tendency: the arithmetic mean, median, and mode. The arithmetic mean is computed only from interval or ratio data by adding the values for all observations of a particular variable and dividing the resulting sum by the number of observations. The median can be computed for all types of data except nominal data by finding the value below which 50 percent of the observations fall. The mode can be computed for any type of data by simply finding the value that occurs most frequently. The arithmetic mean is, by far, the most commonly used measure of central tendency.

In addition to central tendency, researchers often want to have an indication of the dispersion of the data. Measures of dispersion include standard deviation, variance, and range.

validation Process of ascertaining that interviews actually were conducted as specified.

editing Process of ascertaining that questionnaires were filled out properly and completely.

skip pattern Sequence in which later questions are asked, based on a respondent's answer to an earlier question or questions.

coding Process of grouping and assigning numeric codes to the various responses to a question.

KEY TERMS & DEFINITIONS

data entry Process of converting information to an electronic format.

intelligent data entry Form of data entry in which the information being entered into the data entry device is checked for internal logic.

scanning technology Form of data entry in which responses on questionnaires are read in automatically by the data entry device.

machine cleaning of data Final computerized error check of data.

error checking routines Computer programs that accept instructions from the user to check for logical errors in the data.

marginal report Computer-generated table of the frequencies of the responses to each question, used to monitor entry of valid codes and correct use of skip patterns.

one-way frequency table Table showing the number of respondents choosing each answer to a survey question.

cross tabulation Examination of the responses to one question relative to the responses to one or more other questions.

mean Sum of the values for all observations of a variable divided by the number of observations.

median Value below which 50 percent of the observations fall.

mode Value that occurs most frequently.

QUESTIONS FOR REVIEW & CRITICAL THINKING

1. What is the difference between measurement validity and interview validation?

2. Assume that Sally Smith, an interviewer, completed 50 questionnaires. Ten of the questionnaires were validated by calling the respondents and asking them one opinion question and two demographic questions over again. One respondent claimed that his age category was 30–40, when the age category marked on the questionnaire was 20–30. On another questionnaire, in response to the question "What is the most important problem facing our city government?" the interviewer had written, "The city council is too eager to raise taxes." When the interview was validated, the respondent said, "The city tax rate is too high." As a validator, would you assume that these were honest mistakes and accept the entire lot of 50 interviews as valid? If not, what would you do?

3. What is meant by the editing process? Should editors be allowed to fill in what they think a respondent meant in response to open-ended questions if the information seems incomplete? Why or why not?

4. Give an example of a skip pattern on a questionnaire. Why is it important to always follow the skip patterns correctly?

5. It has been said that, to some degree, coding of open-ended questions is an art. Would you agree or disagree? Why? Suppose that, after coding a large number of questionnaires, the researcher notices that many responses have ended up in the "Other" category. What might this imply? What could be done to correct this problem?

6. Describe an intelligent data entry system. Why are data typically entered directly from the questionnaire into the data entry device?

7. What is the purpose of machine cleaning data? Give some examples of how data can be machine cleaned. Do you think that machine cleaning is an expensive and unnecessary step in the data tabulation process? Why or why not?

8. It has been said that a cross tabulation of two variables offers the researcher more insightful information than does a one-way frequency table. Why might this be true? Give an example.

9. Illustrate the various alternatives for using percentages in one-way frequency tables. Explain the logic of choosing one alternative method over another.

10. Explain the differences among the mean, median, and mode. Give an example in which the researcher might be interested in each of these measures of central tendency.

11. Calculate the mean, median, mode, and standard deviation for the following data set:

Respondent	Times Visited Whitehall Mall in Past 6 Months	Times Visited Northpark Mall in Past 6 Months	Times Visited Sampson Mall in Past 6 Months
A	4	7	2
B	5	11	16
C	13	21	3
D	6	0	1
E	9	18	14
F	3	6	8
G	2	0	1
H	21	3	7
I	4	11	9
J	14	13	5
K	7	7	12
L	8	3	25
M	8	3	9

12. Enter the following data into an Excel spreadsheet. Include the column headings (Q1, Q2, and Q3), as well as the numeric values. The definitions of the numeric values are provided at the bottom of the table. Use the Pivot Table feature in Excel (found under the Data option) to cross tabulate the likelihood of purchase (row) by gender (column) and income level (column). What conclusions can you draw about the relationship between gender and likelihood of purchase and that between income and likelihood of purchase?

Respondent	Likelihood of Purchase	Gender	Income
A	5	2	3
B	4	2	3
C	4	2	2
D	3	1	2
E	1	1	2
F	5	2	3
G	5	2	3
H	4	1	3
I	1	1	2
J	1	1	2
K	2	1	1
L	5	2	3

Respondent	Likelihood of Purchase	Gender	Income
M	5	2	3
N	4	1	3
O	3	1	2
P	3	1	2
Q	4	2	3
R	5	2	3
S	2	1	1
T	2	1	1

Likelihood of purchase: very likely = 5, likely = 4, undecided = 3, unlikely = 2, very unlikely = 1
Gender: male = 1, female = 2
Income: under $30,000 = 1, $30,000 to $75,000 = 2, over $75,000 = 3

13. Using data from a newspaper or magazine article, create the following types of graphs:
    a. Line graph
    b. Pie chart
    c. Bar chart

WORKING THE NET

What is statistics? To find out, go to the Web site of the American Statistical Association at *http://www.amstat.org/*. Here you will find many resources by going to the menu items on the left side of the page, including career information, publications, and various links.

REAL-LIFE RESEARCH • 14.1

Taco Bueno

Taco Bueno has recently opened its 15th store in Utah. Currently, the chain offers tacos, enchiladas, and burritos. Management is considering offering a supertaco that would be approximately two and a half times as large as a regular taco and would contain 5 ounces of ground beef. The basic taco simply has spiced ground beef, lettuce, and cheese. Management feels that the supertaco ought to have more toppings. Therefore, a marketing research study was undertaken to determine what those toppings should be. A key question on the survey was, "What, if anything, do you normally add to a taco that you have prepared at home besides meat?" The question is open-ended, and the coding categories that have been established for the question are shown in the table.

Responses	Code
Avocado	1
Cheese (Monterey Jack/cheddar)	2
Guacamole	3
Lettuce	4
Mexican hot sauce	5

Responses	Code
Olive (black/green)	6
Onion (red/white)	7
Peppers (red/green)	8
Pimiento	9
Sour cream	0
Other	X

Questions

1. How would you code the following responses?
   a. I usually add a green, avocado-tasting hot sauce.
   b. I cut up a mixture of lettuce and spinach.
   c. I'm a vegetarian; I don't use meat at all. My taco is filled only with guacamole.
   d. Every now and then, I use a little lettuce, but normally I like cilantro.

2. Is there anything wrong with having a great number of responses in the "Other" category? What problems does this present for the researcher?

PrimeCare

PrimeCare is a group of 12 emergency medical treatment clinics in the Columbus and Toledo, Ohio, markets. The management group for PrimeCare is considering a communications campaign that will rely mainly on radio ads to boost its awareness and quality image in the market. The ad agency of Dodd and Beck has been chosen to develop the campaign. Currently, the plan is to focus on PrimeCare's experienced, front-line health professionals. Two themes for the ad campaign are now being considered. One theme ("We are ready!") focuses primarily on the special training given to PrimeCare's staff, and the second theme ("All the experts—all the time") focuses primarily on PrimeCare's commitment to having the best, trained professionals available at each PrimeCare facility 24/7. Dodd and Beck's research team has conducted a survey of consumers to gauge the appeal of the two campaigns. Overall results and results broken down by gender and by location are shown in the table.

REAL-LIFE RESEARCH • 14.2

	Total	Gender		Location	
		Male	Female	Columbus	Toledo
Total	400	198	202	256	144
	100%	100.0%	100.0%	100.0%	100.0%
Prefer "Ready" campaign	150	93	57	124	26
	37.5%	47.0%	28.2%	48.4%	18.1%
Prefer "All the Time" campaign	250	105	145	132	118
	62.5%	53.0%	71.8%	51.6%	81.9%

Questions

1. Which theme appears to have more appeal overall? Justify your answer.
2. How does the appeal of the campaigns differ between men and women? What is your basis for that conclusion?
3. Are the campaign themes equally attractive to residents of Columbus and Toledo? Why do you say that?

SPSS EXERCISES FOR CHAPTER 14

Exercise #1: Machine Cleaning Data

1. Go to the Wiley Web site at **www.wiley.com/college/mcdaniel** and download the *Segmenting the College Student Market for Movie Attendance* database to SPSS Windows. This database will have several errors for you to correct. In the SPSS Data Editor, go to the *variable view* option and notice the **computer coding** for each variable.

2. Also from the Wiley Web site, download a copy of the *Segmenting the College Student Market for Movie Attendance* questionnaire. Notice the computer coding for each of the variables; which is the same as that in the *variable view* option on the SPSS Data Editor. This information will be important in finding errors in the database.

3. In the SPSS Data Editor, invoke the *analyze/descriptive statistics/frequencies* sequence to obtain frequencies for all of the variables in the database.

4. From the SPSS Viewer *output screen*, determine which variables have input errors. Summarize the errors using the template below as a guide.

Questionnaire Number	Variable Containing error	Incorrect Value	Correct Value

Going back to the *data view* screen of the *SPSS Data Editor*.

5. Another possible source of errors is in question 8. Notice that in this question the sum of the answers should be 100 percent. Create a summated variable for question 8 (Q8a + Q8b + Q8c + Q8d) to check for errors by invoking the *transform/compute* sequence. Now, compute a frequency distribution for Q8sum. The values that are not "100" indicate an input error. (Such an error could be the result of the respondent not totaling percentages to 100, but for this machine cleaning exercise, the assumption is that it is an input error.) Summarize the errors using the template above.

6. Once you have completed summarizing the variables containing errors, go back to the *data view* screen of the *SPSS Data Editor*. Position the cursor on each of the

variables containing errors. Use the *ctrl-f* function to find the questionnaire numbers where the errors occurred. At this point, you will need the corrected database, or the database with no errors. Your professor has access to this database with no errors. After getting the corrected database, finish filling in the table in part (4) above with the correct values. Then make the changes in your database, so that you have a database with no errors. Be sure to resave your database after correcting it for errors.

7. After machine cleaning your data, rerun the *analyze/descriptive statistics/frequencies* sequence to obtain frequencies for your corrected database.

8. You will use the results of this exercise to answer the questions in Exercises #2 and #4.

Exercise #2: Analysis of Data with Frequency Distributions

If you did not complete Exercise #1, you will need the corrected database from your professor. After getting the corrected database, use the *analyze/descriptive statistics/frequencies* sequence to obtain frequency distributions for all of the variables in your database except the questionnaire number (Q No).

If you completed Exercise #1, you will have a corrected database, which consists of frequency distributions for each of the variables in the database.

Answer the following questions.

1. What percentage of all respondents attended at least *1* movie in the past year? _____%

2. What percentage of all respondents *never buy food items* at a movie? _____%

3. Produce a table indicating the percentage of all respondents that consider each of the movie theater items in question 5 of the questionnaire *very important*. List the top 5 movie items in descending order (start with the movie items that have the highest percentage of *very important* responses).

For Example:

Movie Item	Percentage of Respondents
Movie item with the highest percentage	75.0%
Movie item with the 2nd highest percentage, etc.	39.2%

4. What percentage of respondents consider the "newspaper" a *very important* source of information about movies playing at movie theaters? _____%

5. What percentage of respondents consider the "Internet" a *very unimportant* source of information about movies playing at movie theaters? _____%

6. By observing the distribution of responses for Q8a, Q8b, Q8c, and Q8d, which is the most popular *purchase option* for movie theater tickets? _____

7. Produce a table listing in descending order the percentage of respondents that consider each of the movie theater information sources (Q7) *very important*.

surveysolutions XP

For example:

Movie Theater Information Sources	Percentage of Respondents Indicating *Very Important*
Internet	55%
Newspaper	31%

Exercise #3: Analysis of Data with Descriptive Statistics

If you did not complete Exercises #1 or #2, you will need the corrected database from your professor. The objective of this exercise is to analyze data using measures of central tendency and measures of dispersion. To analyze means and standard deviations, use the *analyze/descriptive statistics/descriptives* sequences. To analyze medians and modes, use the *analyze/descriptive statistics/frequencies* sequence, and select *statistics*. You will see the box with all three measures of central tendency (mean, median and mode).

On the questionnaire, question 5 utilizes a 4-point Itemized Rating scale (illustrated below). This scale is balanced and can be assumed to yield interval scale/metric data. Given the preceding, invoke SPSS to calculate the mean and standard deviation for all of the variables in question 5 (Q5a–Q5i).

Very unimportant	Somewhat unimportant	Somewhat important	Very important
1	2	3	4

Answer the following questions.

1. Using only the **mean** for each of the variables, which of the movie theater items was considered "most important"? _____

2. Using only the **standard deviation** for each of the variables, for which question was there the greatest amount of agreement? _____
   Hint: Least amount of dispersion regarding the response to the movie item

3. Questions 4 and 6 utilize multiple-choice questions that yield nonmetric data, but that are ordinal scale. The appropriate measures of central tendency for nonmetric data are the median and the mode.

   a. What is the *median* response for question 4, concerning the amount a person spends on food/drink items at a movie? _____

Never buy food items at movies (0)	Up to $7.49 (1)	$7.50 to $14.99 (2)	$15.00 or more (3)

   b. Concerning question 6, the distance a person would drive to see a movie on a "big screen," what is the *mode* of that distribution of responses?

Zero (0)	1 to 9 miles (1)	11 to 24 miles (2)	25 to 49 miles (3)	50+ miles (4)

4. In this question the objective will be to compare the results of median and mean responses for Q3.
   a. Mean response: _____
   b. Median response: _____
   c. Standard deviation: _____
   d. Minimum response: _____
   e. Maximum response: _____

5. When the responses to a question contain extreme values, the mean response can lie in the upper or lower quartile of the response distribution. In such a case, the median value would be a better indicator of an average response than the mean value. Given the information you obtained from answering #4 above, is the mean or median a better representative of the "average" response to Q3?

   _____

   _____

   _____

Exercise #4: Analysis of Demographic Characteristics Using Charts

If you completed Exercise #1 and/or Exercise #2 you will have the information to complete this exercise.

If you did not complete either Exercise #1 or #2, you will need to get a corrected soft drink database from your professor. After getting the database, use the *analyze/descriptive statistics/frequencies* sequence to obtain frequency distributions for the demographic questions (questions 11–14).

Complete the following.

1. Display the demographic data for each of the four demographic variables in tables.
2. For each demographic variable, illustrate the table results using some type of graphic representation of the data (pie charts, line charts, or bar charts).

Note: Some students who are proficient in Excel may want to paste their databases into an Excel spreadsheet for the geographical depiction of the demographic variables.

STATISTICAL TESTING OF DIFFERENCES AND RELATIONSHIPS

LEARNING OBJECTIVES

1.	To become aware of the nature of statistical significance.
2.	To understand the concept of hypothesis development and how to test hypotheses.
3.	To understand the difference between type I and type II errors.
4.	To be familiar with several of the more common statistical tests of goodness of fit, hypotheses about one mean, hypotheses about two means, and hypotheses about proportions.
5.	To learn about analysis of variance.

Pat Casey, of Weed Waster, is reviewing the results of a product concept test just completed with Marketing Data Visions (MDV). The test involved evaluation of three alternative enhancements to the company's best selling edger/trimmer, the V900. This product currently has 26.4 percent of the market.

The test was done by mall-intercept interviewing in three cities—Los Angeles, Denver, and Chicago. A total of 900 qualified consumers were surveyed—300 in each market. To qualify, consumers had to be homeowners, take care of their yards themselves, and own a power lawn edger/trimmer.

The survey covered current brand of lawn edger/trimmer used, ratings of competitive brands, demographic and psychographic characteristics, and reactions to the new product concepts. The new concepts offered three different approaches to improving the plastic line that does the trimming. The same people were asked about all three new versions of the system. The order of presentation of the new concepts was randomly rotated from survey to survey to avoid any order bias.

As noted above, the survey covered many issues, but the key questions for Casey were the purchase intent questions. Specifically, the approach used for all the purchase intent questions on the survey was, "If an edger with the new system was available at stores where you normally shop and sold for $49.95, how likely would you be to buy it?" The response options were "very likely," "somewhat likely," "undecided," "somewhat unlikely," and "very unlikely." By Casey's calculations, the new product would need a Top 2 box score (sum of the "very likely" and "somewhat likely" responses) of 36 percent to reach the needed sales volume. The Top 2 box scores for the three concepts were as follows: Concept A 38.3 percent, Concept B 35.3 percent, and Concept C 42.4 percent. Casey has framed the issues that must be addressed as follows:

- ☐ Concept C scored the best, but is it possible that the true result for Concept C could be less than the 38 percent target level when sampling error is taken into account?

- ☐ Concept A scored over the 36 percent target level, but is it possible that the true result could be less than 36 percent if sampling error is taken into account?

This chapter shows you how to address these issues, and when you have completed it you should be able to answer Pat's questions. ■

This chapter addresses statistical techniques that can be used to determine whether the observed differences, noted above, are likely to be real differences or whether they are likely attributable to sampling error.

Evaluating Differences and Changes

The issue of whether certain measurements are different from one another is central to many questions of critical interest to marketing managers. Some specific examples of managers' questions follow:

☐ Our posttest measure of top-of-mind awareness is slightly higher than the level recorded in the pretest. Did top-of-mind awareness really increase, or is there some other explanation for the increase? Should we fire or commend our agency?

☐ Our overall customer satisfaction score increased from 92 percent 3 months ago to 93.5 percent today. Did customer satisfaction really increase? Should we celebrate?

☐ Satisfaction with the customer service provided by our cable TV system in Dallas is, on average, 1.2 points higher on a 10-point scale than is satisfaction with the customer service provided by our cable TV system in Cincinnati. Are customers in Dallas really more satisfied? Should the customer service manager in Cincinnati be replaced? Should the Dallas manager be rewarded?

☐ In a recent product concept test, 19.8 percent of those surveyed said they were very likely to buy the new product they evaluated. Is this good? Is it better than the results we got last year for a similar product? What do these results suggest in terms of whether to introduce the new product?

☐ A segmentation study shows that those with incomes of more than $30,000 per year frequent fast-food restaurants 6.2 times per month on average. Those with incomes of $30,000 or less go an average of 6.7 times. Is this difference real—is it meaningful?

☐ In an awareness test, 28.3 percent of those surveyed have heard of our product on an unaided basis. Is this a good result?

These are the eternal questions in marketing and marketing research. Although considered boring by some, statistical hypothesis testing is important because it helps researchers get closer to the ultimate answers to these questions. We say "closer" because certainty is never achieved in answering these questions in marketing research.

Statistical Significance

The basic motive for making statistical inferences is to generalize from sample results to population characteristics. A fundamental tenet of statistical inference is that it is possible for numbers to be different in a mathematical sense but not significantly different in a statistical sense. For example, suppose cola drinkers are asked to try two cola drinks in a blind taste test and indicate which they prefer; the results show that 51 percent prefer one test product and 49 percent prefer the other. There is a mathematical difference in the results, but the difference would appear to be minor and unimportant. The difference probably is well within the range of accuracy of researchers' ability to measure taste preference and thus probably is not significant in a statistical sense. Three different concepts can be applied to the notion of differences when we are talking about results from samples:

☐ *Mathematical differences.* By definition, if numbers are not exactly the same, they are different. This does not, however, mean that the difference is either important or statistically significant.

☐ *Statistical significance.* If a particular difference is large enough to be unlikely to have occurred because of chance or sampling error, then the difference is statistically significant.

☐ *Managerially important differences.* One can argue that a difference is important from a managerial perspective only if results or numbers are sufficiently different. For example, the difference in consumer responses to two different packages in a test market might be statistically significant but yet so small as to have little practical or managerial significance.[1] This issue is discussed in greater detail in the Practicing Marketing Research feature on page 480.

This chapter covers different approaches to testing whether results are statistically significant.

Hypothesis Testing

A **hypothesis** is an assumption or guess that a researcher or manager makes about some characteristic of the population being investigated. The marketing researcher is often faced with the question of whether research results are different enough from the norm that some element of the firm's marketing strategy should be changed. Consider the following situations.

> **hypothesis**
> Assumption or theory that a researcher or manager makes about some characteristic of the population under study.

☐ The results of a tracking survey show that awareness of a product is lower than it was in a similar survey conducted 6 months ago. Are the results significantly lower? Are the results sufficiently lower to call for a change in advertising strategy?

☐ A product manager believes that the average purchaser of his product is 35 years of age. A survey is conducted to test this hypothesis, and the survey shows that the average purchaser of the product is 38.5 years of age. Is the survey result different enough from the product manager's belief to cause him to conclude that his belief is incorrect?

☐ The marketing director of a fast-food chain believes that 60 percent of her customers are female and 40 percent are male. She does a survey to test this hypothesis and finds that, according to the survey, 55 percent are female and 45 percent are male. Is this result sufficiently different from her original theory to permit her to conclude that her original theory was incorrect?

All of these questions can be evaluated with some kind of statistical test. In hypothesis testing, the researcher determines whether a hypothesis concerning some characteristic of the population is likely to be true, given the evidence. A statistical hypothesis test allows us to calculate the probability of observing a particular result if the stated hypothesis is actually true.[2]

There are two basic explanations for an observed difference between a hypothesized value and a particular research result. Either the hypothesis is true and the observed difference is likely due to sampling error, or the hypothesis is false and the true value is some other value.

Steps in Hypothesis Testing

Five steps are involved in testing a hypothesis. First, the hypothesis is specified. Second, an appropriate statistical technique is selected to test the hypothesis. Third, a decision rule is specified as the basis for determining whether to reject or fail to reject (FTR) the null hypothesis H_0. Please note that we did not say "reject H_0 or accept H_0." Although a seemingly small distinction, it is an important one. The distinction will be discussed in greater detail later on. Fourth, the value of the test statistic is calculated and the test is

PRACTICING MARKETING RESEARCH

Why We Need Statistical Tests of Differences

A 13-year-old spent 4½ hours searching through the Internet for a workable definition of statistically significant. He needed the definition for his science class. Finally, he came upon Ask A Scientist©, a feature sponsored by the Argonne National Laboratory, Division of Educational Programs for grades K–12. Dr. Ali Khounsary of the laboratory volunteered to answer the student's question.

Say you have a new drug to treat cancer and you try it on sick rats. You apply the drug to 100 sick rats and notice that 20 get well. Does this mean the drug works? Although it seemingly cured 20 rats, perhaps they could have recovered on their own, without the drug. Now you

test the drug on 200 sick rats, randomly selected. Divide these 200 rats into two groups of 100 each. Treat one group with the actual drug and the other with a fake or placebo drug. The person administering the real and fake drugs will not know which pills are which.

After a while, see how many rats have recovered. If 20 taking the real drug and only 5 from the placebo group are cured, then you would comfortably feel that the drug really works. But if 18 rats taking the placebo actually survived, then you would not be sure that the new drug had any effect because the difference between the two survival rates, 20 on the real drug, 18 on the placebo, is not very big.

Statistical tests provide a basis for determining whether differences are greater or not greater than we would expect due to chance.[3]

---

performed. Fifth, the conclusion is stated from the perspective of the original research problem or question.

Step One: Stating the Hypothesis   Hypotheses are stated using two basic forms: the null hypothesis H_0 and the alternative hypothesis H_a. The null hypothesis H_0 (sometimes called the *hypothesis of the status quo*) is the hypothesis that is tested against its complement, the alternative hypothesis H_a (sometimes called the *research hypothesis of interest*). For more discussion of the null hypothesis see the Practicing Marketing Research feature on page 481. Suppose the manager of Burger City believes that his operational procedures will guarantee that the average customer will wait 2 minutes in the drive-in window line. He conducts research, based on the observation of 1,000 customers at randomly selected stores at randomly selected times. The average customer observed in this study spends 2.4 minutes in the drive-in window line. The null hypothesis and the alternative hypothesis might be stated as follows:

☐   Null hypothesis H_0: Mean waiting time = 2 minutes
☐   Alternative hypothesis H_a: Mean waiting time ≠ 2 minutes

It should be noted that the null hypothesis and the alternative hypothesis must be stated in such a way that both cannot be true. The idea is to use the available evidence to ascertain which hypothesis is more likely to be true.

Step Two: Choosing the Appropriate Test Statistic   As you will see in the following sections of this chapter, the analyst must choose the appropriate statistical test, given the characteristics of the situation under investigation. A number of different statistical tests, along with the situations where they are appropriate, are discussed in this

PRACTICING MARKETING RESEARCH

The Null Hypothesis— Is It a Joking Matter?

Even though the null hypothesis fulfills a legitimate function within the model of scientific discovery, and especially in market research, ever since Karl Popper developed it as a statistical tool of empirical research it has had mixed reviews. Clearly, a bias against the null hypothesis has been observed in the social sciences because measuring no-effects has little practical use, it's believed.

Perhaps that is what led to the following joke about the null hypothesis. A person tumbles into a deep hole. He tries to escape many times but fails. He is exhausted, on the verge of collapse, and finally he mutters, "It must be impossible to get out of here." Then he hears a voice not far away, also muttering in the darkness of the hole. "You are so right. I tried every method you did to get out of this hole. None of them works." The first person, hearing this, is startled. Then he answers with bitterness, "Then why didn't you tell me before now?" The other voice answers, "So who publishes null results?"[4]

---

chapter. Exhibit 15.1 provides a guide to selecting the appropriate test for various situations. All the tests in this table are covered in detail later in this chapter.

Step Three: Developing a Decision Rule   Based on our previous discussions of distributions of sample means, you may recognize that one is very unlikely to get a sample result that is exactly equal to the value of the population parameter. The problem is determining whether the difference, or deviation, between the actual value of the sample mean and its expected value based on the hypothesis could have occurred by chance (5 times out of 100, for example) if the statistical hypothesis is true. A decision rule, or standard, is needed to determine whether to reject or fail to reject the null hypothesis. Statisticians state such decision rules in terms of significance levels.

The significance level (α) is critical in the process of choosing between the null and alternative hypotheses. The level of significance—.10, .05, or .01, for example—is the probability that is considered too low to justify acceptance of the null hypothesis.

Consider a situation in which the researcher has decided that she wants to test a hypothesis at the .05 level of significance. This means that she will reject the null hypothesis if the test indicates that the probability of occurrence of the observed result (for example, the difference between the sample mean and its expected value) because of chance or sampling error is less than 5 percent. Rejection of the null hypothesis is equivalent to supporting the alternative hypothesis.

Step Four: Calculating the Value of the Test Statistic   In this step, the researcher does the following:

☐   Uses the appropriate formula to calculate the value of the statistic for the test chosen.

☐   Compares the value just calculated to the critical value of the statistic (from the appropriate table), based on the decision rule chosen.

☐   Based on the comparison, determines to either reject or fail to reject the null hypothesis H_0.

Step Five: Stating the Conclusion   The conclusion summarizes the results of the test. It should be stated from the perspective of the original research question.

EXHIBIT 15.1	Statistical Tests and Their Uses				
Area of Application	Subgroups or Samples	Level Scaling	Test	Special Requirements	Example
Hypotheses about frequency distribution	One	Nominal	χ^2	Random sample	Are observed differences in the numbers of people responding to three different promotions likely/not likely due to chance?
	Two or more	Nominal	χ^2	Random sample, independent samples	Are differences in the numbers of men and women responding to a promotion likely/not likely due to chance?
Hypotheses about means	One (large sample)	Metric (interval or ratio)	Z test for one mean	Random sample, $n \geq 30$	Is the observed difference between a sample estimate of the mean and some set standard or expected value of the mean likely/not likely due to chance?
	One (small sample)	Metric (interval or ratio)	t test for one mean	Random sample, $n < 30$	Same as for small sample above
	Two (large sample)	Metric (interval or ratio)	Z test for one mean	Random sample, $n \geq 30$	Is the observed difference between the means for two subgroups (mean income for men and women) likely/not likely due to chance?
	Three or more	Metric (interval or ratio)	One-way ANOVA	Random sample	Is the observed variation between means for three or more subgroups (mean expenditures on entertainment for high-, moderate-, and low-income people) likely/not likely due to chance?
Hypotheses about proportions	One (large sample)	Metric (interval or ratio)	Z test for one proportion	Random sample, $n \geq 30$	Is the observed difference between a sample estimate of proportion (percentage who say they will buy) and some set standard or expected value likely/not likely due to chance?
	Two (large sample)	Metric (interval or ratio)	Z test for two proportions	Random sample, $n \geq 30$	Is the observed difference between estimated percentages for two subgroups (percentage of men and women who have college degrees) likely/not likely due to chance?

Types of Errors in Hypothesis Testing

➤ **type I error (α error)** Rejection of the null hypothesis when, in fact, it is true.

Hypothesis tests are subject to two general types of errors, typically referred to as type I error and type II error. A **type I error** involves rejecting the null hypothesis when it is, in fact, true. The researcher may reach this incorrect conclusion because the observed difference between the sample and population values is due to sampling error. The researcher must

FROM THE FRONT LINE

Tips on Significance Testing

Paul Schmiege, Marketing Science, DSS Research

A typical question in the marketing research industry goes something like this: "Last year, the percentage of respondents aware of our brand on an unaided basis was 43.2 percent. This year the corresponding percentage was 47.5 percent. Is this difference significant?" This is not the same as asking, "Is this difference important, is it something that we should act on, should we continue with the same advertising strategy to increase unaided awareness?"

However, you must be careful to distinguish the technical term *statistical significance* from more intuitive terms such as *practical significance* or *importance*. At the heart of its technical meaning, significance in the field of statistics means that the difference is likely greater than we would expect due to sampling error.

In the above example, you only have statistics about samples and not population parameters. Therefore, you can never be entirely certain that a difference between two sample results is a real difference. The difference may only reflect sampling error.

The single most common test in marketing research is the two-sample *t* test. You might not ever see any other test in your entire career. Because the two-sample *t* test is so important, it is good to keep at least two points in mind about it:

- The two-sample *t* test is a two-tailed test. It asks, "Does a significant difference exist?" It does not ask, "Is the first significantly greater than the second?" or "Is the first significantly less than the second?" Consequently, if a significant difference exists you should say, "A statistically significant difference exists, and that observed difference is higher (or lower)."
- The two-sample *t* test is run with the assumption of equal variances. The true standard deviation for the combined populations is unknown, so you "pool" the two-sample standard deviations together to calculate something similar to a weighted average. In academic research, you would first test whether to assume equal or unequal variance, but you will probably never have to do that in the business world.

For any given observed difference, there are sample sizes large enough that the difference will be significant in a two-sample *t* test (sample sizes go in the denominator of the equation). Or to think of it from another perspective, when you start testing with larger and larger sample sizes, smaller and smaller differences become statistically significant, but practical significance remains the same. Is a 0.5 percent increase worth telling management about even if it should happen to be statistically significant? Probably not.

In the end, you have to rely on your expertise and judgment regarding what's important and what's not important for a particular measure in a particular industry. Significance, or nonsignificance, is just another piece of information you use to decide what to recommend to clients.

decide how willing she or he is to commit a type I error. The probability of committing a type I error is referred to as the *alpha* (α) *level.* Conversely, $1 - \alpha$ is the probability of making a correct decision by not rejecting the null hypothesis when, in fact, it is true.

A **type II error** involves failing to reject the null hypothesis when it actually is false. A type II error is referred to as a *beta* (β) *error.* The value $1 - \beta$ reflects the probability of making a correct decision in rejecting the null hypothesis when, in fact, it is false. The four possibilities are summarized in Exhibit 15.2.

type II error (β error)
Failure to reject the null hypothesis when, in fact, it is false.

EXHIBIT 15.2	Type I and Type II Errors	
Actual State of the Null Hypothesis	**Fail to Reject H_0**	**Reject H_0**
H_0 is true	Correct $(1 - \alpha)$	Type I error (α)
H_0 is false	Type II error (β)	Correct $(1 - \beta)$

As we consider the various types of hypothesis tests, keep in mind that when a researcher rejects or fails to reject the null hypothesis, this decision is never made with 100 percent certainty. There is a probability that the decision is correct and there is a probability that the decision is not correct. The level of α is set by the researcher, after consulting with his or her client, considering the resources available for the project, and considering the implications of making type I and type II errors. However, the estimation of β is more complicated and is beyond the scope of our discussion. Note that type I and type II errors are not complementary; that is, $\alpha + \beta \neq 1$.

It would be ideal to have control over n (the sample size), α (the probability of a type I error), and β (the probability of a type II error) for any hypothesis test. Unfortunately, only two of the three can be controlled. For a given problem with a fixed sample size, n is fixed, or controlled. Therefore, only one of α and β can be controlled.

Assume that for a given problem you have decided to set $\alpha = .05$. As a result, the procedure you use to test H_0 versus H_a will reject H_0 when it is true (type I error) 5 percent of the time. You could set $\alpha = 0$ so that you would never have a type I error. The idea of never rejecting a correct H_0 sounds good. However, the downside is that β (the probability of a type II error) is equal to 1 in this situation. As a result, you will always fail to reject H_0 when it is false. For example, if $\alpha = 0$ in the fast-food service time example, where H_0 is mean waiting time = 2 minutes, then the resulting test of H_0 versus H_a will automatically fail to reject H_0 (mean waiting time = 2 minutes) whenever the estimated waiting time is any value other than 2 minutes. If, for example, we did a survey and determined that the mean waiting time for the people surveyed was 8.5 minutes, we would still fail to reject (FTR) H_0. As you can see, this is not a good compromise. We need a value of α that offers a more reasonable compromise between the probabilities of the two types of errors. Note that in the situation in which $\alpha = 0$ and $\beta = 1$, $\alpha + \beta = 1$. As you will see later on, this is not true as a general rule.

The value of α selected should be a function of the relative importance of the two types of errors. Suppose you have just had a diagnostic test. The purpose of the test is to determine whether you have a particular medical condition that is fatal in most cases. If you have the disease, a treatment that is painless, inexpensive, and totally without risk will cure the condition 100 percent of the time. Here are the hypotheses to be tested:

> H_0: Test indicates that you do not have the disease.
>
> H_a: Test indicates that you do have the disease.

Thus,

> $\alpha = P(\text{rejecting } H_0 \text{ when it is true})$
>
> $= (\text{test indicates that you have the disease when you do not have it})$

$$\beta = P(\text{FTR } H_0 \text{ when in fact it is false})$$
$$= P(\text{test indicates that you do not have the disease when you do have it})$$

Clearly, a type I error (measured by α) is not nearly as serious as a type II error (measured by β). A type I error is not serious because the test will not harm you if you are well. However, a type II error means that you will not receive the treatment you need even though you are ill.

The value of β is never set in advance. When α is made smaller, β becomes larger. If you want to minimize type II error, then you choose a larger value for α in order to make β smaller. In most situations, the range of acceptable values for α is .01 to .1.

In the case of the diagnostic test situation, you might choose a value of α at or near .1 because of the seriousness of a type II error. Conversely, if you are more concerned about type I errors in a given situation, then a small value of α is appropriate. For example, suppose you are testing commercials that were very expensive to produce, and you are concerned about the possibility of rejecting a commercial that is really effective. If there is no real difference between the effects of type I and type II errors, as is often the case, an α value of .05 is commonly used.

Accepting H_0 versus Failing to Reject (FTR) H_0

Researchers often fail to make a distinction between accepting H_0 and failing to reject H_0. However, as noted earlier, there is an important distinction between these two decisions. When a hypothesis is tested, H_0 is presumed to be true until it is demonstrated to be likely to be false. In any hypothesis testing situation, the only other hypothesis that can be accepted is the alternative hypothesis H_a. Either there is sufficient evidence to support H_a (reject H_0) or there is not (fail to reject H_0). The real question is whether there is enough evidence in the data to conclude that H_a is correct. If we fail to reject H_0, we are saying that the data do not provide sufficient support of the claim made in H_a—not that we accept the statement made in H_0.

One-Tailed versus Two-Tailed Test

Tests are either one-tailed or two-tailed. The decision as to which to use depends on the nature of the situation and what the researcher is trying to demonstrate. For example, when the quality control department of a fast-food organization receives a shipment of chicken breasts from one of its vendors and needs to determine whether the product meets specifications in regard to fat content, a one-tailed test is appropriate. The shipment will be rejected if it does not meet minimum specifications. On the other hand, the managers of the meat company that supplies the product should run two-tailed tests to determine two factors. First, they must make sure that the product meets the minimum specifications of their customer before they ship it. Second, they want to determine whether the product exceeds specifications because this can be costly to them. If they are consistently providing a product that exceeds the level of quality they have contracted to provide, their costs may be unnecessarily high.

The classic example of a situation requiring a two-tailed test is the testing of electric fuses. A fuse must trip, or break contact, when it reaches a preset temperature or a fire may result. On the other hand, you do not want the fuse to break contact before it reaches the specified temperature or it will shut off the electricity unnecessarily. The test used in the quality control process for testing fuses must, therefore, be two-tailed.

PRACTICING MARKETING RESEARCH

When Statistical Significance Expands into Practical Significance

Statistical significance refers to results that are true and do not represent random sampling fluctuations or chance in a marketing survey. But managerially important differences, also called practical significance, refer to differences that are judged sufficient or impressive enough to warrant changes in your marketing approach. Here's an example from Honda and its new hybrid Civic that combines a gasoline engine and an electric motor. The question pertains to gas mileage.

Honda focused its advertising approach on gas savings. The hybrid Civic uses its electric motor at slow speeds, then switches to a combination of gas and electric motors for higher speeds, such as when you are on the freeways. Consider that the Civic maintains 50 mpg on average with a deviation of ±10 mpg. Then researchers, mulling over their data on all the vehicles used in testing, discover the actual average mpg is 51. Is this statistically significant? Is the 1 mpg difference real? It must be, for it's based on a count and quantification of mileage of all Civic vehicles. Random sampling was not involved in generating this result; it is a population value.

Although this number, then, is statistically significant, the next level question is: does it have practical significance, big enough to motivate the marketing department to change commercials already produced based on a 50 mpg claim?

The quality control department of a fast-food organization would probably do a one-tailed test to determine whether a shipment of chicken breasts met product specifications. However, a two-tailed test would probably be done by the managers of the meat company that supplied the chicken breasts.

Example of Performing a Statistical Test

Income is an important determinant of the sales of luxury cars. Lexus North America (LNA) is in the process of developing sales estimates for the Southern California market, one of its key markets. According to the U.S. Census, the average annual family income in the market is $55,347. LNA has just completed a survey of 250 randomly selected households in the market to obtain other measures needed for its sales forecasting model. The recently completed survey indicates that the average annual family income in the market is $54,323. The actual value of the population mean (μ) is unknown. This gives us two estimates of μ: the census result and the survey result. The difference between these two estimates could make a substantial difference in the estimates of Lexus sales produced by LNA's forecasting model. In the calculations, the U.S. Census Bureau estimate is treated as the best estimate of μ.

LNA decides to statistically compare the census and survey estimates. The statistics for the sample are

$$\overline{X} = \$54,323$$
$$S = \$4,323$$
$$n = 250$$

The following hypotheses are produced:

$$H_0: \mu = \$55,347$$
$$H_a: \mu \neq \$55,347$$

The decision makers at LNA are willing to use a test that will reject H_0 when it is correct only 5 percent of the time ($\alpha = .05$). This is the significance level of the test. LNA will reject H_0 if $|\overline{X} - \$55,347|$ is larger than can be explained by sampling error at $\alpha = .05$.

Standardizing the data so that the result can be directly related to Z values in Exhibit 2 in Appendix 2, we have the following criterion:

Reject H_0 if $\left| \dfrac{\overline{X} - \$55,347}{S/\sqrt{n}} \right|$ is larger than can be explained by sampling error at $\alpha = .05$. This expression can be rewritten as

$$\left| \frac{\overline{X} - \$55,347}{S/\sqrt{n}} \right| > k$$

What is the value of k? If H_0 is true and the sample size is large (≥ 30), then (based on the central limit theorem) X approximates a normal random variable with

$$\text{Mean} = \mu = \$55,347$$
$$\text{Standard deviation} = \frac{S}{\sqrt{n}}$$

That is, if H_0 is true, $(\overline{X} - \$55,347)/(S/\sqrt{n})$ approximates a standard normal variable Z for samples of 30 or larger with a mean equal to 0 and a standard deviation equal to 1.

Exhibit 15.3

Shaded Area Is Significance Level α

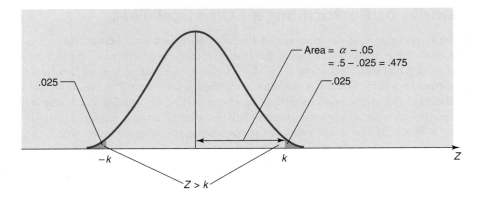

We will reject H_0 if $|Z| > k$. When $|Z| > k$, either $Z > k$ or $Z < -k$, as shown in Exhibit 15.3. Given that

$$P(|Z| > k) = .05$$

the total shaded area is .05, with .025 in each tail (two-tailed test). The area between 0 and k is .475. Referring to Exhibit 2 in Appendix 2, we find that $k = 1.96$. Therefore, the test is

$$\text{Reject } H_0 \text{ if } \left| \frac{\overline{X} - \$55,347}{S/\sqrt{n}} \right| > 1.96$$

and FTR H_0 otherwise. In other words,

$$\text{Reject } H_0 \text{ if } \left| \frac{\overline{X} - \$55,347}{S/\sqrt{n}} \right| > 1.96 \text{ or if } \left| \frac{\overline{X} - \$55,347}{S/\sqrt{n}} \right| < 1.96$$

The question is, is $\overline{X} = \$54,323$ far enough away from $\$55,347$ for LNA to reject H_0? The results show that

$$Z = \frac{\overline{X} - \$55,347}{S/\sqrt{n}}$$

$$= \frac{\$54,323 - \$55,347}{\$4,322/\sqrt{250}} = -3.75$$

Because $-3.75 < -1.96$, we reject H_0. On the basis of the sample results and $\alpha = .05$, the conclusion is that the average household income in the market is not equal to $\$55,347$. If H_0 is true ($\mu = \$55,347$), then the value of $\overline{X}$ obtained from the sample ($\$54,323$) is 3.75 standard deviations to the left of the mean on the normal curve for $\overline{X}$. A value of $\overline{X}$ this far away from the mean is very unlikely (probability is less than .05). As a result, we conclude that H_0 is not likely to be true, and we reject it.

Commonly Used Statistical Hypothesis Tests

A number of commonly used statistical hypothesis tests of differences are presented in the following sections. Many other statistical tests have been developed and are used, but a full discussion of all of them is beyond the scope of this text.

The distributions used in the following sections for comparing the computed and tabular values of the statistics are the Z distribution, the t distribution, the F distribution, and the chi-square (χ^2) distribution. The tabular values for these distributions appear in Exhibits 2, 3, 4, and 5 of Appendix 2.

Independent versus Related Samples

In some cases, one needs to test the hypothesis that the value of a variable in one population is equal to the value of that same variable in another population. Selection of the appropriate test statistic requires the researcher to consider whether the samples are independent or related. **Independent samples** are those in which measurement of the variable of interest in one sample has no effect on measurement of the variable in the other sample. It is not necessary that there be two different surveys, only that the measurement of the variable in one population has no effect on the measurement of the variable in the other population. In the case of **related samples**, measurement of the variable of interest in one sample may influence measurement of the variable in another sample.

If, for example, men and women were interviewed in a particular survey regarding their frequency of eating out, there is no way that a man's response could affect or change the way a woman would respond to a question in the survey. Thus, this would be an example of independent samples. On the other hand, consider a situation in which the researcher needed to determine the effect of a new advertising campaign on consumer awareness of a particular brand. To do this, the researcher might survey a random sample of consumers before introducing the new campaign and then survey the same sample of consumers 90 days after the new campaign was introduced. These samples are not independent. The measurement of awareness 90 days after the start of the campaign may be affected by the first measurement.

> **➤ independent samples**
> Samples in which measurement of a variable in one population has no effect on measurement of the variable in the other.

> **➤ related samples**
> Samples in which measurement of a variable in one population may influence measurement of the variable in the other.

Degrees of Freedom

Many of the statistical tests discussed in this chapter require the researcher to specify degrees of freedom in order to find the critical value of the test statistic from the table for that statistic. The number of degrees of freedom is the number of observations in a statistical problem that are not restricted or are free to vary.

The number of degrees of freedom (d.f.) is equal to the number of observations minus the number of assumptions or constraints necessary to calculate a statistic. Consider the problem of adding five numbers when the mean of the five numbers is known to be 20. In this situation, only four of the five numbers are free to vary. Once four of the numbers are known, the last value is also known (can be calculated) because the mean value must be 20. If four of the five numbers were 14, 23, 24, and 18, then the fifth number would have to be 21 to produce a mean of 20. We would say that the sample has $n - 1$ or 4 degrees of freedom. It is as if the sample had one less observation—the inclusion of degrees of freedom in the calculation adjusts for this fact.

Goodness of Fit

Chi-Square Test

As noted earlier in the text, data collected in surveys are often analyzed by means of one-way frequency counts and cross tabulations.[5] The purpose of a cross tabulation is to study relationships among variables. The question is, do the numbers of responses that fall into the various categories differ from what one would expect? For example, a study might involve partitioning users into groups by gender (male, female), age (under 18, 18 to 35, over 35), or income level (low, middle, high) and cross tabulating on the basis of answers to questions about preferred brand or level of use. The **chi-square** (χ^2) **test** enables the research analyst to determine whether an observed pattern of frequencies corresponds to, or fits, an "expected" pattern.[6] It tests the "goodness of fit" of the observed distribution to an expected distribution. We will look at the application of this technique to test distributions of cross-tabulated categorical data for a single sample and for two independent samples.

> **chi-square test**
>
> Test of the goodness of fit between the observed distribution and the expected distribution of a variable.

Chi-Square Test of a Single Sample Suppose the marketing manager of a retail electronics chain needs to test the effectiveness of three special deals (deal 1, deal 2, and deal 3). Each deal will be offered for a month. The manager wants to measure the effect of each deal on the number of customers visiting a test store during the time the deal is on. The number of customers visiting the store under each deal is as follows:

Deal	Month	Customers per Month
1	April	11,700
2	May	12,100
3	June	11,780
Total		35,580

The marketing manager needs to know whether there is a significant difference between the numbers of customers visiting the store during the time periods covered by the three deals. The chi-square (χ^2) one-sample test is the appropriate test to use to answer this question. This test is applied as follows:

1. Specify the null and alternative hypotheses.

   ☐ Null hypothesis H_0: The numbers of customers visiting the store under the various deals are equal.

   ☐ Alternative hypothesis H_a: There is a significant difference in the numbers of customers visiting the store under the various deals.

2. Determine the number of visitors who would be expected in each category if the null hypothesis were correct (E_i). In this example, the null hypothesis is that there is no difference in the numbers of customers attracted by the different deals. Therefore, an equal number of customers would be expected under each deal. Of course, this assumes that no other factors influenced the number of visits to the store. Under

the null (no difference) hypothesis, the expected number of customers visiting the store in each deal period would be computed as follows:

$$E_i = \frac{TV}{N}$$

where   TV = total number of visits

N = number of months

Thus,

$$E_i = \frac{35,580}{3} = 11,860$$

The researcher should always check for cells in which small expected frequencies occur because they can distort χ^2 results. No more than 20 percent of the categories should have an expected frequency of less than 5, and none should have an expected frequency of less than 1. This is not a problem in this case.

3. Calculate the χ^2 value, using the formula

$$\chi^2 = \sum_{i=1}^{k} \frac{(O_i - E_i)^2}{E_i}$$

where O_i = observed number in ith category

E_i = expected number in ith category

k = number of categories

For this example,

$$\chi^2 = \frac{(11,700 - 11,860)^2}{11,860} + \frac{(12,100 - 11.860)^2}{11,860}$$
$$+ \frac{(11,780 - 11,860)^2}{11,860}$$
$$= 7.6$$

4. Select the level of significance α. If the .05 level of significance (α) is selected, the tabular χ^2 value with 2 degrees of freedom ($k - 1$) is 5.99. (See Exhibit 4 in Appendix 2 for $k - 1 = 2$ d.f., $\alpha = .05$.)

5. State the result. Because the calculated χ^2 value (7.6) is higher than the table value (5.99), we *reject the null hypothesis*. Therefore, we conclude with 95 percent confidence that customer response to the deals was significantly different. Unfortunately, this test tells us only that the overall variation among the cell frequencies is greater than would be expected by chance. It does not tell us whether any individual cell is significantly different from the others.

PRACTICING MARKETING RESEARCH

A Simple Field Application of Chi-Square Goodness of Fit

Say you are a marketing manager and you want to know if an observed pattern of frequencies differs from an expected pattern. The best test for addressing this question is the chi-square test of goodness of fit in which only one categorical variable is involved. Here's how to apply it in a case of packaging color design.

As a marketing manager you have five colors to choose from for your packaging design, but you can only use one. Which one does the market prefer? Obviously, you want to know this before you debut the product. You do a random sampling of 400 consumers and ask them, getting these results:

Package Color	Consumer Preference
Red	70
Blue	106
Green	80
Pink	70
Orange	74
TOTAL	400

The results suggest that people prefer blue, but you need to be sure that this seeming preference for blue is not a chance result. Your null hypothesis posits that all colors are preferred equally, but your alternative hypothesis says they are not equally preferred. In the calculations, note that in terms of the null hypothesis for equal preference for all colors, the expected frequencies for all colors will equal 80. The chi-square value is 11.40 calculated per the standard formula. The results are below.

Because the critical value of chi-square at the 0.5 level of significance (5 percent probability of incorrectly rejecting the null hypothesis) for 4 degrees of freedom is 9.488, you can eliminate the null hypothesis. You can conclude that consumers do not equally prefer all colors but in fact like blue the best. As marketing manager, you can introduce your product in a blue package and do so confidently that it is the best option of those available to you.[7]

Package Color	Observed Frequencies (O)	Expected Frequencies (E)	(O−E)	$\chi^2 = \sum \left(\dfrac{(O-E)^2}{E} \right)$
Red	70	80	100	1.25
Blue	106	80	676	8.45
Green	80	80	0	0.00
Pink	70	80	100	1.25
Orange	74	80	36	0.45
TOTAL	400	400	—	11.40

Chi-Square Test of Two Independent Samples Marketing researchers often need to determine whether there is any association between two or more variables. Before formulation of a marketing strategy, questions such as the following may need to be answered: Are men and women equally divided into heavy-, medium-, and light-user

EXHIBIT 15.4	Data for χ^2 Test of Two Independent Samples

Visits to Convenience Store by Males				Visits to Convenience Stores by Females			
Number X_m	Frequency f_m	Percent	Cumulative Percent	Number X_f	Frequency f_f	Percent	Cumulative Percent
2	2	4.4	4.4	2	5	7.0	7.0
3	5	11.1	15.6	3	4	5.6	12.7
5	7	15.6	31.1	4	7	9.9	22.5
6	2	4.4	35.6	5	10	14.1	36.6
7	1	2.2	37.8	6	6	8.5	45.1
8	2	4.4	42.2	7	3	4.2	49.3
9	1	2.2	44.4	8	6	8.5	57.7
10	7	15.6	60.0	9	2	2.8	60.6
12	3	6.7	66.7	10	13	18.3	78.9
15	5	11.1	77.8	12	4	5.6	84.5
20	6	13.3	91.1	15	3	4.2	88.7
23	1	2.2	93.3	16	2	2.8	91.5
25	1	2.2	95.6	20	4	5.6	97.2
30	1	2.2	97.8	21	1	1.4	98.6
40	1	2.2	100.0	25	1	1.4	100.0

$n_m = 45$ $n_f = 71$

Mean number of visits by males, $\bar{X}_m = \dfrac{\sum X_m f_m}{45} = 11.5$ Mean number of visits by females, $\bar{X}_f = \dfrac{\sum X_f f_f}{71} = 8.5$

categories? Are purchasers and nonpurchasers equally divided into low-, middle-, and high-income groups? The chi-square (χ^2) test for two independent samples is the appropriate test in such situations.

The technique will be illustrated using the data from Exhibit 15.4. A convenience store chain wants to determine the nature of the relationship, if any, between gender of customer and frequency of visits to stores in the chain. Frequency of visits has been divided into three categories: 1 to 5 visits per month (light user), 6 to 14 visits per month (medium user), and 15 and above visits per month (heavy user). The steps in conducting this test follow.

1. State the null and alternative hypotheses.

   ☐ Null hypothesis H_0: There is no relationship between gender and frequency of visits.

   ☐ Alternative hypothesis H_a: There is a significant relationship between gender and frequency of visits.

2. Place the observed (sample) frequencies in a $k \times r$ table (cross-tabulation or contingency table), using the k columns for the sample groups and the r rows for the conditions or treatments. Calculate the sum of each row and each column. Record those totals at the margins of the table (they are called *marginal totals*). Also, calculate the total for the entire table (N).

	Male	Female	Totals
1–5 visits	14	26	40
6–14 visits	16	34	50
15 and above visits	15	11	26
Totals	45	71	116

SPSS JUMP START FOR CHI-SQUARE TEST

Steps that you need to go through to do the chi-square test problem shown in the book are provided below along with the output produced. Use the data set **Chisqex**, which you can download from the Web site for the text.

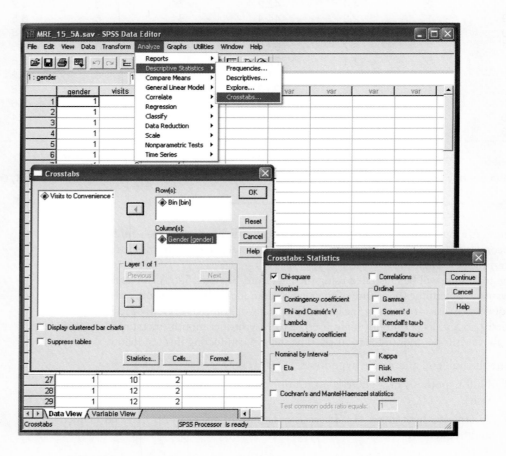

Steps in SPSS

1. Select *Analyze → Descriptive Statistics → Crosstabs.*
2. Move **bin** to Rows.
3. Move **gender** to Columns.

4. Click Statistics.
5. Check box for Chi-square
6. Click Continue.
7. Click OK.

SPSS Output for Chi-Square Test

Crosstabs

Case Processing Summary

	Cases					
	Valid		Missing		Total	
	N	Percent	N	Percent	N	Percent
Bin * Gender	116	100.0%	0	.0%	116	100.0%

Bin * Gender Crosstabulation

Count

		Gender		Total
		Male	Female	
Bin	1-5 visits	14	26	40
	6-14 visits	16	34	50
	15 and above visits	15	11	26
Total		45	71	116

Chi-Square Tests

	Value	df	Asymp. Sig. (2-sided)
Pearson Chi-Square	5.125[a]	2	.077
Likelihood Ratio	5.024	2	.081
Linear-by-Linear Association	2.685	1	.101
N of Valid Cases	116		

a. 0 cells (.0%) have expected count less than 5. The minimum expected count is 10.09.

3. Determine the expected frequency for each cell in the contingency table by calculating the product of the two marginal totals common to that cell and dividing that value by N.

	Male	Female
1–5 visits	$\frac{45 \times 40}{116} = 15.5$	$\frac{71 \times 40}{116} = 24.5$
6–14 visits	$\frac{45 \times 50}{116} = 19.4$	$\frac{71 \times 50}{116} = 30.6$
15 and above visits	$\frac{45 \times 26}{116} = 10.1$	$\frac{71 \times 26}{116} = 15.9$

The χ^2 value will be distorted if more than 20 percent of the cells have an expected frequency of less than 5 or if any cell has an expected frequency of less than 1. The test should not be used under these conditions.

4. Calculate the value of χ^2 using

$$\chi^2 = \sum_{i=1}^{r} \sum_{j=1}^{k} \frac{(O_{ij} - E_{ij})^2}{E_{ij}}$$

where $\quad O_{ij}$ = observed number in the ith row of the jth column

$\quad\quad\quad E_{ij}$ = expected number in the ith row of the jth column

For this example,

$$\chi^2 = \frac{(14 - 15.52)^2}{15.52} + \frac{(26 - 24.48)^2}{24.48} + \frac{(16 - 19.4)^2}{19.4}$$
$$+ \frac{(34 - 30.6)^2}{30.6} + \frac{(15 - 10.09)^2}{10.09} + \frac{(11 - 15.91)^2}{15.91}$$
$$= 5.1$$

5. State the result. The tabular χ^2 value at a .05 level of significance and $(r - 1) \times (k - 1) = 2$ degrees of freedom is 5.99 (see Table 4 of Appendix 2). Because the calculated $\chi^2 = 5.1$ is less than the tabular value, we *fail to reject (FTR) the null hypothesis* and conclude that there is no significant difference between males and females in terms of frequency of visits.

Another chi-square example is provided in the Practicing Marketing Research feature on page 492.

Hypotheses about One Mean

Z Test

> **Z test**
> Hypothesis test used for a single mean if the sample is large enough and drawn at random.

One of the most common goals of marketing research studies is to make some inference about the population mean. If the sample size is large enough ($n \geq 30$), the appropriate test statistic for testing a hypothesis about a single mean is the **Z test**. For small samples ($n < 30$), the t test with $n - 1$ degrees of freedom (where n = sample size) should be used.

Video Connection, a Dallas video store chain, recently completed a survey of 200 consumers in its market area. One of the questions was "Compared to other video stores in the area, would you say Video Connection is much better than average, somewhat better than average, average, somewhat worse than average, or much worse than average?" Responses were coded as follows:

Response	Code
Much better	5
Somewhat better	4
Average	3
Somewhat worse	2
Much worse	1

The mean rating of Video Connection is 3.4. The sample standard deviation is 1.9. How can the management of Video Connection be confident that its video stores' mean rating is significantly higher than 3 (average in the rating scale)? The Z test for hypotheses about one mean is the appropriate test in this situation. The steps in the procedure follow.

1. Specify the null and alternative hypotheses.

    ☐   Null hypothesis H$_0$: $M \leq 3$ ($M =$ response on rating scale).
    ☐   Alternative hypothesis H$_a$: $M > 3$.

2. Specify the level of sampling error (α) allowed. For $\alpha = .05$, the table value of Z(critical) $= 1.64$. (See Exhibit 3 in Appendix 2 for d.f. $= \infty$, .05 significance, one-tail. The table for t is used because $t = Z$ for samples greater than 30.) Management's need to be very confident that the mean rating is significantly higher than 3 is interpreted to mean that the chance of being wrong because of sampling error should be no more than .05 (an α of .05).

3. Determine the sample standard deviation (S), which is given as $S = 1.90$.

4. Calculate the estimated standard error of the mean, using the formula

$$S_{\bar{X}} = \frac{S}{\sqrt{n}}$$

where $S_{\bar{X}} =$ estimated standard error of the mean

In this case,

$$S_{\bar{X}} = \frac{1.9}{\sqrt{200}} = 0.13$$

5. Calculate the test statistic:

$$Z = \frac{(\text{Sample mean}) - \left(\begin{array}{c}\text{Population mean specified} \\ \text{under the null hypothesis}\end{array}\right)}{\text{Estimated standard error of the mean}}$$

$$= \frac{3.4 - 3}{0.13} = 3.07$$

6. State the result. *The null hypothesis can be rejected* because the calculated Z value (3.07) is larger than the critical Z value (1.64). Management of Video Connection can infer with 95 percent confidence that its video stores' mean rating is significantly higher than 3.

t Test

As noted earlier, for small samples ($n < 30$), the ***t* test** with $n - 1$ degrees of freedom is the appropriate test for making statistical inferences. The t distribution also is theoretically correct for large samples ($n \geq 30$). However, it approaches and becomes indistinguishable from the normal distribution for samples of 30 or more observations. Although the Z test is generally used for large samples, nearly all statistical packages use the t test for all sample sizes.

To see the application of the t test, consider a soft drink manufacturer that test markets a new soft drink in Denver. Twelve supermarkets in that city are selected at random,

▶ *t* test
Hypothesis test used for a single mean if the sample is too small to use the Z test.

and the new soft drink is offered for sale in these stores for a limited period. The company estimates that it must sell more than 1,000 cases per week in each store for the brand to be profitable enough to warrant large-scale introduction. Actual average sales per store per week for the test are shown below.

Here is the procedure for testing whether sales per store per week are more than 1,000 cases:

1. Specify the null and alternative hypotheses.

    ☐ Null hypothesis H_0: $\overline{X} \leq 1,000$ cases per store per week ($\overline{X}$ = average sales per store per week)

    ☐ Alternative hypothesis H_a: $X > 1,000$ cases per store per week

Store	Average Sales per Week (X_i)
1	870
2	910
3	1,050
4	1,200
5	860
6	1,400
7	1,305
8	890
9	1,250
10	1,100
11	950
12	1,260

$$\text{Mean sales per week, } \overline{X} = \frac{\sum\limits_{i=1}^{n} X_i}{n} = 1087.1$$

2. Specify the level of sampling error (α) allowed. For $\alpha = .05$, the table value of t(critical) $= 1.796$. (See Exhibit 3 in Appendix 2 for $12 - 1 = 11$ d.f., $\alpha = .05$, one-tail test. A one-tailed t test is appropriate because the new soft drink will be introduced on a large scale only if sales per week are more than 1,000 cases.)

3. Determine the sample standard deviation (S) as follows:

$$S = \sqrt{\frac{\sum\limits_{i=1}^{n} (X_i - \overline{X})^2}{n - 1}}$$

where X_i = observed sales per week in ith store

$\overline{X}$ = average sales per week

n = number of stores

For the sample data,

$$S = \sqrt{\frac{403,822.9}{(12 - 1)}} = 191.6$$

   •

Steps that you need to go through to do the *T* test problem shown in the book are provided below along with the output produced. Use the data set **TTestex**, which you can download from the Web site for the text.

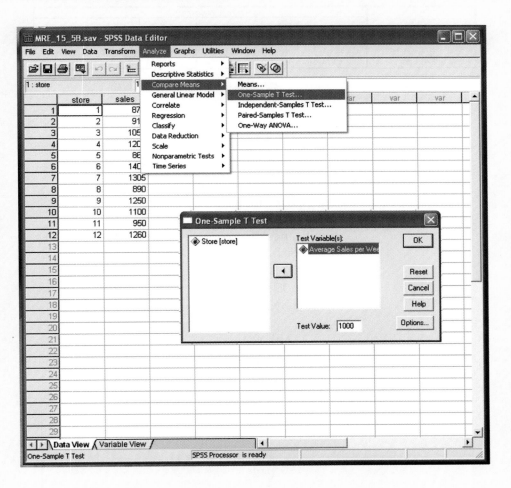

1. Select *Analyze → Compare Means → One-Sample T Test.*
2. Move **sales** to Test Variable(s).
3. Input 1000 after Test Value.
4. Click OK.

SPSS Output for T Test

T-Test

One-Sample Statistics

	N	Mean	Std. Deviation	Std. Error Mean
Average Sales per Week	12	1087.08	191.602	55.311

One-Sample Test

	Test Value = 1000					
					95% Confidence Interval of the Difference	
	t	df	Sig. (2-tailed)	Mean Difference	Lower	Upper
Average Sales per Week	1.574	11	.144	87.083	-34.65	208.82

Note:

SPSS here only lists the significance for a two-tailed test. We need the significance of a one-tailed test, which is half this. 072. .072 is greater than the _ = .05 so fail to reject the null hypothesis.

4. Calculate the estimated standard error of the mean ($S_{\overline{X}}$), using the following formula:

$$S_{\overline{X}} = \frac{S}{\sqrt{n}}$$

$$= \frac{191.6}{\sqrt{12}} = 55.3$$

5. Calculate the t-test statistic:

$$t = \frac{(\text{Sample mean}) - \left(\begin{array}{c}\text{Population mean} \\ \text{under the null hypothesis}\end{array}\right)}{\text{Estimated standard error of the mean}}$$

$$= \frac{1,087.1 - 1000}{55.31} = 1.6$$

6. State the result. *The null hypothesis cannot be rejected* because the calculated value of t is less than the critical value of t. Although mean sales per store per week ($\overline{X} = 1087.1$) are higher than 1,000 units, the difference is not statistically significant, based on the 12 stores sampled. On the basis of this test and the decision criterion specified, the large-scale introduction of the new soft drink is not warranted.

Hypotheses about Two Means

Marketers are frequently interested in testing differences between groups. In the following example of testing the differences between two means, the samples are independent.

The management of a convenience store chain is interested in differences between the store visit rates of men and women. Believing that men visit convenience stores more often than women, management collected data on convenience store visits from 1,000 randomly selected consumers. Testing this hypothesis involves the following steps:

1. Specify the null and alternative hypotheses.
   - ☐ Null hypothesis H_0: $M_m - M_f \leq 0$; the mean visit rate of men (M_m) is the same as or less than the mean visit rate of women (M_f).
   - ☐ Alternative hypothesis H_a: $M_m - M_f > 0$; the mean visit rate of men (M_m) is higher than the mean visit rate of women (M_f).

   The observed difference in the two means (Exhibit 15.4) is $11.49 - 8.51 = 2.98$.

2. Set the level of sampling error (α). The managers decided that the acceptable level of sampling error for this test is $\alpha = .05$. For $\alpha = .05$, the table value of Z(critical) = 1.64. (See Exhibit 3 in Appendix 2 for d.f. = ∞, .05 significance, one-tail. The table for t is used because $t = Z$ for samples greater than 30.)

3. Calculate the estimated standard error of the differences between the two means as follows:

$$S_{X_{m-f}} = \sqrt{\frac{S_m^2}{n_m} + \frac{S_f^2}{n_f}}$$

where

S_m = estimated standard deviation of population m (men)
S_f = estimated standard deviation of population f (women)
n_m = sample size for sample m
n_f = sample size for sample f

Therefore,

$$S_{X_{m-f}} = \sqrt{\frac{(8.16)^2}{45} + \frac{(5.23)^2}{71}} = 1.37$$

Note that this formula is for those cases in which the two samples have unequal variances. A separate formula is used when the two samples have equal variances. When this test is run in SAS and many other statistical packages, two t values are provided—one for each variance assumption.

4. Calculate the test statistic Z as follows:

$$Z = \frac{\left(\begin{array}{c}\text{Difference between means}\\\text{of first and second sample}\end{array}\right) - \left(\begin{array}{c}\text{Difference between means}\\\text{under the null hypothesis}\end{array}\right)}{\text{Standard error of the differences between the two means}}$$

$$= \frac{(11.49 - 8.51) - 0}{1.37} = 2.18$$

Before launching new services designed for families with an annual income of more than $50,000, the bank needs to be certain about the percentage of its customers who meet or exceed this threshold income.

5. State the result. The calculated value of Z (2.18) is larger than the critical value (1.64), so *the null hypothesis is rejected.* Management can conclude with 95 percent confidence ($1 - \alpha = .95$) that, on average, men visit convenience stores more often than do women.

Hypotheses about Proportions

In many situations, researchers are concerned with phenomena that are expressed in terms of percentages.[8] For example, marketers might be interested in testing for the proportion of respondents who prefer brand A versus those who prefer brand B or those who are brand loyal versus those who are not.

Proportion in One Sample

A survey of 500 customers conducted by a major bank indicated that slightly more than 74 percent had family incomes of more than $50,000 per year. If this is true, the bank will develop a special package of services for this group. Before developing and introducing the new package of services, management wants to determine whether the true percentage is greater than 60 percent. The survey results show that 74.3 percent of the bank's customers surveyed reported family incomes of $50,000 or more per year. The procedure for the **hypothesis test of proportions** follows:

➤ **hypothesis test of proportions**
Test to determine whether the difference between proportions is greater than would be expected because of sampling error.

1. Specify the null and alternative hypotheses.
   - ☐ Null hypothesis H_0: $P \leq .60$.
   - ☐ Alternative hypothesis H_a: $P > .60$ ($P =$ proportion of customers with family incomes of $50,000 or more per year).

2. Specify the level of sampling error (α) allowed. For $\alpha = .05$, the table value of Z(critical) $= 1.64$. (See Exhibit 3 in Appendix 2 for d.f. $= \infty$, .05 significance, one-tail. The table for t is used because $t = Z$ for samples greater than 30.)

3. Calculate the estimated standard error, using the value of P specified in the null hypothesis:

$$S_p = \sqrt{\frac{P(1 - P)}{n - 1}}$$

where $P =$ proportion specified in the null hypothesis
$n =$ sample size

Therefore,

$$S_p = \sqrt{\frac{.6(1 - .6)}{35 - 1}} = .084$$

4. Calculate the test statistic as follows:

$$Z = \frac{(\text{Observed proportion} - \text{Proportion under null hypothesis})}{\text{Estimated standard error } (S_p)}$$

$$= \frac{0.7429 - 0.60}{.084} = 1.7$$

The *null hypothesis is rejected* because the calculated Z value is larger than the critical Z value. The bank can conclude with 95 percent confidence ($1 - \alpha = .95$) that more than 60 percent of its customers have family incomes of $50,000 or more. Management can introduce the new package of services targeted at this group.

Two Proportions in Independent Samples

In many instances, management is interested in the difference between the proportions of people in two different groups who engage in a certain activity or have a certain characteristic. For example, management of a convenience store chain had reason to believe, on the basis of a research study, that the percentage of men who visit convenience stores nine or more times per month (heavy users) is larger than the percentage of women who do so. The specifications required and the procedure for testing this hypothesis are as follows.

1. Specify the null and alternative hypotheses:

   ☐ Null hypothesis H$_0$: $P_m - P_f \leq 0$; the proportion of men (P_m) reporting nine or more visits per month is the same as or less than the proportion of women (P_f) reporting nine or more visits per month.

   ☐ Alternative hypothesis H$_a$: $P_m - P_f > 0$; the proportion of men (P_m) reporting nine or more visits per month is greater than the proportion of women (P_f) reporting nine or more visits per month.

   The sample proportions and the difference can be calculated from Exhibit 15.4 as follows:

$$P_m = \frac{26}{45} = .58$$

$$P_f = \frac{30}{71} = .42$$

$$P_m - P_f = .58 - .42 = .16$$

2. Set the level of sampling error α at .10 (management decision). For $\alpha = .10$, the table value of Z(critical) = 1.28. (See Exhibit 3 in Appendix 2 for d.f. = ∞, .10 significance, one-tail. The table for t is used because $t = Z$ for samples greater than 30.)

3. Calculate the estimated standard error of the differences between the two proportions as follows:

$$S_{P_{m-f}} = \sqrt{P(1 - P)\left(\frac{1}{n_m} + \frac{1}{n_f}\right)}$$

where
$$P = \frac{n_m P_m + n_f P_f}{n_m + n_f}$$

P_m = proportion in sample m (men)

P_f = proportion in sample f (women)

n_m = size of sample m

n_f = size of sample f

Therefore,

$$P = \frac{45(.58) + 71(.41)}{45 + 71} = .48$$

and
$$S_{P_{m-f}} = \sqrt{.48(1 - .48)\left(\frac{1}{45} + \frac{1}{71}\right)} = .10$$

4. Calculate the test statistic.

$$Z = \frac{\left(\begin{array}{c}\text{Difference between}\\\text{observed proportions}\end{array}\right) - \left(\begin{array}{c}\text{Difference between proportions}\\\text{under the null hypothesis}\end{array}\right)}{\begin{array}{c}\text{Estimated standard error of the differences}\\\text{between the two means}\end{array}}$$

$$= \frac{(.58 - .42) - 0}{.10} = 1.60$$

5. State the result. *The null hypothesis is rejected* because the calculated Z value (1.60) is larger than the critical Z value (1.28 for $\alpha = .10$). Management can conclude with 90 percent confidence $(1 - \alpha = .90)$ that the proportion of men who visit convenience stores nine or more times per month is larger than the proportion of women who do so.

It should be noted that if the level of sampling error α had been set at .05, the critical Z value would equal 1.64. In this case, we would fail to reject (FTR) the null hypothesis because Z(calculated) would be smaller than Z(critical).

Analysis of Variance (ANOVA)

> **analysis of variance (ANOVA)**
> Test for the differences among the means of two or more independent samples.

When the goal is to test the differences among the means of two or more independent samples, **analysis of variance (ANOVA)** is an appropriate statistical tool. Although it can be used to test differences between two means, ANOVA is more commonly used for hypothesis tests regarding the differences among the means of several (C) independent groups (where $C \geq 3$). It is a statistical technique that permits the researcher to determine whether the variability among or across the C sample means is greater than expected because of sampling error.

The Z and t tests described earlier normally are used to test the null hypothesis when only two sample means are involved. However, in situations in which there are three or more samples, it would be inefficient to test differences between the means two at a time. With five samples and associated means, 10 t tests would be required to test all pairs of means. More important, the use of Z or t tests in situations involving three or more means increases the probability of a type 1 error. Because these tests must be performed for all possible pairs of means, the more pairs, the more tests that must be performed. And the more tests performed, the more likely it is that one or more tests will show significant differences that are really due to sampling error. At an α of .05, this could be expected to occur in 1 of 20 tests on average.

One-way ANOVA is often used to analyze experimental results. Suppose the marketing manager for a chain of brake shops was considering three different services for a possible in-store promotion: wheel alignment, oil change, and tune-up. She was interested in knowing whether there were significant differences in potential sales of the three services.

Sixty similar stores (20 in each of three cities) were selected at random from among those operated by the chain. One of the services was introduced in each of three cities. Other variables under the firm's direct control, such as price and advertising, were kept at the same level during the course of the experiment. The experiment was conducted for a 30-day period, and sales of the new services were recorded for the period.

Average sales for each shop are shown below. The question is, are the differences among the means larger than would be expected due to chance?

A brake shop might use analysis of variance to analyze experimental results with respect to several new services before deciding on a particular new service to offer.

Chicago (Wheel Alignment)		Cleveland (Oil Change)		Detroit (Tune-Up)	
310	318	314	321	337	310
315	322	315	340	325	312
305	333	350	318	330	340
310	315	305	315	345	318
315	385	299	322	320	322
345	310	309	295	325	335
340	312	299	302	328	341
330	308	312	316	330	340
320	312	331	294	342	320
315	340	335	308	330	310
$\overline{X} = 323$		$\overline{X} = 315$		$\overline{X} = 328$	

1. Specify the null and alternative hypotheses.

   ☐ Null hypothesis H_0: $M_1 = M_2 = M_3$; mean sales of the three items are equal.

   ☐ Alternative hypothesis H_a: The variability in group means is greater than would be expected because of sampling error.

2. Sum the squared differences between each subsample mean $(\overline{X}_j)$ and the overall sample mean $(\overline{X}_t)$, weighted by sample size (n_j). This is called the *sum of squares among groups* or among group variation (SSA). SSA is calculated as follows:

$$SSA = \sum_{j=1}^{C} n_j(\overline{X}_j - \overline{X}_t)^2$$

In this example, the overall sample mean is

$$\overline{X}_t = \frac{20(323) + 20(315) + 20(328)}{60} = 322$$

Thus,

$$SSA = 20(323 - 322)^2 + 20(315 - 322)^2 + 20(328 - 322)^2$$
$$= 1720$$

The greater the differences among the sample means, the larger the SSA will be.

3. Calculate the variation among group means as measured by the *mean sum of squares among groups* (MSA). The MSA is calculated as follows:

$$MSA = \frac{\text{Sum of squares among groups (SSA)}}{\text{Degrees of freedom (d.f.)}}$$

where   Degrees of freedom = number of groups $(C) - 1$

In this example,

$$d.f. = 3 - 1 = 2$$

Thus,

$$MSA = \frac{1720}{2} = 860$$

4. Sum the squared differences between each observation (X_{ij}) and its associated sample mean $(\overline{X}_j)$, accumulated over all C levels (groups). Also called the *sum of squares within groups* or *within group variation*, it is generally referred to as the *sum of squared error* (SSE). For this example, the SSE is calculated as follows:

$$SSE = \sum_{j=1}^{C} \sum_{i=1}^{n_j} (X_{ij} - \overline{X}_j)^2$$
$$= (6644) + (4318) + (2270) = 13,232$$

5. Calculate the variation within the sample groups as measured by the mean sum of squares within groups. Referred to as *mean square error* (MSE), it represents an estimate of the random error in the data. The MSE is calculated as follows:

$$MSE = \frac{\text{Sum of squares within groups (SSE)}}{\text{Degrees of freedom (d.f.)}}$$

The number of degrees of freedom is equal to the sum of the sample sizes for all groups minus the number of groups (C):

$$d.f. = \left(\sum_{j=1}^{K} n_j \right) - C$$
$$= (20 + 20 + 20) - 3 = 57$$

Thus,

$$MSE = \frac{13,232}{57} = 232.14$$

As with the Z distribution and t distribution, a sampling distribution known as the *F distribution* permits the researcher to determine the probability that a particular calculated value of F could have occurred by chance rather than as a result of the treatment effect. The F distribution, like the t distribution, is really a set of distributions whose shape changes slightly depending on the number and size of the samples involved. To use the **F test**, it is necessary to calculate the degrees of freedom for the numerator and the denominator.

> ⊳ **F test**
> Test of the probability that a particular calculated value could have been due to chance.

6. Calculate the F statistic as follows:

$$F = \frac{MSA}{MSE}$$
$$= \frac{860}{232.14} = 3.70$$

The numerator is the MSA, and the number of degrees of freedom associated with it is 2 (step 3). The denominator is the MSE, and the number of degrees of freedom associated with it is 57 (step 5).

7. State the results. For an alpha of .05, the table value of F(critical) with 2 (numerator) and 57 (denominator) degrees of freedom is approximately 3.15. (See Exhibit 5 in Appendix 2 for d.f. for denominator = 5, d.f. for numerator = 2, .05 significance.) The calculated F value (3.70) is greater than the table value (3.15), and so *the null hypothesis is rejected.* By rejecting the null hypothesis, we conclude that the variability observed in the three means is greater than expected due to chance.

The results of an ANOVA generally are displayed as follows:

Source of Variation	Sum of Squares	Degrees of Freedom	Mean Square	F Statistic
Treatments	1,720 (SSA)	2 ($C - 1$)	860 (MSA)	3.70 calculated
Error	13,232 (SSE)	57 ($n - C$)	232.14 (MSE)	
Total	14,592 (SST)	59 ($n - 1$)		

p Values and Significance Testing

For the various tests discussed in this chapter, a standard—a level of significance and associated critical value of the statistics—is established, and then the value of the statistic is calculated to see whether it beats that standard. If the calculated value of the statistic exceeds the critical value, then the result being tested is said to be statistically significant at that level.

However, this approach does not give the exact probability of getting a computed test statistic that is largely due to chance. The calculations to compute this probability, commonly referred to as the **p value**, are tedious to perform by hand. Fortunately, they are easy for computers. The p value is the most demanding level of statistical (not managerial) significance that can be met, based on the calculated value of the statistic. Computer statistical packages usually use one of the following labels to identify the probability that the distance between the hypothesized population parameter and the observed test statistic could have occurred due to chance:

> **p value**
> Exact probability of getting a computed test statistic that is due to chance. The smaller the p value, the smaller the probability that the observed result occurred by chance.

☐ p value

☐ ≤ PROB

☐ PROB =

The smaller the p value, the smaller is the probability that the observed result occurred by chance (sampling error).

An example of computer output showing a p value calculation appears in Exhibit 15.6. This analysis shows the results of a t test of the differences between means for two independent samples. In this case, the null hypothesis H_0 is that there is no difference between what men and women would be willing to pay for a new communications service. (The variable name is GENDER, with the numeric codes of 0 for males and 1 for females. Subjects were asked how much they would be willing to pay per month for a new wireless communications service that was described to them via a videotape. Variable ADDEDPAY is their response to the question.) The results show that women are willing to pay an average of $16.82 for the new service and men are willing to pay $20.04. Is this a significant difference? The calculated value for t of −1.328 indicates, via the associated p value of .185, that there is an 18.5 percent chance that the difference is due to sampling error. If, for example, the standard for the test were set at .10 (willing to accept a 10 percent chance of incorrectly rejecting H_0), then the analyst would *fail to reject* H_0 in this case.

EXHIBIT 15.6	**Sample t-Test Output**

Stat.	Grouping: GENDER (pcs. sta)
Basic	Group 1: G_1:1
Stats	Group 2: G_2:0

Variable	Mean G_1:1	Mean G_2:0	t-value	df	P	Valid N G_1:1	Valid N G_2:0
ADDED PAY	16.82292	20.04717	−1.32878	200	.185434	96	106

The purpose of making statistical inferences is to generalize from sample results to population characteristics. Three important concepts applied to the notion of differences are mathematical differences, managerially important differences, and statistical significance.

A hypothesis is an assumption or theory that a researcher or manager makes about some characteristic of the population being investigated. By testing, the researcher determines whether a hypothesis concerning some characteristic of the population is valid. A statistical hypothesis test permits the researcher to calculate the probability of observing the particular result if the stated hypothesis actually were true. In hypothesis testing, the first step is to specify the hypothesis. Next, an appropriate statistical technique should be selected to test the hypothesis. Then, a decision rule must be specified as the basis for determining whether to reject or fail to reject the hypothesis. Hypothesis tests are subject to two types of errors called type I (α error) and type II (β error). A type I error involves rejecting the null hypothesis when it is, in fact, true. A type II error involves failing to reject the null hypothesis when the alternative hypothesis actually is true. Finally, the value of the test statistic is calculated, and a conclusion is stated that summarizes the results of the test.

Marketing researchers often develop cross tabulations, whose purpose usually is to uncover interrelationships among the variables. Usually the researcher needs to determine whether the numbers of subjects, objects, or responses that fall into some set of categories differ from those expected by chance. Thus, a test of goodness of fit of the observed distribution in relation to an expected distribution is appropriate. One common test of goodness of fit is chi square.

Often marketing researchers need to make inferences about a population mean. If the sample size is equal to or greater than 30 and the sample comes from a normal population, the appropriate test statistic for testing hypotheses about means is the Z test. For small samples, researchers use the t test with $n-1$ degrees of freedom when making inferences (n is the size of the sample).

When researchers are interested in testing differences between responses to the same variable, such as advertising, by groups with different characteristics, they test for differences between two means. A Z value is calculated and compared to the critical value of Z. Based on the result of the comparison, they either reject or fail to reject the null hypothesis. The Z test also can be used to examine hypotheses about proportions from one sample or independent samples.

When researchers need to test for differences among the means of three or more independent samples, analysis of variance is an appropriate statistical tool. It is often used for hypothesis tests regarding the differences among the means of several independent groups. It permits the researcher to test the null hypothesis that there are no significant differences among the population group means.

hypothesis Assumption or theory that a researcher or manager makes about some characteristic of the population under study.

type I error (α error) Rejection of the null hypothesis when, in fact, it is true.

type II error (β error) Failure to reject the null hypothesis when, in fact, it is false.

independent samples Samples in which measurement of a variable in one population has no effect on measurement of the variable in the other.

related samples Samples in which measurement of a variable in one population may influence measurement of the variable in the other.

chi-square test Test of the goodness of fit between the observed distribution and the expected distribution of a variable.

Z test Hypothesis test used for a single mean if the sample is large enough and drawn at random.

t test Hypothesis test used for a single mean if the sample is too small to use the Z test.

hypothesis test of proportions Test to determine whether the difference between proportions is greater than would be expected because of sampling error.

analysis of variance (ANOVA) Test for the differences among the means of two or more independent samples.

F test Test of the probability that a particular calculated value could have been due to chance.

p value Exact probability of getting a computed test statistic that is due to chance. The smaller the p value, the smaller the probability that the observed result occurred by chance.

QUESTIONS FOR REVIEW & CRITICAL THINKING

1. Explain the notions of mathematical differences, managerially important differences, and statistical significance. Can results be statistically significant and yet lack managerial importance? Explain your answer.

2. Describe the steps in the procedure for testing hypotheses. Discuss the difference between a null hypothesis and an alternative hypothesis.

3. Distinguish between a type I error and a type II error. What is the relationship between the two?

4. What is meant by the terms *independent samples* and *related samples*? Why is it important for a researcher to determine whether a sample is independent?

5. Your university library is concerned about student desires for library hours on Sunday morning (9:00 A.M.–12:00 P.M.). It has undertaken to survey a random sample of 1,600 undergraduate students (one-half men, one-half women) in each of four status levels (i.e., 400 freshmen, 400 sophomores, 400 juniors, 400 seniors). If the percentages of students preferring Sunday morning hours are those shown below, what conclusions can the library reach?

	Seniors	Juniors	Sophomores	Freshmen
Women	70	53	39	26
Men	30	48	31	27

6. A local car dealer was attempting to determine which premium would draw the most visitors to its showroom. An individual who visits the showroom and takes a test drive is given a premium with no obligation. The dealer chose four premiums and offered each for one week. The results are as follows.

Week	Premium	Total Given Out
1	Four-foot metal stepladder	425
2	$50 savings bond	610
3	Dinner for four at a local steak house	510
4	Six pink flamingos plus an outdoor thermometer	705

Using a chi-square test, what conclusions can you draw regarding the premiums?

7. A market researcher has completed a study of pain relievers. The following table depicts the brands purchased most often, broken down by men versus women. Perform a chi-square test on the data and determine what can be said regarding the cross tabulation.

Pain Relievers	Men	Women
Anacin	40	55
Bayer	60	28
Bufferin	70	97
Cope	14	21
Empirin	82	107
Excedrin	72	84
Excedrin PM	15	11
Vanquish	20	26

8. A child psychologist observed 8-year-old children behind a one-way mirror to determine how long they would play with a toy medical kit. The company that designed the toy was attempting to determine whether to give the kit a masculine or a feminine orientation. The lengths of time (in minutes) the children played with the kits are shown below. Calculate the value of Z and recommend to management whether the kit should have a male or a female orientation.

Boys	Girls	Boys	Girls
31	26	67	9
12	38	67	9
41	20	25	16
34	32	73	26
63	16	36	81
7	45	41	20
		15	5

9. American Airlines is trying to determine which baggage handling system to put in its new hub terminal in San Juan, Puerto Rico. One system is made by Jano Systems, and the second is manufactured by Dynamic Enterprises. American has installed a small Jano system and a small Dynamic Enterprises system in two of its low-volume terminals. Both terminals handle approximately the same quantity of baggage each month. American has decided to select the system that provides the minimum number of instances in which passengers disembarking must wait 20 minutes or longer for baggage. Analyze the data that follow and determine whether there is a significant difference at the .95 level of confidence between the two systems. If there is a difference, which system should American select?

Minutes of Waiting	Jano Systems (Frequency)	Dynamic Enterprises (Frequency)
10–11	4	10
12–13	10	8
14–15	14	14
16–17	4	20
18–19	2	12
20–21	4	6
22–23	2	12

24–25	14	4
26–27	6	13
28–29	10	8
30–31	12	6
32–33	2	8
34–35	2	8
36 or more	2	2

10. Menu space is always limited in fast-food restaurants. However, McDonald's has decided that it needs to add one more salad dressing to its menu for its garden salad and chef salad. It has decided to test-market four flavors: Caesar, Ranch-Style, Green Goddess, and Russian. Fifty restaurants were selected in the North-Central region to sell each new dressing. Thus, a total of 200 stores were used in the research project. The study was conducted for 2 weeks; the units of each dressing sold are shown below. As a researcher, you want to know if the differences among the average daily sales of the dressings are larger than can be reasonably expected by chance. If so, which dressing would you recommend be added to the inventory throughout the United States?

Day	Caesar	Ranch-Style	Green Goddess	Russian
1	155	143	149	135
2	157	146	152	136
3	151	141	146	131
4	146	136	141	126
5	181	180	173	115
6	160	152	170	150
7	168	157	174	147
8	157	167	141	130
9	139	159	129	119
10	144	154	167	134
11	158	169	145	144
13	184	195	178	177
14	161	177	201	151

WORKING THE NET

1. Go to *http://www.ifigure.com/index.html* and click on the highlighted word "article" in the paragraph of text. This will take you to an article that provides examples of the wide range of situations for which online calculators are available. To locate a tool, use the menu or the search box at the top left of the page.

2. Go to *http://www.ifigure.com/math/stat/testing.htm* and review the range of statistical calculators available. Use the *Hypothesis Testing of Means* calculator to address the following problem. The Fort Worth Cats minor league baseball team tracked actual hot dog sales several years ago and found (by dividing actual sales by the total number of attendees) that the average fan consumed 1.2 hot dogs per game. They quit tracking actual sales shortly after that. Now they need to figure out what is happening to hot dog sales. To do this, they took samples of fans at three randomly selected games. Four hundred were sampled at the end of each game, and they got an average consumption figure of 1.4 hot dogs with a standard deviation of .96 hot dogs. Can they conclude that consumption has increased? In the calculator, use:

- 1.4 for the sample value of the mean
- 1.2 for the hypothesized value of the mean
- .96 for the standard deviation
- 1,200 for the sample size

What is your answer?

Experiment with other values of the inputs for the calculator and see how the changes affect the result.

I Can't Believe It's Yogurt

REAL-LIFE RESEARCH • 15.1

Phil Jackson, research manager for I Can't Believe It's Yogurt (ICBIY), is trying to develop a more rational basis for evaluating alternative store locations. ICBIY has been growing rapidly, and historically the issue of store location has not been critical. It didn't seem to matter where stores were located—all were successful. However, the yogurt craze has faded, and some of its new stores and a few of its old ones are experiencing difficulties in the form of declining sales.

ICBIY wants to continue expanding but recognizes that it must be much more careful in selecting locations than it was in the past. It has determined that the percentage of individuals in an area who have visited a frozen yogurt store in the past 30 days is the best predictor of the potential for one of its stores—the higher that percentage, the better.

ICBIY wants to locate a store in Denver and has identified two locations that, on the basis of the other criteria, look good. It has conducted a survey of households in the areas that would be served from each location. The results of that survey are shown below.

Yogurt Store Patronage	Both Areas	Area A	Area B
Have patronized in past 30 days	465	220	245
Have not patronized	535	280	255

Questions

1. Determine whether there is a significant difference at the .05 level between the two areas.
2. Based on this analysis, what would you recommend to ICBIY regarding which of the two areas it should choose for the new store? Explain your recommendation.

New Mexico Power

REAL-LIFE RESEARCH • 15.2

Marc Guerraz is the new marketing research director for New Mexico Power, an investor-owned, vertically integrated electric utility involved in the generation, transmission, distribution, and energy service domains of the electricity industry. Marc was hired to help New Mexico Power transition to a competitive environment for energy services, which will occur in one year. In this environment, customers will be allowed to select their provider of electricity, much as customers now select long-distance telecommunications service from providers such as Sprint, Verizon, and SBC.

One of the crucial questions for New Mexico Power is that of current customer retention. How many current customers will switch to another provider of electric services during the first 6 months of competition? To address this question, Marc and his team designed and fielded a survey in the current service territory of New Mexico Power. They had 500 customers give complete answers to all questions. Initial results indicate that 22 percent of customers would switch. The margin of error is 4 percent, which means that (at the 95 percent confidence level) the actual percentage of customers switching could be as low as 18 percent or as high as 26 percent. New Mexico Power senior management is concerned about this error range of 4 percent, which means that error spans a total of 8 percentage points. Further customer retention efforts must be budgeted now, and New Mexico Power senior management wants firmer numbers on which to base strategies and budgets.

Questions

1. How could the error range be reduced without collecting more data? Would you recommend taking this approach? Why/Why not?
2. Do you think New Mexico Power senior management would find this approach to reducing the error range satisfactory?
3. If 500 more respondents were surveyed and 30 percent of them indicated that they would switch, what would the error range become?

 •

Exercise #1: Analyzing Data Using Cross-tabulation Analysis

Note: Go to the Wiley Web site at *www.wiley.com/college/mcdaniel* and download the *Segmenting the College Student Market for Movie Attendance* database to SPSS windows.

Use the *analyze/descriptive statistics/crosstab* sequence to obtain cross-tabulated results. In addition, click on the "cell" icon and make sure the *observed, expected, total, row, and column* boxes are checked. Then, click on the "statistics" icon and check the *chi-square* box. Once you run the analysis, on the output for the chi-square analysis, you will only need the *Pearson chi-square statistic* to assess whether or not the results of the crosstab are statistically significant.

In this exercise we are assessing whether or not persons who attend movies at movie theaters are demographically different from those who do not. Invoke the crosstab analysis for the following pairs of variables:

    a. Q1 & Q11
    b. Q1 & Q12
    c. Q1 & Q13
    d. Q1 & Q14

Answer questions 1–6 <u>using only the sample data</u>. <u>Do not consider</u> the results of the *chi-square test*.

1. What % of males do not attend movies at movie theaters? _____%

2. What % of all respondents are African American and do not attend movies at movie theaters? _____%

3. What % of respondents not attending movies at movie theaters are in the 19–20 age category? _____%

4. Which classification group is most likely to attend movies at movie theaters? _____

5. Which age category is least likely to attend movies at a movie theater? _____

6. Are Caucasians less likely to attend movie theaters than African Americans? _____

For question 7, the objective is to determine statistically whether, in the population from which the sample data was drawn, there were demographic differences in persons who attend and do not attend movies at movie theaters. We do this by using the results of the *chi-square test for independent samples.*

7. Evaluate the chi-square statistic in each of your crosstab tables. Construct a table to summarize the results. For example:

Variables	Pearson Chi-Square	Degrees of Freedom	Asymp sig.	Explanation
Q1 (attend or not attend movies at movie theaters & Q12 (gender)	2.71	1	.10	We can be 90% confident that based on our sample results, males differ significantly from females in their tendency to attend or not attend movies at movie theaters.

Exercise #2: T/Z Test for Independent Samples

Use the *analyze/compare means/independent samples t-test* sequence to complete this exercise. This exercise compares males and females regarding the information sources they utilize to search for information about movies at movie theaters. SPSS calls the variable in which the means are being computed the *test variable,* and the variable in which we are grouping responses the *grouping variable.*

Note: In statistics, if a sample has fewer than 30 observations or cases, then we invoke a *t* test. If there are 30 or more cases, we invoke a *z* test, as *the t test values and z test values are virtually the same; hence SPSS refers only to a t test.*

Answer the following questions.

The result of the *t* test generates a table of **group statistics**, which is based only on the **sample** data. The other output table generated by the *t* test has statistical data from which we can determine whether or not the sample results can be generalized to the population from which the sample data was drawn. If the *t* test is significant, then we can use the group statistics to determine the specifics of the computed results. For example, a significant *t* test may tell us that males differ from females regarding the importance they place on the newspaper as an information source, but the group statistics tell us "who" considers it most important.

From our *sample data*, can we generalize our results to the population by saying that males differ from females regarding the importance they place on various information sources to get information about movies at movie theaters by:

1. the newspaper (Q7a)?
2. the Internet (Q7b)?
3. phoning in to the movie theater for information (Q7c)?
4. the television (Q7d)?
5. friends or family (Q7e)?

You may want to use the template below to summarize your *t* test results. For example:

Variables	Variance Prob of Sig Diff	Means Prob of Sig Diff	Interpretation of Results
Q12 (gender) & Q7a (newspaper)	.000	.035	96.5% confident that based on our sample results, males differ significantly from females concerning the importance they place on the newspaper as an information source about movies at movie theaters **(means test).** 100% confident that males and females were significantly different regarding the variance of response within each gender **(variance test).**

Exercise #3: ANOVA Test for Independent Samples

Invoke the *analyze/compare means/One-Way ANOVA* sequence to invoke the ANOVA test to complete this exercise. This exercise compares the responses of freshman, sophomores, juniors, seniors, and graduate students to test for significant differences in the importance placed on several movie theater items. For the ANOVA test, SPSS calls the variable in which means are being computed the *independent variable* and the variable in which we are grouping responses the *factor variable*. Be sure to click the *options* icon and check *descriptives* so that the output will produce the mean responses by student classification for the sample data. As with the *t* test, the ANOVA test produces a table of *descriptives* based on sample data. If our ANOVA test is significant, the *descriptives* can be used to determine, for example, which student classification places the most importance on comfortable seats.

Answer the following questions.

From our sample data, can we generalize our results to the population by saying that there are significant differences across the classification of students by the importance they place on the following movie theatre items?

1. video arcade at the movie theater (Q5a)?
2. soft drinks and food items (Q5b)

3. plentiful restrooms (Q5c)

4. comfortable chairs (Q5d)

5. auditorium-type seating (Q5e)

6. size of the movie theater screens (Q5f)

7. quality of the sound system (Q5g)

8. number of screens at a movie theater (Q5h)

9. clean restroom (Q5i)

10. Using only the *descriptive statistics,* which classification group (Q13) places the least amount of importance on clean restrooms (Q5i)? _____

11. Using only the *descriptive statistics,* which classification group (Q13) places the greatest amount of importance on quality of sound system (Q5i)? _____

Summarize the results of your ANOVA analysis using a table similar to the one below.

Variables	Degrees of Freedom	F-Value	Probability of Insignificance	Interpretation of Results
Q5a (importance of a video arcade) & Q13 (student classification)	4,461	12.43	.001	99.9% confident that based on the sample results, students differ significantly by classification concerning the importance placed on there being a video arcade at the movie theater.

surveysolutions XP

BIVARIATE CORRELATION AND REGRESSION

LEARNING OBJECTIVES

1.	To comprehend the nature of correlation analysis.
2.	To understand bivariate regression analysis.
3.	To become aware of the coefficient of determination R^2.
4.	To understand Spearman rank-order correlation.

J oe Eng and his boss, Jennifer Andersen, manage the salesforce for Big Tex Commercial Leasing in Dallas, Texas. They are in the process of doing a careful evaluation of the performance of individual salespersons in their organization. After examining the results for the past two years, Eng believes that *years of experience in the industry* is the best indicator of the volume of sales a salesperson will produce. On the other hand, Andersen believes that *number of calls made* by a salesperson is the best predictor of the sales volume. They have discussed the issue with Will Adams, the analyst who works in their department. He suggested that correlation analysis be used to resolve their debate.

Adams took the data for salespeople who have worked for the company for the last two years and ran two separate correlations. First, for each salesperson, he correlated sales with number of years in the industry. Second, he ran correlations between sales and number of calls made. The correlation coefficient between sales and years in the industry was .27. The correlation coefficient between sales and the number of calls made was .54. His conclusion is that the number of calls made is more closely associated with sales volume produced than years in the industry.

This chapter addresses correlation analysis and related techniques. After you read this chapter, you will be prepared to decide whether Adams' conclusion is correct. If it is, what are the implications for Eng and Andersen? ∎

In this chapter, we will cover techniques that will permit you to evaluate the relationships between two variables.

Bivariate Analysis of Association

> **bivariate techniques**
> Statistical methods of analyzing the relationship between two variables.

> **independent variable**
> Variable believed to affect the value of the dependent variable.

> **dependent variable**
> Variable expected to be explained or caused by the independent variable.

In many marketing research studies, the interests of the researcher and manager go beyond issues that can be addressed by the statistical testing of differences discussed in Chapter 15. They may be interested in the degree of association between two variables. Statistical techniques appropriate for this type of analysis are referred to as **bivariate techniques**. When more than two variables are involved, the techniques employed are known as *multivariate techniques*. Multivariate techniques are discussed in Chapter 17.

When the degree of association between two variables is analyzed, the variables are classified as the **independent** (predictor) **variable** and the **dependent** (criterion) **variable**. Independent variables are those that are believed to affect the value of the dependent variable. Independent variables such as price, advertising expenditures, or number of retail outlets may, for example, be used to predict and explain sales or market share of a brand—the dependent variable. Bivariate analysis can help provide answers to questions such as the following: How does the price of our product affect its sales? What is the relationship between household income and expenditures on entertainment?

It must be noted that none of the techniques presented in this chapter can be used to prove that one variable caused an observed change in another variable. They can be used only to describe the nature of statistical relationships between variables.

The analyst has a large number of bivariate techniques from which to choose. This chapter discusses two procedures that are appropriate for metric (ratio or internal) data—bivariate regression and Pearson's product moment correlation—and one that is appropriate for ordinal (ranking) data—Spearman rank-order correlation. Other statistical procedures that can be used for analyzing the statistical relationship between two variables include the two-group *t* test, chi-square analysis of crosstabs or contingency tables, and ANOVA (analysis of variance) for two groups. All of these procedures were introduced and discussed in Chapter 15.

Bivariate Regression

> **bivariate regression analysis**
> Analysis of the strength of the linear relationship between two variables when one is considered the independent variable and the other the dependent variable.

Bivariate regression analysis is a statistical procedure appropriate for analyzing the relationship between two variables when one is considered the dependent variable and the other the independent variable. For example, a researcher might be interested in analyzing the relationship between sales (dependent variable) and advertising (independent variable). If the relationship between advertising expenditures and sales can be accurately captured by regression analysis, the researcher can use the resulting model to predict sales for different levels of advertising. When the problem involves using two or more independent variables (for example, advertising and price) to predict the dependent variable of interest, multiple regression analysis (discussed in Chapter 17) is appropriate.

Nature of the Relationship

One way to study the nature of the relationship between the dependent and the independent variable is to plot the data in a scatter diagram. The dependent variable Y is plotted on the vertical axis, whereas the independent variable X is plotted on the horizontal axis. By examining the scatter diagram, one can determine whether the relationship between the two variables, if any, is linear or curvilinear. If the relationship appears to be linear or close to linear, linear regression is appropriate. If a nonlinear relationship is shown in the

Exhibit 16.1

Types of
Relationships Found
in Scatter Diagrams

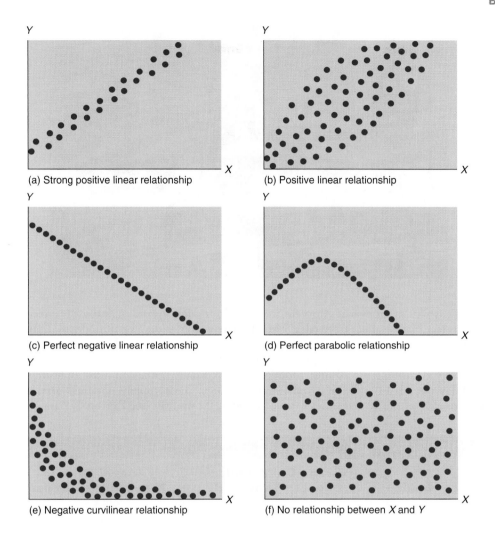

(a) Strong positive linear relationship

(b) Positive linear relationship

(c) Perfect negative linear relationship

(d) Perfect parabolic relationship

(e) Negative curvilinear relationship

(f) No relationship between X and Y

scatter diagram, curve-fitting nonlinear regression techniques are appropriate. These techniques are beyond the scope of this discussion.

Exhibit 16.1 depicts several kinds of underlying relationships between the X (independent) and Y (dependent) variables. Scatter diagrams (a) and (b) suggest a positive linear relationship between X and Y. However, the linear relationship shown in (b) is not as strong as that portrayed in (a); there is more scatter in the data shown in (b). Diagram (c) shows a perfect negative, or inverse, relationship between variables X and Y. An example might be the relationship between price and sales. As price goes up, sales go down. As price goes down, sales go up. Diagrams (d) and (e) show nonlinear relationships between the variables; appropriate curve-fitting techniques should be used to mathematically describe these relationships. The scatter diagram in (f) shows no relationship between X and Y.

Example of Bivariate Regression

Stop 'N Go recently conducted a research effort designed to measure the effect of vehicular traffic past a particular store location on annual sales at that location. To control for other factors, researchers identified 20 stores that were virtually identical on all other variables known to have a significant effect on store sales (for example, square footage, amount of parking, demographics of the surrounding neighborhood). This particular

Bivariate regression analysis can help answer such questions as "How does advertising affect sales?"

analysis is part of an overall effort by Stop 'N Go to identify and quantify the effects of various factors that affect store sales. The ultimate goal is to develop a model that can be used to screen potential sites for store locations and select, for actual purchase and store construction, the ones that will produce the highest level of sales.

After identifying the 20 sites, Stop 'N Go took a daily traffic count for each site over a 30-day period. In addition, from internal records, the company obtained total sales data for each of the 20 test stores for the preceding 12 months (see Exhibit 16.2).

EXHIBIT 16.2	Annual Sales and Average Daily Vehicular Traffic	
Store Number (i)	Average Daily Vehicular Count in Thousands (X_i)	Annual Sales in Thousands of Dollars (Y_i)
1	62	1121
2	35	766
3	36	701
4	72	1304
5	41	832
6	39	782
7	49	977
8	25	503
9	41	773
10	39	839
11	35	893
12	27	588
13	55	957
14	38	703
15	24	497
16	28	657
17	53	1209
18	55	997
19	33	844
20	29	883

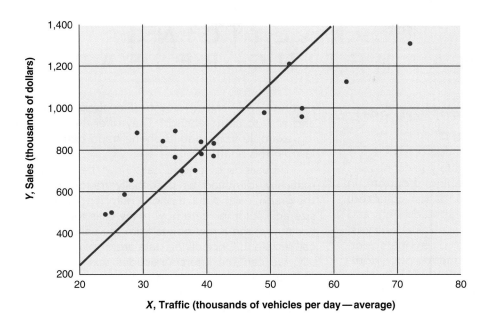

Exhibit 16.3

Scatterplot of Annual Sales by Traffic

A scatterplot of the resulting data is shown in Exhibit 16.3. Visual inspection of the scatterplot suggests that total sales increase as average daily vehicular traffic increases. The question now is how to characterize this relationship in a more explicit, quantitative manner.

Least-Squares Estimation Procedure   The least-squares procedure is a fairly simple mathematical technique that can be used to fit data for X and Y to a line that best represents the relationship between the two variables. No straight line will perfectly represent every observation in the scatterplot. This is reflected in discrepancies between the actual values (dots on the scatter diagram) and predicted values (values indicated by the line). Any straight line fitted to the data in a scatterplot is subject to error. A number of lines could be drawn that would seem to fit the observations in Exhibit 16.3.

The least-squares procedure results in a straight line that fits the actual observations (dots) better than any other line that could be fitted to the observations. Put another way, the sum of the squared deviations from the line (squared differences between dots and the line) will be lower for this line than for any other line that can be fitted to the observations.

The general equation for the line is $Y = a + bX$. The estimating equation for regression analysis is

$$Y = \hat{a} + \hat{b}X + e$$

where $Y =$ dependent variable, annual sales in thousands of dollars

$\hat{a} =$ estimated Y intercept for regression line

$\hat{b} =$ estimated slope of regression line, regression coefficient

$X =$ independent variable, average daily vehicular traffic in thousands of vehicles

$e =$ error, difference between actual value and value predicted by regression line

PRACTICING MARKETING RESEARCH

How Data Visualization Can Help Identify Fraud

Sometimes there is so much data you cannot see the proverbial needle, or meaningful pattern, in the haystack of business information collected. Scrolling numerous pages of spreadsheets and reports, or data mining and statistical analysis, can be time-consuming and often inefficient, leaving you data-rich but information poor, comment Richard Brath and Andrea Brody. Brath is senior director of business development with Oculus Info, and Brody is president of EA Brody Consultants.

"Data visualization has the capacity to present a very large amount of detail on a single screen," they note, and makes relationships easy to see. The approach is well-suited to identifying visual patterns and making statistical analysis "simple and easy to comprehend." They offer the following example from mobile phone fraud data to illustrate this point.

Thousands of phone calls have been automatically identified as potentially fraudulent. In the graph, each dot is a phone number. The dot's size and color indicate how many calls that caller has made; the arrow points from the caller to the call recipient. Once all the data are displayed visually, we can see interconnections that were not obvious before. The special visualization technique helps you make a deeper data analysis.

First, note that around the perimeter of the diagram are clusters of small numbers of calls (typically 1–4), not too suspicious.

Second, in the center, more calls per number or caller are clustered together and may be inherently more suspicious than the ones on the perimeter because they involve a larger network of people within a larger set of possibly fraudulent calls.

Third, note at the bottom of the diagram a pair of red joined dots. The callers indicated by these large dots have phoned each other many times, suggesting that they may share a unique technique known only to themselves, and thus are worthy of suspicion.

Fourth, at the top left, note the label at the center of a small ring that indicates many calls. The caller (at the center) has called numerous people (around the ring's edge). This caller probably is more suspicious than others because many of his or her calls are tagged as fraudulent.[1]

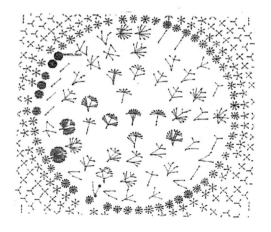

Values for $\hat{a}$ and $\hat{b}$ can be calculated from the following equations:

$$\hat{b} = \frac{\sum X_i Y_i - n\overline{X}\,\overline{Y}}{\sum X_i^2 - n(\overline{X})^2}$$

$$\hat{a} = \overline{Y} - \hat{b}\overline{X}$$

where $\overline{X}$ = mean value of X

         $\overline{Y}$ = mean value of Y

         n = sample size (number of units in the sample)

With the data from Exhibit 16.4, $\hat{b}$ is calculated as follows:

$$\hat{b} = \frac{734{,}083 - 20(40.8)(841.3)}{36{,}526 - 20(40.8)^2} = 14.7$$

The value of $\hat{a}$ is calculated as follows:

$$\hat{a} = \overline{Y} - \hat{b}\overline{X}$$
$$= 841.3 - 14.72(40.8) = 240.9$$

Thus, the estimated regression function is given by

$$\hat{Y} = \hat{a} + \hat{b}X$$
$$= 240.9 + 14.7(X)$$

where $\hat{Y}$ (Y hat) is the value of the estimated regression function for a given value of X.

According to the estimated regression function, for every additional 1,000 vehicles per day in traffic (X), total annual sales will increase by \$14,720 (estimated value of b). The value of $\hat{a}$ is 240.9. Technically, $\hat{a}$ is the estimated value of the dependent variable (Y, or annual sales) when the value of the independent variable (X, or average daily vehicular traffic) is zero.

EXHIBIT 16.4	Least-Squares Computation				
Store	X	Y	X²	Y²	XY
1	62	1,121	3,844	1,256,641	69,502
2	35	766	1,225	586,756	26,810
3	36	701	1,296	491,401	25,236
4	72	1,304	5,184	1,700,416	93,888
5	41	832	1,681	692,224	34,112
6	39	782	1,521	611,524	30,498
7	49	977	2,401	954,529	47,873
8	25	503	625	253,009	12,575
9	41	773	1,681	597,529	31,693
10	39	839	1,521	703,921	32,721
11	35	893	1,225	797,449	31,255
12	27	588	729	345,744	15,876
13	55	957	3,025	915,849	52,635
14	38	703	1,444	494,209	26,714
15	24	497	576	247,009	11,928
16	28	657	784	431,649	18,396
17	53	1,209	2,809	1,461,681	64,077
18	55	997	3,025	994,009	54,835
19	33	844	1,089	712,336	27,852
20	29	883	841	779,689	25,607
Sum	816	16,826	36,526	15,027,574	734,083
Mean	40.8	841.3			

SPSS JUMP START FOR REGRESSION

Steps that you need to go through to do the bivariate regression problem shown in the book are provided below along with the output produced. Use the data set **Bivregex**, which you can download from the Web site for the text.

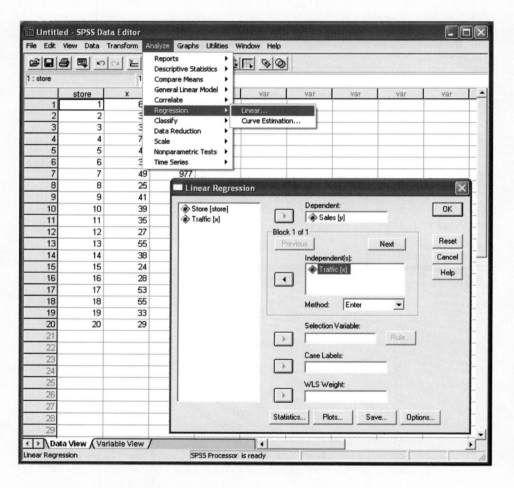

Steps in SPSS

1. Select *Analyze → Regression → Linear*.
2. Move **y** to Dependent.
3. Move **x** to Independent(s).
4. Click OK.

SPSS Output for Regression

Regression

Variables Entered/Removed[b]

Model	Variables Entered	Variables Removed	Method
1	Traffic[a]	.	Enter

a. All requested variables entered.

b. Dependent Variable: Sales

Model Summary

Model	R	R Square	Adjusted R Square	Std. Error of the Estimate
1	.896[a]	.803	.792	97.640

a. Predictors: (Constant), Traffic

ANOVA[b]

Model		Sum of Squares	df	Mean Square	F	Sig.
1	Regression	700255.40	1	700255.399	73.451	.000[a]
	Residual	171604.80	18	9533.600		
	Total	871860.20	19			

a. Predictors: (Constant), Traffic

b. Dependent Variable: Sales

Coefficients[a]

Model		Unstandardized Coefficients		Standardized Coefficients	t	Sig.
		B	Std. Error	Beta		
1	(Constant)	240.857	73.383		3.282	.004
	Traffic	14.717	1.717	.896	8.570	.000

a. Dependent Variable: Sales

Regression Line   Predicted values for Y, based on calculated values for $\hat{a}$ and $\hat{b}$, are shown in Exhibit 16.5. In addition, errors for each observation $(Y - \hat{Y})$ are shown. The regression line resulting from the $\hat{Y}$ values is plotted in Exhibit 16.6.

Strength of Association: R^2   The estimated regression function describes the nature of the relationship between X and Y. Another important factor is the strength of the relationship between the variables. How widely do the actual values of Y differ from the values predicted by the model?

surveysolutions XP

EXHIBIT 16.5		Predicted Values and Errors for Each Observation				
Store	X	Y	$\hat{Y}$	$Y - \hat{Y}$	$(Y - \hat{Y})^2$	$(Y - \overline{Y})^2$
1	62	1,121	1,153.3	−32.2951	1,043	78,232
2	35	766	755.9	10.05716	101	5,670
3	36	701	770.7	−69.6596	4,852	19,684
4	72	1,304	1,300.5	3.537362	13	214,091
5	41	832	844.2	−12.2434	150	86
6	39	782	814.8	−32.8098	1,076	3,516
7	49	977	962.0	15.02264	226	18,414
8	25	503	608.8	−105.775	11,188	114,447
9	41	773	844.2	−71.2434	5,076	4,665
10	39	839	814.8	24.19015	585	5
11	35	893	755.9	137.0572	18,785	2,673
12	27	588	638.2	−50.2088	2,521	64,161
13	55	957	1,050.3	−93.2779	8,701	13,386
14	38	703	800.1	−97.0931	9,427	19,127
15	24	497	594.1	−97.0586	9,420	118,542
16	28	657	652.9	4.074415	17	33,966
17	53	1,209	1,020.8	188.1556	35,403	135,203
18	55	997	1,050.3	−53.2779	2,839	24,242
19	33	844	726.5	117.4907	13,804	7
20	29	883	667.6	215.3577	46,379	1,739
Sum	816	16,826	16,826		171,605	871,860
Mean	40.8	841				

The **coefficient of determination**, denoted by R^2, is the measure of the strength of the linear relationship between X and Y. The coefficient of determination measures the percentage of the total variation in Y that is "explained" by the variation in X. The R^2 statistic ranges from 0 to 1. If there is a perfect linear relationship between X and Y (all

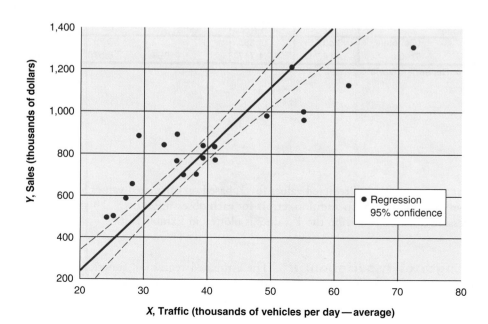

Exhibit 16.6

Least-Squares Regression Line Fitted to Sample Data

the variation in Y is explained by the variation in X), then R^2 equals 1. At the other extreme, if there is no relationship between X and Y, then none of the variation in Y is explained by the variation in X, and R^2 equals 0.

$$R^2 = \frac{\text{Explained variation}}{\text{Total variation}}$$

where

$$\text{Explained variation} = \text{Total variation} - \text{Unexplained variation}$$

The coefficient of determination for the Stop 'N Go data example is computed as follows. [See Exhibit 16.5 for calculation of $(Y - \hat{Y})^2$ and $(Y - \overline{Y})^2$.]

$$R^2 = \frac{\text{Total variation} - \text{Unexplained variation}}{\text{Total variation}}$$

$$= 1 - \frac{\text{Unexplained variation}}{\text{Total variation}}$$

$$= 1 - \frac{\sum_{i=1}^{n} (Y_i - \hat{Y}_i)^2}{\sum_{i=1}^{n} (Y_i - \overline{Y})^2}$$

$$= 1 - \frac{171,605}{871,860} = .803$$

Of the variation in Y (annual sales), 80 percent is explained by the variation in X (average daily vehicular traffic). There is a very strong linear relationship between X and Y.

Statistical Significance of Regression Results   In computing R^2, the total variation in Y was partitioned into two component sums of squares:

$$\text{Total variation} = \text{Explained variation} + \text{Unexplained variation}$$

The total variation is a measure of variation of the observed Y values around their mean $\overline{Y}$. It measures the variation of the Y values without any consideration of the X values.
Total variation, known as the *total sum of squares* (SST), is given by

$$\text{SST} = \sum_{i=1}^{n} (Y_i - \overline{Y})^2 = \sum_{i=1}^{n} Y_i^2 - \left(\frac{\sum_{i=1}^{n} Y_i^2}{n} \right)$$

The explained variation, or the **sum of squares due to regression** (SSR), is given by

▷ **sum of squares due to regression**
Variation explained by the regression.

$$\text{SSR} = \sum_{i=1}^{n} (\hat{Y}_i - \overline{Y})^2 = a \sum_{i=1}^{n} Y_i + b \sum_{i=1}^{n} X_i Y_i - \left(\frac{\sum_{i=1}^{n} Y_i}{n} \right)^2$$

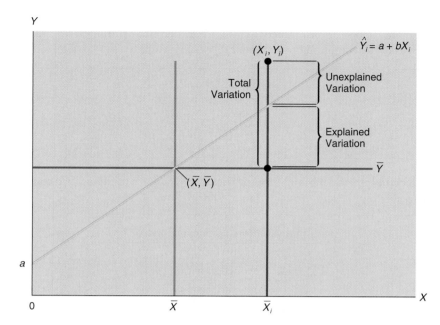

Exhibit 16.7

Measures of Variation in a Regression

Exhibit 16.7 depicts the various measures of variation (that is, sum of squares) in a regression. SSR represents the differences between Y_i (the values of Y predicted by the estimated regression equation) and $\overline{Y}$ (the average value of Y). In a well-fitting regression equation, the variation explained by regression (SSR) will represent a large portion of the total variation (SST). If $Y_i = \hat{Y}_i$ at each value of X, then a perfect fit has been achieved. All the observed values of Y are then on the computed regression line. Of course, in that case, SSR $\neq$ SST.

The unexplained variation, or **error sum of squares** (SSE), is obtained from

➤ **error sum of squares**
Variation not explained by the regression.

$$\text{SSE} = \sum_{i=1}^{n} (Y_i - \hat{Y}_i)^2 = \sum_{i=1}^{n} Y_i^2 - a \sum_{i=1}^{n} Y_i - b \sum_{i=1}^{n} X_i Y_i$$

In studying the relationship between vehicular traffic and sales, the coefficient of determination may be used to measure the percent of the total variation.

In Exhibit 16.7, note that SSE represents the residual differences (error) between the observed and predicted Y values. Therefore, the unexplained variation is a measure of scatter around the regression line. If the fit were perfect, there would be no scatter around the regression line and SSE would be zero.

Hypotheses Concerning Overall Regression   Here we, as the researchers, are interested in hypotheses regarding the computed R^2 value for the problem. Is the amount of variance explained in the result (by our model) significantly greater than we would expect due to chance? Or, as with the various statistical tests discussed in Chapter 15, to what extent can we rule out sampling error as an explanation of the results? Analysis of variance (an F test) is used to test the significance of the results.

An analysis of variance table is set up as shown in Exhibit 16.8. The computer output for our example appears in Exhibit 16.9. The breakdowns of the total sum of squares and associated degrees of freedom are displayed in the form of an analysis of variance (ANOVA) table. We use the information in this table to test the significance of the linear relationship between Y and X. As noted previously, an F test will be used for this purpose. Our hypotheses are as follows:

☐   Null hypothesis H_0: There is no linear relationship between X (average daily vehicular traffic) and Y (annual sales).

☐   Alternative hypothesis H_a: There is a linear relationship between X and Y.

As in other statistical tests, we must choose α. This is the likelihood that the observed result occurred by chance, or the probability of incorrectly rejecting the null hypothesis. In this case, we decide on a standard level of significance: $\alpha = .05$. In other words, if the calculated value of F exceeds the tabular value, we are willing to accept a 5 percent

EXHIBIT 16.8   Analysis of Variance

Source of Variation	Degrees of Freedom	Sum of Squares	Mean Square	F Statistic
Regression (explained)	1	SSR	$MSR = \dfrac{SSR}{1}$	$F = \dfrac{MSR}{MSE}$
Residual (unexplained)	$n-2$	SSE	$MSE = \dfrac{SSE}{n-2}$	
Total	$n-1$	SST		

EXHIBIT 16.9   Regression Analysis Output

STAT. MULTIPLE REGRESS.	Regression Summary for Dependent Variable: Y $R = .89619973$ $R^2 = .80317395$ Adjusted $R^2 = .79223917$ $F(1,18) = 73.451$ $p < .00000$ Std. Error of estimate: 97.640					
$N = 20$	BETA	St. Err. of BETA	B	St. Err. of B	$t(18)$	p-level
Intercpt			240.8566	73.38347	3.282164	.004141
X	.896200	.104570	14.7168	1.71717	8.570374	.000000

chance of incorrectly rejecting the null hypothesis. The value of F, or the F ratio, is computed as follows (see Exhibit 16.9):

$$F = \frac{\text{MSR}}{\text{MSE}}$$
$$= \frac{700{,}255}{9{,}534} = 73.5$$

We will reject the null hypothesis if the calculated F statistic is greater than or equal to the table, or critical, F value. The numerator and denominator degrees of freedom for this F ratio are 1 and 18, respectively. As noted earlier, it was decided that an alpha level of .05 ($\alpha = .05$) should be used.

The table, or critical, value of F with 1 (numerator) and 18 (denominator) degrees of freedom at $\alpha = .05$ is 4.49 (see Table 5 in Appendix 2). Because the calculated value of F is greater than the critical value, we reject the null hypothesis and conclude that there is a significant linear relationship between the average daily vehicular traffic (X) and annual sales (Y). This result is consistent with the high coefficient of determination R^2 discussed earlier.

Hypotheses about the Regression Coefficient b Finally, we may be interested in making hypotheses about b, the regression coefficient. As you may recall, b is the estimate of the effect of a one-unit change in X on Y. The hypotheses are as follows:

☐ Null hypothesis H$_0$: $b = 0$.
☐ Alternative hypothesis H$_a$: $b \neq 0$.

The appropriate test is a t test, and, as you can see from the last line of Exhibit 16.9, the computer program calculates the t value (8.57) and the p value (probability of incorrectly rejecting the null hypothesis of .0000). See Chapter 15 for a more detailed discussion of p values. Given the α criterion of .05, we would reject the null hypothesis in this case.

Correlation Analysis

Correlation for Metric Data: Pearson's Product-Moment Correlation

> **correlation analysis**
> Analysis of the degree to which changes in one variable are associated with changes in another.

Correlation is the degree to which changes in one variable (the dependent variable) are associated with changes in another. When the relationship is between two variables, the analysis is called simple, or bivariate, **correlation analysis**. With metric data, **Pearson's product-moment correlation** may be used.

In our example of bivariate regression, we used the coefficient of determination R^2 as a measure of the strength of the linear relationship between X and Y. Another descriptive measure, called the *coefficient of correlation R*, describes the degree of association between X and Y. It is the square root of the coefficient of determination with the appropriate sign ($+$ or $-$):

> **Pearson's product-moment correlation**
> Correlation analysis technique for use with metric data.

$$R = \pm\sqrt{R^2}$$

The value of R can range from -1 (perfect negative correlation) to $+1$ (perfect positive correlation). The closer R is to ± 1, the stronger the degree of association between X and Y. If R is equal to zero, then there is no association between X and Y.

PRACTICING MARKETING RESEARCH

A Novel Application: Using the Pearson Product-Moment Correlation to Study Sayings in the Gospel of Thomas

Since the 1970s, biblical scholars have been vexed as to whether the Gospel of Thomas used any of the synoptic gospels as a source for its 100 sayings attributed to Jesus. Using the laborious scholarly method respectfully called careful learned consideration, scholars sought to

correlation, Davies created two statistical tables, based on the 100 with no doubtful parallels.

The first table shows the correlations between the sayings found in Thomas that are also found in the gospels to their order in those texts. Davies explains that in both tables, the Degree of Correlation (R) shows the closeness of linear relationship between the two named variables, and that the Reliability of Correlation (p) shows how much R was likely due to chance. That means that the lower p is, the lower it is likely that the correlation R observed was due to chance. N stands for the number of pairs of sayings that Davies analyzed.

Matthew parallels in Thomas to Luke parallels in Thomas	Matthew parallels in Thomas to Mark parallels in Thomas	Luke parallels in Thomas to Mark parallels in Thomas	Matthew parallels in Thomas to Luke parallels in Thomas
$R = .528$ $N = 62$ $p = .0001$	$R = .876$ $N = 29$ $p = .0001$	$R = .709$ $N = 25$ $p = .0001$	$R = .460$ $N = 37$ $p = .004$

compare the order of the quoted sayings in Thomas against that found in the gospels to see if there is a direct relationship. But this is "fundamentally a question for technical statistical analysis," decided Stevan L. Davies, professor of Religious Studies at College Misericordia in Dallas, Pennsylvania, and translator of *The Gospel of Thomas*.

Davies worked with two lists. One had 110 sayings but with some doubtful parallels; the other had 100, with no doubtful parallels. In all he would compare the sayings from Thomas with about 226 other ordered sayings in the gospels. Using the Pearson product-moment

According to Davies, the correlations displayed in the first table are not likely to be due to chance. The sayings used in this first table came from a random list, namely, only those found in Thomas, and are important to the study mainly because they confirm the applicability of the correlation method used.

In the second table, Davies shows how the method demonstrates what the biblical scholars had presumed for 30 years, that there is no statistically significant correlation in the order of the paralleled sayings in Thomas with the order of sayings in the other gospels or even to any source-subset of the gospels.[2]

Mark parallels in Thomas's order to Mark's order	All Matthew parallels in Thomas's order to Matthews' order	All Luke parallels in Thomas's order to Luke's order	Matthew parallels in Thomas's order to Matthews' order	Luke parallels in Thomas's order to Luke's order	Matthew parallels in Thomas's order to Matthews' order	Luke parallels in Thomas's order to Luke's order
$R = .213$ $N = 30$ $p = .258$	$R = .088$ $N = 82$ $p = .431$	$R = .141$ $N = 77$ $p = .221$	$R = .062$ $N = 37$ $p = .714$	$R = .074$ $N = 37$ $p = .663$	$R = .084$ $N = 25$ $p = .689$	$R = .170$ $N = 25$ $p = .415$

If we had not been interested in estimating the regression function, we could have computed R directly from the data for the convenience store example, using this formula:

$$R = \frac{n\Sigma XY - (\Sigma X)(\Sigma Y)}{\sqrt{[n\Sigma X^2 - (\Sigma X)^2][n\Sigma Y^2 - (\Sigma Y)^2]}}$$

$$= \frac{20(734{,}083) - (816)(16{,}826)}{\sqrt{[20(36{,}526) - (816)^2][20(15{,}027{,}574) - (16{,}826)^2]}}$$

$$= .896$$

In this case, the value of R indicates a positive correlation between the average daily vehicular traffic and annual sales. In other words, successively higher levels of sales are associated with successively higher levels of traffic.

surveysolutions XP ●

SPSS JUMP START FOR CORRELATION

Steps that you need to go through to do the correlation problem shown in the book are provided below along with the output produced. Use the data set **Correx**, which you can download from the Web site for the text.

Steps in SPSS

1. Select *Analyze → Correlate → Bivariate*.
2. Move **x** to Variables.
3. Move **y** to Variables.
4. Click OK.

SPSS Output for Correlation

Correlations

Correlations

		Traffic	Sales
Traffic	Pearson Correlation	1	.896**
	Sig. (2-tailed)	.	.000
	N	20	20
Sales	Pearson Correlation	.896**	1
	Sig. (2-tailed)	.000	.
	N	20	20

**. Correlation is significant at the 0.01 level

PRACTICING MARKETING RESEARCH

When Bivariate and Multivariate Correlation Combined Give the Best Picture

Social researchers Douglas Kirby, Karin Coyle, and Jeffrey B. Gould wanted to assess the relationships between conditions of poverty and birthrates among young teenagers in California. They collected data from 1,811 zip codes in which any teenage births had been recorded between 1991 and 1996. They excluded all zip code areas that did not have at least 200 young women aged 15–17 (which they called "young teenage birthrates") to get a sample of 1,192 zip codes.

Their dependent variable was the mean of the yearly birthrates for women in this group. Their independent variables included 19 demographic features, which they culled from a list of 177 social indicators. Of these 19 independent measures, 3 dealt with ethnicity and 16 represented other factors such as education, employment, marital status, income level, and housing status.

Using these data, the researchers calculated the simple bivariate correlation and regression coefficients between young teenage birthrate and the 19 social measures, one at a time. Their bivariate analysis results showed that the number of families living in conditions of poverty in a given zip code was "highly related" to the birthrate among teenagers 15–17. The bivariate correlations, they concluded, "show that a single variable, the proportion of households living below the poverty line, is highly related to the young-teenage birthrate." Bivariate analysis also demonstrated that median household income and the number of homes receiving public assistance are also highly related and that three of the four poverty measures have the largest regression coefficients.

But the researchers wanted to look at a bigger picture of relationships and control for the "correlates" of family poverty level. So they shifted to multivariate correlation to make connections among multiple manifestations of poverty, low educational levels and employment status, and high levels of employment. They found that these factors also have a "large impact" on teenage birthrates. Multivariate correlation showed that the number of families living at or below poverty levels "remained by far the most important predictor" of teenage birthrate.[3]

Similarly, researcher and author Clayton E. Cramer found that the sequential application of bivariate and then multivariate correlation produced the best results in his study of the effectiveness of the Brady Handgun Violence Prevention Act of 1993. Bivariate analysis is easy to perform, Cramer says, and works well for certain types of research problems, such as comparing brands of gun ammunition or suggesting that factor A did not cause factor B or that factor A affected factor B.

But when you tackle "hard social problems" such as those associated with crime and gun control, using only two variables is insufficient for figuring out true causality. "Unlike bivariate correlation analysis, multivariate correlation analysis can help identify some truly subtle relationships—where a 3 percent increase in A may cause a 1 percent increase in B." Multivariate analysis is "a devilishly complex technique," and scientists using it can make legitimate mistakes hard to detect except by other scientists, Cramer says, but application of it produced strong data that the Brady Law had no effect on homicide rates.[4]

SUMMARY

The techniques used to analyze the relationship between variables taken two at a time are called bivariate analyses. Bivariate regression analysis allows a single dependent variable to be predicted from knowledge about a single independent variable. One way to examine the underlying relationship between a dependent and an independent variable is to plot them on a scatter diagram. If the relationship appears to be linear, then linear regression analysis may be used. If it is curvilinear, then curve-fitting techniques should be applied. The general equation for a straight line fitted to two variables is given by

$$Y = a + bX$$

where $Y =$ dependent variable

$X =$ independent variable

$a = Y$ intercept

$b =$ amount Y increases with each unit increase in X

Both a and b are unknown and must be estimated. This process is known as simple linear regression analysis. Bivariate least-squares regression analysis is a mathematical technique for fitting a line to measurements of the two variables X and Y. The line is fitted so that the algebraic sum of deviations of the actual observations from the line is zero and the sum of the squared deviations is less than it would be for any other line that might be fitted to the data.

The estimated regression function describes the nature of the relationship between X and Y. In addition, researchers want to know the strength of the relationship between the variables. This is measured by the coefficient of determination, denoted by R^2. The coefficient of determination measures the percent of the total variation in Y that is "explained" by the variation in X. The R^2 statistic ranges from 0 to 1. An analysis of variance (ANOVA) approach also can be used for regression analysis. The total variation is known as the total sum of squares (SST). The explained variation, or the sum of squares due to regression (SSR), represents the variability explained by the regression. The unexplained variation is called the error sum of squares (SSE).

Correlation analysis is the measurement of the degree to which changes in one variable are associated with changes in another. Correlation analysis will tell the researcher whether the variables are positively correlated, negatively correlated, or independent.

KEY TERMS & DEFINITIONS

bivariate techniques Statistical methods of analyzing the relationship between two variables.

independent variable Variable believed to affect the value of the dependent variable.

dependent variable Variable expected to be explained or caused by the independent variable.

bivariate regression analysis Analysis of the strength of the linear relationship between two variables when one is considered the independent variable and the other the dependent variable.

coefficient of determination Percentage of the total variation in the dependent variable explained by the independent variable.

sum of squares due to regression Variation explained by the regression.

error sum of squares Variation not explained by the regression.

correlation analysis Analysis of the degree to which changes in one variable are associated with changes in another.

Pearson's product-moment correlation Correlation analysis technique for use with metric data.

QUESTIONS FOR REVIEW & CRITICAL THINKING

1. Give an example of a marketing problem for which use of each of the three procedures listed in question 1 would be appropriate.

2. A sales manager of a life insurance firm administered a standard multiple-item job satisfaction scale to all the members of the firm's salesforce. The manager then correlated (Pearson's product-moment correlation) job satisfaction score with years of school completed for each salesperson. The resulting correlation was .11. On the basis of this analysis, the sales manager concluded: "A salesperson's level of education has little to do with his or her job satisfaction." Would you agree or disagree with this conclusion? Explain the basis for your position.

3. What purpose does a scatter diagram serve?

4. Explain the meaning of the coefficient of determination. What does this coefficient tell the researcher about the nature of the relationship between the dependent and independent variables?

5. It has been observed in the past that when an AFC team wins the Super Bowl, the stock market rises in the first quarter of the year in almost every case. When an NFC team wins the Super Bowl, the stock market falls in the first quarter in most cases. Does this mean that the direction of movement of the stock market is caused by which conference wins the Super Bowl? What does this example illustrate?

6. The following table gives data collected by a convenience store chain for 20 of its stores.

Column 1: ID number for each store

Column 2: Annual sales for the store for the previous year in thousands of dollars

Column 3: Average number of vehicles that pass the store each day, based on actual traffic counts for one month

Column 4: Total population that lives within a 2-mile radius of the store, based on 1990 census data

Column 5: Median family income for households within a 2-mile radius of the store, based on 2000 census data

Store ID No.	Annual Sales (thousands of dollars)	Average Daily Traffic	Population in 2-Mile Radius	Average Income in Area
1	$1,121	61,655	17,880	$28,991
2	$ 766	35,236	13,742	$14,731
3	$ 595	35,403	19,741	$ 8,114
4	$ 899	52,832	23,246	$15,324
5	$ 915	40,809	24,485	$11,438
6	$ 782	40,820	20,410	$11,730
7	$ 833	49,147	28,997	$10,589
8	$ 571	24,953	9,981	$10,706
9	$ 692	40,828	8,982	$23,591
10	$1,005	39,195	18,814	$15,703
11	$ 589	34,574	16,941	$ 9,015
12	$ 671	26,639	13,319	$10,065
13	$ 903	55,083	21,482	$17,365
14	$ 703	37,892	26,524	$ 7,532
15	$ 556	24,019	14,412	$ 6,950
16	$ 657	27,791	13,896	$ 9,855
17	$1,209	53,438	22,444	$21,589
18	$ 997	54,835	18,096	$22,659
19	$ 844	32,916	16,458	$12,660
20	$ 883	29,139	16,609	$11,618

Answer the following:
a. Which of the other three variables is the best predictor of sales? Compute correlation coefficients to answer the question.
b. Do the following regressions:
   1. Sales as a function of average daily traffic
   2. Sales as a function of population in a 2-mile radius
c. Interpret the results of the two regressions.

7. Interpret the following:
a. $Y = .11 + .009X$, where Y is the likelihood of sending children to college and X is family income in thousands of dollars. Remember: It is family income in *thousands*.

1. According to our model, how likely is a family with an income of $100,000 to send their children to college?
2. What is the likelihood for a family with an income of $50,000?
3. What is the likelihood for a family with an income of $17,500?
4. Is there some logic to the estimates? Explain.

b. $Y = .25 - .0039X$, where Y is the likelihood of going to a skateboard park and X is age.

1. According to our model, how likely is a 10-year-old to go to a skateboard park?
2. What is the likelihood for a 60-year-old?
3. What is the likelihood for a 40-year-old?
4. Is there some logic to the estimates? Explain.

8. The following ANOVA summary data are the result of a regression with sales per year (dependent variable) as a function of promotion expenditures per year (independent variable) for a toy company.

$$F = \frac{MSR}{MSE} = \frac{34,276}{4,721}$$

The degrees of freedom are 1 for the numerator and 19 for the denominator. Is the relationship statistically significant at $\alpha = .05$? Comment.

WORKING THE NET

1. Go to *http://www.grapentine.com/displayrn.asp?Id=17* for an excellent discussion of the role that collinearity plays in regression analysis. A variety of other statistical issues in a marketing context are discussed at this site.

2. Go to *http://www.grapentine.com/displayrn.asp?Id=54* for a very good discussion of interpretation of the correlation coefficient.

3. Go to *http://www.spss.com/regression/* for discussion of regression applications provided by SPSS.

REAL-LIFE RESEARCH • 16.1

Axcis Athletic Shoes

Fred Luttrell is the new product development manager for Axcis Athletic Shoe Company. He recently completed consumer testing of 12 new shoe concepts. As part of this test, a panel of consumers was asked to rate the 12 shoe concepts on two attributes, overall quality and style. A 10-point scale was used with anchors at 10 = best possible and 1 = worst possible.

The panel of 20 consumers met as a group and came up with the ratings as a group. Fred believes that there is a relationship between the style ratings and the overall quality ratings. He believes that shoes receiving higher ratings on style also will tend to receive higher ratings on overall quality. The ratings results for the 12 shoe concepts are as follows.

Shoe Model	Style Rating	Quality Rating
1	9	8
2	7	7
3	6	8
4	9	9
5	8	7
6	5	5
7	9	7
8	7	9
9	8	6
10	10	9
11	6	5
12	9	10

Questions

1. Which of the statistical procedures covered in this chapter is appropriate for addressing Fred's theory? Why would you choose that technique over the other?

2. Use the technique that you chose to determine whether Fred's theory is supported by the statistical evidence. State the appropriate null and alternative hypotheses. Is Fred's theory supported by the statistical evidence? Why or why not?

REAL-LIFE RESEARCH • 16.2

Find Any Error?

Bloomberg Personal is a monthly investment magazine published for upscale U.S. retail investors. Each issue of *Bloomberg Personal* now includes a section entitled "Global Reach," which gives a brief description of activity in the national stock and bond markets of foreign countries. The performance of foreign financial markets can be useful in gauging current economic conditions for consumers in these foreign countries.

In the December 1997 issue, nine countries were featured, including Japan, Australia, Russia, and China.[5] In addition, an inset box included the following information:

Here's how closely some markets have mirrored the S & P 500 (a stock index of 500 leading firms in the United States) since 1992. The closer the figure is to 1.0, the higher the correlation.

Canada	.62
UK	.41
France	.39
Germany	.37
Italy	.22
Singapore	.19
Chile	.15
Brazil	.14
Philippines	.08
Turkey	−.02

Source: "A Mirror to the World," *Bloomberg Personal,* December 1997. Reprinted by permission.

Questions

1. What other information would be essential to have before you could use these secondary data in a marketing research report?
2. If you had this other information and the precision of measurement was acceptable to you, what is the story these numbers would begin to tell about the linkages between the U.S. stock market and the stock markets of some other nations in the world?

 ● **SPSS EXERCISES FOR CHAPTER 16**

Note: If you did not complete any of the SPSS exercises in Chapter 14, you will need a corrected database from your professor.

Exercise #1: Bivariate Regression

Use the *analyze/regression/linear* sequence to invoke bivariate regression analysis. This exercise attempts to explain the variation in the *number of movies the respondent attends in an average month (Q3)*. Hence, **Q3** is the **dependent variable.** Invoke the bivariate regression procedure for the following pairs of variables:

1. Q3 and Q5d (movie theater item—importance of comfortable chairs)
2. Q3 and Q5e (movie theater item—auditorium type seating)
3. Q3 and Q7a (movie theater information source—newspaper)
4. Q3 and Q7b (movie theater information source—Internet)
5. Q3 and Q7c (movie theater information source—phone in for information)
6. Q3 and Q9 (self-perception of how physically active)
7. Q3 and Q10 (self-perception of how socially active)

Summarize the results of the bivariate regression analysis, by filling in tables similar to the ones below.

Model	Regression coefficient	t	Sig.
Constant			
Q5d			
Q5e, etc.			

Variables	Model R²	Model F-value	Sig.
Q5d			
Q5e, etc.			

1. At the 95 percent level of confidence, which of the regression models (list the pairs of variables) are significant (list the dependent variables)?

   _____

   _____

2. ***Interpretation of the regression coefficients:*** Use the following table to summarize the regression coefficient, *b*, in each of the 7 regression models.

Model	Regression Coefficient *b*	*t*	Sig. of *b*	Interpretation of the Regression Coefficient *b*
Example Q3 & Q5b	.244	4.147	.000	A one-unit increase in Q5b is associated with a .244 increase in monthly movie attendance

3. Using the regression results, compute Y(Q3) if Q5d = 4.   _____

4. Using the regression results, compute Y(Q3) if Q7c = 2.   _____

5. Using the regression results, compute Y(Q3) if Q9 = 3.   _____

6. Which of the 7 models in the bivariate regression analysis explained the most variation in Q3 (*hint: R^2*)?   _____

7. In which of the 7 models does the independent variable's regression coefficient cause the largest change in Q3 for a one unit change in the independent variable?   _____

Exercise #2: Pearson's Product-Moment Correlation

Use the *analyze/correlate/bivariate* sequence to invoke bivariate correlation analysis. This exercise utilizes the metric correlation technique (Pearson's), which requires that both variables in the bivariate analysis be of at least interval measurement scale. The objective of this exercise is to examine the association between various pairs of variables.

Invoke the bivariate correlation procedure utilizing the Pearson coefficient to evaluate the association between the following pairs of variables:

   a. Q3 and Q8a (Purchase Option for movie tickets—Internet)
   b. Q9 (self-perception of how physically active) and Q10 (self-perception of how socially active)
   c. Q8a (Purchase Option for movie tickets—Internet) and Q7b (importance of the Internet as a source of information about movies at movie theaters)
   d. Q5b (Movie Theater Item—importance of soft drinks and food items) and Q9 (self-perception of how physically active)
   e. Q5h (Movie Theater Item—number of screens at a movie theater) and Q10 (self-perception of how socially active)

With the results of the bivariate correlation using the Pearson coefficient, fill in a table similar to the one below.

Variables	Pearson Coefficient (include +/−)	Probability of an insignificant correlation in the population (based on the sample results)	Interpretation of the results

Questions to Answer: (Assume a significant relationship requires at least a **95 percent** level of confidence.)

1. Of the five correlations computed, which pair of variables had the strongest association? _____

2. Of the three correlations computed, which pair of variables had the weakest association? _____

3. Do people who perceive themselves as more physically active have a greater or lesser need for food and drink at a movie theater? _____

4. Are people who use the Internet to purchase movie tickets more or less likely to use the Internet to get information about movies at movie theaters? _____

surveysolutions XP

MULTIVARIATE DATA ANALYSIS

LEARNING OBJECTIVES

→	1.	To define multivariate data analysis.
→	2.	To describe multiple regression analysis and multiple discriminant analysis.
→	3.	To learn about cluster analysis and factor analysis.
→	4.	To gain an appreciation of perceptual mapping.
→	5.	To develop an understanding of conjoint analysis.

Michelle Simpson is director of marketing for Community Wireless Communications, a company that was recently created by the merger of three medium-sized wireless companies. The merger gives Community national coverage. Simpson is in the process of developing market segmentation and product strategies as well as marketing strategies to build the Community brand, which is currently unknown to consumers.

Community has just completed a large national survey that is designed to provide information for the development of product and market segmentation strategies. Simpson has reviewed the cross tabulations from the research firm and is concerned about a number of issues addressed by the study. She is not satisfied with the analysis. The cross tabulations suggest answers to some of her questions but lead to no clear conclusions or direction. She has four general concerns:

- ☐ First, she has certain theories regarding the importance of various product/service attributes and their relative importance. For example, she believes that the range of geographic coverage offered in an area should be the best predictor of how much consumers in the market are willing to pay per month for wireless service. This theory is based on previous research conducted by Community. Simpson has heard from some of her colleagues that multiple regression analysis provides a way to test this theory. However, the research firm that conducted the study is not experienced in the use of this multivariate analysis technique.

- ☐ Second, Simpson is interested in developing a better understanding of the factors that predict whether someone has or does not have wireless telephone service. Half of those surveyed in the recent study have wireless service and half do not. She wants to know how those who have wireless service differ from those who do not have it in regard to the importance they attach to various features of wireless service. She has heard that multiple discriminant analysis can be used to test these differences.

- ☐ Third, she believes that the market can be segmented on the basis of the importance that consumers attach to different features of wireless communications service. If this is true, identifying those "important" features would be very useful in helping him decide how the new service should be positioned and what features to target in her market communications.

- ☐ Finally, Simpson believes that the way consumers feel about some of the attributes of wireless service may be strongly correlated with the way they feel about other attributes. If this is true, then she may be able to build her positioning and communications strategy around clusters of product attributes or features that resonate most strongly with target consumers.

These issues and questions are addressed in this chapter. Multivariate analysis procedures are powerful tools for analyzing various types of marketing research data, and they provide a basis for testing all of the issues of concern to Simpson. ■

Multivariate Analysis Procedures

Advances in computer hardware and software have provided the basis for remarkable developments in the use of powerful statistical procedures for the analysis of marketing research data. These developments have made it possible to analyze large amounts of complex data with relative ease. In particular, multivariate analysis procedures have been extremely significant in this data analysis revolution.

> **multivariate analysis**
> A general term for statistical procedures that simultaneously analyze multiple measurements on each individual or object under study.

The term **multivariate analysis** refers to the simultaneous analysis of multiple measurements on each individual or object being studied.[1] Some experts consider any simultaneous statistical analysis of more than two variables to be multivariate analysis. Multivariate analysis procedures are extensions of the univariate and bivariate statistical procedures discussed in Chapters 15 and 16.

A number of techniques fall under the heading of multivariate analysis procedures. In this chapter, we will consider six of these techniques:

- ☐ Multiple regression analysis
- ☐ Multiple discriminant analysis
- ☐ Cluster analysis
- ☐ Factor analysis
- ☐ Perceptual mapping
- ☐ Conjoint analysis

You may have been exposed to multiple regression analysis in introductory statistics courses. The remaining procedures are newer, less widely studied, or both. Summary descriptions of the techniques are provided in Exhibit 17.1.

EXHIBIT 17.1	Brief Descriptions of Multivariate Analysis Procedures
Multiple regression analysis	Enables the researcher to predict the level of magnitude of a dependent variable based on the levels of more than one independent variable.
Multiple discriminant analysis	Enables the researcher to predict group membership on the basis of two or more independent variables.
Cluster analysis	Is a procedure for identifying subgroups of individuals or items that are homogeneous within subgroups and different from other subgroups.
Factor analysis	Permits the analyst to reduce a set of variables to a smaller set of factors or composite variables by identifying underlying dimensions in the data.
Perceptual mapping	Is appropriate when the goal is to analyze consumer perception of companies, products, brands, and the like.
Conjoint analysis	Provides a basis for estimating the utility that consumers associate with different product features or attributes.

Although awareness of multivariate techniques is far from universal, they have been around for decades and have been widely used for a variety of commercial purposes. Fair Isaac & Co. has built a $70-million business around the commercial use of multivariate techniques.[2] The firm and its clients have found that they can predict with surprising accuracy who will pay their bills on time, who will pay late, and who will not pay at all. The federal government uses secret formulas, based on the firm's analyses, to identify tax evaders. Fair Isaac has also shown that results from its multivariate analyses help in identifying the best sales prospects.

Multivariate Software

The computational requirements for the various multivariate procedures discussed in this chapter are substantial. As a practical matter, running the various types of analyses presented requires a computer and appropriate software. Until the late 1980s, most types of multivariate analysis discussed in this chapter were done on mainframe or minicomputers, because personal computers were limited in power, memory, storage capacity, and range of software available. Those limitations are in the past. Personal computers today have the power to handle just about any problem that a marketing researcher might encounter. Most problems can be solved in a matter of seconds, and a wide variety of outstanding Windows software is available for multivariate analysis. SPSS for Windows is one of the best and surely the most widely used by professional marketing researchers.

It includes a full range of software modules for integrated database creation and management, data transformation and manipulation, graphing, descriptive statistics, and multivariate procedures. It has an easy-to-use graphical interface. Additional information on the SPSS product line can be found at *http://www.spss.com*. A number of other useful resources are available at the SPSS site:

☐ Technical support, product information, FAQs (frequently asked questions), various downloads, and product reviews

☐ Examples of successful applications of multivariate analysis to solve real business problems

☐ Discussions of data mining and data warehousing applications

Multiple Regression Analysis

Researchers use multiple regression analysis when their goal is to examine the relationship between two or more metric predictor (independent) variables and one metric dependent (criterion) variable.[3] Under certain circumstances, described later in this section, nominal predictor variables can be used if they are recoded as binary variables.

Multiple regression analysis is an extension of bivariate regression, discussed in Chapter 16. Instead of fitting a straight line to observations in a two-dimensional space, multiple regression analysis fits a plane to observations in a multidimensional space. The

> **multiple regression analysis**
> Procedure for predicting the level or magnitude of a (metric) dependent variable based on the levels of multiple independent variables.

output obtained and the interpretation are essentially the same as for bivariate regression. The general equation for multiple regression is as follows:

$$Y = a + b_1X_1 + b_2X_2 + b_3X_3 + \cdots + b_nX_n$$

where Y = dependent or criterion variable

   a = estimated constant

   $b_1 - b_n$ = coefficients associated with the predictor variables so that a change of one unit in X will cause a change of b_1 units in Y; values for the coefficients are estimated from the regression analysis

   $X_1 - X_n$ = predictor (independent) variables that influence the dependent variable

For example, consider the following regression equation (in which values for a, b_1, and b_2 have been estimated by means of regression analysis):

$$\hat{Y} = 200 + 17X_1 + 22X_2$$

where $\hat{Y}$ = estimated sales in units

   X_1 = advertising expenditures

   X_2 = number of salespersons

This equation indicates that sales increase by 17 units for every \$1 increase in advertising and 22 units for every one-unit increase in number of salespersons.

Applications of Multiple Regression Analysis

There are many possible applications of multiple regression analysis in marketing research:

☐ Estimating the effects of various marketing mix variables on sales or market share

☐ Estimating the relationship between various demographic or psychographic factors and the frequency with which certain service businesses are visited

☐ Determining the relative influence of individual satisfaction elements on overall satisfaction

☐ Quantifying the relationship between various classification variables, such as age and income, and overall attitude toward a product or service

☐ Determining which variables are predictive of sales of a particular product or service

Multiple regression analysis can serve one or a combination of two basic purposes: (1) predicting the level of the dependent variable, based on given levels of the independent variables, and (2) understanding the relationship between the independent variables and the dependent variable. An application in international research is shown in the Global Research feature on page 549.

coefficient of determination
Measure of the percentage of the variation in the dependent variable explained by variations in the independent variables.

Multiple Regression Analysis Measures

In the discussion of bivariate regression in Chapter 16, a statistic referred to as the **coefficient of determination**, or R^2, was identified as one of the outputs of regression analysis. This statistic can assume values from 0 to 1 and provides a measure of the percentage of

Multiple regression analysis can be used to estimate the relationship between various demographic or psychographic factors and the frequency with which a service business is hired.

the variation in the dependent variable that is explained by variation in the independent variables. For example, if R^2 in a given regression analysis is calculated to be .75, this means that 75 percent of the variation in the dependent variable is explained by variation in the independent variables. The analyst would always like to have a calculated R^2 close to 1. Frequently, variables are added to a regression model to see what effect they have on the R^2 value.

The b values, or **regression coefficients**, are estimates of the effect of individual independent variables on the dependent variable. It is appropriate to determine the likelihood that each individual b value is the result of chance. This calculation is part of the output provided by virtually all statistical software packages. Typically, these packages compute the probability of incorrectly rejecting the null hypothesis of $b_n = 0$.

> **regression coefficients**
> Estimates of the effect of individual independent variables on the dependent variable.

Dummy Variables

In some situations, the analyst needs to include nominally scaled independent variables such as gender, marital status, occupation, and race in a multiple regression analysis. *Dummy variables* can be created for this purpose. Dichotomous nominally scaled independent variables can be transformed into dummy variables by coding one value (for example, female) as 0 and the other (for example, male) as 1. For nominally scaled independent variables that can assume more than two values, a slightly different approach is required. Consider a question regarding racial group with three possible answers: African American, Hispanic, or Caucasian. Binary or dummy variable coding of responses requires the use of two dummy variables, X_1 and X_2, which might be coded as follows:

	X_1	X_2
If person is African American	1	0
If person is Hispanic	0	1
If person is Caucasian	0	0

Potential Use and Interpretation Problems

The analyst must be sensitive to certain problems that may be encountered in the use and interpretation of multiple regression analysis results. These problems are summarized in the following sections.

Collinearity   One of the key assumptions of multiple regression analysis is that the independent variables are not correlated (collinear) with each other.[4] If they are correlated, then the estimated b values (regression coefficients) will be biased and unstable. Conventional wisdom says that this is not a problem if the regression model is intended strictly for purposes of prediction. However, if the goal of the analysis is to determine how each of the predictor variables influences the dependent variable, the possibility that the b values are biased because of **collinearity** becomes a serious problem.

> **collinearity**
> Correlation of independent variables with each other, which can bias estimates of regression coefficients.

The simplest way to check for collinearity is to examine the matrix showing the correlations between each variable in the analysis. One rule of thumb is to look for correlations between independent variables of .30 or greater. If correlations of this magnitude exist, then the analyst should check for distortions of the b values. One way to do this is to run regressions with the two or more collinear variables included and then run regressions again with the individual variables. The b values in the regression with all variables in the equation should be similar to the b values computed for the variables run separately.

There are a number of strategies for dealing with collinearity. Two of the most commonly used strategies are (1) to drop one of the variables from the analysis if two variables are heavily correlated with each other and (2) to combine the correlated variables in some fashion (for example, an index) to form a new composite independent variable, which can be used in subsequent regression analyses.

Causation   Although regression analysis can show that variables are associated or correlated with each other, it cannot prove **causation**. Causal relationships can be confirmed only by other means (see Chapter 8). A strong logical or theoretical basis must be developed to support the idea that there is a causal relationship between the independent variables and the dependent variable. However, even a strong logical base and supporting statistical results demonstrating correlation are only *indicators* of causation.

> **causation**
> Inference that a change in one variable is responsible for (caused) an observed change in another variable.

Scaling of Coefficients   The magnitudes of the regression coefficients associated with the various independent variables can be compared directly only if they are scaled in the same units or if the data have been standardized. Consider the following example:

$$\hat{Y} = 50 + 20X_1 + 20X_2$$

where $\hat{Y}$ = estimated sales volume

X_1 = advertising expenditures in thousands of dollars

X_2 = number of salespersons

At first glance, it appears that an additional dollar spent on advertising and another salesperson added to the salesforce have equal effects on sales. However, this is not true because X_1 and X_2 are measured in different kinds of units. Direct comparison of regression coefficients requires that all independent variables be measured in the same units (for example, dollars or thousands of dollars) or that the data be standardized. *Standardization* is achieved by taking each number in a series, subtracting the mean of the series from the number, and dividing the result by the standard deviation of the series. This

GLOBAL RESEARCH

What Drives Brand Strength?

Multiple regression analysis was used to identify key drivers of brand strength in different countries around the world. Results are summarized in the following table.[5]

Market	Key Drivers of Brand Strength
United States	Offering sound advice Having responsive customer service Having low fees and competitive packages
Japan	Treating you like a valued customer Having a strong reputation
Germany	Having responsive customer service Having a strong reputation
Brazil	Having low fees and competitive packages Having a wide variety of different kinds of product Treating you like a valued customer

process converts any set of numbers to a new set with a mean of 0 and a standard deviation of 1. The formula for the standardization process is as follows:

$$\frac{X_i - \overline{X}}{\sigma}$$

where
X_i = individual number from a series of numbers

$\overline{X}$ = mean of the series

σ = standard deviation of the series

Sample Size   The value of R^2 is influenced by the number of predictor variables relative to sample size.[6] Several different rules of thumb have been proposed; they suggest that the number of observations should be equal to at least 10 to 15 times the number of predictor variables. For the preceding example (sales volume as a function of advertising expenditures and number of salespersons) with two predictor variables, a minimum of 20 to 30 observations would be required.

Example of Multiple Regression Analysis

This sample problem and others in this chapter use data from the research described in the appendix to this chapter. Ed English, the marketing director for United Wireless Communications, believes that five variables are important in determining how much target customers are willing to pay each month to have wireless service. The five items are consumer importance ratings of the following service features: range of coverage, mobility, sound quality, ability to place and receive calls when away from home, and average monthly bill. This hypothesis is based on the results of focus groups and other research conducted by United. All six variables (the dependent variable and five predictor variables) were measured in the survey. The five predictor variables were all measured on a nine-point scale, where 9 means the attribute is "very important" and 1 means the attribute is "very unimportant." The five predictors can be found under question 3 in the survey in the appendix to this chapter.

To test English's hypothesis, the following model was estimated, using multiple regression analysis:

$$\hat{Y} = a + b_1 X_1 + b_2 X_2 + b_3 X_3 + b_4 X_4 + b_5 X_5$$

where
$\hat{Y}$ = dependent variable, amount willing to pay each month to have wireless service (ADDED)

a = constant term, or Y-axis intercept

b_1–b_5 = regression coefficients to be estimated

X_1 = first independent variable, importance rating of range of coverage (RANGE)

X_2 = second independent variable, importance rating of mobility (MOBILITY)

X_3 = third independent variable, importance rating of sound quality (SOUND)

X_4 = fourth independent variable, importance rating of ability to place and receive calls when away from home (PRECEIV)

X_5 = fifth independent variable, importance rating of average monthly bill (AVGBILL)

The estimated regression equation is

$$\hat{Y} = .82 + .44X_1 + .69X_2 + .21X_3 + .45X_4 + 1.44X_5$$

Complete regression results generated with the SPSS software package are shown in Exhibit 17.2. These results provide the following information:

☐ All the regression coefficients (b_1, b_2, and so on) have positive signs. This indicates that higher importance ratings on each of the five independent variables are associated with the willingness to pay more for wireless service, as expected.

☐ The regression coefficient (b) shows the estimated effect of a one-unit increase in each of the associated independent variables on the dependent variable. The estimated unstandardized coefficients are shown under the column labeled "B." The results show, for example, that a one-unit increase in the importance rating of RANGE is associated with a $.44 increase in the amount an individual is willing to pay per month for wireless service. The column labeled "BETA" shows the regression coefficient computed with standardized data. According to these estimates, MOBILITY has a greater effect on the amount prospective customers are willing to pay for the service than does any of the other four independent variables. AVGBILL is second in importance, and RANGE and PRECEIV are tied for third place. Interestingly, according to the model,

SPSS JUMP START FOR MULTIPLE REGRESSION ANALYSIS

Steps that you need to go through to do the Multiple Regression Analysis example shown in this chapter are provided below along with the output produced. Use the data set **Mulregex**, which you can download from the Web site for the text.

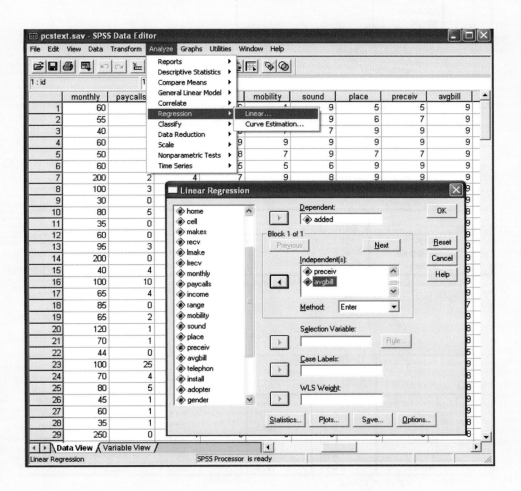

Steps in SPSS

1. Select *Analyze → Regression → Linear*.
2. Move **added** to Dependent.
3. Move **range, mobility, sound, preceiv**, and **avgbill** to Independent(s).
4. Click OK.

SPSS Output for Multiple Regression Analysis

Regression

Variables Entered/Removed[b]

Model	Variables Entered	Variables Removed	Method
1	avgbill, preceiv, sound, mobility, range	.	Enter

a. All requested variables entered.
b. Dependent Variable: added

Model Summary

Model	R	R Square	Adjusted R Square	Std. Error of the Estimate
1	.866[a]	.749	.743	1.486

a. Predictors: (Constant), avgbill, preceiv, sound, mobility, range

ANOVA[b]

Model		Sum of Squares	df	Mean Square	F	Sig.
1	Regression	1282.226	5	256.445	116.085	.000[a]
	Residual	428.569	194	2.209		
	Total	1710.795	199			

a. Predictors: (Constant), avgbill, preceiv, sound, mobility, range
b. Dependent Variable: added

Coefficients[a]

Model		Unstandardized Coefficients		Standardized Coefficients	t	Sig.
		B	Std. Error	Beta		
1	(Constant)	.819	1.667		.491	.624
	range	.441	.104	.211	4.249	.000
	mobility	.687	.065	.522	10.541	.000
	sound	.209	.125	.067	1.667	.097
	preceiv	.449	.123	.206	3.645	.000
	avgbill	1.444	.173	.321	8.329	.000

a. Dependent Variable: added

SOUND has the smallest relative effect on the amount prospective customers are willing to pay.

☐ The adjusted R^2 value is .743, indicating that 74.3 percent of the variation in the amount consumers are willing to pay for wireless service is explained by the variation in the five independent, or predictor, variables.

EXHIBIT 17.2	Regression Summary for Dependent Variable: ADDED

$R = .86573182$ $R^2 = .74949158$ Adjusted $R^2 = .74303518$
$F(95,194) = 116.09$ $p < 0.0000$ Std. error of estimate: 1.4863

	Beta	St. Err of BETA	B	St. Err of B	t(194)	p level
Intercept			0.82	1.67	0.49	0.62
RANGE	0.21	0.05	0.44	0.10	4.25	0.00
MOBILITY	0.52	0.05	0.69	0.07	10.54	0.00
SOUND	0.07	0.04	0.21	0.13	1.67	0.10
PRECEIV	0.21	0.06	0.45	0.12	3.65	0.00
AVGBILL	0.32	0.04	1.44	0.17	8.33	0.00

Multiple Discriminant Analysis

Although **multiple discriminant analysis** is similar to multiple regression analysis,[7] there are important differences. In the case of multiple regression analysis, the dependent variable must be metric; in multiple discriminant analysis, the dependent variable is nominal or categorical in nature. For example, the dependent variable might be usage status for a particular product or service. A particular respondent who uses the product or service might be assigned a code of 1 for the dependent variable, and a respondent who does not use it might be assigned a code of 2. Independent variables might include various metric measures, such as age, income, and number of years of education. The goals of multiple discriminant analysis are as follows:

> **multiple discriminant analysis**
> Procedure for predicting group membership for a (nominal or categorical) dependent variable on the basis of two or more independent variables.

☐ Determine if there are statistically significant differences between the average discriminant score profiles of two (or more) groups (in this case, users and nonusers).

☐ Establish a model for classifying individuals or objects into groups on the basis of their values on the independent variables.

☐ Determine how much of the difference in the average score profiles of the groups is accounted for by each independent variable.

The general discriminant analysis equation follows:

$$Z = b_1 X_1 + b_2 X_2 + \cdots + b_n X_n$$

where $Z = $ discriminant score
$b_1 - b_n = $ discriminant weights
$X_1 - X_n = $ independent variables

The **discriminant score**, usually referred to as the *Z score*, is the score derived for each individual or object by means of the equation. This score is the basis for predicting the group to which the particular object or individual belongs. *Discriminant weights*, often referred to as **discriminant coefficients**, are computed by means of the discriminant analysis program. The size of the discriminant weight (or coefficient) associated with a particular independent variable is determined by the variance structure of the variables in the equation. Independent

> **discriminant score**
> Score that is the basis for predicting to which group a particular object or individual belongs; also called *Z score*.

> **discriminant coefficient**
> Estimate of the discriminatory power of a particular independent variable; also called *discriminant weight*.

PRACTICING MARKETING RESEARCH

Multiple Discriminant Analysis Beats Regression in Certain Applications

Researchers at Georgia Tech highly recommend discriminant analysis as the "preferred method" of study when you are trying to assess the suitability of educational interventions, specifically for students at risk of failing a class or not understanding a subject's concepts.

Edward W. Thomas and his colleagues noted that a course in introductory electromagnetism showed a 30 percent student failure rate. Since this was a prerequisite course for engineering majors, it was cost-inefficient to the school and inconvenient to the students to have such a high failure rate. Was there any way to accurately predict in advance which students might have problems?

Thomas and his team applied discriminant analysis in a case study with more than 1,600 engineering majors to determine the predictors of course performance. They specifically chose discriminant analysis over multiple regression because it handles the data and prediction requirements better. Although the two approaches are similar in assumptions, discriminant analysis uses a categorical dependent variable (i.e., the grade received) and can handle noncontinuous variables (i.e., grades, minority status, gender), which are important issues for this analysis.

The researchers took data from 1,622 students who had enrolled in the course over a five-year period to see what distinguished students who did well from those who did poorly or failed outright. They examined at least eight predictor variables, including ethnic group, gender, major, college, SAT scores, overall grade point average, math grade point average, and how well they did in classes judged predictive of their performance in the electromagnetism course. Then they applied the method to produce information at three levels.

First, although univariate F tests showed that performance ratings in all academic subjects had predictive relevance for performance in electromagnetism, discriminant analysis showed something better: only three of these variables made "significant independent contributions."

Second, this approach yielded a 48 percent successful prediction rate in students who would fail but an 86 percent success rate in predicting those who would do well. Discriminant analysis did much better in identifying successful students than poor ones, possibly because good students have consistent records and poor students have erratic ones, Thomas theorized.

The third application of this methodology was to identify students at risk in future course sections so that targeted educational interventions could be done. Here the success rate at picking out students not at risk was 84 percent, and for those who were at risk, it was 50 percent.

The educators praised discriminant analysis for the way it efficiently reduces data, eliminates nonpredictive variables, more reliably identifies students at risk of course failure, and allows for a more detailed error analysis or prediction than does regression.[8]

---

variables with large discriminatory power (large differences between groups) have large weights, and those with little discriminatory power have small weights.

The goal of discriminant analysis is the prediction of a categorical variable. The analyst must decide which variables would be expected to be associated with the probability of a person or object falling into one of two or more groups or categories. In a statistical sense, the problem of analyzing the nature of group differences involves finding a linear combination of independent variables (the discriminant function) that shows large differences in group means. Multiple discriminant analysis out performs multiple regression analysis in some applications where they are both appropriate as described in the Practicing Marketing Research feature on page 554.

Applications of Multiple Discriminant Analysis

Discriminant analysis can be used to answer many questions in marketing research:

☐ How are consumers who purchase various brands different from those who do not purchase those brands?

☐ How do consumers who show high purchase probabilities for a new product differ in demographic and lifestyle characteristics from those with low purchase probabilities?

☐ How do consumers who frequent one fast-food restaurant differ in demographic and lifestyle characteristics from those who frequent another fast-food restaurant?

☐ How do consumers who have chosen either indemnity insurance, HMO coverage, or PPO coverage differ from one another in regard to healthcare use, perceptions, and attitudes?

Example of Multiple Discriminant Analysis

United's marketing director wants to know if the five importance ratings used in the regression analysis predict whether an individual currently has a wireless telephone. Wireless telephone ownership is captured by question 7 on the survey in the appendix to this chapter. Those who currently have wireless telephones were assigned the code of 1, and those who do not currently have wireless telephones were assigned the code of 0. Previous research conducted by United suggested that the five independent variables (RANGE, MOBILITY, SOUND, PRECEIV, and AVGBILL) should be good predictors of wireless telephone ownership. The following discriminant model was designed to test this hypothesis:

$$Z = b_1X_1 + b_2X_2 + b_3X_3 + b_4X_4 + b_5X_5$$

where

Z = discriminant score

$b_1 - b_5$ = discriminant coefficients or weights

X_1 = first independent variable, importance rating of range of coverage (RANGE)

X_2 = second independent variable, importance rating of mobility (MOBILITY)

X_3 = third independent variable, importance rating of sound quality (SOUND)

X_4 = fourth independent variable, importance rating of ability to place and receive calls when away from home (PRECEIV)

X_5 = fifth independent variable, importance rating of average monthly bill (AVGBILL)

The discriminant analysis results are

$$Z = -.02X_1 + .22X_2 - .36X_3 + .55X_4 - .07X_5$$

These results show that the ability to place and receive calls when away from home (PRE-CEIV) is the most important variable in discriminating between current users and nonusers of wireless telephone service, and range of coverage (RANGE) is the least important variable.

Another important role of discriminant analysis is to classify objects or people. In this example, the goal was to correctly classify consumers into two groups—those that currently have wireless telephone service and those that do not have wireless telephone service. To determine whether the estimated discriminant model is a good predictor, a *classification matrix* (sometimes called a *confusion matrix*) is used. The classification matrix produced for this problem is shown in Exhibit 17.3. This table shows that the model correctly predicted 73.8 percent of current wireless nonusers as nonusers. However, it incorrectly predicted that 33, or 26.2 percent, of the nonusers were users. The model also predicted that 71.6 percent of current wireless users were users but that 28.4 percent were nonusers. Overall, the model correctly classified 73 percent of all respondents as wireless users or nonusers. This is far better than an analyst would expect to do on a chance basis. Thus, the conclusion is that the five independent variables are significant predictors of whether or not a particular individual is a current wireless user.

Statistical tests are available to indicate whether the resulting classification is better than could be expected by chance. When group sizes are unequal and the goal is to correctly predict membership in the two groups, one simple approach is to use the proportional chance criterion. The formula is as follows:

$$C_{PRO} = p^2 - (1 - p)^2$$

where p = proportion of individuals in group 1

         $1 - p$ = proportion of individuals in group 2

In this case, group 1 (nonusers) includes 126 people, or 63 percent of the total (126/200). Calculation of the proportional chance criterion follows:

$$C_{PRO} = .63^2 - (1 - .63)^2$$
$$= 5.397 - .137$$
$$= 5.534, \text{ or } 53.4\%$$

The classification matrix model correctly classified 93 of the nonusers and 53 of the users, for a total of 146 out of 200, or 73 percent, correctly classified. This exceeds the proportional chance criterion of 53.4 percent by a wide margin and shows that the model did a better job than could be expected by chance.

EXHIBIT 17.3   **Classification Matrix (pcstext.sta)**

Rows: Observed classifications
Columns: Predicted classifications

	Percent Correct	G_1:0 p = .63000	G_2:1 p =.37000
G_1:0	73.8	93	33
G_2:1	71.6	21	53
Total	73.0	114	86

SPSS JUMP START FOR MULTIPLE DISCRIMINANT ANALYSIS

Steps that you need to go through to do the Multiple Discriminant Analysis shown in the book are provided below along with the output produced. Use the data set **Muldiscrimex**, which you can download from the Web site for the text.

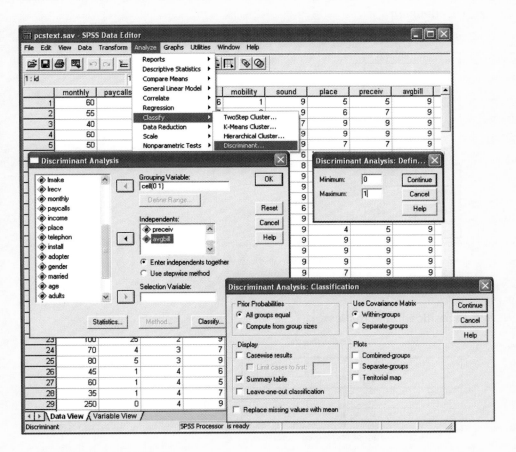

Steps in SPSS

1. Select *Analyze → Classify → Discriminant.*
2. Move **cell** to Grouping Variable.
3. Click Define Range.
4. Set Minimum to 0 and Maximum to 1.
5. Click Continue.
6. Move **range, mobility, sound, preceiv**, and **avgbill** to Independents.
7. Click Classify.

surveysolutions XP

8. Check box for Summary table.
9. Click Continue.
10. Click OK.

Selected SPSS Output for Multiple Discrimination Analysis

Discriminant

Standardized Canonical Discriminant Function Coefficients

	Function 1
range	-.031
mobility	.456
sound	-.338
preceiv	.668
avgbill	.047

Structure Matrix

	Function 1
preceiv	.893
mobility	.768
range	.446
sound	-.202
avgbill	-.029

Pooled within-groups correlations between discriminating variables and standardized canonical discriminant functions

Variables ordered by absolute size of correlation within function.

Classification Statistics

Classification Results[a]

		cell	Predicted Group Membership		Total
			0	1	
Original	Count	0	77	49	126
		1	11	63	74
	%	0	61.1	38.9	100.0
		1	14.9	85.1	100.0

a. 70.0% of original grouped cases correctly classified.

Cluster Analysis

The term **cluster analysis** generally refers to statistical procedures used to identify objects or people that are similar in regard to certain variables or measurements. The purpose of cluster analysis is to classify objects or people into some number of mutually exclusive and exhaustive groups so that those within a group are as similar as possible to one another.[9] In other words, clusters should be homogeneous internally (within cluster) and heterogeneous externally (between clusters).

Procedures for Clustering

A number of different procedures (based on somewhat different mathematical and computer routines) are available for clustering people or objects. However, the general approach underlying all of these procedures involves measuring the similarities among people or objects in regard to their values on the variables used for clustering.[10] Similarities among the people or objects being clustered are normally determined on the basis of some type of distance measure. This approach is best illustrated graphically. Suppose an analyst wants to group, or cluster, consumers on the basis of two variables: monthly frequency of eating out and monthly frequency of eating at fast-food restaurants. Observations on the two variables are plotted in a two-dimensional graph in Exhibit 17.4. Each dot indicates the position of one consumer in regard to the two variables. The distance between any pair of points is positively related to how similar the corresponding individuals are when the two variables are considered together (the closer the dots, the more similar the individuals). In Exhibit 17.4, consumer X is more like consumer Y than like either Z or W.

Inspection of Exhibit 17.4 suggests that three distinct clusters emerge on the basis of simultaneously considering frequency of eating out and frequency of eating at fast-food restaurants:

☐ Cluster 1 includes those people who do not frequently eat out or frequently eat at fast-food restaurants.

☐ Cluster 2 includes consumers who frequently eat out but seldom eat at fast-food restaurants.

☐ Cluster 3 includes people who frequently eat out and also frequently eat at fast-food restaurants.

The fast-food company can see that its customers are to be found among those who, in general, eat out frequently. To provide more insight for the client, the

> **cluster analysis**
> General term for statistical procedures that classify objects or people into some number of mutually exclusive and exhaustive groups on the basis of two or more classification variables.

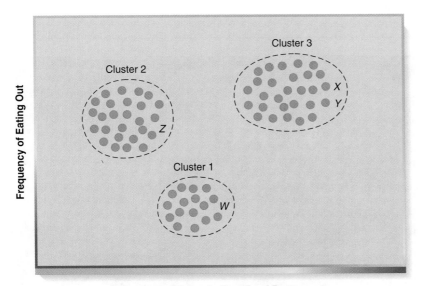

Frequency of Going to Fast Food Restaurants

Exhibit 17.4

Cluster Analysis Based on Two Variables

PRACTICING MARKETING RESEARCH

Birds of a Feather

Marketers use geodemographic *cluster systems* to reach new customers, choose new business locations, target direct mail, and do other tasks. Now the major providers have recently revised their cluster systems to include the most recent census data. Here's an overview of the latest in clustering, and some advice for customers who are buying a *cluster* system.

Consumers want the best value for their money. So do marketers. That's why products that make marketing more efficient are in great demand. Helping companies identify and reach their best prospects is a booming business. One of the most sophisticated tools for capturing customers is the geodemographic segmentation system.

Products such as Claritas's PRIZM, Strategic Mapping's ClusterPLUS 2000, NDS/Equifax's MicroVision, and CACI's ACORN use data from the decennial census and other sources to separate the nation's neighborhoods into similar groups known as clusters.

Cluster systems are based on the premise that birds of a feather tend to flock together. Look at your own neighborhood. The homes and cars are probably of similar size and value. If you could look inside the mailboxes and cupboards, you would probably find many of the same magazines and cereals.

Some cluster systems use catchy names that try to capture the essence of each segment, such as PRIZM's "Blue Blood Estates." Others are more plainly descriptive, such as the "Urban New Families, New Homes" segment of ClusterPLUS 2000.

The idea behind all geodemographic cluster systems is the same. Each system divides neighborhoods into groups based on similarities in income, education, and household type, as well as attitudes and product preferences. But each of the four major cluster systems is dynamic and changeable, and the most recent census data gives them an enormous infusion of new data. Two of the players used census data to completely overhaul their systems, creating new sets of clusters organized in new ways.

To make matters even more complicated, two direct-marketing companies have recently introduced cluster systems that do not start with the census—Metromail's DNA and Trans Union's SOLO. This business can get confusing, but there are ways to decide which system to buy and how to put it to good use.[11]

Clustering people according to how frequently and where they eat out is a way of identifying a particular consumer base. An upscale restaurant can see that its customers fall into cluster 2 and possibly cluster 3 in Exhibit 17.4.

analyst should develop demographic, psychographic, and behavioral profiles of consumers in cluster 3.

As shown in Exhibit 17.4, clusters can be developed from scatterplots. However, this time-consuming, trial-and-error procedure becomes more tedious as the number of variables used to develop the clusters or the number of objects or persons being clustered increases. You can readily visualize a problem with two variables and fewer than 100 objects. Once the number of variables increases to three and the number of observations increases to 500 or more, visualization becomes impossible. Fortunately, computer algorithms are available to perform this more complex type of cluster analysis. The mechanics of these algorithms are complicated and beyond the scope of this discussion. The basic idea behind most of them is to start with some arbitrary cluster boundaries and modify the boundaries until a point is reached where the average interpoint distances within clusters are as small as possible relative to average distances between clusters.

Example of Cluster Analysis

United Wireless Communications wants to explore the issue of market segmentation using the data from the consumer survey. It believes that the market can be segmented on the basis of the eight attribute importance responses (question 3 in the appendix) and that the resulting clusters might be further described on the basis of demographic and usage data.

In order to address this issue, cluster analysis was performed using the K-means cluster analysis procedure. Because cluster analysis does not produce a "best" solution, United experimented with a number of different solutions before choosing a three-cluster solution on the basis of the distinctness of the clusters. The sizes of the three clusters and their average ratings on the eight attribute importance questions are summarized in Exhibit 17.5. Average attribute ratings are also summarized in a line graph in Exhibit 17.6. This solution has the following characteristics:

☐ Cluster 3 is the largest, with 83 respondents, and cluster 2 is the smallest, with 55 respondents.

☐ In regard to attribute importance ratings, clusters 2 and 3 are the most similar. They have almost identical average importance ratings on six of the eight attributes. They do differ significantly in regard to price sensitivity (TELEPHON and INSTALL).

EXHIBIT 17.5	Cluster Sizes and Average Ratings on Attribute Importance Variables		
Variable	Cluster 1 (n = 62)	Cluster 2 (n = 55)	Cluster 3 (n = 83)
RANGE	6.8	8.1	8.2
MOBILITY	4.5	8.1	8.2
SOUND	8.1	8.5	8.5
PLACE	6.7	8.3	8.7
PRECEIV	6.8	8.5	8.6
AVGBILL	8.6	8.4	8.8
TELEPHON	8.1	6.3	8.7
INSTALL	7.2	5.1	8.5

Exhibit 17.6

Average Attribute Importance Ratings for Three Clusters

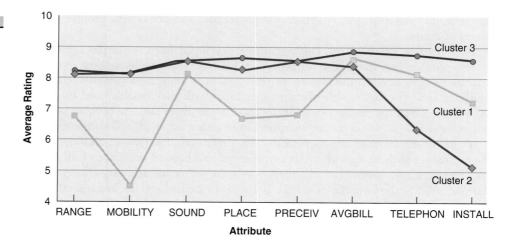

Members of cluster 3 assign a much higher importance to the price of the required equipment and installation/activation charges.

☐ Cluster 1 differs markedly from clusters 2 and 3. In particular, members of this cluster view RANGE, MOBILITY, PLACE, and PRECEIV to be significantly less important than do the members of the other two clusters.

☐ Members of clusters 2 and 3 are the best targets for the new wireless service, based on the importance they place on the RANGE, MOBILITY, PRECEIV, and PLACE variables. In the early stages of product introduction, cluster 3 members represent the most attractive target because of their relative insensitivity to price. Cluster 2 members might be targeted later, assuming that prices fall over time, which is the projected scenario.

The clusters also differ in regard to demographic and usage data. This issue was addressed by cross tabulating cluster membership with the various demographic and usage measures available in the survey.

☐ Cluster 1 individuals are the lightest users of all telephone services. They are about equally likely to be male or female, are least likely (by a narrow margin) to be married, are younger than members of the other groups, and come from households with the largest number of adults.

☐ Cluster 2 individuals are the heaviest users of most telephone services. They are much more likely to be female and are very similar to the members of cluster 3 on most other demographic measures.

☐ Cluster 3 members are between the other two groups in regard to usage of most telephone services. They are more likely to be male than female, are most likely to be married, are older than members of the other groups, and are willing to pay the highest amount, on average, for wireless service.

United's management is, as always, left with the question of what to do based on these findings. Preliminary analysis suggests that the company's initial target should be members of cluster 3, for the reasons just mentioned. Later, as prices fall, an appropriate strategy might be to expand the target to include the members of cluster 2. Members of cluster 1 should be targeted only after United has achieved saturation penetration levels among members of clusters 2 and 3. This plan can be operationalized by more careful analysis of the demographic characteristics of the members of the three clusters and the implementation of a sales and media plan to maximize communication with the most likely prospects.

GLOBAL RESEARCH

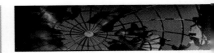

Growing Use of Marketing Research in India

Market research in India has been evolving rapidly to tackle the increasing needs of marketers operating in a complex environment. One of the key evolutions was the development of a socioeconomic system (SEC) of classifying consumers around a decade ago. While SEC is an improvement on income, data from large-scale studies show that further refinement is now needed.

One possible solution is to introduce further levels in the SEC system. This is being done by combining SEC with household expenses to see if a combined system yields better results. The appropriate questions are now being added to large-scale surveys, and the results will be available in the near future.[13]

Factor Analysis

 factor analysis
Procedure for simplifying data by reducing a large set of variables to a smaller set of factors or composite variables by identifying underlying dimensions of the data.

The purpose of **factor analysis** is data simplification.[12] The objective is to summarize the information contained in a large number of metric measures (for example, rating scales) with a smaller number of summary measures, called *factors*. As with cluster analysis, there is no dependent variable.

Many phenomena of interest to marketing researchers are actually composites, or combinations, of a number of measures. These concepts are often measured by means of rating questions. For instance, in assessing consumer response to a new automobile, a general concept such as "luxury" might be measured by asking respondents to rate different cars on attributes such as "quiet ride," "smooth ride," or "plush carpeting." The product designer wants to produce an automobile that is perceived as luxurious but knows that a variety of features probably contribute to this general perception. Each attribute rated should measure a slightly different facet of luxury. The set of measures should provide a better representation of the concept than a single global rating of "luxury."

Several measures of a concept can be added together to develop a composite score or to compute an average score on the concept. Exhibit 17.7 shows data on six consumers who each rated an automobile on four characteristics. You can see that those respondents who gave higher ratings on "smooth ride" also tended to give higher ratings on "quiet ride." A similar pattern is evident in the ratings of "acceleration" and "handling." These four measures can be combined into two summary measures by averaging the pairs of ratings. The resulting summary measures might be called "luxury" and "performance" (see Exhibit 17.8).

EXHIBIT 17.7	Importance Ratings of Luxury Automobile Features			
Respondent	**Smooth Ride**	**Quiet Ride**	**Acceleration**	**Handling**
Bob	5	4	2	1
Roy	4	3	2	1
Hank	4	3	3	2
Janet	5	5	2	2
Jane	4	3	2	1
Ann	5	5	3	2
Average	4.50	3.83	2.33	1.50

EXHIBIT 17.8	Average Ratings of Two Factors	
Respondent	Luxury	Performance
Bob	4.5	1.5
Roy	3.5	1.5
Hank	3.5	2.5
Janet	5.0	2.0
Jane	3.5	1.5
Ann	5.0	2.5
Average	4.25	1.92

Factor Scores

Factor analysis produces one or more factors, or composite variables, when applied to a number of variables. A *factor*, technically defined, is a linear combination of variables. It is a weighted summary score of a set of related variables, similar to the composite derived by averaging the measures. However, in factor analysis, each measure is first weighted according to how much it contributes to the variation of each factor.

In factor analysis, a factor score is calculated on each factor for each subject in the data set. For example, in a factor analysis with two factors, the following equations might be used to determine factor scores:

$$F_1 = .40A_1 + .30A_2 + .02A_3 + .05A_4$$
$$F_2 = .01A_1 + .04A_2 + .45A_3 + .37A_4$$

where F_1–F_n = factor scores
A_1–A_n = attribute ratings

With these formulas, two factor scores can be calculated for each respondent by substituting the ratings she or he gave on variables A_1 through A_4 into each equation. The coefficients in the equations are the factor scoring coefficients to be applied to each respondent's ratings. For example, Bob's factor scores are computed as follows:

$$F_1 = .40(5) + .30(4) + .02(2) + .05(1) = 3.29$$
$$F_2 = .01(5) + .04(4) + .45(2) + .37(1) = 2.38$$

In the first equation, the factor scoring coefficients, or weights, for A_1 and A_2 (.40 and .30) are large, whereas the weights for A_3 and A_4 are small. The small weights on A_3 and A_4 indicate that these variables contribute little to score variations on factor 1 (F_1). Regardless of the ratings a respondent gives to A_3 and A_4, they have little effect on his or her score on F_1. However, variables A_3 and A_4 make a large contribution to the second factor score (F_2), whereas A_1 and A_2 have little effect. These two equations show that variables A_1 and A_2 are relatively independent of A_3 and A_4 because each variable takes on large values in only one scoring equation.

The relative sizes of the scoring coefficients are also of interest. Variable A_1 (with a weight of .40) is a more important contributor to factor 1 variation than is A_2 (with a smaller weight of .30). This finding may be very important to the product designer when evaluating the implications of various design changes. For example, the product manager might want to improve the perceived luxury of the car through product redesign or advertising. The product manager may know, based on other research, that a certain expenditure on redesign will result in an improvement of the average rating on "smooth ride" from 4.3 to 4.8. This research may also show that the same expenditure will produce a half-point improvement in ratings on "quiet ride." The factor analysis shows that perceived luxury will be enhanced to a greater extent by increasing ratings on "smooth ride" than by increasing ratings on "quiet ride" by the same amount.

Factor Loadings

The nature of the factors derived can be determined by examining the **factor loadings**. Using the scoring equations presented earlier, a pair of factor scores (F_1 and F_2) are calculated for each respondent. Factor loadings are determined by calculating the correlation (from $+1$ to -1) between each factor (F_1 and F_2) score and each of the original ratings variables. Each correlation coefficient represents the loading of the associated variable on the particular factor. If A_1 is closely associated with factor 1, the loading or correlation will be high, as shown for the sample problem in Exhibit 17.9. Because the loadings are correlation coefficients, values near $+1$ or -1 indicate a close positive or negative association. Variables A_1 and A_2 are closely associated (highly correlated) with scores on factor 1, and variables A_3 and A_4 are closely associated with scores on factor 2. Stated another way, variables A_1 and A_2 have high loadings on factor 1 and serve to define the factor; variables A_3 and A_4 have high loadings on and define factor 2.

> **factor loading**
> Correlation between factor scores and the original variables.

Naming Factors

Once each factor's defining variables have been identified, the next step is to name the factors. This is a somewhat subjective step, combining intuition and knowledge of the variables with an inspection of the variables that have high loadings on each factor. Usually, a certain consistency exists among the variables that load highly on a given factor. For instance, it is not surprising to see that the ratings on "smooth ride" and "quiet ride" both load on the same factor. Although we have chosen to name this factor "luxury," another analyst, looking at the same result, might decide to name the factor "prestige."

Number of Factors to Retain

In factor analysis, the analyst is confronted with a decision regarding how many factors to retain. The final result can include from one factor to as many factors as there are variables. The decision is often made by looking at the percentage of the variation in the

EXHIBIT 17.9	Factor Loadings for Two Factors	
	Correlation with	
Variable	Factor 1	Factor 2
A_1	.85	.10
A_2	.76	.06
A_3	.06	.89
A_4	.04	.79

FROM THE FRONT LINE

Secrets to Finding the Right Number of Factors

Mike Foytik, Chief Technical Officer, DSS Research

Say you need to develop a key driver's analysis using multiple regression to determine the relative importance of 20 different satisfaction items such as friendliness of customer service reps, how quickly people can get through to a rep, or the speed with which their problem is resolved. You need this analysis to determine overall customer satisfaction (a dependent variable). Then collinearity between the 20 predictors is likely, and factor analysis offers a way to deal with it.

The preferred method for extracting and rotating factors is SPSS, Principal Components Analysis with Varimax rotation, if the results are to be used in a statistical model like the one described above. It is easy to run factor analysis in SPSS, but the art in selecting a factor analysis solution is to determine the appropriate number of factors to retain. Textbooks provide certain statistical guidelines, and a lot of common sense lies behind these guidelines, but we have found that they tend to produce solutions with too few factors for many practical problems.

Multicollinearity, random noise, and measurement error run rampant through data produced by even the most carefully designed questionnaires. The greater the multicollinearity, the more difficult it is to find the uncorrelated (orthogonal) factors we need for regression analysis. Measurement error can cause large numbers of variables to clump together in a factor unless more factors are extracted. Too few factors may cause explained variance to fall below 70 percent; this calls into question the use of factor analysis as a data reduction technique if 30 percent or more of the unique variation is lost in the solution.

We often start with looser criteria (set eigenvalue in SPSS to 0.7 or even 0.65 rather than the standard 1.0). If the last factor does not load highly on any variable (i.e., a loading of 0.5 or greater), don't use the last factor as a predictor in your regression model. Let the regression results determine whether a factor is "significant." If a factor is found to be a statistically significant predictor of the dependent variable (overall satisfaction), then keep it. If the factor is not statistically significant, either drop the variables that loaded highest on that factor or change the criteria used for extraction and rerun the factor analysis.

Repeat the process of running factor analysis followed by subsequent statistical modeling (e.g., regression, logit, etc.) until a stable solution is found where all factors are significant predictors. If all the factors are significant and interpretable (make sense), you have found the solution.

original data that is explained by each factor. In this case, the first and second factors explain a total of 92.5 percent of the variability in the four measures (see Exhibit 17.10). The last two factors explain only 7.5 percent of the variation and contribute little to the objective of data simplification.

There are many different decision rules for choosing the number of factors to retain. Probably the most appropriate decision rule is to stop factoring when additional factors no longer make sense. The first factors extracted are likely to exhibit logical consistency; later factors are usually harder to interpret, for they are more likely to contain a large amount of random variation.

EXHIBIT 17.10	Percentage of Variation in Original Data Explained by Each Factor

Factor	Percent of Variation Explained
1	55.0
2	37.5
3	4.8
4	2.7

Example of Factor Analysis

Once again, we refer to the United survey results for an example of factor analysis. In this instance, United is interested in determining or identifying attributes that go together. As suggested earlier, this will permit United to identify clusters of benefits that are associated in the minds of target customers and to design market communications that speak to these related benefits. As you may recall, factors identified via factor analysis represent underlying supervariables constructed from pieces of the original input variables.

After experimenting with several different solutions, we settled on the three-factor solution as the "best" solution, based on statistical and interpretability criteria. Factor analysis procedures produce a number of different types of output. One key type of output is the matrix of factor loadings. Factor loadings, as noted earlier, are the simple correlations between each of the original input variables and each factor, or supervariable, identified in the analysis. The factor loadings for the three-factor solution to this problem are shown in Exhibit 17.11. Information on the proportion of the total variance in the original eight input variables explained by each factor is provided at the bottom of the table. These data show that the three factors explain 72 percent of the variance in the eight original input variables. An interpretation of the factors follows:

☐ Factor 1 loads heavily or correlates on the following input variables: RANGE, MOBILITY, PLACE, and PRECEIV. We conclude that "staying in touch" is an appropriate name for this factor; different analysts might look at these results and come up with somewhat different names for the factor. However, given the four variables on which this factor loads, it clearly has something to do with the ability to reach and be reached by other people at all times.

EXHIBIT 17.11	Factor Loadings (Varimax raw) (pcstext.sta) Extraction: Principal Components

	Factor 1	Factor 2	Factor 3
RANGE	0.70	−0.10	0.39
MOBILITY	0.83	−0.09	0.07
SOUND	0.03	0.03	0.96
PLACE	0.85	0.19	−0.12
PRECEIV	0.91	−0.02	0.02
AVGBILL	−0.04	0.69	0.29
TELEPHON	−0.01	0.83	−0.11
INSTALL	0.06	0.77	0.02
Proportion of total variance	0.34	0.23	0.15

- ☐ Factor 2 correlates or loads on the variables AVGBILL, TELEPHON, and IN-STALL. A quick review indicates that all of these variables have something to do with cost; therefore, we simply call this the "cost" factor.

- ☐ Factor 3 correlates strongly with only one of the original input variables—SOUND. Therefore, we call it the "sound quality" factor.

This analysis suggests, for example, that it would be logical to send consumers information about RANGE, MOBILITY, PLACE, and PRECEIV issues in the same mailing. The analysis might also provide useful direction for the design of initial market communications.

Perceptual Mapping

> **perceptual mapping**
> Procedure for producing visual representations of consumer perceptions of products, brands, companies, or other objects.

Perceptual mapping, as the name suggests, involves the production of perceptual maps. Perceptual maps are visual representations of consumer perceptions of a product, brand, company, or any other object in two or more dimensions. Ordinarily, such maps show the extremes of the dimensions on the ends of the X and Y axes. Exhibit 17.12 shows a sample perceptual map. Assuming that "good value" and "fast service" are features that target what customers want in restaurants of this type, the analyst can clearly see that restaurant B is in the best position (high on good value and fast service), and restaurant D is in the worst position (high on poor value and slow service).

A number of different approaches are used to develop perceptual maps, including factor analysis, multidimensional scaling, discriminant analysis, and correspondence analysis. One approach, built around factor analysis, is discussed in the following section.[14]

Example of Perceptual Mapping

The results in the factor analysis example discussed earlier were based on a survey in which respondents rated only one automobile on a number of characteristics of interest. In many situations, management needs ratings data on a competitive set of products. For example, each respondent might be asked to rate several different automobiles on a number of different attributes or characteristics.

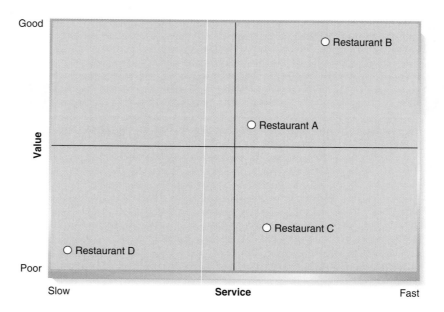

Exhibit 17.12

Sample Perceptual Map

EXHIBIT 17.13	Factor Scores for Four Automobile Concepts			
Attribute	Cadillac Seville	Lincoln Continental	BMW 540	Chrysler 300 M
Smooth ride	4.50	4.17	2.00	1.67
Quiet ride	3.83	3.50	1.83	1.83
Acceleration	2.33	4.00	4.17	2.17
Handling	1.50	3.83	4.00	1.83
Score 1	3.07	2.87	1.53	1.22
Score 2	1.71	3.17	3.57	1.66

The basic format for any factor analysis is a correlation matrix, which shows the correlation for each pair of variables. In the case of the problem presented in the previous section, the format is a 4-by-4 matrix of correlations.

If ratings data were obtained for several automobiles, a separate set of factor scores could be calculated for each model. Factor scores could be calculated for each factor, for each individual, and for each automobile rated. Averaging these factor scores across all individuals or groups of individuals would produce an average score for each product. These average factor scores would represent the coordinate positions of the automobiles in a perceptual map.[15]

Exhibit 17.13 shows the average attribute ratings for four automobiles. Factor scores for each automobile, calculated with the scoring equations introduced earlier, are also shown in this table. These factor scores are plotted in the perceptual map shown in Exhibit 17.14. This perceptual map is based on the average factor scores taken across all subjects. It shows that the Lincoln Continental and the Cadillac Seville are seen as being more luxurious than the BMW 540 and the Chrysler 300, and the Lincoln Continental and the BMW 540 are seen as offering a higher level of performance than the Chrysler 300 and the Cadillac Seville.

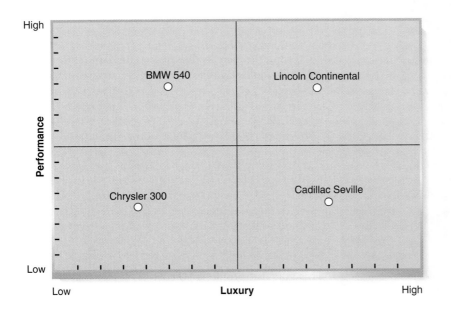

Exhibit 17.14

Perceptual Map of Average Factor Scores for Four Automobile Concepts

Conjoint Analysis

> **conjoint analysis**
> Procedure used to quantify the value that consumers associate with different levels of product/service attributes or features.

Conjoint analysis is a popular multivariate procedure used by marketers to help determine what features a new product or service should have and how it should be priced. It can be argued that conjoint analysis has become popular because it is a more powerful, more flexible, and often less expensive way to address these important issues than is the traditional concept testing approach.[16]

Conjoint analysis is not a completely standardized procedure.[17] A typical conjoint analysis application involves a series of steps covering a variety of procedures; it is not a single procedure as is, for example, regression analysis. Fortunately, conjoint analysis is not difficult to understand, as we demonstrate in the following example concerning the attributes of golf balls.

Example of Conjoint Analysis

Put yourself in the position of a product manager for Titleist, a major manufacturer of golf balls. From focus groups recently conducted, past research studies of various types, and your own personal experience as a golfer, you know that golfers tend to evaluate golf balls in terms of three important features or attributes: average driving distance, average ball life, and price.

You also recognize a range of feasible possibilities for each of these features or attributes, as follows:

Conjoint analysis could be used by a manufacturer of golf balls to determine the three most important features of a golf ball and which ball meets the most needs of both consumer and manufacturer.

1. Average driving distance
   - ☐ 10 yards more than the golfer's average
   - ☐ Same as the golfer's average
   - ☐ 10 yards less than the golfer's average

2. Average ball life
   - ☐ 54 holes
   - ☐ 36 holes
   - ☐ 18 holes

3. Price per ball
   - ☐ $2.00
   - ☐ $2.50
   - ☐ $3.00

From the perspective of potential purchasers, the ideal golf ball would have the following characteristics:

- ☐ Average driving distance—10 yards above average
- ☐ Average ball life—54 holes
- ☐ Price—$2.00

From the manufacturer's perspective, which is based on manufacturing cost, the ideal golf ball would probably have these characteristics:

- ☐ Average driving distance—10 yards below average
- ☐ Average ball life—18 holes
- ☐ Price—$3.00

This golf ball profile is based on the fact that it costs less to produce a ball that travels a shorter distance and has a shorter

PRACTICING MARKETING RESEARCH

Off-Beat Conjoint Analysis: How It Helped Marriott Design a New Hotel

It was the early 1980s and the Marriott Corporation was experiencing a slowdown in growth and suitable sites for new hotels. It wanted to develop a new concept for a hotel chain for business and pleasure travelers not satisfied with the then current hotel offerings. Marriott engaged a team of market researchers, including Jerry Wind and Paul E. Green, both of the Wharton School at the University of Pennsylvania, to do a research study.

It would be a large-scale consumer study involving 601 consumers (263 midlevel business, 83 high-end business, and 255 nonbusiness travelers) drawn from four metropolitan areas (Atlanta, Dallas, San Francisco, and Chicago). Suburban areas and small towns were selected randomly within these areas, and potential respondents were screened by telephone for income, hotel preferences, and frequency and type of trips they took. Respondents got $35 for participating.

Wind, Green, and their colleagues called their method a hybrid categorical conjoint analysis. Its advantage was that it simplified data collection but still kept individual differences in utility functions. Their study encompassed 50 attributes, ranging from two to eight levels, thus making it a very complex trade-off study. The study results, it was hoped, would provide specific guidelines for picking target market segments and designing a new hotel to match consumer demands.

The researchers first administered a questionnaire (which they called a univariate self-explicated evaluation) to solicit consumer preferences. Respondents got a set of seven cards, one at a time; each card dealt with seven facets of hotel facilities and asked for their preferences. The team analyzed the data to generate individual utility functions and then used a computer simulation model to identify any new concept formulations. Later on, the team generated a "multifaceted evaluation of 'complete' hotel offerings" as the second phase. For hotel location analysis, the team asked respondents to rank a number of possible hotel locations using a 100-point allocation.

The core of the analysis centered on computing consumer utility functions for the hotel amenity-price evaluation. The research result was "extremely detailed guidelines" for the selection of about 200 hotel features. The practical result was the introduction in 1983 of three test hotels called Courtyard by Marriott. In 1987, there were 90, and by 2003, 450 worldwide. The Courtyard by Marriott hotel concept was a success, thanks largely to the conjoint analysis.[18]

life. The company confronts the eternal marketing dilemma: the company would sell a lot of golf balls but would go broke if it produced and sold the ideal ball from the golfer's perspective. However, the company would sell very few balls if it produced and sold the ideal ball from the manufacturer's perspective. As always, the "best" golf ball from a business perspective lies somewhere between the two extremes.

A traditional approach to this problem might produce information of the type displayed in Exhibit 17.15. As you can see, this information does not provide new insights regarding which ball should be produced. The preferred driving distance is 10 yards above average, and the preferred average ball life is 54 holes. These results are obvious without any additional research.

EXHIBIT 17.15	Traditional Nonconjoint Rankings of Distance and Ball Life Attributes		
Average Driving Distance		**Average Ball Life**	
Rank	Level	Rank	Level
1	275 yards	1	54 holes
2	250 yards	2	36 holes
3	225 yards	3	18 holes

Considering Features Conjointly   In conjoint analysis, rather than having respondents evaluate features individually, the analyst asks them to evaluate features conjointly or in combination. The results of asking two different golfers to rank different combinations of "average driving distance" and "average ball life" conjointly are shown in Exhibits 17.16 and 17.17.

As expected, both golfers agree on the most and least preferred balls. However, analysis of their second through eighth rankings makes it clear that the first golfer is willing to trade off ball life for distance (accept a shorter ball life for longer distance), while the second golfer is willing to trade off distance for longer ball life (accept shorter distance for a longer ball life).

This type of information is the essence of the special insight offered by conjoint analysis. The technique permits marketers to see which product attribute or feature potential customers are willing to trade off (accept less of) to obtain more of another attribute or feature. People make these kinds of purchasing decisions every day (for example, they may choose to pay a higher price for a product at a local market for the convenience of

EXHIBIT 17.16	Conjoint Rankings of Combinations of Distance and Ball Life for Golfer 1		
	Ball Life		
Distance	54 holes	36 holes	18 holes
275 yards	1	2	4
250 yards	3	5	7
225 yards	6	8	9

EXHIBIT 17.17	Conjoint Rankings of Combinations of Distance and Ball Life for Golfer 2		
	Ball Life		
Distance	54 holes	36 holes	18 holes
275 yards	1	3	6
250 yards	2	5	8
225 yards	4	7	9

shopping there). Another conjoint analysis application is provided in the Practicing Marketing Research feature on page 571.

Estimating Utilities   The next step is to calculate a set of values, or *utilities,* for the three levels of price, the three levels of driving distance, and the three levels of ball life in such a way that, when they are combined in a particular mix of price, ball life, and driving distance, they predict a particular golfer's rank order for that particular combination. Estimated utilities for golfer 1 are shown in Exhibit 17.18. As you can readily see, this set of numbers perfectly predicts the original rankings. The relationship among these numbers or utilities is fixed, though there is some arbitrariness in their magnitude. In other words, the utilities shown in Exhibit 17.18 can be multiplied or divided by any constant and the same relative results will be obtained. The exact procedures for the estimation of these utilities are beyond the scope of this discussion. They are normally calculated by using procedures related to regression, analysis of variance, or linear programming.

The trade-offs that golfer 1 is willing to make between "ball life" and "price" are shown in Exhibit 17.19. This information can be used to estimate a set of utilities for "price" that can be added to those for "ball life" to predict the rankings for golfer 1, as shown in Exhibit 17.20.

This step produces a complete set of utilities for all levels of the three features or attributes that successfully capture golfer 1's trade-offs. These utilities are shown in Exhibit 17.21.

Simulating Buyer Choice   For various reasons, the firm might be in a position to produce only 2 of the 27 golf balls that are possible with each of the 3 levels of the 3 attributes. The possibilities are shown in Exhibit 17.22. If the calculated utilities for golfer

EXHIBIT 17.18	Ranks (in parentheses) and Combined Metric Utilities for Golfer 1—Distance and Ball Life		
	Ball Life		
Distance	**54 holes** **50**	**36 holes** **25**	**18 holes** **0**
275 yards	(1) 150	(2) 125	(4) 100
250 yards	(3) 110	(5) 85	(7) 60
225 yards	(6) 50	(8) 25	(9) 0

EXHIBIT 17.19	Conjoint Rankings of Combinations of Price and Ball Life for Golfer 1		
	Ball Life		
Price	**54 holes**	**36 holes**	**18 holes**
$2.00	1	2	4
$2.50	3	5	7
$3.00	6	8	9

EXHIBIT 17.20	Ranks (in parentheses) and Combined Metric Utilities for Golfer 1—Price and Ball Life

	Ball Life		
	54 holes	36 holes	18 holes
Price	50	25	0
$2.00	(1)	(2)	(4)
	70	45	20
$2.50	(3)	(5)	(7)
	55	30	5
$3.00	(6)	(8)	(9)
	50	25	0

EXHIBIT 17.21	Complete Set of Estimated Utilities for Golfer 1

Distance		Ball Life		Price	
Level	Utility	Level	Utility	Level	Utility
275 yards	100	54 holes	50	$1.25	20
250 yards	60	36 holes	25	$1.50	5
225 yards	0	18 holes	0	$1.75	0

EXHIBIT 17.22	Ball Profiles for Simulation

Attribute	Distance Ball	Long-Life Ball
Distance	275	250
Life	18	54
Price	$2.50	$3.00

1 are applied to the 2 golf balls the firm is able to make, then the results are the total utilities shown in Exhibit 17.23. These results indicate that golfer 1 will prefer the ball with the longer life over the one with the greater distance because it has a higher total utility. The analyst need only repeat this process for a representative sample of golfers to estimate potential market shares for the 2 balls. In addition, the analysis can be extended to cover other golf ball combinations.

The three steps discussed here—collecting trade-off data, using the data to estimate buyer preference structures, and predicting choice—are the basis of any conjoint analysis application. Although the trade-off matrix approach is simple, useful for explaining conjoint analysis, and effective for problems with small numbers of attributes, it is currently not widely used. An easier and less time-consuming way to collect conjoint data is to have respondents rank or rate product descriptions on a paper questionnaire or to use PC-based interviewing software that applies certain rules to determine what questions and product profiles to present to each respondent based on his or her previous answers.

PRACTICING MARKETING RESEARCH

Modeling of Modern Mailings

Multivariate techniques are often used by direct-mail firms to "score" lists and eliminate people with a very low probability of responding. There are a number of reasons for this. First, the budget available may not cover the cost of mailing or phoning every person in a database. Second, the budget may be big enough, but contacting every person in the database will not be profitable. Third, perhaps some customers in a database are so profitable that they should be contacted many times in a given time period, while others should be contacted only once or twice. The bottom line is that some customers and prospects in a database are less likely to respond to direct mail or telemarketing offers than others.

Multivariate modeling allows the marketer to "score" the customer or prospect in terms of their probability of responding. Models predicting probability of response are built on results of past mailing campaigns. Of course, we need certain information about each person in the database used for the past campaign or campaigns to do the necessary analysis. Some of the information that we might have is date the person first entered the database, source of the customer (direct mail, print, broadcast, etc.), date of their most recent purchase, total dollar purchases to date, total number of purchases to date, number of times they were mailed to, products or services purchased in the past, and various demographic characteristics.

With data like those indicated above, a statistician could build a model in the following steps:

- ☐ Obtain the names and records of all persons who responded to the mailing.

- ☐ Divide responders into two groups.

- ☐ Draw a random sample of nonresponders and divide that sample into two groups.

- ☐ Create a "calibration sample" that consists of half of the responders and half of the nonresponders.

- ☐ Create a "validation sample" that includes the other half of the responders and the other half of the sample of nonresponders.

- ☐ Use the calibration file to build the predictive model or scoring equation. A regression model might be used to estimate a scoring equation that would look something like this:

$$Y = a + b_1X_1 + b_2X_2 + b_3X_3 + b_nX_n$$

Y = the probability of response. The X's represent the importance of each variable selected to be included in the model in predicting likelihood to respond. The b's are the weights assigned to each variable in the modeling process.

- ☐ Apply the scoring equation to all of the records in the validation file. This means that every record in the validation file will now have a "predicted or expected" likelihood of responding (purchasing) that ranges from zero to one. The average of all the predicted probabilities should equal the average response rate for the mailing.

- ☐ Sort all of the records in the validation file in descending order of their estimated probability of response.

- ☐ Divide the sorted file into 10 equal groups or deciles and calculate the actual response rate for each decile. If the model is poor then the actual response rate for each decile will be similar to the average overall response rate for the mailing. In other words, the modeling process wasn't able to find segments, measured in deciles, that did better or worse than average. If the model did well, the top decile would show a response rate greater than the response rate of the second decile, which will be greater than the response rate of the third decile, and so on. The greater the spread between the top (best) and the bottom (worst) decile, the better the model.

If the results are good, then we can, for example, decide to eliminate deciles with estimated response rates below some threshold level that we choose. In this manner, we can use multivariate analysis to help us save resources and focus on the people in our list with a higher probability of responding.[19]

EXHIBIT 17.23	Estimated Total Utilities for the Two Sample Profiles				
	Distance Ball		Price		
Attribute	Level	Utility	Level	Utility	
Distance	275	100	250	60	
Life	18	0	54	50	
Price	$2.50	5	$3.00	0	
Total utility	105	110			

As suggested earlier, there is much more to conjoint analysis than has been discussed in this section. However, if you understand this simple example, then you understand the basic concepts that underlie conjoint analysis.

Limitations of Conjoint Analysis

Like many research techniques, conjoint analysis suffers from a certain degree of artificiality. Respondents may be more deliberate in their choice processes in this context than in a real situation. The survey may provide more product information than respondents would get in a real market situation. Finally, it is important to remember that the advertising and promotion of any new product or service can lead to consumer perceptions that are very different from those created via descriptions used in a survey.

SUMMARY

Multivariate analysis refers to the simultaneous analysis of multiple measurements on each individual or object being studied. Some of the more popular multivariate techniques include multiple regression analysis, multiple discriminant analysis, cluster analysis, factor analysis, perceptual mapping, and conjoint analysis.

Multiple regression analysis enables the researcher to predict the magnitude of a dependent variable based on the levels of more than one independent variable. Multiple regression fits a plane to observations in a multidimensional space. One statistic that results from multiple regression analysis is called the coefficient of determination, or R^2. The value of this statistic ranges from 0 to 1. It provides a measure of the percentage of the variation in the dependent variable that is explained by variation in the independent variables. The b values, or regression coefficients, indicate the effect of the individual independent variables on the dependent variable.

Whereas multiple regression analysis requires that the dependent variable be metric, multiple discriminant analysis uses a dependent variable that is nominal or categorical in nature. Discriminant analysis can be used to determine if statistically significant differences exist between the average discriminant score profiles of two (or more) groups. The technique can also be used to establish a model for classifying individuals or objects into groups on the basis of their scores on the independent variables. Finally, discriminant analysis can be used to determine how much of the difference in the average score profiles of the groups are accounted for by each independent variable. The discriminant score, called a Z score, is derived for each individual or object by means of the discriminant equation.

Cluster analysis enables a researcher to identify subgroups of individuals or objects that are homogeneous within the subgroup, yet different from other subgroups. Cluster analysis requires that all independent variables be metric, but there is no specification of a dependent variable. Cluster analysis is an excellent means for operationalizing the concept of market segmentation.

The purpose of factor analysis is to simplify massive amounts of data. The objective is to summarize the information contained in a large number of metric measures such as rating scales with a smaller number of summary measures called factors. As in cluster analysis, there is no dependent variable in factor analysis. Factor analysis produces factors, each of which is a weighted composite of a set of related variables. Each measure is weighted according to how much it contributes to the variation of each factor. Factor loadings are determined by calculating the correlation coefficient between factor scores and the original input variables. By examining which variables load heavily on a given factor, the researcher can subjectively name that factor.

Perceptual maps can be produced by means of factor analysis, multidimensional scaling, discriminant analysis, or correspondence analysis. The maps provide a visual representation of how brands, products, companies, and other objects are perceived relative to each other on key features such as quality and value. All the approaches require, as input, consumer evaluations or ratings of the objects in question on some set of key characteristics.

Conjoint analysis is a technique that can be used to measure the trade-offs potential buyers make on the basis of the features of each product or service available to them. The technique permits the researcher to determine the relative value of each level of each feature. These estimated values are called utilities and can be used as a basis for simulating consumer choice.

KEY TERMS & DEFINITIONS

multivariate analysis General term for statistical procedures that simultaneously analyze multiple measurements on each individual or object under study.

multiple regression analysis Procedure for predicting the level or magnitude of a (metric) dependent variable based on the levels of multiple independent variables.

coefficient of determination Measure of the percentage of the variation in the dependent variable explained by variations in the independent variables.

regression coefficients Estimates of the effect of individual independent variables on the dependent variable.

collinearity Correlation of independent variables with each other, which can bias estimates of regression coefficients.

causation Inference that a change in one variable is responsible for (caused) an observed change in another variable.

multiple discriminant analysis Procedure for predicting group membership for a (nominal or categorical) dependent variable on the basis of two or more independent variables.

discriminant score Score that is the basis for predicting to which group a particular object or individual belongs; also called Z score.

discriminant coefficient Estimate of the discriminatory power of a particular independent variable; also called *discriminant weight*.

cluster analysis General term for statistical procedures that classify objects or people into some number of mutually exclusive and exhaustive groups on the basis of two or more classification variables.

factor analysis Procedure for simplifying data by reducing a large set of variables to a smaller set of factors or composite variables by identifying underlying dimensions of the data.

factor loading Correlation between factor scores and the original variables.

perceptual mapping Procedure for producing visual representations of consumer perceptions of products, brands, companies, or other objects.

conjoint analysis Procedure used to quantify the value that consumers associate with different levels of product/service attributes or features.

QUESTIONS FOR REVIEW & CRITICAL THINKING

1. Distinguish between multiple discriminant analysis and cluster analysis. Give several examples of situations in which each might be used.

2. What purpose does multiple regression analysis serve? Give an example of how it might be used in marketing research. How is the strength of multiple regression measures of association determined?

3. What is a dummy variable? Give an example using a dummy variable.

4. Describe the potential problem of collinearity in multiple regression. How might a researcher test for collinearity? If collinearity is a problem, what should the researcher do?

5. A sales manager examined age data, education level, a personality factor that indicated level of introvertedness/extrovertedness, and level of sales attained by the company's 120-person salesforce. The technique used was multiple regression analysis. After analyzing the data, the sales manager said, "It is apparent to me that the higher the level of education and the greater the degree of extrovertedness a salesperson has, the higher will be an individual's level of sales. In other words, a good education and being extroverted cause a person to sell more." Would you agree or disagree with the sales manager's conclusions? Why?

6. The factors produced and the results of the factor loadings from factor analysis are mathematical constructs. It is the task of the researcher to make sense out of these factors. The following table lists four factors produced from a study of cable TV viewers. What label would you put on each of these four factors? Why?

		Factor Loading
Factor 1	I don't like the way cable TV movie channels repeat the movies over and over.	.79
	The movie channels on cable need to spread their movies out (longer times between repeats).	.75
	I think the cable movie channels just run the same things over and over and over.	.73
	After a while, you've seen all the pay movies, so why keep cable service.	.53
Factor 2	I love to watch love stories.	.76
	I like a TV show that is sensitive and emotional.	.73
	Sometimes I cry when I watch movies on TV.	.65
	I like to watch "made for TV" movies.	.54

Factor 3   I like the religious programs on TV
(negative correlation). −.76
I don't think TV evangelism is good. .75
I do not like religious programs. .61

Factor 4   I would rather watch movies at home than go
to the movies. .63
I like cable because you don't have to go out
to see the movies. .55
I prefer cable TV movies because movie theaters
are too expensive. .46

7. The following table is a discriminant analysis that examines responses to various attitudinal questions from cable TV users, former cable TV users, and people who have never used cable TV. Looking at the various discriminant weights, what can you say about each of the three groups?

		Discriminant Weights		
		Users	**Formers**	**Nevers**
Users				
A19	Easygoing on repairs	−.40		
A18	No repair service	−.34		
A7	Breakdown complainers	+.30		
A5	Too many choices	−.27		
A13	Antisports	−.24		
A10	Antireligious	+.17		
Formers				
A4	Burned out on repeats		+.22	
A18	No repair service		+.19	
H12	Card/board game player		+.18	
H1	High-brow		−.18	
H3	Party hog		+.15	
A9	VCR preference		+.16	
Nevers				
A7	Breakdown complainer			−.29
A19	Easygoing on repairs			+.26
A5	Too many choices			+.23
A13	Antisports			+.21
A10	Antireligious			−.19

8. The following table shows regression coefficients for two dependent variables. The first dependent variable is willingness to spend money for cable TV. The independent variables are responses to attitudinal statements. The second dependent variable is stated desire never to allow cable TV in their homes. By examining the regression coefficients, what can you say about persons willing to spend money for cable TV and those who will not allow cable TV in their homes?

	Regression Coefficients
Willing to Spend Money for Cable TV	
Easygoing on cable repairs	−3.04
Cable movie watcher	2.81

Comedy watcher	2.73
Early to bed	−2.62
Breakdown complainer	2.25
Lovelorn	2.18
Burned out on repeats	−2.06
Never Allow Cable TV in Home	
Antisports	0.37
Object to sex	0.47
Too many choices	0.88

WORKING THE NET

1. Go to *http://www.dobney.com/Conjoint/CnjtDemo.htm* and go through their interactive demonstration of conjoint analysis. In particular, use the simulation tool they provide to estimate share for digital cameras with different features and pricing. This should give you some idea of why conjoint analysis, in its various forms, has become so popular.

2. Can conjoint analysis be used to determine the type of new house a person may choose? Go to *http://www.sawtooth.com/news/sawtoothnews/newsarch/basics.htm* to see how you would approach this problem.

REAL-LIFE RESEARCH • 17.1

Satisfaction Research for Pizza Quik

The Problem: Pizza Quik is a regional chain of pizza restaurants operating in seven states in the Midwest. Pizza Quik has adopted a Total Quality Management (or TQM) orientation.[20] As part of this orientation, the firm is committed to the idea of market-driven quality. That is, it intends to conduct a research project to address the issue of how its customers define quality and to learn from the customers themselves what they expect in regard to quality.

Research Objectives: The objectives of the proposed research are:

- ☐ To identify the key determinants of customer satisfaction

- ☐ To measure current customer satisfaction levels on those key satisfaction determinants

- ☐ To determine the relative importance of each key satisfaction determinant in deriving overall satisfaction

- ☐ To provide recommendations to management regarding where to direct the company's efforts

Methodology: The first objective was met by means of qualitative research. A series of focus groups were conducted with customers to determine which attributes of Pizza Quik's product and service are most important to them. Based on this analysis, the following attributes were identified.

- ☐ Overall quality of food

- ☐ Variety of menu items

- ☐ Friendliness of Pizza Quik's employees

- ☐ Provision of good value for the money

- ☐ Speed of service

In the second stage of the research, central-location telephone interviews were conducted with 1,200 randomly selected individuals who had purchased or eaten at a Pizza

Quik restaurant (in the restaurant or take-out) in the past 30 days. Key information garnered in the survey included:

☐ Overall rating of satisfaction with Pizza Quik on a 10-point scale (1 = poor and 10 = excellent)

☐ Rating of Pizza Quik on the five key satisfaction attributes identified in the qualitative research, using the same 10-point scale as for overall satisfaction

☐ Demographic characteristics

Results and Analysis: Extensive cross tabulations and other traditional statistical analyses were conducted. A key part of the analysis was to estimate a regression model with overall satisfaction as the dependent variable and satisfaction with key product and service attributes as the predictors. The results of this analysis were:

$$S = .48X_1 + 13X_2 + .27X_3 + .42X_4 + .57X_5$$

where

S = overall satisfaction rating
X_1 = rating of food quality
X_2 = rating of variety of menu
X_3 = rating of friendliness of employees
X_4 = rating of value
X_5 = rating of speed of service

Average ratings on the 10-point scale for overall satisfaction and the five key attributes were:

$S = 7.3$
$X_1 = 6.8$
$X_2 = 7.7$
$X_3 = 8.4$
$X_4 = 6.9$
$X_5 = 8.2$

The regression coefficients provide estimates of the relative importance of the different attributes in determining overall satisfaction. The results show that X_5 (rating of speed of service) is the most important driver of overall satisfaction. The results indicate that a one-unit increase in average rating on speed of service will produce an increase of .57 in average satisfaction rating. For example, the current average rating on speed of service is 8.2. If, by providing faster service, Pizza Quik could increase this rating to 9.2, then it would expect the average satisfaction rating to increase to 7.87. X_1 (rating of food quality) and X_4 (rating of value) are not far behind speed of service in their effect on overall satisfaction according to the regression estimates. At the other extreme, X_2 (rating of variety of menu) is least important in determining overall satisfaction, and X_3 (rating of friendliness of employees) is in between in importance.

The performance ratings provide a different picture. According to the average ratings, customers believe Pizza Quik is doing the best job on X_3 (friendliness of employees) and the worst job on X_1 (food quality).

Questions

1. Plot the importance and performance scores in a matrix. One axis would be importance from low to high, and the other would be performance from low to high.

2. Which quadrant should you pay the most attention to? Why?

3. Which quadrant or quadrants should you pay the least attention to? Why?

4. Based on your analysis, where would you advise the company to focus its effort? What is the rationale behind this advice?

REAL-LIFE RESEARCH • 17.2

Custom Car Wash Systems

Custom Car Wash Systems offers car wash franchises throughout the United States. Currently, 872 car washes franchised by Custom are in operation. As part of its service to franchisees, Custom runs a national marketing and advertising program.

Carl Bahn is the senior vice president in charge of marketing for Custom. He is currently in the process of designing the marketing and advertising campaigns for the upcoming year. Bahn believes that it is time for Custom to take a more careful look at user segments in the market. Based on other analyses, he and his associates at Custom have decided that the upcoming campaign should target the heavy user market. Through other research, Custom has defined "heavy car wash users" as those individuals who have their cars washed at a car wash facility three or more times per month on average. "Light users" are defined as those who use such a facility less than three times a month but at least four times a year. "Nonusers" are defined as those who use such a facility less than four times per year. Bahn and his associates are currently in the process of attempting to identify those factors that discriminate between heavy and light users. In the first stage of this analysis, Custom conducted interviews with 50 customers at 100 of its locations for a total of 5,000 interviews. Cross tabulation of the classification variables with frequency of use suggests that four variables may be predictive of usage heaviness: vehicle owner age, annual income of vehicle owner, age of vehicle, and socioeconomic status of vehicle owner (based on an index of socioeconomic variables).

Custom retained a marketing research firm called Marketing Metrics to do further analysis for the company. Marketing Metrics evaluated the situation and decided to use multiple discriminant analysis to further analyze the survey results and identify the relative importance of each of the four variables in determining whether a particular individual is a heavy or light user. The firm obtained the following results:

where
$$Z = .18X_1 + .53X_2 - .49X_3 + .93X_4$$

X_1 = age of vehicle owner

X_2 = annual income of vehicle owner

X_3 = age of vehicle

X_4 = socioeconomic status of owner (as measured by an index in which a higher score means higher status)

Questions

1. What would you tell Bahn about the importance of each of the predictor variables?

2. What recommendations would you make to him about the type of people Custom should target, based on its interest in communicating with heavy users?

Appendix: Wireless Communications Data Set

This appendix includes a description of a data set obtained from an actual survey done for a client in the wireless communications business. The client is referred to as United Wireless. Here, you will also find descriptions of the research objectives, the methodology used, and the physical layout of the data set.

Research Objectives

The objectives of the research were as follows:

- ☐ To determine the likelihood of purchasing the new wireless communications service at various monthly service charges and equipment costs.
- ☐ To measure the importance of various wireless communications service attributes.
- ☐ To determine expected usage patterns and usage heaviness for the new wireless service.
- ☐ To determine usage heaviness of existing residential and long-distance telephone services.
- ☐ To measure current expenditures on local and long-distance services.
- ☐ To determine, for purposes of market segmentation, the demographic characteristics of likely purchasers and nonpurchasers.

Methodology

A summary description of the methodology employed for this research follows:

- ☐ *Sample size.* 200 consumers
- ☐ *Qualified respondents.* Individuals 18 years of age or older from households with annual incomes of $30,000 or more
- ☐ *Sample area.* National probability sample
- ☐ *Sample type.* Random sample based on random digit dialing
- ☐ *Sampling error.* ±7.1 percent with 95 percent confidence
- ☐ *Data-collection method.* All surveying was done by means of central-location telephone interviewing, using a computer-assisted approach. Interviewing was supervised and unobtrusively monitored. All interviewing was conducted from a central-location telephone interviewing facility.
- ☐ *Interview length.* Surveys averaged 10 minutes in length.
- ☐ *Survey timing.* All interviewing was conducted during February 2000.
- ☐ *Questionnaire.* A copy of the questionnaire employed for the study follows this methodology summary.

Description of the Data Set

The description of the data set is keyed to the questionnaire. The data are available on the CD-ROM in the back of this textbook in two formats: ASCII and .dbf. The ASCII file has the name unitedwireless.TXT, and the other file has the name unitedwireless.dbf. The unitedwireless.dbf file can be directly imported into most statistical packages by using the import feature.

The locations of the numerical representations of the responses to each question for the ASCII file are shown in parentheses throughout the questionnaire. The variable names for the .dbf file are shown in the left margin in capital letters. If you employ the import feature of the statistical package you are using, these names should be correctly imported with the data and will appear at the top of the column containing the data for the particular question.

Wireless Survey

ADDED

1. Before we begin the next exercise, how much more would you be willing to pay each month to receive wireless service? This is in addition to what you are currently paying for basic telephone service to your home. **ENTER THE AMOUNT. TYPE "0" FOR NOTHING, "5" FOR $5, ETC.**

_____ Additional amount willing to pay to receive wireless service (4–6)

2. Considering the phone service that you currently have, please indicate the probability that you will purchase one of the new wireless services presented as an **addition** to your existing service.

Indicate your likelihood to purchase each wireless service on a 0 to 100 scale, where 0 means you are not at all likely to purchase that telephone service and 100 means you are extremely likely to purchase that telephone service for your home.

W25100

a. How likely would you be to purchase the new wireless service if your monthly service charge was $25 and the cost of the telephone was $100?

_____ Likelihood to purchase (7–9)

W500

b. How likely would you be to purchase the new wireless service if your monthly service charge was $50 and the cost of the telephone was $0?

_____ Likelihood to purchase (10–12)

3. Now I would like for you to rate several attributes on their level of importance to you when selecting telephone service. For each factor, use a 9-point scale, where 9 means the attribute is "**very important**" (VI) and 1 means the attribute is "**very unimportant**" (VU) to you when selecting local telephone service. How important is . . . **READ LIST AND ROTATE**

	Attributes	VI								VU	
RANGE	Range of coverage	9	8	7	6	5	4	3	2	1	(13)
MOBILITY	Mobility	9	8	7	6	5	4	3	2	1	(14)
SOUND	Sound quality (sound and static)	9	8	7	6	5	4	3	2	1	(15)
PLACE	Ability to place calls when away from home	9	8	7	6	5	4	3	2	1	(16)
PRECEIV	Ability to place and receive calls when away from home	9	8	7	6	5	4	3	2	1	(17)
AVGBILL	Average monthly telephone bill	9	8	7	6	5	4	3	2	1	(18)
TELEPHON	Price of telephone equipment	9	8	7	6	5	4	3	2	1	(19)
INSTALL	Installation/activation charges	9	8	7	6	5	4	3	2	1	(20)

CAR

4. If you purchased wireless service, what percentage of your calls (made and received) on the wireless service would be from your car? **ENTER A PERCENTAGE FROM 0 TO 100**

_____ Percentage of wireless calls from your car (21–23)

MET

5. What percentage of calls using wireless service would be within the Orlando metropolitan area?

_____ Percentage of wireless calls within metropolitan area (24–26)

HOME

6. And what percentage of your wireless calls would be made in and around your home or neighborhood?

_____ Percentage of wireless calls in and around the home (27–29)

And now, I have just a few questions concerning telephone usage in your household.

CELL

7. Do you own or use a wireless phone?

(30)
1   YES
2   NO

MAKES

8. Considering the local telephone calls of all members of your household for a **typical day**, how many calls would you say your household MAKES in a typical day?

_____ Number of calls MADE by household per day (31–32)

RECV   **9.** How many calls would you say your household receives in a typical day?

           _____ Number of calls RECEIVED by household per day (33–34)

LMAKE   **10.** Now considering the number of long-distance calls of all members of your household for a **typical week**, how many long-distance calls would you say your household MAKES in a typical week?

           _____ Number of long-distance calls MADE by household per week (35–36)

LRECV   **11.** How many long-distance calls would you say your household receives in a typical week?

           _____ Number of long-distance calls RECEIVED by household per week (37–38)

MONTHLY   **12.** How much is your average monthly telephone bill, including **local and long-distance charges**?

           _____ Average monthly telephone bill (39–41)

PAYCALL   **13.** How often do you use a pay telephone for personal calls in a typical month?

           _____ Number of pay telephone calls per mo. (42–43)

GENDER   **14.** INDICATE GENDER BY OBSERVATION

       (44)
       1   MALE
       2   FEMALE

MARRIED   **15.** Are you married?

       (45)
       1   YES
       2   NO
       3   Refused

AGE   **16.** Which of the following categories includes your age?

       (46)
       1   18–24
       2   25–34
       3   35–44
       4   45–54
       5   55–64
       6   65 and older
       7   Refused

ADULTS   **17.** How many adults age 18 and over are currently living in your household including yourself?

           _____ Number of adults (47)

CHILDREN   **18.** Do you have any children age 18 and under currently living in your household?

       (48)
       1   YES
       2   NO
       3   RF

INCOME   **19.** Which of the following categories includes the total annual income of all members of your household before taxes?

       (49)
       1   Less than $35,000
       2      $35,000–$49,999
       3      $50,000–$74,999
       4      $75,000 or more
       5   DK/RF

Thanks for participating.

Name _____ Telephone _____

Address _____

Interviewer # _____ Length of interview _____

Source: Courtesy of DSS Research.

Role of Marketing Research in the Organization and Ethical Issues

Marketing Research across the Organization

1. The question of data interpretation is not fully resolved in business today. Someone must still look at the data and decide what they really mean. Often this is done by the people in marketing research. Defend the proposition that persons in engineering, finance, and production should interpret all marketing research data when the survey results affect their operations. What are the arguments against this position?

2. Marketing research data analysis for a large electric utility found that confidence in the abilities of the repairperson is customers' primary determinant of their satisfaction or dissatisfaction with the electric utility. Armed with these findings, the utility embarked on a major advertising campaign extolling the heroic characteristics of the electric utility repairperson. The repairpeople hated the campaign. They knew that they couldn't live up to the customer expectations created by the advertising. What should have been done differently?

3. When marketing research is used in strategic planning, it often plays a role in determining long-term opportunities and threats in the external environment. Threats, for example, may come from competitors' perceived future actions, new competitors, governmental policies, changing consumer tastes, or a variety of other sources. Management's strategic decisions will determine the long-term profitability, and perhaps even the survival, of the firm. Most top managers are not marketing researchers or statisticians; therefore, they need to know how much confidence they can put into the data. Stated differently, when marketing researchers present statistical results, conclusions, and recommendations, they must understand top management's tolerance for ambiguity and imprecision. Why? How might this understanding affect what marketing researchers present to management? Under what circumstances might the level of top management's tolerance for ambiguity and imprecision shift?

Ethical Dilemma

Branding the Black Box in Marketing Research

Marketing research discovered branding in the mid-1980s, and it experienced phenomenal growth in the 1990s and it continues today. Go to virtually any large marketing research firm's Web site, and you'll see a vast array of branded research products for everything from market segmentation to customer value analysis—all topped off with a diminutive ^{SM}, ^{TM}, or $^{®}$. Here's just a sample: MARC's Designor^{SM}, Market Facts' Brand Vision$^{®}$, Maritz Research's 80/20$^{®}$ Relationship Manager, and Total Research's TRBC^{TM}, a scale bias correction algorithm.

A common denominator across some of these products is that they are proprietary, which means the firms won't disclose exactly how they work. That's why they're also known pejoratively as black boxes. A black box method is proprietary—a company is able to protect its product development investment. And if customers perceive added value in the approach, suppliers can charge a premium price to boot. (Black boxes and brand names are not synonymous. Almost all proprietary methods have a clever brand name, but there are also brand names attached to research methods that are not proprietary.)

At least two factors have given rise to this branding frenzy. First, competitive pressures force organizations to seek new ways to differentiate their product offerings from those of their competitors. Second, many large research companies are publicly held, and publicly held companies are under constant pressure to increase sales and profits each quarter. One way to do this is to charge a premium price for services. If a company has a proprietary method for doing a marketing segmentation study, presumably it can charge more for this approach than another firm using publicly available software such as SPSS or SAS. Ironically, it is possible that some black boxes are perfectly standard software such as SPSS and SAS; but if their proponents won't say how they work, or which techniques are used, these methods are still black boxes.

Questions

1. Is the use of branded black box models unethical?

2. Should marketing research suppliers be forced to explain to clients how their proprietary models work?

3. Should firms be required by law to conduct validity and reliability tests on their models to demonstrate that they are better than nonproprietary models?

Source: Terry Grapentine, "You Can't Take Human Nature Out of Black Boxes," *Marketing Research* (Winter 2001), p. 21.

 ● **SPSS EXERCISES FOR CHAPTER 17**

Exercise #1: Multivariate Regression

This exercise uses Multivariate Regression to explain and predict how many movies a respondent attends in a month.

1. Go to the Web site for the text and download the Movie database.

2. Open the database in SPSS and view the variables under Variable View. We will be using the independent variables Q2 Q4 Q6 Q8a Q8b Q8c Q8d Q9 Q10 Q12 and Q13 to predict the dependent variable Q3.
   We are including the variables Q4 and Q6 as is. Strictly speaking, is this proper? What might you want to do instead and why? Why might you decide to leave a variable in bins instead? Would it ever be proper to use a variable like Q11 as is?

3. Go to Analyze → Descriptive Statistics → Descriptives and move Q3 Q2 Q4 Q6 Q8a Q8b Q8c Q8d Q9 Q10 Q12 and Q13 to the Variable(s) box and click OK. Multivariate techniques require that every variable have a legitimate value. If a respondent did not answer every question, then the analyst must either ignore the observation entirely or impute estimates for the missing values. The default for statistical software is to ignore those observations automatically. We will not do imputation for this exercise.

   a. What will the sample size be for later multivariate techniques?
   b. Is this sample size large enough for multivariate regression?
   c. What would some possible problems be if the sample size were not large enough?
   d. Are the minimum and maximum values for each variable within the proper range? A value that is out of range would indicate either a data input error or a user-defined missing value like "Refused" or "Don't Know." Data input errors should be corrected or deleted. User-defined missing values should be declared in SPSS.
   e. Are all the variables within the proper range?

4. Go to Analyze → Regression → Linear.
   Move Q3 to Dependent.
   Move Q2 Q4 Q6 Q8a Q8b Q8c Q8d Q9 Q10 Q12 Q13 to Independent(s).
   Change Method to Stepwise.
   Click OK.

   a. Which independent variables did the stepwise regression select? Why not the rest?
   b. Is each variable chosen significant?
   c. Are the variables that have not been chosen necessarily insignificant?
   d. Is the model significant?
   e. Does this method guarantee that you get the "best" model?

5. Go to Analyze → Descriptive Statistics → Descriptives and remove Q6 Q8a Q8b Q8c Q8d Q9 Q10 and Q12 from the Variable(s) box, so that only Q3 Q2 Q4 and Q13 remain in the box and then click OK.
   What is the sample size now?

6. Go to Analyze → Regression → Linear.
   Move Q3 to Dependent.
   Remove Q6 Q8a Q8b Q8c Q8d Q9 Q10 and Q12 from Independent(s) so that only Q2 Q4 and Q13 remain.
   Change Method to Enter.
   Click OK.

   a. How and why does this model differ from the model based on stepwise regression?
   b. Which model is better?

Interpretation

1. How does stated importance affect the number of times one attends movies?
2. How does spending money on snacks affect the number of times one attends movies?
3. How does student classification affect the number of times one attends movies?
4. If a sophomore thought that going to the movies was somewhat important and typically spent $12 on snacks, how many times per month would he or she attend movies based on this model?
5. Do any of the variables, according to the results, appear to have an effect on the number of times one attends movies, or does it seem that other factors not covered in this survey are driving movie attendance?

Exercise #2: Factor Analysis

This exercise uses Factor Analysis to explore how survey respondents consider various aspects of a theater visit.

1. Go to the Web site for the text and download the Movie database.
2. Open the database in SPSS and view the variables under Variable View. Notice that question 5 has 10 importance rating items.
3. Go to Analyze → Descriptive Statistics → Descriptives and move Q5a through Q5i to the Variable(s) box and click OK.

   a. Which item is the most important?
   b. Which item is the least important?

Multivariate techniques require that every variable have a legitimate value. If a respondent did not answer every question, then the analyst must either ignore the observation entirely or impute estimates for the missing values. The default for statistical software is to ignore those observations automatically. We will not get involved with imputation for this exercise.

a. What will the sample size be for later multivariate techniques?
b. Is this sample size large enough for factor analysis?
c. What would some possible problems be if the sample size were not large enough?
d. It is a good idea to check that the minimum and maximum values for each variable are within the proper range. A value that is out of range indicates either a data input error or a user-defined missing value such as "Refused" or "Don't Know." Data input errors should be corrected or deleted. User-defined missing values should be declared in SPSS.
e. Are all the variables within the proper range?

4. Go to Analyze → Descriptive Statistics → Descriptives and move Q5a through Q5i to the Variables box and click OK.
Examine the resulting correlations matrix.

a. Other than the 1's down the main diagonal of the matrix, what is the highest correlation in absolute value?
b. Does any variable "just not fit" with the others?
c. Does multicollinearity appear to exist among some of the items?

5. Go to Analyze → Data Reduction → Factor.
Move Q5a through Q5i to the Variables box.
Click the Rotation button, place a check in front of "Varimax," and click Continue.
Click the Options button.
Place a check in front of "Sorted by size."
Place a check in front of "Suppress absolute values less than" and set the value after it to .25.
Click Continue.
Click OK.
SPSS produces a lot of output Factor Analysis. It is possible to create much more output than we have generated here by setting various subcommands and options.

a. How many factors did SPSS create?
b. Why did it stop at that number?
c. How could you change the defaults to create a different number of factors?
d. Go to the output entitled Total Variance Explained. How much variance was explained in this Factor Analysis?
e. Go to the output entitled Rotated Component Matrix. Why are some elements in this matrix blank?
f. Do the components or factors make sense?
g. Can you identify a common theme for each component or factor?

Interpretation

1. Is this a good factor solution? Why do you say that?
2. How might you create a better factor solution?
3. What understanding has this analysis helped you gain about how movie-goers perceive their movie-going experience?
4. What recommendations would you give a manager of a movie house based on this analysis?

COMMUNICATING THE RESEARCH RESULTS AND MANAGING MARKETING RESEARCH

LEARNING OBJECTIVES

1.	To become aware of the primary purposes of a research report.
2.	To learn how to organize and prepare a research report.
3.	To learn how to make a personal presentation.
4.	To understand the effective use and communication of marketing research information.
5.	To understand what clients want from a marketing research supplier or department.
6.	To learn some of the key managerial functions in running a marketing research supplier organization.
7.	To see what marketing research departments are doing to gain a more strategic role in the corporation.
8.	To examine how corporations are measuring the contribution of marketing research to the organization.

Rising oil and gas prices affect every aspect of the U.S. economy as businesses, farming enterprises, and households look for ways to reduce energy bills. Electricity, diesel, and gasoline are the traditionally dominant fuel sources. However, propane is a safe and cost-effective alternative that has not yet achieved its full potential. The Propane Education & Research Council (PERC) has made significant inroads in the effort to increase awareness of propane as an alternative resource. Recently, it has focused its efforts on the agricultural industry.

PERC has a lot riding on its assessment of market potential, and providing funding for the right idea could turn the tide for propane the way the light bulb did for electricity. With hundreds of possible projects vying for limited funding, PERC's challenge is to evaluate the impact of each project on the propane market, prioritize it, and demonstrate its value to the propane producers funding the organization. It's a process that requires great insight into market needs and motivators.

To help simplify the process and provide a solid basis for their investment decisions, PERC turned to St. Louis-based Osborn & Barr Communications. The agency developed a series of research projects that eventually helped PERC prioritize and fund new technologies that could change the nature of farming. A comprehensive, user-friendly research matrix now allows PERC to identify and quantify market potential for new agricultural technologies such as thermal agriculture, crop drying, engines, food safety, waste treatment, and other agriculture production areas.

In phase one of the research, Osborn & Barr provided an initial evaluation of the attitudes of agricultural producers and propane retailers toward propane for agricultural applications. A total of 750 growers/producers reflecting the estimated universe of growers/producers were interviewed about their energy use and perceptions of various fuel sources. The study showed that producers/growers estimate they spend an average of $32,813 per year on energy resources for their operations. Propane and electricity were rated similarly for customer service, environmental friendliness, and availability. However, propane was considered to be much/somewhat better than electricity in terms of cost and energy efficiency by 31 percent and 29 percent of the respondents, respectively.

Armed with information about grower/producer attitudes toward propane use in general, the next step was to be able to accurately evaluate the funding requests submitted to PERC. Osborn & Barr developed a proposal for a comprehensive research project that covered the top 33 commodities tracked by the U.S. Department of Agriculture. The goal of the research was to clearly define the size and scope of the total agricultural market from almond growers to wheat growers and beef producers to turkey producers.

The in-depth quantitative and qualitative research provided by Osborn & Barr puts PERC in a better position to evaluate the likelihood of success for new or improved propane agriculture technology. The research will be the foundation for assessing marketing potential and disbursing funding for new propane projects. "As we developed the structure of the report, we did not aim to tell PERC where they should invest, but instead wanted to provide them with the appropriate information to make the best decisions," says Jeff Whetstine, account executive, Osborn & Barr.[1]

What is the role of the research report? Whetstine says, "let the data speak for itself." Should researchers go beyond this to making recommendations? How do clients decide whether or not to use research reports?

In addition to discussing communicating the research results, we will discuss the process of managing marketing research. We will also examine managing a research supplier company and a research department in large organizations. ■

The Research Report

A good researcher is anticipating the report almost from the time she writes the proposal for a project, before she even has the business. The genesis of the report and the researcher's thinking are the objectives provided by the client in the request for proposal (RFP). Along with any background information provided with the RFP or developed as part of the process of preparing the proposal, the objectives give the researcher insight into the client's thinking and needs. What problem/opportunity is the client organization facing? What resources and competencies can it bring to bear on the problem or opportunity? What decisions is the client facing, and what information is it going to need to make those decisions in the most effective manner? If the researcher does not get a handle on these issues, then that failure will be reflected in the resulting proposal, and she probably will not get the job to begin with.

Given that we are about to write the report, we have to assume that the researcher did understand the client's needs and wrote a proposal, including a detailed methodology, that resonated with the client to the extent that she was chosen to do the work over the other competitors.

The research objectives, the decisions to be made based on the research, and a vision of the analysis and the report to be written should have guided the researcher through the design and execution of the research. For a survey-based project, the development of the questionnaire, in particular, should have been based on continuous reference to the research objectives. Now, we have the data, it has been cross tabulated, statistical testing has been performed, extensive statistical analysis has been conducted, and the researcher and her team have spent time sifting through all of this information and relating it back to the original objectives and the decisions associated with those objectives. This process could go on and on, but deadlines in the schedule push the process to a conclusion, often faster than we would like.

The researcher has a tremendous amount of information—piles of crosstabs, reams of statistical analyses, tons of notes, and an assortment of other pieces of information. The challenge is: How to package all of this in a coherent report that efficiently and effectively communicates the key findings and the decision implications of those findings? We like to think of this process as one of trying to figure out how to tell a story. Before you can tell a story, you have to have a pretty good idea of where the story is going to end up. All the analysis brings one to that conclusion. Once you know or have ascertained the key points that you want to make, it becomes much easier to map out what you need to get across to your readers to bring them to that same conclusion.

Organizing the Report

The traditional research report follows an outline like the one below:

1. **Title Page.** The title page should be dominated by the name of the project. Other elements that should be included are the name of the client organization, name of the research firm, and date of the report.

2. **Table of Contents.** This should not exceed one page and should list the major sections of the report along with the page numbers on which they start. It is a convenience for the reader and, often, the researcher in that it permits quick reference for finding specific information in the report.

3. **Executive Summary.** This is perhaps the most difficult part of the report to write because it must succinctly cover the key findings and any recommendations that flow from those findings. Not all reports include recommendations. Whether they include

recommendations depends on the nature of the research, what is expected from the research firm, and what the research found. However, all research reports should include key findings. What makes it tough to do the executive summary is that it should be short (two to four pages at a maximum), and many researchers find it very difficult to summarize the massive amount of information available to them in just two to four pages. It is easy to be long winded, but it is difficult to be compact in your summarization. The executive summary should not summarize every single finding but should focus on those findings that are important and relevant to the goals of the research.

4. **Background.** The background sets the context for the research and addresses such things as the overall goal of the research, the decisions that need to be made, the company's strength and weaknesses regarding the issue in question, and other similar information. It should not be more than one or two pages. Again, it is often difficult to compress a lot of information down to its essentials.

5. **Methodology.** Here we should discuss how the research was done and why it was done that way. Issues that need to be addressed include who was interviewed, why did we interview those people, how were they interviewed (for example, telephone survey, mail survey, Internet survey, or some hybrid of these methods), why were they interviewed in that manner, how were people selected, what type of sampling methodology did we use, whether the sample is a representative sample, how many people did we interview, how were the completed surveys processed, what special statistical procedures were used and why did we use those procedures, and so forth. It is not necessary that this section be long—one to two pages is appropriate. If it is necessary to address some technical elements of the methodology in a more extensive manner, then more detailed information on, for example, statistical procedures used should be provided in an appendix.

6. **Findings.** This is typically the longest section of the report and should summarize results for almost every question on the survey.

7. **Appendixes.** This final section of the report provides a number of supporting items such as a copy of the questionnaire, a set of cross tabulations for every question on the survey (client can look up specific issues not addressed in the findings), and other supporting material such as detailed technical information on special research procedures and techniques.

Interpreting the Findings

The most difficult task for individuals who are writing a research report for the first time is interpreting the findings to arrive at conclusions and then using these conclusions to formulate recommendations. The **executive summary** is the portion of the report that explains what the research found, what the data mean, and what action, if any, should be taken, based on the research. The difficulties of this process are completely understandable, given that the marketing researcher is often inundated with piles of computer printouts, stacks of questionnaires, hundreds of pages of cross tabulations, the results of hundreds of statistical tests, pages and pages of statistical analysis printouts, and a scratch pad full of notes on the project. There is, however, a systematic method that the researcher can follow to draw conclusions.

The research objectives and background stated early in the marketing research process should serve as the primary guide for interpreting findings and drawing conclusions. These objectives should have been stated as specifically as possible, perhaps even with an explicit priority rank for each objective. Although the questionnaire should have been designed to touch on all facets of the objectives, specific bits of information about any one objective may be spread across the questionnaire. Computer printouts often contain information in statistical order rather than in the order in which managers will

executive summary
Portion of a research report that explains why the research was done, what was found, what those findings mean, and what action, if any, management should undertake.

FROM THE FRONT LINE

How to Write a Good Report

Michelle Dodd, Director of Client Services, DSS Research

A good report starts with a good proposal. The researcher must have a clear understanding of the real issue or decision at hand and, subsequently, what underlying questions the client must have answered in order to make the best decision. This understanding must then be translated into an effective questionnaire, which will provide answers to those key questions.

Put yourself in the mindset of your client. What kind of report would you want to read? How long would you want it to be? The report should start with a brief description of the project background, objectives, and methodology for those readers who are less familiar with the study. Next, you want a powerful yet concise executive summary. If the reader goes no further than the executive summary, what key pieces of information should he or she take away?

At a minimum, the executive summary should address each of the key research questions and provide a recommendation regarding the decision at hand. It should also cover any other critical findings that you believe are worthy of the client's attention. You need to tell a story, not just dispense numbers. Yes, this is quite subjective, which is why writing the report is as much art as it is science.

Moving past the executive summary, you should include detailed findings from the study, which typically come in the form of graphs and tables. Questions answered should be grouped by topic and reported in order of descending importance, which will most likely not end up matching the exact order of the questionnaire. You are looking for findings that have managerial implications, not just those that are merely statistically significant or different. Including a "slide takeaway" on each page is ideal. These takeaways should consist of a few sentences that tell the story on each page and provide the key information on which the reader should focus.

The final key to writing a good report is style and literary consistency. The report should be written in consistent font and point size, and in the present tense, and abbreviations and capitalization should be consistent throughout.

---

use the data. Consequently, the researcher's first task is to pull together all the printouts and results that pertain to each of the various objectives. A system will evolve as the researcher focuses attention on the objectives one at a time.

For example, assume that Burger King is reconsidering its breakfast menu. An objective of its breakfast research study is "to determine the feasibility of adding (1) bagels and cream cheese, (2) a western omelette, or (3) French toast." All cross tabulations and one-dimensional tables referring to these food items should be brought together. Generally, the researcher first examines the one-dimensional tables to get the overall picture—that is, understand which of the three breakfast items was most preferred. Next, cross tabulations are analyzed to obtain a better understanding of the overall data—that is, to get a clear view of which age group is most likely to prefer French toast.

conclusions
Generalizations that answer the questions raised by the research objectives or otherwise satisfy the objectives.

Conclusions are generalizations that answer the questions raised by the research objectives or otherwise satisfy the objectives. These conclusions are derived through the process of *induction,* or generalizing from small pieces of information. The researcher should try to merge the information and then paraphrase it in a few descriptive statements that generalize the results. In short, the conclusion of a research report should be a statement or series of statements that communicate the results of the study to the reader but would not necessarily include any of the data derived from the statistical analysis.

Format of the Report

The format and preparation of marketing research reports have changed dramatically over the last 15 years. The pressure to find more efficient and effective ways to communicate research results has pushed researchers toward a heavy reliance on presentation software to tell their stories. Microsoft's PowerPoint totally dominates the market today.

A typical marketing research report tells its story with pictures or graphics. This is what clients expect and what the researcher is expected to deliver. It is not unusual for clients to specify that they want graphics-based reports in their RFPs. Research reports that might have included 50 or more pages of text and a handful of graphs in the past are now presented in a limited amount of text, perhaps just a few pages if it were all strung together, and 20 or 30 pages of graphs and tables. This approach enables time-pressed executives to quickly grasp the story and the key findings and move ahead to conclusions and recommendations. Most clients today just want a copy of the PowerPoint presentation instead of a long, detailed traditional report.

Graphics, text boxes, bulleted lists, and the like are used to interpret the meaning of various graphs. Examples of pages from a report prepared using presentation software are provided in Exhibits 18.1 through 18.6.

Formulating Recommendations

Recommendations are gained from the process of deduction. The marketing researcher applies the conclusions to specific areas in order to make suggestions for marketing strategies or tactics. A recommendation usually focuses on how the client can gain a differential advantage. A *differential advantage* is a true benefit offered by a potential marketing mix that the target market cannot obtain anywhere else (for example, American Airlines having exclusive U.S. carrier landing rights at a foreign airport).

In some cases, a marketing researcher must refrain from making specific recommendations and instead fall back on more general ones. For example, the marketing researcher might not have sufficient information about the resources and experience base of the company or about the decision maker to whom the report is being directed. Or the researcher may have been notified that the recommendations will be determined by the decision maker. Under these circumstances, the researcher offers conclusions and stops at that point.

> **recommendations**
> Conclusions applied to marketing strategies or tactics that focus on a client's achievement of differential advantage.

Exhibit 18.1

Sample Bulleted List from Executive Summary

Satisfaction with all customer service characteristics increased in 2007 compared to the results of 2006.

- *Representative was courteous, friendly, and concerned*—94% (93% in 2007 and 91% in 2006)
- *Representative understood coverage and benefits*—91% (82% in 2007 and 71% in 2006)
- *Automated menu was easy to understand*—90% (87% in 2007 and 90% in 2006)
- *Representative provided accurate response*—88% (83% in 2007 and 84% in 2006)
- *Representative answered the phone promptly*—87% (84% in 2007 and 82% in 2006)
- *Representative was easily reached*—85% (82% in 2007 and 83% in 2006)
- *Representative resolved issue during the call*—78% (71% in 2007 and 82% in 2006)
- *Representative followed up if needed*—47% (16% in 2007 and 14% in 2006)

Exhibit 18.2

Sample Presentation of Customer Satisfaction Results
2007 Sample Size = 901

Overall Survey Results	2007	2006	2005
Overall Satisfaction with Ranch and Home (excellent/very good/good)	89%	85%	81%
Overall Satisfaction with Customer Services Contact (excellent/very good/good)	87%	82%	79%
Overall Satisfaction with Claims Processing (excellent/very good/good)	82%	76%	71%
Likelihood to Continue (very likely/somewhat likely)	93%	87%	85%
Willingness to Recommend (very willing/somewhat willing)	88%	83%	78%
Overall Performance (improved in the past 12 months)	15%	8%	6%

Loyalty Index:
Three indicators of customer satisfaction are satisfaction with the company, likelihood to continue, and willingness to recommend. By combining these three indicators, the degree of customer loyalty can be inferred. By analyzing a customer's overall satisfaction, likelihood to continue, and likelihood to recommend, customer loyalty can be predicted. Based on our analysis, the following results were generated:

- Loyal—17% (13% in 2006)
- Favorable—68% (61% in 2006)
- Vulnerable—10% (17% in 2006)
- At risk—5% (9% in 2006).

Loyal customers = responded excellent to overall satisfaction, very likely to continue, and very willing to recommend.

Favorable customers = chose a favorable response for each of the three indicators, but not the most favorable in each case.

Vulnerable customers = did not consistently rate any of the three indicators favorably or unfavorably.

At-risk customers = chose an unfavorable response for all three indicators.

The final report, whether written or personal or both, represents the culmination of the research effort. The quality of the report and its recommendations often determine whether a research user will return to a supplier. Within a corporation, an internal report prepared by a research department may have less impact, but a history of preparing excellent reports may lead to merit salary increases and, ultimately, promotion for a research staff member.

The Presentation

Clients may expect a presentation of the research results. A presentation serves many purposes. It requires that the interested parties assemble and become reacquainted with the research objectives and methodology. It also brings to light any unexpected events or findings and highlights the research conclusions. In fact, for some decision makers in the

Overall Satisfaction with Ranch and Home
(percent responding excellent, very good, or good)

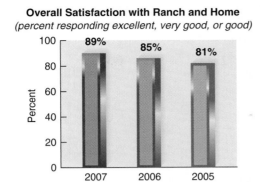

Ranch and Home's Service
(past 12 months)

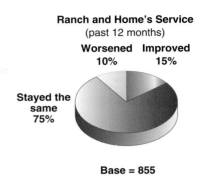

Worsened 10% Improved 15%

Stayed the same 75%

Base = 855

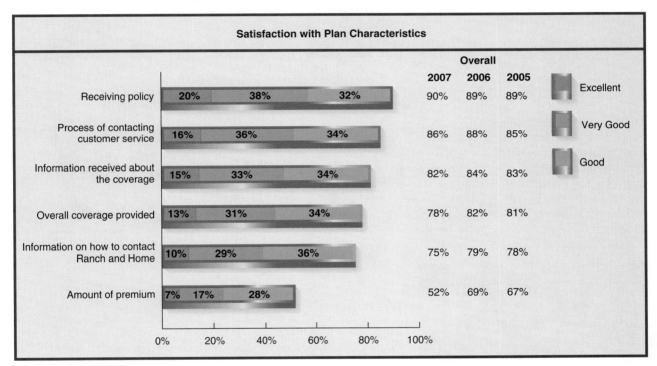

Satisfaction with Plan Characteristics

				Overall			
				2007	2006	2005	
Receiving policy	20%	38%	32%	90%	89%	89%	Excellent
Process of contacting customer service	16%	36%	34%	86%	88%	85%	Very Good
Information received about the coverage	15%	33%	34%	82%	84%	83%	Good
Overall coverage provided	13%	31%	34%	78%	82%	81%	
Information on how to contact Ranch and Home	10%	29%	36%	75%	79%	78%	
Amount of premium	7%	17%	28%	52%	69%	67%	

0%   20%   40%   60%   80%   100%

Exhibit 18.3

Multiple Graphs on a Page Tell a Story

company, the presentation will be their *only* exposure to the findings; they will never read the report. Other managers may only skim the written report, using it as a memory-recall trigger for points made in the presentation. In short, effective communication in the presentation is absolutely critical.

Presentation Materials

We recommend the use of two aids for a presentation:

1. *Visuals.* The PowerPoint presentation. The slides should be succinct and relevant. The format should generally follow that of the report.

2. *Copies of the final report.* The report serves as physical evidence of the research. Its comprehensive nature should make clear that it includes much detail that was omitted in the personal presentation. It should be made available to interested parties at the end of the presentation.

Exhibit 18.4

Graphs and Tables on the Same Page Maximize Communication

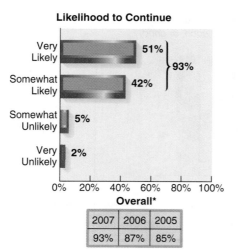

Likelihood to Continue

- Very Likely — 51%
- Somewhat Likely — 42%
- Somewhat Unlikely — 5%
- Very Unlikely — 2%

} 93%

0% 20% 40% 60% 80% 100%

Overall*

2007	2006	2005
93%	87%	85%

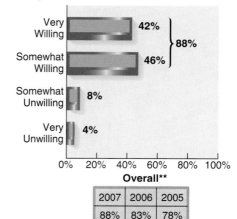

Willingness to Recommend Ranch and Home

- Very Willing — 42%
- Somewhat Willing — 46%
- Somewhat Unwilling — 8%
- Very Unwilling — 4%

} 88%

0% 20% 40% 60% 80% 100%

Overall**

2007	2006	2005
88%	83%	78%

* Percent responding *very likely/somewhat likely*
** Percent responding *very willing/somewhat willing*

Primary Reason for Selecting Ranch and Home***
(top five reasons)

	2007	2006
It was the most affordable option	24%	22%
It was the only choice I could find	22%	24%
I was already doing business with your agent for other coverage	21%	27%
It offered the best value	13%	15%
It offered the most comprehensive coverage	10%	13%

An analysis of the likelihood of joining a health club based on income may yield a recommendation that focuses on how the client can gain a differential advantage over its competitors.

Making a Presentation

An effective presentation is tailored to the audience. It takes into account the receivers' frame of reference, attitudes, prejudices, educational background, and time constraints. The speaker must select words, concepts, and illustrative figures to which the audience can relate. A good presentation allows time for questions and discussion.

One reason presentations are sometimes inadequate is that the speaker lacks an understanding of the barriers to effective communication. A second factor is that the speaker fails to recognize or admit that the purpose of many research reports is persuasion. *Persuasion* does not imply stretching or bending the truth, but rather using research findings to reinforce conclusions and recommendations. In preparing a presentation, the researcher should keep the following questions in mind:

- ☐ What do the data really mean?
- ☐ What impact do they have?
- ☐ What have we learned from the data?
- ☐ What do we need to do, given the information we now have?
- ☐ How can future studies of this nature be enhanced?
- ☐ What could make this information more useful?

Exhibit 18.5

Different Types of Graphs and Tables Convey a Lot of Information Quickly

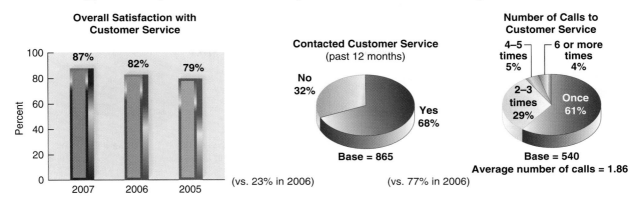

Overall Satisfaction with Customer Service

87% (2007)
82% (2006)
79% (2005)

(vs. 23% in 2006)

Contacted Customer Service
(past 12 months)

No 32%
Yes 68%

Base = 865

(vs. 77% in 2006)

Number of Calls to Customer Service

4–5 times 5%
6 or more times 4%
2–3 times 29%
Once 61%

Base = 540
Average number of calls = 1.86

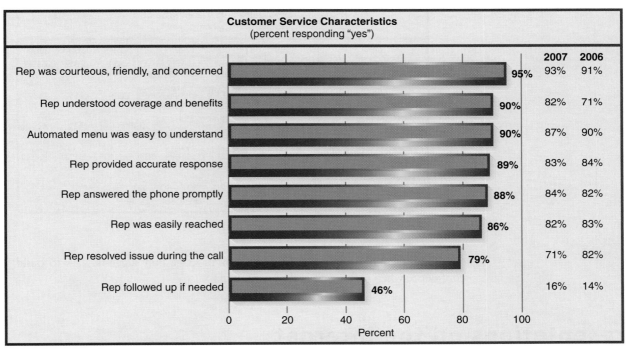

Customer Service Characteristics
(percent responding "yes")

		2007	2006
Rep was courteous, friendly, and concerned	95%	93%	91%
Rep understood coverage and benefits	90%	82%	71%
Automated menu was easy to understand	90%	87%	90%
Rep provided accurate response	89%	83%	84%
Rep answered the phone promptly	88%	84%	82%
Rep was easily reached	86%	82%	83%
Rep resolved issue during the call	79%	71%	82%
Rep followed up if needed	46%	16%	14%

Percent

Reasons Customer Service was Contacted
(top six reasons)

	2007	2006
To obtain coverage information	41%	38%
To obtain claim problem/resolution information	36%	40%
To inquire about how to file a claim	33%	34%
To determine claim status	26%	28%
To get information on policy renewal	24%	24%
To request a new policy	18%	27%

Exhibit 18.6

Multiple Measures on a Single Satisfaction Item Conveyed on a Single Page

Overall Satisfaction with Claim Process*

79% (2007), 76% (2006), 72% (2005)

(vs. 46% in 2006)

*Percent responding *excellent*, *very good*, or *good*

Customer Filed Claim
(past 12 months)

No 57%   Yes 43%

Base = 852   (vs. 54% in 2006)

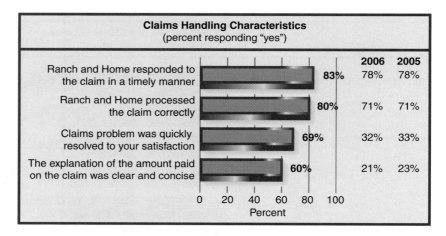

Claims Handling Characteristics (percent responding "yes")		2006	2005
Ranch and Home responded to the claim in a timely manner	83%	78%	78%
Ranch and Home processed the claim correctly	80%	71%	71%
Claims problem was quickly resolved to your satisfaction	69%	32%	33%
The explanation of the amount paid on the claim was clear and concise	60%	21%	23%

The Practicing Marketing Research box on page 603 suggests ways to build your confidence when making an oral presentation.

Presentations on the Internet

With PowerPoint, publishing presentations to the Web is easier than ever. Publication to the Web enables individuals to access the presentation, regardless of where they are or when they need to access it. In addition, researchers can present results at multiple locations on the Internet. The steps are very simple:

1. Open your presentation in PowerPoint. To see what your slides will look like on the Web, choose "Web Page Preview" from the "File" menu. After you have made any edits, choose "Save as Web Page" from the same menu.

2. The "Save As" dialog box allows you to change the title of your presentation to whatever you want displayed in the title bar of your visitor's browser.

3. The "Publish" button takes you to the "Publish as Web Page" dialog box, where you can customize your presentation.

4. The "Web Options" dialog box lets you specify the way your published file will be stored on the Web server and whether to update internal links to these files automatically.

PRACTICING MARKETING RESEARCH

Presenting More Confidently

Seize the opportunity. A key building block for developing confidence as a speaker is to speak, and speak often. Seize every opportunity you can, personally and professionally, to speak in public.

Use the "as if" principle. If your goal is to be a persuasive presenter, then start acting "as if" you are. Dress, speak, and behave like a confident speaker.

Realize you are an expert. If you have been asked to give a presentation, then there is probably a reason. Namely, people perceive you to be an expert or an authority on a subject, and they want to hear what you have to say. Trust yourself as a presenter, and you'll project confidence.

Meet your audience before you present. A good way to build confidence is to arrive early and, as guests enter the room, introduce yourself, shake hands, and look them in the eye. This will help you get rid of your nervousness, and it sets the stage for a relaxed, natural delivery.

Visualize your success. Before you present, mentally walk yourself and your emotions through your presentation. See yourself speaking with confidence and poise; hear yourself speaking with eloquence; feel your energy as you stand before an enthusiastic audience.

Make anxiety your ally. Anxiety is natural for most people before a presentation. This is nature's way of preparing you for action. You need to learn to use it effectively. Those jittery feelings provide the basis for a dynamic presentation— they increase your energy, heighten your awareness, and sharpen your intellect.

Rehearse, rehearse, rehearse. Rehearsal helps you to get to the point where you can make a presentation without thinking about doing it. It familiarizes your mind and body with the mechanics of presenting and frees you to focus on the message, not the way you deliver it.

Remember that your audience wants you to succeed. Remember that you and your audience are on the same team, moving together toward a solution. When you give a winning presentation, they win too.[2]

Creating good research that will be acted upon by clients requires effective management of the marketing research function. In the remaining portion of the chapter we address managing a marketing research firm (supplier) and managing a research department in a client firm such as McDonald's or Procter & Gamble.

Marketing Research Supplier Management

What Do Clients Want?

Managing a marketing research supplier organization involves understanding what clients want and expect, maintaining good communications with the client, effectively managing the research process, and good time management, cost management, and client profitability management. If a marketing research department in a large organization is conducting its own research, then it will also face these same managerial issues. If it farms out its research, then good management requires selecting the right vendor. A research department must also try to become less of an "order-taker" and play a greater role in the marketing decision-making process within the organization. First, we will discuss managing a marketing research supplier organization and then describe additional managerial issues associated with managing a marketing research department.

Market Directions, a marketing research firm in Kansas City, Missouri, asked marketing research clients across the United States to rate the importance of several statements about research companies and research departments. Replies from a wide range of industries are summarized in the following top-10 list:

1. Maintains client confidentiality.
2. Is honest.
3. Is punctual.
4. Is flexible.
5. Delivers against project specifications.
6. Provides high-quality output.
7. Is responsive to the client's needs.
8. Has high quality-control standards.
9. Is customer-oriented in interactions with client.
10. Keeps the client informed throughout a project.[3]

The two most important factors, confidentiality and honesty, are ethical issue, which were covered earlier in the text. The remaining issues relate to managing the research function and maintaining good communication.

Communication

The key to good supplier–client relations is excellent communication. Every project should have a liaison who serves as a communication link between the supplier and the client. In large firms, this individual may be an account executive or project manager, while in small firms, he or she may be an owner or partner. But, whatever the job title, the liaison must communicate accurately, honestly, and frequently with the client.

Before a project begins, the communication liaison should go over the project objectives, methodology, and timing with the client to make certain that there are no misunderstandings. The client should then sign off on the questionnaire, thereby agreeing that the questionnaire is sufficient to gather the raw data needed to accomplish the research objectives.

John Colias, vice president of MARC Research, says the following about communication between a research supplier and its client:

> **research management**
> Overseeing the development of excellent communication systems, data quality, time schedules, cost controls, client profitability, and staff development.

When a company hires a market research firm to design a study, the supplier must operate as part of the team of researchers and marketers. To be an effective member of the team, the supplier must also intimately understand the marketing questions. This understanding results from interactive dialogue among the researcher, marketer, and the supplier about the marketing questions and business decisions. Such a dialogue crystallizes the research objectives into concrete deliverables that directly influence business decisions.[4]

The liaison must ascertain how often the client wants progress reports. At a minimum, these reports should be issued weekly. The report should cover the status of the project, unusual problems encountered, and, if it is a cost-plus project, expenses incurred to date. *Cost-plus* refers to actual costs plus an additional markup to cover overhead.

Cost-plus projects are typically found in situations where a research department of a large corporation, such as Ford Motors, conducts a project for another department.

Managing the Research Process

Research management has seven important goals beyond excellent communication: building an effective organization, assurance of data quality, adherence to time schedules, cost control, client profitability management, and staff management and development.

Organizing the Supplier Firm Traditionally, most marketing research firms were organized around functions. Large suppliers, for example, may have separate departments for sampling, questionnaire programming, field, coding, tabulation, statistics, and sales. Even the client service staff may be separate from those who manage projects and write questionnaires and reports. Each of these departments has a head who is expert in the functions of that department and manages work assignments within the department. Projects flow from department to department.

A functional form of organization allows technical people to perform backroom tasks such as programming and data analysis and the "people people" to handle project management and client contact. It provides for knowledgeable supervision, so that, for example, beginners in tabulation are working under the direction of veteran experts. It permits the development of good work processes and quality standards, so that tasks are performed consistently. It lets the difficulty of a given project be matched with the skill of the person doing it, so that routine work is given to junior staff and the most complex tasks are reserved for the expert. This matching of work and skill levels leads to happier staff and lower project costs.

Yet functional organizations are not without their problems. Department staff can become focused on the execution of their task, to the detriment of the whole process and the client. Departmental standards and scheduling policies may take on lives of their own, optimizing the efficiency and quality of a department's work but making timely completion of the whole project difficult. By becoming removed from client contact, departments can become inwardly oriented, viewing clients as problems rather than the source of their livelihood. Interdepartmental communication and scheduling can become time-consuming and flawed, as project managers or operations schedulers negotiate each project's schedule with a series of independent department heads. Each department may feel that it is performing perfectly, yet the whole process viewed from the outside can seem rigid, bureaucratic, and ineffective.

In response to problems like these, some companies are organizing by teams. They are breaking up functional departments and organizing their staff into units based around client groups or research types. These teams include people with all or most of the skills necessary to complete a study from beginning to end. A typical team might include several client service/project management people, a field director, a questionnaire programmer, and a tab specwriter. Staff are frequently cross-trained in multiple functions. The team is almost always headed by a senior staff member with a client service or project management background.

There are many variations on this theme. Within the teams, work may remain specialized (the specwriter does the tables), or there can be extensive cross-training (everyone does tables). Highly specialized functions (such as statistical analysis) that are carried out by one or two experts may remain as functional departments, available to all. A hybrid approach is also possible, where some functions are moved within the teams, while others (such as field management) remain as separate departments.

Because each client group controls its own resources, scheduling and communication are easier. With no department heads or central scheduling to go through, the group

PRACTICING MARKETING RESEARCH

Doing High-Quality Work—On Time

Here are seven tips on time management for marketing management project research directors.

Manage expectations. Most job descriptions for project directors mention writing skills, facility with mathematics, organizational ability, and experience with presentations, but managing expectations may be the most critical skill to master. If you're pretty sure that the work will be done by Thursday, don't say you're "shooting for Wednesday." You're better off promising Friday and giving yourself a chance to be a hero.

Think about priorities. When the client has a crisis, sometimes you just have to drop everything and help out. Clients are, after all, the ones paying our salaries. Even without a crisis, however, it doesn't hurt to think about your priorities. The time-management books suggest concentrating on the most important tasks only, and ignoring the others until they too join the "most important" list. If you don't mind a messy desk, this is pretty good advice.

Think about leverage. What if the client is not in crisis mode, but you still have 10 things to do? Concentrate first on the tasks that require contributions from others. If the interviewers are waiting for your briefing or the data processing people are waiting for your codes, then everyone's work is backing up.

Provide regular updates. It is amazing how many games of voice-mail tag can be avoided by filling out a simple form. Set up a form that you can fax or e-mail every day explaining how many interviews have been finished, where the incidence is coming out, how you are doing on interview length, and whatever other facts your client requires. If you are working with 10 field services on a study, get them to fill out update forms too—this saves you another 10 calls a day.

Be on the lookout for problems. A statistician I worked with used to say, "All lists are bad"—actually, he used a stronger term—"the trick is to find out why this particular list is bad." Project directing is problem solving. Incidence estimates will be off, questionnaires will be too long, respondents will be uncooperative, and lists will be, uh, bad. Spending a little extra time on instructions, briefings, and safety checks today will save a lot of extra work tomorrow.

When you discover a problem, let the client know quickly. You can stick a problem in a folder for a day or two, but it's not likely to solve itself. The sooner the client hears about the problem, the sooner he or she can adjust schedules or budgets. In my experience, you can almost always go back to a client—once—to discuss changes in specifications, schedules, and budgets. But you need to bring these issues up early, when your client still has some flexibility. Surprises at the 11th hour are both painful and time-consuming for everyone.

If you need to bring up a problem, don't be afraid to suggest some solutions as well. Suggesting solutions will help to solve the issue quickly and efficiently. As a general rule, the range of possible solutions is not hard to come up with. The following should cover about 80 percent of all of the possible problems:

☐ Order more sample.
☐ Change the screening criteria.
☐ Raise the incentives.
☐ Rebrief the interviewers.
☐ Reschedule the focus groups.
☐ Reduce the number of interviews.
☐ Lengthen the interviewing schedule.
☐ Increase the budget.

The challenge is in getting beyond the issue of who is to blame and determining which solution will work best this time.[6]

head directly prioritizes the work of everyone working on his or her projects.

Technical and operations personnel become closer to clients and more aligned with their needs. By reducing the organizational distance between the client and these staff members, it is easier for them to appreciate the client's situation and focus on serving his or her needs.

Staff may develop more flexibility and broader skills. Cross-training and cross-assignment of work are easier when all the people involved report to the same person.[5]

Data Quality Management   Perhaps the most important objective of research management is to ensure the quality or integrity of the data produced by the research process. You have probably heard announcers on television say, "The poll had a margin of error of 3 percent." Some problems and implicit assumptions are associated with this statement. First, you learned in the discussion of sampling error in Chapter 12 that this statement is missing an associated level of confidence. In other words, how confident are the pollsters that the poll has a margin of error of 3 percent? Are they 68.26 percent confident, 95.44 percent confident, 99.74 percent confident, or confident at some other level? Second, this statement does not make clear that the margin of error applies only to *random sampling error.* The implicit, or unstated, assumption is that there are no other sources of error, that all other sources of error have been effectively dealt with by the research design and procedures, or that all other sources of error have been effectively randomized by taking summary measures across the entire sample. By definition, error is random when there are just as many errors in one direction as in the other direction, leaving overall measures, such as averages, unaffected. Marketing research managers can help assure high-quality data by having policies and procedures in place to minimize sources of error (see Chapter 6).

Effective time management is becoming increasingly important in all aspects of professional life. One requirement of research management is to keep a project on the schedule specified by the client.

Managers must also have in place procedures to ensure the careful proofing of all text, charts, and graphs in written reports and other communications provided to the client. Mistakes may mislead a client into making the wrong decision. Suppose the data suggest purchase intent at 25 percent but the report shows 52 percent; this typographical mistake could easily lead to an incorrect decision. If the client finds even small mistakes, the credibility of the researcher and all of the research findings may be brought into serious question. The rule of thumb is to never provide information to the client that has not been very carefully checked.

Time Management   A second goal of research management is to keep the project on schedule. Time management is important in marketing research because clients often have a specified time schedule that they must meet. For example, it may be absolutely imperative that the research results be available on March 1 so that they can be presented at the quarterly meeting of the new product committee. The findings will affect whether the test product will receive additional funding for development.

Two problems that can play havoc with time schedules are inaccuracies in estimates of the incidence rate and the interview length. A lower-than-expected incidence rate will require more interviewing resources than originally planned to get the job done on time. If the research manager does not have idle resources to devote to the project, then it will take longer to complete. The same is true for a longer-than-anticipated interview.

Recall that the *incidence rate* is the percentage of persons or households out of the general population that fit the qualifications to be interviewed in a particular study. Often, estimates of incidence rate are based not on hard-and-fast data but on data that are incomplete, known to be relatively inaccurate, or dated. Incidence rate problems cannot only increase the amount of time required to complete the sample for the project but also negatively affect the costs of the data collection phase of the research.

The project manager must have early information regarding whether or not a project can be completed on time. If a problem exists, the manager must first determine whether anything can be done to speed up the process. Perhaps training additional interviewers would help expedite completion of the survey. Second, the researcher must inform the client that the project is going to take longer than expected. The researcher can then explore with the client whether a time extension is possible or what changes the client might be willing to make to get the project completed on the original time schedule. For example, the client might be willing to reduce the total sample size or shorten the length of the interview by eliminating questions that are judged to be less critical. Thus, it is very important that the system be structured so that both the researcher and the client are alerted to potential problems within the first few days of the project.

Time management, like cost control, requires that systems be put in place to inform management as to whether or not the project is on schedule. Policies and procedures must be established to efficiently and quickly solve schedule problems and promptly notify the client about the problem and potential solutions. In the Practicing Marketing Research feature, Joshua Libresco, executive vice president of OSR Group, a marketing research firm in San Rafael, California, offers several tips on how overworked marketing research project directors can better manage their time and still provide high-quality work. A second box explains how to do quality work in a timely manner.

Cost Management   In comparison to data quality and time management, cost management is straightforward. All it requires is adherence to good business practices, such as procedures for cost tracking and control. In particular, good procedures for cost control include the following elements:

- ☐ Systems that accurately capture data-collection and other costs associated with the project on a daily basis.

- ☐ Daily reporting of costs to the communication liaison. Ideally, reports should show actual costs in relation to budget.

- ☐ Policies and practices in the research organization that require the liaison to communicate the budget picture to clients and to senior managers at the research company.

- ☐ Policies and practices that quickly identify overbudget situations and then find causes and seek solutions.

If the project is over budget because the client provided information that proved to be erroneous (for example, incidence rate, interview length), then it is imperative that the client be offered options early in the process: a higher cost, smaller sample size, shorter interview, or some combination of these. If the firm waits until the project is complete to communicate this problem to the client, the client is likely to say, "You should have told me sooner—there is nothing I can do now." In this situation, the firm will probably have to swallow the cost overrun.

Michael Mitrano, a partner in Transition Strategies Corporation, a management consulting firm, discusses managing a marketing research firm for profitability in the following Practicing Marketing Research feature.

Client Profitability Management

While marketing research departments may be able to focus on doing "on demand" projects for internal clients, marketing research suppliers have to think about profitability. The old adage that 20 percent of the clients generate 80 percent of the profits is often true.

PRACTICING MARKETING RESEARCH

Managing a Marketing Research Firm for Profitability

Good financial systems are very helpful in managing for profitability, but they aren't sufficient. Even more important, in my experience, is business focus. There are some very profitable businesses in this industry that have fairly basic financial information, and many companies with extensive financial data and even more extensive losses. The key is what you do with the information you have.

Owners of most profitable research companies manage them for profit. That doesn't mean they are bad researchers, or ruthless, or cheap. It does mean that the CEO or partners recognize that they are running a business first and foremost. How does this show?

- [ ] They hold senior staff accountable for project or account profitability in a firm but fair way.
- [ ] They accept unfavorable financial information and act on it, rather than trying to argue it away or change the metric so that unprofitable activity looks profitable.
- [ ] They are willing to make the hard decisions to let people go who can't deliver acceptable sales or manage a study on budget. They will make the even harder decision to exit a client relationship that can't be made profitable rather than hanging on forever in hope.
- [ ] They know what their findings and recommendations are worth to clients, and price to that value rather than looking solely at cost.
- [ ] They believe in the value of their company's work and the fairness of its prices, and don't back down quickly when faced with price pressure.[7]

Custom Research Incorporated (CRI), of Minneapolis, realized a few years back that it had too many clients—or too few good ones.[8] The company divided its clients into four categories based on the client's perceived value to CRI's bottom line (see Exhibit 18.7). Only 10 of CRI's 157 customers fell into the most desirable category (generating a high dollar volume and a high profit margin). Another 101 customers contributed very little to the top or bottom line. In short, CRI was spending too much time and too many valuable employee resources on too many unprofitable customers.

In assessing which customers to keep, CRI calculated the profit for each one by subtracting all direct costs and selling expenses from the total revenues brought into CRI by that customer for the year. That is, CRI asked, "What costs would we not incur if this customer went away?" The cut-off points for high and low scores were purely subjective; they corresponded to CRI's goals for profit volume and profit margin. CRI management decided that it had to systematically drop a large number of old customers and carefully screen potential new customers. CRI's screening questions for new customers are shown in Exhibit 18.8.

Using the customers analysis, CRI went from 157 customers and $11 million in revenue to 78 customers and $30 million in revenue. Most importantly, profits more than doubled. Managers had calculated they'd need to reap about 20 to 30 percent more business from some two dozen companies to help make up for the roughly 100 customers they planned to "let go" within 2 years. This was accomplished by building a close personal relationship with the clients that remained. The process involved CRI's researching the industry, the client company, and its research personnel to fully understand the client's needs. For each client, CRI created a Surprise and Delight plan to deliver a

Exhibit 18.7

CRI's Client Profitability Analysis

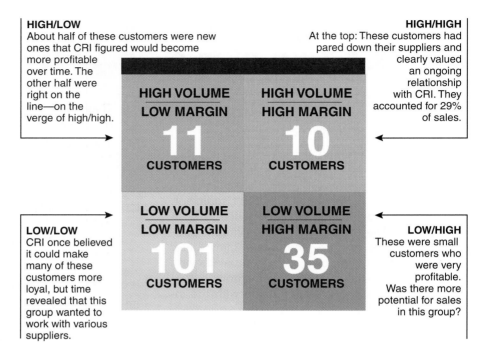

HIGH/LOW
About half of these customers were new ones that CRI figured would become more profitable over time. The other half were right on the line—on the verge of high/high.

HIGH/HIGH
At the top: These customers had pared down their suppliers and clearly valued an ongoing relationship with CRI. They accounted for 29% of sales.

HIGH VOLUME LOW MARGIN
11 CUSTOMERS

HIGH VOLUME HIGH MARGIN
10 CUSTOMERS

LOW VOLUME LOW MARGIN
101 CUSTOMERS

LOW VOLUME HIGH MARGIN
35 CUSTOMERS

LOW/LOW
CRI once believed it could make many of these customers more loyal, but time revealed that this group wanted to work with various suppliers.

LOW/HIGH
These were small customers who were very profitable. Was there more potential for sales in this group?

EXHIBIT 18.8	Screening Questions Used by CRI and the Rationale for Each Question
Question	**Rationale**
How did you hear about us?	A bad answer: "I found you in the Yellow Pages." Unlike many companies, CRI doesn't ask this question so that it can decide how to divvy up the marketing dollars. "If someone finds us in the Yellow Pages, they have no reason to use us over anyone else," CRI cofounder Judy Corson explains. A good answer: "A colleague of mine worked with you at another company."
What kind of work is it (in terms of industry or scope)?	More than anything, the answer reveals whether the caller is trying to price a quick, one-time project or one that's totally outside CRI's realm. If so, the caller is referred to an indirect competitor.
What's your budget?	That's akin to asking someone how much money he or she makes, but the prospect's response to a ballpark guess on the cost of the project helps CRI ascertain what the client has in mind.
What are your decision criteria?	CRI knows that it doesn't fare well in blind bidding or in drawn-out, committee-style decisions, so it's interested in dealing with callers who have some level of decision-making power—and assiduously avoids getting involved in anything that smells like a bidding war.
Whom are we competing against for your business?	CRI likes to hear the names of its chief rivals, a half-dozen large companies, including the M/A/R/C Group, Market Facts, and Burke Marketing Research.
Why are you thinking of switching?	"There's a two-edged sword here," explains cofounder Jeff Pope. "Clients that are hard to break into are better because they don't switch too easily. But you need a way to get in—so a legitimate need for a new supplier is OK." Each month only 2 or 3 of 20 to 30 callers answer enough questions correctly to warrant more attention. So why spend time with the rest? "Do unto others. . . . You never know where people will go."

Source: Susan Greco, "Choose or Lose," *INC.* (December 1998), pp. 57–59, 62–66.

"value-added" bonus to the client. For example, Dow Brands received some complimentary software that CRI knew the company needed. This one-on-one relationship marketing has been the key to CRI's success.

Staff Management and Development

The primary asset of any marketing research firm is its people. Proprietary techniques and models can help differentiate a marketing research company, but eventually its success depends on the professional nature of its staff and their determination to deliver a quality product. Consequently, recruiting and retaining a competent, enthusiastic staff are crucial and constant management challenges.

Kathleen Knight is president and CEO of BAIGlobal, Incorporated, a Tarrytown, New York, marketing research firm. She offers several suggestions for staff development in a research firm:

1. *Create an environment that encourages risk taking, experimentation, and responsibility.* The benefits to the research firm, such as new service development, new techniques, and business growth, outweigh any potential risks. However, employees need to feel that they will be supported in taking risks. New ideas and different business approaches need to be treated with respect and given room to develop.

2. *Foster recognition and accountability.* Recognize good effort and reward it. One of the best forms of reward is visibility within the company. Make sure that everyone knows when an outstanding job was done and that excellence matters.

3. *Provide job autonomy within a certain structure.* Marketing research is a technical science, and the numbers have to add up. But it also is a business, and projects have to generate money to pay the bills. Within these boundaries, there are many different ways to get the job done. Let employees put their personal stamp on a project and they will feel like true partners in their work.

4. *Attract and support people with entrepreneurial attitudes.* Set business goals and management parameters; then let the staff determine the path to take to get the job done. This allows each person to leverage his or her own abilities and achieve the highest level of success.

5. *Connect rewards to a business result.* Providing open financial data to researchers seems to create a business consciousness that is exciting for all. Often, very talented researchers know little about the financial dynamics of the industry. They welcome the chance to learn and thus become more accountable for bottom-line results.

6. *Open your financial books.* Research firms can provide senior employees with full financial information to let them know how well they are doing across the months and years. The bottom line is the best aggregate measure of performance—individually, as a group, and as a firm. Opening the books establishes a common mission and goal across the organization.

7. *Offer diversity within your organization.* It's fun and exciting to learn new products, serve new clients, and work with a new research team. A chance at a new position is often the spark someone needs to really do well within a firm. And the possibility of this kind of job change seems to add to the satisfaction that employees feel. If you pay attention to individuals and create a career path across disciplines within your organization, it's more likely that talented researchers will stay.

8. *Provide clear promotional paths.* Employees like to know how they can advance and want to feel some control over their careers. Clear criteria and expectations go a long way toward helping researchers feel comfortable. In the marketing research business,

FROM THE FRONT LINE

Tips for Managing Difficult Clients

Tammy Austin, VP Marketing, DSS Research

Anyone who has worked in the business of marketing research knows that it is a gratifying process to work with clients—most of them, at least. Managing difficult clients can be stressful but rewarding when handled properly. Here are some tips for turning potentially disastrous projects into successful ones.

- **Listen.** Listen carefully to your client about the project. This allows you to identify client needs and understand their objectives. Ask questions calmly and pay attention to their answers. Recognizing different viewpoints will often prevent any aggressive conduct from a client.

- **Keep detailed notes.** Document all specifications and milestones for both parties, so that everything is detailed in writing and can be used later as a reference. Keep detailed records of all communication with difficult clients and of steps taken to address their concerns. Write an action plan to prevent any future issues or misunderstandings. Maintain a log of items to be addressed (based on the schedule and ad hoc client requests) and who should deal with them and by when. Competent recordkeeping is critical in keeping the client focused, and it helps you address any unanticipated issues. Depending on the project, hold weekly or monthly review meetings of the issues log (these can be conference calls) to keep the communication lines open and the project on track.

- **Be flexible.** You may have to compromise to work out satisfying outcomes for your client.

- **Take the client's point of view.** Be proactive and focus on client needs. Try to see things from their point of view and speak their language. Using procedural/methodological terminology can be confusing to clients and can interfere with good communication.

- **Solve problems.** Don't blame the client; look for solutions. The ultimate priority is to agree on a mutually beneficial solution rather than win an argument.

- **Follow up.** Follow up on problem resolution to make sure the client is content. Even if you do not want repeat business from this client, you don't want them to have negative feelings toward your company. The marketing research industry is small, and problems left unsolved or solved unprofessionally can damage your company's reputation.

the best training is as an apprentice, working with senior researchers doing interesting work. Talented people will grow and prosper where the expectations are that senior managers will be mentors, that junior staff will learn, and that excellent work produced together will lead to everyone's career advancement.[9]

Managing a Marketing Research Department

When a marketing research department decides to not do the research in-house, then a research supplier must be selected. A second global issue facing research departments is the role they will play, if any, in management decision making. Finally, more and more companies are trying to determine what amount of return they are earning on the marketing research formation. Each of these issues is discussed below.

Selecting the Right Marketing Research Suppliers

Once the nature, scope, and objectives of the project have been determined, the second step is to assess the capabilities of alternative suppliers. Some research vendors have a particular area of specialization. There are firms that specialize in advertising or customer satisfaction research, while there are others who are devoted to a particular technique (for example, conjoint analysis or market segmentation) or data-collection method (for example, mall intercepts, mail surveys, or Internet surveys).

A research department manager should beware of firms committed to a particular technique and/or data-collection method, as they are more likely to "force" the department's research project into their particular model, rather than tailor the research to fit the specific needs of the research department's project.

Research department managers must consider the size of the firms in their decision. The size of the vendor is an extremely important decision criterion. It is important not to overwhelm a small firm with an enormous project, and, conversely, a small project may not get the proper attention at a large firm.

The general rule is to favor the smallest firm consistent with the scope of the project. However, any project that is 30 percent or more of a marketing research supplier's annual revenues may be too large for that firm to handle effectively.

The research department manager should establish, up front, the individual who will be managing the project. It should be determined in advance who would be responsible for the day-to-day management of the project; that is, will it be the person who "sold" the project or a project director hundreds of miles away? If the contact becomes unavailable, will competent support staff be available?

The research department manager needs to become acquainted with the backgrounds of the potential vendors. There are some general questions that every potential vendor should be asked to determine the stability of the company and its qualifications to complete the project in a satisfactory manner. These questions would include:

☐ How long has the vendor been in business?

☐ For what other companies has the vendor conducted research projects? Remember it is imperative to request references and check them for each firm.

☐ What are the academic backgrounds and experience of those persons who will be working on the project, that is, the project director, field director, data processing manager, and so forth? Does the composition of the project team strike the right balance between top-level management and technical researchers and analysts?

☐ Does the success of the project depend on the capabilities of a subcontractor? If the marketing research supplier will be subcontracting any elements of the project, it is important that the subcontractor and his or her qualifications be identified.

Also, the research manager should review the quality control standards of each potential vendor. The validity of the results of any research project is dependent on the quality control measures practiced by the vendor. For example, on telephone studies, what are the procedures with respect to callbacks, monitoring, and validation? It is prudent to avoid firms that do not practice generally accepted practices in their operations.

The reputations of the firms must be considered in the decision. Reputation is important, but a department should not pay a larger premium for it. However, there may be situations that require the services of a prestigious research firm because a company plans to publicize the results, or use them in advertisements, so having the best reputation available may actually be a good investment. For example, Dell touts its standings in J.D. Power Customer Satisfaction surveys.

Finally, a manager should avoid letting price be the sole determining factor in the selection. When reviewing proposals, price should be the last item to be considered.[10]

Moving Marketing Research into a Decision-Making Role

A more strategic managerial question regarding the marketing research department is the role and importance of marketing research in the managerial decision-making process. The researchers' challenge is to shed their long-held traditional role as a support function, one that reacts to requests from project and new product development managers and then focuses on producing the numbers but not on their meaning to the business.

"There's a gap between what research believes it's capable of providing and what top management perceives it can get from research," says Larry Stanek, senior associate of the Hartman Group, located in Bellevue, Washington. "Researchers believe they have answers critical to decision-making, while management views research as having the data but maybe not the insight to drive business."[11]

Experts agree that, to earn the ear of senior management, researchers must move beyond the task of simply crunching numbers and churning out results; they need to understand the underlying business issues at stake and adjust the information they gather and how they analyze it. They also must reach out to other departments, building relationships and a better understanding of the issues companywide.

Experts also suggest that researchers should spend more time discussing the decisions that need to be made with the results before designing and conducting a study—to avoid a that's-nice-to-know-but-I-really-need-this-*other* information response from management. And when it comes to reporting results, researchers must translate the numbers into specific recommendations and even link the findings to other data that management typically uses to make decisions. Not surprisingly, researchers agree that securing a seat at the table not only demands strong analytical abilities, but also so-called softer skills in persuasion, communication, and presentation.

"I strongly emphasize that while [the research managers and associates] may be in my official marketing research department—it's my insistence that they view themselves as members of the business team" first and foremost, says Daryl Papp, Lilly's director of U.S. market research. He adds that about half of his department comprises professionals who come from areas of marketing other than research for a several-year "broadening assignment" to learn about the company's businesses. Papp believes that having marketing researchers sit side by side with other colleagues who aspire to high-level management helps contribute to the business-oriented mentality in his department.[12]

Most firms rely on marketing research departments to provide data to the brand marketing and sales teams so that successes can be achieved in many areas, including new product launches, brand management and stewardship, the efficiency of marketing operations, and advertising effectiveness. In this context, the marketing researcher participates on a team charged with accomplishing an objective for the firm. The great majority of a firm's marketing research activities fall into this category. At this stage, the question of whether the objective or initiative has merit is already decided. The marketing researcher helps the team make decisions about the most efficient and effective ways to spend its limited marketing funds to achieve the greatest result. This is not limited to new product initiatives. These activities include tracking studies, usage and attitude studies, copy testing and advertising research, sales promotion evaluation, sales analysis, strategic positioning studies, and many more.[13]

In order to influence senior management, the marketing researcher needs to move beyond fulfilling research assignments designed to avoid failure or enable success. When marketing researchers look beyond already-generated ideas and already-created products, services, ads, or distribution channels, their strategic value increases. And this begins to attract management's attention. Management places high value on this activity because companies need growth, which has become exceedingly hard to achieve. At its best, marketing research redefines business strategy by using data in novel ways to create a sustainable competitive advantage (see Exhibit 18.9).[14]

Measuring Marketing Research's Return on Investment (ROI) The old view of marketing as an art form disappeared long ago. In its place is the notion of strict accountability. Marketing expenditures become investments, with performance measures coming from the world of finance. So it has become increasingly fashionable in large corporations to demand that marketing research prove its worth. The approach that is gaining in popularity is ROI. Recall that ROI is simply the after-tax income from an investment divided by the dollar amount of the investment. Several arguments can be made against using ROI to measure the value of marketing research to an organization.

> **First**, ROI is theoretically flawed because it divides the profit return by the expenditure instead of subtracting it. All reputable bottom-line metrics, such as profit, cash flow, payback, and shareholder value, subtract expenditure from income. Dividing one into the other distorts the result.

EXHIBIT 18.9 A Researcher's Route to the Table

	Area of Influence	Key Contribution	How
On the Management Radar	Transforming the Business	Discovering new and better business strategies	Innovating with data.
	Discovering Opportunities	Finding new opportunities or products to become passionate about	Using data to spot the next trend. Assessing failures and learning from them. Helping creators to innovate through better input from the marketplace.
Below the Management Radar	Enabling Success	Serving as a passionate member of the team	Researching the market and customers to improve marketing for existing products. Using research to achieve greatest leverage at lowest cost. Overcoming obstacles to shorten time lines, finding conclusions faster.
	Avoiding Failure	Remaining objective so team passion can be channeled into the right initiatives	At minimum, preventing the firm from making errors. Proving the potential of great new ideas. Quickly and accurately predicting marketplace success.

Source: John Huppertz, "Passion vs. Dispassion," *Marketing Research* (Summer 2003), p. 21.

Second, ROI was invented to compare alternative uses of capital, based on their projected percentage return on that capital. Market research, however, is usually a stream of costs that continue for the purposes of comparison in each and every year. Market research (MR) is rarely an investment in the true sense of the word.

Third, improving ROI tends to suboptimize expenditure. Most investments have diminishing profit returns. The early profits give the greatest ROI, but maximizing productivity (i.e., total profit return) requires more expenditure beyond that. Would you rather, at the same low level of risk, have a 100 percent return on $2 or an 80 percent return on $1,000? This objection arises directly from the division rather than subtraction anomaly.

Fourth, ROI usually focuses on the short term and does not consider the effects on the marketing asset (brand equity) or the dynamic development of marketing over longer time periods.

Fifth, the purpose of the ROI ratio is to compare alternative expenditures. Research is not really an alternative to the elements of the marketing mix it should control. Such a comparison does not contrast like with like. Internal information, such as the management accounts or budgets, is a closer comparison as it fights with marketing metrics for space on the dashboard used by top management to help drive the business. And yet when did anyone call for the ROI on the internal accounting function?[15]

Despite the negatives, the growing popularity of ROI deserves further examination into how it can be operationalized. Two approaches are ROI Lite and ROI Complete created by Dawn Lesh, president of New York-based A. Dawn Lesh International, and Diane Schmalensee, president of Schmalensee Partners in Chestnut Hill, Massachusetts.[16]

ROI Lite.   To measure ROI Lite, MR asks the client for two estimates during preproject planning:

1.   The anticipated dollar value of the decision that will be based on the research.

2.   The anticipated increase in confidence of making the "right" decision. For example, instead of saying a decision is worth $10 million, a client might say it's worth $8 million to $12 million. Or a client could say he or she expects his or her confidence to rise 40 to 60 percent.

With the answers to these questions, MR can calculate the expected ROI Lite using the following formula.

$$\text{ROI Lite} = \frac{\$ \text{ Value} \times \text{Increased Confidence}}{\text{Cost of Research}}$$

For example, assume a firm has to decide which of five creative approaches to use in a $2 million advertising campaign.

☐   Since it is uncertain how the advertising will affect sales, the firm decides to use the $2 million campaign cost as the value estimate.

☐   No one knows which of the five approaches is best, so the confidence of randomly picking the best one is only 20 percent.

☐   The firm believes that after the research it will be 80 percent confident of making the best decision (an increase of 60 percent).

☐   The cost of the copy testing is $250,000.

$$\text{ROI Lite} = \frac{\$2\text{M} \times 60\%}{\$250\text{K}} = \frac{\$1.2\text{M}}{\$250\text{K}} = 480\%$$

This ROI Lite discussion can help determine how much to invest in the research. If the dollar value of a decision is small or the expected decrease in uncertainty is low, then the budget should be kept small. After the research is completed, MR meets again with the client to revise the ROI Lite estimate in light of what was learned.

ROI Complete   ROI Complete is similar to ROI Lite except that it adds the concept of the likelihood of taking action. MR and the client discuss the estimated likelihood of taking action with and without the research. If the firm usually acts without research, then MR may not be able to raise the likelihood of acting, and the firm should not spend much money on the research. However, if the firm seldom acts without research, then the research is more valuable.

The following equation is used:

$$\text{ROI Complete} = \frac{\$ \text{ Value} \times \text{Increased Confidence} \times \text{Increased Likelihood of Acting}}{\text{Cost of Research}}$$

For example, suppose the decision is whether or not to enter a new market.

☐   Costs (including research, manufacturing, and marketing) are estimated to be $20 million, and potential revenue is estimated at $50 million in the first year. The client and MR agree to use the first year's net income of $30 million as the expected dollar value. (Note that a few sophisticated MR departments calculate the net present value of the continuing revenue stream, but we have kept the example simple.)

☐   The executives know that entering a new market is risky. They are only 10 percent confident of making the right decision without research. With the research, they estimate that they will be 70 percent confident—an increase of 60 percent.

☐   The executives often act without research. The estimated likelihood of acting without research (based on past history) is 50 percent. They expect this would rise to 80 percent after the research—an increase of 30 percent.

☐   The cost of the research is $1 million.

☐   The firm decides to go forward with the research because there will be an anticipated positive 540 percent ROI by the end of the first year.

$$\text{ROI Complete} = \frac{\$30\text{M} \times 60\% \times 30\%}{\$1\text{M}} = \frac{\$5.4\text{M}}{\$1\text{M}} = 540\%$$

After the research is completed, MR and the client recalculate ROI.

What if the research says the firm should not enter the market? In that case, the research still has a positive ROI since it saves the firm from investing in a losing venture. Using the previous example, suppose that the research made the firm 80 percent certain it would lose its $20 million investment. Before the research, the firm was 50 percent likely to act and make a losing decision, which means the return on the research is 800 percent:

$$\text{Actual ROI} = \frac{\$20\text{M} \times 80\% \times 50\%}{\$1\text{M}} = \frac{\$8\text{M}}{\$1\text{M}} = 800\%$$

What if the research convinces the firm to avoid the market it originally preferred (as shown above) but to invest in an alternative market that would generate a new profit of $30 million in the first year? Assume the firm is 70 percent confident that the alternative is the best one (an increase of 60 percent since it had only 10 percent confidence in it before the research). Also assume that the research increases the likelihood of actually entering a new market by 30 percent. Then the ROI is even higher:

$$\text{Actual ROI} = \frac{(\$20\text{M} \times 80\% \times 50\%) + (\$30\text{M} \times 60\% \times 30\%)}{\$1\text{M}}$$

$$= \frac{\$8\text{M} + \$5.4\text{M}}{\$1\text{M}} = 1{,}340\%$$

What if the client decides not to act even though the research projects a positive outcome? This often happens when there are changes in leadership or other uses for the capital. In that case, ROI is 0 percent, but the postresearch discussion makes clear that this is the client's choice and not MR's fault.

It's not always easy to ask clients how likely they are to take action. Sometimes firms commission research simply to bless a decision that has already been made. Or firms may expect the research to increase their knowledge without necessarily leading to action. Examples of this would be new segmentation research or customer satisfaction tracking. In these cases, the likelihood of acting and the dollar value would depend entirely on what was learned. One MR director said, "Just like estimating the return on IT investments, there are so many assumptions necessary that you can never be sure your estimate will be close. For some kinds of exploratory research, you don't know until you're done whether or not it will produce anything of financial value." Because these discussions are difficult, some MR groups prefer to use ROI Lite rather than ROI Complete.[17]

SUMMARY

The six primary sections of a contemporary marketing research report are, in order: the table of contents, background and objectives, executive summary, methodology, findings, and appendixes with supporting information.

The primary objectives of the marketing research report are to state the specific research objectives, explain why and how the research was done, present the findings of the research, and provide conclusions and recommendations. Most of these elements are contained in the executive summary. The conclusions do not necessarily contain statistical numbers derived from the research but rather generalize the results in relation to the stated objectives. Nor do conclusions suggest a course of action. This is left to the recommendations, which direct the conclusions to specific marketing strategies or tactics that would place the client in the most positive position in the market.

The marketing research report of today makes heavy use of graphics to present key findings. For most researchers, PowerPoint is the software of choice for creating research reports. In terms of mechanics, reports minimize the use of words, feed information to clients in "minibites," and make extensive use of bulleted charts and graphics. In addition to the written report which is often nothing more than a copy of the PowerPoint presentation, a presentation of research results is often required. It is common for research reports to be published on the Internet by the client or by the researcher at the client's request. This has the advantage of making the results available to individuals worldwide in the client's organization. The Internet can also be used to support simultaneous presentation of the research results in multiple locations.

Supplier research marketing management has five important goals beyond excellent communication: creation of an effective organization, assurance of data quality, adherence to time schedules, cost control, client profitability management, and staff management and development. Many research firms are transitioning to a team-based organization from the traditional functional organizational structure. Marketing research managers can help assure high-quality data by attempting to minimize sources of error. Time management requires a system to notify management of potential problems and policies to solve behind-schedule problems both efficiently and quickly. Cost management demands good cost-tracking and cost control processes. Client profitability management requires that the marketing research supplier determine how much each client contributes to the researcher's overall profitability. Unprofitable clients should be dropped; marginally profitable clients should be developed into high-profit clients or dropped. The supplier should use relationship marketing to build a solid, increasingly profitable long-term relationship with clients identified as high-profit contributors. Finally, staff management and development requires that employees be encouraged to take risks and assume responsibility, be recognized for a job well done, and be offered job autonomy, financial rewards tied to business results, new challenges, and a clear career path.

Managing a marketing research department requires the same skills as managing a research supplier organization if the department is conducting its own research projects. If not, it must develop skills in selecting the right research supplier. This includes assessing competing supplier capabilities and reviewing the quality controls of each supplier. Strategically, research departments often attempt to become more than simply data gatherers. They want to become part of the decision process as well. Many companies are now measuring the ROI on marketing research. This tool, applied to marketing research, is controversial.

KEY TERMS & DEFINITIONS

executive summary Portion of a research report that explains why the research was done, what was found, what those findings mean, and what action, if any, management should undertake.

conclusions Generalizations that answer the questions raised by the research objectives or otherwise satisfy the objectives.

recommendations Conclusions applied to marketing strategies or tactics that focus on a client's achievement of differential advantage.

research management Overseeing the development of excellent communication systems, data quality, time schedules, cost controls, client profitability, and staff development.

QUESTIONS FOR REVIEW & CRITICAL THINKING

1. What are the roles of the research report? Give examples.

2. Distinguish among findings, conclusions, and recommendations in a research report.

3. Why should research reports contain executive summaries? What should be contained in an executive summary?

4. Describe four different ways a manager can help ensure high data quality.

5. What policies need to be put in place to assure that research projects are handled in a timely manner? What steps should be taken if a project falls behind schedule?

6. How can a research supplier develop its employees?

7. Should every firm conduct a client profitability study? Why?

8. What should marketing research do in order to play a more strategic role in the organization?

9. Assume that a company is trying to determine whether to enter a new market. The estimated first year's revenue is $2.2 million. Because management knows a little about this market, they are 20 percent confident that they can make the right decision without research. With research, they will be 80 percent confident. The estimated likelihood of moving into the market without research is 40 percent. This would rise to 80 percent after the research. The cost of the research is $400,000. What is the ROI after the first year?

WORKING THE NET

1. Go to *http://www.gallup.com* and examine some of the special reports on American opinions, such as those found under "Social Issues and Policy." Do these reports meet the criteria discussed in the text for good marketing research reports? Why or why not?

2. Go to *http://www.presentersuniversity.com*. Describe the different ways this organization can help an individual become a more effective speaker.

3. Go to *www.worldopinion.com* or *www.Quirks.com* find an article on managing marketing research firms. Summarize this article for the class.

REAL-LIFE RESEARCH • 18.1

Benson Research Deals with Growth

Barry Benson started his research company in 1987 in Allentown, Pennsylvania. He began with a few local clients and two employees. Interviewers were hired as subcontractors and were paid only when his clients paid Barry. In order to make ends meet, he opened several mall locations and set up a focus group facility. By taking in work as a field service as well as a full-service research company he began to grow. In 1990, his sales reached $1 million, and he had 20 employees. Today the firm has 238 employees, including over 100 full-time interviewers who work in the firm's phone room.

Barry's growth slowly led to the creation of a functional organization structure. This seemed to happen as much by chance as by design. For example, to get control over the 15 client service/salespeople, they were put into a separate department. The same thing happened with questionnaire design and programming, advanced analytics, database management, and so forth.

Barry's company has grown beyond his wildest dreams, yet all is not well in the organization. Recently, he lost a number of key people, and morale seems to be low throughout the company. Some clients have complained about late projects and unsatisfactory reports. Barry feels that some departments view clients as sources of problems rather than as the source of their livelihood. Barry has also noticed that interdepartmental communication has become very time-consuming. He has seen project managers bargaining with department heads of the tabbing department to get their project moved in front of others. Client service/sales personnel have complained about selling research and then not being able to get it done in a timely manner.

Questions

1. Barry is considering reorganizing. What should he do?
2. What are the advantages of keeping a functional organizational structure? What are the disadvantages?
3. What might he gain from a team structure? Are there any risks in moving to this form of organization?

TouchWell Tracking Research

TouchWell is a large health plan in a major metropolitan area in the western United States. TouchWell has been buffeted by all of the problems experienced by managed care organizations, including the following:

☐   Fierce competition from other plans

☐   Financial concerns associated with rising medical costs on the one hand and pressure to keep premiums low on the other hand

☐   The stream of negative publicity about HMOs and managed care plans

However, TouchWell has managed to continue to grow during this period through aggressive marketing to both business decision makers, who make choices among group health insurance plans for their employees, and consumers. Its marketing programs have been guided by an equally aggressive marketing research program. Senior managers at TouchWell are convinced that they could make better decisions if they had the information necessary to make those decisions. Their research program has included a mix of qualitative and quantitative research covering market segmentation, product testing, communications testing, and tracking research (sometimes referred to as attitude, awareness, and usage—AA&U—research).

A high-level presentation to TouchWell's senior management by Alpha Research, covering four waves of tracking research, follows. The presentation includes key measurements from the tracking research, such as unaided plan awareness, general impressions of HMOs, reasons for negative impressions, and impressions of TouchWell and key competitors.

TouchWell believes that maintaining high plan awareness is an important part of the process of selling to both business decision makers and consumers. Impressions of HMOs in general provide management with some idea of the context in which they are selling their product, and specific impressions of TouchWell and its major competitors provide measures of image.

TouchWell Tracking Research

**Summary of Findings from
2005 and 2007**

prepared by Alpha Research

Background

■ The information summarized in this report is based on telephone surveys conducted by Alpha Research in 2005 and 2007
■ Two waves of research were conducted in each year:
  ➤ 2005—March and October.
  ➤ 2007—January and November.
■ In all the waves of research, separate samples and survey instruments were used for:
  ➤ Consumers with group health coverage through an employer who were the decision makers for group health coverage for the household.
  ➤ Individuals from companies that offer group health coverage to their employees who make decisions regarding coverage for their companies.
■ Random samples were used for all surveys. Sample sizes were as follows:
  ➤ 2005 Pretest—Business (400), Consumer (500).
  ➤ 2005 Posttest—Business (400), Consumer (400).
  ➤ 2007 Pretest—Business (400), Consumer (400).
  ➤ 2007 Posttest—Business (400), Consumer (400).

Consumers: Unaided Plan Awareness

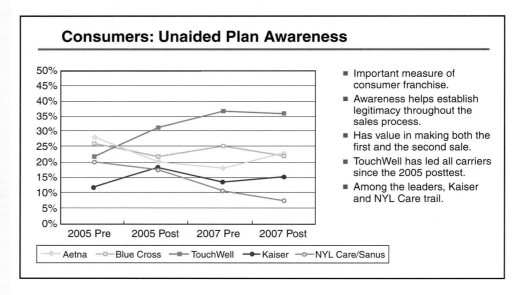

■ Important measure of consumer franchise.
■ Awareness helps establish legitimacy throughout the sales process.
■ Has value in making both the first and the second sale.
■ TouchWell has led all carriers since the 2005 posttest.
■ Among the leaders, Kaiser and NYL Care trail.

Business Decision Makers: Unaided Plan Awareness

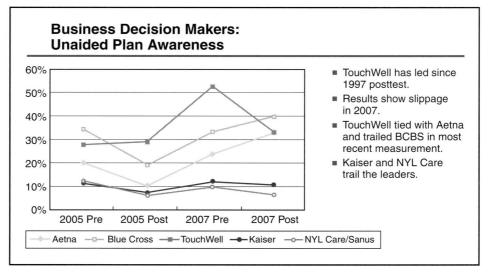

■ TouchWell has led since 1997 posttest.
■ Results show slippage in 2007.
■ TouchWell tied with Aetna and trailed BCBS in most recent measurement.
■ Kaiser and NYL Care trail the leaders.

Consumers: Impression of HMOs

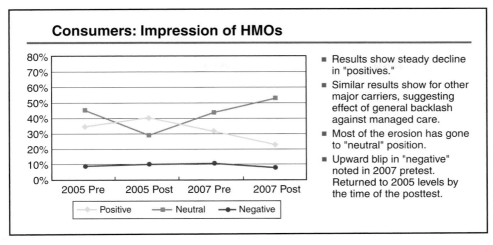

- Results show steady decline in "positives."
- Similar results show for other major carriers, suggesting effect of general backlash against managed care.
- Most of the erosion has gone to "neutral" position.
- Upward blip in "negative" noted in 2007 pretest. Returned to 2005 levels by the time of the posttest.

Business Decision Makers: Impression of HMOs

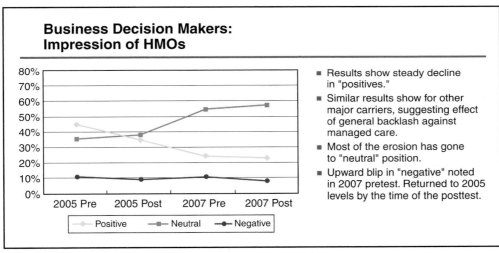

- Results show steady decline in "positives."
- Similar results show for other major carriers, suggesting effect of general backlash against managed care.
- Most of the erosion has gone to "neutral" position.
- Upward blip in "negative" noted in 2007 pretest. Returned to 2005 levels by the time of the posttest.

Decision Makers and Consumers: Reasons for Negative Impressions

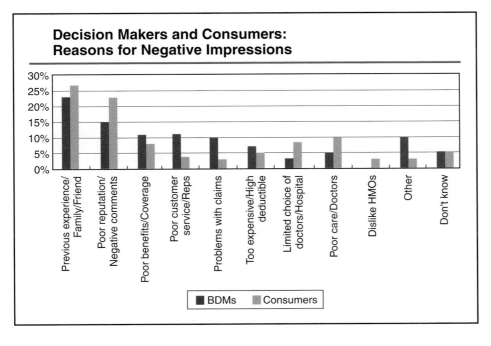

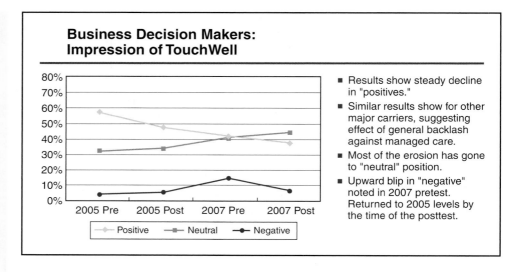

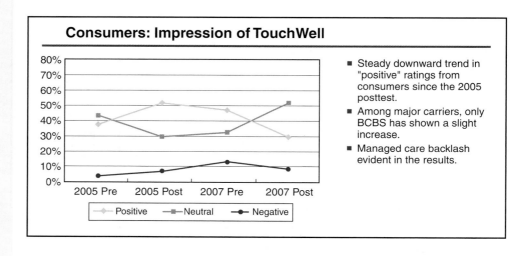

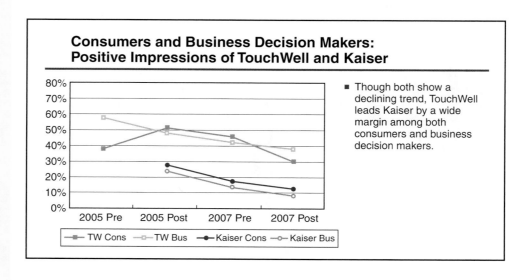

Questions

1. Comment on the general quality of the presentation. Are the slides easy to understand? Do they effectively convey key information? What suggestions would you have for improving this presentation?

2. Comment on the content of the slides regarding unaided plan awareness for both consumers and business decision makers. What are the implications for TouchWell?

3. What do the slides show with respect to the image or impressions that consumers and business decision makers have regarding HMOs? How have these impressions changed over time? What are the major reasons for negative impressions of HMOs among business decision makers and consumers?

4. What has happened to TouchWell's image over the four waves of research? How do these changes differ for business decision makers and consumers?

PHOTO CREDITS

Chapter 1: Page 2: Kim Jangwook/Gamma-Presse, Inc. Page 6: Jennifer Todd/DSS Research. Page 9: PhotoDisc, Inc./Getty Images. Page 10: Rex F. May. Page 12: PhotoDisc, Inc./Getty Images.

Chapter 2: Page 24: Digital Vision/Getty Images. Page 29: Jennifer Todd/DSS Research. Page 37: Nick Keane/she UK/Retna. Page 39: Foote, Cone & Belding-Chicago/Gatorade. Page 45: PhotoDisc, Inc./Getty Images. Page 53: Digital Vision/Getty Images.

Chapter 3: Page 60: Elle Wagner/Copyright John Wiley & Sons, Inc. Page 70: Jennifer Todd/DSS Research. Page 73: PhotoDisc, Inc./Getty Images.

Chapter 4: Page 90: Elle Wagner/Copyright John Wiley & Sons, Inc. Page 100: Royalty free/Corbis Images. Page 111: Copyright John Wiley & Sons, Inc.

Chapter 5: Page 126: Hilary Newman & Elle Wagner/Copyright John Wiley & Sons, Inc. Page 132: Spencer Grant/PhotoEdit. Page 137: DILBERT reprinted by permission of United Features Syndicate, Inc. Page 149: Jennifer Todd/DSS Research.

Chapter 6: Page 162: ThinkStock/Index Stock. Pages 166: PhotoDisc, Inc./Getty Images. Page 174: Courtesy In-Touch Survey Systems, Inc. Page 191: Jennifer Todd/DSS Research.. Page 193: Norbert Schwerin/The Image Works.

Chapter 7: Page 204: Nick Dolding/PhotoDisc, Inc./Getty Images. Page 218: The PreTesting Co., Tenafly, NJ.

Chapter 8: Page 232: Digital Vision/Getty Images. Page 247: PhotoDisc, Inc./Getty Images. Page 250 (top): Corbis Digital Stock. Page 250 (bottom): Corbis Digital Stock. Page 253: Copyright John Wiley & Sons, Inc.

Chapter 9: Page 264: Digital Vision/Getty Images. Page 272: Copyright John Wiley & Sons, Inc. Page 273: Jennifer Todd/DSS Research. Page 274: Copyright John Wiley & Sons, Inc. Page 281: Mark Richards/PhotoEdit.

Chapter 10: Page 292: Digital Vision/Getty Images. Page 294: American Cancer Society. Page 307: Corbis Stock Market. Page 313: YMCA of Greater Cincinnati.

Chapter 11: Page 328: Mark Leibowitz/Masterfile. Page 331: Copyright John Wiley & Sons, Inc. Page 338: PhotoDisc, Inc./Getty Images. Page 358: Jennifer Todd/DSS Research. Page 359: Alex Farnsworth/The Image Works.

Chapter 12: Page 372: Digital Vision/Getty Images. Page 381: PhotoDisc, Inc./Getty Images. Page 386: Jennifer Todd/DSS Research. Page 389: PhotoDisc, Inc./Getty Images. Page 391: PhotoDisc, Inc./Getty Images.

Chapter 13: Page 402: Stewart Cohen/Index Stock. Page 410: PhotoDisc, Inc./Getty Images. Page 414: Corbis Digital Stock. Page 423: Image State.

Chapter 14: Page 432: Justin Sullivan/Getty Images News and Sport Services. Page 436: PhotoDisc, Inc./Getty Images. Page 449: Corbis Digital Photo. Page 454: Jennifer Todd/DSS Research. Page 464: Corbis Stock Market.

Chapter 15: Page 476: Altrendo/Getty Images, Inc. Page 483: Jennifer Todd/DSS Research. Page 486: PhotoDisc, Inc./Getty Images. Page 502: PhotoDisc, Inc./Getty Images. Page 505: PhotoDisc, Inc./Getty Images.

Chapter 16: Page 518: Shiva Twin/Taxi/Getty Images. Page 522: Michael Milia/Retna. Page 530: PhotoDisc, Inc./Getty Images.

Chapter 17: Page 544: Courtesy Samsung Electronics America. Page 549: PhotoDisc, Inc./Getty Images. Page 562: PhotoDisc, Inc./Getty Images. Page 568: Jennifer Todd/DSS Research. Page 572: PhotoDisc, Inc./Getty Images.

Chapter 18: Page 592: Digital Vision/Getty Images. Page 596: Jennifer Todd/DSS Research. Page 600: Andrew Carruth/Retna. Page 607: PhotoDisc, Inc./Getty Images. Page 612: Jennifer Todd/DSS Research.

Questions

1. Comment on the general quality of the presentation. Are the slides easy to understand? Do they effectively convey key information? What suggestions would you have for improving this presentation?

2. Comment on the content of the slides regarding unaided plan awareness for both consumers and business decision makers. What are the implications for TouchWell?

3. What do the slides show with respect to the image or impressions that consumers and business decision makers have regarding HMOs? How have these impressions changed over time? What are the major reasons for negative impressions of HMOs among business decision makers and consumers?

4. What has happened to TouchWell's image over the four waves of research? How do these changes differ for business decision makers and consumers?

PHOTO CREDITS

APPENDIX ONE

Comprehensive Cases

A
**Biff Targets an Online Dating Service
for College Students**

B
**Freddy Favors Fast Food and
Convenience for College Students**

C
**Superior Online Student Travel—
A Cut Above**

D
**Rockingham National
Bank Visa Card Survey**

A-2 | APPENDIX 1 | Comprehensive Cases

Comprehensive Case A

Biff Targets an Online Dating Service for College Students

Biff Henderson, a distant cousin of Bif Henderson of the *David Letterman Show*, graduated from the California state system three years ago. Being a bit shy, Biff had decided that the best way to meet girls was through an online dating service. His hits and misses during his college days led him to think that there must be a better way for college students to hook up. The big, generic services like Match.com and Yahoo Personals didn't meet his needs. Also, speed dating at Starbucks and name swapping at the Apple Store were unsuccessful.

Biff decided that if the big online services weren't right for him they must not be right for thousands of other college students as well. A little secondary research indicated that there are about 2.5 million subscribers to online dating services nationwide and this number is expected to double in the next few years. By utilizing scientifically derived compatibility tests and demographic preferences, a person can quickly filter through numerous candidates to find the person or persons whom they would most like to contact. Biff liked the idea of targeting only college students in order to attract singles looking for a more defined dating pool.

Biff decided that to become a member of his new service the person had to be enrolled in a college or university. He didn't necessarily have to be a full-time student, but he did have to be currently enrolled. A single student will be able to search by region, specific university, and/or by major field of study. A unique feature that Biff is considering will be called "Biff's Bashes." These will be all-inclusive spring break and summer week-long vacations to places like Cancun or Daytona Beach. Biff will provide airfare, hotel, ground transportation, five dinners, three lunches, and nightly mixers with music. "Biff's Bashes" will be open only to members of his online service.

Biff wonders about the demand for his "bashes" as well as what college students would ideally like to see in an online dating service. For example, might they also be interested in single cycling or weekend hiking trips? While virtually all college students may be surfing the net for love, there are a tiny minority that may be predators or dangerous criminals. Biff is therefore thinking about offering background checks for an additional fee. Another service might be bodyguards or escorts for singles meeting for the first time. Biff felt that this service might be desirable for students living in large cities that aren't completely comfortable with dating online.

Biff decided that what was needed was some good marketing research.

ONLINE DATING SERVICE FOR COLLEGE STUDENTS

S1. Which of the following categories includes your age?
1 Under 18—THANK AND TERM
2 18–20
3 21–25
4 26–30
5 31 or older
6 Refused—THANK AND TERM

S2. Are you currently enrolled as a full-time or part-time student in any of the following types of institutions?
1 Community college
2 Junior college / two-year program
3 University / four-year program
4 None of the above—THANK AND TERM

Q1. How familiar are you with the concept of online dating services, where people pay a membership fee to post a profile and picture online and can then search through profiles/pictures of members of the opposite sex for the purpose of meeting people to date?
   5 Extremely familiar
   4 Very familiar
   3 Somewhat familiar
   2 Not too familiar
   1 Not at all familiar

Q2. How interested are you in the general concept of an online dating service as a way of meeting members of the opposite sex? HOW ABOUT SAME SEX?
   5 Extremely interested
   4 Very interested
   3 Somewhat interested
   2 Not too interested
   1 Not at all interested

Q3. Which of the following dating services are you aware of? Please select all that apply.
ROTATE LIST A–J.
   A Match.com
   B Yahoo! Personals
   C PerfectMatch.com
   D AmericanSingles.com
   E eHarmony.com
   F FriendFinder.com
   G Date.com
   H Speed dating
   I Apple Store
   J Great Expectations
   K None of the above—SKIP TO Q7

(INCLUDE ALL MENTIONS FROM Q3)

Q4. Which of the following dating services have you ever tried?
   A Match.com
   B Yahoo! Personals
   C PerfectMatch.com
   D AmericanSingles.com
   E eHarmony.com
   F FriendFinder.com
   G Date.com
   H Speed dating
   I Apple Store
   J Great Expectations
   K None of the above—SKIP TO Q7

(ASK Q5 FOR ALL MENTIONS IN Q4)

Q5. Overall, how satisfied are you with your experience with (ANSWER FROM Q4)?
   5 Completely satisfied
   4 Very satisfied
   3 Somewhat satisfied
   2 Not too satisfied
   1 Not at all satisfied

(ASK FOR ALL Q4 MENTIONS RATED A "1" OR "2" IN Q5)

Q6. Why are you less than satisfied with your experience with (ANSWER FROM Q3)? Please select all answers that apply. ROTATE A–J.
   A Small/limited selection of members of the opposite sex
   B Too large/overwhelming selection of members of the opposite sex
   C Poor quality selection of members of the opposite sex
   D Cost/fees too high

E   Members not honest in their profile/picture
F   Bad experiences on dates
G   No personality/compatibility test included in membership
H   No organized social events included in membership
I   No criminal background check included in membership
J   Requires too much time
K   Other (please specify)_____

Q7. A new online dating service may be introduced in the near future. Membership in this service would be limited to those enrolled in a college or university (full or part time) and students would be able to search by region, specific university and/or by major field of study. Members would also be able to utilize a compatibility test and demographic preferences to filter through numerous candidates to find the person or persons who they would most like to contact.

How interested are you in this particular concept of an online dating services as a way of meeting members of the opposite sex?
5   Extremely interested
4   Very interested
3   Somewhat interested
2   Not too interested—SKIP TO Q14
1   Not at all interested—SKIP TO Q14

Q8. What would be an appropriate monthly fee for this basic service?
1   $1–$5
2   $6–$10
3   $11–$15
4   $16–$20
5   $21–$25
6   $26–$30
7   More than $30

Q9. How important is it that all members pass a criminal background check prior to being allowed to join the online service?
5   Extremely important
4   Very important
3   Somewhat important
2   Not too important
1   Not at all important

Q10. How interested would you be in having a bodyguard or escort accompany you on your first date with a member of the opposite sex?
5   Extremely interested
4   Very interested
3   Somewhat interested
2   Not too interested
1   Not at all interested

Q11. In addition to the services described earlier, this new online dating service may also include some organized social events, such as spring break and summer week-long vacations to places like Cancun or Daytona Beach. Members would be provided with airfare, hotel accommodations, ground transportation, five dinners, three lunches, and nightly mixers with music. These social events would be open only to members of the online dating service.

If you were a member of this online dating service, how likely would you be to participate in this type of organized social event?
5   Extremely likely
4   Very likely
3   Somewhat likely
2   Not too likely
1   Not at all likely

Q12. This new online dating service may also include some shorter organized social events, such as single cycling or weekend hiking trips. These social events would be open only to members of the online dating service.

If you were a member of this online dating service, how likely would you be to participate in this type of organized social event?

5 Extremely likely
4 Very likely
3 Somewhat likely
2 Not too likely
1 Not at all likely

Q13. What other organized social events would you be likely to participate in? Please mark all that apply.

A Movie night
B Game night
C Happy hour
D Dinner at a local restaurant
E Volunteer work
F Other (please specify)_____

SKIP TO END

Q14. Would you be more interested in this online dating service if it also included any of the following additional benefits?

	Much more interested	Somewhat more interested	No more interested
A All-inclusive week-long trips during spring break and summer to places like Cancun or Daytona Beach	3	2	1
B Single cycling or weekend hiking trips	3	2	1
C Happy hours, game nights, movie nights, etc.	3	2	1
D Mandatory criminal background check for members	3	2	1
E Bodyguard/escort service on first dates	3	2	1

Those are all of our questions. Thank you for your help!

Exercises

1. Using secondary data from the Internet and the "Real People-Real Data" database determine if Biff should move forward with his project.

2. If the new service is a "go," prepare a detailed marketing plan (see Appendix Two) of what should be offered to give Biff a competitive advantage.

Comprehensive Case B

Freddy Favors Fast Food and Convenience for College Students

Freddy Bender shared a college dorm room with Jack Mendenhall throughout his four-year tenure at a large northeastern university. They were not only roommates but best friends as well. Freddy, having a solid quantitative background, helped Jack prepare for exams in statistics and marketing research. After graduation, Freddy put in eight years as a loan officer with CitiBank in New York, whereas Jack moved to California to work in his father's venture capital firm, Mendenhall Partners.

Freddy is a fast-food junkie, or as it is called in the business, a "heavy user." His love of fast food has always been coupled with a desire to be in the business. Freddy knows that college students often fall into the "heavy user" category. A little secondary research revealed that almost half of all college students (46 percent) say that they ate fast food one or two times in the prior week. Three in ten (28 percent) say they ate it three to five times in that same period, while 13 percent claim to have eaten it five or more times![1] College students spend $4.8 billion per year at fast-food restaurants.[2]

Freddy's dream is to open a chain of fast-food restaurants coupled with a convenience store on or near major college campuses. The notion is to carry a limited line of convenience goods and serve quality fast food in a Starbuck's-like atmosphere with comfy sofas, chairs, and WiFi. Freddy knows that price is paramount but that variety and quality are important to college students.

Further research showed that a limited version of Freddy's ideas had worked extremely well for Tedeschi Food Shops Inc., operator of Tedeschi Food Shops, Li'l Peach, and Store 24. Store 24 is the chain's primary store brand in college markets, such as Boston and the areas around the University of New Hampshire and the University of Connecticut. "In our stores, we seem to be students' destination for lunch, dinner and late-dinner/early-breakfast," said Joe Hamza, director of marketing. Fresh, quality foods have made these stores destinations for students, Hamza said. "Students also look at quick in-and-out and at variety—healthy, vegetarian, ethnic, ready-to-eat, or heat-and-eat meals—as big variables."[3]

Indeed, Store 24 was an early observer of the low-carb trend and offers vegetarian options and ethnic foods, such as sushi, Italian, and Middle Eastern dishes like tabouli and hummus. "These kids are diverse ethnically and look at these dishes as a vegetarian or healthy alternative to the steak and cheese," Hamza said. "Our growth comes from the innovative items, not from the turkey or roast beef sandwiches."[4]

A telephone call to Jack Mendenhall, Freddy's college roommate, resulted in a very receptive attitude to provide venture capital. Jack said, "Bring me a viable marketing plan, and we will provide the funds for the first 10 restaurants. If these prove successful, additional funding won't be a problem." Freddy was elated!

Freddy knew that marketing research would be necessary before he could build his marketing plan. He needed answers to a number of questions. These included: Is a Starbuck's-like atmosphere desirable? What type of fast food should be offered? Should the quality/price point be above, below, or at the level of the national chains? What is the best mix of convenience goods to carry for college students? Is there some other service or product that the stores can offer to build foot traffic and loyalty?

FAST FOOD AND CONVENIENCE FOR COLLEGE STUDENTS

S1. What is your current age?

1   Under 18—THANK AND TERM
2   18
3   19
4   20
5   21
6   22
7   23–25
8   26–30
9   31 or older

S2. Are you currently enrolled in any of the following types of institutions?
1   Junior college
2   Community college/two-year program
3   University/four-year program
4   None of the above—THANK AND TERM

Q1. How many times have you visited a **fast food** restaurant in the last seven days? Please do not include restaurants where you were served by a waiter or waitress.
1   None/zero—SKIP TO Q8
2   One time
3   Two times
4   Three times
5   Five times
6   Five or more times

Q2. For which of the following meal types did you eat fast food in the last seven days? Please mark all that apply.
A   Breakfast
B   Lunch
C   Afternoon snack
D   Dinner
E   Evening/late night snack
F   Other

Q3. Many fast food restaurants offer combo meals or value meals, which typically include a main dish, a side dish and a drink for a discounted price. How often do you buy combo or value meals, when they are available, versus purchasing single items a la carte?
1   Always
2   Often
3   Seldom
4   Never

Q4. How important are each of the following factors when deciding with fast food restaurant to visit? ROTATE FACTORS.
A   Taste
B   Convenience of location
C   Price
D   Healthy food choices available
E   Food quality
F   Cleanliness of restaurant
G   General atmosphere of restaurant
H   Ethnic food choices available
I   Vegetarian food choices available
J   Freshness of the food
    5   Extremely important
    4   Very important
    3   Somewhat important
    2   Not too important
    1   Not at all important

Q5. When you visit fast food restaurants, how often do you stay and eat the food in the restaurant versus getting it to go or going through the drive-through window?
1   Always—SKIP TO Q8
2   Often
3   Seldom
4   Never

Q6. If a fast food restaurant had comfortable sofas and chairs, where you could socialize with friends, and wireless Internet connection, how likely would you be to stay and cat your food there rather than getting it go or going through the drive-through window?
5   Extremely likely
4   Very likely

>   3   Somewhat likely
>   2   Not too likely
>   1   Not at all likely

Q7. Why do you say that? Please be as specific as possible.

_____

Q8. How many times have you purchased/consumed the following convenient foods in the last seven days?
A   Candy bar
B   Chips or pretzels
C   Microwavable frozen meal like Hungry Man or Lean Cuisine
D   Hot Pocket
E   Ramen Noodles
F   Microwavable popcorn
G   Ice cream
H   Soup
I   Bagel or donut
J   Cookie
K   Pre-packaged/ready-to-eat salad
L   Fruit
M   Pre-made, refrigerated sandwich
>   1   None/zero
>   2   One time
>   3   Two times
>   4   Three times
>   5   Four times
>   6   Four or more times

(IF Q1=1, CONTINUE, ALL OTHERS, SKIP TO END)

Q9. Why have you not visited any fast food restaurants in the last seven days? Please select all that apply. ROTATE FACTORS.
A   Don't like the taste of fast foods
B   Inconvenience of locations
C   Price
D   Healthy food choices not available
E   Poof food quality
F   Poor cleanliness of restaurants
G   Poor general atmosphere of restaurants
H   Ethnic food choices not available
I   Vegetarian food choices not available
J   Lack of freshness of the food
K   Atypical week—I usually do eat some fast food in a typical week
L   Other

Q10. If a fast food restaurant had comfortable sofas and chairs, wireless Internet connection, and a variety of fresh, healthy American and ethnic food choices and convenience items, how likely would you be to visit?
5   Extremely likely
4   Very likely
3   Somewhat likely
2   Not too likely
1   Not at all likely

Q11. Why do you say that? Please be as specific as possible.

_____

Thank you. Those are all of our questions.

_____

Exercise

Using your "Real People-Real Data" database plus secondary information that you find on the Internet, build a marketing plan (see Appendix Two) for Freddy to take to Jack.

Notes

1. "Fast Fact" (Fast Food), *Youth Market Alert*, November 1, 2004.
2. Barbara Grondin Francella, "The College Try: Around the Clock Value and Variety are the Way to Students' Hearts and Stomachs," *Convenience Store News* (August 23, 2004).
3. Ibid.
4. Ibid.

Comprehensive Case C

Superior Online Student Travel—A Cut Above

Over 41 million people purchase travel online. Consumers are most satisfied with their ability to book airfares online. Consider the following percentages of online travel users:

Booking airfare online: 43 percent

Obtaining general destination information: 39 percent

Making lodging arrangements: 36 percent

Renting a car online: 33 percent

Making entertainment arrangements: 31 percent[1]

Mary Ann Johnson knew that, with limited funds and fairly high levels of customer satisfaction, such as shown above, she couldn't compete with the likes of Travelocity, Orbitz, or Expedia. Her only hope was to find a niche market from which to launch her online travel site. Previous experience with Sabre and Orbitz gave Mary Ann a good working knowledge of the online travel business.

Mary Ann found that several firms were already serving the college market such as Student City and Student Universe. Student City seemed to emphasize spring break and party time, whereas Student Universe focused on student airfares. While Mary Ann didn't want to ignore either of these offerings, she felt that a different approach might prove successful.

Mary Ann wondered if her partnering with several universities to offer educational trips to various international destinations, led by a professor, for credit would have an appeal. Her idea was to highlight 10 or more trips in the summer and 5 over the Christmas break. The trips would be offered by a major field of study. For example, an art major might sign up for a trip featuring the Picasso Museum, Rodin Museum, and the Louvre in Paris, the Uffizi in Florence, and the museums of the Vatican in Rome. The tour would be led by an art history professor and would result in three college credits.

Similarly, a marketing major would find a tour that visited Nestlé, the World Trade Organization, and Solomon Skis in Switzerland, Carrefour (the huge department store chain) in Paris, Airbus in Toulouse, and Volkswagen in Germany. At each business, the global marketing manager would discuss the firm's global marketing strategy. The tour would be led by a marketing professor.

All tours would be all inclusive, except lunches, and would feature a day of sightseeing and a half-day free time.

Mary Ann had the contracts and the know-how to set up the tours. Her concern was determining what tours should be offered and the demand for the tours. She knew that she would offer student airfares, student forums (but she was unsure of the topics), rail passes, discounts to college-oriented hotels and hostels, and travel insurance on her Web site. Beyond this, she wasn't sure. A big question was whether to offer spring break packages. Although very profitable, might these clash with her positioning as an education-oriented online travel service? If she did decide to feature spring break, what should the package include, and what destinations should be featured?

ONLINE STUDENT TRAVEL

S1. What is your current age?
1   Under 18—THANK AND TERM
2   18
3   19
4   20
5   21
6   22
7   23–25
8   26–30
9   31 or older

S2. Are you currently enrolled in any of the following types of institutions?
1   Junior college
2   Community college/two-year program
3   University/four-year program
4   None of the above—THANK AND TERM

Q1. Which of the following online travel purchase sites are you aware of? Please mark all that apply.
A   Travelocity
B   Expedia
C   Orbitz
D   Sabre
E   Student City
F   Student Universe
G   Cheap Tickets
H   None of the above—SKIP TO Q8

(INCLUDE MENTIONS FROM Q1)

Q2. Which online travel purchase sites have you **ever used**?
A   Travelocity
B   Expedia
C   Orbitz
D   Sabre
E   Student City
F   Student Universe
G   Cheap Tickets
H   None of the above—SKIP TO Q8

(INCLUDE MENTIONS FROM Q2)

Q3. Which online travel purchase sites have you used in the **past year**?
A   Travelocity
B   Expedia
C   Orbitz
D   Sabre
E   Student City
F   Student Universe

G   Cheap Tickets
H   None of the above—SKIP TO Q8

(INCLUDE MENTIONS FROM Q3. ASK FOR EACH TRAVEL SITE.)

Q4. What did you use the online travel site for? Please select all that apply for each travel site used.
A   Travelocity
B   Expedia
C   Orbitz
D   Sabre
E   Student City
F   Student Universe
G   Cheap Tickets
  A   Obtain general destination information
  B   Book a <u>spring break</u> travel package (including two or more of airfare, lodging/cruise and car rental)
  C   Book a <u>non-spring break</u> travel package (including two or more of airfare, lodging/cruise and car rental)
  D   Book airfare
  E   Book lodging
  F   Book car rental
  G   Book a cruise
  H   Purchase entertainment tickets
  I   Other (please specify)_____

Q5. Did this travel site offer you a student discount on your purchase(s)?
A   Travelocity
B   Expedia
C   Orbitz
D   Sabre
E   Student City
F   Student Universe
G   Cheap Tickets
  1   Yes
  2   No
  3   Don't know

Q6. In general, do you prefer to purchase all-inclusive travel packages, that include your airfare, lodging and meals or do you prefer to purchase each item separately?
1   Prefer all-inclusive packages
2   Prefer to purchase items separately

Q7. Why do you say that? Please be as specific as possible.

Q8. Have you ever participated in a study-abroad program, where you obtain college credits by taking a class at a university in a foreign country?
1   Yes
2   No

Q9. Please consider the following concept that could be offered through an online travel site: Educational trips to various international destinations, led by a professor, offered for three class credits at your college or university. All tours would be all-inclusive (except lunches) and feature a day of sightseeing and a half-day of free time. Trips would be offered during the summer break and/or Christmas break and would be organized by major fields of study (i.e. marketing, art, etc.). The cost would be comparable to the price for a regular three-credit class and would be approximately two weeks in length. ??? Two examples could be as follows:

1) A trip for art majors including the Picasso Museum, Rodin Museum, and the Louvre in Paris, the Uffizi in Florence, and the museums of the Vatican in Rome, led by an art history professor.

2) A trip for marketing majors including a tour that visited Nestle, the World Trade Organization, and Solomon Skis in Switzerland, Carrefour (the huge department store chain) in Paris, Airbus in

Toulouse, and Volkswagen in Germany to learn about each firm's global business strategy, led by a marketing professor.

How interested would you be in earning college credits through an educational trip abroad, such as those described above?

5   Extremely interested
4   Very interested
3   Somewhat interested
2   Not too interested
1   Not at all interested

Q10. Why do you say that? Please be as specific as possible.

_____

(IF Q9=2 OR 1, SKIP TO Q13)

Q11. Each package would include student airfare, student forums, rail passes (if applicable), discounts to college-oriented hotels and hostels, and travel insurance. What else, if anything, should these package include? Please be as specific as possible.

_____

Q12. How interested would you be in visiting each of the following destinations on an educational trip? Please mark all that apply.

A   Africa
B   Asia
C   Australia
D   Central America
E   Europe
F   Middle East
G   South America

    5   Extremely interested
    4   Very interested
    3   Somewhat interested
    2   Not too interested
    1   Not at all interested

Q13. In your opinion, should this online travel site offer spring break packages in addition to these educational trips?

1   Yes
2   No—SKIP TO Q16

Q14. How interested would you be in each of the following spring break destinations? ROTATE A–P.

A   Cancun, Mexico
B   Cabo San Lucas, Mexico
C   Cozumel, Mexico
D   South Padre Island, TX
E   Daytona Beach, FL
F   Key West, FL
G   Acapulco, Mexico
H   Myrtle Beach, SC
I   Bahamas
J   Lake Havasu, AZ
K   Mazatlan, Mexico
L   Puerto Vallarta, Mexico
M   Las Vegas, NV
N   Panama City, FL
O   South Beach, FL
P   Jamaica
Q   New York, NY
R   Chicago, IL

S   Telluride, CO
    5   Extremely interested
    4   Very interested
    3   Somewhat interested
    2   Not too interested
    1   Not at all interested

Q15. What should a spring break package include? Please mark all that apply.
    A   Airfare
    B   Lodging/hotel
    C   Car rental
    D   Some meals at your hotel (i.e. breakfast and lunch or breakfast and dinner each day)
    E   All meals at your hotel (breakfast, lunch and dinner each day)
    F   Alcoholic drink vouchers good at your hotel
    G   Discounted club admission
    H   Discounted entertainment tickets
    I   Shuttle bus to and from the airport
    J   Food vouchers good at any local restaurant
    K   Other (please specify)_____

Q16. Which of the following best describes your major area of study?
    1   Architecture
    2   Business Administration
    3   Education
    4   Engineering
    5   Law/Public Safety
    6   Liberal Arts
    7   Nursing
    8   Science
    9   Social Work
    10 Urban and Public Affairs
    11 Other

Thank you. Those are all of our questions.

Exercise

Using secondary data from the Internet and the "Real People—Real Data" database, advise Mary Ann on constructing her website and marketing plan (see Appendix Two).

Note

1. "Consumers Going Online Before Going on the Road," *PR Newswire,* (June 28, 2005).

Comprehensive Case D

Rockingham National Bank Visa Card Survey

Company Background   Rockingham National Bank, located in Chicago, Illinois, is attempting to expand the market for its Visa card. It is examining certain target groups to determine its ability to penetrate the credit card market with special offers.

Purpose of the Study The purpose of this research study is to evaluate how teachers in Illinois will respond to specific credit card promotional offers. Specifically, the questionnaire was designed to achieve the following objectives:

☐ Develop a demographic, psychographic, credit card ownership, and credit card usage profile of teachers.

☐ Determine the likelihood that teachers would respond to several different concepts for a credit card offer.

☐ Determine which demographic, psychographic, attitudinal, credit card ownership, and credit card usage variables are the best predictors of likelihood to respond to the concept credit card offers.

☐ Make predictions regarding the likely level of response to a credit card offer to the teacher market.

☐ Identify those features most likely to induce teachers to respond to a credit card offer.

Research Approach All data were collected by means of central-location telephone interviewing from the Ameridata facility in Arlington, Texas, by experienced Ameridata interviewers.

The interviews were conducted with software-driven interfaces to virtually eliminate tabulation errors. All interviewing was supervised and monitored by Ameridata personnel.

The geographic area covered was the state of Illinois. The sample was selected following the criteria for a simple random sample; qualified respondents were individuals licensed to teach in Illinois. A total of 400 interviews were completed.

ROCKINGHAM BANK CREDIT CARD SURVEY OF TEACHERS

(ASK TO SPEAK TO RESPONDENT LISTED ON THE SAMPLE SHEET. IF ANOTHER MEMBER OF THE HOUSEHOLD IS WILLING TO DO THE SURVEY, THANK the person for his or her WILLINGNESS, BUT EXPLAIN THAT you NEED TO COMPLETE THE INTERVIEW WITH THE LISTED RESPONDENT.)

Hello, my name is _____ with Ameridata Research, an independent marketing research firm. I would like to ask you a few questions about credit card usage. First, let me assure you this is not a sales call, you will not be contacted again, and my questions will only take a few minutes of your time. (READ ONLY IF NEEDED) Let me assure you that this is not a sales call; we are only conducting research on credit card usage and are interested in your opinions about credit cards.

1. First of all, please tell me whether you strongly agree, agree, neither agree nor disagree, disagree, or strongly disagree with each of the following statements (READ LIST; ROTATE):

	SA	A	NAD	D	SD	DK
a. Money may not be everything, but it's got a big lead over whatever is second.	5	4	3	2	1	6
b. Money can't buy happiness.	5	4	3	2	1	6
c. It is important for me to be fashionable and chic.	5	4	3	2	1	6
d. I buy things even though I can't afford them.	5	4	3	2	1	6
e. I make only the minimum payments on my credit cards.	5	4	3	2	1	6
f. I sometimes buy things to make myself feel better.	5	4	3	2	1	6
g. Shopping is fun.	5	4	3	2	1	6
h. During the last three years, my financial situation has gotten worse.	5	4	3	2	1	6

		SA	A	NAD	D	SD	DK
i.	I am satisfied with my present financial situation.	5	4	3	2	1	6
j.	Buying things gives me a lot of pleasure.	5	4	3	2	1	6
k.	You can tell a lot about people by the credit cards they use.	5	4	3	2	1	6
l.	I attach great importance to money.	5	4	3	2	1	6
m.	I attach great importance to credit cards.	5	4	3	2	1	6
n.	I attach great importance to material possessions.	5	4	3	2	1	6
o.	I generally read all offers that I receive through the mail just to know what they are about.	5	4	3	2	1	6

2. Please tell me which of the following credit cards you carry with you. Do you carry . . . (PROBE FOR VISA OR MASTERCARD)

    1 Visa? (ASK FOR NUMBER OF VISA CARDS) _____

    2 MasterCard? (ASK FOR NUMBER OF MASTERCARDS) _____

    3 Discover?

    4 American Express?

    5 Optima?

    6 AT&T Universal?

    7 GM?

    8 Ford?

    9 None (SKIP TO Q.11)

3. Which card do you use the most often? (PROBE FOR ONE ANSWER ONLY; IF RESPONDENT IS UNABLE TO GIVE ONLY ONE RESPONSE, TAKE THE FIRST RESPONSE GIVEN)

    1 Visa

    2 MasterCard

    3 Discover

    4 American Express

    5 Optima

    6 AT&T Universal

    7 GM

    8 Ford

    9 DON'T KNOW (SKIP TO Q.11)

(IF "VISA" OR "MASTERCARD" IS MENTIONED IN Q.3, ASK Q.4. OTHERWISE, SKIP TO Q.11)

4. Which bank issued this Visa/MasterCard?

    [MASTERCARD ISSUERS]

    1 Associates National Bank

    2 Chase Manhattan

    3 Citibank

    4 Credit union issued

    5 First Bank

    6 Household

    7 MBNA

    8 Other

    9 DK

    [VISA ISSUERS]

    1 Associates National Bank

    2 Bank of America

    3 Citibank

    4 Credit union issued

    5 First Bank

    6 Household

    7 MBNA

    8 Other

    9 DK

5. Why do you use [ANSWER FROM Q.3] most often?

  1 Convenience
  2 Only card owned/carried
  3 Interest rate
  4 Wide acceptance
  5 Cash back
  6 Cash rebate
  7 Billing cycle/grace period
  8 No annual fee
  9 Issued by a local bank
10 Corporate/business card
11 Credit limit
12 Itemized bill
13 It's a Gold Card.
14 Rebate toward automobile purchase
15 Relationship with organization sponsoring card (IF YES, "Which organization?")
16 Other

6. What is the interest rate on the balances that you carry on the card you use most often?

  1 Less than 8 percent
  2 8–8.9 percent
  3 9–9.9 percent
  4 10–10.9 percent
  5 11–11.9 percent
  6 12–12.9 percent
  7 13–13.9 percent
  8 14–14.9 percent
  9 15–15.9 percent
10 16–16.9 percent
11 17–17.9 percent
12 18–18.9 percent
13 19–19.9 percent
14 20 percent or more

7. What is your credit limit on the card you can use the most?

_____ Credit limit

8. Is the card you use most often a Gold Card?

  1 Yes
  2 No
  3 DK

9. Does the card you use most often . . . (READ LIST)

	Yes	No	DK
Charge an annual fee?	1	2	3
Offer cash rebates/cash back on purchases?	1	2	3
Offer extended warranties on products you buy?	1	2	3
Offer buyer protection policies on products you buy (to replace the product if damaged, lost, or stolen)?	1	2	3
Offer a photo credit card?	1	2	3

10. Besides a lower interest rate, what feature or features would a new card need to have to convince you to obtain it?

  1 No annual fee
  2 Preapproved
  3 Rebate/cash back/free offers
  4 Business/corporate card
  5 Gold Card
  6 High credit limit

7   Wide acceptance

8   Other

11. Have you received any credit card offers in the past year?

1   Yes   (CONTINUE)

2   No   SKIP TO Q.17)

3   DK   (SKIP TO Q.17)

12. Approximately how many credit offers have you received in the past year?

_____ Number of offers received

13. Have you responded to any of these offers?

1   Yes   (CONTINUE)

2   No   (SKIP TO Q.16)

3   DK   (SKIP TO Q.17)

14. To which offer or offers did you respond?

1   Visa

2   MasterCard

3   Discover

4   American Express

5   Optima

6   AT&T Universal

7   GM

8   Ford

9   Other

15. Why did you respond [to this offer/these offers]? (ASK FOR EACH RESPONSE IN Q.14)

1   No annual fee

2   Preapproved

3   Interest rate

4   Build credit rating

5   Convenience/emergencies

6   Rebate/cash back/free offers

7   Business/corporate card

8   Gold Card

9   Credit limit

10   Travel

11   Grocery shopping

12   Wide acceptance

13   Other

(SKIP TO Q.17)

16. Why didn't you respond to any of the offers? (PROBE)

1   Interest rate too high

2   Have too many credit cards

3   Credit card balances too high

4   Credit limit

5   Interest rate confusing

6   Do not use credit cards

7   Do not need any more credit cards

8   Not preapproved/fear of being turned down

9   Other

10   DK

17. Have you closed or stopped using any credit cards in the past year?

1   Yes   (CONTINUE)

2   No   (SKIP TO Q.20)

3   DK   (SKIP TO Q.20)

18. Which card or cards have you stopped using?

1   Visa

2   MasterCard

3   Discover

    4   American Express
    5   Optima
    6   AT&T Universal
    7   Other

19. Why have you stopped using this card? (ASK FOR EACH RESPONSE IN Q.18)
    1   Interest rate
    2   Annual fee
    3   Own too many credit cards
    4   Balance too high
    5   Billing problems
    6   Never used it
    7   Limited acceptance
    8   Consolidation of debt
    9   Other

20. Would you say that your attitudes toward the use of credit cards have changed in the past year?
    1   Yes   (CONTINUE)
    2   No   (SKIP TO Q.22)
    3   DK   (SKIP TO Q.22)

21. (IF "YES" IN RESPONSE TO Q.20, ASK) How have your attitudes changed? (PROBE)

22. In comparison with a year ago, would you say you are using your credit cards . . . (READ LIST)
    1   Less often?
    2   About the same?
    3   More often?
    4   DK

23. In comparison with a year ago, which of the following statements is true in regard to your total credit card balances? (READ LIST)
    1   They are less.
    2   They are about the same.
    3   They are greater.
    4   DK

24. Now, I would like to find out how you feel about a particular credit card offer. We are not making this offer to you today—we are only interested in how you feel about the offer. (READ LIST OF OFFER FEATURES. RESPONDENTS WILL BE ASKED about ONE OF THE FOLLOWING SCENARIOS—100 FOR EACH SCENARIO)

	Preapproved	Application
6.0% Intro APR		
9.9% Intro APR		

☐ You receive [an application/a preapproved application] for a Limited Edition Visa card.
☐ There is no annual fee.
☐ It has a [9.9 /6.0] percent initial APR through March 2004.
☐ After that, the APR will be 16.9 percent.
☐ You can immediately transfer balances from other cards up to your credit limit—you can do this through March 2004 with no cash advance fees.
☐ It has a credit limit of up to $5,000.

25. On a scale of 0 to 100, where 0 is not at all likely and 100 is extremely likely, how likely would you be to respond to this offer?
    _____ Likelihood

26. What, if anything, do you particularly LIKE about this offer? (PROBE: "Anything else?")
    1   No annual fee
    2   Good interest rate
    3   Good offer in general
    4   Features/benefits
    5   Ability to transfer balances

      6   Credit limit
      7   Appealing offer in general
      8   Advantages over other offers
      9   MasterCard/Visa brand
     10 Identifies you as a professional
     11 Prestige of Limited Edition's name
     12 Other

27. What, if anything, do you particularly DISLIKE about this offer? (PROBE: "Anything else?")
      1   Interest rate too high
      2   Don't use credit cards
      3   Interest rate confusing
      4   Not competitive with current card
      5   Interest rate change after March
      6   No reason
      7   Other
      8   DK

28. Is the interest rate in the Visa credit card offer clear and understandable?
      1   Yes
      2   No
      3   DK/NS

29. Using a scale of 1 to 10, where 1 is poor and 10 is excellent, please tell me how you would rate the following product features in the Visa credit card offer that was just described. (ROTATE TO REFLECT INTRODUCTORY PERCENTAGE RATE AND BEING PREAPPROVED/HAVING TO APPLY)
_____ No annual fee
_____ 9.9/6.0 percent introductory rate through March 2004
_____ 16.9 percent APR after March 2004
_____ Being preapproved/receiving an application
_____ Ability to transfer balances from other cards
_____ Credit limit of up to $5,000

30. Do you consider this Visa credit card offer to be better than, about the same as, or worse than . . .

	Better	Same	Worse	DK
Discover Card?	1	2	3	4
American Express Optima Card?	1	2	3	4
AT&T Universal Card?	1	2	3	4
GM or Ford Card?	1	2	3	4
Other MasterCard/Visa for teaching professionals?	1	2	3	4
Credit card you use most often?	1	2	3	4

31. (IF BETTER OR WORSE IN Q.30, ASK) Why do you feel that way? (PROBE)

32. In evaluating a credit card offer, how important are the following things to you? Please use a 1 to 10 scale, where 1 is very unimportant and 10 is very important. How important is . . . ? (READ LIST AND ROTATE)
_____ Being preapproved?
_____ Interest rate?
_____ Annual fee?
_____ Credit limit?
_____ Billing cycle/grace period?
_____ Reputation of issuer?
_____ Extended warranty/buyer protection?
_____ No charges if monthly balance is paid?
_____ Cash advance?
_____ Financing payment plan?
_____ 24-hour service for lost or stolen cards?
_____ Ability to transfer balances from other cards?
_____ Rebates?
Finally, just a few questions to help us classify your responses.

33. (INDICATE SEX OF RESPONDENT)
    1   Male
    2   Female

34. Are you currently married or not married?
    1   Married
    2   Not married
    3   RF

35. Which of the following categories includes your age? Are you . . .
    1   18–24?
    2   25–34?
    3   35–44?
    4   45–54?
    5   55–64?
    6   65 or over?
    7   RF

36. What is the highest level of education completed by the primary wage earner in your household?
    1   Less than high school graduate
    2   High school graduate
    3   Some college
    4   College graduate
    5   Any postgraduate work
    6   RF

37. What is your occupation? (PROBE FOR TYPE OF BUSINESS, ETC.)

38. (IF MARRIED) What is your spouse's occupation? (PROBE FOR TYPE OF BUSINESS, ETC.)

39. Which of the following categories includes the total annual income of all the working members of your household before taxes?
    1   Under $15,000
    2   $15,000–$24,999
    3   $25,000–$39,999
    4   $40,000–$54,999
    5   $55,000–$69,999
    6   $70,000 or more
    7   DK
    8   RF

That concludes our survey, and I would like to thank you for taking the time to assist us.

NAME _____

TELEPHONE (_____) _____

INTERVIEWER NUMBER_____

Exercises

1. Use the survey results to respond to each research objective specified at the beginning of the case.
2. How are those who use Visa or MasterCard most often different from those who use American Express most often?
3. Describe respondents' attitudes toward credit limits.
4. Discuss credit card offers and the teachers' responses. Also, discuss credit card closings.
5. How did respondents react to the new credit card proposals?
6. Use multivariate statistics to determine the strongest predictors of response to the new credit card offers.

APPENDIX TWO

Considerations in Creating a Marketing Plan

I. MARKETING OVERVIEW

- ☐ What is the mission of the firm?
- ☐ What business are we in?
- ☐ What are the strategic goals of the organization?
- ☐ What do we sell?
- ☐ What are our target markets?
- ☐ What are the basic assumptions implicit in this plan?

II. OBJECTIVES

- ☐ Sales goals
- ☐ Profit goals
- ☐ Customer-service goals

III. SITUATION ANALYSIS

- ☐ Is a strategic window opening or closing?
- ☐ What are our competitive advantages?
- ☐ Are these competitive advantages sustainable and can we protect them?

A. Potential Internal Strengths and Weaknesses
- ☐ Managerial knowledge and capabilities
- ☐ Technology (internal)
- ☐ Employee attitudes
- ☐ Employee productivity
- ☐ Competitive intelligence
- ☐ Ability to produce quality products and services
- ☐ Marketing skills
- ☐ Quality control procedures
- ☐ Research and development skills
- ☐ Financial strength
- ☐ Management Information System

B. Potential External Opportunities and Threats
- ☐ Understanding of social/cultural values in the marketplace
- ☐ Understanding changing demographics
- ☐ Economic climate
- ☐ Understanding emerging technology
- ☐ Availability of natural resources
- ☐ Comprehension of the political and legal environment
- ☐ Understanding our competitors

C. Creation of Contingency Plans
- ☐ Take advantage of opportunities
- ☐ Mitigate threats

IV. MARKETING STRATEGY

A. Target Market Strategy
- ☐ Target market defined demographically and psychographically
- ☐ Forecasted change in size and growth rate of the target market
- ☐ Who is the decision maker?
- ☐ What is their decision process?
- ☐ Needs of the target market
- ☐ How do they view our products/services versus the competition?
- ☐ What does the target market want from us?
- ☐ Who are our best customers?

☐ Are some customers not profitable?
☐ How loyal are our customers?

B. Marketing Mix
  ☐ Is the marketing mix fully integrated in order to achieve the marketing objectives?
  1. Product/Service
    ☐ What are our major product/service offerings?
    ☐ What benefits do they offer?
    ☐ Profitability of each item in our product/service mix
    ☐ What is our brand equity?
    ☐ Scope, quality, and gaps in the product line
    ☐ Perceptions of our warranty
    ☐ Quality of our packaging
    ☐ Effectiveness of our new product development
    ☐ Service quality?
  2. Price
    ☐ How does target market view price versus value?
    ☐ Are we above/below or at the price level of our competition?
    ☐ How price sensitive is the target market?
    ☐ Discounts?
    ☐ Geographic price differences?
    ☐ Profitability per product/service
    ☐ Methods of payment
    ☐ Bundling considerations?
    ☐ Leasing options?
  3. Distribution
    ☐ Do we have effective supply chain management?
    ☐ Where does the target market expect to buy our product?
    ☐ Are we using the most efficient modes of transportation?
    ☐ Are customers satisfied with our delivery time?
    ☐ Are our warehouses/distribution centers strategically located and cost effective?
    ☐ Quality of order fulfillment
    ☐ How are channels evolving and what does this mean for us?
  4. Promotion
    ☐ Do we have an effective integrated marketing communications (IMC) plan?
    ☐ What is our positioning strategy and unique selling proposition and are they communicated properly in the IMC plan?
    ☐ Is our message resulting in increased sales?
    ☐ Advertising media used and effectiveness of the mix
    ☐ Advertising timing strategies
    ☐ Advertising agency functions and relationship with our organization
    ☐ Effectiveness of each sales promotion activity
    ☐ Objectives of each sales promotion activity
    ☐ Sales call effectiveness
    ☐ Frequency of sales calls on key accounts? Other accounts?
    ☐ How is salesforce organized and compensated?
    ☐ How are prospects identified and then forwarded to the sales force?
    ☐ Do we have adequate geographic sales coverage?
    ☐ Effectiveness of sales management

☐ Quality of our public relations program
☐ Components of our public relations program and their contribution to IMC.

V. IMPLEMENTATION, EVALUATION, AND CONTROL
☐ Resources necessary to implement the plan (budgets)
☐ Timing and order of activities
☐ Other required data to implement the plan
☐ Assigning authority and responsibility
☐ Projected outcomes in terms of sales and market share
☐ Criteria for determining the success of the plan
☐ Timing of evaluations

APPENDIX THREE

Statistical Tables

EXHIBIT 1	Random Digits								
63271	59986	71744	51102	15141	80714	58683	93108	13554	79945
88547	09896	95436	79115	08303	01041	20030	63754	08459	28364
55957	57243	83865	09911	19761	66535	40102	26646	60147	15702
46276	87453	44790	64122	45573	84358	21625	16999	13385	22782
55363	07449	34835	15290	76616	67191	12777	21861	68689	03263
69393	92785	49902	58447	42048	30378	87618	26933	40640	16281
13186	29431	88190	04588	38733	81290	89541	70290	40113	08243
17726	28652	56836	78351	47327	18518	92222	55201	27340	10493
36520	64465	05550	30157	82242	29520	69753	72602	23756	54935
81628	36100	39254	56835	37636	02421	98063	89641	64953	99337
84649	48968	75215	75498	49539	74240	03466	49292	36401	45525
63291	11618	12613	75055	43915	26488	41116	64531	56827	30825
70502	53225	03655	05915	37140	57051	48393	91322	25653	06543
06426	24771	59935	49801	11082	66762	94477	02494	88215	27191
20711	55609	29430	70165	45406	78484	31639	52009	18873	96927
41990	70538	77191	25860	55204	73417	83920	69468	74972	38712
72452	36618	76298	26678	89334	33938	95567	29380	75906	91807
37042	40318	57099	10528	09925	89773	41335	96244	29002	46453
53766	52875	15987	46962	67342	77592	57651	95508	80033	69828
90585	58955	53122	16025	84299	53310	67380	84249	25348	04332
32001	96293	37203	64516	51530	37069	40261	61374	05815	06714
62606	64324	46354	72157	67248	20135	49804	09226	64419	29457
10078	28073	85389	50324	14500	15562	64165	06125	71353	77669
91561	46145	24177	15294	10061	98124	75732	00815	83452	97355
13091	98112	53959	79607	52244	63303	10413	63839	74762	50289
73864	83014	72457	22682	03033	61714	88173	90835	00634	85169
66668	25467	48894	51043	02365	91726	09365	63167	95264	45643
84745	41042	29493	01836	09044	51926	43630	63470	76508	14194
48068	26805	94595	47907	13357	38412	33318	26098	82782	42851
54310	96175	97594	88616	42035	38093	36745	56702	40644	83514
14877	33095	10924	58013	61439	21882	42059	24177	58739	60170
78295	23179	02771	43464	59061	71411	05697	67194	30495	21157
67524	02865	39593	54278	04237	92441	26602	63835	38032	94770
58268	57219	68124	73455	83236	08710	04284	55005	84171	42596
97158	28672	50685	01181	24262	19427	52106	34308	73685	74246
04230	16831	69085	30802	65559	09205	71829	06489	85650	38707
94879	56606	30401	02602	57658	70091	54986	41394	60437	03195
71446	15232	66715	26385	91518	70566	02888	79941	39684	54315
32886	05644	79316	09819	00813	88407	17461	73925	53037	91904
62048	33711	25290	21526	02223	75947	66466	06332	10913	75336
84534	42351	21628	53669	81352	95152	08107	98814	72743	12849
84707	15885	84710	35866	06446	86311	32648	88141	73902	69981
19409	40868	64220	80861	13860	68493	52908	26374	63297	45052
57978	48015	25973	66777	45924	56144	24742	96702	88200	66162
57295	98298	11199	96510	75228	41600	47192	43267	35973	23152
94044	83785	93388	07833	38216	31413	70555	03023	54147	06647
30014	25879	71763	96679	90603	99396	74557	74224	18211	91637
07265	69563	64268	88802	72264	66540	01782	08396	19251	83613
84404	88642	30263	80310	11522	57810	27627	78376	36240	48952
21778	02085	27762	46097	43324	34354	09369	14966	10158	76089

EXHIBIT 2 | **Standard Normal Distribution: Z-values**

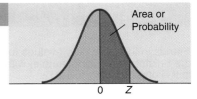

Area or Probability

Entries in the table give the area under the curve between the mean and Z standard deviations above the mean. For example, for Z = 1.25, the area under the curve between the mean and Z is .3944.

Z	.00	.01	.02	.03	.04	.05	.06	.07	.08	.09
.0	.0000	.0040	.0080	.0120	.0160	.0199	.0239	.0279	.0319	.0359
.1	.0398	.0438	.0478	.0517	.0557	.0596	.0636	.0675	.0714	.0753
.2	.0793	.0832	.0871	.0910	.0948	.0987	.1026	.1064	.1103	.1141
.3	.1179	.1217	.1255	.1293	.1331	.1368	.1406	.1443	.1480	.1517
.4	.1554	.1591	.1628	.1664	.1700	.1736	.1772	.1808	.1844	.1879
.5	.1915	.1950	.1985	.2019	.2054	.2088	.2123	.2157	.2190	.2224
.6	.2257	.2291	.2324	.2357	.2389	.2422	.2454	.2486	.2518	.2549
.7	.2580	.2612	.2642	.2673	.2704	.2734	.2764	.2794	.2823	.2852
.8	.2881	.2910	.2939	.2967	.2995	.3023	.3051	.3078	.3106	.3133
.9	.3159	.3186	.3212	.3238	.3264	.3289	.3315	.3340	.3365	.3389
1.0	.3413	.3438	.3461	.3485	.3508	.3531	.3554	.3577	.3599	.3621
1.1	.3643	.3665	.3686	.3708	.3729	.3749	.3770	.3790	.3810	.3830
1.2	.3849	.3869	.3888	.3907	.3925	.3944	.3962	.3980	.3997	.4015
1.3	.4032	.4049	.4066	.4082	.4099	.4115	.4131	.4147	.4162	.4177
1.4	.4192	.4207	.4222	.4236	.4251	.4265	.4279	.4292	.4306	.4319
1.5	.4332	.4345	.4357	.4370	.4382	.4394	.4406	.4418	.4429	.4441
1.6	.4452	.4463	.4474	.4484	.4495	.4505	.4515	.4525	.4535	.4545
1.7	.4554	.4564	.4573	.4582	.4591	.4599	.4608	.4616	.4625	.4633
1.8	.4641	.4649	.4656	.4664	.4671	.4678	.4686	.4693	.4699	.4706
1.9	.4713	.4719	.4726	.4732	.4738	.4744	.4750	.4756	.4761	.4767
2.0	.4772	.4778	.4783	.4788	.4793	.4798	.4803	.4808	.4812	.4817
2.1	.4821	.4826	.4830	.4834	.4838	.4842	.4846	.4850	.4854	.4857
2.2	.4861	.4864	.4868	.4871	.4875	.4878	.4881	.4884	.4887	.4890
2.3	.4893	.4896	.4898	.4901	.4904	.4906	.4909	.4911	.4913	.4916
2.4	.4918	.4920	.4922	.4925	.4927	.4929	.4931	.4932	.4934	.4936
2.5	.4938	.4940	.4941	.4943	.4945	.4946	.4948	.4949	.4951	.4952
2.6	.4953	.4955	.4956	.4957	.4959	.4960	.4961	.4962	.4963	.4964
2.7	.4965	.4966	.4967	.4968	.4969	.4970	.4971	.4972	.4973	.4974
2.8	.4974	.4975	.4976	.4977	.4977	.4978	.4979	.4979	.4980	.4981
2.9	.4981	.4982	.4982	.4983	.4984	.4984	.4985	.4985	.4986	.4986
3.0	.4986	.4987	.4987	.4988	.4988	.4989	.4989	.4989	.4990	.4990

EXHIBIT 3   t-Distribution

Entries in the table give *t*-values for an area or probability in the upper tail of the *t*-distribution. For example, with 10 degrees of freedom and a .05 area in the upper tail, $t_{.05} = 1.812$.

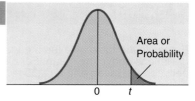

Area or Probability

Degrees of Freedom	Area in Upper Tail				
	.10	.05	.025	.01	.005
1	3.078	6.314	12.706	31.821	63.657
2	1.886	2.920	4.303	6.965	9.925
3	1.638	2.353	3.182	4.541	5.841
4	1.533	2.132	2.776	3.747	4.604
5	1.476	2.015	2.571	3.365	4.032
6	1.440	1.943	2.447	3.143	3.707
7	1.415	1.895	2.365	2.998	3.499
8	1.397	1.860	2.306	2.896	3.355
9	1.383	1.833	2.262	2.821	3.250
10	1.372	1.812	2.228	2.764	3.169
11	1.363	1.796	2.201	2.718	3.106
12	1.356	1.782	2.179	2.681	3.055
13	1.350	1.771	2.160	2.650	3.012
14	1.345	1.761	2.145	2.624	2.977
15	1.341	1.753	2.131	2.602	2.947
16	1.337	1.746	2.120	2.583	2.921
17	1.333	1.740	2.110	2.567	2.898
18	1.330	1.734	2.101	2.552	2.878
19	1.328	1.729	2.093	2.539	2.861
20	1.325	1.725	2.086	2.528	2.845
21	1.323	1.721	2.080	2.518	2.831
22	1.321	1.717	2.074	2.508	2.819
23	1.319	1.714	2.069	2.500	2.807
24	1.318	1.711	2.064	2.492	2.797
25	1.316	1.708	2.060	2.485	2.787
26	1.315	1.706	2.056	2.479	2.779
27	1.314	1.703	2.052	2.473	2.771
28	1.313	1.701	2.048	2.467	2.763
29	1.311	1.699	2.045	2.462	2.756
30	1.310	1.697	2.042	2.457	2.750
40	1.303	1.684	2.021	2.423	2.704
60	1.296	1.671	2.000	2.390	2.660
120	1.289	1.658	1.980	2.358	2.617
∞	1.282	1.645	1.960	2.326	2.576

Reprinted by permission of Biometrika Trustees from Table 12, Percentage Points of the *t*-Distribution, by E. S. Pearson and H. O. Hartley, *Biometrika Tables for Statisticians*, Vol. 1, 3rd Edition, 1966.

EXHIBIT 4	Chi-Square Distribution

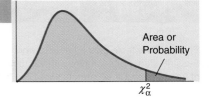

Area or Probability

χ_α^2

Entries in the table give χ_α^2 values, where α is the area or probability in the upper tail of the chi-square distribution. For example, with 10 degrees of freedom and a .01 area in the upper tail, χ_α^2 23.2093.

Degrees of Freedom	Area in Upper Tail									
	.995	.99	.975	.95	.90	.10	.05	.025	.01	.005
1	.0000393	.000157	.000982	.000393	.015709	2.70554	3.84146	5.02389	6.63490	7.87944
2	.0100251	.0201007	.0506356	.102587	.210720	4.60517	5.99147	7.37776	9.21034	10.5966
3	.0717212	.114832	2.15795	.351846	.584375	6.25139	7.81473	9.34840	11.3449	12.8381
4	.206990	.297110	.484419	.710721	1.063623	7.77944	9.48773	11.1433	13.2767	14.8602
5	.411740	.554300	.831211	1.145476	1.61031	9.23635	11.0705	12.8325	15.0863	16.7496
6	.675727	.872085	1.237347	1.63539	2.20413	10.6446	12.5916	14.4494	16.8119	18.5476
7	.989265	1.239043	1.68987	2.16735	2.83311	12.0170	14.0671	16.0128	18.4753	20.2777
8	1.344419	1.646482	2.17973	2.73264	3.48954	13.3616	15.5073	17.5346	20.0902	21.9550
9	1.734926	2.087912	2.70039	3.32511	4.16816	14.6837	16.9190	19.0228	21.6660	23.5893
10	2.15585	2.55821	3.24697	3.94030	4.86518	15.9871	18.3070	20.4831	23.2093	25.1882
11	2.60321	3.05347	3.81575	4.57481	5.57779	17.2750	19.6751	21.9200	24.7250	26.7569
12	3.07382	3.57056	4.40379	5.22603	6.30380	18.5494	21.0261	23.3367	26.2170	28.2995
13	3.56503	4.10691	5.00874	5.89186	7.04150	19.8119	22.3621	24.7356	27.6883	29.8194
14	4.07468	4.66043	5.62872	6.57063	7.78953	21.0642	23.6848	26.1190	29.1413	31.3193
15	4.60094	5.22935	6.26214	7.26094	8.54675	22.3072	24.9958	27.4884	30.5779	32.8013
16	5.14224	5.81221	6.90766	7.96164	9.31223	23.5418	26.2962	28.8454	31.9999	34.2672
17	5.69724	6.40776	7.56418	8.67176	10.0852	24.7690	27.5871	30.1910	33.4087	35.7185
18	6.26481	7.01491	8.23075	9.39046	10.8649	25.9894	28.8693	31.5264	34.8053	37.1564
19	6.84398	7.63273	8.90655	10.1170	11.6509	27.2036	30.1435	32.8523	36.1908	38.5822
20	7.43386	8.26040	9.59083	10.8508	12.4426	28.4120	31.4104	34.1696	37.5662	39.9968
21	8.03366	8.89720	10.28293	11.5913	13.2396	29.6151	32.6705	35.4789	38.9321	41.4010
22	8.64272	9.54249	10.9823	12.3380	14.0415	30.8133	33.9244	36.7807	40.2894	42.7958
23	9.26042	10.19567	11.6885	13.0905	14.8479	32.0069	35.1725	38.0757	41.6384	44.1813
24	9.88623	10.8564	12.4011	13.8484	15.6587	33.1963	36.4151	39.3641	42.9798	45.5585
25	10.5197	11.5240	13.1197	14.6114	16.4734	34.3816	37.6525	40.6465	44.3141	46.9278
26	11.1603	12.1981	13.8439	15.3791	17.2919	35.5631	38.8852	41.9232	45.6417	48.2899
27	11.8076	12.8786	14.5733	16.1513	18.1138	36.7412	40.1133	43.1944	46.9630	49.6449
28	12.4613	13.5648	15.3079	16.9279	18.9392	37.9159	41.3372	44.4607	48.2782	50.9933
29	13.1211	14.2565	16.0471	17.7083	19.7677	39.0875	42.5569	45.7222	49.5879	52.3356
30	13.7867	14.9535	16.7908	18.4926	20.5992	40.2560	43.7729	46.9792	50.8922	53.6720
40	20.765	22.1643	24.4331	26.5093	29.0505	51.8050	55.7585	59.3417	63.6907	66.7659
50	27.9907	29.7067	32.3574	34.7642	37.6886	63.1671	67.5048	71.4202	76.1539	79.4900
60	35.5346	37.4848	40.4817	43.1879	46.4589	74.3970	79.0819	83.2976	88.3794	91.9517
70	43.2752	45.4418	48.7576	51.7393	55.3290	85.5271	90.5312	95.0231	100.425	104.215
80	51.1720	53.5400	57.1532	60.3915	64.2778	96.5782	101.879	106.629	112.329	116.321
90	59.1963	61.7541	65.6466	69.1260	73.2912	107.565	113.145	118.136	124.116	128.299
100	67.3276	70.0648	74.2219	77.9295	82.3581	118.498	124.342	129.561	135.807	140.169

EXHIBIT 5 | F-Distribution

Entries in the table give F_α values, where α is the area or probability in the upper tail of the F-distribution. For example, with 12 numerator degrees of freedom, 15 denominator degrees of freedom, and a .05 area in the upper tail, $F_{.05} = 2.48$.

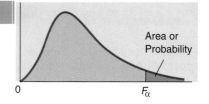

Area or Probability

0   F_α

Table of $F_{.05}$ Values

Numerator Degrees of Freedom

	1	2	3	4	5	6	7	8	9	10	12	15	20	24	30	40	60	120	∞
1	161.4	199.5	215.7	224.6	230.2	234.0	236.8	238.9	240.5	241.9	243.9	245.9	248.0	249.1	250.1	251.1	252.2	253.3	254.3
2	18.51	19.00	19.16	19.25	19.30	19.33	19.35	19.37	19.38	19.40	19.41	19.43	19.45	19.45	19.46	19.47	19.48	19.49	19.50
3	10.13	9.55	9.28	9.12	9.01	8.94	8.89	8.85	8.81	8.79	8.74	8.70	8.66	8.64	8.62	8.59	8.57	8.55	8.53
4	7.71	6.94	6.59	6.39	6.26	6.16	6.09	6.04	6.00	5.96	5.91	5.86	5.80	5.77	5.75	5.72	5.69	5.66	5.63
5	6.61	5.79	5.41	5.19	5.05	4.95	4.88	4.82	4.77	4.74	4.68	4.62	4.56	4.53	4.50	4.46	4.43	4.40	4.36
6	5.99	5.14	4.76	4.53	4.39	4.28	4.21	4.15	4.10	4.06	4.00	3.94	3.87	3.84	3.81	3.77	3.74	3.70	3.67
7	5.59	4.74	4.35	4.12	3.97	3.87	3.79	3.73	3.68	3.64	3.57	3.51	3.44	3.41	3.38	3.34	3.30	3.27	3.23
8	5.32	4.46	4.07	3.84	3.69	3.58	3.50	3.44	3.39	3.35	3.28	3.22	3.15	3.12	3.08	3.04	3.01	2.97	2.93
9	5.12	4.26	3.86	3.63	3.48	3.37	3.29	3.23	3.18	3.14	3.07	3.01	2.94	2.90	2.86	2.83	2.79	2.75	2.71
10	4.96	4.10	3.71	3.48	3.33	3.22	3.14	3.07	3.02	2.98	2.91	2.85	2.77	2.74	2.70	2.66	2.62	2.58	2.54
11	4.84	3.98	3.59	3.36	3.20	3.09	3.01	2.95	2.90	2.85	2.79	2.72	2.65	2.61	2.57	2.53	2.49	2.45	2.40
12	4.75	3.89	3.49	3.26	3.11	3.00	2.91	2.85	2.80	2.75	2.69	2.62	2.54	2.51	2.47	2.43	2.38	2.34	2.30
13	4.67	3.81	3.41	3.18	3.03	2.92	2.83	2.77	2.71	2.67	2.60	2.53	2.46	2.42	2.38	2.34	2.30	2.25	2.21
14	4.60	3.74	3.34	3.11	2.96	2.85	2.76	2.70	2.65	2.60	2.53	2.46	2.39	2.35	2.31	2.27	2.22	2.18	2.13
15	4.54	3.68	3.29	3.06	2.90	2.79	2.71	2.64	2.59	2.54	2.48	2.40	2.33	2.29	2.25	2.20	2.16	2.11	2.07
16	4.49	3.63	3.24	3.01	2.85	2.74	2.66	2.59	2.54	2.49	2.42	2.35	2.28	2.24	2.19	2.15	2.11	2.06	2.01
17	4.45	3.59	3.20	2.96	2.81	2.70	2.61	2.55	2.49	2.45	2.38	2.31	2.23	2.19	2.15	2.10	2.06	2.01	1.96
18	4.41	3.55	3.16	2.93	2.77	2.66	2.58	2.51	2.46	2.41	2.34	2.27	2.19	2.15	2.11	2.06	2.02	1.97	1.92
19	4.38	3.52	3.13	2.90	2.74	2.63	2.54	2.48	2.42	2.38	2.31	2.23	2.16	2.11	2.07	2.03	1.98	1.93	1.88
20	4.35	3.49	3.10	2.87	2.71	2.60	2.51	2.45	2.39	2.35	2.28	2.20	2.12	2.08	2.04	1.99	1.95	1.90	1.84
21	4.32	3.47	3.07	2.84	2.68	2.57	2.49	2.42	2.37	2.32	2.25	2.18	2.10	2.05	2.01	1.96	1.92	1.87	1.81
22	4.30	3.44	3.05	2.82	2.66	2.55	2.46	2.40	2.34	2.30	2.23	2.15	2.07	2.03	1.98	1.94	1.89	1.84	1.78
23	4.28	3.42	3.03	2.80	2.64	2.53	2.44	2.37	2.32	2.27	2.20	2.13	2.05	2.01	1.96	1.91	1.86	1.81	1.76
24	4.26	3.40	3.01	2.78	2.62	2.51	2.42	2.36	2.30	2.25	2.18	2.11	2.03	1.98	1.94	1.89	1.84	1.79	1.73
25	4.24	3.39	2.99	2.76	2.60	2.49	2.40	2.34	2.28	2.24	2.16	2.09	2.01	1.96	1.92	1.87	1.82	1.77	1.71
26	4.23	3.37	2.98	2.74	2.59	2.47	2.39	2.32	2.27	2.22	2.15	2.07	1.99	1.95	1.90	1.85	1.80	1.75	1.69
27	4.21	3.35	2.96	2.73	2.57	2.46	2.37	2.31	2.25	2.20	2.13	2.06	1.97	1.93	1.88	1.84	1.79	1.73	1.67
28	4.20	3.34	2.95	2.71	2.56	2.45	2.36	2.29	2.24	2.19	2.12	2.04	1.96	1.91	1.87	1.82	1.77	1.71	1.65
29	4.18	3.33	2.93	2.70	2.55	2.43	2.35	2.28	2.22	2.18	2.10	2.03	1.94	1.90	1.85	1.81	1.75	1.70	1.64
30	4.17	3.32	2.92	2.69	2.53	2.42	2.33	2.27	2.21	2.16	2.09	2.01	1.93	1.89	1.84	1.79	1.74	1.68	1.62
40	4.08	3.23	2.84	2.61	2.45	2.34	2.25	2.18	2.12	2.08	2.00	1.92	1.84	1.79	1.74	1.69	1.64	1.58	1.51
60	4.00	3.15	2.76	2.53	2.37	2.25	2.17	2.10	2.04	1.99	1.92	1.84	1.75	1.70	1.65	1.59	1.53	1.47	1.39
120	3.92	3.07	2.68	2.45	2.29	2.17	2.09	2.02	1.96	1.91	1.83	1.75	1.66	1.61	1.55	1.50	1.43	1.35	1.25
∞	3.84	3.00	2.60	2.37	2.21	2.10	2.01	1.94	1.88	1.83	1.75	1.67	1.57	1.52	1.46	1.39	1.32	1.22	1.00

Table of $F_{.01}$ Values

	Numerator Degrees of Freedom																			
	1	2	3	4	5	6	7	8	9	10	12	15	20	24	30	40	60	120	∞
1	4052	4999.5	5403	5625	5764	5859	5928	5982	6022	6056	6106	6157	6209	6235	6261	6287	6313	6339	6366
2	98.50	99.00	99.17	99.25	99.30	99.33	99.36	99.37	99.39	99.40	99.42	99.43	99.45	99.46	99.47	99.47	99.48	99.49	99.50
3	34.12	30.82	29.46	28.71	28.24	27.91	27.67	27.49	27.35	27.23	27.05	26.87	26.69	26.60	26.50	26.41	26.32	26.22	26.13
4	21.20	18.00	16.69	15.98	15.52	51.21	14.98	14.80	14.66	14.55	14.37	14.20	14.02	13.93	13.84	13.75	13.65	13.56	13.46
5	16.26	13.27	12.06	11.39	10.97	10.67	10.46	10.29	10.16	10.05	9.89	9.72	9.55	9.47	9.38	9.29	9.20	9.11	9.06
6	13.75	10.92	9.78	9.15	8.75	8.47	8.26	8.10	7.98	7.87	7.72	7.56	7.40	7.31	7.23	7.14	7.06	6.97	6.88
7	12.25	9.55	8.45	7.85	7.46	7.19	6.99	6.84	6.72	6.62	6.47	6.31	6.16	6.07	5.99	5.91	5.82	5.74	5.65
8	11.26	8.65	7.59	7.01	6.63	6.37	6.18	6.03	5.91	5.81	5.67	5.52	5.36	5.28	5.20	5.12	5.03	4.95	4.86
9	10.56	8.02	6.99	6.42	6.06	5.80	5.61	5.47	5.35	5.26	5.11	4.96	4.81	4.73	4.65	4.57	4.48	4.40	4.31
10	10.04	7.56	6.55	5.99	5.64	5.39	5.20	5.06	4.94	4.85	4.71	4.56	4.41	4.33	4.25	4.17	4.08	4.00	3.91
11	9.65	7.21	6.22	5.67	5.32	5.07	4.89	4.74	4.63	4.54	4.40	4.25	4.10	4.02	3.94	3.86	3.78	3.69	3.60
12	9.33	6.93	5.95	5.41	5.06	4.82	4.64	4.50	4.39	4.30	4.16	4.01	3.86	3.78	3.70	3.62	3.54	3.45	3.36
13	9.07	6.70	5.74	5.21	4.86	4.62	4.44	4.30	4.19	4.10	3.96	3.82	3.66	3.59	3.51	3.43	3.34	3.25	3.17
14	8.86	6.51	5.56	5.04	4.69	4.46	4.28	4.14	4.03	3.94	3.80	3.66	3.51	3.43	3.35	3.27	3.18	3.09	3.00
15	8.68	6.36	5.42	4.89	4.56	4.32	4.14	4.00	3.89	3.80	3.67	3.52	3.37	3.29	3.21	3.13	3.05	2.96	2.87
16	8.53	6.23	5.29	4.77	4.44	4.20	4.03	3.89	3.78	3.69	3.55	3.41	3.26	3.18	3.10	3.02	2.93	2.84	2.75
17	8.40	6.11	5.18	4.67	4.34	4.10	3.93	3.79	3.68	3.59	3.46	3.31	3.16	3.08	3.00	2.92	2.83	2.75	2.65
18	8.29	6.01	5.09	4.58	4.25	4.01	3.84	3.71	3.60	3.51	3.37	3.23	3.08	3.00	2.92	2.84	2.75	2.66	2.57
19	8.18	5.93	5.01	4.50	4.17	3.94	3.77	3.63	3.52	3.43	3.30	3.15	3.00	2.92	2.84	2.76	2.67	2.58	2.49
20	8.10	5.85	4.94	4.43	4.10	3.87	3.70	3.56	3.46	3.37	3.23	3.09	2.94	2.86	2.78	2.69	2.61	2.52	2.42
21	8.02	5.78	4.87	4.37	4.04	3.81	3.64	3.51	3.40	3.31	3.17	3.03	2.88	2.80	2.72	2.64	2.55	2.46	2.36
22	7.95	5.72	4.82	4.31	3.99	3.76	3.59	3.45	3.35	3.26	3.12	2.98	2.83	2.75	2.67	2.58	2.50	2.40	2.31
23	7.88	5.66	4.76	4.26	3.94	3.71	3.54	3.41	3.30	3.21	3.07	2.93	2.78	2.70	2.62	2.54	2.45	2.35	2.26
24	7.82	5.61	4.72	4.22	3.90	3.67	3.50	3.36	3.26	3.17	3.03	2.89	2.74	2.66	2.58	2.49	2.40	2.31	2.21
25	7.77	5.57	4.68	4.18	3.85	3.63	3.46	3.32	3.22	3.13	2.99	2.85	2.70	2.62	2.54	2.45	2.36	2.27	2.17
26	7.72	5.53	4.64	4.14	3.82	3.59	3.42	3.29	3.18	3.09	2.96	2.81	2.66	2.58	2.50	2.42	2.33	2.23	2.13
27	7.68	5.49	4.60	4.11	3.78	3.56	3.39	3.26	3.15	3.06	2.93	2.78	2.63	2.55	2.47	2.38	2.29	2.20	2.10
28	7.64	5.45	4.57	4.07	3.75	3.53	3.36	3.23	3.12	3.03	2.90	2.75	2.60	2.52	2.44	2.35	2.26	2.17	2.06
29	7.60	5.42	4.54	4.04	3.73	3.50	3.33	3.20	3.09	3.00	2.87	2.73	2.57	2.49	2.41	2.33	2.23	2.14	2.03
30	7.56	5.39	4.51	4.02	3.70	3.47	3.30	3.17	3.07	2.98	2.84	2.70	2.55	2.47	2.39	2.30	2.21	2.11	2.01
40	7.31	5.18	4.31	3.83	3.51	3.29	3.12	2.99	2.89	2.80	2.66	2.52	2.37	2.29	2.20	2.11	2.02	1.92	1.80
60	7.08	4.98	4.13	3.65	3.34	3.12	2.95	2.82	2.72	2.63	2.50	2.35	2.20	2.12	2.03	1.94	1.84	1.73	1.60
120	6.85	4.79	3.95	3.48	3.17	2.96	2.79	2.66	2.56	2.47	2.34	2.19	2.03	1.95	1.86	1.76	1.66	1.53	1.38
∞	6.63	4.61	3.78	3.32	3.02	2.80	2.64	2.51	2.41	2.32	2.18	2.04	1.88	1.79	1.70	1.59	1.47	1.32	1.00

ENDNOTES

Chapter 1

1. Brian Maraone, "Ready to Get Behind the Wheel," *Quirk's Marketing Research Review* (July 2003), pp. 66–69.
2. *www.marketingpower.com* (May 31, 2005).
3. "U.S. Automakers Lag in Hybrid Sales," *www.consumeraffairs.com* (April 26, 2005).
4. "Understanding Discontinuous Opportunities," *Marketing Research* (Fall 1999), p. 9.
5. *www.marketingpower.com* (May 31, 2005).
6. Todd Wasserman, "Duracell Looks to Sink Zinc," *Brandweek* (May 16, 2005), p. 8.
7. "Kids Get Their Wish," *www.heinz.com* (June 1, 2005).
8. "Kraft Introduces New Products for South Beach Diet," *www.kraft.com/newsroom* (January 7, 2005).
9. *www.correctcraft.com* (June 2, 2005).
10. "Why Some Customers Are More Equal Than Others," *Fortune* (September 19, 1994), pp. 215–224.
11. Sunil Gupta, Donald Lehmann, and Jennifer Ames Stuart, "Valuing Customers," *Journal of Marketing Research* (February 2004), pp. 7–18.
12. "Cast Your Net," *Marketing News* (November 24, 2003), pp. 15–19.
13. "Sony Unveils Business Strategy for New Aiwa Products," *Kyodo News* (January 8, 2003).
14. Michael Fielding, "Resorts' email Alerts Revive Flat Business on Slopes," *Marketing News* (March 1, 2005), pp. 17–18.
15. Christopher DeAngelis, "Trends in Data Collection," CASRO Conference: Chicago, IL (November 19, 2004). Projections for 2006 by the authors.
16. Dana James, "Precision Decision," *Marketing News* (September 27, 1999), pp. 23–24.
17. Christine Wright-Isak and David Prensky, "Early Marketing Research: Science and Application," *Marketing Research* (Fall 1993), pp. 16–23.
18. Percival White, *Market Analysis: Its Principles and Methods*, 2nd ed. (New York: McGraw-Hill, 1925).
19. Much of this section is taken from David W. Steward, "From Methods and Projects to Systems and Process: The Evolution of Marketing Research Techniques," *Marketing Research* (September 1991), pp. 25–34.
20. William D. Neal, "Getting Serious about Marketing Research," *Marketing Research* (Summer 2002), pp. 24–28.
21. Gail Gaboda, "For Business Travelers, There's No Place Like Home," *Marketing News* (September 15, 1997), pp. 19–20. Reprinted by permission of the American Marketing Association.
22. "I Want My Satellite Radio," *Quirk's Marketing Research Review* (May 2005), p. 74.

Chapter 2

1. Sarah Ellison, "P&G Chief's Turnaround Recipe: Find Out What Women Want," *Wall Street Journal* (June 1, 2005), pp. A1, A16.
2. "Top 50 U.S. Marketing Research Firms," *Marketing News* (June 15, 2005), p. H4.
3. Ibid.
4. Jack Honomichl, "Strong Progress," *Marketing News* (June 15, 2005), pp. H3, H57.
5. "New CMO Says Wal-Mart Will Reach More Customers," *Brandweek* (May 2, 2005), p. 5.
6. "Top 50. U.S. Marketing Research Firms," pp. H6–H12.
7. Ibid.
8. Barton Le, Soumya Saklani, and David Tatterson, "Top Prospects: State of the MR Industry," *Marketing News* (June 10, 2002), pp. 12–13.
9. *Inside Research* (May 2004).
10. "Kraft's Miracle Whip Targets Core Consumers with '97 Ads," *Advertising Age* (February 3, 1997), p. 12.
11. Data provided by Mary Klupp, Futures Research Manager, Ford Motor Company.
12. The information on users and suppliers is from a speech entitled, "Where in the World Are We?" presented by Merrill Dubrow, CEO, M/A/R/C Research (January 31, 2005).
13. Catherine Arnold, "Self Examination," *Marketing News* (February 1, 2005), pp. 55–56.
14. Jerry Thomas, "The Dot.Com Meltdown," *Marketing News* (March 4, 2002).
15. These ethical theories are from: Catherine Rainbow, "Descriptions of Ethical Theories and Principles," *www.bio.davidson.edu/people/Kabernd/Indep/carainbow.htm* (June 22, 2005).
16. David Haynes, "Respondent Goodwill Is a Cooperative Activity," *Quirk's Marketing Research Review* (February 2005), pp. 30–32.

17. "New York State Sues Survey Firm for Allegedly Tricking Students," *Wall Street Journal* (August 30, 2002), p. B4.
18. Shelby Hunt, Lawrence Chonko, and James Wilcox, "Ethical Problems of Marketing Researchers," *Journal of Marketing Research* (August 1984), p. 314. Reprinted by permission of the American Marketing Association
19. Terry Grapentine, "You Can't Take the Human Nature Out of Black Boxes," *Marketing Research* (Winter 2004), pp. 20–22.
20. "The Code of Marketing Research Standards," *www.mra-net.org/pdf/expanded_code.pdf* (June 29, 2005).
21. Diane Bowers, "New Requirement for Research: Privacy Assurance and Professional Accountability." *CASRO Journal* (2002), pp. 115–116.
22. *http://www.export.gov* (June 29, 2005).
23. "Professional Researcher Certification," *http://www.mra-net.org* (June 29, 2005).
24. Paul Green, Abba Krieger, and Yoram Wind, "Survey Methods Help to Clear Up Legal Questions, "*Marketing News* (September 16, 2002).
25. "Coke sets Accord over Rigged Test," *International Herald Tribune* (August 4, 2003), p. 10; "Coke Agrees to Pay Burger King $10 Million to Resolve Dispute," *Wall Street Journal* (August 4, 2003), p. B6; "How Coke Officials Beefed Up Results of Marketing Test," *Wall Street Journal* (August 20, 2003), pp. A1, A6; "Coke Fountain Chief Steps Down Amid Furor over Burger King Test," *Wall Street Journal* (August 26, 2003), p. B4.

Chapter 3

1. Ann Breese and Donald Bruzzone, "A Definite Impact," *Quirk's Marketing Research Review* (April 2004), pp. 22–31.
2. "Meet the Aggregators," *Brandweek* (May 30, 2005), p. 25.
3. Karole Friemann, "6 Steps During Initiation Critical to Efficacy," *Marketing News* (January 20, 2003), p. 14.
4. Paul Conner, "Defining the Decision Purpose of Research," *Marketing News* (June 9, 1997), p. H15. Reprinted by permission of the American Marketing Association.
5. Diane Schmalensee and Dawn Lesh, "How to Make Research More Actionable," *Marketing Research* (Winter 1998/Spring 1999), pp. 23–26. Reprinted with permission from *Marketing Research*, published by the American Marketing Association.
6. "CEOs Use Technology to Gather Information, Build Customer Loyalty," *Wall Street Journal* (October 26, 2004), p. B1.
7. Carol Graff, "Working with Difficult Internal Clients," *Quirk's Marketing Research Review* (December 2001), pp. 70–74.
8. Joseph Rydholm, "What Do Clients Want from a Research Firm?" *Marketing Research Review* (October 1995), p. 82.
9. Fred Luthans and Janet K. Larsen, "How Managers Really Communicate," *Human Relations 39* (1986), pp. 161–178; and Harry E. Penley and Brian Hawkins, "Studying Interpersonal Communication in Organizations: A Leadership Application," *Academy of Management Journal 28* (1985), pp. 309–326.
10. Rohit Deshpande and Scott Jeffries, "Attitude Affecting the Use of Marketing Research in Decision Making: An Empirical Investigation," in *Educators' Conference Proceedings*, Series 47, edited by Kenneth L. Bernhardt et al. (Chicago: American Marketing Association, 1981), pp. 1–4.
11. Rohit Deshpande and Gerald Zaltman, "Factors Affecting the Use of Market Information: A Path Analysis," *Journal of Marketing Research 19* (February 1982), pp. 14–31; Rohit Deshpande, "A Comparison of Factors Affecting Researcher and Manager Perceptions of Market Research Use," *Journal of Marketing Research 21* (February 1989), pp. 32–38; Hanjoon Lee, Frank Acito, and Ralph Day, "Evaluation and Use of Marketing Research by Decision Makers: A Behavioral Simulation," *Journal of Marketing Research 24* (May 1987), pp. 187–196; and Michael Hu, "An Experimental Study of Managers' and Researchers' Use of Consumer Market Research," *Journal of the Academy of Marketing Science 14* (Fall 1986), pp. 44–51.
12. Rohit Deshpande and Gerald Zaltman, "A Comparison of Factors Affecting Use of Marketing Information in Consumer and Industrial Firms," *Journal of Marketing Research 24* (February 1987), pp. 114–118.
13. "Frozen Pizza Industry Leaves Consumers Wanting More," *Quirk's Marketing Research Review* (February 2004), p. 61.

Chapter 4

1. Kevin Kelleher, "66,207,896 Bottles of Beer on the Wall," *Business 2.0* (January/February 2004), pp. 47–49.
2. John Goodman and David Beinhacker, "By the Numbers," *Quirk's Marketing Research Review* (October 2003), pp. 18, 82.
3. "The Information Gold Mine," *Business Week E. Biz* (July 26, 1999), p. EB18.
4. "A Potent New Tool for Selling Database Marketing," *Business Week* (September 5, 1994), pp. 56–62.
5. Julie Schlosser, "Looking for Intelligence in Ice Cream," *Fortune* (March 17, 2003), pp. 114–120.

6. Joan Raymond, "Home Field Advantage," *American Demographics* (April 2001), pp. 34–36.

7. "Interview with Mike Foytik, DSS Research," conducted by Roger Gates (November 29, 2000). Reprinted by permission.

8. This section is adapted from Nick Wingfield, "A Marketer's Dream," *Wall Street Journal* (December 7, 1998), p. R20.

9. "What've you Done for Us Lately?" *Business Week* (April 23, 1999), pp. 24–34.

10. "Looking for Patterns," *Wall Street Journal* (June 21, 1999), pp. R16, R20.

11. *www.privacy.org* (March 24, 2005).

12. "The Great Data Heist," *Fortune* (May 16, 2005), pp. 66–75.

13. "Choice Point to Exit Non-FCRA, Consumer-Sensitive Data Markets," (*www.choicepoint.com*) (March 4, 2005).

14. "Citi Notifies 3.9 Million Customers of Lost Data," *MSNBC.com* (June 7, 2005).

15. Julia Boorstin, "What's the Government Doing?" *Fortune* (May 16, 2005), p. 75.

16. "On My Mind: The Privacy Hoax: Consumers Say They Care about Internet Privacy But Don't Act That Way. Let the Market Rule," *Forbes* (October 14, 2002), pp. 42–44.

17. Donna Gillin and Jane Sheppard, "The Fallacy of Getting Paid for Your Opinions," *Marketing Research* (Fall 2003), p. 8.

18. This section is from *http://www.lib.berkeley.edu/TeachingLib/Guides/Internet/Strategies.html*

19. Ibid.

20. Adapted from: "Evaluating Web Pages: Techniques to Apply and Questions to Ask," from *http://www.lib.berkeley.edu/TeachingLib/Guide/Internet/evaluate.html* (May 9, 2005).

21. The section on GIS has been updated by Joshua Been, University of Texas at Arlington.

22. Case Study—Avon Products (November 2004) *http://www.tactician.com/News/News_CS_AVON1104.asp*

23. "Turning a Map into a Layer Cake of Information," *New York Times*, January 20, 2000, Thursday, Late Edition—Final, Section G; Page 1, Column 1, Circuits, 2132 words, by CATHERINE GREENMAN.

24. Amy Cortese, "Is Your Business in the Right Spot? *Business 2.0* (May 2004), pp. 76–77.

25. "Googling to the Max—Exercises," Part I of Research Quality Web Searching, *The Teaching Library* (Spring 2005), University of California, Berkeley.

Chapter 5

1. Deborah Ball, Sarah Ellison, and Janet Adamy, "Just What You Need!" *Wall Street Journal* (October 28, 2004), pp. B1, B8.

2. Alison Stein Wellner, "The New Science of Focus Groups," *American Demographics* (March 2003), pp. 29–33.

3. "Focus Groups Illuminate Quantitative Research," *Marketing News* (September 23, 1996), p. 41.

4. For an article on blending qualitative and quantitative research, see Rebecca Quarles, "Blurring the Traditional Boundaries Between Qualitative and Quantitative Research," *CASRO Journal* (1999), pp. 47–50.

5. John Houlahan, "In Defense of the Focus Group," *Quirk's Marketing Research Review* (October 2003), pp. 16, 84. The 2005 estimates are the authors'.

6. "Motives Are as Important as Words When Group Describes a Product," *Marketing News* (August 28, 1987), p. 49.

7. Houlahan, "In Defense of the Focus Group," p. 84.

8. Alison Stein Wellner, "The New Science of Focus Groups," *American Demographics* (March 2003), pp. 29–33.

9. Ibid., p. 32.

10. Peter Tuckel, Elaine Leppo, and Barbara Kaplan, "Focus Groups under Scrutiny," *Marketing Research* (June 1992), pp. 12–17; see also "Break These Three Focus Group Rules," *Quirk's Marketing Research Review* (December 1999), pp. 50–53.

11. Ken Berwitz, "Not So Stupid, Recruiting Tricks," *Quirk's Marketing Research Review* (December 2002), pp. 40–43.

12. Vauhini Vara, "Researchers Mine Web for Focus Groups," *Wall Street Journal* (November 17, 2004), p. B3E.

13. Marilyn Rausch, "Qualities of a Beginning Moderator," *Quirk's Marketing Research Review* (December 1996), p. 24. Reprinted by permission of *Quirk's Marketing Research Review*; also see: Tom Neveril, "Ten Qualities for Qualitative Researchers," *Quirk's Marketing Research Review* (June 2004), pp. 18–21.

14. Jim Eschrich, "Establishing a Comfort Level," *Quirk's Marketing Research Review* (April 2002), pp. 44–47.

15. Yvonne Martin Kidd, "A Look at Focus Group Moderators Through the Client's Eyes," *Quirk's Marketing Research Review* (May 1997), pp. 22–26. Reprinted by permission of *Quirk's Marketing Research Review*.

16. Murray Simon, "Are the Days Getting Shorter or Are the Discussion Guides Getting Longer?" *Quirk's Marketing Research Review* (June 2003), p. 122.

17. Dennis Rook, "Out of Focus Groups," *Marketing Research* (Summer 2003), pp. 10–15.

18. Naomi Henderson, "First the Bad News. . . . What's the Best Way to Report Negative Qualitative Data to Clients?" *Marketing Research* (Winter 2003), p. 40.

19. B. G. Yovoich, "Focusing on Consumers' Needs and Motivations," *Business Marketing* (March 1991), pp. 13–14. Reprinted with permission of *Business Marketing*. Copyright Crain Communications Inc., 1991.

20. Ibid.
21. Ibid.
22. Kate Maddox, "Virtual Panels Add Real Insight for Marketers," *Advertising Age* (June 29, 1998), pp. 34, 40; and "Turning the Focus Online," *Marketing News* (February 28, 2000), p. 15; see also "The Hows, Whys, Whens and Wheres of Online Focus Groups," *MRA Alert* (December 1999), p. 21.
23. Hy Mariampolski and Pat Sabena, "Qualitative Research Develops in China," *Quirk's Marketing Research Review* (December 2002), pp. 44–49.
24. Mary Beth Solomon, "Is 'Internet Focus Group' an Oxymoron?" *Quirk's Marketing Research Review* (December 1998), pp. 35–38. Reprinted by permission.
25. *www.channelM2* (July 2005).
26. Naomi Henderson, "Art and Science of Effective In-Depth Qualitative Interviews," *Quirk's Marketing Research Review* (December 1998), pp. 24–31; reprinted by permission; "Dangerous Intersections," *Marketing News* (February 28, 2000), p. 18; and "Go In-Depth with Depth Interviews," *Quirk's Marketing Research Review* (April 2000), pp. 36–40.
27. Henderson, "Art and Science of Effective in Depth Qualitative Interviews," p. 26.
28. Gerald Berstell and Denise Nitterhouse, "Asking All the Right Questions," *Marketing Research* (Fall 2001), pp. 15–20.
29. Jennifer Haid, "Understand the Mind of the Market," *Quirk's Marketing Research Review* (December 2004), pp. 26–31.
30. Ronald Lieber, "Storytelling: A New Way to Get Closer to Your Customer," *Fortune* (February 3, 1997), pp. 102–110; see also "Marketers Seek the Naked Truth in Consumers' Psyches," *Wall Street Journal* (May 30, 1997), pp. B1, B13; for details on Zaltman's technique see: Gwendolyn Catchings-Castello, "The ZMET Alternative," *Marketing Research* (Summer 2000), pp. 6–12.
31. Case prepared by Dr. Mark Peterson's MS for Marketing Research Class, University of Texas at Arlington.
32. Steve August and Kimberly Daniels August, "Online In-depth Proves Its Promise," *Quirk's Marketing Research Review* (May 2005), pp. 48–51.

Chapter 6

1. "Dudes: Do I Look Fat in This Survey?" *Brandweek* (April 18, 2005), p. 20.
2. "Research Department As Bellwether?" *Quirk's Marketing Research Review* (June 2005), p. 8.
3. Patricia E. Moberg, "Biases in Unlisted Phone Numbers," *Journal of Adverting Research* 22 (August–September 1982), p. 55.
4. Reprinted with permission from the *Respondent Cooperation and Industry Image Survey* (New York: Council for Marketing and Opinion Research, 2003), p. 2.
5. Caterina Gerlotto, "Learning on the Go," *Quirk's Marketing Research Review* (November 2003), pp. 42–45.
6. *www.mrsi.com/instore.html* (June 11, 2005).
7. David Whitlark and Michael Gearts, "Phone Surveys: How Well Do Respondents Represent Average Americans" *Marketing Research* (Fall 1998), pp. 13–17; see also. "This Is Not a Sales Call," *Quirk's Marketing Research Review* (May 2000), pp. 32–34.
8. Ibid.
9. Al Fitzgerald, "Conducting Telephone Research in the Age of Consumer Advocacy," *Quirk's Marketing Research Review* (October 2003), pp. 60–64.
10. Amanda Durkee, "First Impressions Are Everything in B-to-B Telephone Surveys," *Quirk's Marketing Research Review* (March 2005), pp. 30–32.
11. For a high-tech variation of the self-administered questionnaire, see John Weisberg, "The MCAPI Primer," *Quirk's Marketing Research Review* (February 2003), pp. 24–34; also see Karl Feld and Steven Wygant, "E-interviewers Add Human Touch to Web-based Research," *Quirk's Marketing Research Review* (July–August 2000), pp. 36–41.
12. For information on building a panel, see Brian Wansink and Seymour Sudman, "Building a Successful Convenience Panel," *Marketing Research* (Fall 2002), pp. 23–27.
13. "Research Department As Bell Wether" *Quirk's* (June 2005).
14. "How Cool Is That?" *Smart Money* (June 2005), p. 13.
15. Kurt Knapton and Steve Myers, "Demographics and Online Survey Response Rates," *Quirk's Marketing Research Review* (January 2005), pp. 58–68.
16. Chris Yalonis, "The Revolution in e-Research," *CASRO Marketing Research Journal* (1999), pp. 131–133; "The Power of On-line Research," *Quirk's Marketing Research Review* (April 2000), pp. 46–48; Bil MacElroy, "The Need for Speed," *Quirk's Marketing Research Review* (July–August 2002), pp. 22–27; Cristina Mititelu, "Internet Surveys: Limits and Beyond Limits," *Quirk's Marketing Research Review* (January 2003), pp. 30–33; Nina Ray, "Cybersurveys Come of Age," *Marketing Research* (Spring 2003), pp. 32–37; "Online Market Research Booming, According to Survey," *Quirk's Marketing Research Review* (January 2005); and Roger Gates, "Internet Data Collection So Far," speech given to Kaiser Permanente (May 2005).

17. Dennis Gonier, "The Research Emperor Gets New Clothes," *CASRO Marketing Research Journal* (1999), pp. 109–114.
18. Gates, "Internet Data Collection So Far."
19. Lee Smith, "Online Research's Time Has Come as a Proven Methodology," *CASRO Journal* (2002), pp. 45–50.
20. Bill MacElroy, "International Growth of Web Survey Activity," *Quirk's Marketing Research Review* (November 2000), pp. 48–51.
21. Raymond Pettit and Robert Monster, "Expanding Horizons: Web-Enabled Technologies Helping Globalize Marketing Research," *Quirk's Marketing Research Review* (November 2001), pp. 42–38.
22. Jerry Thomas, CEO, Decision Analyst (June 2005).
23. *www.surveysampling.com* (June 14, 2005).
24. "SurveySpot: A Researcher's Best Friend," at *www.surveysampling.com* (June 13, 2005).
25. Jerry Thomas, CEO, Decision Analyst, provided the information to the authors on June 10, 2005.
26. Bill Ahlhauser, "Introductory Notes on Web Interviewing," *Quirk's Marketing Research Review* (July 1999), pp. 20–26.
27. "Industry Split over Net Research Group," *Marketing News* (June 5, 2000), pp. 5, 8.
28. SurveySpot Panel, April 2004.
29. Joseph Rydholm, "The Theme Is Fun," *Quirk's Marketing Research Review* (July–August 2004), pp. 38–.

Chapter 7

1. Joseph Pereira, "Spying on the Sales Floor," *Wall Street Journal* (December 21, 2004), pp. B1, B4.
2. E. W. Webb, D. T. Campbell, K. D. Schwarts, and L. Sechrest, *Unobtrusive Measures: Nonreaction Research in the Social Sciences* (Chicago: Rand McNally, 1966), pp. 113–114.
3. Alison Stein Wellner, "Watch Me Now," *American Demographics* (October 2002), pp. S1–S8; and Robert Kozinets, "The Field Behind the Screen: Using Netnography for Marketing Research in Online Communities," *Journal of Marketing Research* (February 2002), pp. 61–72.
4. See Clynton Taylor, "What's All the Fuss About?" *Quirk's Marketing Research Review* (December 2003), pp. 40–45.
5. Wellner, "Watch Me Now,"
6. "P&G's Teaching an Old Dog New Tricks," *Fortune* (May 31, 2004), p. 172.
7. Ron Welty, "21st Century Mystery Shopping," *Quirk's Marketing Research Review* (January 2005), pp. 78–81.
8. Newl Templin, republished with permission of *The Wall Street Journal* "Undercover with a Hotel Spy," *Wall Street Journal* (May 12, 1999), pp. B1, B12; permission conveyed through Copyright Clearance Center, Inc.; and Celina Abernathy, Sonic Drive-in.
9. Donal Dinoon and Thomas Garavan, "Ireland: The Emerald Isle," *International Studies of Management and Organization* (Spring/Summer 1995), pp. 137–164. Reprinted by permission from M. E. Sharpe, Inc., Armonk, NY 10504.
10. Rebecca Gardyn, "What's on Your Mind?" *American Demographics* (April 2000), pp. 31–33.
11. Ibid.
12. John Cacioppo and Richard Petty, "Physiological Responses and Advertising Effects," *Psychology and Marketing* (Summer 1985), pp. 115–126; and Jack Shimell, "Testing Ads Using Galvanic Skin Response Measurements," *Quirk's Marketing Research Review* (March 2002), pp. 46–55.
13. Michael Eysenek, "Arousal, Learning, and Memory," *Psychological Bulletin 83* (1976), pp. 389–404.
14. James Grant and Dean Allman, "Voice Stress Analyzer Is a Marketing Research Tool," *Marketing News* (January 4, 1988), p. 22.
15. Glen Brickman, "Uses of Voice-Pitch Analysis," *Journal of Advertising Research 20* (April 1980), pp. 69–73; Ronald Nelson and David Schwartz, "Voice-Pitch Analysis," *Journal of Advertising Research 19* (October 1979), pp. 55–59; and Nancy Nighswonger and Claude Martin, Jr., "On Using Voice Analysis in Marketing Research," *Journal of Marketing Research 18* (August 1981), pp. 350–355.
16. Andy Raskin, "A Face Any Business Can Trust," *Business 2.0* (December 2003), pp. 58–60.
17. Ibid.
18. *www.pretesting.com* (June 2005).
19. Jon Gertner, "Our Ratings, Ourselves," *New York Times* (April 10, 2005), p. D12.
20. Linda Dupree and John Bosarge, "Media on the Move: How to Measure In-and-Out-of-Home Media Consumption," *AC Nielsen Trends & Insights.* Downloaded on March 9, 2005.
21. Laurence Gold, "The Coming of Age of Scanner Data," *Marketing Research* (Winter 1993), pp. 20–23.
22. The material on Information Resources Incorporated is from its public relations department on its Web site (May 17, 2005).
23. "IRI Enhances BehaviorScan," *IRI News Release* (October 29, 2001).
24. IRI Web site, "Custom Store Tracking," April 4, 2003.
25. IRI Web site, "Syndicated Store Tracking," April 4, 2003.

26. Marco Vriens and Michael Grigsby, "Building Profitable Online Customer-Brand Relationships," *Marketing Management* (November–December 2001), pp. 35–39.
27. Rich Bruner, "The Decade In Online Advertising," *www.doubleclick.com* (April 2005).
28. Ibid.
29. Ibid.
30. Ann D'Innocenzio, "Stores Putting Data from Loyalty Cards to Work," *Fort Worth Star Telegram* (March 25, 2003), p. 12C.
31. "DoubleClick Research—In-Direct Response to Online Advertising: Best Practices in Measuring Response over Time—Continental Airlines Case Study *www.doubleclick.net* (July 2004).

Chapter 8

1. Thomas D. Cook and Donald T. Campbell, *Experimentation: Design Analysis Issues for Field Settings* (Chicago: Rand McNally, 1979).
2. See Claire Selltiz et al., *Research in Social Relations*, rev. ed. (New York: Holt, Rinehart and Winston, 1959), pp. 80–82.
3. A good example of a laboratory experiment is described in Caroll Mohn, "Simulated-Purchase 'Chip' Testing vs. Trade-Off Conjoint Analysis—Coca-Cola's Experience." *Marketing Research* (March 1990), pp. 49–54.
4. A. G. Sawyer, "Demand Artifacts in Laboratory Experiments in Consumer Research," *Journal of Consumer Research 2* (March 1975), pp. 181–201; and N. Giges, "No Miracle in Small Miracle: Story Behind Failure," *Advertising Age* (August 1989), p. 76.
5. John G. Lynch, "On the External Validity of Experiments in Consumer Research," *Journal of Consumer Research 9* (December 1982), pp. 225–239.
6. For a more detailed discussion of this and other experimental issues, see Thomas D. Cook and Donald T. Campbell, "The Design and Conduct of Quasi-Experiments and True Experiments in Field Settings," in M. Dunnette, ed., *Handbook of Industrial and Organizational Psychology* (Skokie, IL: Rand McNally, 1978).
7. Ibid.
8. For further discussion of the characteristics of various types of experimental designs, see Donald T. Campbell and Julian C. Stanley, *Experimental and Quasi-Experimental Design for Research* (Chicago: Rand McNally, 1966); see also Richard Bagozzi and Youjar Ti, "On the Use of Structural Equation Models in Experimental Design," *Journal of Marketing Research 26* (August 1989), pp. 225–270.
9. Thomas D. Cook and Donald T. Campbell, *Quasi-Experimentation: Design and Analysis Issues for Field Settings* (Boston: Houghton Mifflin, 1979), p. 56.
10. T. Karger, "Test Marketing as Dress Rehearsals," *Journal of Consumer Marketing 2* (Fall 1985), pp. 49–55; Tim Harris, "Marketing Research Passes Toy Marketer Test," *Advertising Age* (August 24, 1987), pp. 1, 8; and John L. Carefoot, "Marketing and Experimental Designs in Marketing Research: Uses and Misuses," *Marketing News* (June 7, 1993), p. 21; and Jim Miller and Sheila Lundy, "Test Marketing Plugs into the Internet," *Consumer Insights* (Spring 2002), p. 23.
11. Jay Klompmaker, G. David Hughes, and Russell I. Haley, "Test Marketing in New Product Development," *Harvard Business Review* (May–June 1976), p. 129; and N. D. Cadbury, "When, Where and How to Test Market," *Harvard Business Review* (May–June 1985), pp. 97–98.
12. G. A. Churchill, Jr., *Basic Marketing Research*, 4th ed. (Fort Worth, TX: Dryden Press, 2001), pp. 144–145.
13. P. Melvin, "Choosing Simulated Test Marketing Systems." *Marketing Research 4*, no. 3 (September 1992), pp. 14–16.
14. Jay Klompmaker, G. David Hughes, and Russell I. Haley, "Test Marketing in New Product Development," *Harvard Business Review* (May–June 1976), p. 129; and N. D. Cadbury, "When, Where and How to Test Market," *Harvard Business Review* (May–June 1985), pp. 97–98.
15. Joseph Rydholm, "To Test or Not to Test," *Quirk's Marketing Research Review* (February 1992), pp. 61–62.
16. "Test Marketing Is Valuable, but It's Often Abused," *Marketing News* (January 2, 1987), p. 40.
17. "Guide to Test Market Selection and Planning," *Creative Media* (2000).
18. G. Scott Thomas, "ACBJ Study: Galveston Nation's Best Test Market," American City Business Journals, *bizjournals* (2005), *www.bizjournals.com/specials/test_marketing/story1.html*
19. Rita J. Runyon, "South Bend ADI: An Ideal Test Market," TRC Entertainment (2004), at: *http://celebrity-network.net/trc/business.htm*
20. "McDonald's Test-Markets Spam," *Pacific Business News-Honolulu* (June 11, 2002), American City Business Journals, at: *www.bizjournals.com/pacific/stories/2002/06/10/daily22.html*
21. "Reduced Nicotine Cigarettes Reach Indiana," WISH-TV, Indianapolis, IN (January 27, 2003), at: *www.wishtv.com/global/story.asp?s=1100154&ClientType=Printable*
22. Bruce Schreiner, "B & W Test Markets New Cigarette," *Washington Post* (November 5, 2001), at: *www.washingtonpost.com/wp-srv/aponline/20011105/aponline194356_000.htm*
23. Ratna Bhushan, "Southside Story," *Financial Daily* (February 21, 2002), at: The Hindu Business Line, Internet Edition, *www.blonnet.com/catalyst/2002/02/21/stories/2002022100010100.htm*

24. Jim Miller, "Global Research: Evaluating New Products Globally; Using Consumer Research to Predict Success," *PDMA Visions* Magazine (October 2002), at: *www.pdma.org/visions/print.php?doc=oct02/research3.html*

Chapter 9

1. "Target and Costco Rated Most Fun to Shop," *Quirk's Marketing Research Review* (February 2005), pp. 8, 64.
2. Rob Kroenitt, Leah Spalding, Brian Cooper, and Liz Le, "Making the Link," *Marketing Research* (Spring 2005), pp. 21–25.
3. An excellent article on secondary data proxies and constructs is: Mark B. Houston, "Assessing the Validity of Secondary Data Proxies for Marketing Constructs," *Journal of Business Research* (February 2004), pp. 154–161.
4. Adapted from Brian Toyne and Peter G. P. Walters, *Global Marketing Management: A Strategic Perspective* (Boston: Allyn & Bacon, 1989), p. 201. Used with permission of Allyn & Bacon.
5. F. N. Kerlinger, *Foundations of Behavioral Research*, 3rd ed. (New York: Rinehart and Winston, 1986), p. 403; see also Mel Crask and R. J. Fox, "An Exploration of the Internal Properties of Three Commonly Used Research Scales," *Journal of the Marketing Research Society* (October 1987), pp. 317–319.
6. Adapted from Claire Selltiz, Laurence Wrightsman, and Stuart Cook, *Research Methods in Social Relations*, 3rd ed., (New York: Holt Rinehart and Winston, 1976), pp. 164–168.
7. Martin Weinberger, "Seven Perspectives on Consumer Research," *Marketing Research* (December 1989), pp. 9–17. Reprinted by permission of the American Marketing Association.
8. Bill MacElroy, "The Anonymity Gradient," *Quirk's Marketing Research Review* (October 1997), pp. 34–35. Reprinted by permission.
9. See David Hardesty and William Bearden, "The Use of Expert Judges in Scale Development: Implications for Improving Face Validity of Measures of Unobservable Constructs," *Journal of Business Research* (February 2004), pp. 98–107.
10. See Edward McQuarrie, "Integration of Construct and External Validity by Means of Proximal Similarity: Implications for Laboratory Experiments in Marketing," *Journal of Business Research* (February 2004), pp. 142–153.
11. Craig Bailey, "Examine Ways to Maximize Surveys," *Marketing News* (October 28, 2002), p. 46.
12. This case was developed from: Qimei Chen, "Shelly Rodgers, and William D. Wells, 'Better Than Sex,'" *Marketing Research* (Winter 2004), pp. 16–21.

Chapter 10

1. "Not Everyone Understands Political Labels," *Quirk's Marketing Research Review* (May 2005), p. 12.
2. See Brian Sternthal and C. Samuel Craig, *Consumer Behavior: An Information Processing Perspective* (Englewood Cliffs, NJ: Prentice Hall, 1982), pp. 157–162; see also Barbara Loken and Ronald Hoverstad, "Relationships between Information Recall and Subsequent Attitudes: Some Exploratory Findings," *Journal of Consumer Research*, 12 (September 1985), pp. 155–168.
3. Robert E. Smith and William Swinyard, "Attitude Behavior Consistency: The Impact of Product Trial versus Advertising," *Journal of Marketing Research 20* (August 1983), pp. 257–267.
4. See Richard Lutz, "The Rise of Attitude Theory in Marketing," in Harold Kassarjian and Thomas Robertson, eds., *Perspectives in Consumer Behavior*, 4th ed. (Upper Saddle River, NJ: Prentice Hall, 1991), pp. 317–339.
5. The first five factors are taken from John Mowen and Michael Minor, *Consumer Behavior*, 5th ed. (Upper Saddle River, NJ: Prentice Hall, 1998), p. 263.
6. Linda F. Alwitt and Ida E. Berger, "Understanding the Link between Environmental Attitudes and Consumer Product Usage: Measuring the Moderating Rise of Attitude Strength," in Leigh McAlister and Michael Rothschild, eds., *Advances in Consumer Research*, Vol. 20 (Provo, UT: Association for Consumer Research, 1992), pp. 194–198.
7. Kunal Gupta, Jamie Baker-Prewitt, and Jeff Miller, "Scaling: The Never Ending Debate," *CASRO Journal* (2001), pp. 125–129.
8. Thomas T. Semon, "Numbers, Like Matches, Can Be Dangerous," *Marketing News* (March 26, 2001), p. 8.
9. For an excellent discussion of the semantic differential, see Charles E. Osgood, George Suci, and Percy Tannenbaum, *The Measurement of Meaning*, (Urbana: University of Illinois Press, 1957).
10. Ibid., pp. 140–153, 192, 193; see also William D. Barclay, "The Semantic Differential as an Index of Brand Attitude," *Journal of Advertising Research 4* (March 1964), pp. 30–33.
11. Theodore Clevenger, Jr., and Gilbert A. Lazier, "Measurement of Corporate Images by the Semantic Differential," *Journal of Marketing Research 2* (February 1965), pp. 80–82.
12. Sabra Brock, "Marketing Research in Asia: Problems, Opportunities, and Lessons," *Marketing Research* (September 1989), pp. 44–51. Reprinted by permission of the American Marketing Association.
13. Michael J. Etzel, Terrell G. Williams, John C. Rogers, and Douglas J. Lincoln, "The Comparability of Three Stapel Forms in a Marketing Setting," in Ronald F. Bush and Shelby D. Hunt, eds., *Marketing Theory: Philosophy of Science Perspectives* (Chicago: American Marketing Association, 1982), pp. 303–306.

14. Diane Schmalensee, "Wording Matters," *Marketing Research* (Winter 2003), pp. 48–49.

15. An excellent article on purchase intent is: Pierre Chandon, Vicki Morwitz, and Werner Reinartz, "Do Intentions Really Predict Behavior? Self Generated Validity Effects in Survey Research," *Journal of Marketing* (April 2005), pp. 1–14.

16. Frederick Reichheld, "The One Number That You Need to Grow," *Harvard Business Review* (December 2003), pp. 46–57.

17. Albert Bemmaor, "Predicting Behavior from Intention-to-Buy Measures: The Parametric Case," *Journal of Marketing Research* (May 1995), pp. 176–191.

18. We use a more conservative set of weights than those recommended by Linda Jamieson and Frank Bass, "Adjusting Stated Intention Measures to Predict Trial Purchase of New Products: A Comparison of Models and Methods," *Journal of Marketing Research* (August 1989), pp. 336–345.

19. Gupta et al., "Scaling," p. 126.

20. William O. and Richard G. Netemeyer, *Handbook of Marketing Scales*, 2nd ed. (Newbury Park, CA: Sage Publications, 1999), pp. 1–9.

21. Brian Engelland, Bruce Alford, and Ron Taylor, "Cautions and Precautions on the Use of Borrowed Scales in Marketing Research," *Proceedings: Society for Marketing Advances* (November 2001).

22. J. A. Krosnick, and L. R. Fabrigar, "Designing Rating Scales for Effective Measurement in Surveys," in L. Lybert, M. Collins, L. Decker, E. Deleeuw, C. Dippo, N. Schwarz, and D. Trewing, eds., *Survey Measurement and Process Quality* (New York: Wiley-Interscience, 1997). Also see Madhubalan Viswanathan, Seymore Sudman and Michael Johnson, "Maximum Versus Meaningful Discrimination in Scale Response: Implications for Validity Measurement of Consumer Perceptions bout Products," *Journal of Business Review* (February 2004), pp. 108–124.

23. Keith Chrzan and Joey Michaud, "Response Scales for Customer Satisfaction Research," *Quirk's Marketing Research Review* (October 2004), pp. 50–55.

24. This section is based on James H. Myers and Mark I. Alpert, "Determinant Buying Attitudes: Meaning and Management," *Marketing Management* (Summer 1997), pp. 50–56.

25. Tim Glowa, "Measuring Consumer Attitudes: What Is Your Scale Really Telling You?" *Quirk's Marketing Research Review* (October 2002), pp. 34–38.

26. William Wells and Leonard Lo Scruto, "Direct Observation of Purchasing Behavior," *Journal of Marketing Research* (August 1996), pp. 42–51.

27. Tim Glowa and Sean Lawson, "Satisfaction Measurement: Is It Worth It?" *Quirk's Marketing Research Review* (October 2000), pp. 32–38.

28. Lois Koch and John Chisholm, "Profitable Insights," *Quirk's Marketing Research Review* (October 2004), pp. 36–42.

Chapter 11

1. Ellen Byron, "How Coach Won a Rich Purse by Inventing New Uses for Bags," *Wall Street Journal* (November 17, 2004), pp. A1, A13.

2. Stephen Hellebusch, "To Double Code or Single Code," *Quirk's Marketing Research Review* (December 2003), pp. 16–18.

3. Kyle Langley, "Ask the Right Questions," *Quirk's Marketing Research Review* (May 2005), pp. 68–71.

4. Alexa Smith, "Ask Overlooked Questions for Greater Insights," *Marketing News* (September 15, 2003), pp. 27–28.

5. Randall Thomas, "Not Sure About Don't Know," *Quirk's Marketing Research Review* (May 2003), pp. 54–57.

6. Nanci Glassman and Myron Glassman, "Screening Questions," (Fall 1998), pp. 276–230. Reprinted with permission from the American Marketing Association.

7. *www.CMOR.org* (June 15, 2005).

8. Lynn Newmann, "That's a Good Question," *American Demographics* (June 1995), pp. 10–15. Reprinted from *American Demographics* magazine with permission. Copyright © 1995, Cowles Business Media, Ithaca, New York.

9. *www.sawtooth.com* (June 15, 2005).

10. Joseph Marinelli and Anastasia Schleck, "Collecting, Processing Data for Marketing Research Worldwide," *Marketing News* (August 18, 1997), pp. 12, 14.

11. Internal company documents supplied to the authors by M/A/R/C, Inc.

12. Ibid.

Chapter 12

1. For excellent discussions of sampling, see Seymour Sudman, *Applied Sampling*, (New York: Academic Press, 1976); and L. J. Kish, *Survey Sampling* (New York: John Wiley and Sons, 1965).

2. Lee J. Bain and Max Engelhardt, *Introduction to Probability and Mathematical Statistics*, 2nd ed., (Boston: PWS-Kent Publishing Company, 1992), pp. 158–161.

3. "Report of the President's Blue Ribbon Panel on the Census," American Statistical Association, 2003; Brad Edmondson, "The Cliffhanger Census," *American Demographics* (January 1998), p. 2.

4. "Do-Not-Call Households," Survey Sampling International (June 8, 2004), at: *www.surveysampling.com/ssi_id=TS&page_id=donotcall&catID=18&subname=donotcall&subid=0&archive=0.* "Do Not Call Registry Is Working Well," Harris Interactive, The Harris Poll #10 (February 13, 2004), at: *www.harrisinteractive.com/harris_poll/printerfirned/index.asp?PID=439*

5. S. Sudman, *Applied Sampling*, pp. 63–67.

6. G. J. Glasser and G. D. Metzger, "Random-Digit Dialing as a Method of Telephone Sampling," *Journal of Marketing Research 9* (February 1972), pp. 59–64; and S. Roslow and L. Roslow, "Unlisted Phone Subscribers Are Different," *Journal of Advertising 12* (August 1972), pp. 59–64.

7. Charles D. Cowan, "Using Multiple Sample Frames to Improve Survey Coverage, Quality, and Costs," *Marketing Research* (December 1991), pp. 66–69.

8. James McClove and P. George Benson, *Statistics for Business and Economics* (San Francisco: Dellen Publishing, 1988), pp. 184–185; and "Probability Sampling in the Real World," *CATI NEWS* (Summer 1993), pp. 1, 4–6; Susie Sangren, "Survey and Sampling in an Imperfect World," *Quirk's Marketing Research Review* (April 2000), pp. 16, 66–69.

9. R. J. Jaeger, *Sampling in Education and the Social Sciences*, (New York: Longman, 1984), pp. 28–35.

10. "Nearly One in Ten U.S. Adults Use Wireless Phones Exclusively and Landline Displacement Expected to Grow," Harris Interactive (June 27, 2005), at: *www.harrisinteractive.com/news/allnewsbydate.asp?NewsID=943*

11. Jaeger, *Sampling in Education and the Social Sciences.*

12. "Web Industry Trends: Half of Online U.S. Hispanics Now Have Broadband at Home, New AOL/Roper Hispanic Survey Finds," (July 21, 2005), at: *www.internetadsales.com/modules/news/article.php?storyid=5864*

13. Lewis C. Winters, "What's New in Telephone Sampling Technology?" *Marketing Research* (March 1990), pp. 80–82; and *A Survey Researcher's Handbook of Industry Terminology and Definitions* (Fairfield, CT: Survey Sampling, Inc., 1992), pp. 3–20.

14. Dick McCullough, "Lessons from Florida: Looking at the Election Debacle from a Research Perspective," *Quirk's Marketing Research Review* (March 2001), pp. 36–39.

15. For discussions of related issues, see John E. Swan, Stephen J. O'Connor, and Seug Doug Lee, "A Framework for Testing Sampling Bias and Methods of Bias Reduction in a Telephone Survey," *Marketing Research* (December 1991), pp. 23–34; Charles D. Cowan, "Coverage Issues in Sample Surveys: A Component of Measurement Error," *Marketing Research* (June 1991), pp. 65–68; and S Sangren, "Survey and Sampling in an Imperfect World," pp. 16, 66–69.

16. For an excellent discussion of stratified sampling, see William G. Cochran, *Sampling Techniques*, 2nd ed. (New York: John Wiley and Sons, 1963); and Sangren, "Survey and Sampling in an Imperfect World," pp. 16, 66–69.

17. Sudman, *Applied Science*, pp. 110–121.

18. Ibid.

19. Earl R. Babbie, *The Practice of Social Research*, 2nd ed. (Belmont, CA: Wadsworth Publishing, 1979), p. 167.

20. "Convenience Sampling Outpacing Probability Sampling" (Fairfield, CT: Survey Sampling, Inc. March 1994), p. 4.

21. Leo A. Goodman, "Snowball Sampling," *Annuals of Mathematical Statistics 32* (1961), pp. 148–170.

22. Douglas Rivers, "Fulfilling the Promise of the Web," *Quirk's Marketing Research Review* (February 2000), pp. 34–41.

23. Roger Gates and Michael Foytik, "Implementing an HRA on the Internet: Lessons Learned," Society of Prospective Medicine (October 1998).

24. Beth Clarkson, "Research and the Internet: A Winning Combination," *Quirk's Marketing Research Review* (July 1999), pp. 46–51.

25. Rundhata Parmar, "Net Research Is Not Quite Global," *Marketing News 37*, no. 5 (March 3, 2003), pp. 51–52. "Chinese Internet Users Reach 103 Mln," Chongqing Daily News Group (July 22, 2005), at: *http://english.big5.cqnews.net/system/2005/07/22/000502828.shtml*

26. Gates and Foytik, "Implementing an HRA on the Internet."

Chapter 13

1. Tom McGoldrick, David Hyatt, and Lori Laffin., "How Big Is Big Enough?" *Marketing Tools* (May 1998), pp. 54–58; and Russell V. Lenth, "Some Practical Guidelines for Effective Sample Size Determination," *The American Statistician* (August 2001), pp. 187–193.

2. McGoldrick et al., "How Big Is Big Enough?" pp. 54–58.

3. Jason Ball, "Simple Rules Shape Proper Sample Size," *Marketing News 38*, no. 2 (February. 1 2004), p. 38. "P:SNAP 2005 to Cover 21,300 Consumers across 247 Categories," Agencyfaqs! News Bureau (July 21, 2005), at: *www.agencyfaqs.com/news/stories/2005/07/21/12084.html.* "New DFW International Airport Traveler Poll Shows Passengers Overwhelmingly Want Southwest Airlines Here—And We Agree," PR Newswire (July 8, 2005), at: *http://biz.yahoo.com/prnews/050708/daf012.html?.V=16*

4. McGoldrick et al., "How Big Is Big Enough?" pp. 54–58.

5. Thomas T. Semon, "Save a Few Bucks on Sample Size, Risk Millions in Opportunity Loss," *Marketing News* (January 3, 1994), p. 19. Reprinted by permission the American Marketing Association.

6. Lafayette Jones, "A Case for Ethnic Sampling," *Promo* (October 1, 2000), p. 12.

7. Thomas T. Semon, "Nonresponse Bias Affects All Survey Research," *Marketing News 38*, no. 12 (July 15, 2004), p. 7.

8. Wim F. de Heer and Ger Moritz, "Workshop on Respondent Issues: Sampling, Weighting, and Nonresponse. Data Quality Problems in Travel Surveys. An International Overview," TRB Transportation Research Circular E–C008: Transport Surveys: Raising the Standard (2000), at: *http://gulliver.trb.org/publications/circulars/ec008/workshop_c.pdf*

9. Joni Montez, "Web Surveys as a Source of Nonresponse Explication," (April 2003), Paper presented at the annual meeting of the American Educational Research Association, Chicago, IL.

10. Craig A. Mertler, "Patterns of Response and Nonresponse from Teachers to Traditional and Web Surveys," *Practical Assessment, Research & Evaluation* (2003), at: *http://pareonline.net/getvn.asp?v=8&n=22*

11. Gang Xu, "Estimating Sample Size for a Descriptive Study in Quantitative Research," *Quirk's Marketing Research Review* (June 1999), pp. 14, 52–53.

12. Susie Sangren, "A Simple Solution to Nagging Questions about Survey, Sample Size and Validity," *Quirk's Marketing Research Review* (January 1999), pp. 18, 53.

13. Stephen J. Hellebusch, "Infotainment Polls Give MR a Bad Rap," *Marketing News 38*, No. 2 (February 1, 2004), p. 35. Nick Panagakis, "How Accurate Are Call-in Polls? *Illinois Issues*, No. 31 (March 1992), at: *www.lib.niu.edu/ipo/ii920330.html*

14. Gang Xu, "Estimating Sample Size for a Descriptive Study in Quantitative Research."

15. For discussions of these techniques, see Bill Williams, *A Sampler on Sampling* (New York: John Wiley & Sons, 1978); and Richard Jaeger, *Sampling in Education and the Social Sciences* (New York: Longman, 1984).

16. Survey Sampling, Inc., "Estimate Sample Size with Precision," *The Frame* (January 1999), p. 1.

17. David Anderson, Dennis Sweeney, and Thomas Williams, *Statistics for Business and Economics*, 4th ed. (St. Paul, MN: West Publishing, 1990), pp. 355–357.

Chapter 14

1. Joe Murphy et al., "A System for Detecting Interviewer Falsification," Conference Proceeding, American Association for Public Opinion Research 59th Annual Conference (May 16, 2004), pp. 1–16, at *www.rti.org/abstract.cfm?pubid=2563*

2. Joseph Rydholm, "Dealing with Those Pesky Open-Ended Responses," *Quirk's Marketing Research Review* (February 1994), pp. 70–79.

3. Raymond Raud and Michael A. Fallig, "Automating the Coding Process with Neural Networks," *Quirk's Marketing Research Review* (May 1993), pp. 14–16, 40–47.

4. For information on semiotics, see Paul Cobley, Litza Jansz, and Richard Appignanesi, *Introducing Semiotics* (Melbourne, Australia: Totem Books, 1997); Marcel Danesi, *Of Cigarettes, High Heels and Other Interesting Things: An Introduction to Semiotics* (New York: St. Martin's Press, 1998); and Umberto Eco, *Semiotics and the Philosophy of Languages* (Bloomington: Indiana University Press, 1986).

5. *Content Analyst Report 1*, No. 2 (July 1, 2004), at: *www.contentanalyst.com/update/report02/feature.html*

6. Joseph Rydholm, "Scanning the Seas: Scannable Questionnaires Give Princess Cruises Accuracy and Quick Turnaround," *Quirk's Marketing Research Review* (May 1993), pp. 38–42.

7. "Cross Tabulation," Custom Insight (2005), at: *www.custominsight.com/articles/crosstab-sample.asp.*

8. Jayavel Sounderpandian, *Market Research and Using Microsoft® Excel*, Cincinnati, OH: SouthWestern College Publishing, 1999.

9. Carl James Schwarz, "Graphical Design," Course Notes for Statistics-301 (1998), at: *www.math.sfu.ca/~cschwarz/Stat-301/Handouts/node7.html*

10. Ibid.

11. Ibid.

12. Michael Friendly, Gallery of Data Visualization (December 31, 2002), at: *www.math.yorku/SCS/Gallery/images/coxcomb.gif.*

Chapter 15

1. Hank Zucker, "What Is Significance?" *Quirk's Marketing Research Review* (March 1994), pp. 12, 14; Gordon A. Wyner, "How High Is Up?" *Marketing Research* (Fall 1993), pp. 42–43; Gordon A. Wyner, "The 'Significance' of Marketing Research," *Marketing Research* (Fall 1993), pp. 43–45; and Patrick M. Baldasare and Vikas Mittel, "The Use, Misuse and Abuse of Significance," *Quirk's Marketing Research Review* (November 1994), pp. 16, 32.

2. Dr. Ali Khounsary, "What Is Statistically Significant?" *Ask a Scientist*, Mathematics Archives (1999), Argonne National Laboratory, Department of Energy, at: *www.newton.dep.anl.gov/askasci/math99/math99052.htm*

3. Thomas T. Semon, "Probability a Perennial Problem for Gamblers—and Also for Researchers." *Marketing News* (January 1999), p. 11.

4. J.M. Cortina and R.G. Folger, "When Is It Acceptable to Accept a Null Hypothesis: No Way, Jose?" *Organizational Research Methods 1*, No. 3 (1998), pp. 334–350.

5. Thomas Exter, "What's Behind the Numbers," *Quirk's Marketing Research Review* (March 1997), pp. 53–59.

6. Tony Babinec, "How to Think about Your Tables," *Quirk's Marketing Research Review* (January 1991), pp. 10–12. For a discussion of these issues, see Gopal K. Kanji, *100 Statistical Tests* (London: Sage Publications, 1993), p. 75.

7. P. K. Viswanathan, "Glimpses into Application of Chi-Square Tests in Marketing," at: *http://davidmlane.com/hyperstat/viswanathan/chi_square_marketing.html*

8. Gary M. Mullet, "Correctly Estimating the Variances of Proportions," *Marketing Research* (June 1991), pp. 47–51.

Chapter 16

1. Richard Brath, Andrea Brody, "Finding the Needle in the Haystack: Using Data Visualization to Spot Patterns and Anomalies in Business Data," *DM Review* (October 2003), at: *www.dmreview.com*

2. Stevan L. Davies, "Statistical Correlation Analysis of the Order of Sayings in Thomas and in the Synoptics," [no date given], at: *www.misericordia.edu/users/davies/thomas/correl.htm*

3. Douglas Kirby et al., "Manifestations of Poverty and Birthrates among Young Teenagers in California Zip Code Areas," *Family Planning Perspectives 33*, No. 2 (March–April 2001), reprinted by The Alan Guttmacher Institute, at: *www.guttmacher.org/pubs/journals/3306301.html*

4. Clayton E. Cramer, "Antigunners Admit Brady Failed," and "Is Gun Control Reducing Murder Rates?" (August 2000), at: *www.claytoncramer.com*

5. "A Mirror to the World," *Bloomberg Personal* (December 1997), p. 49.

Chapter 17

1. For an excellent and highly understandable presentation of all the multivariate techniques presented in this chapter, see Joseph Hair, Rolph Anderson, Ron Tatham, and William Black, *Multivariate Data Analysis,* 5th ed. (New York: Prentice Hall, 1998); see also Charles J. Schwartz, "A Marketing Research's Guide to Multivariate Analysis," *Quirk's Marketing Research Review* (November 1994), pp. 12–14.

2. Joseph R. Garber, "Deadbeat Repellant," *Forbes* (February 14, 1994), p. 164.

3. For a thorough discussion of regression analysis, see Norman Draper and Harry Smith, *Applied Regression Analysis* (New York: John Wiley & Sons, 1966).

4. Charlotte H. Mason and William D. Perreault, Jr., "Collinear Power and Interpretation of Multiple Regression Analysis," *Journal of Marketing Research* (August 1991), pp. 268–280; Doug Grisaffe, "Appropriate Use of Regression in Customer Satisfaction Analyses: A Response to William McLauchlan," *Quirk's Marketing Review* (February 1993), pp. 10–17; and Terry Clark, "Managing Outliers: Qualitative Issues in the Handling of Extreme Observations in Market Research," *Marketing Research* (June 1989), pp. 31–45.

5. Michael Lieberman, "Key Driver Analysis," *Quirk's Marketing Research Review* (February 2001), p. 51.

6. See Hair et al., *Multivariate Data Analysis,* p. 46.

7. William D. Neal, "Using Discriminant Analysis in Marketing Research: Part 1," *Marketing Research* (September 1989), pp. 79–81; William D. Neal, "Using Discriminant Analysis in Marketing Research: Part 2," *Marketing Research* (December 1989), pp. 55–60; and Steve Struhl, "Multivariate and Perceptual Mapping with Discriminant Analysis," *Quirk's Marketing Research Review* (March 1993), pp. 10–15, 43.

8. Edward W. Thomas et al., "Using Discriminant Analysis to Identify Students at Risk," FIE (Frontiers in Education) 1996 Conference, Salt Lake City, UT, (1996), at: *http://fie.engrng.pitt.edu/fie96/papers/141.pdf*

9. See Girish Punj and David Stewart, "Cluster Analysis in Marketing Research: Review and Suggestions for Application," *Journal of Market Research 20* (May 1983), pp. 134–138; and G. Ray Funkhouser, Anindya Chatterjee, and Richard Parker, "Segmenting Samples," *Marketing Research* (Winter 1994), pp. 40–46.

10. Susie Sangren, "A Survey of Multivariate Methods Useful for Market Research," *Quirk's Marketing Research Review* (May 1999), pp. 16, 63–69.

11. Susan Mitchell, "Birds of a Feather," *American Demographics 17*, no. 2 (February 1995), pp. 40–42.

12. This section is based on material prepared by Glen Jarboe, University of Texas at Arlington; see also Paul Green, Donald Tull, and Gerald Albaum, *Research for Marketing Decision*, 5th ed., (Englewood Cliffs, NJ: Prentice Hall, 1998), pp. 553–573.

13. Ashok, "Highly Classified," *Quirk's Marketing Research Review* (November 2001), p. 53.

14. For a complete discussion of the production of perceptual maps using factor analysis, see Glen Urban and John Hauser, *Design and Marketing of New Products*, 2nd ed. (Englewood Cliffs, NJ: Prentice Hall, 1993), pp. 233–241; for a more concisely formatted discussion, see Glen Urban, John Hauser, and Mikhilesh Dholakia, *Essentials of New Product Management,* (Englewood Cliffs, NJ: Prentice Hall, 1987), pp. 57–58, 105–119; and

for a humorous look at perceptual mapping see "Company Brief: House of Widsor," *The Economist* (August 29, 1992), p. 53.

15. Susie Li, "Exploring Marketing Ideas with Perceptual Maps," *Quirk's Marketing Research Review* (November 2001), pp. 16, 79–83.

16. Dick Wittink and Phillipe Cattin, "Commercial Use of Conjoint Analysis: An Update," *Journal of Marketing* (July 1989), pp. 91–96; see also Rajeev Kohli, "Assessing Attribute Significance in Conjoint Analysis: Nonparametric Tests and Empirical Validation," *Journal of Marketing Research* (May 1988), pp. 123–133.

17. Examples of current issues and applications are provided in Richard Smallwood, "Using Conjoint Analysis for Price Optimization," *Quirk's Marketing Research Review* (October 1991), pp. 10–13; Paul E. Green, Abba M. Krieger, and Manoj K. Agarwal, "Adaptive Conjoint Analysis: Some Caveats and Suggestions," *Journal of Marketing Research* (May 1991), pp. 215–222; Paul E. Green and V. Srinivasan, "Conjoint Analysis in Marketing: New Developments with Implications for Research and Practice," *Journal of Marketing Research Review* (October 1990), pp. 3–19; Joseph Curry, "Determining Product Feature Price Sensitivities," *Quirk's Marketing Research Review* (November 1990), pp. 14–17; Gordon A. Wyner, "Customer-Based Pricing Research," *Marketing Research* (Spring 1993), pp. 50–52; Steven Struhl, "Discrete Choice Modeling Comes to the PC," *Quirk's Marketing Research Review* (May 1993), pp. 12–15, 36–41; Steven Struhl, "Discrete Choice: Understanding a Better Conjoint. . . . ," *Quirk's Marketing Research Review* (June–July 1994), pp. 12–15, 36–39; Bashir A. Datoo, "Measuring Price Elasticity," *Marketing Research* (Spring 1994), pp. 30–34; Gordon A. Wyner, "Uses and Limitations of Conjoint Analysis—Part 1," *Marketing Research* (June 1992), pp. 12–44; and Gordon A. Wyner, "Uses and Limitations of Conjoint Analysis—Part II," *Marketing Research* (September 1992), pp. 46–47; Yilian Yuan and Gang Xu, "Conjoint Analysis in Pharmaceutical Marketing Research," *Quirk's Marketing Research Review* (June 2001), pp. 18, 54–61; and Bryan Orme, "Assessing the Monetary Value of Attribute Levels with Conjoint Analysis: Warnings and Suggestions," *Quirk's Marketing Research Review* (May 2001), pp. 16, 44–47.

18. Jerry Wind, Paul E. Green, et al., "Courtyard by Marriott: Designing a Hotel Facility with Consumer–Based Marketing Models," Chapter 12 (Courtyard by Marriott), Adventures in Conjoint Analysis: A Practitioner's Guide to Trade-Off Modeling and Applications (unpublished manuscript: 2003) at: *www-marketing.wharton.upenn.edu/people/faculty/green-monograph.html*

19. David Shepard, "Modeling a Modern Mailing," *Marketing Tools* (November–December 1994), pp. 4–7. Reprinted by permission.

20. See Robert Eng, "Is the Market Research Industry Failing Its TQM Clients?" *Quirk's Marketing Research Review* (October 1996), pp. 24, 36–38.

Chapter 18

1. Tammy Donelson, "Evaluating the Impact Of a Great Idea," *Quirk's Marketing Research Review* (May 2005), pp. 36–39.

2. Darlene Price and John Messerschmitt, "Try These Eight Power Points for Presenting More Confidently," *Presentations* (August 1999), p. 84.

3. Joseph Rydholm, "What Do Clients Want from a Research Firm?" *Quirk's Marketing Research Review* (October 1996), p. 80.

4. John Walters and John Colias, "The Simple Secret to Effective Market Research," *CASRO Journal* (2002), pp. 65–66.

5. The material on organizing a supplier firm is from: Michael Mitrano, "Supplier Side: Organizing Your Company—Are Project Teams the Answer?" *Quirk's Marketing Research Review* (April 2002), pp. 20, 68.

6. Joshua Libresco, reprinted with permission from *Marketing News*, published by the American Marketing Association, from "Advice for the Juggler" (January 4, 1999), pp. 13, 23.

7. Michael Mitrano, "Managing for Profitability," *Quirk's Marketing Research Review* (March 2002), pp. 24, 76.

8. Susan Greco, "Choose or Lose." Reprinted with permission from *Inc.* magazine, February 2001. Copyright 1998 by Gruner & Jahr USA Publishing.

9. Kathleen Knight, "Finding and Retaining Research Staff: A Perspective," *Quirk's Marketing Research Review* (February 1998), pp. 18, 54. Reprinted by permission.

10. This section is adapted from Richard Snyder, *Quirk's Marketing Research Review* (November 2002), pp. 62–65.

11. Dana James, "Establish Your Place at the Table," *Marketing News* (September 16, 2002), pp. 1, 19–20.

12. Ibid.; also see Natalie Jobity and Jeff Scott, "Practices Make Perfect—Improving Research and Consulting Through Collaboration," *CASRO Journal* (2002), pp. 19–24.

13. John Huppertz, "Passion vs. Dispassion," *Marketing Research* (Summer 2003), pp. 17–21.

14. Ibid.

15. Tim Ambler, "Differing Dimensions," *Marketing Research* (Fall 2004), pp. 8–13.

16. This section of ROI is from: A. Dawn Lesh and Diane Schmalensee, "Measuring Returns of Research," *Marketing Research* (Fall 2004), pp. 22–27.

17. Ibid.

GLOSSARY

ad hoc mail surveys Questionnaires sent to selected names and addresses without prior contact by the researcher; sometimes called *one-shot mail surveys*.

after-only with control group design True experimental design that involves random assignment of subjects or test units to experimental and control groups, but no premeasurement of the dependent variable.

allowable sampling error Amount of sampling error the researcher is willing to accept.

analysis of variance (ANOVA) Test for the differences among the means of two or more independent samples.

applied research Research aimed at solving a specific, pragmatic problem—better understanding of the marketplace, determination of why a strategy or tactic failed, or reduction of uncertainty in management decision making.

appropriate time order of occurrence Change in an independent variable occurred before an observed change in the dependent variable.

attitude Enduring organization of motivational, emotional, perceptual, and cognitive processes with respect to some aspect of a person's environment.

audit Examination and verification of the sales of a product.

balanced scales Measurement scales that have the same number of positive and negative categories.

basic, or pure, research Research aimed at expanding the frontiers of knowledge rather than solving a specific, pragmatic problem.

before and after with control group design True experimental design that involves random assignment of subjects or test units to experimental and control groups and pre- and postmeasurements of both groups.

BehaviorScan Scanner-based research system that can manipulate the marketing mix for household panels in geographically dispersed markets and then electronically track consumer purchases.

bivariate regression analysis Analysis of the strength of the linear relationship between two variables when one is considered the independent variable and the other the dependent variable.

bivariate techniques Statistical methods of analyzing the relationship between two variables.

cartoon test A projective test in which the respondent fills in the dialogue of one of two characters in a cartoon.

case analysis Reviewing information from situations that are similar to the current one.

causal research Research designed to determine whether a change in one variable likely caused an observed change in another.

causal studies Research studies that examine whether the value of one variable causes or determines the value of another variable.

causation Inference that a change in one variable is responsible for (caused) an observed change in another variable.

census Collection of data obtained from or about every member of the population of interest.

central limit theorem Idea that a distribution of a large number of sample means or sample proportions will approximate a normal distribution, regardless of the distribution of the population from which they were drawn.

central-location telephone interviews Interviews conducted by calling respondents from a centrally located marketing research facility.

chance variation The difference between the sample value and the true value of the population mean.

chi-square test Test of the goodness of fit between the observed distribution and the expected distribution of a variable.

closed-ended questions Questions that require the respondent to choose from a list of answers.

cluster analysis General term for statistical procedures that classify objects or people into some number of mutually exclusive and exhaustive groups on the basis of two or more classification variables.

cluster sample Probability sample in which the sampling units are selected from a number of small geographic areas to reduce data collection costs.

coding Process of grouping and assigning numeric codes to the various responses to a question.

coefficient of determination Measure of the percentage of the variation in the dependent variable explained by variations in the independent variables.

collinearity Correlation of independent variables with each other, which can bias estimates of regression coefficients.

comparative scales Measurement scales in which one object, concept, or person is compared with another on a scale.

computer-assisted telephone interviews (CATI) Central-location telephone interviews in which interviewers enter respondents' answers directly into a computer.

conclusions Generalizations that answer the questions raised by the research objectives or otherwise satisfy the objectives.

concomitant variation Statistical relationship between two variables.

concurrent validity Degree to which another variable, measured at the same point in time as the variable of interest, can be predicted by the measurement instrument.

confidence interval Interval that, at the specified confidence level, includes the true population value.

confidence level Probability that, a particular interval will include the true population value; also called *confidence coefficient*.

conjoint analysis Procedure used to quantify the value that consumers associate with different levels of product/service attributes or features.

constant sum scales Measurement scales that ask the respondent to divide a given number of points, typically 100, among two or more attributes, based on their importance to him or her.

constitutive definition Statement of the meaning of the central idea or concept under study, establishing its boundaries; also known as *theoretical*, or *conceptual, definition*.

constructs Specific types of concepts that exist at higher levels of abstraction.

construct validity Degree to which a measurement instrument represents and logically connects, via the underlying theory, the observed phenomenon to the construct.

consumer drawings Projective technique in which respondents draw what they are feeling or how they perceive an object.

consumer orientation The identification of and focus on the people or firms most likely to buy a product and the production of a good or service that will meet their needs most effectively.

contamination Inclusion in a test of a group of respondents who are not normally there—for example, buyers from outside the test market who see an advertisement intended only for those in the test area and enter the area to purchase the product being tested.

content validity Representativeness, or sampling adequacy, of the content of the measurement instrument.

convenience samples Nonprobability samples based on using people who are easily accessible.

convergent validity Degree of correlation among different measurement instruments that purport to measure the same construct.

cookie A text file placed on a user's computer in order to identify the user when she or he revisits the Web site.

cooperation rate Percentage of qualified persons contacted that will agree to complete the survey.

correlation analysis Analysis of the degree to which changes in one variable are associated with changes in another.

criterion-related validity Degree to which a measurement instrument can predict a variable that is designated a criterion.

crosstabulation Examination of the responses to one question relative to the responses to one or more other questions.

custom research firms Companies that carry out customized marketing research to address specific projects for corporate clients.

data entry Process of converting information to an electronic format.

data mining The use of statistical and other advanced software to discover nonobvious patterns hidden in a database.

database marketing Marketing that relies on the creation of a large computerized file of customers' and potential customers' profiles and purchase patterns to create a targeted marketing mix.

decision support system (DSS) An interactive, personalized information management system, designed to be initiated and controlled by individual decision makers.

dependent variable Variable expected to be explained or caused by the independent variable.

depth interviews One-on-one interviews that probe and elicit detailed answers to questions, often using nondirective techniques to uncover hidden motivations.

descriptive function The gathering and presentation of statements of fact.

descriptive studies Research studies that answer the questions who, what, when, where, and how.

design control Use of the experimental design to control extraneous causal factors.

determinant attitudes Those consumer attitudes most closely related to preferences or to actual purchase decisions.

diagnostic function The explanation of data or actions.

dichotomous questions Closed-ended questions that ask the respondents to choose between two answers.

discriminant coefficient An estimate of the discriminatory power of a particular independent variable; also called *discriminant weight*.

discriminant score Score that is the basis for predicting to which group a particular object or individual belongs; also called *Z-score*.

discriminant validity Measure of the lack of association among constructs that are supposed to be different.

discussion guide Written outline of topics to be covered during a focus group discussion.

disguised observation Process of monitoring people who do not know they are being watched.

disproportional, or optimal, allocation Sampling in which the number of elements taken from a given stratum is proportional to the relative size of the stratum and the standard deviation of the characteristic under consideration.

door-to-door interviews Interviews conducted face to face with consumers in their homes.

editing Process of ascertaining that questionnaires were filled out properly and completely.

electroencephalograph (EEG) Machine that measures electrical pulses on the scalp and generates a record of electrical activity in the brain.

equivalent form reliability Ability of two very similar forms of an instrument to produce closely correlated results.

error checking routines Computer programs that accept instructions from the user to check for logical errors in the data.

error sum of squares Variation not explained by the regression.

ethics Moral principles or values, generally governing the conduct of an individual or group.

ethnographic research Study of human behavior in its natural context, involving observation of behavior and physical setting.

evaluative research Research done to assess program performance.

executive interviews Industrial equivalent of door-to-door interviewing.

executive summary Portion of a research report that explains why the research was done, what was found, what those findings mean, and what action, if any, management should undertake.

experience surveys Discussions with knowledgeable individuals, both inside and outside the organization, who may provide insights into the problem.

experiment Research approach in which one variable is manipulated and the effect on another variable is observed.

experimental design Test in which the researcher has control over and manipulates one or more independent variables.

experimental effect Effect of the treatment variable on the dependent variable.

exploratory research Preliminary research conducted to increase understanding of a concept, to clarify the exact nature of the problem to be solved, or to identify important variables to be studied.

external validity Extent to which causal relationships measured in an experiment can be generalized to outside persons, settings, and times.

F test Test of the probability that a particular calculated value could have been due to chance.

face validity Degree to which a measurement seems to measure what it is supposed to measure.

factor analysis Procedure for simplifying data by reducing a large set of variables to a smaller set of factors or composite variables by identifying underlying dimensions of the data.

factor loading Correlation between factor scores and the original variables.

field experiments Tests conducted outside the laboratory in an actual environment, such as a marketplace.

field management companies Firms that provide such support services as questionnaire formatting, screener writing, and coordination of data collection.

field service firms Companies that only collect survey data for corporate clients or research firms.

finite population correction factor (FPC) An adjustment to the required sample size that is made in cases where the sample is expected to be equal to 5 percent or more of the total population.

focus group Group of 8 to 12 participants who are led by a moderator in an in-depth discussion on one particular topic or concept.

focus group facility Research facility consisting of a conference room or living room setting and a separate observation room with a one-way mirror or live audiovisual feed.

focus group moderator Person hired by the client to lead the focus group; this person should have a background in psychology or sociology or, at least, marketing.

frame error Error resulting from an inaccurate or incomplete sampling frame.

galvanic skin response (GSR) Change in the electric resistance of the skin associated with activation responses; also called *electrodermal response.*

garbologists Researchers who sort through people's garbage to analyze household consumption patterns.

geographic information system (GIS) Computer-based system that uses secondary and/or primary data to generate maps that visually display various types of data geographically.

goal orientation A focus on the accomplishment of corporate goals; a limit set on consumer orientation.

graphic rating scales Measurement scales that include a graphic continuum, anchored by two extremes.

group dynamics Interaction among people in a group.

hermeneutic research Research that focuses on interpretation through conversations.

history Intervention, between the beginning and end of an experiment, of outside variables or events that might change the dependent variable.

hypothesis A conjectural statement about a relationship between two or more variables that can be tested with empirical data.

hypothesis test of proportions Test to determine whether the difference between proportions is greater than would be expected because of sampling error.

independent samples Samples in which measurement of a variable in one population has no effect on measurement of the variable in the other.

independent variable Variable believed to affect the value of the dependent value.

individual depth interviews One-on-one interviews that probe and elicit detailed answers to questions, often using nondirective techniques to uncover hidden motivations.

InfoScan Custom Store Tracking Scanner-based data system that collects information on consumer packaged goods.

instant analysis Moderator debriefing, offering a forum for brainstorming by the moderator and client observers.

instrument variation Changes in measurement instruments (e.g., interviews or observers) that might affect measurements.

intelligent data entry Form of data entry in which the information being entered into the data entry device is checked for internal logic.

Interactive Marketing Research Organization (IMRO) Organization dedicated to the development, dissemination, and implementation of interactive marketing research concepts, practice, and information.

internal consistency reliability Ability of an instrument to produce similar results when used on different samples during the same time period to measure a phenomenon.

internal database A collection of related information developed from data within the organization.

internal validity Extent to which competing explanations for the experimental results observed can be ruled out.

interrupted time-series design Research in which repeated measurement of an effect "interrupts" previous data patterns.

interval estimates Interval or range of values within which the true population value is estimated to fall.

interval scales Scales that have the characteristics of ordinal scales, plus equal intervals between points to show relative amounts; they may include an arbitrary zero point.

interviewer error, or interviewer bias Error that results from the interviewer's influencing—consciously or unconsciously—the respondent.

itemized rating scales Measurement scales in which the respondent selects an answer from a limited number of ordered categories.

judgment samples Nonprobability samples in which the selection criteria are based on the researcher's personal judgment about representativeness of the population under study.

laboratory experiments Experiments conducted in a controlled setting.

Likert scales Measurement scales in which the respondent specifies a level of agreement or disagreement with statements expressing either a favorable or an unfavorable attitude toward the concept under study.

longitudinal study Study in which the same respondents are resampled over time.

low-ball pricing Quoting an unrealistically low price to secure a firm's business and then using some means to substantially raise the price.

machine cleaning of data Final computerized error check of data.

mail panels Precontacted and pre-screened participants who are periodically sent questionnaires.

mall-intercept interviews Interviews conducted by intercepting mall shoppers (or shoppers in other high-traffic locations) and interviewing them face to face.

management decision problem A statement specifying the type of managerial action required to solve the problem.

marginal report Computer-generated table of the frequencies of the responses to each question, used to monitor entry of valid codes and correct use of skip patterns.

marketing The process of planning and executing the conception, pricing, promotion, and distribution of ideas, goods, and services to create exchanges that satisfy individual and organizational objectives.

marketing concept A business philosophy based on consumer orienta-

tion, goal orientation, and systems orientation.

marketing mix The unique blend of product/service, pricing, promotion, and distribution strategies designed to meet the needs of a specific target market.

marketing research The planning, collection, and analysis of data relevant to marketing decision making and the communication of the results of this analysis to management.

marketing research aggregator A company that acquires, catalogs, reformats, segments, and resells reports already published by large and small marketing research firms.

marketing research objective A goal statement, defining the specific information needed to solve the marketing research problem.

marketing research problem A statement specifying the type of information needed by the decision maker to help solve the management decision problem and how that information can be obtained efficiently and effectively.

marketing strategy A plan to guide the long-term use of a firm's resources based on its existing and projected internal capabilities and on projected changes in the external environment.

maturation Changes in subjects occurring during the experiment that are not related to the experiment but which may affect subjects' response to the treatment factor.

mean Sum of the values for all observations of a variable divided by the number of observations.

measurement Process of assigning numbers or labels to persons, objects, or events in accordance with specific rules for representing quantities or qualities of attributes.

measurement error Systematic error that results from a variation between the information being sought and what is actually obtained by the measurement process.

measurement instrument bias Error that results from the design of the questionnaire or measurement instrument; also known as *questionnaire bias*.

median Value below which 50 percent of the observations fall.

mode Value that occurs most frequently.

mortality Loss of test units or subjects during the course of an experiment, which may result in a nonrepresentativeness.

multidimensional scales Scales designed to measure several dimensions of a concept, respondent, or object.

multiple-choice questions Closed-ended questions that ask the respondent to choose among several answers; also called *multichotomous questions.*

multiple discriminant analysis Procedure for predicting group membership for a (nominal or categorical) dependent variable on the basis of two or more independent variables.

multiple regression analysis Procedure for predicting the level or magnitude of a (metric) dependent variable based on the levels of multiple independent variables.

multiple time-series design Interrupted time-series design with a control group.

multivariate analysis A general term for statistical procedures that simultaneously analyze multiple measurements on each individual or object under study.

mystery shoppers People who pose as consumers and shop at a company's own stores or those of its competitors to collect data about customer–employee interactions and to gather observational data; they may also compare prices, displays, and the like.

neural network A computer program that mimics the processes of the human brain and thus is capable of learning from examples to find patterns in data.

newsgroup An Internet site where people can read and post messages devoted to a specific topic.

nominal scales Scales that partition data into mutually exclusive and collectively exhaustive categories.

nonbalanced scales Measurement scales that are weighted toward one end or the other of the scale.

noncomparative scales Measurement scales in which judgment is made without reference to another object, concept, or person.

nonprobability sample A subset of a population in which the chances of selection for the various elements in the population are unknown.

nonresponse bias Error that results from a systematic difference between those who do and those who do not respond to a measurement instrument.

nonsampling error All error other than sampling error; also called *measurement error.*

normal distribution Continuous distribution that is bell-shaped and symmetric about the mean; the mean, median, and mode are equal.

observation research Systematic process of recording patterns of occurrences or behaviors without normally communicating with the people involved.

one-group pretest–posttest design Pre-experimental design with pre- and postmeasurements but no control group.

one-shot case study design Pre-experimental design with no pretest observations, no control group, and an after-measurement only.

one-way frequency table Table showing the number of respondents choosing each answer to a survey question.

one-way mirror observation Practice of watching behaviors or activities from behind a one-way mirror.

online focus groups Focus groups conducted via the Internet.

open-ended questions Questions to which the respondent replies in her or his own words.

open observation Process of monitoring people who know they are being watched.

operational definition Statement of precisely which observable characteristics will be measured and the process for assigning a value to the concept.

opportunity identification Using marketing research to find and evaluate new opportunities.

optical scanning Form of data entry in which responses on questionnaires are read in automatically by the data entry device.

ordinal scales Scales that maintain the labeling characteristics of nominal scales and have the ability to order data.

p **value** Exact probability of getting a computed test statistic that is due to chance. The smaller the *p* value, the smaller the probability that the observed result occurred by chance.

paired comparison scales Measurement scales that ask the respondent to pick one of two objects in a set, based on some stated criteria.

Pearson's product moment correlation Correlation analysis technique for use with metric data.

people meters Components of a microwave computerized rating system, used to measure national TV audiences, that transmits demographic information overnight.

People Reader Machine that simultaneously records the respondent's reading material and eye reactions.

perceptual mapping Procedure for producing visual representations of consumer perceptions of products, brands, companies, or other objects.

photo sort Projective technique in which a respondent sorts photos of different types of people, identifying those people who she or he feels would use the specified product or service.

physical control Holding constant the value or level of extraneous variables throughout the course of an experiment.

pilot studies Surveys using a limited number of respondents and often employing rigorous sampling techniques than are employed in large, quantitative studies.

point estimate Particular estimate of a population value.

population Entire group of people about whom information is needed; also called *universe* or *population of interest.*

population distribution Frequency distribution of all the elements of a population.

population specification error Error that results from incorrectly defining the population or universe from which a sample is chosen.

population standard deviation Standard deviation of a variable for the entire population.

portable people meter Device worn by people that measures the radio and TV programming to which the participant was exposed during the day.

predictive function Specification of how to use descriptive and diagnostic research to predict the results of a planned marketing decision.

predictive validity Degree to which a future level of a criterion variable can be forecast by a current measurement scale.

pre-experimental designs Designs that offer little or no control over extraneous factors.

pretest Trial run of a questionnaire.

primary data New data gathered to help solve the problem under investigation.

probability sample A subset of a population that can be assumed to be a representative cross section because every element in the population has a known nonzero chance of being selected.

processing error Error that results from the incorrect transfer of information from a survey document to a computer.

profession Organization whose membership is determined by objective standards, such as an examination.

professionalism Quality said to be possessed by a worker with a high level of expertise, freedom to exercise judgment, and the ability to work independently.

programmatic research Research conducted to develop marketing options through market segmentation, market opportunity analyses, or consumer attitude and product usage studies.

projective test Technique for tapping respondents' deepest feelings by having them project those feelings into an unstructured situation.

proportional allocation Sampling in which the number of elements selected from a stratum is directly proportional to the size of the stratum relative to the size of the population.

proportional property of the normal distribution Feature that the number of observations falling between the mean and a given number of standard deviations from the mean is the same for all normal distributions.

pupilometer Machine that measures changes in pupil dilation.

purchase intent scales Scales used to measure a respondent's intention to buy or not buy a product.

push polling Style of research gathering in which zealous political supporters deride one candidate to lead voters to support the other candidate.

Q-sorting Measurement scale employing a sophisticated form of rank ordering using card sorts.

qualitative research Research whose findings are not subject to quantification or quantitative analysis.

quantitative research Research that uses mathematical analysis.

quasi-experiments Studies in which the researcher lacks complete control over the scheduling of treatments or must assign respondents to treatments in a nonrandom manner.

questionnaire Set of questions designed to generate the data necessary to accomplish the objectives of the research project; also called an *interview schedule* or *survey instrument.*

quota samples Nonprobability samples in which quotas, based on demographic or classification factors selected by the researcher, are established for population subgroups.

random-digit dialing Method of generating lists of telephone numbers at random.

random error, or random sampling error Error that results from chance variation.

randomization Random assignment of subjects to treatment conditions to ensure equal representation of subject characteristics.

rank-order scales Measurement scales in which the respondent compares two or more items and ranks them.

Rapid Analysis Measurement System (RAMS) Hand-held device that

allows respondents to record how they are feeling by turning a dial.

ratio scales Scales that have the characteristics of interval scales, plus a meaningful zero point so that magnitudes can be compared arithmetically.

recommendations Conclusions applied to marketing strategies or tactics that focus on a client's achievement of differential advantage.

recruited Internet sample Sample group recruited to ensure representativeness of a target population.

refusal rate Percentage of persons contacted who refused to participate in a survey.

regression coefficients Estimates of the effect of individual independent variables on the dependent variable.

regression to the mean Tendency of subjects with extreme behavior to move toward the average for that behavior during the course of an experiment.

related samples Samples in which measurement of a variable in one population may influence measurement of the variable in the other.

reliability Degree to which measures are free from random error and, therefore, provide consistent data.

request for proposal (RFP) A solicitation sent to marketing research suppliers inviting them to submit a formal proposal, including a bid.

research design The plan to be followed to answer the marketing research objectives.

research management Overseeing the development of excellent communication systems, data quality, time schedules, cost controls, client profitability, and staff development.

research panel A group of individuals who agree to participate in a series of research studies over time.

research proposal A document developed, usually in response to an RFP, that states the research objectives, research design, time line, and cost.

research request An internal document used by large organizations that describes a potential research project, its benefits to the organization, and estimated costs; it must be

formally approved before a research project can begin.

response bias Error that results from the tendency of people to answer a question incorrectly through either deliberate falsification or unconscious misrepresentation.

return on quality Management objective based on the principles that (1) the quality being delivered is at a level desired by the target market and (2) that level of quality must have a positive impact on profitability.

rule Guide, method, or command that tells a researcher what to do.

sample Subset of all the members of a population of interest.

sample design error Systematic error that results from an error in the sample design or sampling procedures.

sample distribution Frequency distribution of all the elements of an individual sample.

sampling Process of obtaining information from a subset of a larger group.

sampling distribution of the mean Theoretical frequency distribution of the means of all possible samples of a given size drawn from a particular population; it is normally distributed.

sampling distribution of the proportion Relative frequency distribution of the sample proportions of many random samples of a given size drawn from a particular population; it is normally distributed.

sampling error Error that occurs because the sample selected is not perfectly representative of the population.

sampling frame List of population elements from which units to be sampled can be selected or a specified procedure for generating such a list.

scale Set of symbols or numbers so constructed that the symbols or numbers can be assigned by a rule to the individuals (or their behaviors or attitudes) to whom the scale is applied.

scaled-response questions Closed-ended questions in which the response choices are designed to capture the intensity of the respondent's feeling.

scaling Procedures for assigning numbers (or other symbols) to properties of an object in order to impart some numerical characteristics to the properties in question.

scanning technology Form of data entry in which responses on questionnaires are read in automatically by the data entry device.

screened Internet sample Self-selected sample group in which quotas are imposed, based on some desired sample characteristics.

screeners Questions used to identify appropriate respondents.

secondary data Data that have been previously gathered.

selection bias Systematic differences between the test group and the control group due to a biased selection process.

selection error Error that results from incomplete or improper sampling procedures or not following appropriate procedures.

selective research Research used to test decision alternatives.

self-administered questionnaires Questionnaires filled out by respondents with no interviewer present.

semantic differential scales Measurement scales that examine the strengths and weaknesses of a concept by having the respondent rank it between dichotomous pairs of words or phrases that could be used to describe it; the means of the responses are then plotted as a profile, or image.

sentence and story completion tests Projective tests in which respondents complete sentences or stories in their own words.

simple random sample Probability sample selected by assigning a number to every element of the population and then using a table of random numbers to select specific elements for inclusion in the sample.

simulated test market (STM) Use of survey data and mathematical models to simulate test market results at a much lower cost; also called *pretest market*.

situation analysis Studying the decision-making environment within which the marketing research will take place.

skip pattern Sequence in which questions are asked, based on a respondent's answer to an earlier question or questions.

snowball samples Nonprobability samples in which additional respondents are selected based on referrals from initial respondents.

split-half technique Method of assessing the reliability of a scale by dividing the total set of measurement items in half and correlating the results.

spurious association A relationship between a presumed cause and a presumed effect that occurs as a result of an unexamined variable or set of variables.

SSL (secure socket layer) technology Computer encryption system that secures sensitive information.

stability Lack of change in results from test to retest.

standard deviation Measure of dispersion calculated by subtracting the mean of the series from each value in a series, squaring each result, summing the results, dividing the sum by the number of items minus 1, and taking the square root of this value.

standard error of the mean Standard deviation of a distribution of sample means.

standard normal distribution Normal distribution with a mean of zero and a standard deviation of one.

Stapel scales Measurement scales that require the respondent to rate, on a scale ranging from 15 to 25, how closely and in what direction a descriptor adjective fits a given concept.

static-group comparison design Pre-experimental design that utilizes an experimental and a control group, but where subjects or test units are not randomly assigned to the two groups and no premeasurements are taken.

statistical control Adjusting for the effects of confounded variables by statistically adjusting the value of the dependent variable for each treatment condition.

statistical power Probability of not making a Type II error.

storytelling Projective technique in which respondents are required to tell stories about their experiences, with a company or product, for example; also known as the *metaphor technique*.

strategic partnership An alliance formed by two or more firms with unique skills and resources to offer a new service for clients, provide strategic support for each firm, or in some other manner create mutual benefits.

stratified sample Probability sample that is forced to be more representative through simple random sampling of mutually exclusive and exhaustive subsets.

structured observation Study in which the observer fills out a questionnaire-like form on each person or event observed or counts the number of times a behavior or activity occurs.

sum of squares due to regression Variation explained by the regression.

supervisor's instructions Written directions to the field service firm on how to conduct the survey.

surrogate information error Error that results from a discrepancy between the information needed to solve a problem and that sought by the researcher.

survey objectives Outline of the decision-making information sought through the questionnaire.

survey research Research in which an interviewer interacts with respondents to obtain facts, opinions, and attitudes.

syndicated service research firms Companies that collect, package, and sell the same general market research data to many firms.

systematic error, or bias Error that results from problems or flaws in the execution of the research design; sometimes called *nonsampling error*.

systematic sampling Probability sampling in which the entire population is numbered and elements are selected using a skip interval.

systems orientation The creation of systems to monitor the external environment and deliver the desired marketing mix to the target market.

***t* test** Hypothesis test used for a single mean if the sample is too small to use the *Z* test.

temporal sequence An appropriate causal order of events.

test market Testing of a new product or some element of the marketing mix using an experimental or quasi-experimental design.

test–retest reliability Ability of the same instrument to produce consistent results when used a second time under conditions as similar as possible to the original conditions.

testing effect Effect that is a byproduct of the research process itself.

third-person technique Projective technique in which the interviewer learns about respondents' feelings by asking them to answer for a third party, such as "your neighbor" or "most people."

traffic counters Machines used to measure vehicular flow over a particular stretch of roadway.

treatment variable Independent variable that is manipulated in an experiment.

true experimental design Research using an experimental group and a control group, to which test units are randomly assigned.

Type I error (α error) Rejection of the null hypothesis when, in fact, it is true.

Type II error (β error) Failure to reject the null hypothesis when, in fact, it is false.

unidimensional scales Scales designed to measure only one attribute of a concept, respondent, or object.

unrestricted Internet sample Self-selected sample group consisting of anyone who wishes to complete an Internet survey.

unstructured observation Study in which the observer simply makes notes on the behavior or activity being observed.

validation Process of ascertaining that interviews actually were conducted as specified.

validity The degree to which what the researcher was trying to measure was actually measured.

variable A symbol or concept that can assume any one of a set of values.

videoconferencing Televising a focus group session at a focus group facility or company site so that more staff can view customer opinions.

voice pitch analysis Studying changes in the relative vibration frequency of the human voice to measure emotion.

word association test Projective test in which the interviewer says a word and the respondent must mention the first thing that comes to mind.

Z test Hypothesis test used for a single mean if the sample is large enough and drawn at random.

INDEX